Governing Nonprofit Organizations

Governing Nonprofit Organizations

Federal and State Law and Regulation

Marion R. Fremont-Smith

**The Belknap Press of
Harvard University Press**

Cambridge, Massachusetts, and London, England

First Harvard University Press paperback edition, 2008.

Library of Congress Cataloging-in-Publication Data

Fremont-Smith, Marion R.
  Governing nonprofit organizations : federal and state law and regulation /
Marion R. Fremont-Smith.
    p.   cm.
  Includes bibliographical references and index.
  ISBN 978-0-674-01306-3 (cloth: alk. paper)
  ISBN 978-0-674-03045-9 (pbk.)
  1. Nonprofit organizations—Law and legislation—United States.   I. Title.

KF1388.F74 2004
346.73′064—dc22   2003063933

Contents

Preface

This volume is a natural outgrowth of my first book, *Foundations and Government: State and Federal Law and Supervision,* published in 1965. Growth in the sense that it covers not just foundations but the entire range of nonprofit charities; and growth in the scope of events it describes that have occurred since the mid-sixties, events that have markedly changed the nonprofit charitable sector itself and the role of government in its regulation. The slight variation in the subtitles of the two works reflects these changes: what was then more modestly termed "supervision" is now forthrightly called regulation, and federal regulation is now listed first in recognition that the Internal Revenue Service is the sole effective regulator in all but a few states.

In the 1960s, and for many years thereafter, I believed that regulation of charities was the proper province of state government, even suggesting federal subsidies to support state programs that met minimum federal standards and reliance on state attorneys general to do the regulating. I would not advocate such measures now for two reasons. The first is a practical one: in 1964 there were ten states actively regulating charities and now, forty years later, there is only one more. The second is more basic: namely, the important change in the nature of federal regulation that has made it more suitable to police charities. Exempt organizations are no longer the stepchildren of the Service; the entire structure of the exempt organizations division has been radically altered so that it is no longer a branch avoided by Service personnel. Rather, TE/GE is staffed by specialists at the national level and for the most part in the regions who view their role as assuring that exempt charitable organizations continue to make the contributions to our society that are the rationale for the special status they are afforded in the tax system.

This would not alone be enough, if Congress had not also provided the framework for meaningful regulation. The first step was enactment of the private foundations rules, and more recently the excess benefit limitations, designed in each instance to correct specific instances of "wrongdoing," not by withdrawing exemption and letting the wrongdoers continue in office but by imposing sanctions on them directly and on those who approved their actions. In addition, the role of regulator has broadened in scope to encompass support programs designed to improve compliance.

There are many reasons for these changes: recognition within the charitable sector as well as within the government of the limitations inherent in reliance on loss of exemption as a sole sanction; the growth and importance of the sector in the economy; and a less obvious, but fundamental, change that came about after passage of the Freedom of Information Act in 1966. For the first time, decisions on tax matters were not the sole province of a small group of tax practitioners who had formerly served in the government. It was possible for the broad community of organizations across the country and their advisors to learn the nature of the problems their counterparts were facing and the rationale used by the Service in the individual rulings it issued. Members of the bar were also able to identify issues needing study or revision, and call these to the attention of the Service as a group and not as partisans of individual clients.

In advocating the IRS as the principal regulator, I do not mean to belittle the role of the states. The state courts and the state attorneys general possess the unique ability to correct abuses through remedies individually framed to meet specific situations. Their power to deal with obsolete, impracticable, or wasteful purposes and with restrictions on administration that prevent charities from fulfilling a meaningful role in society could not be easily replicated at the federal level. What is needed and what, as of the close of 2003 still had not been accomplished, is the ability of federal and state regulators to communicate freely on pending matters so that their efforts are complementary. There have never been similar constraints on the sharing of information between the IRS and state revenue departments, making the failure to accomplish this change difficult to comprehend. But even greater information sharing will not make state regulation easier; more likely it will impose a greater burden on already pressed state regulators. In those states in which little or no attention is paid to the regulation of charitable fiduciary behavior (as opposed to regulation of charitable fund-raising) one can nonetheless hope that information on wrongdoing provided by the Service will be an impetus for increased state activity, particularly in cases in which the unique equity powers of the state courts to remove trustees and order restitution will preserve charitable assets in ways not available to federal regulators.

During the forty-five years since I was introduced to the law of charity, a new legal field has emerged, formally acknowledged with the inauguration in 2002 of the American Law Institute project on Principles of the Law of Nonprofit Organizations. This new interest of the academic community in the study of nonprofit organizations and philanthropy has led to a vast increase in the number and range of courses being offered across the disciplines in colleges and universities, and has brought new analyses to international philanthropy. The result can only be improvement in the operation and regulation of the sector.

My experience as regulator of, commentator on, and advisor to charities has provided a unique opportunity to appreciate the essential contributions charities make to our society, as well as the necessity of a strong regulatory regime that assures the public of the integrity of the sector. Without that assurance, charities will not continue to receive the degree of support now provided by government and the private sector. My hope in publishing this study is that it will contribute to a better understanding of the importance of framing meaningful rules for the governance of charities, rules that encourage their freedom of operation while assuring that they are not being used for private purposes, as well as appreciation of the proper role of government in enforcing these rules and the ways in which both the law and regulation can be improved.

There are many individuals whose encouragement and assistance over the years I wish to acknowledge, beginning with Edward J. McCormack, Jr., Attorney General of the Commonwealth of Massachusetts from 1958 to 1962, who in 1959 appointed me an assistant attorney general and director of the Division of Public Charities in his office and charged me to make it a model of state regulation. F. Emerson Andrews, founding president of The Foundation Center, editor of The Foundation Directory, and director of the program on philanthropy at the Russell Sage Foundation, was a true mentor during the time I was writing that first book and a subsequent one on corporate philanthropy under the auspices of the Foundation. The partners of Choate, Hall and Stewart, past and present, afforded me a unique opportunity to learn about the charitable sector from different perspectives—as a practicing attorney, a trustee and director of individual charities, large and small, and of organizations formed to support the sector, as well as a consultant to state and federal governments. From my first day at the firm, W. Arthur Dupee, Jesse Fillman, and G. D'Adelot Belin were unfailing supporters, and it is with deep gratitude that I honor their memory.

Professors Harvey Dale and Joel Fleishman, then chairman and president respectively of what was in 1996 an anonymous funder, now identifiable as The Atlantic Philanthropies, suggested that I undertake the study that is now embodied in this book. Profound thanks to them and Atlantic Philanthropies, which has generously underwritten the project. I am also indebted to Harvey and Joel for introducing me to Professor Mark Moore, director of the then newly formed Hauser Center for Nonprofit Organizations at Harvard, who has made a home for me at the Center, thereby providing an intellectually stimulating and always challenging environment in which I have conducted my research.

Among my colleagues at the Hauser Center, in addition to Mark, I wish to thank Derek Bok, Shawn Bowen, Peter Frumkin, Peter Dobkin Hall, Liz Keating, Chris Letts, Bill Ryan, the other faculty members, and the Center's support staff, particularly Guy Keeley and Corinne Locke. I have been especially fortunate to work with two of the Faculty Fellows of the Center, Professors Martha Minow in her seminar on nonprofit organizations and Dan Halperin in his course on tax-exempt organizations at Harvard Law School.

My research assistants at Harvard have provided exceptional support. Andras Kosaras has been a true collaborator in the final year and a half of this study, giving meticulous attention to the citations and sources and wise observations on the law of nonprofits. His predecessors, Adam Morris, Tim Freiermuth, and Nathaniel O'Connell, each made distinct, invaluable contributions to the research. I have had remarkable assistance from a dedicated group of law student researchers: in particular I wish to acknowledge the contributions of Michael Arlein and Jonathan Lever, Mike for his comprehensive research that formed the basis for Chapter 4 and Table 3, and Jon for his equally comprehensive work that is reflected in the materials in Chapter 6 and Table 1. Luisa Grillo-Chope and Slade Sullivan provided additional research materials, of great importance to the study. Jackie Corliss, my assistant at Choate, Hall and Stewart, deserves special thanks for making it possible for me to hold two part-time positions without slighting either. Galli Aizenman of The Atlantic Philanthropies has been a source of encouragement, which I acknowledge with thanks. Good fortune led me to Michael Aronson at Harvard University Press, who has been a calm, enthusiastic supporter of my work, and to Richard Audet for his painstaking editing of the manuscript.

I have received invaluable help from a number of my fellow exempt organization enthusiasts, both scholars and legal practitioners. They are among my most discerning critics: John Simon and Tom Troyer, whose friendships date to the 1960s; and Evelyn Brody, Jill Horwitz, Steve Schwarz, Amy Segal, Catharine Wells, and the members of the New York Nonprofit Forum, who provided discerning comments on portions of the manuscript. In its preparation I have been accorded the gracious cooperation of many former and present officials of the federal government, and of the assistant attorneys general and other charity regulators in almost every state and of their staffs. Their interest and concern with improving the administration of the nonprofit sector merit great appreciation. I particularly want to thank Evelyn Petscheck,

Marc Owens, Steve Miller, Dave Jones, Cathy Livingston, Jim McGovern, and Susan Brown in Washington, and state charity regulators Richard Allen, Karl Emerson, Karen Kunstler Goldman, Belinda Johns, Jamie Katz, and Dan Moore.

In a group of acknowledgments such as this, it is traditional to name last those who really come first, and I am not one to flout tradition. Yet in all respects it is my family who deserve foremost recognition for their patience, their great good humor, and the inspiration they provide. It is a big family: my children, Beth Johnsey, Keith Miller, Brad Miller; their spouses, Bob Johnsey, Mary Miller, Jennifer Hosmer; my grandchildren, Evan, Samantha, Caroline, Austin, Lauren, and Julia Miller. My stepchildren, Paul, Chris, Nan, Deborah, and Frances, and their spouses, children, and grandchildren add to the fullness of my life and keep vibrant for all of us the memory of their father, Paul Fremont-Smith. Paul was at the heart of this extended family for thirty-nine years from the date of our marriage in 1961 until his death in 2000. His love, his empathy, and his unwavering support of my career are behind all I have been able to accomplish.

Governing Nonprofit Organizations

1

The Nonprofit Sector in the Twenty-First Century

The 1.4 million charitable, religious, scientific, educational, and cultural organizations that comprise what is generally considered the "nonprofit" sector[1] hold assets worth more than $2 trillion[2] and receive annually an estimated $241 billion in support from individuals, corporations, and foundations.[3] Both the size of the sector and the extent of the support it receives from the general public reflect recognition of the contributions of the sector to society.

These contributions are evident in almost every aspect of American life—whether they are provided by religious institutions, schools and colleges, human and social resource agencies, cultural and arts organizations, medical and scientific research facilities, or humanitarian organizations. In addition to the specific contributions, the sector serves as a counterbalance to government and to the private realm, supplementing their public and private activities, filling in the gaps in services that neither meet, while using its unique position to innovate in delivering services and providing facilities for the general good.

A distinguishing feature of the nonprofit sector is the freedom within which its component entities are allowed to operate. The vast number of organizations that comprise the sector, including almost all churches and organizations with receipts of $25,000 or less, are under no duty to account to any governmental agency on a regular basis. The rest operate largely without

1. Table 22, "Tax-Exempt Organizations and Other Entities Listed on the Exempt Organization Business Master File, by Type of Organization and Internal Revenue Code Section, Fiscal Years 1999–2002," in *2002 IRS Data Book,* and Lester M. Salamon, *America's Nonprofit Sector: A Primer,* 22, 44 (New York: Foundation Center, 2d ed., 1999).

2. Paul Arnsberger, "Charities and Other Tax-Exempt Organizations, 1999," in *IRS Statistics of Income Bulletin* (Fall 2002); Melissa Ludlum, "Domestic Private Foundations and Charitable Trusts, 1999," in *IRS Statistics of Income Bulletin* (Fall 2002).

3. AAFRC (Association of American Fundraising Counsel) Trust for Philanthropy, *Giving USA 2003.*

1

supervision by any state official and with minimal oversight by the federal government, oversight, moreover, that is generally limited to assuring that they meet the conditions for exemption from federal taxes. Governments require no accountings of the methods by which nonprofit organizations pursue their missions nor make any attempt to assure that charitable assets are used effectively or efficiently.

In part this failure to provide meaningful regulation has been justified on the grounds that, because they are formed to "do good," the people who run nonprofit organizations will likewise "do good"; they will not profit at the organization's expense nor be reckless in their management of its assets. The general public has held to this belief despite evidence surfacing from time to time that charitable funds have been diverted to private hands or frittered away through bad management or negligent risk-taking. One cannot assume, however, that the public will continue to tolerate misdeeds or mismanagement of charitable funds. The wise course, therefore, is to provide a sufficient degree of regulation of charities to assure the public of the integrity of the sector, yet that it not be so draconian as to limit its freedom to meet changing needs and fulfill its public-serving roles.

The subject of this book is the legal structures society has adopted to hold trustees, directors, and managers of nonprofit, charitable organizations accountable and the ways in which they can be improved. It starts from a premise that the sector is a vital component of our democratic society and that it must be allowed the greatest degree of freedom to operate, consistent with the need to assure the public of its integrity. The law has traditionally required that fiduciaries act with loyalty, diligence, and prudence—that they assure that charitable funds not be chained to the needs of the past but rather be directed to the solution of contemporary problems and the formulation of methods for meeting the needs of the future. The law has also formulated regimes designed to assure that charities comply with these legal standards. By virtue of our federal system of government, charity regulation in the United States is a dual regime, with both the states and the federal government prescribing rules of behavior and enforcing those rules separately. Accordingly the two regimes are treated separately, while the areas in which they overlap and in which the regulators can or should cooperate are described.

This chapter contains a description of the current status of the sector, noting particularly how it has changed in recent decades. Chapter 2 provides a brief history of the laws governing charities from their earliest roots. Succeeding chapters describe the laws that govern the behavior of charitable fiduciaries. These are followed by descriptions of the manner in which the states and the federal government enforce these rules and the circumscribed rights of individuals to do so. A final chapter contains evaluations and suggestions for change.

The Legal Meaning of Charity

The primary focus of this study is that group of organizations forming the principal part of the nonprofit sector whose purposes are considered in law to be "charitable." The word "charitable" in this context encompasses a wide range of activities that aim to improve or uplift mankind, while the word "charity" is used to describe an organization established to carry out those purposes. The word "nonprofit" is also used to distinguish charitable organizations from their counterparts in the for-profit world by virtue of the fact that there are no "owners" of their assets or their earnings. Although in common parlance charity is often associated exclusively with relief of the poor, the needy, or the distressed, its legal meaning is far broader and one that constantly expands to meet changing concepts of what is of benefit to the public.

The concept of charity existed in early cultures and has formed an important part of the entire Judeo-Christian tradition. Organizations with charitable purposes are to be found in early Egyptian, Greek, and Roman records. The Ptolemies endowed a library in Alexandria; Plato bequeathed funds to support his academy after his death; and in the early centuries A.D. in Rome, private associations for relief of the poor, educational institutions, hospitals, foundling asylums, and old people's homes were established. Charity, in the form of foundations for the benefit of the needy, was a part of the earliest Islamic tradition. In the Middle Ages the Church became the chief dispenser of charity, and its role in the field of philanthropy has continued to be a dominant one. During the Reformation in England the guilds and companies replaced the Church as the administrator of many charitable gifts. A wave of philanthropy arose among the new middle classes leading to the establishment of permanent funds, usually trusts, for specific charitable objects administered by private individuals or corporations. Philanthropic societies and associations also developed and multiplied following the industrial revolution, and they have remained an important segment of society in the United States since its earliest days.

There has always been a problem describing the universe of "charities." Each of the broad general categories that comprise the legal definition—religious, charitable, scientific, literary, educational—is specified in section 501(c)(3) of the Internal Revenue Code. Under state law these organizations are considered to be "public charities." The legal definition actually has two components. The purposes of a charitable organization must fit within a category of legally recognized purposes that are broadly described as "of public benefit," and the benefit must extend to an indefinite class of beneficiaries, not specific individuals. The word "public" in this context is often misconstrued. Charities are public in the sense that their activities are devoted to benefiting the public at large. There can be no such thing as a private charity in law, since a trust or corporation devoted to benefiting one or a few named individuals, even if its stated purpose is to ease their suffering or to improve their mind (or any other legally charitable purpose), is not considered to be a charity.[4]

The meaning of the term "public charity" was further clouded with passage of the Tax Reform Act of 1969, which divided the universe of organizations described in section 501(c)(3) of the Internal Revenue Code into two distinct categories: private foundations and all other organizations described in that section. Private foundations were singled out in the act for separate, restrictive treatment on the theory that they were not responsive to the public, as were churches, governmental instrumentalities, schools, hospitals, and organizations primarily dependent upon support from the general public—in short, all of the remaining organizations described in that section.

Nomenclature is further confused by attempts to describe the universe of charities. In recognition that charities comprise that part of the American economy not controlled by private business nor by government, this universe is variously called the "third sector," the "independent sector," the "philanthropic sector," the "charitable sector," and, toward the end of the twentieth century, "civil society." In countries other than the United States and Great Britain, nonprofit organizations are commonly referred to as "nongovernmental organizations" or NGOs, and the sector is defined by that term. Each of these titles captures an important characteristic of the sector, but no one title accurately summarizes the entirety of the activities carried on by its constituents.

Size and Characteristics of the Nonprofit Sector

The American "nonprofit" sector is commonly considered to be comprised of those corporations, associations, trusts, and other legal entities that have been granted exemption from income tax by the Internal Revenue Service.

4. "The terms 'public charity' and 'private charity' are sometimes used . . . For the purposes of the law of charitable trusts it is believed confusing to use these two phrases . . . The words 'charitable' and 'public' are synonymous." George G. Bogert and George T. Bogert, *The Law of Trusts and Trustees*, §362 (St. Paul: West Group, 3d ed., 1977).

There are thirty-two categories of tax-exempt entities listed in the Internal Revenue Code, encompassing almost 1.6 million organizations.[5] However, since churches and church-related organizations as well as organizations with receipts of less than $25,000 are not required to file for exemption, the number is in fact larger. The number of churches that are not included in the IRS Master Files was estimated to be 354,000 in 1998, while there are no reliable estimates of the number of small organizations.[6] Nonetheless, most scholars rely on the IRS universe as providing the broadest definition of the nonprofit sector. The term "nonprofit" is also used in a narrower sense to refer to both the "religious, charitable, scientific, educational" organizations described in section 501(c)(3) and the "social welfare" organizations described in section 501(c)(4) of the Internal Revenue Code. Those organizations qualifying for exemption under section 501(c)(3) of the Code are actually referred to by the Service, except in rare circumstances, as charities, thereby recognizing that they almost invariably meet the definition in the nontax laws governing charitable trusts and corporations.[7] The National Center on Charitable Statistics uses the terms "charitable" and "nonprofit" interchangeably when describing its research on this smaller subset of tax-exempt organizations, and that precedent is followed in this study.[8]

In his *America's Nonprofit Sector: A Primer,* Lester Salamon identifies the "nonprofit sector" as the broader category of all tax-exempt entities, while the narrower group of 501(c)(3) and select 501(c)(4) organizations are called "public-serving" nonprofit organizations.[9] The *Nonprofit Almanac,* published by Independent Sector, distinguishes between the "nonprofit sector" and the smaller "independent sector."[10] The former includes all tax-exempt entities and the latter is described as comprising "501(c)(3), 501(c)(4) and religious organizations," although religious organizations, while they are not required to obtain a ruling as to exempt status, are described in and exempt under section 501(c)(3).

Charitable organizations are typically subdivided into categories according to their purposes. In 1985 the National Center for Charitable Statistics published the National Taxonomy of Exempt Entities (NTEE) in order to stan-

5. Table 22, in *2002 IRS Data Book.*

6. Murray S. Weitzman and Linda M. Lampkin, *The New Nonprofit Almanac and Desk Reference,* Table 1.1, at 4–5 (New York: Jossey-Bass, 2002).

7. See, for example, Arnsberger, "Charities and Other Tax-Exempt Organizations, 1999."

8. National Center for Charitable Statistics, available at *www.nccs.urban.org.*

9. Salamon, *America's Nonprofit Sector: A Primer,* 22–25.

10. Weitzman and Lampkin, *New Nonprofit Almanac,* xxvii, 7; Virginia Ann Hodgkinson et al., *Nonprofit Almanac 1996–1997,* 23–25, 37 (New York: Jossey-Bass, 1996).

dardize and assist in the analysis of the charitable sector.[11] The NTEE divides the nonprofit universe into twenty-six groups under ten broad categories:

Category	No. of groups
I. Arts, culture, and humanities	1
II. Education	1
III. Environment and animals	2
IV. Health	4
V. Human services	8
VI. International, foreign affairs	1
VII. Public, societal benefit	6
VIII. Religion related	1
IX. Mutual/membership benefit	1
X. Unknown, unclassified	1

In 1995 the Internal Revenue Service incorporated the NTEE into the government's economic classification system, the North American Industry Classification System (NAICS), in an attempt to promote uniformity.

In 2002 the organizations described in sections 501(c)(3) and 501(c)(4), other than churches and small organizations, in the IRS Master File constituted 1.05 million (66%) of the 1.58 million organizations that received tax-exemption under the federal tax code. This included 909,574 section 501(c)(3) organizations and 137,526 section (c)(4) social welfare organizations.[12] In the 1997 Master File, there were 692,524 501(c)(3) and 141,776 (c)(4) organizations, or approximately 63% of the 1.32 million organizations that received tax-exemption determination under the federal tax code.[13] Twenty years earlier, in 1977, there were an estimated 276,000 501(c)(3) entities and 130,000 social welfare organizations, representing 51% of the 790,000 organizations then considered exempt from income tax.[14] In sharp contrast, in 1940 the Internal Revenue Service files listed 12,500 exempt organizations, while in 1950 the number had grown to 50,000.

In the 2002 IRS Master File, the number of organizations exempt under section 501(c) other than (c)(3) and (c)(4) organizations were as follows:[15]

11. National Center for Charitable Statistics, *Guide to the National Taxonomy of Exempt Entities (NTEE)*, available at *nccs.urban.org/ntee-cc*.

12. Table 22, in *2002 IRS Data Book*.

13. Table 22, "Tax-Exempt Organizations and Other Entities Listed on the Exempt Organization Business Master File, by Type of Organization and Internal Revenue Code Section, Fiscal Years 1997–2000," in *2000 IRS Data Book*.

14. Weitzman and Lampkin, *New Nonprofit Almanac,* Table 1.1, at 4–5.

15. Table 22, in *2002 IRS Data Book*.

c1	Federal instrumentalities	88
c2	Title-holding companies	6,998
c5	Labor and agricultural organizations	62,246
c6	Trade associations	83,712
c7	Social clubs	68,175
c8	Fraternal beneficiary societies	80,193
c9	Voluntary employees' beneficiary associations	13,173
c10	Fraternal orders and associations	23,096
c11	Teachers' retirement funds	15
c12	Benevolent life insurance associations	6,553
c13	Cemetery companies	10,424
c14	Credit unions	4,471
c15	Small mutual insurance companies	1,608
c16	Corporations to finance crop operations	24
c17	Supplemental unemployment benefit trusts	477
c18	Employee-funded pension trusts	1
c19	Veterans' organizations	35,227
c20	Legal services organizations (no longer exempt)	—
c21	Black lung trusts	28
c22	Multiemployer pension plans	—
c23	Veterans' associations founded prior to 1880	2
c24	Certain pension trusts	1
c25	Holding companies for pensions	1,274
c26	High-risk health insurance organizations	9
c27	Workers' compensation reinsurance organizations	10

The nonprofit sector constituted 5.8% of all legal entities in the United States in 1997. The public and private sectors respectively represented 0.3% and 93.9% of all organizations. From 1977 to 1997 the number of 501(c)(3) and (c)(4) organizations grew at an average annual rate of 4.7%, outpacing both the government (0.4%) and business (2.9%) sectors.[16]

After adjusting for inflation, revenue growth of the nonprofit sector between 1977 and 1997 increased by 144%—approximately twice the 81% growth rate of the national economy.[17] When considered as contributors to the gross domestic product, according to the Bureau of Economic Analysis' summary of income and product accounts by sector, as of the close of 2002 the total compensation paid to employees of nonprofit institutions that primarily serve individuals was $500 billion, or 4.7% of the nation's total gross domestic product estimated at $10.6 trillion, as compared to the business

16. Weitzman and Lampkin, *New Nonprofit Almanac*, Table 1.1, Figure 1.2, at 4–5, 12.

17. Lester M. Salamon, "The Resilient Sector: The State of Nonprofit America," in *The State of Nonprofit America*, 31 (Lester M. Salamon ed., Washington, D.C.: Brookings Institution Press, 2002).

sector's GDP of $8.9 trillion (84%) and the public sector's GDP of $1.2 trillion (11.3%).[18]

The nonprofit sector draws revenue from three principal sources: private payments; government funds; and private giving. Private payments are payments that organizations receive for their services, together with membership fees, dues, and sales of products. Private payments furnish the majority of nonprofit income, with slight variations between 46% in 1977 and 47% in 1997 of total receipts. During the same period the greatest increase in income came from government funds, usually in the form of grants and contracts. In 1977 the government accounted for 27% of nonprofit income and in 1997, 33%. Government support of the nonprofit sector increased 195%, accounting for 37% of the sector's growth from 1977 to 1997, while fees and charges increased 145%. Finally, although private giving increased 90% during this period, its relative share of total giving dropped from 27% to 20%.[19]

There also have been important shifts in the composition of private giving since 1977. Although gifts from individuals remained the largest source of private giving, the amount from this source declined from 84% in 1977 to 76% in 2002. In contrast, income from foundations increased at a rate almost double that of all giving. In 1977 foundations furnished just under 6% of all gifts. In 2002, foundations provided 11% of private gifts. Bequests accounted for 8% of giving in 2002, up from 6% in 1977, while corporate giving to charitable organizations was 5% of private contributions in 2002, up from 4% in 1977. Thus the relative decrease in private giving to the nonprofit sector was almost entirely due to a reduction in gifts from individuals.[20]

These statistics indicate that the rise in government spending did not presage a decline in nongovernmental charitable activities. On the contrary, the field of private philanthropy has been constantly increasing, fostered chiefly by government action in the form of exemption from taxation, the granting of tax incentives to donors and investors, and the use of these organizations to carry out government-funded activities under contracts or grants or indirectly through vouchers.

The increase in private payments is particularly important. It occurred during the late 1990s at a time when the pace of government spending slowed, particularly in the field of social welfare. Spurred in part by this change, charities turned to the business arena to compensate for the loss of funding. This was manifested in many ways. Charities increased the scale of related activities that would produce income, exemplified by the growth of museum shops,

18. Table 1.7, "Gross Domestic Product by Sector," National Income and Product Accounts Tables, Bureau of Economic Analysis, available at *www.bea.doc.gov.*

19. Salamon, "The Resilient Sector," Table 1-6, at 31.

20. AAFRC Trust for Philanthropy, *Giving USA 2003.*

the increase in licensing arrangements for intellectual property as well as the "good name" of the organization on affinity credit cards, and the sale or exchange of mailing lists. Hospitals, and then other charities, created taxable subsidiaries to carry on not only taxable unrelated activities, but activities that, if conducted by the parent organizations, would be exempt from income tax. The incentive in many instances was the ability to attract capital not otherwise available. In others, it was a means of providing additional compensation to the charity's officers in the form of higher salaries and the ability to share in profits.

Current Challenges for Specific Components of the Sector

Religious Organizations

The Internal Revenue Service estimated in 1998 that there were approximately 354,000 religious organizations in existence, including churches and other religious entities.[21] However, these organizations are exempt from the registration and filing requirements applicable to other charities, making it impossible to obtain statistics as to the exact size and composition of this component of the nonprofit sector. Furthermore, Congress has placed severe restrictions on the ability of the Service to audit religious organizations, thereby permitting them to operate with less accountability than any other group. The problems that religious entities pose for regulators include determining whether a particular organization is a valid charity rather than a scheme to avoid tax, exemplified by attempts of families to declare themselves churches in the 1980s, by instances of private inurement such as that revealed in the case of Jim and Tammy Faye Bakker in 1989, and more recently by the participation of churches in political campaigns.[22]

Health Care Organizations

Health care organizations account for the largest amount of assets and receive over half of the revenue of the sector, while expending 54.3% of wages and salaries.[23] In addition to hospitals, this universe encompasses nursing homes, health maintenance organizations, drug treatment centers, and home health care agencies. Starting in the 1990s, major fluctuations in size and composition have characterized the field, with for-profit firms moving into

21. Weitzman and Lampkin, *New Nonprofit Almanac*, Table 1.1, at 4–5.
22. See Chapter 2.
23. Weitzman and Lampkin, *New Nonprofit Almanac*, Table 2.8 and Table 4.2, at 46–47, 96–97.

activities, notably operation of hospitals and other health care facilities, previously conducted almost exclusively by nonprofit organizations and for-profit entities changing to nonprofit. The conversion of nonprofit hospitals and health insurance organizations to for-profit status and the proliferation of joint ventures with for-profit entities were the most notable developments during this period. These changes put pressures on the organizations and on regulators to define the parameters of nonprofit activity. State regulators have had to assure that a fair price was received from the sale of charitable assets, that there was no improper self-dealing, and that the proceeds of conversions remained devoted to charitable purposes. For the federal regulators, conversions raised the question of the application of the excess benefit prohibitions under section 4958, and joint ventures posed questions as to the continuing exempt status of the nonprofit organizations entering into such arrangements.

Educational Organizations

This part of the nonprofit sector is comprised of approximately 30,000 organizations providing education for almost 20% of all students in colleges and universities and 10% of students in elementary and high schools, as well as an uncounted number of organizations providing specialized training of all sorts.[24] They rely for support on tuition, endowment income, and contributions, principally from graduates. Government aid is provided primarily in the form of scholarship grants and research contracts. Educational organizations compete with state institutions and, more recently, with for-profit corporations, particularly in the areas of distance learning and continuing education. There have been some conversions but not nearly on the scale as those in the health care field. For state regulators of fiduciary duties, educational organizations do not present unique problems, although because these organizations hold the largest amount of endowment assets, the management and expenditure of these funds require particular scrutiny. At the federal level, the issue of discrimination in admissions has been particularly important, as has been the taxation of certain business activities.

Human and Social Service Organizations

The provision of human and social services by nonprofit organizations since the 1960s has depended in great part on government support and, as a result, the amount and scope of services have fluctuated with changes in govern-

---

24. Donald M. Steward et al., "Education and Training," in *State of Nonprofit America*, 107.

ment policy. Moreover, the nature of government funding changed, particularly with the change in welfare programs from providing direct cash support to recipients to funding programs such as child care and job training. This led in turn to a proliferation of new organizations that are small, often undercapitalized, and lacking a base of private donors to tide them over when public funding declines. As noted by Smith, since government now relies on these new community organizations to provide vital public services, the capacity of these agencies to fulfill their public expectations has become a major policy and management issue. This intensifies pressures on nonprofit governance, with many agencies not equipped to meet the demands.[25]

A review of press reports of wrongdoing by charitable fiduciaries conducted in 2003 produced evidence that some of these new organizations were formed by individuals who intended to and did use them for private benefit, resulting in diversion of substantial sums. In other cases, inexperience and lack of care resulted in losses and failures. In both instances, state and federal regulators played an important role in identifying behavior that was either criminal or involved breaches of fiduciary duty, requiring government intervention to restore funds and impose sanctions on the wrongdoers.[26]

Arts and Cultural Organizations

This group of charities includes music, theatrical performance, visual arts and exhibitions, broadcasting, print media, and what DiMaggio characterized as "presenting organizations," which encompasses universities, churches, museums, and local art agencies that sponsor cultural events on an occasional basis.[27] This area of the nonprofit sector is one in which for-profit entities have traditionally operated parallel to their nonprofit counterparts, often making it difficult for policymakers to differentiate between the two other than on the basis of their form of organization. Otherwise, arts and cultural organizations do not pose unique problems for state regulators.

For the Internal Revenue Service, the rationale for exemption has been that arts and cultural organizations serve an educational function and are subject to the nondistribution constraint in regard to profits. The problems

25. Steven Rathgeb Smith, "Social Services," in *State of Nonprofit America*, 149–186.

26. Marion R. Fremont-Smith and Andras Kosaras, "Wrongdoing by Officers and Directors of Charities: A Survey of Press Reports 1995–2002," 42 *Exempt Organization Tax Review* 25 (2003).

27. Paul DiMaggio, "Nonprofit Organizations in the Production and Distribution of Culture," in *The Nonprofit Sector: A Research Handbook*, 199 (Walter W. Powell ed., New Haven: Yale University Press, 1987).

posed are not different from those presented by any organization reliant on fees for services. It was, however, a challenge by the Service to the exemption of a theater company that tested the propriety of exempt organizations entering into joint ventures with for-profit investors, a challenge that was lost when the Tax Court held in 1980 that exemption would not be lost by virtue of this activity.[28] The case signaled the start of the ever-expanding growth of joint venture arrangements to provide revenue, which occurred in almost all parts of the charitable sector.

Foundations and Other Grantmakers

Historical data as to the growth in the number of foundations and the value of their assets are incomplete. However, directories of known foundations published from time to time beginning in 1915 give some indication of their development, particularly of the larger ones. According to the records of the Foundation Center, as of January 2003 there were 130 foundations then in existence that had been created in 1900 or before.[29] The Treasury Department's 1964 study of foundations reported that at the end of 1962 there were 15,000 foundations with $16.3 billion of total assets.[30] In 1977 there were 22,152 foundations holding assets worth $30.37 billion. As of 2001 the number had grown to 61,180 holding assets of $480 billion and making grants of more than $30.5 billion.[31]

These figures for foundation grants do not include grants from a new configuration of donor-advised grant-making organizations commonly referred to as "gift funds." The first of these funds was created in 1992 when Fidelity Investment Company established the Fidelity Charitable Gift Fund, a publicly supported charity that served as a vehicle for investors in the company's mutual funds to receive immediate, full deductions for their contributions together with the ability over time to "advise" as to which organizations the funds should be disbursed. Community foundations had long ago established donor-advised funds, but they had not attracted much attention. The concept of the Fidelity Charitable Gift, however, proved immensely attractive: in 2001 and 2002 it received $1 billion in contributions, second only to

28. Plumstead Theatre Society, Inc. v. Commissioner, 74 T.C. 1324 (1980), aff'd, 675 F.2d 244 (9th Cir. 1982); see Chapter 5.

29. Telephone interview with Foundation Center staff (January 15, 2003); see also The Foundation Center, *The Foundation Center Yearbook*, ch. 5 (2002).

30. Staff of Treasury Department, *Report on Private Foundations*, 89th Cong., 1st Sess., 82 (Senate Finance Committee, February 2, 1965).

31. The Foundation Center, *The Foundation Center Yearbook* (2002); *fdncenter.org/fc_stats/grantmakerinfo.html*.

the Salvation Army in the amount of private donations received by charities in those years; in 2002 it held $2.4 billion in assets, representing 70% of all assets held by twelve commercial donor-advised funds.[32] The problems faced by regulators from this new configuration arose from the fact that they operate as grant-making foundations yet are not subject to the limitations on private foundations, and from the question of whether the distinction between donor advice and donor direction was blurred in some instances so that the legitimacy of deductions was brought into question.

A resurgence of criticism of foundations in 2003 was reminiscent of the concerns expressed in the 1960s that had resulted in the imposition of severe restrictions on the manner in which they operated and the amounts they were required to expend currently. The criticism was directed toward payments of excessive compensation and benefits to foundation trustees as publicized by state regulators and congressmen; there were also calls to raise the payout rate from the 5% mandated in the Internal Revenue Code on the basis that the current rate had resulted in the growth of foundations at the expense of grantees. As more fully described in Chapter 2, the debate between grantors and grantees was rancorous, and the divisions were unlikely to be easily resolved.

How Extensive Is Wrongdoing in the Sector?

Despite newspaper reports and statements by critics of charities and by government regulators suggesting that there is widespread dereliction of duty by the managers and directors of nonprofit charitable organizations, the extent of wrongdoing has always been difficult to determine. This is due in part to the failure of all but a handful of states to police fiduciary behavior. Their inaction left regulation, by default, to the Internal Revenue Service, which, until recently, had few meaningful tools for correcting misbehavior.

This lack of information as to extent of wrongdoing is also attributable to the nature of the regulatory process, which provides privacy during the investigatory stages and relies in many instances on threat of litigation to force settlement of disputes, the terms of which are rarely disclosed to the public. Finally, the press seldom reports the outcomes of litigation, so the terms of most of the cases that are settled subsequent to the filing of a suit are similarly not made available to the public.

32. Nicole Lewis and Meg Sommerfeld, "Donations to Big Groups Rose 13% in 2000," *Chronicle of Philanthropy*, November 1, 2001, at 35; Elizabeth Greene et al., "The Tide Turns: Donations to Big Charities Lag in Uncertain Economic Climate," *Chronicle of Philanthropy*, October 31, 2002, at 28; Marni D. Larose and Brad Wolverton, "Donor-Advised Funds Experience Drop in Contributions, Survey Finds," *Chronicle of Philanthropy*, May 15, 2003, at 7.

A study of wrongdoing by charitable fiduciaries, conducted by this author and Kosaras that was published in 2003, revealed 152 organizations whose fiduciaries were accused of criminal or civil wrongdoing. The study reviewed newspaper reports of breaches of duty published between 1995 and 2002 by Lexis/Nexis, a service that disseminates articles from 13,111 English-language news sources, including the daily newspapers from all of the major American cities.[33]

Of the 152 incidents, 98 entailed criminal activity, 48 entailed breaches of the duties of loyalty and prudence—self-dealing, failing to carry out the mission of the charity, and negligent management of assets—while six fell into both categories. Included were cases involving Adelphi University, the Allegheny Health system in Pennsylvania, the United Ways of Santa Clara and the National Capital Area (Washington, D.C., and the surrounding suburbs), the Foundation for New Era Philanthropy, the International Olympic Committee and its Utah affiliate, and the Bishop Estate, each of which received nationwide attention.

Acknowledging the limitations of the study, we drew several conclusions about the nature of wrongdoing in the charitable sector and the effectiveness of government regulatory efforts. The small number of reported incidents, 152 occurring over a period of seven years from a universe of an estimated 1.4 million organizations, reinforces an initial impression that there is serious underreporting, and that privacy provisions in federal and state law prevent an untold number of incidents from coming to light.

The fact that the number of criminal cases far exceeded the number of those involving breach of fiduciary duty can be attributed to the preponderance of regulatory tools to correct criminal behavior and the greater funding of state and federal agencies prosecuting crimes.[34] As to the 54 instances in which individuals and organizations were alleged to have breached the fiduciary duties of loyalty and prudence, the smaller total number and the fewer federal cases are confirmation that these duties are defined under state, not federal, laws and that, with a few exceptions, the states have neither the funds nor the personnel to pursue cases of this nature.

Human service agencies were significantly involved in both types of wrongdoing: 56 of the 104 criminal cases and 20 of the 54 breach of duty cases. Of note was the fact that only one church-related organization was involved in a case in which breach of fiduciary duty was alleged, while there were seven churches and church-related organizations among the criminal

33. Fremont-Smith and Kosaras, "Wrongdoing by Officers and Directors of Charities."
34. In the following analysis the six cases that involved both criminal and civil wrongdoing are included in the totals for both categories.

cases. Four foundations were implicated in criminal cases and five in civil cases, casting some doubt on congressional charges made during 2002 and 2003 of widespread abuses on the part of these organizations.[35]

A relatively large number of cases involved charges of misuse of federal and state funds by charities. Of the 104 criminal cases, 32 implicated organizations that received a preponderance of funding from federal and state programs, while 11 of the 54 organizations among the civil cases received funding from government programs.

The survey results also indicated a large number of officers charged with wrongdoing, 132, compared with the 38 directors and trustees implicated. These numbers lend support to the conclusion of Gibelman and Gelman in an earlier study that the root cause of wrongdoing is a failure of governance.[36] However, in regard to the civil cases involving breaches of fiduciary duty, as noted in Chapter 4 the laws in many of the states afford such a high degree of protection to board members that it is very difficult for an attorney general to build a successful case involving breach of duties. On the other hand, the outcomes of the fiduciary duty cases demonstrate the important role state regulation can play in protecting charitable funds, whether by terminating or reorganizing charities or by removing and replacing fiduciaries who have breached their duties.

This study, and others like it, cannot lay to rest allegations of pervasive wrongdoing in the sector. However, it does lend support to the view that wrongdoing is not as widespread as some have claimed, and that draconian remedies are not warranted at this time.

Policy Issues Facing the Nonprofit Sector in the Twenty-First Century

At the start of the twenty-first century, one of the most important issues facing the sector was what Weisbrod was the first to characterize as the growing convergence of the nonprofit and the for-profit sectors.[37] Hansmann first questioned the rationale for tax exemption and other privileges for nonprofits

---

35. Harvey Lipman and Ian Wilhelm, "Pressing Foundations to Give More," *Chronicle of Philanthropy,* May 29, 2003, at 7; Grant Williams, "Making Philanthropy Accountable," *Chronicle of Philanthropy,* June 26, 2003, at 23.

36. Margaret Gibelman and Sheldon R. Gelman, "Very Public Scandals: Nongovernmental Organizations in Trouble," 12 *Voluntas* 49 (2001); Margaret Gibelman and Sheldon R. Gelman, "Should We Have Faith in Faith-Based Social Services?" 13 *Nonprofit Management and Leadership* 49 (2002).

37. Burton A. Weisbrod, *The Voluntary Nonprofit Sector: An Economic Analysis* (Lexington, Mass.: Lexington Books, 1977).

that rely for support solely on receipts for the services they provide, noting the difficulties of differentiating them from their counterparts in the for-profit sector.[38] The issue continued to be debated while the reliance of the sector on fees for services increased markedly. Congress entered the debate in 1986 when it voted to withhold exemption from Blue Cross Blue Shield and other organizations that provided commercial-type insurance.

In 1998 Weisbrod catalogued the increase in commercial activities conducted by nonprofit organizations and pointed to the ambiguity of their effect on pursuit of mission. He concluded that nonprofit commercialization did not inexorably require major reform of the sector, its activities, or its revenue sources. Rather, he suggested directions for change, particularly consideration of the effect of changes in public policy relating to grants, contracts, or tax subsidies that lead to increased commercial activities, arguing for avoidance of sweeping reforms of nonprofit finance mechanisms that do not recognize the diversity of the sector, as well as close regulation of conversions.[39]

Hill and Mancino also raised concern about the convergence of the tax-exempt and the taxable sectors, citing as examples the conversion of hospitals from nonprofit to for-profit status, the increased number of for-profit schools offering education for all ages, and of joint ventures with private investors, as well as widespread use of royalty agreements between exempt organizations and taxable entities involving many activities, particularly those relating to intellectual property.[40]

There is no definite information about the extent of this new "business" activity carried on by tax-exempt charities. Some evidence can be gleaned from the IRS statistics on sources of revenue for the sector. Steuerle in 2000 reported on a survey of a panel of 6,000 nonprofit organizations that filed Form 990 in 1993 and 1998, in which the number of taxable subsidiaries grew by more than 50%, from 1,449 in 1993 to 2,244 in 1998, while the

38. Henry Hansmann, "Economic Theories of Nonprofit Organization," in *The Nonprofit Sector: A Research Handbook*, 27–42; see also Henry Hansmann, *The Ownership of Enterprise* (Cambridge, Mass.: Belknap Press, 1996); Henry Hansmann, "The Role of Nonprofit Enterprise," 89 *Yale Law Journal* 835 (1980).

39. Burton A. Weisbrod, *To Profit or Not to Profit: The Commercial Transformation of the Nonprofit Sector*, 287–305 (Cambridge: Cambridge University Press, 1998); see also Burton A. Weisbrod, *The Nonprofit Economy* (Cambridge, Mass.: Harvard University Press, 1988); Burton A. Weisbrod, *The Voluntary Nonprofit Sector: An Economic Analysis* (Lexington, Mass.: Lexington Books, 1977).

40. Frances R. Hill and Douglas M. Mancino, *Taxation of Exempt Organizations*, ¶1.01 (New York: Warren, Gorham & Lamont, 2002); Frances R. Hill, "Targeting Exemption for Charitable Efficiency: Designing a Nondiversion Constraint," 56 *Southern Methodist University Law Review* 675 (2003).

number of organizations with one or more taxable subsidiaries increased 35%. He reported that the level of unrelated taxable income has not changed very much, with about a third of organizations reporting net taxable losses, but attributed this to the way in which organizations classify income and expenses in order to keep taxable income small.[41] In 1999 charities reported $4 billion in unrelated business income, a drop of $125 million from that reported in 1998. After deductions, the income subject to tax was $380 million, paid by 4,340 charities. This was not a significant change from the data used by Steuerle in his study.[42]

Steuerle also described another panel of 130,000 organizations that filed Form 990 returns in 1993 and 1998, in which 66% reported an increase in the amount of commercial income, with the increase most prevalent among higher education organizations and hospitals where commercial income rose in three out of four of these types of organizations. He acknowledged that this growth may reflect a rapidly expanding health sector that generates most of its revenue from hospital fees for service.[43]

In addition, there was evidence in the late 1990s of an increase in the creation of taxable subsidiaries of nonprofit organizations to conduct activities related to the organization's charitable purposes, activities that, if carried on directly by the organization, would not be subject to income tax. The areas in which exempt organizations were conducting these activities as taxable enterprises included low-income and other rental housing, distance learning and executive education, biotechnology, business start-ups, information systems, and sales operations conducted by commercial organizations for exempt charities, particularly on the Internet. Steuerle noted that if these types of activities increased significantly, they could call into question the tax exemption of certain segments of the nonprofit world, and possibly that of the entire sector. One possibility he posed would be that entity-based exemption might be transformed into a system that imposed different tax regimes on activities depending on their level of social value.[44]

Salamon characterized these changes as a move to the market, pointing to them as examples of the resilience of the nonprofit sector, in the face of an increasingly competitive environment. Called upon to make fundamental changes in the way they operated, nonprofit organizations were able to do so. What was involved, Salamon noted, was "not simply the importation of

41. Eugene Steuerle, "When Nonprofits Conduct Exempt Activities as Taxable Enterprises," in *Urban Institute-Hauser Center Emerging Issues in Philanthropy Brief* (November 2000).

42. Margaret Riley, "Unrelated Business Income Tax Returns, 1999," in *IRS Statistics of Income Bulletin* (Spring 2003).

43. Steuerle, "When Nonprofits Conduct Exempt Activities."

44. Id.

'business methods' into nonprofit organizations, although that is sometimes how it is portrayed."[45] Rather, he observed that businesses themselves had incorporated management approaches associated with nonprofit work, particularly the emphasis on organizational mission, the ethos of service to clients, and the need to imbue staff with a sense of purpose beyond the maximization of profit. In short, the changes involved movement by both sectors toward each other.

Examples of the resilience of the nonprofit sector also noted by Salamon were its growth in the latter part of the twentieth century, its successful pursuit of public funds, the revolution in fund-raising techniques, its success in meeting political competition, and the emergence of an effective organizational infrastructure. Noting that all of these changes posed great risk for the continued viability of the sector, he pointed to the need for a revised rationale for its existence, increased public understanding of those qualities in the sector that make it worth preserving, and adjustments in public policy designed to assure that the sector's commitments to community benefit and charitable purpose are reinforced.[46]

Government supports the nonprofit sector in two basic ways. One is by assuring its viability by granting privileges to its component organizations and their donors, as well as direct financial support in the form of grants and contracts. The second is by assuring its integrity by enacting laws prescribing the behavior of the organizations that comprise the sector and the individuals who manage them, and granting powers to government agencies to enforce these laws. Changes in the nonprofit sector demand continuous assessment of the effectiveness of government regulation. The chapters that follow represent an attempt to provide the groundwork for making those assessments.

45. Salamon, "The Resilient Sector," 6; see also Dennis R. Young and Lester M. Salamon, "Commercialization, Social Ventures, and For-Profit Competition," in *State of Nonprofit America*, 423–446.

46. Salamon, "The Resilient Sector," 45, 48–52; see also Steuerle, "When Nonprofits Conduct Exempt Activities"; Hill and Mancino, *Taxation of Exempt Organizations*, ¶1.01.

2

A Brief History of the
Law of Charities

This chapter provides an overview of the origins of the laws that govern the creation, administration, and regulation of charities, tracing their development from earliest times to the present. Succeeding chapters contain detailed descriptions of these laws and in certain instances additional historical background necessary for an understanding of their source and impact.

Introduction

There is no clear-cut body of American law that can be called "the law of charity." Relevant law is to be found in the first instance in the law of trusts, but it is also contained in the laws relating to corporations, state and federal tax laws, the law of decedents' estates, and the entire field of property law. It was under the law of uses, the forerunner of the present law of trusts, however, that the legal concept of charity originated, and a study of government regulation of charities must start with this branch of the law.

Theoretically, the acquisition of legal status as a charity is not necessary in order to perform philanthropic works. However, organized charity has grown and developed because society has granted privileges not accorded to private enterprises to those institutions meeting certain requirements. The best known of these benefits is, of course, exemption from taxation; but equally important from an historical standpoint is the relation of certain rules of law limiting the right to hold private property. Thus charitable entities are granted existence in perpetuity, the right to accumulate income, and the privilege of having their purposes revised if they become obsolete. The legal requirements for classification under law as a charity have developed through the centuries and are still in flux.

Evolution of Charities in Early Society

The emergence of charities as legal entities was closely tied to religious philosophy and the development of the concepts of wills, testamentary dispositions, and corporate entities. Even before the right to make wills and testaments developed, the practice of leaving property in perpetuity to other than paternal heirs was encouraged for religious purposes in both Egypt and Chaldea.[1] The Greeks first developed a concept of a "living legal heir" to whom property could be given in perpetuity during a person's life with the consent of his natural heirs. In the first century B.C. the Roman law modified this concept to declare that associations were at one and the same time "sentient reasonable beings" and "immutable undying persons," and by the first century A.D. they were permitted to receive bequests.[2]

From A.D. 96 to A.D. 180, these associations, or foundations as they were called, were greatly encouraged throughout the Roman Empire. Cities and towns were accorded the right to accept funds by bequest, and gradually the motive behind these donations shifted from honoring the gods to helping the underprivileged. The funds of these foundations were confiscated during the reigns of the thirty "barracks emperors" from A.D. 192 to A.D. 324. Constantine recognized the need for the state to assist the causes formerly aided by the foundations. By edict he reiterated the legal rights of the Christian Church as an association whose property could be neither alienated by any individual nor used within the Church for purposes other than those designated by the donor. Thereafter the Church was utilized as the medium for the distribution of all public funds for the underprivileged, and all individuals were encouraged by the state to make donations to the Church for charitable purposes.[3] These gifts, called *piae causae,* were administered by the bishop of the church where the donor was domiciled. As large amounts of wealth were amassed by the local churches, abuses in the management and disbursement of funds became increasingly prevalent.

An attempt was made to rectify the situation at the time of the revision of the Roman law in 550 and the enactment of the *Corpus Juris Civilis* (the Code, Digest, and Statutes of Justinian). The aim was to place the Church foundations on legal bases more appropriate to the changing society of the times. Ecclesiastical foundations were declared legal persons of an ecclesiastical nature whose personality derived from the Church but had a legal capacity of their own.[4] A comprehensive list of safeguards was enacted to protect the foundations and keep them socially useful. The bishops were given appointive and supervisory power over administration of the funds, and were

---

1. Ernest W. Hollis, "Evolution of the Philanthropic Foundation," 20 *Educational Record* 575, 578 (1939).

2. Id. at 576.

3. P. W. Duff, "The Charitable Foundations of Byzantium," in *Cambridge Legal Essays* 83, 84 (Percy H. Winfield et al. eds., Cambridge: W. Heffer and Sons, 1926).

4. Hollis, "Evolution of the Philanthropic Foundation," 579.

directed to keep "a watchful eye over them to remove those who were negligent and in such case to appoint other trustees who had the true fear of God."[5] The bishops, in turn, were responsible to their superiors, and the actions of the entire hierarchy were reviewable by the citizens, who were empowered to make a judicial complaint if a testator's intention was not fulfilled.[6] Provision was made for the selection of a similar cause if the original purpose of a gift should lose its social utility,[7] and rules were laid down concerning the investment and management of funds, including the leasing and mortgaging of property. A gift was to revert to a donor or his heirs if not made effective within a certain period, and the Church was prohibited from permanently alienating any property given it.

The managers were also accorded the right to act as guardians, or to appoint and supervise guardians, for all legally incompetent persons under their care. These prerogatives gave great power to the Church throughout the entire period of the Middle Ages.[8]

Islamic Foundations

In the seventh century Mohammed recommended the establishment of what is the Islamic equivalent of the charitable foundation or trust.[9] The *vaqf*, as this institution is called, developed independently of Roman and Anglo-Saxon equivalents, but the similarities between the two are striking. A *vaqf* may be established for any purpose recognized as laudable by Islam and the religion of the founder. It is characterized by perpetuity, but accumulation of income is forbidden. The founder may appoint himself the first *mutawali*, or trustee, and assign to himself a remuneration, commonly 10% of income, which cannot be above that which he appoints for subsequent trustees.

The three recognized categories of usages are a man's duty to his own family, the maintenance of God's worship according to the tenets of Islam, and charities in the English sense, including works of public utility. The first usage is, of course, contrary to the Western concept of a charitable trust and reflects the influence of Islamic philosophy and culture.

The primary difference between the *vaqf* and the charitable trust or foundation, however, is that the *vaqf* has remained under religious sanction; no

5. Comment, "Supervision of Charitable Trusts," 21 *University of Chicago Law Review* 118, 119 (1953).

6. Id.

7. Hollis, "Evolution of the Philanthropic Foundation," 580.

8. Id. at 581.

9. F. Emerson Andrews, "On the Nature of the *Vaqf*," *Foundation News*, September 1964, at 8–9.

secular law relating to its position in society similar to that in the West has developed. The number of *vaqfs* in existence today is reported to be considerable in the Islamic countries of the Middle East, and some are said to have great wealth.[10]

Charities in England

Roman concepts of charities were carried to England and can be found in the laws that developed there, although they received the distinctive imprint of the Anglo-Saxon legal system that developed during the period of the Reformation. The Saxon kings followed the Roman practice and gave to the local bishops the duty of supervision of charitable gifts as well as the religious institutions that administered them.

The word "corporation" came into use in Saxon times to describe religious institutions and monastic orders as well as religious persons. The parson of a parish or an order of friars was regarded as a corporation by prescription and was therefore a separate legal entity that could exist in perpetuity. Present-day corporate concepts have their roots in these early views.

A system of ecclesiastical courts developed in England following the Norman Conquest in 1066. Starting from their special jurisdiction in respect to pious causes, these courts gradually developed general jurisdiction over all testamentary matters. During this period, under the protection of the ecclesiastic courts, charitable gifts acquired three distinct characteristics that still survive: (1) the privilege of indefinite existence; (2) the privilege of validity even if the gift is in general terms, so long as its objective is exclusively charitable; and (3) the privilege of obtaining fresh objects if those laid down by the founder become incapable of execution, known today as the doctrine of cy pres.

The power of the Church and the ecclesiastical courts was challenged after 1066 in a struggle that lasted four hundred years. Although the conflict was political and economic, its repercussions in the law resulted in the eventual extinction of the jurisdiction of the ecclesiastical courts and in the curtailment of the charity holdings of the Church. Henry II (1154–1189) decreed that the bishops and abbots held their possessions "of the king and were answerable to the king's justice." Thus the Crown was recognized in law as guardian of the revenues of all vacant bishoprics and patron of all char-

---

10. Further information on the legal aspects of the *vaqf* is to be found in Seymour Vesey-Fitzgerald, *Muhammadan Law* (Cambridge: Oxford University Press, 1931); see also H. A. R. Gibb and Harold Bowen, *Islamic Society and the West*, vol. 1, pts. 1 and 2 (London: Oxford University Press, 1950); Murat Çizakça, *A History of Philanthropic Foundations: The Islamic World from the Seventh Century to the Present* (Istanbul: Boğaziçi University Press, 2000).

ity funds. The Church corporations held land by a form of tenure called *frankalmoign* under which they rendered no service to any superior lord. By the time of Henry VIII these holdings amounted to an estimated one-third to as much as one-half of the entire wealth of England.[11]

In an attempt to curtail this general power of the Church, statutes were enacted, starting with Magna Charta (1215), that limited gifts of land to charitable corporations. These statutes were called acts of mortmain, since their purpose was to prevent land from coming to a "dead hand." Section 32 of Magna Charta forbade freemen to alienate "so much of his land as will render the residue insufficient to secure the service due to his Lord."[12] Section 36 forbade a "dodge" whereby after tenants gave land to a religious house and thereby discharged it from service, it was deeded back to themselves. The Statute de Viris Religioses of 1279[13] attempted a general prohibition against the holding of land in mortmain and removed the right of the overlord to grant licenses for such alienation. These statutes did not prevent the transfer; they denied the right of the corporation to hold the land if it was claimed by the overlord of the donor. If the overlord did not exercise this right within one year, his overlord might take it within the next half year, and so on, the ultimate right devolving to the Crown.

Development of Trusts

Conveyances to religious corporations were not the sole method of making charitable gifts; during this same period (following the Norman invasion) a new form of conveyance known as the use developed. The origin of this method of conveyance, which was the precursor of the modern trust, is not clear. Maitland suggests that it first appeared in the thirteenth century when lands were conveyed to individuals who agreed to hold them for the use of the Franciscan friars, whose order did not allow the holding of property, either individually or communally.[14]

At this time uses were not recognized by the courts and therefore were not enforceable, so that the practice was not considered to violate the vows of poverty. Following the enactment of the early mortmain statutes, the device of conveyances to an individual for the use of a religious corporation became common. In fact, it was so common that in 1391 Parliament enacted a new

11. William A. Orton, "Endowments and Foundations," in *Encyclopaedia of the Social Sciences*, vol. 5, at 531 (New York: The Macmillan Co., 1931).

12. Amherst D. Tyssen, *The Law of Charitable Bequests*, 2 (London: Sweet and Maxwell, 1888).

13. Stat. 7 Edw. 1 (1279).

14. Frederic William Maitland, *Equity*, 25 (Cambridge: The University Press, 2d ed., 1936).

mortmain statute that specifically prohibited the practice of granting the use of lands to religious corporations. Scott notes that "the cestui que use (or beneficiary) in these cases had no enforceable interest in the property conveyed, but the danger that the feoffee (or title holder) would carry out his moral obligation was so great, and the result of his doing so was regarded as so subversive of public policy, that Parliament felt compelled to interpose."[15]

The period from 1200 to 1400 has been characterized as the first in the development of uses and trusts.[16] The second historical period in the development of uses, and thus of charitable trusts, began early in the fifteenth century when the Courts of Chancery in England began to enforce the conveyance to uses.

Scott has said that the present-day trust would never have developed had it not been for the more or less accidental circumstance that in England in the fifteenth century, and for four hundred years afterward, there were separate courts of law and equity.[17] The term "equity" is used in law to describe a system of jurisdiction as well as the principles and standards of that system. The standards are based on the concepts of justice and fairness, and their development in the English legal system, notes Maitland, sprang from the "old idea that when ordinary justice fails there is a reserve of extra-ordinary justice which the king can exercise . . . In civil cases men made their way to the king's Chancellor begging him in piteous terms to intervene 'for the love of God and in the way of charity.' It is not of any defect in the material law that they complain; but somehow or other they cannot get justice."[18]

Today in the United States there are no longer separate courts of equity; but certain forms of remedies, which developed in the Courts of Chancery, are referred to as "equitable" and are interpreted and enforced according to the doctrines of equity based on precedents that originally developed in those courts. Equity jurisdiction provides such remedies as rescinding contracts, canceling or reforming instruments, requiring performance of contracts, remedying misrepresentation, concealment, or mistake, preventing illegal actions by means of injunction, and, in the field of trust law, defining rights of parties and the means of enforcing them.

The powers of the courts that are called equitable were first exercised by the Common Law Courts. In the early fourteenth century, however, these courts became more rigid and their equity powers disappeared. When injus-

15. Austin W. Scott and William F. Fratcher, *The Law of Trusts*, §1.3 (Boston: Little, Brown, 4th ed., 1987).

16. Id., §1.2.

17. Id., §1.

18. Frederic William Maitland, *Collected Papers*, vol. 3, at 334–335 (H. A. L. Fisher ed., Cambridge: The University Press, 1911).

tices arose from the application of the strict rules of law by the Common Law Courts, resort was taken to Parliament or the King's Council for relief.[19] Gradually, these petitions were referred to the Chancellor, who was usually an ecclesiastic, and in time the Court of Chancery began to exercise equity jurisdiction, becoming an established court of the realm by 1422. This court based its decisions on ethical principles, not legal precedents. Its procedure was more flexible than that of the Common Law Courts; and its freedom from fixed forms of action and its power to enforce a defendant's duties, not merely to uphold a plaintiff's rights, made it particularly suited to assuming jurisdiction over uses.

By the mid-fifteenth century, the Chancellors were interfering to enforce on the trustee his duties and to protect the interest of the beneficiaries. Uses were assignable and descendable. They were employed not only to avoid the restrictions on ecclesiastic corporations, but also to circumvent creditors, to defeat certain claims of the feudal lords, and to prevent the confiscation of property, a consequence of conviction for high treason. In time, Parliament acted to prevent most of these evasions, and the primary purpose for the use soon came to be to secure the effect of devises of land.[20]

The English feudal laws did not permit testamentary disposition of land; they required that land descend according to the laws of primogeniture. The great landowners, however, wanting to make broader testamentary disposi-tions, employed the use to circumvent the legal restriction through the de-vice of enfeoffing to the use of such persons as a man might designate by will. It has been said that at the time of the reign of Henry V (1413–1422), the greater part of the land in England was held in use.[21] It was, of course, during this period that the system of feudal tenure was disintegrating. Its demise was hastened by the confusion with respect to title resulting from the widespread employment of the use.

An attempt to stem the tide and correct the abuses and obscurities arising from uncontrolled employment of uses was made by Henry VIII through the passage of the Statute of Uses in 1535.[22] This act did not outlaw the use en-tirely, but merely declared that the legal title as well as the beneficial interest passed to the *cestui que use* (the person who had the use). The intent was that the use should no longer be merely an equitable interest protected by Chan-cery, but should be an ordinary legal interest subject to the jurisdiction of the law courts. The act, therefore, removed the possibility of devising land, a re-sult highly unsatisfying to the majority of landowners in Parliament who suc-

19. H. V. Holdsworth, "The Early History of Equity," 13 *Michigan Law Review* 293 (1915).
20. Maitland, "Trust and Corporation," in *Collected Papers*, 335.
21. Scott and Fratcher, *Law of Trusts*, §1.3.
22. Stat. 27 Hen. 8, ch. 10 (1535).

ceeded in changing it five years later with passage of the Statute of Wills.[23] This statute authorized devises of certain important categories of land, although it expressly excepted devises to bodies politic or corporate.

The Statute of Uses was of great importance in the development of English law, particularly the law of conveyancing. It cleared away the obscurities of titles that had arisen during the previous centuries; and, by forcing the enactment of the Statute of Wills, it eased the transition period that marked the end of feudalism. It did not, however, mean the extinguishment of the use or trust as a device for the disposition of property. Both the common law judges and the Chancellors acted to continue the possibility of creating beneficial interests separate from legal title. The Statute of Uses was strictly construed. Active, as opposed to passive, trusts, where the trustees had duties to perform beyond merely holding title, continued to be recognized in equity, as were trusts for a period of years and a use that was placed upon a prior use. Thus the main lines of development of the modern law of trusts were clearly laid out, and the groundwork prepared for the development of the modern law of charitable trusts.

Restrictions on Charitable Gifts

The period that marked the development of the trust was coterminous with the period of struggle between the Crown and the Church; it was also characterized by an increasing interest in secular charitable activities.[24] As early as 1391, the mortmain statute, which prohibited grants of the use of land to religious corporations, contained a restriction on the holding of land without license of the Crown by all civil corporations and municipalities.[25] Such a restriction was included because the effect of granting lands to guilds, fraternities, and municipal corporations "had come to be regarded as equally detrimental to the rights of the overlord."[26]

The years 1300 to 1500 saw the creation of the great nonmonastic charitable associations such as the Oxford and Cambridge colleges for the promotion of education and the establishment of hospitals for the maintenance of the sick, indigent, or infirm.[27] Many charitable gifts were administered by the guilds. Charitable uses and trusts, constituted for the administration of chari-

23. Stat. 32 Hen. 8, ch. 1 (1540).

24. For a detailed, scholarly study of this subject, see W. K. Jordan, *Philanthropy in England, 1480–1660* (New York: Russell Sage Foundation, 1959).

25. Stat. 15 Rich. 2, ch. 5 (1391).

26. George W. Keeton, *The Modern Law of Charities*, 171 (London: Sir Isaac Pitman and Sons, 1962).

27. John P. Davis, *Corporations*, ch. 7 (New York: Capricorn, 1961).

table gifts, appeared with increasing frequency from the reign of Henry VI (1422–1460) onward.

The Courts of Chancery assumed jurisdiction over these charitable gifts, but in so doing they preserved the privileges that had been conferred by the ecclesiastical courts in Norman times, thereby offering the encouragement of the state to charitable benefactions.[28] Records of the Court of Chancery for this period are meager, but it is clear that the Chancellor was issuing subpoenas for the enforcement of charitable uses from the early part of the fifteenth century. Suits were usually brought by inhabitants of a town or parish in behalf of themselves and the other inhabitants or parishioners. In some cases they were in the name of the poor of a town or parish, and in a few cases they were brought by the Attorney General.[29] Reference to the "Attorney General" of England appears in 1461, initially appointed by the King only for specific matters but by the fifteenth century an Attorney General served for the Crown on a regular basis.[30] Relief was granted by means of orders of the court compelling trustees to restore funds taken improperly, or by injunctions forbidding trustees to commit acts not authorized by the terms of the agreement to uses.

By the middle of the fourteenth century many of the monastic institutions that had been the chief dispensers of charity were beginning to decay. The long and inexorable process of deterioration of monasticism was far advanced well before the advent of the Reformation. This was true throughout western Europe, but perhaps most dramatically so in England where, almost a generation prior to the Dissolution, the monastic framework was in decline, contributions were drying up, and many foundations were so reduced in numbers that the spiritual offices required by the monastic rule could not be maintained.[31]

The formal dissolution of the monasteries from 1541 to 1560 added to the increase of poverty in fifteenth- and sixteenth-century England, which was caused primarily by economic upheavals, the growth of towns, changes in agricultural methods, and the extension of commerce. In 1414 an important statute was passed that attempted to correct and repair the decay and disappearance of a large number of endowed foundations for the relief of the poor.[32] The ecclesiastical authorities were ordered to inquire into the manner of founding of such institutions and to make reparations. Jordan observes,

28. Keeton, *Modern Law of Charities,* 3.

29. Scott and Fratcher, *Law of Trusts,* §348.2; Jordan, *Philanthropy in England,* 119.

30. "Attorney General," in *The New Encyclopedia Britannia* (15th ed., 1988); see also Attorney General's Review of the Year (2001/2002), available at *www.lslo.gov.uk.*

31. Jordan, *Philanthropy in England,* 58.

32. Stat. 2 Hen. 5, ch. 3 (1414).

"There is, however, little evidence that the statute was given full effect or that the calamitous decay of medieval charitable institutions, already far advanced, was significantly retarded."[33]

Restraints were imposed on the creation of trusts for religious purposes during the reign of Henry VIII by the passage in 1531–1532 of a statute that reiterated the mortmain doctrine denying corporations the right to hold land without license and prohibited the creation of trusts for religious uses of more than twenty years.[34] Jordan notes: "From this day forward, indeed, the whole weight of law as well as of policy was exerted to mould the charities of England to secular ends and to assist donors in creating the great charitable institutions which were so profoundly to alter the structure of the English society."[35]

The far-reaching social changes of the sixteenth century had a profound and direct impact on the law of charities. The Reformation and the social and economic upheavals of the century had important consequences not only for the relation between charitable trusts and public welfare services but also for the law of charity. Unemployment and vagrancy were prevalent, the guild system of apprenticeship was breaking down, and the welfare and educational services, provided by the Church before the Reformation, were interrupted. Something had to be found to take their place. The refounding of grammar schools under new deeds, the Elizabethan Poor Law, and the Statute of Charitable Uses of 1601 "to redress the Misemployment of Lands Goods and Stocks of Money heretofore given to Charitable Uses" were the answer. The latter statute was passed at practically the same time as the Statute for Relief of the Poor and formed part of a concerted plan for dealing with the economic and social problems of the day.[36]

The Statute of Charitable Uses

The Statute of Charitable Uses, also referred to as the Statute of Elizabeth, enacted in 1601,[37] has been described as "the starting point of the modern law of charities."[38] There can be no doubt that it profoundly influenced development of the concept of charitable purposes in England and the United

33. Jordan, *Philanthropy in England,* 114–115.
34. Stat. 23 Hen. 8, ch. 10 (1532).
35. Jordan, *Philanthropy in England,* 115.
36. *Report of the Committee on the Law and Practice Relating to Charitable Trusts,* Cmnd. 8710, at 18 (London: Her Majesty's Stationery Office, 1952). This report, prepared under the chairmanship of Lord Nathan, and commonly referred to as the "Nathan Report," contained the results of a study made by a parliamentary committee of charitable trusts in England and its recommendations for new legislation.
37. Stat. 43 Eliz. 1, ch. 4 (1601).
38. Keeton, *Modern Law of Charities,* 10.

States, and that it stimulated the rapid growth of charitable trusts in England immediately following its enactment.

The purpose of the statute was to create a code for the encouragement and organization of private almsgiving. Accordingly, there were two specific objects. The first was to provide a method for correcting the abuses in the administration of charitable gifts that had been multiplying in the previous period. The second was to encourage further gifts to charity "by listing a great variety of specific charitable purposes, and thus removing the uncertainties that had arisen with the Reformation."[39]

The preamble enumerated the purposes for which charitable gifts had heretofore been made:

> some for relief of aged, impotent and poor people, some for maintenance of sick and maimed soldiers and mariners, schools of learning, free schools, and scholars in universities, some for repair of bridges, ports, havens, causeways, churches, seabanks and highways, some for education and preferment of orphans, some for or towards relief, stock or maintenance for houses of correction, some for marriages of poor maids, some for supportation, aid and help of young tradesmen, handicraftsmen and persons decayed, and others for relief or redemption of prisoners or captives, and for aid or ease of any poor inhabitants concerning payments of fifteens, setting out of soldiers and other taxes.[40]

Henry Allen Moe[41] has pointed out the similarity between this list of purposes and the fourteenth-century poem *The Vision of Piers the Plowman* of William Langland, wherein anxious (and rich) merchants are counseled by Truth to obtain remission of sins and a happy death by using their fortunes:

> And therewith repair hospitals,
> help sick people,
> mend bad roads,
> build up bridges that had been broken down,
> help maidens to marry or to make them nuns,
> find food for prisoners and poor people,
> put scholars to school or to some other craft,
> help religious orders, and
> ameliorate rents or taxes.[42]

39. *Report of the Committee on the Law and Practice Relating to Charitable Trusts*, 18.

40. Stat. 43 Eliz. 1, ch. 4 (1601).

41. Henry Allen Moe in a statement to the Select (Cox) Committee to Investigate Tax-Exempt Foundations, quoted in Jordan, *Philanthropy in England*, 112.

42. William Langland, *The Vision of Piers the Plowman*, 114 (W. W. Skeat et al. trans., London: Chatto and Windus, 1931).

Historians believe that this similarity reflects the fact that the definitions of charitable purposes that were well established by 1601 were those known in the fourteenth century, whether or not there was a direct borrowing from the poem,[43] and support for this view is to be found in the reports of cases on charitable trusts in Chancery during the fifteenth century.[44]

A major omission in the Statute of 1601 that reflected the temper of the times was that of gifts for religion other than the repair of churches. The mention of education is also scanty, leading to the conclusion that the statute was not an attempt at a definition of charity, but an enumeration of some of the charitable purposes that had become the subject of benefactions. There is no evidence that the courts in the seventeenth century treated the list as comprehensive, and only in later centuries did the device of regarding the preamble to the statute as a definition of charitable purposes occur. The importance of the "definition" lay not in the exact list, but in the fact that it implied the necessity of some form of public benefit.[45]

The body of the statute provided for the appointment of ad hoc commissioners to inquire into allegations of negligence, maladministration, and diversion of charitable funds by reason of which property was not being employed according to the intent of the donors. The commissioners were to be appointed by the Chancellor, and were to include the bishop and chancellor of the diocese and other persons of good and sound behavior. They were given the power to "enquire by oath of twelve lawful men," as well as by other means. They could, accordingly, impanel juries, summon and hear witnesses, and make reviews of the current status of all known charitable funds in a given region. They were empowered to make decrees that would be valid until undone or altered by the Chancellor. Persons aggrieved by these decrees were given a right of appeal to the Chancellor, who might make such decrees as "should be thought to stand in equity and good conscience according to the true intent and meaning of the donors and founders."[46]

At first the commissions were created at frequent intervals. During the first year of the act, forty-five commissions were established, and before 1700 more than 1,000 investigations were made; but during the eighteenth century they were rarely formed, and by 1803 the practice had died out.[47] Nevertheless, the main object of the statute was accomplished. The growth of charitable trusts in the period immediately following enactment of the statute has been described as "a torrent." Jordan states:

43. Keeton, *Modern Law of Charities*, 4.
44. Scott and Fratcher, *Law of Trusts*, §1.
45. *Report of the Committee on the Law and Practice Relating to Charitable Trusts*, 18.
46. Scott and Fratcher, *Law of Trusts*, §348.2.
47. *Report of the Committee on the Law and Practice Relating to Charitable Trusts*, 18.

The consequence [of the work of the commissioners] was that charitable funds were on the whole administered with quite astonishing probity and skill and that a tradition of the highest fidelity in the discharge of duty was quickly established. This fact in itself lent powerful encouragement to substantial men considering benefactions and accounts in no small part for the huge sums vested in charitable trusts during the last two generations of our period.[48]

Two other statutes of the Elizabethan era contributed to the reframing and molding of the law of charities to the purposes of the state. In 1572 an act was passed to assist benefactors who wished to found hospitals and almshouses; it provided that a gift in a will should be "good and available in law despite the misnaming, misreciting or not true naming or reciting" of the intended foundation.[49] In 1597 an "Act for erecting of hospitals or abiding and working houses for the poor" gave power to donors to give or bequeath lands in fee simple by simply enrolling a deed in Chancery without having to secure a special royal license or act of Parliament to achieve incorporation, so long as the yearly value of the endowment was at least £10.[50] The preamble to this statute includes a list of charitable purposes identical with that in the Statute of Charitable Uses of 1601.

The enactment of these statutes has been described as part of a concerted plan for dealing with the economic and social problems of the day. The philosophy behind the legislation was thought to be that of a partnership between private charity and the state "in which the state filled in gaps left by charity rather than charity filling in gaps left by the state; and this has continued down to the changed situation of our own day."[51]

In the two centuries following the enactment of the Statute of Charitable Uses of 1601 the number of charities being founded rapidly increased. The Statute was interpreted by the courts as rendering valid in equity devises in trust or otherwise to charitable corporations, a practice that had previously been prohibited by the Statute of Wills.[52] Then in 1695–1696 the Statute of Mortmain empowered the Crown to grant licenses to schools, colleges, and other bodies politic or incorporated for "other good and public uses," per-

---

48. Jordan, *Philanthropy in England*, 117.

49. Stat. 14 Eliz. 1, ch. 11 (1572).

50. Stat. 39 Eliz. 1, ch. 5 (1597).

51. *Report of the Committee on the Law and Practice Relating to Charitable Trusts*, 8; see also Keeton, *Modern Law of Charities*, 11; Lester M. Salamon, "The Resilient Sector: The State of Nonprofit America," in *The State of Nonprofit America*, 11 (Lester M. Salamon ed., Washington, D.C.: Brookings Institution Press, 2002).

52. Scott and Fratcher, *Law of Trusts*, §362.2.

mitting them to hold land free from liability of forfeiture to either the Crown or the mesne lord.[53]

The Role of the Attorney General and the Charity Commission

With the decline of the use of commissions provided for in the Statute of Charitable Uses, it fell to the Attorney General, representing the Crown as *parens patriae* with a prerogative right, to protect all charitable trusts. Procedure before the nineteenth century was slow and costly, and rarely were abuses called to the attention of the Attorney General or the courts.[54] Individuals were unwilling to apprise the Attorney General of malpractices because they were liable to pay the costs if he instituted proceedings and was defeated.

A limited improvement was undertaken with the enactment of Gilbert's Act in 1786, which required that returns of trusts for the benefit of the poor be made under pain of penalty to the clerk of Parliament by the ministers or church wardens of the parish where the trust was to operate.[55] Some returns were made, but compliance with the act was sparse. A similar fate befell the Charitable Donations Registration Act of 1812,[56] which provided that all charitable trusts should be registered with the clerk of the peace of the county, city, or town wherein the beneficiaries were situated. However, notes Keeton, this act "was very generally ignored."[57] Another act of 1812 also attempted to simplify the procedure for redress against maladministration by way of information initiated by the Attorney General.[58] The act was limited to actions against trustees at the suit of beneficiaries, and did not provide a notable improvement over the existing method.

The most important development in the nineteenth century was the creation by Parliament in 1819 of a Charities Commission, known originally as the Brougham Commission, to investigate and record all charitable trusts in England and Wales. The impetus for this move came from the efforts of Lord Brougham and his associates to improve public education, and from the findings of his Committee of Inquiry on the Education of the Lower Orders, which had been created in 1816, that many trusts for educational purposes were being badly misused or neglected. By the act of 1819[59] the Commis-

---

53. Stat. 7 & 8 Will. 3, ch. 37 (1695–1696); see also Keeton, *Modern Law of Charities*, 171.
54. *Report of the Committee on the Law and Practice Relating to Charitable Trusts*, 19.
55. Return of Charitable Donations Act, Stat. 26 Geo. 3, ch. 58 (1786).
56. Stat. 52 Geo. 3, ch. 102 (1812).
57. Keeton, *Modern Law of Charities*, 13.
58. Charities Procedure Act, Stat. 52 Geo. 3, ch. 101 (1812).
59. Stat. 59 Geo. 3, ch. 91 (1819).

sioners were authorized to give evidence to the Attorney General, who would commence proceedings for correction of abuses. Charitable trustees were empowered to apply to court for amendment of their statutes or regulations where they gave insufficient powers. The Brougham Commission and its successors conducted their inquiries for nineteen years, and the sixty volumes of their reports revealed many cases of malversation of charitable funds.

Brougham's initial bill providing for the creation of the Charities Commission had met with some opposition in Parliament, and the government succeeded in removing from the scope of the Commission's inquiry the universities and principal public schools. Even with this exclusion, however, much valuable work was accomplished. The level of administration of charitable trusts improved,[60] and the information in the reports persuaded Parliament of the need for some regular form of supervision.

In 1835 a Select Committee was constituted to examine the reports of the Commission and make recommendations for further legislation. At this time the Commission had completed its work in only twenty-eight counties. Keeton states: "The Committee made two major recommendations: (1) the establishment of administrative control over charitable trusts by an independent body, without, however, removing the final jurisdiction of the courts; (2) the institution of legal changes to permit the broadening of charitable trusts that were too narrow in operation and, in some instances, the transfer of funds to objects more socially appropriate."[61] This second recommendation was in effect a request for extension of the cy pres doctrine, which had been narrowly employed by the courts. Nonetheless, the "stubborn, influential, and strongly entrenched resistance of some of the most important charities to any form of control"[62] resulted in the failure of Parliament to enact any corrective legislation for eighteen years, although thirteen bills were introduced during those years.

The Charitable Trusts Act finally became law in 1853.[63] It provided for the creation of a permanent Board of Charity Commissioners, which was given authority to examine into all charities in England and Wales as to their objects and management and the value of their property, and to require all trustees to furnish accounts and statements.[64] The Commissioners were not subordinate to any government department. Two were normally full-time professional and salaried appointments, and the third was usually a member of Parliament

---

60. Keeton, *Modern Law of Charities*, 15; *Report of the Committee on the Law and Practice Relating to Charitable Trusts*, 19.

61. Keeton, *Modern Law of Charities*, 17.

62. Id. at 18.

63. Stat. 16 & 17 Vict., ch. 137 (1853).

64. Scott and Fratcher, *Law of Trusts*, §391.

who answered parliamentary questions and introduced bills for the Commissioners. The act also provided for the creation of two new institutions, the Office of Trustee of Charitable Lands and the Office of Trustee of Charitable Funds. In the latter, title to charitable funds could be vested without cost to the trustees, thereby obviating the problems and expense arising from a change in trustees.

In 1860 the powers of the Commissioners were broadened to allow them to apply the cy pres doctrine for the administration of any charity with an annual income of less than £50.[65] The exercise of these quasi-judicial powers was subject to review on appeal by the Court of Chancery, which interpreted them narrowly to apply only to the machinery for carrying out a testator's intent, not to reforming the originally stated charitable purpose. For example, in *In re Weir Hospital*,[66] the court rejected a scheme that the Commissioners had approved for the joint administration of the funds of two inadequately endowed medical colleges in London. In 1899 the jurisdiction of the Board of Charity Commissioners over educational endowments was transferred to the Board of Education.[67]

The Board of Charity Commissioners operated under the powers of the acts of 1853 and 1860 for a century. The Commissioners exercised few active supervisory powers over trustees and functioned chiefly to receive complaints on abuses of administration, correcting them where possible under their own powers and referring others to the Attorney General for action. The requirement for filing accounts was largely ignored.

The mortmain provisions were changed during this period, primarily by the Mortmain and Charitable Uses Acts of 1888 and 1891, which repealed most of the earlier legislation.[68] The act of 1888 prohibited acquisition of land by a corporation through mortmain except under license from the Crown or under statute; trusts of land for charitable uses were required to be made by deed to take effect at once, and had to be made at least twelve months before the death of the donor. The act of 1891 permitted devises of land in trust to a charitable corporation provided the land was sold within one year from the testator's death, unless the court or the Charity Commissioners had extended the period or had authorized retention when the land was to be used for the charity's purposes.

---

65. Charitable Trusts Act, Stat. 23 & 24 Vict., ch. 136 (1860).
66. [1910] 2 Ch. 124.
67. Board of Education Act, Stat. 62 & 63 Vict., ch. 33 (1899).
68. Stat. 51 & 52 Vict., ch. 42 (1888); Stat. 54 & 55 Vict., ch. 73 (1891).

Regulation of Charities after 1950

The laws governing charities and the regulatory scheme remained essentially unchanged until 1950 when Parliament established a Committee on the Law and Practice relating to Charitable Trusts. Its report, commonly called the Nathan Report, was presented by the Prime Minister to Parliament in December 1952.[69] It contained an excellent summary of the history of charity law and the activities of the Commissioners. The Nathan Committee made extensive recommendations for legislative change, most of which were incorporated in an act of 1960, which replaced the Charities Acts of 1853 to 1939.[70]

In addition to repealing most of the prior legislation on charities, the act abolished certain technicalities with regard to transfers of property, repealed all previous mortmain legislation, and extended the doctrine of cy pres. It provided for a new administrative system that enlarged the supervisory powers of the Charity Commissioners and created a new relationship between them and Parliament designed to facilitate the introduction of new legislation. It also required the registration of all charities other than those in three categories: small charities, defined as those with incomes of less than £10,000; excepted charities, which includes scouts and guides, armed forces groups, and some religious charities that are registered with their own umbrella or support group; and exempt charities, which includes universities, housing associations, and charitable industrial and provident societies, all of which receive significant government funding and are thus considered to be adequately supervised by the funding agency.[71]

In 1992 Parliament passed legislation based on recommendations of a special commission that were embodied in a 1987 report to Parliament. The Woodfield Report[72] had recommended expanding the number of charities required to register with the Charity Commission, as well as requiring audited financial reports from certain charities and the filing of annual reports with the Commission. These recommendations were adopted as part of the Charities Act of 1992, together with provisions facilitating the ability of small charities to merge or terminate.[73]

---

69. *Report of the Committee on the Law and Practice Relating to Charitable Trusts*, 19.

70. Stat. 8 & 9 Eliz. 2, ch. 58 (1960).

71. Id.

72. Sir Philip Woodfield et al., *Efficiency Scrutiny of the Supervision of Charities: Report of the Home Secretary and the Economic Secretary to the Treasury* (London: Her Majesty's Stationery Office, 1987).

73. Charities Act, 1992, ch. 41.

In September 2002 the Strategy Unit of the Cabinet Office, convened at the request of the Prime Minister to review the law and regulatory structure governing the charitable sector, issued a report containing sixty-one recommendations designed to modernize the law, encourage growth in the sector, improve performance, and strengthen government regulation.[74] Among the recommendations dealing with regulation were a number designed to strengthen the powers of the Charity Commission. These included extending registration requirements to include the large number of excepted charities while raising the threshold for registration to exempt a larger number of small charities, and requiring annual reporting from registered charities. The Strategy Unit suggested that the Commission, working with the sector, should conduct and publish performance reviews of different subsectors, develop information services to meet the needs of donors and users of charity services, and regulate solicitation of charitable funds. The report also recommended that the number of Charity Commissioners be enlarged to reflect a wider range of stakeholders and that, in order to more clearly indicate its purpose, the Charity Commission be renamed the Charity Regulation Authority.[75] The report had the strong support of the Prime Minister, and it was expected that its recommendations would be adopted after a period of consultation.

Developments in Substantive Charity Law after 1601

The description of the law of charities in England since the enactment of the Statute of Charitable Uses has centered chiefly on legislative enactments and the regulatory scheme. The legal doctrines that shaped and defined the nature of charitable trusts and corporations had been laid down and accepted prior to the passage of that act: the right to existence in perpetuity; the doctrine that a charitable trust will not fail for want of a trustee, because of uncertainty as to the precise object or the mode of its application, or as the result of an imperfect trust provision; the legal meaning of charity; and the cy pres doctrine. These concepts all became part of the established law in the early days of the Court of Chancery, much of it being adopted from doctrines developed in the ecclesiastical courts.

After the sixteenth century the Chancery Court became more and more similar to the Common Law Courts. The rule developed that "equity follows the law," and decisions came to be based on precedent. In the 1870s the

74. Strategy Unit Report, Cabinet Office, *Private Action, Public Benefit: A Review of Charities and the Wider Not-for-Profit Sector* (September 2002), available at *www.strategy-unit.gov.uk*.
75. Id. at 93–97.

entire English legal system was reformed. The old distinctions between Common Law Courts and Equity Courts were abolished, and all courts received the right, where necessary, to use both kinds of law. In a legal system that is based on precedent and "judge-made law," as is the Anglo-American, it is inevitable and desirable that certain concepts be modified over a period of time as the cases on a specific subject multiply. In the field of charity law in England, the development was toward a narrowing and restriction of some of the early concepts, particularly the definition of charity and the doctrine of cy pres.

The Nathan Committee in its 1952 report criticized the rigidity of the courts and the Charity Commissioners in ruling on the validity of charitable purposes and recommended that the legal definition be restated. This suggestion, however, was rejected by Parliament, although the Charities Act of 1960 repealed the preamble to the Statute of Elizabeth of 1601 that had still been in force, thereby leaving the definition of charity entirely to the courts. This decision was severely criticized by Keeton, who characterized court intervention in this area as "probably the worst exhibition of the operation of the technique of judicial precedent which can be found in the law reports."[76] Questioning whether the new act would inspire the judiciary to introduce coherence into this branch of the law, he concluded, "In deciding what is, and what is not a charity, the courts are really making decisions upon questions of public policy which, in an age of rapid social change, are of steadily increasing importance. It is, therefore, inevitable that decisions upon what is, and what is not a charity should be frequent, and should provoke criticism."[77]

The Prime Minister's 2002 report reiterated the criticism in the 1952 report of charity regulation and recommended that the traditional four "heads" of the definition of charity be broadened to ten to more accurately reflect the range of organizations that were or should be charitable. The four purposes were those recited in the *Pemsel* case of 1891,[78] namely relief of poverty (more specifically including the aged, impotent, or poor), advancement of education, advancement of religion, and other purposes beneficial to the community. The new categories finally were to include social and community advancement, the advancement of culture, arts, and heritage, the advancement of amateur sport, the promotion of human rights, conflict resolution and reconciliation, and the advancement of environmental protection and improvement. In addition, relief of poverty would be broadened to include "prevention." As to the catchall "other purposes beneficial to the

76. Keeton, *Modern Law of Charities*, 165.
77. Id.
78. Commissioners for Special Purposes of Income Tax v. Pemsel, 1891 App. Cas. 531.

community," the report stressed that the principle of public benefit should remain an essential requirement of charitable status.[79] Each of the newly defined purposes were ones that the Charity Commission had been slow to recognize; in contrast, they constitute valid charitable purposes under federal and state law in the United States.

The 2002 report addressed several problem areas that were the subject of debate in the United States. One was whether organizations that charge fees for the provision of services could be considered charities. The report concluded that charging fees that are affordable to large sections of the population would not affect the public character of a charity, but that it must provide access for those who would be excluded because of the fees, giving as an example an independent school that charged high fees but made provision for those who could not meet the payments. Noting that there was no ongoing review of charities after registration, the report recommended that the Charity Commission undertake periodic review of existing organizations to assure that they remained in compliance with the public character test.[80] Two other recommendations that dealt with issues then being debated in the United States were (1) that charities should be allowed to conduct substantial unrelated business activities, termed "trading," without having to conduct them through a subsidiary; and (2) that charities should be permitted to engage in political activities as a means of fulfilling their charitable purpose.[81]

It was noted earlier that the doctrine of cy pres originated with the Romans and was subsequently adopted by the English ecclesiastical courts. The term itself is Norman-French and means either "near this" *(ici près)* or "as near as possible" *(aussi-près comme possible)* to the declared object. A 1959 study suggested that the doctrine originally was given a liberal interpretation in accord with the first definition, but that through the years it came to have the second meaning.[82]

As developed by the English courts, the doctrine of cy pres was used where a clear charitable intention was expressed, but the mode or purpose specified by the donor was or became impossible to carry out. During the nineteenth century the courts refused to apply the doctrine unless clear impossibility was shown. This requirement was relaxed for educational trusts by the Endowed Schools Act of 1869,[83] which empowered an independent commission (and later the Charity Commissioners), subject to court review, to adopt new

---

79. Strategy Unit Report, *Private Action, Public Benefit*, 36–43.

80. Id. at 41–42.

81. Id. at 43–44.

82. L. A. Sheridan and V. T. Delany, *The Cy Pres Doctrine*, 2 (London: Sweet and Maxwell, 1959).

83. Stat. 32 & 33 Vict., ch. 56 (1869).

schemes in such manner as might render educational endowments most conducive to the advancement of the education of boys and girls. These powers were transferred in 1899 to the Board of Education, and they are now vested in the Ministry of Education.

An even broader power was granted to the Secretary of State to frame schemes for the government and management of educational endowments in Scotland.[84] However, the power of the Charity Commissioners to frame schemes for other than educational trusts, initially authorized by the Charitable Trusts Act of 1860, was very narrowly interpreted by the courts, and the requirements of impossibility or impracticality were strictly construed.[85] Requests for extension of the doctrine are to be found in legal literature, particularly in the Reports of the Charity Commissioners from 1857 to 1894, but Parliament took no action until 1960.

There were also certain situations where it was held that the Crown, not the courts, had the power to make dispositions cy pres. This right, called the prerogative power, was based on the supervisory power of the Crown, as *parens patriae,* over all charities. It was thought to have originated from the sovereign's power to ensure justice to all his subjects. In time it came to be administered by the Lord Chamberlain acting in his administrative capacity.[86] The prerogative cy pres power was applied in three types of cases: (1) where there was a gift directly "to charity" with no further specific purpose; (2) where there was an outright gift for a specified object of charity involving a charitable institution that failed because the institution did not exist at the death of the testator, or subsequently ceased to operate, and a general intention in favor of charity was evidenced; and (3) where the object of the gift was illegal or was void as contrary to public policy (usually a gift for a forbidden religion). The property subject to the power of prerogative cy pres was held by the court pending a direction "by the sign manual" of the King, made at the suggestion of the Attorney General.[87] The doctrine of prerogative cy pres, though still in existence in England today, has been narrowed in its application and is only rarely cited as the basis of court action.[88]

The Nathan Committee devoted considerable attention to the need to liberalize the cy pres doctrine and extend its application, recommendations that were embodied in the Charities Act of 1960. In 1987 a new commission to

---

84. Stat. 45 & 46 Vict., ch. 59 (1882), now Stat. 9 & 10 Geo. 6, ch. 72, §§115–134 (1946).

85. Keeton, *Modern Law of Charities,* chs. 9, 10.

86. Sheridan and Delany, *Cy Pres Doctrine,* 65.

87. Tyssen, *Law of Charitable Bequests,* 211–214; see also George G. Bogert and George T. Bogert, *The Law of Trusts and Trustees,* §432 (St. Paul: West Group, 3d ed., 1977); Scott and Fratcher, *Law of Trusts,* §399.

88. Sheridan and Delany, *Cy Pres Doctrine,* 65.

review charity law concluded that, "although the cy pres doctrine might need to be redefined in statute in a rather looser way, or relaxations introduced specifically for small charities," there was no immediate need for legislation. Rather, the Charity Commission was urged to review its precedent systems and the guidance given to its staff with the aim of promoting a "flexible and imaginative approach, consistent with due regard for the donor's wishes."[89] However, the 1992 Charities Act in sections 43 and 44 did adopt a proposal to permit application of cy pres for small trusts.[90]

Charitable Corporations

The earliest forerunners of the modern business corporation were the ecclesiastic and charitable organizations and the municipalities, guilds, and universities of early England. Since the Reformation, the trust has been the predominant English form of organization for charitable activities and remains so today. Part of the explanation lies in the nature of the development of the corporation in England. Although these early charitable organizations had some attributes in common with the present-day corporation, not until the middle of the sixteenth century did the important attributes of modern corporations begin to develop. The first large business corporations in England were the foreign trading companies formed during the period of exploration and colonization in the sixteenth and seventeenth centuries. Created by royal charter or special act of Parliament, these companies were granted the privilege of exploring and trading with certain lands across the seas. The East India Company, chartered in 1600, and the Hudson Bay Company, chartered in 1670, are examples.

In the eighteenth century the privileges of incorporation, usually with monopoly rights, were granted by special acts of Parliament to certain groups to protect or promote the use of improved processes or inventions or to encourage the development of the natural resources of localities.[91] Stock companies became a popular form of organization for business enterprises, and with them came the concept of transferable shares of stock.

The rapid rise in economic activity during the nineteenth century caused a demand for legislation permitting the formation of companies offering limited liability to their shareholders. Starting in 1855, Parliament passed a series of acts that permitted general incorporation for certain purposes. Thus there was a transition from the concept of specific government sanction and the

89. *Charities: A Framework for the Future,* Cmnd. 694, at 37 (White Paper prepared by the Secretary of State for the Home Department) (London: Her Majesty's Stationery Office, 1989).

90. Charities Act, 1992, ch. 41.

91. Davis, *Corporations,* 260.

grant of a privilege to incorporate for purposes of community benefit to the concept of a wide grant of power to individuals freely to form associations for their private benefit. This change paralleled the growth of individualism as a political concept and the decline in the powers of the sovereign.

The business motive completely overshadowed the place of charitable enterprises in this development. The Companies Act of 1867 did permit incorporation for nonpecuniary ends. However, since the state was the source of power to create corporations whereas the creator of a charitable trust was afforded great freedom, the trust form continued to be preferred. Moreover, incorporation did not have the advantage of relieving managers of charitable funds of the supervision of the Charity Commissioners or the courts.[92] Unlike the law of charities as it developed in the United States, the English law did not make distinctions as to the nature of ownership of property between the corporation and the trust. Tyssen, discussing the nature of a devise to a charitable corporation, describes a situation wherein land was devised to a corporation without any expression of trust, "but as the corporation existed solely for charitable purposes, this was held equivalent to a devise upon a charitable trust."[93]

The Charities Act of 1960 contains the following definitions:

- "charity" means any institution, corporate or not, which is established for charitable purposes and is subject to the control of the High Court in the exercise of the court's jurisdiction with respect to charities.
- "charity trustees" means the persons having the general control and management of the administration of a charity.
- "trusts," in relation to a charity, means the provisions establishing it as a charity and regulating its purposes and administration, whether those provisions take effect by way of trust or not, and in relation to other institutions, has a corresponding meaning.[94]

Accordingly, it can be said that there has always been a single "law of charities" in England. Historical accident, however, has led to a different situation in this country.

Unlike the situation in the United States, incorporation of charities was rare. There was no specific legislation governing their creation; rather, the rare incorporated charity was formed under the rules for business corpora-

---

92. Ernst Freund, "Legal Aspects of Philanthropy," in *Intelligent Philanthropy*, 156, 175 (Ellsworth Fans et al. eds., Chicago: University of Chicago Press, 1930).

93. Incorporate Society v. Richards, 1 Dr. War. 258, cited in Tyssen, *Law of Charitable Bequests*, 10.

94. Stat. 8 & 9 Eliz. 2, ch. 58, §§45(1), 46(1) (1960).

tions, which often were not appropriate. In addition, corporate charities were subject to two regulatory regimes, that of the Charity Commission and of the Companies House, a situation characterized by one commentator as an "unwelcome regulatory burden."[95] The possibility of enacting legislation authorizing a charity-specific form of incorporation was considered by a Company Law Review Steering Group. Its final report, issued in June 2001, also recommended legislation authorizing a new corporate form.[96] The proposal was subsequently considered by an Advisory Group established by the Charity Commissioners, which recommended adoption of legislation authorizing a new form, to be called a Charitable Incorporated Organisation (CIO), that would differ from the Company Law proposal only in minor respects.[97] The September 2002 Strategy Unit Report to the Cabinet endorsed the Charity Commission's proposal to permit creation of Charitable Incorporated Organisations as an alternative form to a Company Limited by Guarantee. Incorporation as a CIO would limit members' liability but would contain an explicit statement of trustees' duty of care consistent with that applicable to trustees of charitable trusts.[98]

On July 16, 2003, the Government published its response to the Strategy Unit review, reflecting comments in 1,100 responses from the voluntary sector and consultations with other parties.[99] All but one of the Strategy Unit proposals were endorsed, although the Government recommended three modifications: adding two additional charitable purposes to the original list of ten, "promoting animal welfare" and "providing social housing," as well as adding "science" to the category that had originally joined together advancement of culture, arts, and heritage. The Government also recommended that the threshold for registration with the Charity Commission be set at £5,000, not £10,000, but that charities that did not meet the threshold could register voluntarily. Rejected was the Strategy Unit's proposal that charities be allowed to trade directly, rather than as under existing law through a dedicated trading subsidiary. The Government expressed concern that the proposed change would "offend the principle of a level playing field with private sector businesses."[100]

95. Debra Morris, "A Step Closer to a New Legal Structure for Charities," 34 *Exempt Organization Tax Review* 235 (2001).

96. The Company Law Review Steering Group, *Modern Company Law: For a Competitive Economy,* 86–88 (June 2001).

97. Advisory Group to the Charity Commission, *Charitable Incorporated Organisation* (Spring 2001), available at *www.charity-commission.gov.uk/enhancingcharities/incorporg.asp.*

98. Strategy Unit Report, *Private Action, Public Benefit,* 57–58.

99. The Home Office, *Charities and Not-for-Profits: A Modern Legal Framework* (July 2003), available at *www.homeoffice.gov.uk/docs2/charitiesnotforprofits.pdf.*

100. Id., §3.34.

Despite its strong endorsement of reform, the Government provided no timetable for implementing the recommendations. However, prior to the release of the Government response, the Charity Commission on June 23, 2003, issued a public statement of its role and approach to regulating charities, articulating seven principles governing the Commission's work: accountability, independence, proportionality, fairness, consistency, diversity and equality, and transparency.[101] The stated purpose of the principles was to modernize regulation within the current legal framework, while "looking forward to the further opportunities to develop the sector provided by the forthcoming Charities Bill."[102]

Charities in the United States

In colonial America an atmosphere favorable to the creation of charitable trusts and institutions was fostered by the encouragement of philanthropic activities under English law, the teaching of charity by the churches, and the needs of the settlers. Miller notes:

> The colonists did not debate the question of public versus private responsibility . . . Public and private philanthropy were so completely intertwined as to become almost indistinguishable. The law itself reflected a pragmatic approach to the solving of social problems through philanthropy. Colonial assemblies went out of their way to remove obstacles in the way of charities. The courts, valuing social betterment above legal technicalities, asserted a permissive charity doctrine that supported donors' benevolent intentions, even when the formulation of their plans was clearly imperfect.[103]

Following the Revolution, there was a rise in nationalistic sentiment and antagonism to all things British. The effect on the law of the new country was the adoption in state constitutions or statutes of provisions aimed at retaining the framework of English jurisprudence "cleansed of what [legislators] considered to be its most undesirable elements," particularly all vestiges of royal power and prerogative.[104] These enactments generally provided for the adoption of all English statutes made in aid of or to supply defects of the common

---

101. Charity Commission, *The Charity Commission and Regulation* (June 2003), available at *www.charity-commission.gov.uk/tcc/pdfs/regstance.pdf*.

102. Charity Commission, "Charity Commission Re-defines Its Role as Regulator," PR/40/ 03 (June 23, 2003), available at *www.charity-commission.gov.uk*.

103. Howard S. Miller, *The Legal Foundations of American Philanthropy, 1776–1844*, xi (Madison: State Historical Society of Wisconsin, 1961).

104. Id.

law enacted prior to 1607 (the time of the first settlement in Virginia), and not inconsistent with the philosophy of the new democracy.

Development of the Law of Charitable Trusts

The applicability of these provisions to charitable trusts was not questioned in the majority of states, which consistently upheld their validity, although the doctrine of prerogative cy pres was rejected. As new states entered the union, they followed the lead of the early states, primarily Massachusetts, whose constitution had provided for adoption of the common law and English statutes,[105] or Connecticut, which had enacted legislation in 1702 specifically upholding charitable trusts.[106]

Charitable trusts were exempted from local taxation, and the courts adopted an attitude of liberality to the legal meaning of charity. Incorporation by special act of the legislature was the usual method of establishing schools, hospitals, religious groups, and other operating charitable institutions. Fear of the rise in power of the Church led to passage of restrictions on the holding of property by charitable, particularly religious, corporations, and in some states the legislature was on occasion reluctant to grant charters to these groups.[107] A policy of encouraging charity predominated, however, and as incorporation for business purposes increased, so did incorporation for charitable ventures of all types.

The development of charitable uses did not parallel that of England, however, for eight states rejected the doctrine of charitable trusts. In these states the only method of devoting money to charitable purposes was through gifts either to established charitable corporations or to trustees who were directed to form a corporation within the period of the Rule Against Perpetuities.[108]

The first difficulty occurred in Virginia, where all English statutes and acts of Parliament were specifically repealed in 1792. The problem arose from an erroneous determination by the Supreme Court of the United States that the law of charitable trusts had its origins in, and was based upon, the Statute of Charitable Uses of 1601, and that with the repeal of that statute by Virginia in 1792, any trust without beneficiaries who were definitely named was invalid. This opinion, delivered by Chief Justice Marshall in the case of *Trustees*

---

105. Mass. Const. ch. 6, §6 (1780).

106. Conn. Gen. Stat. §45a-514, §47-2; see also Peter Dobkin Hall, *Inventing the Nonprofit Sector,* 13–25 (Baltimore: John Hopkins University Press, 1992).

107. Miller, *Legal Foundations of American Philanthropy,* 19.

108. For a detailed discussion of this history, see Thomas E. Blackwell, "The Charitable Corporation and the Charitable Trust," 24 *Washington University Law Quarterly* 1 (1938); Edith L. Fisch, *The Cy Près Doctrine in the United States* (New York: Matthew Bender, 1950).

of *Philadelphia Baptist Association v. Hart's Executors*,[109] was based on false and incomplete historical evidence and on the dicta in certain English cases that led to the impression that charitable trusts for indefinite beneficiaries did not exist in England prior to the enactment of the Statute of Elizabeth.[110] Scott characterized the case as based on "historical error," adding the following comment: "It is astonishing how frequently courts rely on the words of other courts not merely as indications of the law but as proof of facts. The words that fall from judges are seldom a sound foundation for historical research."[111]

The *Hart* case was followed in Virginia, Maryland, the District of Columbia, and West Virginia for nearly one hundred years; and it influenced the development of charitable trusts in New York, Michigan, Wisconsin, and Minnesota. It had this effect despite the fact that twenty-five years later the Supreme Court reversed itself in *Vidal v. Girard's Executors*,[112] holding that charitable trusts should be afforded recognition in the United States regardless of statutes abolishing English law.

In the interval between the decision in the *Hart* case and the *Girard* case, the Supreme Court ruling had aroused great interest, both in the United States and England, and stimulated further research into the early history of equity jurisdiction. The result was the definite establishment of the fact that charitable trusts had been recognized by the English courts prior to 1601. In the *Girard* case, the Supreme Court was asked to determine the validity of a charitable trust created in the will of Stephen Girard for the establishment of a school or college for orphan children in Philadelphia. The decision would be based on the law of Pennsylvania, where the Statute of Elizabeth had been previously declared to be of no force. The Court declared that the lack of effect of the Statute of Elizabeth in Pennsylvania was immaterial, since equity had inherent jurisdiction independent of the Statute of Elizabeth or of the prerogative power to sustain, because of their charitable purposes, trusts that would otherwise be invalid. Warren noted, "Few cases ever more keenly interested the general public or brought it more closely in contact with the court."[113] However, the interest was not sufficient to persuade

---

109. 17 U.S. (4 Wheat.) 1 (1819).

110. Scott and Fratcher, *Law of Trusts*, §348.3.

111. Id.

112. 43 U.S. (2 How.) 127 (1844).

113. Charles Warren, *The Supreme Court in United States History*, vol. 2, at 398 (Boston: Little, Brown, 1926), quoted in Miller, *Legal Foundations of American Philanthropy*, 38, who added that this interest in the case was due more to the fame of counsel than to the points of law at stake. These noted counsel were Daniel Webster for the heirs of Stephen Girard, and Horace Binney representing the city of Philadelphia.

either the courts or the legislatures in Virginia, Maryland, the District of Columbia, or West Virginia, which persisted in holding to the rule of the *Hart* case.

In New York charitable trusts were declared invalid because of judicial interpretation of the codification of the law of trusts made there originally in 1789.[114] This first code contained no English statutes, thereby repealing by implication the Statute of Elizabeth. A second codification of the laws enacted in 1829 abolished all uses and trusts of land except those specifically authorized or modified therein.[115] It contained no mention of charitable trusts, leaving the state with no clear policy as to their validity. The Court of Chancery held in 1844 that the act of 1829 implied no ban on charitable trusts.[116] The decision was severely criticized six years later, however, by the New York Supreme Court, which held that no trusts could be recognized unless specifically authorized by statute.[117] In 1853 in the case of *Williams v. Williams*[118] a charitable trust of personal property was upheld on the grounds that jurisdiction over charities existed independently of statute, but this case was not followed. Zollmann described it as "the last ray of light preceding a total eclipse."[119]

The attitude of the New York courts for the next fifty years was summarized in a decision of 1866,[120] which stated that the intention of the legislature to abolish all charitable trusts was evidenced by the repeal of the Statute of Elizabeth and the omission of charitable purposes from the revision of 1829. In the opinion of the court, it was better policy to limit charitable gifts to those charitable corporations that were regulated by statute than to allow "every private citizen the right to create a perpetuity for such purposes as to him seem good, and to endow it with more than corporate powers and more than corporate immunity."[121]

In 1891 the failure of a legacy of almost $4 million left by Governor Samuel J. Tilden to found a free library in New York City[122] led to a public reaction against the ban on charitable trusts that culminated in the passage of the "Tilden Act" in 1893.[123] This act declared that charitable trusts should there-

114. Jones and Varrick Laws of New York, 1789.

115. Rev. Stat. of New York, 1829, at 727.

116. Shotwell v. Mott, 2 Sand. Ch. 46 (N.Y. 1844).

117. Yates v. Yates, 9 Barb. Ch. 324 (N.Y. 1850).

118. 8 N.Y. 525 (1853).

119. Carl F. G. Zollmann, *American Law of Charities*, 31 (Milwaukee: Bruce Publishing Co., 1924).

120. Bascom v. Albertson, 34 N.Y. 584 (1866).

121. Id. at 615; see also Scott and Fratcher, *Law of Trusts*, §348.3.

122. Tilden v. Green, 28 N.E. 880 (N.Y. 1891).

123. Acts of 1893, ch. 701, codified at N.Y. Real Prop. Law, §113; N.Y. Pers. Prop. Law, §12.

after be valid. Subsequent amendments restored to New York the entire doctrine of charitable trusts, which received thereafter favorable construction in the courts.[124] However, the New York code of 1828 had been copied in Michigan, Wisconsin, and Minnesota, and not until the early years of the twentieth century did the validity of charitable trusts come to be generally recognized in those states.[125]

Today charitable trusts are upheld in all the states, either by court decision or legislative enactment, but the early decisions affected the entire development of the law of charities in this country, particularly the legal status of property held by charitable corporations and the acceptance of the cy pres doctrine. It is likely that the early decision rejecting the law of charitable trusts has also served to enhance a bias against the trust form that is based on a misunderstanding of the rules governing trustees and the liabilities to which they may be subject. It is common to describe trust law as strict and the liabilities of trustees as exceedingly harsh, particularly when compared with the powers of corporate directors and the more lenient standards to which they are held. This is certainly the case if one is looking at trust law as it existed at the start of the twentieth century.

Trust law changed drastically, however, particularly after the adoption of Restatement (Second) of the Law of Trusts (1959). Grantors were given the power to exculpate trustees, to relax the rules against self-dealing, to broaden investment powers, to permit delegation of powers, and, in many jurisdictions, to relieve trustees from intrusive court supervision. In fact, charitable trusts that are created inter vivos have fewer reporting requirements than their corporate counterparts and are not subject to the rules governing corporate procedures.[126] It is unfortunate, therefore, that the perceptions have persisted and, in a number of instances, have found their way into the case law. Karst commented on this situation as follows:

> A distinction which gives such great weight to organizational form rather than operational need carries a substantial burden of justification, and as yet that burden has not been met . . . [T]here is no good reason for making different rules for the managers of two large foundations simply because one is a corporation and the other a trust. The law should recognize that the charitable trust and the charitable corporation have more in common with each other than each has with its private counterpart. The important differences among charities relate not to

124. Zollmann, *American Law of Charities*, 35.

125. Peter Dobkin Hall, "A Historical Overview of the Private Nonprofit Sector," in *The Nonprofit Sector: A Research Handbook,* 3 (Walter W. Powell ed., New Haven: Yale University Press, 1987).

126. See Chapters 3 and 4 for detailed descriptions of these laws.

their form but to their function. In the area of fiduciary duties, a law of charities is needed.[127]

More than forty years later, that law has not emerged. However, the American Law Institute in 2002 approved a project to draft a Principles of the Law of Nonprofit Organizations, naming Professors Evelyn Brody and Alan Feld as the Reporters and appointing a committee of advisors. Clearly, reconciliation of the laws of trusts and corporations as applied to charities is an important issue for the project to address.

Charitable Purposes

American case law dealing with the definition of "charitable purposes" has evolved over time to reflect changed perceptions of "public benefit." State courts have been far more liberal than their English counterparts, so there has been far less controversy and little impetus to broaden the definition by means of statutes. Thus Restatement (Third) of the Law of Trusts, which was adopted in May 2001, defined charitable purposes to include the four "heads" of the English definition of charity, relating to poverty, education, religion, and other purposes beneficial to the community,[128] while adding promotion of health and governmental or municipal purposes.[129]

Some commentators have questioned the importance of the state law definition of charity, noting the overriding consideration of tax exemption and the consequent deference to the definition of charitable purposes in the Internal Revenue Code. State tax law also becomes of abiding importance, most particularly in regard to property tax exemptions.[130] Where the definitions matter is in determining the validity of gifts and bequests in regard to charitable corporations as well as charitable trusts and, probably of greatest importance, in connection with application of the doctrines of cy pres and deviation.

An issue of wide general import, particularly in the years after World War II, has been the validity of charities established for the benefit of a limited class defined by race, ethnicity, gender, or religion and the consequent question of whether they would have to be modified on the grounds that they violated public policy. Under trust law principles, restrictions will be upheld unless they involve invidious discrimination. Under this doctrine the courts have in recent years uniformly declared that exclusions based on race or na-

127. Kenneth L. Karst, "The Efficiency of the Charitable Dollar: An Unfulfilled State Responsibility," 73 *Harvard Law Review* 433, 436 (1960).
128. Commissioners for Special Purposes of Income Tax v. Pemsel, 1891 App. Cas. 531.
129. Restatement (Third) of the Law of Trusts, §28.
130. See Chapter 3.

tional origin are invalid, with some cases taking a similar position in regard to gender. Although the support of efforts to promote affirmative action have been considered charitable in some instances, they came under attack in the late 1990s, with the matter unresolved as of the end of 2003.[131]

There were two other far-reaching developments in the substantive laws affecting charities. The first was the adoption of the Uniform Management of Institutional Funds Act (UMIFA) in 1972 and its subsequent widespread enactment by the states. The second was the adoption by the ALI of the Modern Prudent Investor Rule as part of the Restatement (Third) of the Law of Trusts in 1990 and the subsequent incorporation of its principles by the Commissioners on Uniform Laws in the Uniform Prudent Investor Act in 1994. UMIFA modified trust law rules applicable to the investment and administration of endowment funds of charitable corporations by permitting application of a total return approach to investing, broadening the ability of "institutions" to release restrictions on the application of endowment funds, and relaxing of the liability of fiduciaries in making investments. The Restatement's Modern Prudent Investor Rule reflected similar acceptance of modern investment theory and practice, and relaxed limits on the ability of trustees to delegate their powers. These changes are described in detail in Chapter 4.

By the end of the twentieth century the cy pres doctrine and its companion doctrine of deviation had been adopted by statute, case law, or dictum in forty-nine states. The trend in the case law has been to broaden the circumstances in which cy pres can be applied, as well as to move away from strict adherence to the original intent of the donor in the framing of schemes. Similarly, the doctrine of deviation, which applies in instances in which the original purposes are still attainable, but the method for carrying them out has been impracticable, is being relied on in cases in which the court is reluctant to adopt the cy pres doctrine. In fact, there has been evidence of confusion between the two, with the courts describing some applications as cy pres that were more appropriately treated as deviations. The doctrines assumed great importance during the decade of the 1990s in which a large number of charitable hospitals sold their assets to for-profit corporations and then sought court approval of a plan for the use of the proceeds.[132]

Charitable Corporations

The influence of the New York and Virginia attitude toward charitable trusts and the development of the business corporation to a position of predomi-

---

131. Restatement (Third) of Trusts, §28, Reporter's Notes, cmt. f; see also Chapter 3.
132. See also Chapter 6 on conversions.

nant importance in American business law combined to make inevitable the greater use of the corporate form in the United States than in England for all types of charitable activities.

Development of the corporation in America paralleled that in England, but with the growth of the continent and the expansion of the American economy, the American corporation soon overtook its English predecessor. In the colonies corporate rights were conferred by the issue of "letters patent" or charters from either the Crown or the Royal Governors acting for the Crown. The power was also delegated in some instances to the colonial assemblies.

The most numerous group of private corporations in the colonies were those for religious worship. Charitable and educational institutions usually were chartered under religious auspices, although some were the result of private bequests. One of the earliest corporate charters was granted by act of the Massachusetts General Court in 1756 to "The Feoffees of the Grammar School of the Town of Ipswich to administer a private bequest in the interest of public education there." Similar acts can be found in the records of the assemblies of Virginia, New Jersey, and Connecticut.[133] General acts for incorporation for charitable purposes preceded those for business purposes in some instances. For example, New York passed a general incorporation act for religious purposes in 1784, and adopted the first act permitting general incorporation for business purposes in the United States in 1811.[134]

By 1850 general corporation laws were common throughout the United States, and in the latter half of the nineteenth century, statutory restrictions on the size and activity of corporations were gradually removed. Incorporation by special act died out, so that by 1900 all but four states had adopted constitutional amendments prohibiting incorporation for business purposes by special acts.[135] Where special acts for business corporations are permitted today, they are limited in application to special forms of corporations, and are only rarely used.

Charitable corporations were considered to be quite different from business corporations. The commentators, following the English cases, described charitable corporations as those founded for the administration of charitable trusts:

> A charitable corporation is merely a trustee or agent selected by the donor of the charity for the purpose of administering funds given for chari-

---

133. Joseph S. Davis, *Essays in the Earlier History of American Corporations,* vol. 1, at 75 (Cambridge: Harvard University Press, 1917).

134. 1811 N.Y. Laws ch. 67.

135. Abram Chayes, "Introduction," in Davis, *Corporations,* xi–xii.

table purposes, and the beneficiaries are frequently the public, or parties outside of the corporation. The principles of law applicable to charitable corporations differ, on this account, from those which apply to ordinary business corporations.[136]

However, in those states that refused to uphold the validity of charitable trusts, it was necessary to devise a different theory concerning the nature of ownership of property by a charitable corporation. Some courts, desirous of upholding charitable gifts, went out of their way to state that a gift to a charitable corporation created no trust but was an absolute gift to the corporation to be used for the purposes for which it was chartered.

Problems arose, however, when a testator bequeathed property to a charitable corporation to be used for only one of its stated corporate purposes, or when he provided that the property should be held in perpetuity and only the income expended. To hold that gifts of this nature were trusts would be to defeat the gift. On the other hand, if the gift were declared absolute, the restrictions could not be enforced, since an absolute owner of property cannot be restricted in its use. Some cases, accordingly, held that no trust was created and that the restrictions were only precatory. Others held that while no true or technical trust was created, the question of enforcement did not depend on this, and the court would enforce the restriction. This is now the accepted view in most states.[137]

There is still no unanimity among the states as to the description of this type of ownership. The cases are almost evenly divided between those that describe the relationship as a trust and those that do not.[138] In the first edition of the Restatement of Trusts, an introductory note to Chapter II on charitable trusts states: "When property is given to a charitable corporation a charitable trust is not created." This note was not included in the second edition of the Restatement published in 1959, and in its stead the following comment was inserted:

> Where property is given to a charitable corporation, particularly where restrictions are imposed by the donor, it is sometimes said by the courts that a charitable trust is created and that the corporation is a trustee. It is sometimes said, however, that a charitable trust is not created. This is a mere matter of terminology. The important question is whether and to

---

136. Victor Morawetz, *A Treatise on the Law of Private Corporations,* §4 (Boston: Little, Brown, 1886).

137. St. Joseph's Hospital v. Bennett, 22 N.E.2d 305 (N.Y. 1939), rev'g 8 N.Y.S.2d 922 (1939); Zollmann, *American Law of Charities,* 326; Scott and Fratcher, *Law of Trusts,* §348.1.

138. See Scott and Fratcher, *Law of Trusts,* §348.1, for citations.

what extent the principles and rules applicable to charitable trusts are applicable to charitable corporations.[139]

Unfortunately, the matter has not always been treated as one of terminology alone. On some occasions the language of decisions from states that did not recognize charitable trusts has been used as authority in states that have always considered them valid.

The Restatement (Third) of Trusts, on charitable purposes, contains a different basis for distinction:

> An outright devise or donation to a nonproprietary hospital or university or other charitable institution, expressly or impliedly to be used for its general purposes, is charitable, but does not create a trust as that term is used in this Restatement. A disposition to such an institution for a specific purpose, however, such as to support medical research, perhaps on a particular disease, or to establish a scholarship fund in a certain field of study, creates a charitable trust of which the institution is the trustee for purposes of the terminology and rules of this Restatement.[140]

This formulation, regrettably, will cause still further confusion, particularly in those jurisdictions in which the nonprofit corporation law or other state laws look to trust law for the definitions of charitable purposes.[141]

In addition to the changes in trust law that are applicable to charitable corporations and the changes in the definition of charitable purposes, there were two important developments in the laws governing charitable corporations during the period after the end of World War II. The first was the codification of the laws governing the creation and administration of corporations and the second was the limitation of the liabilities of their officers and directors. The first development began with the formulation in 1952 of a Model Nonprofit Corporation Act by the Business Section of the American Bar Association and its subsequent revision in 1987 (RMNCA).[142] The revision was based in large part on the California nonprofit corporation act, which classified nonprofits into three categories: public benefit, mutual benefit, and religious corporations, with provisions relating to organization, termination, and the duties of directors suited to their differences.[143] The standards adopted for the

139. Restatement (Second) of Trusts, §348 cmt. f.

140. Restatement (Third) of Trusts, §28 cmt. a.

141. See, for example, Banner Health System v. Long, 663 N.W.2d 242 (S.D. 2003); In re Roxborough Memorial Hospital, No. 555, 17 Fiduciary Rptr. 2d 412 (Pa. C.P., Orphans' Ct. Div., September 30, 1997).

142. Revised Model Nonprofit Corporation Act (1987) (RMNCA); see also Lizabeth A. Moody, "The Who, What, and How of the Revised Model Nonprofit Corporation Act," 16 *Northern Kentucky Law Review* 251 (1989).

143. Nonprofit Corporation Law, Cal. Corp. Code, div. 2.

duties of care and loyalty were similar to, but not as lenient as, those found in the business corporation laws in the various states. As of the end of 2002 the RMNCA or a statute based on similar concepts had been adopted in twenty-three states. The provisions of the act and of the statutes in the remaining states are described in detail in Chapters 3 and 4.

The second major development was a marked relaxation of the standards under which directors would be held to account—under the duties of loyalty and care—with the courts and the state legislatures ultimately opting for the corporate standards and the business judgment rule. Signaling the trend was the case of *Stern v. Lucy Webb Hayes National Training School*[144] (commonly referred to as the "Sibley Hospital" case) in which the Federal District Court for the District of Columbia ruled that business corporate law, not trust law, governed the behavior of directors of a charitable corporation. The case was followed in a number of jurisdictions, and its holding was codified in the laws of several states. Accompanying this relaxation of the duties of care and loyalty was the adoption of statutes in a vast majority of the states authorizing charities to indemnify their directors and officers, to pay their legal fees, and to purchase liability insurance to cover claims against them. Finally, both Congress and the states adopted a vast number of statutes protecting charity volunteers from suit. Taken together, these measures created an environment in which it would be nearly impossible to hold a charitable fiduciary liable for breach of duty except in the most egregious circumstances, often only if criminal behavior were involved. Chapter 4 contains a detailed description of these developments and current law.

State Regulation of Charities

Philanthropy in the United States has been claimed by one writer to be "our freest enterprise,"[145] and this phrase does emphasize what the dominant policy of the federal government and the individual states toward charitable activities has been since colonial times. With the exception of the restrictive legislation regarding charitable trusts that has been described, the enactment of legislation in a few states designed to protect heirs against complete or unreasoned disinheritance in favor of charity, and minor restrictions on the holdings of charitable corporations, the great body of legislation and court decisions has been directed toward the removal of restrictions on charitable funds and toward the grant of almost complete freedom of action to the managers and directors of these funds.

Regulation of charities was the exclusive province of the states until enact-

---

144. 381 F. Supp. 1003 (D.D.C. 1974).

145. Edward C. Jenkins, *Philanthropy in America,* 5 (New York: Association Press, 1950).

ment of federal tax laws in the early years of the twentieth century. The power to ensure proper application of charitable funds rests with the attorney general in each state, and from the earliest days of the republic there are reported cases in which the attorney general participated, with most involving the validity of charitable gifts and the application of the cy pres doctrine. The secretary of state or other official charged with overseeing the creation of corporations did have power to determine whether a particular corporation met the statutory requirements for a charitable corporation and in some jurisdictions exercised this power to limit the number of charitable corporations that could be formed.[146] The power to correct wrongdoing by charitable fiduciaries, however, was rarely invoked before World War II. No measures comparable to those in England establishing the Brougham Commission or the Board of Charity Commissioners were ever enacted in the states, and it was only after the mid-1900s that any state official attempted to actively supervise charitable activity.

As more fully described in Chapter 6, in the late 1950s and early 1960s a handful of states adopted legislation requiring certain charities to register and file annual financial reports with the attorney general. The rationale was based on the fact that an attorney general could not adequately carry out his common law duties as supervisor of charitable funds without knowledge of the charities subject to his jurisdiction and the nature and extent of their financial dealings. By 1965 there were ten states with regulatory programs, several of them based on a Uniform Act that had been adopted by the Commissioners on Uniform State Laws in 1954.[147]

Although federal regulation of charities expanded after 1950, there was little if any coordination between state and federal activities. The Tax Reform Act of 1969 did include three provisions designed to encourage and enhance state regulation of charities, in recognition that the powers held by state equity courts were better suited to correcting the behavior of charitable fiduciaries than those held by the Internal Revenue Service. Specifically, Congress recognized that the sole sanction available to the Service was revocation of tax exemption, a sanction that in some circumstances was meaningless and in all cases did not prevent wrongdoers from continuing to manage the charity. One of the measures in the Tax Reform Act of 1969 was a provision permitting the IRS to disclose information on tax-exempt charities to state charity officials. The second permitted abatement of the confiscatory private foundation termination tax if it could be demonstrated that state officials had taken action to preserve the charity's assets, while the third required all

146. Norman I. Silber, *A Corporate Form of Freedom: The Emergence of the Modern Nonprofit Sector,* 20–23 (Boulder: Westview Press, 2001).

147. See Marion R. Fremont-Smith, *Foundations and Government,* chs. 8, 9 (New York: Russell Sage Foundation, 1965), for descriptions of these state programs as constituted in 1964.

foundations to provide the appropriate state official with a copy of their Form 990s.

None of these provisions were to meet the expectations of the draftsmen; in many instances state regulatory programs that had focused primarily on foundation activities were curtailed, while in Iowa and Washington they were discontinued. Interest in charity regulation in all but a few states turned to regulation of those charities that solicited funds from the general public. The increase in this activity at the state level paralleled an increase in activities by the state attorneys general and secretaries of state in consumer protection, in this case from misleading and deceptive communications as to the application of charitable contributions.

In 1974 thirty-one states were actively regulating the solicitation of funds for charitable purposes by charities and for-profit organizations presenting themselves to the public as charities. By 2003 the number had grown to thirty-nine.[148] In contrast, in 1970 there were ten states in which certain charities were required to register and report on all of their activities, not just soliciting charities, and in which the attorney general attempted with varying degrees of commitment to regulate the behavior of fiduciaries in respect to conflicts of interest and negligent behavior. In 2003 there were still only eleven states with registration and reporting statutes, although attorneys general in several others were attempting to regulate fiduciary behavior and were actively regulating conversions. These eleven states included New York, California, Illinois, Michigan, and Ohio, which meant that the vast majority of charities nationwide were subject to a regulatory scheme. Nonetheless, wide discrepancies in the regulatory climate encouraged forum-shopping and facilitated evasion of regulation, limiting the ability of these states to correct many abuses.[149]

One marked improvement in state regulation was achieved in the early 1980s when representatives of the National Association of Attorneys General (formed in 1907) and the National Association of State Charity Officials (NASCO) (1979) began to coordinate their activities and sought to develop closer relations with the IRS. NASCO developed and supported adoption of a uniform registration form for soliciting charities, and it has cooperated with the IRS to improve the federal information-reporting forms. Interested members of the general public are invited to participate in an open session at their annual meetings to discuss common problems, and the organization maintains a website with links to the charity officers in each state.[150]

---

148. See Appendix, Table 1, Column 15.
149. See Chapter 6.
150. See *www.nasconet.org*.

Federal Regulation of Charities: The Internal Revenue Code

The first federal income tax, enacted in 1894, contained an exemption for any corporation or association organized exclusively for religious, educational, or charitable purposes.[151] Although this statute was declared unconstitutional by the United States Supreme Court in 1895,[152] subsequent enactments of the income tax code have all contained exemptions derived from this wording. The Corporation Excise Act of 1909 contained a provision to the effect that the tax did not apply "to any corporation or association organized or operated exclusively for religious, educational, or charitable purposes, no part of the net income of which inures to the benefit of any private stockholder or individual."[153] The legislative history behind this enactment is sparse. Dale relates its first appearance as part of an amendment offered by Senator Augustus O. Bacon of Georgia on July 2, 1909, to the effect that its provisions "shall not apply to any corporation or association organized and operated for religious, charitable or educational purposes, no part of the profit of which inures to the benefit of any private stockholder or individual, but all of the profit of which is in good faith devoted to the said religious, charitable, or educational purpose."[154] Although the amendment was tabled, it reemerged several days later in the same language, and on July 6, 1909, the amendment was adopted with a change suggested by Senator Bacon that added the word "exclusively" after the phrase "organized and operated." Prior to its enactment by the Senate the anti-inurement language was later changed by substituting the phrase "net income" for the word "profit," and by deleting the final clause. There is no explanation in the Conference Committee Report of the change nor can one be found in any other sources.

The language of the 1909 act, with the addition of the word "scientific," was repeated in the Tariff Act of 1913[155] and again in the acts of 1916[156] and 1918.[157] In the Revenue Act of 1921, the word "literary" was added to the list of permitted purposes,[158] while the phrase "or the prevention of cruelty to children or animals" was added in 1918.[159] In 1934 the limitation on lobby-

151. Internal Revenue Act of 1894, ch. 349, §32, 28 Stat. 509, 556 (1894).

152. Pollock v. Farmers' Loan & Trust Co., 158 U.S. 601 (1895).

153. Corporation Tax Act of 1909, ch. 6, 36 Stat. 11 (1909), codified at I.R.C. §501(c)(3).

154. Harvey Dale, "Reflections on Inurement, Private Benefit, and Excess Benefit Transactions" (2001) (on file with author).

155. Tariff Act of 1913, ch. 16, §II(G)(a), 38 Stat. 114, 172 (1913).

156. Revenue Act of 1916, ch. 463, 39 Stat. 756 (1916).

157. Revenue Act of 1918, ch. 18, §231(6), 40 Stat. 1057, 1076 (1918).

158. Revenue Act of 1921, ch. 136, §231(6), 42 Stat. 227 (1921).

159. Revenue Act of 1918, ch. 18, §231(6), 40 Stat. 1057, 1076 (1918).

ing first appeared in the statute,[160] although it had been regarded as grounds for denial of exemption by regulations and decisions prior to that time. The prohibition on intervening in political campaigns was not added to the Code until 1954 when it was introduced by Senator Lyndon B. Johnson as an amendment to the Revenue Act of 1954, reflecting his reaction to allegations that funds provided by a charitable foundation were used to help finance the campaign of an opponent in a primary election.[161] The phrase was further refined in 1987 with the addition of the phrase "in opposition to" any candidate.[162]

The next addition to the list of exempt purposes in Code section 501(c)(3) was not made until 1976 when an amendment added to the list of purposes "or to foster national or international amateur sports competition (but only if no part of its activities involve the provision of athletic facilities or equipment)."[163] The limitation was designed to assure that exemption under section 501(c)(3) would not be available to social clubs and similar organizations that provide facilities and equipment for their members.[164] This limitation effectively prevented the establishment of organizations formed to raise funds to support athletes participating in the Olympics and other international competitions. In response to public protest, in 1982 Congress added section 501(j) to the Code, which modified section 501(c)(3) to permit exemption under that section to "qualified amateur sports organizations,"[165] defined as organizations that are organized and operated primarily to conduct national or international competition in sports or to support and develop amateur athletes for national or international competition even if they provided facilities or equipment.[166]

Exemptions similar to those in section 501(c)(3) were included in the Estate and Gift Tax Laws of 1916[167] and 1926[168] and in the 1924 Excise Tax Law taxing "admissions."[169] Today these provisions are found in the Internal Revenue Code of 1986 in section 170(c) describing organizations eligible to

160. Revenue Act of 1934, ch. 277, §101(6), 48 Stat. 680, 700 (1934).

161. 100 Cong. Rec. 9604 (1954).

162. Omnibus Budget Reconciliation Act of 1987, Pub. L. No. 100-203, §10711(a)(2), 101 Stat. 1330, 1330-464 (1987).

163. Tax Reform Act of 1976, Pub. L. No. 94-455, §1313(a), 90 Stat. 1520, 1730 (1976).

164. Joint Committee on Taxation, *General Explanation of the Tax Reform Act of 1976*, 94th Cong., 2d Sess., 423–424 (1976).

165. Tax Equity and Fiscal Responsibility Act of 1982, Pub. L. No. 97-248, §286(a), 96 Stat. 324, 569–570 (1982).

166. I.R.C. §501(j)(2); see also Gen. Couns. Mem. 39,775 (July 15, 1988).

167. Revenue Act of 1916, ch. 463, 39 Stat. 756, 777 (1916).

168. Revenue Act of 1926, ch. 27, 44 Stat. 1, 69 (1926).

169. Revenue Act of 1924, ch. 234, §500, 43 Stat. 253, 320 (1924).

receive contributions that may be deducted for income tax purposes, in section 642(c) relating to income taxes, and in sections 2055, 2016, 2532, and 2601 relating to estate, gift, and generation-skipping taxes.[170]

Section 501(c)(3) provides for exemption for organizations with purposes that are considered in substantive law to be "charitable." However, some organizations that are exempt under section 501(c)(4) of the Code, which describes organizations operated exclusively for the promotion of "social welfare," also referred to in the regulations as civic organizations and local associations of employees, may be considered charities under state law.[171] The important distinctions between the two sections are that social welfare organizations are not eligible to receive tax-deductible contributions but they are permitted to lobby without limit. Section 504, enacted in 1976, prohibits an organization that loses exemption under section 501(c)(3) because of excessive lobbying from qualifying for exemption under section 501(c)(4).[172]

Tax exemption is also granted to more than twenty other categories of organizations. Thus subsection (c)(1) of section 501 describes instrumentalities of the United States organized under Acts of Congress; subsection (c)(2) confers exemption on organizations holding title to property for other exempt organizations; subsection (c)(4), as noted above, describes civic leagues, social welfare organizations, and local associations of employees established and operated for the promotion of community welfare or for charitable, educational, or recreational purposes; subsection (c)(5) covers labor, agricultural, and horticultural organizations; subsection (c)(6) describes business leagues, chambers of commerce, real estate boards, and other organizations that seek to improve business conditions of one or more lines of business; subsection (c)(7) grants exemption to social and recreational clubs; subsections (c)(8) through (c)(12) and (c)(14) through (c)(17) describe lodges, mutual benefit associations established for varying groups of individuals, cooperative banks, and insurance companies; and subsection (c)(13) refers to certain cemetery companies, while subsections (c)(19) and (c)(23) apply to veterans associations. The remaining sections describe various entities that provide unemployment and other benefits and pensions as well as specific categories of title-holding companies.

It was during the mid-1940s, a period during which the number of exempt organizations grew rapidly and there were widespread press reports of abuse of their status, that Congress looked at and then enacted measures that ultimately were designed to limit the behavior of charitable fiduciaries. The first

170. I.R.C. §170(c); §642(c); §2055, §2016; §2532; §2601.
171. I.R.C. §501(c)(4); see also Treas. Reg. §1.501(c)(4)-1.
172. I.R.C. §504, codified by Tax Reform Act of 1976, Pub. L. No. 94-455, §1307(a)(2), 90 Stat. 1520, 1721–1722 (1976).

restrictive legislation, passed in 1944, however, merely required certain exempt organizations, principally foundations, to file returns disclosing their financial affairs.[173] The stated purpose of the requirement was to provide information to the Internal Revenue Service and the Congress that would serve as the basis for additional legislation.[174]

Much of the growth in the number of charities in the years after the end of World War II was attributed to the increase in individual income tax rates during and after the war, which led some tax planners, seeking ways to reduce taxes, to manipulate charitable organizations for private purposes. The methods employed involved novel transactions between charities and businesses. Three operations concerned the Service: (1) the creation of corporations commonly known as feeders that operated as businesses but distributed all of their profits to a charitable organization and claimed tax exemption for themselves on the basis of the "destination" of their income; (2) exempt organizations that engaged in exempt activities but also carried on income-producing activities that were not in furtherance of their charitable programs; and (3) organizations established for charitable purposes but subject to varying degrees of control by private interests whereby the accumulated income or earnings of the charity could be used to business or personal advantage.[175]

Prior to 1950 the Internal Revenue Service had directed its regulatory activities in regard to charities toward assuring that the basic requirements for tax exemption were met at the time an organization was established. The Service had questioned whether exemption was available for an organization that raised funds through the conduct of business activities unrelated to carrying on its exempt purpose and limited its charitable activities to distributing the net income to other charities. In 1924 the Supreme Court had held that a certain amount of business activity was not sufficient to constitute grounds for revocation of exemption, regardless of whether or not the activity was related to the exempt activities of the organization so long as the destination of its income was charity.[176] This remained the law until passage of the Tax Reform Act of 1950 in which Congress enacted Code section 502 denying exemption to feeder corporations.[177] This amendment reflected in part a reaction to several court decisions upholding the exemption for feeder corporations, particularly a Tax Court decision that had granted exemption to a

173. Revenue Act of 1943, ch. 63, §117, 58 Stat. 21, 36 (1944).

174. H.R. Rep. No. 871, 78th Cong., 1st Sess. (1944).

175. Norman Sugarman and Harlan Pomeroy, "Business Income of Exempt Organizations," 44 *Virginia Law Review* 424, 427 (1960).

176. Trinidad v. Sagrada Orden de Predicadores, 263 U.S. 578 (1924).

177. I.R.C. §502 (1954), codified by Revenue Act of 1950, ch. 994, §301(b), 64 Stat. 906, 949 (1950).

charity that operated a pasta factory and whose sole charitable activity was distributing the net income from the business to New York University.[178]

In the late 1940s Congress started receiving complaints from the private sector that small businesses were being hurt by unfair competition from the so-called feeder organizations and that private foundations were being used for private benefit. In response, the Interstate and Foreign Commerce Committee revealed the results of an investigation of the activities of a business organization that had been charged with taking advantage of a controlled foundation's tax-exempt status to accumulate large amounts of income for subsequent use in the acquisition of other enterprises and for financing business transactions on a preferential basis.[179]

The investigation led to enactment in 1950 of four restrictions on the activities of exempt charities:

1. A tax was imposed on the net income of activities not substantially related to the tax-exempt purposes of a charity that were regularly carried on.[180]
2. Feeder organizations, meaning organizations whose primary purpose was carrying on a trade or business for profit, were denied exemption regardless of the fact that all of their income was payable to a charitable organization.[181]
3. Certain charities would lose exemption if they accumulated income unreasonably or if they invested accumulated income in such a manner as to jeopardize the carrying out of their charitable purposes.[182]
4. Certain charities would lose exemption if they entered into self-dealing transactions with their creators and substantial contributors and related parties. Among the prohibited transactions were loans, sales for other

---

178. C. F. Mueller Co., 13 T.C. 922 (1950), rev'd, 190 F.2d 120 (3d Cir. 1951).

179. Investigation of Closing of Nashua, N.H. Mills and Operations of Textron, Incorporated: Hearings before the Senate Subcommittee of the Committee on Interstate and Foreign Commerce, 80th Cong., 2d Sess., pts. 1 and 2 (1948, 1949). Comment, "The Modern Philanthropic Foundation: A Critique and a Proposal," 59 Yale Law Journal 477 (1950), contains a summary of this investigation and of the activities of Royal Little and Textron, Inc., that served to bring the problem before Congress. See also "A Correction to the Textron Story," 59 Yale Law Journal 1121 (1950).

180. I.R.C. §§512–514 (1954), codified by Revenue Act of 1950, ch. 994, §301(a), 64 Stat. 906, 948 (1950).

181. I.R.C. §502 (1954), codified by Revenue Act of 1950, §301(b).

182. I.R.C. §504 (1954), codified by Revenue Act of 1950, §301(a) (repealed by Tax Reform Act of 1969, Pub. L. No. 91-172, §101, 83 Stat. 487, 527 (1969)).

than fair market value, and payments of excessive compensation to disqualified persons.[183]

The limitations described in paragraphs 3 and 4 were applicable only to a category of tax-exempt charities that later came to be defined in section 509 of the Code as "private foundations."[184] In the 1950 act, churches, schools, hospitals, and charities supported by contributions from the public were exempted from the new restrictions.[185] As a practical matter, this meant that the provisions were applicable only to organizations that fit the common parlance definition of foundations.

The Revenue Act of 1964 added to the Code another set of restrictions on private foundations that were potential donees of gifts from donors who by virtue of having made large charitable contributions during the prior ten years qualified for an unlimited charitable deduction.[186] Under the new limitation the deduction was not available if the donee was a private foundation, and if during the contribution year, the three prior, and the three succeeding years, it had entered into what were described as "disqualifying transactions." These included any loans to the donor, any but minimal sales or purchases of securities from or to a related donor, and payment of unreasonable compensation or provision of services to a donor. This legislation presaged changes in the Code that were ultimately adopted as part of the Tax Reform Act of 1969.

Until 1954 there had been no requirement that an organization claiming tax exemption obtain a determination from the Internal Revenue Service that it was entitled to that status, although, as a practical matter, with the exception of churches, almost all organizations that relied on contributions from individuals and corporations did obtain a ruling from the Service affirming their exempt status in order to assure donors of the organization's eligibility to receive deductible contributions. In 1954 the Treasury promulgated regulations under which organizations seeking exemption were required to file an application for exemption and receive a determination of exempt status prior to operating.[187] Like the provisions enacted in 1950, "public organizations" received more lenient treatment than private foundations. Thus newly formed operating institutions, including religious organizations, schools,

---

183. I.R.C. §503 (1954), codified by Revenue Act of 1950, §301(a) (repealed by Tax Reform Act of 1969, §101).

184. I.R.C. §509, codified by Tax Reform Act of 1969, Pub L. No. 91-172, §101, 83 Stat. 487, 527 (1969).

185. I.R.C. §503 (1954).

186. I.R.C. §170(g)(4), codified by Revenue Act of 1964, Pub. L. No. 88-272, §209(b), 78 Stat. 19 (1964).

187. Treas. Reg. §1.501(c)(3)-1(b)(6).

hospitals, and publicly supported charities, were entitled to a tentative advance ruling as to their status. Foundations, however, were required to have "operated" for one year before becoming eligible to receive a ruling. Furthermore, if an income tax return was due during the year, a new foundation was required to file an income tax return as a taxable entity even though the exemption, if granted, would apply retroactively to the date of creation and contributions made during the first year would be deductible.

The effect of this ruling was to bifurcate the test for exemption into two separate parts, which became known as the "organizational" and the "operational" tests. They were so referred to in regulations issued in 1959 that set forth the requirements for exemption.[188] These tests remain the basis for eligibility for exemption under section 501(c)(3).[189]

The requirement that foundations operate for a year before becoming entitled to receive a determination of exemption proved unworkable in that donors, reluctant to have their contributions disallowed, merely waited until the end of its first year to fund the organization so that it would have little or no activity during its first year of existence. In December 1963 the Service announced rescission of the twelve-month operational requirement if the organization could show affirmatively and in sufficient detail in its exemption application and supporting documents that it was "clearly exempt" within the requirements of the law under which exemption was claimed.[190]

Deductibility of Contributions

The distinction between organizations that are considered private foundations and other organizations described in section 501(c)(3) first appeared in the Revenue Act of 1943, which contained a provision requiring certain exempt organizations to file annual information returns.[191] The act excluded from the filing requirements churches and other religious organizations, schools and colleges, and certain publicly supported organizations. In the Revenue Act of 1950 this same group of charities was excluded from the prohibitions contained in sections 503 and 504 against self-dealing and unreasonable accumulations of income, as well as from expanded information reporting requirements.[192]

The distinction between public charities and private foundations was also

188. Treas. Reg. §1.501(c)(3)-1(a) (T.D. 6391) (1959).
189. See Chapter 5.
190. Rev. Proc. 63-30, 1963-2 C.B. 769 (1963).
191. Revenue Act of 1943, ch. 63, §117, 58 Stat. 21, 36 (1944); see also H.R. Rep. No. 871, 78th Cong., 1st Sess., 24–25 (1944).
192. Revenue Act of 1950, ch. 994, 64 Stat. 906 (1950).

made in the Code sections pertaining to the availability of the income tax deduction for charitable contributions.[193] Section 23(o) of the 1939 Code limited the amount of deductible charitable contributions to 20% of adjusted gross income (AGI).[194] The 1954 Code retained this limitation but added a provision permitting deduction of an additional 10% for contributions to three categories of organizations: (1) churches and conventions of churches; (2) educational organizations, but limited to schools having a student body, faculty, curriculum, and campus as set forth in section 503(b)(2); and (3) hospitals.[195] The reason given in the committee report was that this provision would aid these institutions "in obtaining additional funds they need, in view of their rising costs and the relatively low rate of return they are receiving on endowment funds."[196] In 1956 medical research organizations were added to the favored category, but only if the contribution was spent by the donee for medical research purposes during the five-year period beginning with the date of contribution.[197] In 1962 endowment funds established to support state colleges or universities were added to the favored list.[198]

In 1964 Congress again added to the category of organizations eligible to receive deductions up to 30% of AGI to include governmental units and organizations that normally received a substantial part of their support (exclusive of income received in the exercise or performance of their charitable, educational, or other purpose or function constituting the basis for exemption under section 501(a)) from a governmental unit, or from direct or indirect contributions from the general public.[199] The explanation for the change was based not as it had been with the previous amendments on the needs of the donee organizations, but rather to encourage gifts that would result in immediately spendable receipts of contributions for charitable organizations, in contrast to gifts to foundations that would hold the assets for extended periods of time and in the meanwhile use the funds for investment.[200] Regulations interpreting this amendment were issued in 1966.[201] They set forth a mechanical and a facts and circumstances test that were subsequently

---

193. I.R.C. §170.

194. I.R.C. §23(o) (1939).

195. I.R.C. §170 (1954) (as amended by H.R. 8300, 83d Cong., 2d Sess. (1954)).

196. S. Rep. No. 1622, 83d Cong., 2d Sess., 29 (1954); H.R. Rep. No. 1337, 83d Cong., 2d Sess., 25 (1954).

197. Act of August 7, 1956, Pub. L. No. 84-1022, §1, 70 Stat. 1117, 1117–1118 (1956).

198. Act of October 23, 1962, Pub. L. No. 87-858, §2(a), 76 Stat. 1134 (1962).

199. I.R.C. §170(b)(1)(A)(v), (vi), codified by Revenue Act of 1964, Pub. L. No. 88-272, §209(a), 78 Stat. 19 (1964).

200. S. Rep. No. 830, 88th Cong., 2d Sess., 58 (1964).

201. T.D. 6900, 1966-1 C.B. 72.

adopted as part of the regulations under section 509, which was added by the Tax Reform Act of 1969 to define private foundations.[202]

Section 170 was also amended in 1964 to permit a five-year carryforward for excess contributions of cash and appreciated property to public charities.[203] It was not until 1984 that a similar carryforward for gifts to private foundations was added.[204] Of great importance to donors was the ability to deduct gifts of appreciated property at their fair market value on the date of the gift rather than at their cost, if it was lower.[205]

In addition to defining private foundations, the Tax Reform Act of 1969 also contained provisions increasing the percentage limitation on deductions for gifts of cash to public charities to 50% of adjusted net income and added two additional classes of organizations to the favored list: (1) private operating foundations[206] and (2) private foundations that, in the tax year after the receipt of the gift, distribute an amount equal to the gift to public charities.[207] Section 170 was also amended to permit a deduction for gifts of appreciated property to "public charities" equal to 30% of the donor's contribution base[208] while gifts of appreciated property to private foundations continued to be deductible only to the extent of the donor's basis, and the total amount that could be deducted was limited to 20% of the contribution base.[209] This 20% limit on gifts of appreciated property was raised to 30% during the years between 1984 and 1994[210] and then made permanent in 1998.[211] In addition, donors to foundations were permitted to deduct the full market value of contributions of stock for which market quotations were readily available so long as the total amount of the stock contributed did not exceed 10% in value of all outstanding stock of the corporation.[212]

Unlike gifts from individuals, contributions from business corporations are

202. Treas. Reg. §1.509(a)-3.

203. I.R.C. §170(b), amended by Revenue Act of 1964, Pub. L. No. 88-272, §209(c), 78 Stat. 19, 45 (1964).

204. I.R.C. §170(b)(1)(D), codified by Deficit Reduction Act of 1984, Pub. L. No. 98-369, §301(c)(1), 98 Stat. 494, 779 (1984).

205. LO 1118, II-2 C.B. 148 (1923); see also Treas. Reg. §1.170A-1(c)(1).

206. I.R.C. §170(b)(i)(A)(vii), §170(b)(1)(E)(i), codified by Tax Reform Act of 1969, Pub L. No. 91-172, §201(a)(1), 83 Stat. 487 (1969).

207. I.R.C. §170(b)(i)(A)(vii), §170(b)(1)(E)(i)–(ii), codified by Tax Reform Act of 1969, §201(a)(1).

208. I.R.C. §170(b)(1)(C)(i), codified by Tax Reform Act of 1969, §201(a)(1).

209. I.R.C. §170(b)(1)(D)(i).

210. I.R.C. §170(e)(5), codified by Deficit Reduction Act of 1984, Pub. L. No. 98-369, §301(b), 98 Stat. 494, 778 (1984).

211. I.R.C. §170(e)(5)(D), repealed by Act of October 21, 1998, Pub. L. No. 105-277, §1004, 112 Stat. 2681 (1998).

212. I.R.C. §170(e)(5).

deductible up to 10% of taxable income, with no distinction as to whether or not the donee is a private foundation.[213] A provision to increase the cap to 20% over a twelve-year period starting with taxable years beginning in 2004 was contained in a bill passed by the House in September 2003, although there was no comparable provision in the Senate version of the act that had been approved the prior spring.[214]

Federal Reporting and Disclosure Requirements

Annual reporting by exempt organizations was not required until 1942 when the Treasury Department imposed a requirement that annual information returns be filed by all tax-exempt organizations.[215] The two-page form covered tax year 1941. It included three questions, an income statement, and a balance sheet, although schedules were required for some items. Some organizations protested the Treasury's authority to impose such a requirement, and compliance was poor. In 1943 the Treasury sought specific statutory authority to require reports of financial status from most categories of exempt organizations.[216]

Today Form 990 consists of six pages with forty-five pages of instructions, and two schedules, Schedule A, which consists of six pages with fourteen pages of instructions, and Schedule B, which consists of seven pages with two pages of instructions. It has been revised a number of times with input from the charitable sector, and in 2002 the Service embarked on a major project to permit electronic filing, with the aim of having it available by 2004 (for fiscal year 2003).[217] A review of the changes in the form over the years mirrors the changes in Code requirements for tax exemption, as well as the regulatory thrust of the Service. Thus questions about related organizations appeared in the 1990s, while in 2002 the Service announced that it would require greater detail about fund-raising activities than it had previously.[218] The enactment of intermediate sanctions on excess benefit transactions required a major addition to the information required by the Service. Since the 1980s when an in-

213. I.R.C. §170(b)(2), amended by Economic Recovery Tax Act of 1981, Pub. L. No. 97-34, §263(a), 95 Stat. 172, 264–265 (1981). Prior to 1981, the limit was 5%.

214. Charitable Giving Act of 2003, H.R. 7, §103, 108th Cong., 1st Sess. (2003); CARE Act of 2003, S. 476, 108th Cong., 1st Sess. (2003).

215. T.D. 5125, 1942-1 C.B. 101; T.D. 5177, 1942-2 C.B. 123.

216. Revenue Act of 1943, ch. 63, §117, 58 Stat. 21, 36 (1944); see also Michael McGreevy, "Review of Rulings and Forms for Reporting," in *Proceedings of the New York University Sixth Biennial Conference on Charitable Foundations*, 191 (1963).

217. Carolyn Wright LaFon, "IRS Director, Staff Hold Press Conference to Discuss EO Division Initiatives," 2002 *Tax Notes Today* 50-3 (March 14, 2002).

218. Ann. 2002-87, 2002-39 I.R.B. 624.

creasing number of states began to permit filing of the federal return to meet state reporting requirements, the Service has cooperated with state regulators to help meet their information needs.[219]

Information returns filed by exempt organizations were first made available to the public in 1950 when Form 990-A was published.[220] This form consisted of four pages, the first two of which contained information required by the Treasury for its purposes, and the latter two of which contained information required by Congress to be disclosed to the public. Not open for public inspection were the detailed schedules of "other income," depreciation, depletion, miscellaneous expenses, the names of the recipients of contributions, and the answers to a series of questions relating to the organization and operation of the organization. Revisions of the form were made in seven of the twelve years between 1950 and 1962, reflecting primarily the Treasury's attempts to obtain information required from foundations under the terms of the Revenue Acts of 1950 and 1954.

Late in 1962, following publication of the first Patman Report and the Treasury Department study of private foundations, the department concluded that it had statutory authority to disclose to the public all information required on Form 990-A other than the names of contributors. This decision was first published in the Federal Register on December 29, 1962;[221] it became effective shortly thereafter and the form was modified to reflect the change.[222] A number of new questions were also added to the form, which reflected the influence of the Patman investigation, notably a request for detailed information relating to all cases in which the foundation owned more than 10% of any class of stock of a company. Several commentators noted at the time that the expanded reporting requirements were frequently ignored and that many returns were inadequately filled out.[223]

At the time that information returns were made public, the failure to file carried a criminal penalty of a maximum of one year's imprisonment and a $10,000 fine.[224] The Service was reluctant to invoke such a strong sanction, and in 1965 the Treasury recommended to Congress that it enact a provision

219. See Chapters 6 and 7.

220. Revenue Act of 1950, ch. 994, §341, 64 Stat. 906, 960 (1950), codifying I.R.C. §6033(b).

221. 27 Fed. Reg. 12,953 (1962).

222. Treas. Reg. §1.6033-1(a), amended by T.D. 6645, 1963-1 C.B. 269.

223. National Council of Community Foundations, Inc., Memorandum to Members, at 3–4 (New York, September 5, 1962); McGreevy, "Review of Rulings and Forms for Reporting," 175, 199; Mitchell Rogovin, "Tax Exemption: Current Thinking within the Service," in *Proceedings of the New York University Twenty-second Annual Institute on Federal Taxation*, 248 (1964).

224. I.R.C. §7203 (1954).

imposing a penalty of $10 per day for each day of delay to a maximum of $5,000, with a similar penalty for officers, directors, or trustees responsible for filing returns if, after notice from the Service of failure to make a complete and timely return, the defect was not remedied within a specific time.[225]

Other forms have been devised by the Service over the years to conform with Code changes. Thus Form 990T was formulated to obtain information concerning unrelated business income and, because this is an income tax, the return is not an information return and therefore not subject to the disclosure requirements.

Congressional Investigations of Charities prior to 1969

The foregoing chronology of the adoption of provisions of the Internal Revenue Code and the regulations thereunder contains references to periods during which congressional interest in the operation of charities led to changes in the manner in which they were regulated by the Internal Revenue Service. During these same periods various congressional committees and subcommittees conducted other investigations of charities that were well reported in the press and thereby influenced public opinion, even though they did not always lead to legislative changes.

Prior to World War II there was only one brief period during which Congress demonstrated specific interest in charitable activity. Congressional attention appears to have been first attracted in 1910 when a bill was introduced in the Senate to incorporate The Rockefeller Foundation. Between 1889 and 1907 Congress by special act had granted corporate charters to thirty-four charitable organizations, including the Carnegie Institution in Washington and the General Education Board. Despite the fact that the charter for the foundation was in almost all respects identical to that granted in 1903 to the General Education Board, the bill to establish The Rockefeller Foundation was debated during three successive sessions of Congress. It was branded as an indefinite scheme for perpetuating vast wealth in the name of a man whose corporate holdings were at that moment under attack by the federal government as illegal monopolies. The controversy generated such heat that the Rockefeller interests abandoned their attempts to obtain a federal charter, and the foundation was incorporated with no protest in New York state in April 1913.[226]

225. Staff of Treasury Department, *Report on Private Foundations*, 89th Cong., 1st Sess. (Senate Finance Committee, February 2, 1965).

226. Marion R. Fremont-Smith, "Governance Models for the Digital Opportunity Investment Trust," in *A Digital Gift to the Nation*, 95, 101 (Lawrence K. Grossman and Newton N. Minow eds., New York: Century Foundation Press, 2001).

The Walsh Commission

Two years after the debate over the charter for The Rockefeller Foundation, Congress created a Commission on Industrial Relations, which proceeded to investigate the role of foundations in the economy. It was composed of representatives of labor, employers of labor, and members of Congress, all appointed by the President with the advice and consent of the Senate. The Walsh Commission, as it became known, published a report in 1916 in which it charged that the concentration of wealth in the large foundations, such as Carnegie and Rockefeller, was being used by industrial magnates to gain control of the universities and, thereby, the social and educational side of American life.[227] The majority of the members recommended enactment of legislation requiring federal charters for the incorporation of all nonprofit organizations with more than one function and funds of more than $1 million; limitations on the size, income, and life of them; and creation of rigid supervisory procedures.[228]

Various reasons for this attack have been propounded, including fear that a proposal by The Rockefeller Foundation to investigate industrial relations would be a whitewash of big business in its controversies with labor; a reaction to changes in foundation grant-making from institution-building to support of educational studies, particularly in the social sciences; and the general industrial unrest that had led to trust-busting and union battles.[229] Feelings against monopolies and the accumulation of vast wealth symbolized by the names of Carnegie and Rockefeller were high. It was therefore natural that liberals would denounce foundations as the instruments of this wealth and its corporate structure.[230]

This brief period of interest was unique. Congress took no action on the Walsh Commission's recommendations. Suspicion of large foundations did surface from time to time, but there were no changes in the tax laws nor enactment of any other provisions limiting charitable activities until after World War II.

In 1942 Treasury representatives had proposed limitations on the business activity of foundations to the Ways and Means Committee, but the

227. Commission on Industrial Relations, *Industrial Relations: Final Report and Testimony*, S. Doc. No. 415, 64th Cong., 1st Sess. (1916).

228. Id. at 85.

229. Joseph C. Kiger, *Operating Principles of the Larger Foundations*, 85–86 (New York: Russell Sage Foundation, 1954).

230. Harold M. Keele, "Government's Attitude toward Foundations," 33 *Michigan State Bar Journal* 9, 18 (October 1954).

Committee recommended no action at that time.[231] Charitable activities were next considered by the Committee in 1947, in a series of hearings focusing on the business activities of foundations, although, again, Congress took no action.[232]

In 1948 the Senate Committee on Interstate and Foreign Commerce, as part of an investigation into the economic situation of the textile industry in New Hampshire, reviewed the operations of an industrialist, Royal Little, who was charged with using tax-exempt foundations created by him to finance several of his business ventures.[233] The Committee report contained a description of the methods by which Mr. Little was able to obtain risk capital for certain ventures and to buy at substantially reduced prices both stock and fixed assets of certain companies he wanted to acquire. It was also charged that he had entered into leaseback arrangements on other property at high rentals that were deductible by the business companies and provided additional capital for the foundation to reinvest in other ventures.

The Committee report recommended an amendment to the Internal Revenue Code to prevent a recurrence of this type of arrangement by requiring that no trust receive tax exemption "unless during the taxable year it has actually paid to its charitable beneficiary 85% of its gross income received in such taxable year."[234] A bill incorporating this provision was introduced in Congress during the 1949 session but was not adopted.[235] The investigation served to focus attention on charitable activities, a focus that culminated in the enactment as part of the Tax Reform Act of 1950 of major changes in the Code, in particular, passage of the unrelated business income tax, the tax on feeder corporations, and provisions limiting accumulation of income and prohibiting self-dealing by foundations.

The Cox and Reece Committees

Despite the far-reaching changes embodied in the 1950 tax reform legislation, foundations remained a direct target of three extensive congressional

231. Revenue Revision of 1942: Hearings before the House Committee on Ways and Means, 77th Cong., 2d Sess., vol. 1 (1942).

232. Revenue Revisions, 1947–1948: Hearings before the House Committee on Ways and Means, 80th Cong., 1st Sess., pt. 5 (1948).

233. Hearings before the Senate Committee on Interstate and Foreign Commerce, 80th Cong., 2d Sess. (1948); Committee on Interstate and Foreign Commerce, *Report*, S. Rep. No. 101, 81st Cong., 1st Sess. (1949). For a summary, see Note, "The Modern Philanthropic Foundation: A Critique and a Proposal," 59 *Yale Law Journal* 477 (1950).

234. Committee on Interstate and Foreign Commerce, *Report*, S. Rep. No. 101, at 23–24.

235. S. 1408, 81st Cong., 1st Sess. (1949).

investigations conducted between 1952 and 1965. The first of these was undertaken by a Select Committee to Investigate and Study Educational and Philanthropic Foundations and Other Comparable Organizations Which Are Exempt from Federal Taxation, established by the House of Representatives in 1952 and named after its chairman, Representative E. E. Cox of Georgia. The Committee was charged with investigating whether these organizations were using their resources "for purposes other than the purposes for which they were established and especially to determine which such foundations and organizations are using their resources for un-American and subversive activities or for purposes not in the interest or tradition of the United States."[236]

The Cox Committee sent questionnaires to more than 1,500 organizations, interviewed 200 persons, and communicated by mail with an additional 200 individuals. It held public hearings on eighteen days between November 18 and December 30, 1952, at which thirty-nine witnesses testified. Fifty-four of the larger foundations responded to a special questionnaire that provided unprecedented information on foundations, which was used as the basis for a study of the operating principles of foundations that was published in 1954.[237]

The final report of the Cox Committee was supportive of foundations, characterizing them as a "vital and essential factor in our progress."[238] Although the Committee found evidence of infiltration by subversives, most of it was attributable to mistakes that were made without sufficient knowledge. The Committee concluded that the overall record of foundations was good and made only two recommendations relating to accountability: (1) public accounting should be required of all foundations; and (2) the Ways and Means Committee should reexamine pertinent tax laws to assure that they are drawn so as to encourage "the free-enterprise system with its rewards from which private individuals may make gifts to these meritorious institutions."[239] Congress did not take action on the recommendations, in part because public disclosure of information returns from foundations had been authorized in the Revenue Act of 1950[240] and implemented by the subsequent Treasury revisions of Form 990-A.

---

236. Select (Cox) Committee to Investigate and Study Educational and Philanthropic Foundations and Other Comparable Organizations Which Are Exempt from Federal Income Taxation, *Final Report*, H.R. Rep. No. 2514, at 2, 82d Cong., 2d Sess. (1953).

237. Kiger, *Operating Principles of the Larger Foundations*. The appendix to the volume contains a copy of the questionnaire.

238. Select (Cox) Committee, *Final Report*, 4–5.

239. Id. at 13.

240. I.R.C. §6033(b), codified by Revenue Act of 1950, ch. 994, §341, 64 Stat. 906, 960 (1950).

In July 1953 Congress adopted a resolution establishing another special committee to investigate foundations, this time under the chairmanship of Congressman B. Carroll Reece of Tennessee, who had been a member of the Cox Committee and sponsored the resolution.[241] The Special Committee to Investigate Tax-Exempt Foundations and Comparable Organizations was charged with examining issues similar to those that the Cox Committee had studied but with the added charge of looking into political purposes, propaganda, or attempts to influence legislation. The Reece Committee held public hearings in sixteen sessions during the spring of 1954, receiving testimony from five general witnesses and three members of the Committee staff.[242] They charged that great changes had occurred in America in the direction of socialism and collectivism and that these changes were aided through a "'diabolical conspiracy' of foundations and certain educational and research organizations."[243] The Committee members were apparently divided in their attitude toward the content of the hearings, as well as their conduct, and the final report was signed by only three of the five members, with one of them in effect negating his signature by submitting a statement that reaffirmed his views as expressed in the Cox Committee report.[244]

The report concluded with fourteen findings charging that foundations had power and influence so great that they might control a large part of the American economy, and that they were characterized by interlocking control by a professional class of administrators. Although the Committee stated that foundation activity was clearly desirable when operating in the natural sciences and making direct donations to religious, educational, scientific, and other institutional donees, it found that foundation activities in the social sciences were cause for alarm, particularly since the research was empirical, as opposed to theoretical, and thereby threatened the basic moral, religious, and governmental principles of the country. It stated that foundations had displayed a distinct tendency to favor political opinions to the left, had led education toward the promotion of collectivism, had affected foreign policy and education in things international, and, finally, had directly supported "subversion."[245]

241. H.R. Res. No. 217, 83d Cong., 1st Sess. (adopted July 27, 1953).

242. Special (Reece) Committee to Investigate Tax-Exempt Foundations and Comparable Organizations: Hearings before the House of Representatives, 83d Cong., 2d Sess., pts. 1 and 2 (1954).

243. F. Emerson Andrews, *Philanthropic Foundations,* 345 (New York: Russell Sage Foundation, 1956).

244. Statement by Congressman Angier L. Goodwin of Massachusetts (reprinted in Andrews, *Philanthropic Foundations,* 346).

245. Special (Reece) Committee to Investigative Tax-Exempt Foundations and Comparable Organizations, *Report,* H.R. Rep. No. 2681 (1954).

The report contained a review of the testimony received at the hearings, as well as a 189-page appendix that consisted of an alphabetical listing and detailed discussion of persons or agencies "whose names had appeared in the body of the Report in a distinctive kind of type indicating that they had been cited by the Attorney General of the United States or by various other government agencies for having associations and affiliations of a questionable character."[246]

The majority's conclusions have been characterized as relatively mild in light of its findings.[247] They specifically did not recommend the abolition of all foundations or the removal of their tax-exempt status. They did recommend a continuing investigation of what they considered unfinished work. Specifically, they suggested that the manpower of the Internal Revenue Service be increased so that foundation activity could be watched more closely; that there be full public access to Form 990-As; and that a ten-to-twenty-five-year limit be placed on the life of all foundations. They further recommended that the accumulations provision of the Internal Revenue Code be amended to give foundations two to three years in which to distribute each year's income, but requiring all income to be paid out within that period and all capital gains to be treated as income and subject to the rule on accumulations. Finally, they recommended that restrictions be placed on corporation-controlled foundations, and that the denial of exemption for engaging in subversive or political activity be made retroactive unless the trustees and directors resigned forthwith.[248]

Congress took no action on the recommendations of the Reece Committee, nor was there any evidence that they were being taken seriously by any considerable part of the general public.[249] In 1962 Waldemar A. Neilsen wrote that the two congressional investigations of the 1950s had "not achieved much." He characterized the Reece Committee as "the most totally mismanaged Congressional investigation of the McCarthy period," which had caused the larger foundations to become exceedingly cautious in their programs, a development that he seriously criticized.[250]

The Patman Committee

A third congressional investigation of foundations was begun in 1961, six years after the release of the Reece Committee report. The impetus for this

---

246. Id. at 227.

247. Andrews, *Philanthropic Foundations,* 345.

248. Special (Reece) Committee, *Report.*

249. Andrews, *Philanthropic Foundations,* 346–347.

250. Waldemar A. Neilsen, "How Solid Are the Foundations?" *New York Times,* October 21, 1962, at 27.

investigation came from Congressman Wright Patman of Texas who, as chairman of the Select Committee on Small Business of the House of Representatives, conducted a preliminary survey of foundation activity as an individual member in 1961, on the basis of which he persuaded Congress of the need for an investigation of the impact of tax-exempt foundations on the American economy. His survey had entailed requests for financial information from more than 500 foundations and from the Internal Revenue Service, data that was analyzed by his staff during 1962. The congressman charged that the Internal Revenue Service files were inadequate and that it had been a struggle to obtain information from the foundations.

The results of this initial survey were contained in an interim report released in December 1962 that contained detailed financial statistics for 534 foundations together with information relating to certain holdings of the Ford Foundation. The report charged laxness and irresponsibility on the part of the Internal Revenue Service; violations of law and regulations by many foundations; withdrawal of almost $7 billion from taxation in the years between 1951 and 1960, a number that represented the total receipts of 534 of an estimated 45,124 foundations; a rapidly increasing concentration of economic power in foundations, which was characterized as far more dangerous than any past concentration of economic power; and the possession by foundation-controlled enterprises of sufficient money and competitive advantage to eliminate the small businessman. The report charged that there might be thousands of foundations operating without knowledge of the Treasury.[251]

The report concluded with a call for an immediate moratorium on foundation tax exemptions, and enactment of seventeen legislative measures to limit the business operations of foundations; control accumulations of income by limiting foundations to a twenty-five-year life and require current distributions of income sufficient to assure total distribution at the end of the twenty-five-year period; restrict the deductibility of contributions; and limit private benefits.[252]

The congressman also recommended measures to increase federal regulation, including consideration of establishing a separate regulatory agency for the supervision of foundations, public disclosure of all matters relating to granting and revoking tax exemption, greater disclosure of amounts spent by foundations on lobbying, political activities, and advertising, expansion of field audits, and stiff penalties and revocation of exemption for improper or insufficient reporting.[253] Several of these proposals were similar to those

251. Select House Committee on Small Business, Chairman's (Patman) Report, *Tax-Exempt Foundations and Charitable Trusts: Their Impact on Our Economy*, First Installment, 87th Cong., 2d Sess., at 2 (December 31, 1962).

252. Id.

253. Id.

made by the Reece Committee; a majority of them have continued to surface in the years since 1962.

The Patman Committee preliminary report received widespread coverage in the press and led to the appointment of a White House Task Force to study whether changes were needed within the Internal Revenue Service or whether new legislation was warranted.[254] In the summer of 1963 the Treasury named an advisory group of private individuals interested in and directly concerned with private foundations to provide information on their operations and investment practices.

There was also an immediate reaction within the Internal Revenue Service. In 1961, prior to publication of the Patman Report, but clearly in anticipation of its release, the Service instituted a program to encourage and improve voluntary compliance, which included revision of reporting forms and increased audits. Revisions of Form 990-A were made again in 1962 and 1963, scheduled audits for exempt organizations were increased from 2,000 to 10,000 per year, and a Master File of exempt organizations was to be compiled from responses to a questionnaire sent to all organizations on the Service records. The Service also established an Exempt Organization Council composed of representatives of various branches of the Service that would make recommendations to the Commissioner regarding the administration of exempt organizations.

A second installment of the Patman Report was released in October 1963.[255] Of 407 pages, 324 consisted of exhibits, correspondence, and documents pertaining to the business transactions of a number of foundations, including three controlled by a New York industrialist that in fact were in the process of being dissolved. This was followed by a third installment of the Patman Report in March 1964.[256] It contained three pages of text describing the "Destructive Effect on Our Tax Base" of the disposition of the estate of Alfred I. DuPont and the Nemours Foundation and 326 pages of related tables and exhibits, all designed to demonstrate the manner in which property escapes taxation.

The Patman Committee held public hearings in the summer of 1964, at which the Secretary of the Treasury, the former Commissioner of Internal Revenue, and the Acting Chairman of the Securities and Exchange Commission were called as witnesses. At its conclusion the subcommittee issued a re-

---

254. *Foundation News,* November 1962, at 5.

255. Patman Committee, *Tax-Exempt Foundations and Charitable Trusts,* Second Installment, 88th Cong., 1st Sess. (Comm. Print, October 16, 1963).

256. Patman Committee, *Tax-Exempt Foundations and Charitable Trusts,* Third Installment, 88th Cong., 2d Sess. (Comm. Print, March 20, 1964).

port containing a summary of the findings and recommendations from the earlier reports.[257]

The next public announcements from the Patman Committee came in December 1966 when Installment 4 of the congressman's report to his committee was issued.[258] Installment 5 followed in April 1967,[259] and the Committee held another series of hearings in October and November of that year that focused almost exclusively on the activities of an organization called Americans Building Constitutionally, the purpose of which was tax reduction.[260] Three other installments of the congressman's report were published, one in March 1968,[261] and another in June 1969.[262] The last of the reports, released in August 1972,[263] was issued on behalf of the Subcommittee on Domestic Finance of the Committee on Banking and Currency and came after passage of the Tax Reform Act of 1969, which contained restrictions on private foundations, many of which had been recommended by the Patman Committee.

The Patman investigation had elements of the best and the worst use of congressional investigatory power. Reforms in the Internal Revenue Service procedure for dealing with tax-exempt organizations were long overdue, and although the need had been recognized by Service personnel before the start of the investigation, publicity generated by the hearings and reports did accelerate their implementation. On the other hand, the reports, the congressman's statements, and some of the charges made at the public hearings went beyond the area of the subcommittee's mandate, which was to consider the impact of foundations on small business. One member of the subcommittee objected that the failure to afford to foundations any public opportunity to refute the charges made against them, or to place their justifications on the printed record, amounted to "an indictment without even being advised that

257. Tax-Exempt Foundations—Their Impact on Small Business: Hearings before the Subcommittee No. 1 on Foundations of the Select House Committee on Small Business, 88th Cong., 2d Sess. (1964).

258. Patman Committee, *Tax-Exempt Foundations and Charitable Trusts*, Fourth Installment, 89th Cong., 2d Sess. (Comm. Print, December 21, 1966).

259. Patman Committee, *Tax-Exempt Foundations and Charitable Trusts*, Fifth Installment, 90th Cong., 1st Sess. (Comm. Print, April 28, 1967).

260. Tax-Exempt Foundations—Their Impact on Small Business: Hearings before the Subcommittee on Small Business of the House Select Committee, 90th Cong., 1st Sess. (1967).

261. Patman Committee, *Tax-Exempt Foundations and Charitable Trusts*, Sixth Installment, 90th Cong., 2d Sess. (Comm. Print, March 26, 1968).

262. Patman Committee, *Tax-Exempt Foundations and Charitable Trusts*, Seventh Installment, 91st Cong., 1st Sess. (Comm. Print, June 30, 1969).

263. House Committee on Banking, Finance, and Urban Affairs, Subcommittee Chairman's (Patman) Report, *Tax-Exempt Foundations and Charitable Trusts*, Eighth Installment, 92d Cong., 2d Sess. (Comm. Print, August 1972).

a party is under indictment or possibly to be indicted."[264] Furthermore, the recommendations were inconsistent and confusing, in many cases based on mistakes of fact, the most egregious of which being the assertion that there were 45,124 foundations in existence at the end of 1960[265] when, in fact, this was the number of Form 990-As filed by all organizations using the form. Both the Treasury and the Foundation Library Center estimated that there were approximately 15,000 foundations in existence at the end of 1961.[266]

1965 Treasury Department Report on Private Foundations

Partly in response to the Patman Reports, the Senate Finance Committee and the House Ways and Means Committee in January 1964 requested the Treasury to prepare a report on the adequacy of the 1950 amendments to the Internal Revenue Code in remedying abuses by exempt organizations, and whether new abuses had developed since then and new legislation was needed. In response the Treasury conducted a survey of approximately 1,300 foundations picked by a random sampling method to include all foundations with assets of $10 million or more, 25% of those with assets from $1 million to $10 million, 10% of those in the $100,000 to $1 million range, and 5% of the remaining foundations. Information from the IRS and the Foundation Center was used to identify the participants in the survey who were asked a series of questions relating to the nature of their assets, the composition of their board, and details of self-dealing transactions between the foundation and its board, officers, contributors, and related parties.

The results of this study were released on February 2, 1965.[267] The report also contained results of its survey, an appraisal of the place and value of foundations in the country, and analysis and recommendations for reform of the tax laws. In response to the charge that the use of foundations to dispense funds resulted in undue delay in the transfer of benefits to society, the Treasury concluded that it had "considerable force," but was capable of solution by a legislative measure of special designation and limited scope.[268] The charge that foundations were becoming a disproportionately large segment of the national economy was characterized as lacking factual basis, as was the assertion that foundation lives should be limited.[269]

264. 108 Cong. Rec. 16,996 (1962) (Representative William H. Avery).

265. Chairman's (Patman) Report, *Tax-Exempt Foundations and Charitable Trusts*, Third Installment, at v.

266. McGreevy, "Review of Rulings and Forms for Reporting," 175, 200.

267. Staff of Treasury Department, *Report on Private Foundations*, 89th Cong., 1st Sess. (Senate Finance Committee, February 2, 1965).

268. Id. at 13.

269. Id. at 13–14.

The report's response to a third criticism of foundations, that they represented a dangerous concentration of economic and social power, was that for the present the matter was being amply met by foundations themselves. The report concluded with recommendations responding to six specific problems, but concluded that there was no need for a separate regulatory agency, so long as appropriate amendments to the tax laws were enacted.[270]

The six specific problems identified by the Treasury were (1) self-dealing, (2) delay in benefit to charity, (3) foundation involvement in business, (4) family use of foundations to control corporate and other property, (5) conduct of financial transactions unrelated to charitable functions, and (6) the need to broaden foundation management. The Treasury recommended an absolute ban on self-dealing for substantial contributors and foundation managers; denial of an income tax deduction for donations of an interest in property over which the donor and related parties retained control until either the foundation disposed of the asset or devoted the property to active charitable operations, or the donor control was terminated; and a prohibition against a foundation holding more than 20% of the stock of a business unrelated to the foundation's charitable activities. A fourth recommendation designed to further limit donor influence provided that after a foundation had been in existence for twenty-five years, its donor and related parties could comprise no more than 25% of the managing board, and the newly constituted board would be empowered to dissolve the foundation and distribute its assets. In regard to accumulation of income, the report recommended that foundations be required to spend all of their income no later than the year after which it was received, and be required to spend the equivalent of income if assets included non-income-producing property. The question of appropriate sanctions was not addressed, although the issue had been raised with the advisory committee during the course of its meetings.[271]

Tax Reform Act of 1969

Tax reform was a major item on the congressional agenda at the start of 1969. The Ways and Means Committee held hearings in February on a bill,[272] which contained provisions designed to curtail what were perceived as foundation abuses and relied heavily on the recommendations contained in the 1965 Treasury Report. The first witness was Congressman Patman, who called for a 20% tax on the income of foundations, a limit on private foundation ownership of more than 3% of the outstanding stock of any corporation,

---

270. Id. at 14.
271. Id. at 14–18.
272. H.R. 13270, 91st Cong., 1st Sess. (1969).

and annual distribution of all foundation income. Representatives from a number of the larger foundations, as well as the Foundation Center and the Council on Foundations, also testified, some favoring congressional action and others arguing that the matter should be left to state regulation. Of concern to a number of the witnesses was the recommendation that foundation ownership of businesses be limited.

While the Patman Committee's and the Treasury Department's recommendations were directed to regulating foundations' control of businesses and their failure to provide immediate benefit to society, the 1969 hearings also addressed the political activities of certain foundations. As described by Troyer, "Disquiet about foundations—already present in the Ways and Means Committee at least as early as 1963 . . . grew gradually to a deepening sense of distrust among the Ways and Means members as the week of hearings proceeded."[273] Troyer noted the anger that occasionally was generated after certain testimony, giving as an example that of Congressman John Rooney (D-N.Y.), who recounted his opponent's use of a foundation he controlled in his campaign to unseat Rooney.[274] "Little could carry fear more directly to the heart of an incumbent Member of Congress; and the rule against any foundation expenditure 'to influence the outcome of any specific political campaign' doubtless received powerful thrust then and there."[275]

Troyer attributed other foundation-grant restrictions adopted by Congress, "primarily at least," to Committee questioning of McGeorge Bundy about Ford Foundation grants, in particular grants to members of Senator Robert Kennedy's staff, support to the Congress on Racial Equality for voter registration in a heavily contested mayoral election in Cleveland, and allegations of lax supervision of certain grants made in New York City.[276]

> Bundy's appearance in the Ways and Means hearings doubtless had its part in stimulating Committee member antagonism toward foundations. He was smarter and more articulate than most people—by a considerable distance—and if he made any effort to conceal his sense of those capacities in his testimony, its effect was limited.
>
> It would be quite wrong, though, to attribute the Committee's mounting distrust of, and hostility toward foundations to Bundy alone. The Members knew that the Treasury Report detailed a considerable

273. Thomas A. Troyer, "The 1969 Private Foundation Law: Historical Perspective on Its Origins and Underpinnings," in *Conference: Private Foundations Reconsidered—Policies and Alternatives, Old and New*, 26 (New York University School of Law, National Center on Philanthropy and the Law, 1999).

274. Id. at 27.

275. Id.

276. Id.

number of specific examples of foundation activities falling far short of prompt and single-minded devotion to charitable works, and they had been told that the Treasury survey had revealed more such examples. Moreover, whatever their personal feelings about Congressman Patman, by 1969 the massive publicity generated by his investigations and reports surely contributed to their strong sense that all was not well in the foundation field.[277]

Simon in his retrospective analysis of the 1969 legislation confirms these observations, while placing them within the larger climate in which Congress was acting, and within what he described as an assault against private foundations, with attacks coming from all sides, including those from the populist left represented by Patman and by Senator Albert Gore Sr. of Tennessee; from opponents of racial integration, including George Wallace; and from some academics.[278]

The Senate Finance Committee approved an amended version of the House bill, which contained most of the provisions affecting foundations, but added one that would have limited the life of any foundation to forty years.[279] In debate on the floor of the Senate, this provision was removed, replaced by one requiring a mandatory payout that was set initially at 6%, but was to be adjusted periodically to reflect changes in Treasury yields. Rather than the 20% tax on foundation income recommended by Patman, or the 7.5% excise tax in the original bill, the final version provided for a 4% excise tax on foundation income, which was characterized as an "audit fee" that would cover the cost of increased audit activity of tax-exempt organizations by the IRS.[280]

The substantive provisions of the Tax Reform Act affecting what were thereafter legally designated as "private foundations" are described in Chapter 5. They represented a landmark in the history of government regulation of charity, containing strict limitations that went to the heart of foundation administration. Of even wider import for the entire charitable sector was the fact that the act changed the sanctions for noncompliance, imposing meaningful penalties in the form of excise taxes not only on the charities themselves, but on their fiduciaries and, in the case of the self-dealing provisions, on the persons who profited from the self-dealing rather than on the foundations themselves, thereby preserving charitable assets for future public benefit.

277. Id. at 28–29.

278. John G. Simon, "The Regulation of American Foundations: Looking Backward at the Tax Reform Act of 1969," 6 *Voluntas* 243, 243–244 (December 1995).

279. S. Rep. No. 91-552, 91st Cong., 1st Sess. (1969).

280. Joint Committee on Taxation, *General Explanation of Tax Reform Act of 1969* (JCS-16-70), 29 (December 3, 1970).

One of the most disquieting revelations that emerged from the 1969 tax-writing process was the lack of cohesion among the charitable sector. The foundation community found itself divided between those who fought against greater federal regulation and a larger group that recognized that there were abuses to be corrected and that Congress would look to the IRS to do the correcting. In addition, the charitable sector itself was divided between foundations on the one hand and the remaining universe of charities that became known in common parlance as "public charities." During the course of passage of the act, the position of a large segment of the public charity universe was that of self-defense, with many organizations signaling to Congress that it could do as it wanted to private foundations, but should leave the rest of the sector, by implication the good part, alone. It was only after the act became fully effective that this group came to realize that the 4% tax on the net income of all foundations served primarily to reduce the amount they would receive as grants, and that the expenditure responsibility provisions posed limits on their operations. Above all, the entire universe of charities was forced to acknowledge an atmosphere of hostility to philanthropy that had not been manifest for many years, and to recognize that it could be successfully countered only if the component parts of the sector joined as one and became actively involved in lobbying for their common interests.

Reactions to the Tax Reform Act from the Nonprofit Sector

The Peterson Commission

In April 1969 a group of citizens, initially gathered together by John D. Rockefeller III, had formed a private Commission on Foundations and Private Philanthropy (known informally as the Peterson Commission after the name of its chairman, Peter G. Peterson, president of Bell and Howell) to address the issues then being considered by Congress. The Commission had sixteen members, none of whom had a direct relationship with foundations, and a staff of five. Studies were commissioned from scholars and members of the nonprofit community, initially with the intent that they would be available before the hearings of the Senate Finance Committee scheduled for the fall. Although the Commission was not prepared to issue a report by that time, Peterson did present testimony at the scheduled hearings, indicating approval of limits on foundation business holdings, and support for a required minimum annual payout that would have been in the range of 6% to 8% of the value of a foundation's assets. This was viewed as a means for improving foundation investment practices in addition to its providing immediate public benefit.[281]

The final recommendations of the Peterson Commission and the studies it generated were published in 1970 after passage of the Reform Act.[282] The recommendations were grouped into two major parts: recommendations to foundations to improve practices and communications among them, and recommendations to government, which included recommendations relating to tax policy and administration. The group called for establishment of a national Advisory Board on Philanthropy composed of ten to fifteen private individuals, appointed by the President, and granted governmental powers to obtain information about philanthropy. Its role was to evaluate performance of charities and of government regulation, and propose incentives for charitable giving and improvements in the sector. Coming as it did after passage of the Tax Reform Act of 1969, the report itself did not generate wide interest. However, the Commission played an important role as spokesman for the sector during the deliberations on the act, and undoubtedly mitigated the effect of the proposals before Congress that would have been most restrictive.

The Filer Commission

In 1973, as Congress was again ready to consider proposals to reduce tax incentives for charitable giving, another commission was formed, again with impetus from John D. Rockefeller III. Its chairman was John Filer, president of a national life insurance company, and the twenty-six commissioners included members of the academic community, civic and business leaders, a union representative, a judge, and the president of a major private foundation. Chief of staff for the commission was Leonard Silverstein, a Washington-based tax attorney with extensive experience in matters relating to tax-exempt organizations and private philanthropy. The Commission obtained reports from more than eighty-one individuals and organizations, almost all of which were published, together with its recommendations, by the U.S. Treasury as Research Papers. These studies covered a wide range of topics, and presented an unparalleled picture of the sector, its history, the scope of its activities, its strengths, and its weaknesses. They remain an invaluable source for historians, public policy experts, and tax planners.

281. Commission on Foundations and Private Philanthropy, *Foundations, Private Giving, and Public Policy* (Chicago: University of Chicago Press, 1970).

282. Id. at 126–168.

The recommendations of the Filer Commission were far-reaching.[283] They covered three major areas:

1. Broadening the base of philanthropy by enacting a deduction for nonitemizers and a double deduction for individuals with incomes of less than $15,000, and otherwise increasing tax incentives for contributions.
2. Improving the philanthropic process, including requiring all charities other than churches to publish annual reports; changing the 4% excise tax on foundations to an audit fee based on the cost of regulation; relaxing the expenditure responsibility requirements for private foundations; changing the payout rate to a flat 5%; and making the lobbying limits on public charities the same as those applicable to business and trade associations.
3. Retaining the Internal Revenue Service as the principal regulating agency for tax-exempt organizations; instituting federal regulation of interstate solicitations while urging more effective state regulation of intrastate fund-raising; amending the Internal Revenue Code to provide sanctions more appropriate than loss of tax exemption as well as providing for administrative or judicial review of the principal existing sanction of revocation of exemption; and establishing a permanent quasi-governmental national commission on the nonprofit sector with power to monitor and support the sector, acting as its spokesman before Congress, the executive branch, and the public.

During the course of the Filer Commission's deliberations, representatives of a number of grantee organizations, including a number of advocacy groups, protested the composition of the Commission, particularly the fact that it was not responsive to disenfranchised populations. Calling themselves the Donee Group, these representatives met with the Filer Commission and obtained from it financial support to conduct a separate study. The Donee Group ultimately prepared its own set of recommendations that were published as part of the final Filer Commission papers. The Donee Group recommendations included opposition to the Filer Commission's proposal to permit deductions for gifts of appreciated property; support of a 6% payout rate for foundations; and calls to limit donor control of foundations, place a limit on fund-raising costs, and establish a national regulatory body for charity to take over the regulatory role of the IRS.[284]

283. "Commission on Private Philanthropy and Public Needs Commentary on Commission Recommendations," in Department of Treasury, Commission on Private Philanthropy and Public Needs, *Research Papers*, vol. 1, pt. 1, at 3–48 (1977).

284. "Private Philanthropy: Vital and Innovative or Passive and Irrelevant—The Donee Group Report and Recommendations," in *Research Papers*, vol. 1, pt. 1, at 49–85.

As described in succeeding sections of this chapter, many of the recommendations of the Filer Commission and the Donee Group were adopted by Congress or by the sector itself. However, the Filer Commission's final recommendation—the establishment of a permanent national commission to represent and advocate for philanthropy—met with disapproval by a large number of the leaders of the sector who feared and opposed any extension of government regulation.[285] Nonetheless, the recommendation contributed to a growing understanding of the need of the sector to have a national voice in policymaking as well as wider-based public support.

While the recommendation of the Filer Commission to establish a quasi-governmental agency to oversee and encourage the nonprofit sector met with general disapproval, it did provide the impetus for creation of a new non-governmental organization, the purpose of which was to fill the supporting role envisioned by the Commission. The new organization, Independent Sector, was established in 1980 through the merger of two existing non-profits, the National Council on Philanthropy and the Coalition of National Voluntary Organizations.

Under the leadership of John Gardner as chairman and Brian O'Connell as president, Independent Sector set about to become the spokesman for the nonprofit sector, as well as its leader in improving practices and increasing giving and volunteering. Starting with fifty members, it had over 600 members five years later and its funding was assured. At the end of 2000 the membership was 700, including almost all of the national organizations representing the various components of the sector. Independent Sector's lobbying efforts have been unusually successful. It has also submitted amicus briefs to the United States Supreme Court on issues affecting solicitation of funds for charitable purposes, and has conducted nationwide educational efforts to increase the amount of charitable giving.

At the same time that Independent Sector was being formed, the role of the Donee Group was taken on by the National Committee for Responsive Philanthropy under the leadership of Pablo Eisenberg, who had been the principal spokesman for the Donee Group. The Committee has continued the focus of the Donee Group as critic of foundations, corporate giving programs, and United Ways, with support from more than 200 members.

Prior to 1969 there had been a number of national organizations representing the various components of the charitable sector. They included the Council on Foundations, the Council for Advancement and Support of Edu-

---

285. Eleanor L. Brilliant, *Private Charity and Public Inquiry: A History of the Filer and Peterson Commissions,* 130–131 (Bloomington: Indiana University Press, 2000).

cation, the American Hospital Association, the National Health Council, Catholic Charities, and Lutheran Services in America. Most of these developed more active lobbying programs and, working together as members of Independent Sector, have had a more influential role in the framing of legislation affecting the sector than had been the case prior to 1970. This will be evident in the succeeding sections of this chapter.

Congressional Activity after the Tax Reform Act of 1969

No issues relating to the operations of exempt organizations have received the same degree of interest and attention from Congress as that generated by the Patman investigations. Nor have any lasted as long or produced as much printed information. Of the issues that have been the subject of congressional investigations and hearings in the years between 1970 and 2002, private foundations remained on the agenda, joined by consideration of a number of other issues, including political and lobbying activities, competition with small business, and the audit of churches.

Private Foundations

The impact of the Tax Reform Act of 1969 on private foundations was the subject of extensive hearings before the Subcommittee on Foundations of the Senate Finance Committee in 1974 and 1976,[286] and led to the amendment of section 4940 to reduce the excise tax on foundation income from 4% to 2%[287] as well as to change the payout rate for foundations to a fixed 5% of asset value.[288] In 1983 the House of Representatives also reviewed the effect of the Tax Reform Act of 1969 on private foundations, but no additional legislative enactments ensued.[289] No investigations have been conducted as to their activities, and it was generally believed that the provisions of the 1969

286. Private Foundations: Hearings before the Subcommittee on Foundations of the Senate Committee on Finance, 93d Cong., 2d Sess. (1974); Impact of Current Economic Crisis on Foundations and Recipients of Foundation Money: Hearings before the Subcommittee on Foundations of the Senate Committee on Finance, 93d Cong., 2d Sess (1974); Tax Reform Act of 1975, Part 5: Hearings before the Senate Committee on Finance, 94th Cong., 2d Sess. (1976).

287. Revenue Act of 1978, Pub. L. No. 95-600, §520(a), 92 Stat. 2763, 2884 (1978).

288. Tax Reform Act of 1976, Pub. L. No. 94-455, §1303, 90 Stat. 1520, 1715 (1976).

289. Tax Rules Governing Private Foundations, Part 1: Hearings before the Subcommittee on Oversight of the House Committee on Ways and Means, Serial 98-32, 98th Cong., 1st Sess. (1983); Tax Rules Governing Private Foundations, Part 2: Hearings before the Subcommittee on Oversight of the House Committee on Ways and Means, Serial 98-33, 98th Cong., 1st Sess. (1983).

Act had corrected the abuses perceived by Congress at the time, with the exception of the payout rate, which continued to be an issue of contention. In 1984, in response to charges that foundations were incurring excessive administrative expenses that were included in determining their minimum distribution amounts, the Code was amended to limit the amount of such expenses that could be counted against the 5% payout requirement to .65% of the foundation's asset value.[290] The limit was imposed for a five-year test period,[291] and the Treasury and the IRS were directed to study its operation and recommend whether it should be extended.[292] This study, which was released in early 1990, recommended that the limit be allowed to terminate, a conclusion accepted by the legislature.[293]

In the spring of 2003, Congress again addressed the question of whether foundation administrative costs were excessive and should be curbed. A provision was included in a House bill that would have reduced the excise tax on foundations from 2% to 1% and would have excluded administrative expenses from the computation of qualifying distributions.[294] The proposal divided the charitable sector, and efforts were made to achieve a compromise.[295] The version passed by the House in September 2003 would limit, rather than eliminate, the amount of expenses that could be included in determining compliance with the payout rule by excluding general overhead expenses and placing a cap on management salaries and excessive travel expenses.[296] There were a number of drawbacks to the compromise, notably uncertainty as to the scope of the amounts to be included and the application of the caps, and it was clear that neither side was wholly satisfied with the outcome. The rift between grantors and grantees mirrored that which occurred during the deliberations of the Filer Commission.

---

290. I.R.C. §4942(g)(4), codified by Deficit Reduction Act of 1984, Pub. L. No. 98-369, §304, 98 Stat. 494, 782-783 (1984).

291. I.R.C. §4942(g)(4)(F).

292. H.R. Conf. Rep. No. 861, 98th Cong., 2d Sess., at 1087 (1984).

293. Department of Treasury, *Grant-Making Administrative Expenses Study* (January 1990), reprinted in 90 *Tax Notes Today* 31-16 (February 7, 1990).

294. Charitable Giving Act of 2003, H.R. 7, §105, 108th Cong., 1st Sess. (introduced May 7, 2003).

295. Michael Klausner, "For Foundation Payout Rates, Time Isn't Money," *Stanford Social Innovation Review* (Spring 2003), at 51; Harvey Lipman and Ian Wilhelm, "Pressing Foundations to Give More," *Chronicle of Philanthropy*, May 29, 2003, at 7; Fred Stokeld, "Foundation Reps Look for Compromise on Administrative Expenses Dispute," 2003 *Tax Notes Today* 157-2 (August 14, 2003).

296. Charitable Giving Act of 2003, H.R. 7, §105, 108th Cong., 1st Sess. (September 17, 2003).

Lobbying by Public Charities

Political activities and lobbying received congressional attention in the mid 1970s. The limitations on lobbying were the subject of hearings in the House in 1972 and 1976[297] and in the Senate in 1976.[298] At issue was the imprecision of the Code provision prohibiting public charities from engaging in substantial lobbying. The outcome was the enactment of section 501(h), which permits public charities other than churches to elect to have an expenditure test apply to determine compliance with the "substantial" test.[299] The act also attempted to close a perceived loophole by prohibiting an organization that lost its exemption under section 501(c)(3) from obtaining exemption under section 501(c)(4).[300]

In 1987 the Senate Subcommittee on Oversight reconsidered the effectiveness of the limitation on lobbying by public charities and the provisions of section 501(h).[301] This led to a consensus within Congress that they were ineffective in curbing these activities by certain organizations and that the sanction of revocation of exemption for an isolated political campaign activity was in some instances too harsh; moreover, for some organizations the sanction was meaningless in that they would disband in all events after the campaign they were formed to support or oppose was concluded. The outcome was enactment of section 4912, which imposed excise taxes on organizations and their managers for the year in which the organization lost its exemption by reason of having conducted substantial lobbying.[302]

Unfair Competition with Small Businesses

Allegations of unfair competition between charities and small businesses received the attention of Congress during the 1980s. This interest was gener-

---

297. Legislative Activity by Certain Types of Exempt Organizations: Hearings before the Subcommittee on Oversight of the House Committee on Ways and Means, 92d Cong., 2d Sess. (1972); Influencing Legislation by Public Charities: Hearings before the Subcommittee on Oversight of the House Committee on Ways and Means, 94th Cong., 2d Sess. (1976).

298. Tax Reform Act of 1975, Part 7: Hearings before the Senate Committee on Finance, 94th Cong., 2d Sess. (1976).

299. I.R.C. §501(h), codified by Tax Reform Act of 1976, Pub. L. No. 94-455, §1307(a), 90 Stat. 1520, 1720–1721 (1976).

300. I.R.C. §504, codified by Tax Reform Act of 1976, Pub. L. No. 94-455, §1307(a)(2), 90 Stat. 1520, 1721–1722 (1976).

301. Lobbying and Political Activities of Tax-Exempt Organizations: Hearings before the Subcommittee on Oversight of the House Committee on Ways and Means, Serial 100-15, 100th Cong., 1st Sess. (1987).

302. I.R.C. §4912, codified by Omnibus Budget Reconciliation Act of 1987, Pub. L. No. 100-203, §10714(a), 101 Stat. 1330, 1330-470 to 1330-472 (1987).

ated by reports from the Small Business Administration to the effect that charities were benefiting unduly at the expense of small businesses. In September 1986 the chairman of the Ways and Means Committee requested Congressman J. J. Pickle, chairman of the Subcommittee on Oversight, to conduct a comprehensive review of the tax treatment of commercial and other income-producing activities of tax-exempt organizations. The Subcommittee issued a set of sixteen questions, which it termed its framework for review, and commissioned the General Accounting Office (GAO) to provide information on the competition issue.

The results of the GAO study appeared in a Briefing Report that was made public in February 1987.[303] It served as a resource during hearings held by the Subcommittee on Oversight over five days in June 1987.[304] Nearly a year later, on March 31, 1988, the Subcommittee released a set of preliminary discussion options relating to the unrelated business income tax (UBIT) and requested public comments.[305] They included substitution of a "directly related" test for the current "substantially related" one, determining whether each income-producing activity standing alone was tax-exempt, or retaining the current test but imposing tax on twelve specific activities "whose nature and scope are inherently commercial, rather than charitable." Each of the twelve had been the target of a segment of the business community. Ten options were suggested that dealt with other aspects of the UBIT provisions, and the report concluded with recommendations to meet the need for increased reporting and improved IRS administration. The Subcommittee reported receiving over 400 comments that were subsequently made public.[306]

The final report of the Pickle Subcommittee contained a detailed review of the current law, and summarized testimony from the hearings and public comments, giving particular attention to the Treasury's recommendation that the existing form of the tax be retained, while increasing IRS oversight and making technical changes to the law in connection with the allocation of expenses, the definition of a controlled subsidiary, and exclusions from income for research activities and from partnerships.[307]

303. General Accounting Office, *Competition between Taxable Businesses and Tax-Exempt Organizations* (GAO/GGD-87-40BR) (February 1987).

304. The Unrelated Business Income Tax, Parts 1–3: Hearings before the Subcommittee on Oversight of the House Committee on Ways and Means, Serial 100-26, 100-27, 100-28, 100th Cong., 1st Sess. (1987).

305. Subcommittee on Oversight, House Committee on Ways and Means, Press Release No. 16 (March 31, 1988); see also Subcommittee on Oversight, House Committee on Ways and Means, *Report on Recommendations on the Unrelated Business Income Tax (UBIT)*, 100th Cong., 2d Sess. (1988).

306. Subcommittee on Oversight, *Report on Recommendations on the Unrelated Business Income Tax (UBIT)*.

307. Id.

The report concluded that the "substantially related" test to determine which business activities would not be subject to income tax should be retained and that additional studies based on better reporting and meaningful data were needed before there was a major overhaul of the law, but that in the meantime certain areas could be clarified and strengthened. Among the activities that were targeted as needing attention were gift shops, bookstores, catalog and mail order activities, activities related to sale of medical equipment and devices, drugs, and laboratory testing, fitness activities, travel and tour services, ancillary food sales, veterinary activities, hotel facility activities, sales of condominiums and time-sharing units, affinity credit cards and similar merchandise, and theme or amusement park activities. In addition, the Subcommittee recommended repeal of the convenience exception, modification of the royalty exclusion, and expansion of the definition of control for purposes of taxing income of a subsidiary. Other changes related to the allocation of expenses and the computation of advertising income. Improved regulation by the IRS, increased and improved reporting provisions, and more accurate disclosure of nondeductibility of return benefit payments by donors were also supported.[308]

Despite the amount of attention to the issue of competition and the effectiveness of the UBIT provisions, Congress took no immediate action in response to the recommendations of the Subcommittee. During the ensuing years, legislation was passed to modify the rules relating to corporate sponsorships and sales and exchange of mailing lists. It was not until 1997, however, that the standard for determining control of a taxable subsidiary was changed as recommended by the Pickle Subcommittee.[309] During the interim, as described below, the IRS did respond to almost all of the other issues raised by the Subcommittee.

CORPORATE SPONSORSHIPS. The issue of payments by business to charities in exchange for public acknowledgment of the payment came to public attention during the 1990s after the Service held that payments for the right to sponsor certain college athletic events, including the Mobil Cotton Bowl and the John Hancock Bowl, were for advertising rights subject to the tax on unrelated business and not charitable contributions as the donors claimed.[310] Affected companies and charities turned to Congress to obtain legislation exempting these payments from tax, but a provision to

308. Id.

309. I.R.C. §512(b)(13)(D), amended by Taxpayer Relief Act of 1997, Pub. L. No. 105-34, §1041(a), 111 Stat. 788, 938–939 (1997).

310. Priv. Ltr. Rul. 91-47-007 (August 16, 1991); Priv. Ltr. Rul. 92-31-001 (October 22, 1991).

this effect enacted in 1992 was vetoed.[311] The Service then issued proposed guidelines designed to clarify the circumstances under which sponsorship payments would be taxable and followed this with a proposed regulation section 1.513-4 that followed the guidelines in most respects. Before the regulation was made final, Congress enacted a new section 513(i) that contained more lenient standards for determining exemption from tax.[312] New proposed regulations reflecting the amendment changes were issued on January 22, 1993, but again were subjected to severe criticism.[313] Final regulations, which were not issued until April 2002, were responsive to the protests from the affected organizations.[314]

ROYALTIES. Another issue that garnered congressional attention and was resolved only after passage of legislation was the taxation of mailing list rentals and exchanges. As with sponsorship payments, the Service took the position that receipts from these sources were not in the nature of royalties that were exempt from UBIT, but rather were payments for services. In response to protests from affected charities, in 1986 Congress reversed the Service's position in regard to exchanges and rentals among charities and veterans organizations of lists of their own members and donors.[315] The Service continued to attempt to tax exchanges and rentals involving charities and other organizations until, after a series of defeats in the courts, in December 1999 it announced that it would no longer pursue the matter and directed its agents to settle outstanding cases.[316] However, the definition of royalties and thus the scope of the exemption continued to be a difficult issue for the Service, affecting the treatment of payments from affinity credit cards.

COMMERCIAL INSURANCE. In 1986 Congress enacted section 501(m) of the Code, which denied exemption to organizations that provide commercial-type insurance as a substantial part of their activities.[317] Aimed primarily at Blue Cross Blue Shield and similar health insurance providers,

311. H.R. 11, §7303, 102d Cong., 2d Sess. (1992) (vetoed on November 5, 1992).

312. I.R.C. §513(i), codified by Taxpayer Relief Act of 1997, Pub. L. No. 105-34, §965, 111 Stat. 788, 893–894 (effective after December 31, 1997).

313. 58 Fed. Reg. 5687 (1993).

314. 67 Fed. Reg. 20,433 (2002) (T.D. 8991) (effective April 25, 2002, for payments solicited or received after December 31, 1997).

315. I.R.C. §513(h)(1)(B), codified by Tax Reform Act of 1986, Pub. L. No. 99-514, §1601(a), 100 Stat. 2085, 2766–2767 (1986).

316. See Chapter 5; see also Memorandum from Director, Exempt Organizations Division, to Acting EO Area Managers (December 16, 1999).

317. I.R.C. §501(m), §833, codified by Tax Reform Act of 1986, Pub. L. No. 99-514, §1012(a), (b), 100 Stat. 2085, 2390–2394 (1986).

the revocation of exemption resulted in a number of these organizations being treated as charities under state law while being fully taxable business corporations for federal tax purposes, one of the rare instances in which this anomaly affected a large part of the charitable sector.

Standards for Exemption of Hospitals

The Internal Revenue Service has had difficulty establishing the requirements under which a hospital would qualify for exemption, particularly after the enactment of Medicare and Medicaid, which transformed the base of hospital revenues from reliance on contributions from the public, government grants, and fees for services from those able to pay to almost total reliance on payments from third parties. In an early ruling, exemption was conditioned on a hospital's providing free care to those unable to pay.[318] In 1969 the Service adopted a community benefit standard that could be met even though free care was not provided if the hospital operated an emergency room available to all.[319] This position was modified in 1983 to permit a hospital to demonstrate that operation of an emergency room would duplicate other emergency services available in the community.[320]

In July 1991 the Ways and Means Committee held hearings to review the basis for exemption of hospitals,[321] and to consider the provisions of two bills that would have codified additional requirements for exemption and imposed new sanctions for noncompliance.[322] Treasury representatives testified that community benefit was a more appropriate standard for determining exemption than one based on the amount of charity care being provided or other more specific requirements. It also voiced objections to the proposed sanctions that were based on mechanical tests tied to the value on a hospital's tax exemption, or would provide for a temporary loss of exemption along with certain intermediate sanctions. The Treasury suggested that intermediate

318. Rev. Rul. 56-185, 1956-1 C.B. 202.

319. Rev. Rul. 69-545, 1969-2 C.B. 117.

320. Rev. Rul. 83-157, 1983-2 C.B. 94.

321. Tax-Exempt Status of Hospitals, and Establishment of Charity Care Standards: Hearing before the Subcommittee on Oversight of the House Committee on Ways and Means, Serial 102-73, 102d Cong., 1st Sess. (1992). Prior to the hearing the GAO had conducted a survey of the provision of health care in five states and concluded that the criteria for exemption would need revision if Congress wished to encourage hospitals to provide charity care and other community services. General Accounting Office, *Nonprofit Hospitals: Better Standards Needed for Tax Exemption* (GAO/HRD-90-84) (May 1990).

322. Charity Care and Hospital Tax-Exempt Status Reform Act of 1991, H.R. 790, 102d Cong., 1st Sess. (1991); H.R. 1374, 102d Cong., 1st Sess. (1991).

sanctions similar to those imposed on private foundations would be more appropriate and far easier to administer.[323] Neither bill was passed, and the issue was not revisited by Congress in succeeding years. However, in the following year the Service published new audit guidelines for hospitals, which indicated that it would be increasing its attention to the issues that were addressed in the proposed legislation.[324]

Regulation of Church Activities

CHURCH AUDITS. Regulation of churches and church-affiliated organizations has been a particularly difficult area for Congress as well as for the Internal Revenue Service, as much because of the constitutional considerations as the sensitivity of Congress in regard to matters of religion, and as a result the rules applicable to churches are far more lenient than those for all other charities. For example, the determination of exemption for churches is essentially automatic in that they are under no obligation to file an application for exemption and receive a determination of eligibility. Furthermore, they are exempt from filing annual information returns and until 1969 were exempt from the tax on unrelated business income. In 1969 Congress enacted section 7605(c), which was designed to protect churches from unnecessary audits.[325] Then, in 1983, as a result of protests that the Service was being overly intrusive in its examining of churches, the Senate Subcommittee on Oversight conducted an examination of IRS audit procedures for religious organizations.[326] This led to the enactment of section 7611, which contained parts of section 7605(c) with new limits on the ability of the Service to conduct audits of churches.[327]

TELEVISION MINISTRIES. The Subcommittee on Oversight of the House Ways and Means Committee held a hearing in October 1987 on the effectiveness of the federal tax rules applicable to a category of religious organiza-

---

323. Tax-Exempt Status of Hospitals, and Establishment of Charity Care Standards: Hearing before the Subcommittee on Oversight of the House Committee on Ways and Means, Serial 102-73, 102d Cong., 1st Sess. (1992).

324. Audit Guidelines for Hospitals, Ann. 92-83, 1992-22 I.R.B. 59.

325. I.R.C. §7605(c), codified by Tax Reform Act of 1969, Pub L. No. 91-172, §121(f), 83 Stat. 487, 548 (1969).

326. Church Audit Procedures Act: Hearing before the Subcommittee on Oversight of the Senate Finance Committee, S. Hrg. 98-481, 98th Cong., 1st Sess. (1983).

327. I.R.C. §7611, codified by Deficit Reduction Act of 1984, Pub. L. No. 98-369, §1033(a), 98 Stat. 494, 1034–1039 (1984).

tions that were engaged in television ministries.[328] The press had called general attention to the activities of certain "televangelists" with large followings who were reported to be receiving large amounts of contributions that were not in all circumstances being applied for their charitable purposes. The press had focused on the activities of the PTL (Praise the Lord) Ministry and its leaders, Jim and Tammy Faye Bakker, who were offering partnerships in a vacation park and retreat that the PTL was building in South Carolina.[329]

The hearings focused on the effectiveness of self-regulation by ministries, especially in preventing diversion of funds to ministry insiders; the Service's difficulty in monitoring the tax compliance of ministries, given the limits on church audits and IRS reporting requirements for churches; and ongoing investigations of ministries by the Service. At the close of the hearings, the Internal Revenue Service agreed to provide the Subcommittee with quarterly status reports on its audit activities in connection with the televangelists. The first report, submitted in February 1988, covered the fourth quarter of 1987.[330] Congressman Pickle on November 2, 1988, requested a summary for the prior year, which was submitted by the IRS on December 5, 1988.[331] It covered the period between October 1987 and October 1988. The results of the report, released by the congressman, indicated that the Service had conducted six examinations of prominent televangelists, with two of them involving criminal inquiries. In most cases they involved diversion of funds from the organization to insiders who failed to report the payments as income. The case involving the Bakkers was not identified in the reports, but Jim Bakker was convicted of mail and wire fraud in October 1989, fined $500,000, and sentenced to forty-five years in prison, a sentence that was subsequently reduced to eight years. He was released in 1994.[332]

In June 1988 the IRS revised the Internal Revenue Manual to reflect procedures for collecting information for the quarterly reports to the Oversight

328. Federal Tax Rules Applicable to Tax-Exempt Organizations Involving Television Ministries: Hearing before the Subcommittee on Oversight of the House Committee on Ways and Means, Serial 100-43, 100th Cong., 1st Sess. (1988).

329. See, for example, William E. Schmidt, "TV Minister Calls His Resort 'Bait' for Christianity," *New York Times,* December 24, 1985, at A8.

330. "Service Recommends Prosecution of Television Evangelists," 88 *Tax Notes Today* 51-1 (March 7, 1988) (reprinting letter from IRS to Chairman Pickle).

331. "Pickle Releases IRS Televangelist Report," 88 *Tax Notes Today* 245-8 (December 7, 1988) (reprinting IRS report).

332. Ronald Smothers, "Ex-Television Evangelist Bakker Ends Prison Sentence for Fraud," *New York Times,* December 2, 1994, at A18.

Subcommittee.[333] No public reports were published after the one that covered the fourth quarter of 1988.[334] The reporting requirement was discontinued in 1994.

CHURCH SUPPORT OF CANDIDATES FOR PUBLIC OFFICE. Controversy over the prohibition against church participation in political campaigns came to the fore in late 1995 when the IRS revoked the exemption of a church that had placed a full-page advertisement in *USA Today* and the *Washington Times* four days before the 1992 election urging the public not to vote for Bill Clinton, and noting that it would accept tax-deductible donations to pay for the advertisement. The church appealed the revocation, but the Internal Revenue Service was upheld in the district court and, subsequently, in the court of appeals in a unanimous decision.[335]

In reaction several bills were introduced in Congress in 2001 and 2002 that would have permitted churches to participate in political campaigns on behalf of or in opposition to any candidate for public office, so long as the participation was not a substantial part of their activities.[336] Although such legislation was strongly supported by a number of conservative organizations, it was reported that a large number of clergy were opposed. Only one bill was brought before the House of Representatives, which failed of passage in the fall of 2002.[337]

Relief for Victims of the Terrorist Attacks of September 2001

The scope of exempt purposes became a subject of public and congressional concern in the aftermath of the terrorist attacks on September 11, 2001. Contributions to aid the victims came in at an unprecedented rate, and charities were faced immediately with the questions of to whom and under what circumstances they could disburse the contributions. Rulings issued

333. Internal Revenue Service, "Quarterly Activity Reports on Evangelist-Related Cases," MS CR 7(10)G-56, Manual Transmittal 7(10)00-148 (June 1, 1988); see also "Reporting Guidelines on Evangelist-Related Cases Provided," 91 *Tax Notes Today* 109-62 (May 17, 1991) (reprinting Internal Revenue Manual).

334. "Pickle Releases IRS Report on Tax-Evading Televangelists," 89 *Tax Notes Today* 59-16 (March 15, 1989) (reprinting IRS report).

335. Branch Ministries, Inc. v. Rossotti, 40 F. Supp. 2d 15 (D.D.C. 1999), aff'd, 211 F.3d 137 (D.C. Cir. 2000).

336. Houses of Worship Political Speech Protection Act, H.R. 2357, 107th Cong., 1st Sess. (2001); Bright-Line Act of 2001, H.R. 2931, 107th Cong., 2d Sess. (2001).

337. Houses of Worship Political Speech Protection Act, H.R. 2357, 107th Cong., 1st Sess. (2001).

by the Internal Revenue Service in connection with aid to the victims of the Oklahoma City bombing in 1995 had held that the Code required that beneficiaries be part of an "indefinite" class and that relief of the "distressed" could only be provided upon demonstration of financial need.[338] These guidelines were restated and expanded in the Service's 1999 *Continuing Professional Education Text*.[339]

Critics of these guidelines noted that the Service apparently relied on the definition of "needy" found in the regulations under section 170 of the Code, which limits the deductibility of contributions by businesses of inventory and other equipment to qualified charities that provide care of the ill, needy, or infants. Korman called attention to the inappropriateness of this application and the mistaken confluence of charitable class with "need."[340]

Immediately following the attacks, the Service issued an announcement summarizing the existing rulings and the establishment of expedited procedures for handling requests for exemption from new organizations formed to provide disaster relief. On November 8, the Ways and Means Oversight Committee convened hearings to investigate responses to the disaster.[341] The director of the IRS Exempt Organizations Division reiterated existing standards, in particular that payments to victims and their families must be based on need and that distributions pro rata were inappropriate.[342] This statement generated wide criticism from the media as well as from several relief organizations that had already made pro rata distributions among beneficiaries.[343] Then on December 10, the Commissioner of Internal Revenue announced what amounted to a new set of guidelines to the effect that distributions would be proper if made in good faith based on reasonable objectives.[344]

The Victims of Terrorism Tax Relief Act of 2001 was enacted in January

338. Internal Revenue Service, *IRS Guidance Letter for Relief Efforts in Oklahoma City* (August 25, 1995).

339. Ruth Rivera Huetter and Marvin Friedlander, "Disaster Relief and Emergency Hardship Programs," *1999 IRS Continuing Professional Education Text,* 219–242.

340. Rochelle Korman, "Charitable Class and Need: Whom Should Charities Benefit?" in *Conference: Defining Charity—A View from the 21st Century* (New York University School of Law, National Center on Philanthropy and the Law, 2002).

341. Response by Charitable Organizations to the Recent Terrorist Attacks: Hearing before the Subcommittee on Oversight of the House Committee on Ways and Means, Serial 107-47, 107th Cong., 1st Sess. (2001).

342. Id. (testimony of Steven T. Miller, Director, Exempt Organizations, Tax Exempt/Government Entities Division).

343. See, for example, Diana B. Henriques and David Barstow, "A Nation Challenged: Charity; Victims' Funds May Violate U.S. Tax Laws," *New York Times,* November 12, 2001, at B1.

344. Notice 2001-78, 2001-50 I.R.B. 576.

2002.[345] It provided in section 104 a one-time exception to the existing rules by permitting charities to make payments to victims of the September 11 attacks or of anthrax "if made in good faith using a reasonable and objective formula which is consistently applied." The explanation provided by the Joint Committee on Taxation stated more specifically that in making payments under this provision, charities would not be required to make a specific assessment of need so long as the good faith requirements were met and that victims and their families are deemed to be a charitable class to whom lump-sum pro rata distributions could be made without taking specific financial needs into account.[346] Section 104 of the act also addressed the ability of private foundations to make payments to the employees of businesses related to the foundation who were victims of the attacks, another issue that had needed clarification.

Public controversy over the disbursement of relief funds did not abate, centering around the propriety of pro rata payments, coordination of lists of victims among the charities, and the question of whether donations were to be distributed immediately or a portion reserved to meet future needs or future disasters.[347]

As part of these investigations, the Ranking Minority Member of the Senate Committee on Finance requested the General Accounting Office to investigate and report on the response of charities to the September 11 attacks. The GAO released an Interim Report in September 2002.[348] It found that thirty-five of the larger charities reported raising an estimated aggregate of $2.7 billion since the date of the attacks, noting however that with more than 300 charities involved in collecting funds, it was difficult to obtain a more precise set of figures. The GAO also found that two-thirds of the amount re-

345. Victims of Terrorism Tax Relief Act of 2001, Pub. L. No. 107-134, §104(a)(1), 115 Stat. 2427, 2431 (2002).

346. Joint Committee on Taxation, *Technical Explanation of the "Victims of Terrorism Tax Relief Act of 2001" as Passed by the House and Senate on December 20, 2001* (JCX-93-01) (December 21, 2001).

347. Victoria B. Bjorklund, "Reflections on September 11 Legal Developments," in *September 11: Perspectives from the Field of Philanthropy*, 11 (Foundation Center, 2002); Susan Rosegrant, "Giving in the Wake of Terror: The Charitable Response to the Attacks of September 11" (Case Study, Practice of Philanthropy and Nonprofit Leadership, John F. Kennedy School of Government, Harvard University, 2002); Robert A. Katz, "A Pig in a Python: How the Charitable Response to September 11 Overwhelmed the Law of Disaster Relief," 36 *Indiana Law Review* 251 (2003).

348. General Accounting Office, *September 11: Interim Report on the Response of Charities* (GAO-02-1037) (September 3, 2002); General Accounting Office, *September 11: More Effective Collaboration Could Enhance Charitable Organizations' Contributions in Disasters* (GAO-03-259) (December 2002).

ported to have been collected by the large charities had been distributed for aid to the families of those killed or injured, for those more indirectly affected through loss of jobs or homes, and for disaster relief workers. In the vast majority of instances, direct uniform payments were made to identified victims, with the Red Cross reporting average payments of $54,000 per family.

Although several measures were in place at the federal, state, and local levels to help address fraud, and relatively few cases had been reported, the GAO concluded that it was too soon to determine the full extent to which fraud had occurred. The investigators also found that although initially there was little coordination among the relief agencies, a degree of coordination had been achieved. The report concluded by identifying two issues that required attention for the future: (1) obtaining information as to the amount of charitable funds that were collected and distributed, to whom and for what purposes; and (2) better coordination of the relief efforts, including consideration of the role the federal government might play in such efforts and what trade-offs might be involved, such as loss of flexibility in, and independence of, the charitable sector.[349]

The response of charities to the terrorist attacks was the subject of another congressional investigation, this time in connection with allegations that charities had financed terrorist organizations. The Subcommittee on International Trade and Finance of the Senate Banking, Housing, and Urban Affairs Committee held hearings in both 2001 and 2002.[350] In the fall of 2002 three bills were introduced in the Senate and the House that would have suspended the tax exemption of and denied any deductions for contributions to any organization designated as terrorist or terrorist-related by an executive order or under the authority of the Immigration and Nationality Act, the International Emergency Economic Powers Act, or the United Nations Participation Act.[351] The bills also provided that no groups could use any judicial proceeding to challenge a terrorist designation, suspension from tax-exempt status, or the denial of a deduction. This provision was included in the CARE Act of 2003, which was passed by the Senate in April 2003, as well as in H.R. 7, which was adopted by the House in September 2003.[352]

349. Id.

350. The Role of Charities and NGOs in the Financing of Terrorist Activities: Hearings before the Subcommittee on International Trade and Finance of the Senate Committee on Banking, Housing, and Urban Affairs, 107th Cong., 2d Sess. (2002); Hawala and Underground Terrorist Financing Mechanisms: Hearings before the Subcommittee on International Trade and Finance of the Senate Committee on Banking, Housing, and Urban Affairs, 107th Cong., 1st Sess. (2001).

351. H.R. 5603, 107th Cong., 2d Sess. (2002); S. 3081, 107th Cong., 2d Sess. (2002); S. 3082, 107th Cong., 2d Sess. (2002).

352. CARE Act of 2003, S. 476, §208, 108th Cong., 1st Sess. (2003); Charitable Giving Act of 2003, H.R. 7, §201, 108th Cong., 1st Sess. (2003).

The Effectiveness of the IRS as Regulator

The effectiveness of the IRS as the regulator of exempt organizations has been a separate subject of congressional interest, particularly in connection with the reform and restructuring of the IRS that was enacted in 1998, although it also received congressional attention in 1974 when a new Office of Employee Plans and Exempt Organizations, headed by an Assistant Commissioner, was established as part of the Employee Retirement Income Security Act of that year. This marked a major change in the regulation of charities, removing it from administration by personnel versed in tax collection to those interested in maintaining the integrity of the tax-exempt sector.[353]

During congressional consideration of the reform and restructuring of the Service between 1995 and 1997, there was concern that the separate administration of the exempt organization rules would be dismantled. However, this was not to be the case and, as more fully described in Chapter 7, the office of Assistant Commissioner, Tax Exempt and Government Entities, was created to administer a separate, dedicated division regulating exempt organization and employee plan activity. Chapter 7 contains a description of its composition and activities in relation to charities.

Congress has also addressed allegations of political influence in the regulation of exempt organizations. In the 1970s there were three investigations of attempted misuse of the Service for political and ideological purposes. A summary of these investigations, reported in a study prepared for the Filer Commission in 1975, concluded as follows:

> The Service has not been totally immune to improper political or partisan influences, but that on the whole its resistance to such influences— even from the White House—seems to be unusually strong. Perfection cannot realistically be expected of any government agency in the face of powerful congressional or White House pressures. However, apart from the aberrations of the early Cold War era which affected the Service equally with the rest of the nation, the instances in which the Service may fairly be regarded as having succumbed to partisan or ideological bias appear to be few. Moreover, the Service's pride in the public evidence from the Watergate-related investigations that successive Commissioners adhered to the tradition of nonpartisan objectivity despite strong contrary pressures, can only have reinforced the institutional strength of that tradition.[354]

353. David Ginsburg et al., "Federal Oversight of Private Philanthropy," in Department of Treasury, Commission on Private Philanthropy and Public Needs, *Research Papers,* vol. 5, pt. 1, at 2575, 2621 (1977); see also Chapter 7.

354. Ginsburg, "Federal Oversight of Private Philanthropy," 2618.

Most recently a Joint Committee study of undue influence on the Service, required by the Restructuring and Reform Act of 1998, which was released in 2000, found no credible evidence (1) that the IRS delayed or accelerated issuance of determination letters to tax-exempt organizations based on the nature of the organizations' perceived views; (2) that the forwarding of certain applications to the national office was the result of a deliberate effort by IRS employees to subject organizations with views that opposed the Clinton administration to more intense scrutiny; (3) that tax-exempt organizations were selected for examination or that the IRS altered the manner in which it conducted examinations based on the views of the organizations; (4) that Clinton administration officials intervened in the selection of or failure to select certain exempt organizations for examination; or (5) that the IRS systematically used information items such as press reports or letters from members of Congress or taxpayers to identify for examination exempt organizations that espoused views opposed to the political views of the Clinton administration.[355]

The Joint Committee had also been charged with investigating allegations of employee misconduct with respect to exempt organizations. It identified eight instances of alleged IRS employee misconduct, but found no substantial evidence of undue influence. The report contains a valuable description of IRS procedures for handling determinations and audits, as well as the functioning of its internal controls, and Appendix B contains a detailed description of the laws limiting political campaign activities and lobbying.[356]

Major Expansion of Federal Regulation: Intermediate Sanctions for Excess Benefit Transactions

In 1996 Congress enacted limitations on the financial benefits that fiduciaries may receive from the organizations they serve.[357] These limitations represented the most far-reaching provisions regulating the operation of charities adopted since exemption was granted in the first income tax laws. Although the private foundation provisions enacted in 1969 had a profound effect on the administration of this group of charities, private foundations comprise only 6.5% of the charitable sector.[358] In contrast, intermediate sanctions apply

355. Joint Committee on Taxation, *Report of Investigation of Allegations Relating to Internal Revenue Service Handling of Tax-Exempt Organization Matters* (JCS-3-00) (March 2000).
356. Id.
357. I.R.C. §4958, codified by Taxpayer Bill of Rights Act 2, Pub. L. No. 104-168, §1311, 110 Stat. 1452, 1475–1479 (1996).
358. Murray S. Weitzman and Linda M. Lampkin, *The New Nonprofit Almanac and Desk Reference*, 125, Table 5.1 (New York: Jossey-Bass, 2002).

to all other organizations exempt under section 501(c)(3), a universe that was estimated in 2002 by the IRS to consist of 910,000 organizations.[359] These provisions also apply to organizations exempt under section 501(c)(4), which does include certain organizations that are considered charities under state law. Just as the private foundation provisions forced major changes in the way that group of organizations was operated, it is anticipated that prohibitions against excess benefit transactions will force trustees and directors of public charities to revise their operating procedures and pay heightened attention to any transaction that entails self-dealing. Because of the impact of these provisions and of their easy acceptance in Congress, they are described here in a separate section.

These new provisions are commonly referred to as "intermediate sanctions," a phrase that connotes the nature of the penalties that may be imposed for certain transactions. They are more appropriately described as "excess benefit transactions," the transactions that the legislation is designed to curtail. An excess benefit transaction is one in which a disqualified person receives from the charity an amount of money or other property that is greater than its fair market value. The rules apply to sales and exchanges between a charity and a disqualified person and to payment of compensation to a disqualified person. Disqualified persons include all fiduciaries and other persons in a position to exercise substantial influence over the organization in question. The sanctions are similar to those applicable in the case of private foundation self-dealing, namely excise tax on the disqualified person and in certain circumstances on the managers of the charity. The sanction is denominated "intermediate" to signify that it lies between no action and the "ultimate" sanction of revocation of exemption.

The impetus for the enactment of the excess benefit transactions provisions came from the Internal Revenue Service itself, specifically from recommendations of a Penalty Task Force established by the Service in November 1987, which suggested that the Service seek legislation providing sanctions similar to those in Chapter 42 governing private foundations to permit correction without revocation of exemption.[360] In 1993 the Commissioner of Internal Revenue recommended enactment of provisions of this nature to Congress during hearings of the Subcommittee on Oversight of the Committee on Ways and Means.[361] Legislation drafted by the Treasury to effect this change

359. Id.

360. Executive Task Force, Commissioner's Penalty Study, Internal Revenue Service, *Report on Civil Tax Penalties,* ch. 9, sec. III (1989).

361. Tax Administration of Public Charities Exempt under Section 501(c)(3): Hearings before the Subcommittee on Oversight of the House Committee on Ways and Means, Serial 103-39, 103d Cong., 1st Sess. (1993).

was submitted to Congress in 1996 and, with the support of many leaders of the charitable sector, the bill was enacted as part of the Taxpayers Bill of Rights 2 of 1996. The substance of the provisions and greater detail as to the legislative history are described in Chapter 5.

The legislative process that led to the final enactment of the excess benefit provisions was unique in the relative absence of opposition by the public and within Congress, although when they were initially suggested certain segments of the sector did raise objections, particularly to the possibility of extending them to apply to all instances of private benefit rather than self-dealing transactions. Although the IRS issued both temporary and proposed regulations before adopting them in final form, public comments on their content focused on technical aspects.[362] Thus the history of the enactment of the excess benefit transactions provisions stands as the exception to the more usual atmosphere of confrontation that has been present during other periods when amendment of the provisions affecting charities has been the subject of congressional and administrative activity.

Other Changes in Substantive Laws after 1970

The foregoing sections describe changes in the laws affecting charities that came about directly from congressional investigations and subsequent enactments. However, federal tax law is also created through the promulgation of administrative rulings and in court decisions. This section describes the development of federal tax law affecting charities that was formulated in the cases, Treasury regulations, and Internal Revenue Service rulings rather than through amendments of the Internal Revenue Code.

Changing Parameters of the Definition of Charitable Purposes

The definition of charitable purposes and the parameters of the requirements for exemption that define a charity pose problems for the Service that are at times difficult to resolve. Included in the definition are the requirements that the beneficiaries of a charity form an indefinite class and that a purpose cannot be charitable if it is illegal or against fundamental public policy. Determination of exemption is further complicated by the fact that the prohibition against intervention in campaigns for public office and the limitations on lobbying were engrafted onto the basic common law rules.

The parameters of the definition of exempt purposes were established in

362. 63 Fed. Reg. 41,486 (August 4, 1998) (proposed regulations); 66 Fed. Reg. 2144 (January 1, 2001) (temporary regulations); 67 Fed. Reg. 3076 (January 23, 2002) (final regulations).

1959 in the regulations issued under section 501(c)(3). These regulations adopted what was described specifically as the common law definition of charity for determining the meaning of each of the purposes recited in that section.[363] Most important, they incorporated the concept that the meaning of charity was not static, but was meant to evolve over time to reflect changing circumstances and changing views of public benefit. In addition to adopting the common law definition of charity, the 1959 regulations actually expanded the scope of charitable activity by permitting exemption to be granted to groups engaging in various forms of social activism under the heading "promotion of social welfare by organizations designed to accomplish any of the traditional purposes or by lessening neighborhood tensions, eliminating prejudice and discrimination, defending human and civil rights secured by law or combating community deterioration and juvenile delinquency."[364] Under this formulation exemptions had been granted prior to 1969 to a voter registration group and to an organization formed to make program-related investments. In the years after 1969, the scope of charitable purposes was broadened in connection with the requirements for exemption of hospitals, environmental groups, legal aid and public interest law firms, human and civil rights organizations, and for a wide range of arts organizations.[365] This sensitivity to change on the part of the Internal Revenue Service is in marked contrast to that of the English Charity Commission, which has resisted broadening the concept of charity to such a degree that in 2002 widespread support had been generated for adding new specific purposes to the general categories in the definition of charity in order to make it relevant.[366]

Application of the Public Policy Doctrine to Definitions of Charitable Purposes

Undoubtedly the most important development in the definition of charity since 1970 was the application of the common law rule that a charitable purpose is not valid if it is against public policy when the Service denied exemption to private schools that discriminated on the basis of race. This decision led to great public debate and was only resolved years later by a 1983 decision of the Supreme Court.[367]

The dispute first arose in 1967 during the turmoil over desegregation with an announcement by the Service that tax exemption would be denied to any

363. Treas. Reg. §1.501(c)(3)-l(d)(2) (T.D. 6391) (1959).
364. Id.
365. See Chapter 5.
366. Strategy Unit Report, *Private Action, Public Benefit*, 36–43, available at *www.strategy-unit.gov.uk*.
367. Bob Jones University v. United States, 461 U.S. 574 (1983).

racially discriminatory private schools that received state aid.[368] In response, parents of black public school students in Mississippi sued to enjoin the Service from granting exemptions or allowing charitable contributions to any discriminatory school within the state, regardless of whether it received state aid.[369] While the litigation was pending, the Service announced that it was extending the prohibition to church-related schools.[370] The Service's position was upheld in the case of *Green v. Connally*,[371] in which a three-judge district court enjoined the IRS from recognizing the exempt status of any private school in Mississippi that had a policy of racial discrimination on the basis that exemption was not available for organizations that conducted activities that were illegal or against public policy.

The Service announced its compliance with the trial court decision in a news release,[372] and soon thereafter published a revenue ruling in which it reiterated its new position based on the rationale of the court.[373] In 1975 this ruling was expanded to include discrimination on the basis of color and national origin within the scope of the prohibition.[374]

In 1978 the Service announced a proposed revenue ruling that provided a stricter standard for tax exemption under which exemption would be denied not only to schools with discriminatory policies but also to those with an insignificant number of minority students that were formed or expanded at or about the time of desegregation of the public schools in the community.[375] Congress responded to this proposal by passing legislation denying funds under the 1980 appropriations act for the formulation or enforcement of the proposed rule.[376] This measure effectively prevented the Service from implementing the procedures in the proposed ruling, and the matter seemed to be in a stalemate.[377]

368. IRS News Release (August 2, 1967).

369. Green v. Kennedy, 309 F. Supp. 1127 (D.D.C.), appeal dismissed sub nom. Cannon v. Green, 398 U.S. 956 (1970).

370. Rev. Rul. 75-231, 1975-1 C.B. 159.

371. 330 F. Supp. 1150 (D.D.C.), aff'd sub nom. Coit v. Green, 404 U.S. 997 (1971).

372. IRS News Release (July 7, 1970).

373. Rev. Rul. 71-447, 1971-2 C.B. 230; see also Rev. Rul. 75-231, 1975-1 C.B. 158.

374. Rev. Rul. 75-50, 1975-2 C.B. 587.

375. 43 Fed. Reg. 37,296 (1978).

376. Treasury Appropriations Act of 1980, Pub. L. No. 96-74, 93 Stat. 559 (1979). The Dornan amendment provided that "[n]one of the funds available under [the] Act may be used to carry out [the IRS proposals]." Id., §615, 93 Stat. 559, 577. The Ashbrook amendment provided that funds may not be used "to formulate or carry out any rule, policy, procedure, guideline, regulation, standard, or measure which would cause the loss of tax-exempt status to private, religious, or church-operated schools." Id., §103, 93 Stat. 559, 562.

377. Thomas McCoy and Neal E. Devins, "Standing and Adverseness in Challenges of Tax Exemptions for Discriminatory Private Schools," 52 *Fordham Law Review* 441, 461–462 (1984).

During this same period the courts were adjudicating cases involving the revocation of the tax exemption of two educational organizations, Bob Jones University and Goldsboro Christian Schools, Inc., on the grounds that they discriminated on the basis of race. In 1980 the Court of Appeals for the Fourth Circuit upheld the Service's revocation of the exemptions,[378] and the Supreme Court consolidated the two cases and granted certiorari.[379] In 1982, before the case was argued, the Reagan administration, which had just taken office, announced that the Service would no longer revoke or deny tax-exempt status for segregated schools without congressional authorization.[380] Contemporaneously, the Justice Department withdrew its brief in the Bob Jones case and asked the court to vacate it as moot.[381] In the face of strong public protest to these actions, the administration thereupon submitted the matter for resolution to the Congress, proposing legislation that would have given the Service authority to carry out its announced policy.[382] This was done with the expectation that the measure would not be adopted, which was the case.[383] Following the Justice Department's withdrawal from the Bob Jones case, the Court of Appeals enjoined the Service from restoring exempt status to any racially discriminatory school and appointed independent counsel to support the original position of the Service in the court proceedings.

The decision of the Supreme Court was rendered on May 24, 1983. It reaffirmed the Service's reliance on common law definitions of charity to hold that schools that discriminated on the basis of race, whether or not church-related, were not entitled to tax exemption. It found that the term "charitable" as used in the Internal Revenue Code encompassed education and required that a charity serve a public purpose, thereby precluding it from actions that violated public policy. This decision laid the matter to rest as far as Congress was concerned, although the success of the tax regulators in prohibiting segregation was open to question.[384]

The Service and the courts have also been called upon to rule as to another aspect of discrimination, namely the validity of measures designed to support disadvantaged minorities. The Service has ruled that granting preferences to Native Americans would not be grounds for denial of exemption, although it

378. Bob Jones University v. United States, 639 F.2d 147 (4th Cir. 1980).

379. 454 U.S. 892 (1981).

380. IRS News Release (January 8, 1982).

381. Bob Jones University v. United States, 461 U.S. 574, 585 (1983).

382. Letter from President Ronald Reagan to the President of the Senate and the Speaker of the House Transmitting Proposed Legislation, 18 *Weekly Comp. Pres. Doc.* 37 (January 18, 1982).

383. See 128 Cong. Rec. S111 (daily ed. January 28, 1982) (remarks of Senator Bradley); id. at S108 (remarks of Senator Hart).

384. Frances R. Hill and Douglas M. Mancino, *Taxation of Exempt Organizations,* ¶7.02 (New York: Warren, Gorham & Lamont, 2002).

also stated that this position should not be interpreted as an endorsement of an affirmative action rationale.[385] In line with this position, the Service also ruled that, although publicly supported educational organizations are prohibited from administering scholarship programs that discriminate on the basis of race, independent trusts or foundations with those purposes were not necessarily prevented from obtaining exemption.[386] The Service had also ruled that a trust that limited benefits to students of the Caucasian race was not entitled to exemption.[387] However, it retreated from this position in 1983, rejecting use of a per se rule and adopting instead a facts and circumstances test to determine whether any specific trust or fund violated public policy.[388]

As of 2002 the law remained unclear as to whether public policy prohibited discrimination on bases other than that of race or national origin in education. Notably, the question of gender discrimination was also unresolved. Hill and Mancino[389] suggested that the future course of the law on this question may well be shaped by the Supreme Court's 1996 decision in *United States v. Virginia*,[390] in which the court held that the exclusion of women from admission to Virginia Military Academy constituted a violation of the equal protection clause. In this case, however, the school was a state university so that the state action doctrine came into play along with the public policy doctrine. This limitation is described below.

State Action Limitations on Charitable Purposes: The Subsidy Theory

In addition to the limitations on charitable purposes imposed by virtue of the public policy doctrine, a denial of exemption may under certain circumstances involve an unconstitutional deprivation of the First Amendment rights of free speech and freedom to petition, and the equal protection of the laws inherent in the due process clause of the Fifth Amendment. These constitutional prohibitions, however, extend only to actions by the state so that, to determine a claim that these rights were violated, one must first demonstrate that the state is involved in the action being challenged. State action is obvious in the case mentioned above of a state university, namely Virginia Military Academy.

385. Gen. Couns. Mem. 36,363 (August 7, 1975).
386. Gen. Couns. Mem. 39,117 (January 13, 1984).
387. Gen. Couns. Mem. 37,462 (March 17, 1978).
388. Gen. Couns. Mem. 39,082 (December 1, 1983); see also Gen. Couns. Mem. 39,117 (January 13, 1984).
389. Hill and Mancino, *Taxation of Exempt Organizations,* ¶7.05[3].
390. 518 U.S. 515 (1996).

However, state action can also be present in less direct ways, one of which is through the provision of subsidies to nongovernmental entities. Examples would be grants to charities or contracts with them to provide certain products. The question of whether the grant of tax exemption itself, and the corollary allowance of deductions for contributions to some organizations, are government subsidies has been the subject of extensive debate by legal and economic scholars, but not with consensus. However, the issue was resolved at least in regard to the power of Congress to regulate tax-exempt organizations in a 1983 decision of the Supreme Court, *Regan v. Taxation with Representation of Washington*.[391] The question before the Court was whether the limitation on lobbying in section 501(c)(3) was a violation of an organization's constitutional right to free speech. In holding that the limitation was valid, the Court found that:

> Both tax exemptions and tax deductibility are a form of subsidy that is administered through the tax system. A tax exemption has much the same effect as a cash grant to the organization of the amount of tax it would have to pay on its income. Deductible contributions are similar to cash grants of the amount of a portion of the individual's contributions. The system Congress has enacted provides this kind of subsidy to nonprofit civic welfare organizations generally, and an additional subsidy to those charitable organizations that do not engage in substantial lobbying. In short, Congress chose not to subsidize lobbying as extensively as it chose to subsidize other activities that nonprofit organizations undertake to promote the public welfare.[392]

The Court noted that the defendant organization, TWR, was not denied the ability to exercise its right of free speech in that it could divide its activities between two organizations, one to conduct educational activities that would be exempt under section 501(c)(3) and eligible to receive tax-deductible contributions, and the other exempt under section 501(c)(4) that could conduct unlimited lobbying activities although without deductibility for contributions.

TWR had also claimed that the lobbying limitation violated the equal protection clause in that taxpayers are permitted to deduct contributions to exempt veterans organizations that are permitted to lobby without limit, but not to organizations exempt under section 501(c)(4). In rejecting this contention, the Court held that Congress's decision not to subsidize the exercise of a fundamental right does not infringe the right. "The issue in this case is

391. 461 U.S. 540 (1983).
392. Id. at 544.

not whether TWR must be permitted to lobby, but whether Congress is required to provide it with public money with which to lobby."[393]

Lobbying

The limitations on lobbying have also caused controversy outside of Congress. Section 501(h), which permitted public charities to elect a mechanical test to determine the amount of their lobbying expenses, was enacted in 1976, but it was not until November 5, 1986, that Treasury published proposed regulations.[394] The delay was attributed to a flood of major tax legislation requiring more immediate attention than the lobbying regulations and to the difficulty of reaching consensus on the definitions.[395] In all events, the proposed draft quickly attracted severe criticism, particularly its definitions of grassroots lobbying and the rules for allocating expenses between those for activities that were permitted as educational and those that were subject to the statutory limits. McGovern noted that approximately 200 organizations signed a position statement submitted by Independent Sector requesting that the proposed regulations be immediately withdrawn. Similar requests were made by a number of other national organizations, and the Service received more than 5,000 individual comments.[396]

Soon after the proposed regulations were published, Congressman Pickle began another investigation of lobbying and political activities. His hearings in March 1987 concluded with a Subcommittee report that the restrictions in the Code reflected sound tax policy but that the regulations were too complex and at times too inexact.[397] Other congressmen questioned the rules, including Dan Rostenkowski, the chairman of the House Ways and Means Committee, who asked that they be withdrawn and that the Service consult with representatives of the public and private sector regarding revisions.[398]

In response to Rostenkowski's suggestion, a Commissioner's Exempt Organizations Advisory Group was established in June 1987. The group met in

393. Id. at 551.

394. 51 Fed. Reg. 40,211 (November 5, 1986).

395. James J. McGovern et al., "The Revised Lobbying Regulations—A Difficult Balance," 41 *Tax Notes* 1425, 1427 (1988).

396. Id.

397. Subcommittee on Oversight, House Committee on Ways and Means, *Report and Recommendations on Lobbying and Political Activities by Tax-Exempt Organizations*, WMCP 100-12, 100th Cong., 1st Sess. (1987).

398. Lobbying and Political Activities of Tax-Exempt Organizations: Hearings before the Subcommittee on Oversight of the House Committee on Ways and Means, Serial 100-15, 100th Cong., 1st Sess. (1987).

September 1987 and February 1988 and, although it discussed a wide range of matters affecting the exempt organization community, the principal focus was on the lobbying regulations. New proposed regulations were published on December 23, 1988, containing revisions consonant with many of the most serious objections raised to the first set.[399] These were ultimately published in final form in August 1990.[400] Despite the long delay, the outcome reflected well on the Service and the exempt sector and provided an example of cooperation that was hoped to be replicated following the establishment in 2000 of a new Advisory Committee as part of the restructuring and reform of the IRS.[401]

UBIT and Commercial Activities

Despite the failure of Congress to act immediately on its recommendations to reform the unrelated business income tax (UBIT), the 1988 report of the Subcommittee of the Ways and Means Committee (the "Pickle Committee") clearly had an impact on the administration of the UBIT provisions by the IRS. In the years following release of the Pickle Report, the IRS directed its audit activity toward all of the areas in which the Subcommittee had recommended a tightening of the rules. This was the case particularly in regard to museum shops, college book stores, travel tours, and royalty agreements. Of even wider import, however, has been the Service's response to the problems generated by increased business activities of exempt organizations. These were noted by the Pickle Committee, but have increased rapidly in the years following its deliberations.[402]

The health care field, which accounted for 49% of the total gross receipts of the charitable sector in 1997,[403] was the first area in which the traditional range of services was broadened to encompass what came to be characterized as "commercial" activities. Some of these activities were related to exempt purposes but others were either subject to UBIT or were conducted by tax-exempt subsidiary organizations or, increasingly during the 1990s, by for-profit subsidiaries. These developments posed problems for the regulators: (1) whether the nature of the arrangements between an exempt organization and its co-venturers imposed obligations on the charity that were

399. 53 Fed. Reg. 51,826 (December 23, 1988).

400. 55 Fed. Reg. 35,579 (August 31, 1990) (T.D. 8308).

401. See Chapter 7.

402. See generally Burton A. Weisbrod, ed., *To Profit or Not to Profit: The Commercial Transformation of the Nonprofit Sector* (Cambridge: Cambridge University Press, 1998).

403. Weitzman and Lampkin, *The New Nonprofit Almanac and Desk Reference,* 125, Table 4.2.

inconsistent with the requirement that it operate exclusively for public benefit or resulted in impermissible private inurement or private benefit; and (2) whether there was a limit to the amount of business activity, related or unrelated, that if exceeded, constituted grounds for loss of exemption on the basis that the organization was no longer operated primarily for exempt purposes.

The first problem for the tax regulators arose in the 1980s when exempt organizations, looking for ways to increase revenue in the face of cutbacks in government support, turned to private investors to provide capital to expand their activities. This occurred at a time when a large number of hospitals were reorganizing their corporate structures to create a parent organization that controlled a number of subsidiary corporations and partnerships, some tax-exempt and others not, with private investors as shareholders or partners in the taxable ventures. Initially, the Service ruled that exemption would be lost if a charity became a general partner in a partnership with for-profit entities or private individuals. This position was abandoned in the early 1980s, but the Service continued to hold that exemption would be lost if a charity entered into a joint venture with a for-profit entity unless the activities of the joint venture furthered the charity's exempt purposes and the charity maintained control of the taxable entity. During the mid-to-late 1990s, the government litigated the validity of a number of joint venture arrangements, particularly ones involving hospitals and health care insurers. The outcome was watched closely as much for its impact in the health care field as in the larger exempt sector in which joint ventures had long been used to finance low-cost housing, but were increasingly being used by universities and arts organizations as well as by a wide range of charities looking to increase revenue through Internet activities.[404]

The second problem facing regulators arose in part from the uncertainty as to whether the Internal Revenue Code limits the amount of commercial activity, both related and unrelated, beyond which an organization will no longer be entitled to tax exemption. Although commentators and representatives from small businesses continued to criticize the amount of commercial activity conducted by the sector, implying that there was a limit, there is no firm basis in the law for such a position. As of the end of 2002 neither the Congress nor the Service had addressed the question directly, but the issue would continue to receive attention as "commercial activities" continued to increase.[405]

404. See Chapter 5.
405. Id.

Regulation of Public Companies and Auditing Firms in 2002 and 2003

The exposure of widespread breaches of fiduciary duty—and in some instances criminal conduct—on the part of the directors and officers of public business corporations that came to light in 2002 had no direct impact on charities, but it was clear that it would influence charity regulators and the sector itself in the years ahead. Congressional response to the disclosures was swift and came in the form of the Sarbanes-Oxley Act, signed on July 30, 2002.[406] The act imposed new obligations on corporate officers and directors, increased disclosure requirements to the Securities and Exchange Commission, enlarged the agency's powers, imposed new and increased criminal penalties on corporate officials who violated the rules, and established a new structure for oversight of public accounting firms under the general supervision of the SEC. One of the provisions that could be applied to charities in the future, particularly those over a certain size, requires the chief executive officer and the chief financial officer to certify that each quarterly and annual report does not contain an untrue statement of a material fact or omit to state one, that it fairly represents the company's condition, and that the signing officers have designed internal controls to assure that proper information is provided to them. The act also requires that only independent directors serve on audit committees, that these directors establish procedures to assure that they are personally available to employees who have questions about the company's behavior, and that the audit committee be empowered to retain independent counsel.

Finally, the act established a five-member body, under the supervision of the SEC, to which all firms conducting audits for public company clients are required to register. The board was empowered to establish accounting standards, inspect firms for compliance, and conduct investigations and disciplinary proceedings as required. It was granted power to impose a wide range of sanctions, including temporary suspension or permanent revocation of registration for companies and their officers, temporary or permanent limitations on the activities of subject firms or persons, and imposition of civil fines in amounts between $100,000 and $15,000,000.[407]

One section of the act as originally approved by the House but deleted in the final version approved by the Conference Committee was directed specifically at relationships with exempt organizations. This provision would have required corporations and their executive officers to inform the SEC

---

406. Sarbanes-Oxley Act of 2002, Pub. L. No. 107-204, 116 Stat. 745 (2002).
407. Id.

about their relationships with "philanthropic organizations." Disclosure would be required if a director, an executive officer, or any member of their immediate families was a director or officer of a nonprofit organization, and if contributions were made during the last five years by any of them to the organization in excess of $10,000 as well as any other activity undertaken by them that provided a material benefit to the nonprofit organization, including lobbying on its behalf.[408]

In January 2003 New York Attorney General Eliot Spitzer released the text of a bill he had drafted that would apply certain provisions of the Sarbanes-Oxley Act to all New York charities. The bill would have required corporate charities to have an independent audit committee and, unless the by-laws prohibited it, an executive committee. It would also have imposed new financial reporting provisions and certification requirements and reduce the extent to which nonprofits could indemnify officers and directors in the event of suit.[409] In response to objections from the charitable sector, the proposals were modified in August 2003 to make them less burdensome to smaller charities.[410] In September 2003 the attorney general announced that he believed further study was needed before he would seek enactment.[411]

Treasury Department Anti-Terrorist Financing Guidelines

Following the September 11, 2001 terrorist attacks the government closed three of the five largest international Islamic humanitarian organizations operating in the United States and froze approximately $8 million of their assets.[412] The administration also sought congressional action to permit it to expand its efforts to stop transfer of money to terrorist organizations. The Victims of Terrorism Tax Relief Act, passed in December 2001, amended section 6103 of the Internal Revenue Code to permit disclosure of tax returns and return information available to government law enforcement agencies outside of the Treasury for the purpose of investigating or responding to

408. H.R. 3763, §7(2) (as passed by House of Representatives on April 24, 2002).

409. Office of New York Attorney General, Press Release, "Spitzer Proposes Reforms of State Corporate Accountability Laws," January 23, 2003; see also S. 4836, 2002–2003 Reg. Sess. (2003).

410. Fred Stokeld, "Legislation to Apply Sarbanes-Oxley to New York Nonprofits Revised," 2003 *Tax Notes Today* 152-1 (August 7, 2003).

411. National Association of Attorneys General and National Association of State Charity Officials, 2003 Annual Charitable Trust and Solicitations Seminar (Brooklyn, September 15, 2003).

412. Hanna Rosin, "U.S. Raids Offices of 2 Muslim Charities; Groups Accused of Funding Terror," *Washington Post*, December 16, 2001, at A28.

terrorist incidents, threats, and activities.[413] At the time of the bill's passage, the Treasury announced that it was considering whether it would need more authority to stop the misuse of charities by terrorist organizations. On August 1, 2002, the department announced that it would not ask for more authority, nor would it be making any proposals to modify the Code to block the financing of the activities of terrorists through charities.[414]

The validity of the Treasury's seizure of the assets of two foundations was challenged and, in both instances, upheld by the federal appellate courts.[415] The founder of one of the charities, after having been detained for a year and a half, was deported in July 2003 on the basis that he had overstayed his visa.[416] The leader of Benevolence International Foundation, another of the Islamic charities whose assets had been seized in 2001, was indicted in October 2002 on conspiracy and racketeering charges, alleging that the charity was a financial front for the terrorist activities of Osama bin Laden.[417] In February 2003 the defendant, Enaam Arnaout, agreed to a plea bargain, admitting to having illegally funneled donations to rebel fighters in Chechnya and Bosnia, with the prosecutors dropping all charges related to alleged financial links to Al Qaeda or terrorism.[418] In sentencing Arnaout to eleven years and four months in prison for defrauding donors, the judge was reported to have noted that prosecutors had never established that he supported terrorism, but that he had misled both the charity's donors and recipients by diverting as much as $400,000 to buy uniforms, boots, and tents for soldiers.[419]

In November 2002 the Treasury released a "voluntary set of best practices guidelines for U.S.-based charities to follow to reduce the likelihood that

413. Victims of Terrorism Tax Relief Act of 2001, Pub. L. No. 107-134, §201, 115 Stat. 2427, 2440 (2002).

414. The Role of Charities and NGOs in the Financing of Terrorist Activities: Hearing before the Subcommittee on International Trade and Finance of the Senate Committee on Banking, Housing, and Urban Affairs, 107th Cong., 2d Sess. (2002) (statement of Kenneth W. Dam, Deputy Secretary, Department of Treasury).

415. Holy Land Foundation for Relief and Development v. Ashcroft, 333 F.3d 156 (D.C. Cir. 2003); Global Relief Foundation, Inc. v. O'Neill, 315 F.3d 748 (7th Cir. 2002).

416. Rachel L. Swarns, "Threats and Responses: A Michigan Case—U.S. Deports Charity Leader in Visa Dispute," *New York Times,* July 15, 2003, at A11.

417. Eric Lichtblau, "Threats and Responses: The Money Trail—U.S. Indicts Head of Charity in Qaeda Financing," *New York Times,* October 10, 2002, at A6.

418. Eric Lichtblau, "Threats and Responses: The Money Trail—Charity Leader Accepts a Deal in a Terror Case," *New York Times,* February 11, 2003, at A1.

419. John Mintz, "Head of Muslim Charity Sentenced; Ill. Man Diverted Funds to Militants; No Proof of Terror Link, Judge Says," *Washington Post,* August 19, 2003, at A2.

charitable funds will be diverted to finance terrorist activities."[420] The Treasury Department press release issued with the guidelines stated that they had been developed at the request of Muslim groups concerned about future government action and faced with declining contributions.[421] The guidelines were divided into three major sections entitled "Governance," "Disclosure/ Transparency," and "Anti-Terrorist Financing Procedures." The section on governance contained specific provisions to be included in governing instruments dealing with composition of the board (requiring at least three members, meeting at least three times annually with the majority of members attending in person) and conflicts of interest. In addition, the guidelines stated that the board should be an independent governing body, specifying that a charity whose directly or indirectly compensated board members constituted more than one-fifth of the board or of the executive committee will not be considered to have an independent governing body.

In the section dealing with disclosure the Treasury Department advised charities to make publicly available a list of board members and salaries paid, as well as a list of the five highest paid employees and the salaries and direct or indirect benefits they receive. The guidelines "suggested" that charities provide annual reports and annual financial statements, and information when soliciting funds, restating provisions legally required under the Internal Revenue Code and the laws in a number of states. Similarly, provisions relating to financial practices followed generally accepted procedures for audits with the exception of a requirement to publish and make available for public inspection an audited financial statement if the charity's total annual gross income exceeded $250,000. Again, this provision has a counterpart under the laws of a number of states, but with different thresholds.

The final section contained detailed procedures to be used to identify potential grantees, including conducting a reasonable search of public information to determine whether the potential grantee is or has been implicated in any questionable activity, and verifying that it does not appear on any government list identifying it as having links to terrorism or money laundering, and

---

420. "U.S. Department of the Treasury Anti-Terrorist Financing Guidelines: Voluntary Best Practices for U.S.-based Charities" (November 7, 2002), available at *www.treas.gov/press/releases/docs/tocc.pdf*.

421. Office of Public Affairs, U.S. Department of the Treasury, "Response to Inquiries from Arab American and American Muslim Communities for Guidance on Charitable Best Practices," PO-3607 (November 7, 2002); see also Alan Cooperman, "In U.S., Muslims Alter Their Giving; Those Observing Islamic Tenet Want to Aid Poor but Fear Prosecution," *Washington Post*, December 7, 2002, at A1.

requiring the foreign recipient to certify that it is not linked to any entities on the lists.[422]

The relationship between the guidelines and federal tax law was described by a former director of the IRS exempt organization division as "ambiguous," particularly in light of the fact that they were issued by the Treasury, the same agency charged with promulgating regulations for the IRS.[423] Others noted that some of the guidelines recited current law requirements applicable to all charities, and others appeared to reiterate the expenditure responsibility rules for private foundations, in effect extending them to publicly supported charities. Thus labeling the guidelines as "voluntary" was at the least misleading.[424] The guidelines also reflected a trend toward imposing restrictions on board composition and board procedures that are required by laws in only three states, although they have appeared with increasing frequency in settlement agreements as conditions imposed by the IRS and state attorneys general. The Treasury's action in issuing the guidelines affirmed the trend toward limiting the ability of charities to choose the rules under which they would operate and standards of behavior to which they would be held.

On May 5, 2003, the IRS requested public comment on how to preclude the diversion of charitable assets for noncharitable purposes without diminishing the important role of worldwide charitable organizations. The announcement stated that the request was made in response to the identification of situations in which charities had provided significant funding to terrorists. The Service asked respondents to identify specific practices and safeguards already being used to prevent asset diversions, including practices introduced since September 11, 2001, together with comments on the difficulties charities encountered in monitoring international grants. It also requested comments on the Treasury's Anti-Terrorist Financing Guidelines.[425]

Among the responses, InterAction and Independent Sector, acting jointly, and the Council on Foundations called for the withdrawal of the Treasury Department guidelines in their entirety, with the former urging continued reliance on existing laws and regulations, no change in reporting forms, and action by the government to produce a consolidated list of blocked organizations and individuals that charities could rely on in making

422. "U.S. Department of the Treasury Anti-Terrorist Financing Guidelines."

423. "Guidelines for Charities on Terrorist Funding May Be Costly, Impractical, Say EO Reps," 2002 *Tax Notes Today* 224-5 (November 20, 2002).

424. Id.

425. Ann. 2003-29, 2003-20 I.R.B. 928.

grants.[426] The ABA Section on Taxation submitted comments from its exempt organization committee requesting precedential guidance similar to that provided by Treasury to assist financial institutions to avoid terrorist financing and other forms of fraud, as well as issuance of a "fail safe" procedure that would protect charities that were in compliance with its provisions.[427]

Conclusion

This summary demonstrates the flexibility of the law over many centuries to adjust to changing circumstances and changing needs while retaining basic concepts, such as the importance of charitable activity. It is also striking to see the parallel development of charity law in England and the United States, where there is more that is similar than different, and to find that present-day challenges are very much alike, despite the fact that it is the tax law in the United States that provides the impetus for and the situs of regulation as opposed to the English system in which tax considerations are subordinate.

The fact that the tax laws drive the regulation of charities today is less surprising than the transformation of those laws and the way in which they are administered that has taken place since the enactment of the income tax in the early twentieth century. What occurred was in fact the transformation of a part of the Internal Revenue Service from a tax-collecting agency to one with broad power to control fiduciary behavior. By including in the Internal Revenue Code standards of behavior for fiduciaries developed under the common law to assure loyalty and prevent recklessness in the handling of charitable assets, Congress imposed on the Service a set of goals that would never have been considered part of the taxing function as recently as 1950. To a certain degree, this occurred because of the failure on the part of the states to fulfill their traditional role in regulating charities. But in larger part, the tax laws developed in tandem with the growth of the charitable sector, a growth that was attributable in large part to the tax benefits provided to charities and their donors. The changes adopted in the late 1990s—notably the excess

426. Independent Sector and InterAction, "Public Comment on 'International Activities and International Grantmaking by Domestic 501(c)(3) Organizations,'" 2003 *Tax Notes Today* 141-17 (July 23, 2003). In their submission InterAction is identified as an alliance of more than 160 international development and humanitarian nongovernmental organizations operating in every developing country to overcome poverty, exclusion, and suffering. Independent Sector is described as a national coalition of over 700 nonprofit organizations, with a mission of promoting, strengthening, and advancing the nonprofit and philanthropic community to foster private initiatives for the public good.

427. Section of Taxation, American Bar Association, "Comments on International Charitable Activities," 2003 *Tax Notes Today* 137-37 (July 17, 2003).

benefit limitations on public charities—completed the transformation of the regulatory function, a transformation that was just beginning to be understood at the start of the new century.

A second important element in this legal history is the overriding role of the Congress in directing the course of charity regulation, an influence that has been far more pervasive than any initiatives made by the executive branch. Similarly, congressional influence has been stronger than that of the courts with the important exception, however, of the courts' application of the public policy doctrine to the definition of charitable purposes. In regard to this issue, the response of the Congress, the courts, and the presidency to the decision of the IRS to withhold exemption from private schools with racially discriminatory policies is an episode that deserves greater attention from scholars, pitting as it did the three branches against each other and demonstrating the extent to which Congress was willing to go to try to overturn a court decision through its appropriation powers.

Finally, it is instructive to trace the changes in the nature of the charges made against charities over the years. The swings mirror public attitudes, but certain themes do recur—the populist distrust of large amounts of property being dispensed for public purposes without public control, the fear of conservatives that charitable funds are being used to support liberal causes, the opposing fears expressed by liberals, and the concern of business that charities receive unfair benefits at their expense. The pervasiveness of these views is not to be underestimated as one evaluates the laws and regulation of charity and considers ways in which they may be made more effective.

3

Creation, Administration, and Termination of Charities

Charities are usually created in one of two legal forms: corporations or trusts, with the corporation being the most common form utilized in the United States since the mid-twentieth century. Charities can also be created informally as voluntary associations, but this form is rarely used because, like partnerships, each member of the association will be subject to personal liability for the debts of the association.[1]

A new legal form, called a limited liability company (LLC), was developed in the 1990s and by the end of the decade had been recognized by the legislatures in all of the states; it afforded the protections from liability of a corporation together with the tax advantages arising from treatment as a pass-through entity that are afforded to partnerships. Since the substantive rules applicable to LLCs are the same as those applicable to corporations, they are not treated separately here.[2]

The historical roots of the laws relating to charities are to be found in the law of trusts as it developed in the Courts of Chancery in England. This is a well-defined body of law, of which the law of charitable trusts forms a distinctive part. The corporation developed as a legal form separate and distinct from that of the trust, but many of the trust principles governing fiduciary

---

1. This common law rule has been superseded in eleven states that have enacted the Uniform Unincorporated Nonprofit Association Act. Under the act, voluntary associations are granted powers to hold property and to incur liability in the name of the association and to limit the liability of members. Uniform Unincorporated Nonprofit Association Act, §§4, 6 (1996).

2. The Internal Revenue Service in 1999 ruled that limited liability companies would be eligible for tax exemption if they were wholly owned by another exempt organization, but in such cases they would be disregarded for tax purposes. Ann. 99-102, 1992-2 C.B. 545. In 2000 the Service further ruled that LLCs meeting twelve conditions designed to assure that they would be organized and operated exclusively for exempt purposes would be eligible for exemption. For tax purposes these LLCs are treated as corporations. Richard A. McCray and Ward L. Thomas, "Limited Liability Companies as Exempt Organizations," *2000 IRS Continuing Professional Education Text*, 111.

behavior have been applied to charitable corporations so that an understanding of trust principles is necessary to an understanding of the law of charitable corporations.

Different sets of laws govern the creation and administration of charitable trusts and charitable corporations, and they are described separately. However, the definition of charitable purposes, which was developed as part of the early law of trusts, applies to both forms of organizations. Accordingly, the first section of this chapter describes the parameters of the definition of charity under state law, including the state tax provisions.[3] This is followed by a description of the requirements governing the creation, administration, and termination of charities formed as trusts, while the succeeding section describes the parallel requirements for charitable corporations. All trustees and directors of charities are subject to a set of duties designed to assist them in governing their organizations and to make them accountable for their actions. Those duties that govern the details of administration are described in this chapter while the duties of loyalty and care are the subject of Chapter 4. The final section of this chapter describes the doctrines of cy pres and deviation under which courts may modify charitable purposes or methods of administration that become obsolete or impracticable of fulfillment.

Charitable Purposes

State Law Definitions

The functions that a charity may perform are enumerated in the statement of purposes in its articles of organization or deed of trust. They are governed by a body of laws referred to as the law of charitable dispositions. This law is to be found in the court decisions in the various states, and in the statutes governing the creation of charitable corporations and the establishment of trusts. Historically, in England charitable dispositions had to conform to strict standards of public policy dictated by the Crown. However, in the United States, the laws governing charitable purposes give wide latitude to a donor to choose the objects of his beneficence. The philosophy underlying this attitude has been described as an outgrowth of the basic political philosophy of the American colonies, which viewed the function of government as that of preserving liberties, not of imposing burdens. As Clark notes, "High on the

---

3. Provisions granting exemption from tax for charitable organizations use the same common law definition found in state law, as interpreted, however, by the federal courts. This body of law is described in Chapter 5.

list of liberties was the right of every owner to control his property unaffected by governmental intrusion."[4] Although this absolute view of property rights has been modified considerably since the seventeenth century, the position of supremacy of the settlor of a charitable trust has remained. It is justified today, not on the basis of the natural rights of an owner of property, but because of the benefits that have been conferred on society by the practice of philanthropy.[5]

The extent of the freedom given to donors to choose charitable purposes is seen most clearly in attempts to frame a definition of those charitable purposes that the law recognizes as valid. As more fully described in Chapter 2, the starting point in the case law for such a definition is usually considered to be the preamble to the Statute of Charitable Uses of 1601, which contained an enumeration of the charitable purposes for which property had been given and which were to be henceforth protected by the state:

> some for relief of aged, impotent and poor people, some for mainte-
> nance of sick and maimed soldiers and mariners, schools of learning, free
> schools, and scholars in universities, some for repair of bridges, ports,
> havens, causeways, churches, seabanks and highways, some for educa-
> tion and preferment of orphans, some for or towards relief, stock or
> maintenance for houses of correction, some for marriages of poor maids,
> some for supportation, aid and help of young tradesmen, handicrafts-
> men and persons decayed, and others for relief or redemption of prison-
> ers or captives, and for aid or ease of any poor inhabitants concerning
> payments of fifteens, setting out of soldiers and other taxes.[6]

Some early cases state that a purpose is not valid if not specifically referred to in this statute,[7] but since the early eighteenth century, courts in both England and the United States have generally regarded the enumeration as descriptive or illustrative. The prevailing rule of construction today is that in determining what purposes are charitable, the courts are to be guided not by the letter of the Elizabethan statute but by its manifest spirit and reason; and they are to consider not what uses are within its words, but what uses are embraced by its meaning and purposes.[8]

---

4. Elias Clark, "Charitable Trusts, the Fourteenth Amendment and the Will of Stephen Girard," 66 *Yale Law Journal* 979, 995 (1957); see also Howard S. Miller, *The Legal Foundations of American Philanthropy, 1776–1844,* at xi (Madison: State Historical Society of Wisconsin, 1961).

5. Clark, "Charitable Trusts," 996.

6. 43 Eliz. 1, ch. 4 (1601).

7. Sanderson v. White, 35 Mass. (18 Pick.) 328, 333 (1836).

8. Drury v. Inhabitants of Natick, 92 Mass. (10 Allen) 169, 177 (1865).

From time to time, judges have attempted to frame definitions of charity and charitable purposes. The problems inherent in such a task are illustrated in Lord Macnaghten's opinion in the leading English case of *Commissioners for Special Purposes of Income Tax v. Pemsel:*

No doubt the popular meaning of the words "charity" and "charitable" does not coincide with their legal meaning; and no doubt it is easy enough to collect from the books a few decisions which seem to push the doctrine of the Court to the extreme, and to present a contrast between the two meanings in an aspect almost ludicrous. But still it is difficult to fix the point of divergence, and no one as yet has succeeded in defining the popular meaning of the word "charity." . . . How far then, it may be asked, does the popular meaning of the word "charity" correspond with its legal meaning? "Charity" in its legal sense comprises four principal divisions: trusts for the relief of poverty; trusts for the advancement of education; trusts for the advancement of religion; and trusts for other purposes beneficial to the community, not falling under any of the preceding heads. The trusts last referred to are not the less charitable in the eye of the law, because incidentally they benefit the rich as well as the poor, as indeed every charity that deserves the name must do either directly or indirectly.[9]

One of the most widely quoted definitions of a charitable trust from the United States cases is that of Chief Justice Gray in *Jackson v. Phillips:*

A charity, in the legal sense, may be more fully defined as a gift, to be applied consistently with existing laws, for the benefit of an indefinite number of persons, either by bringing their minds or hearts under the influence of education or religion, by relieving their bodies from disease, suffering or constraint, by assisting them to establish themselves in life, or by erecting or maintaining public buildings or works or otherwise lessening the burdens of government.[10]

The Restatement (Second) of the Law of Trusts, adopted by the American Law Institute in 1959, declared that a charitable trust is one devoted to charitable purposes, and then amplified: "A purpose is charitable if its accomplishment is of such social interest to the community as to justify permitting property to be devoted to the purpose in perpetuity."[11] A revision of this section, adopted in 2001, added the phrase "and to justify the various other special

9. 1891 App. Cas. 531, 583.
10. 96 Mass. (14 Allen) 539, 556 (1867).
11. Restatement (Second) of the Law of Trusts, §368 cmt. b (1959).

privileges that are typically allowed to charitable trusts," referring to the relaxation of rules against perpetual existence and accumulations of income, as well as leniency in matters of interpretation.[12]

Both the Restatement (Second) and (Third) enumerate five broad sectors of activity similar to those in Justice Gray's definition, but conclude: "There is no fixed standard to determine what purposes are of such social interest to the community [as to justify treating them as charitable]; the interests of the community vary with time and place."[13]

Scott has said, "The truth of the matter is that it is impossible to frame a perfect definition of charitable purposes. There is no fixed standard to determine what purposes are charitable."[14] Nevertheless, Clark's description indicates the attitude of the American courts toward charitable uses, an attitude that existed at the end of the twentieth century as well as in 1960:

> The courts have found no way to make an effective classification [of valid charitable purposes]. Purposes worthy of community support are as diffuse as the winds. They vary with time . . . Because of this constant flux, attempts to formalize the community benefit into abstract rules inevitably degenerate into a listing of ad hoc responses to particular situations. The courts have clearly perceived these dangers and have adjusted to them by accepting as charitable those trusts which benefit a group larger than the settlor's immediate family and friends and which are not affirmatively absurd, obscene, illegal, excessively selfish or specifically offensive to some considerable segment of the population.[15]

Both Restatements enumerate five specific purposes and a sixth "catchall" category. The five are relief of poverty, advancement of education, advancement of religion, promotion of health, and governmental or municipal purposes. The sixth describes "other purposes that are beneficial to the community."[16] However, the commentaries to Restatement (Third) expanded their scope, reflecting both judicial decisions rendered since publication of Restatement (Second) and the opinion of the American Law Institute as to what the law should be.[17] Thus the comment on clause (b), "advancement of edu-

12. Restatement (Third) of the Law of Trusts, §28 cmt. a (2003).

13. Restatement (Second) of Trusts, §368 cmt. b; Restatement (Third) of Trusts, §28 cmt. a; see also Austin W. Scott and William F. Fratcher, *Law of Trusts*, §368 (Boston: Little, Brown, 4th ed., 1987).

14. Scott and Fratcher, *Law of Trusts*, §368.

15. Clark, "Charitable Trusts," 997–998; see also Elias Clark, "The Limitation on Political Activities: A Discordant Note in the English Law of Charities," 46 *Virginia Law Review* 439, 443 (1960).

16. Restatement (Second) of Trusts, §368; Restatement (Third) of Trusts, §28.

17. Restatement (Third) of Trusts, §28.

cation," changed the formulation to "advancement of knowledge or education" and gave as examples establishing libraries and museums, preparing and disseminating publications, and providing citizenship training.[18] Promotion of physical training, which had been included under clause (b) in Restatement (Second),[19] was moved to clause (f), "other purposes beneficial to the community."[20] Under the sixth (catchall) category, Restatement (Second) included providing vacations and moderate-cost homes for working girls as examples,[21] whereas Restatement (Third) cites providing low-cost housing and lending money to help individuals enter a certain profession or business venture.[22]

Purposes that are illegal or will involve illegal acts are not considered charitable. Thus Restatement (Second) states that dissemination of information that violates a statute is not charitable, giving as examples providing instruction on overthrowing the government and on birth control.[23] Restatement (Third) modified this comment as follows:

> A trust to provide instruction in the performance of a criminal act or to induce the commission of such acts is not charitable, although a trust to support the dissemination of literature advocating or explaining the nature and societal benefits of conduct or procedures that are illegal in the state (e.g., assisted suicide) would ordinarily be an educational and thus a charitable purpose.[24]

A trust to disseminate controversial ideas and unpopular causes is valid if the general purposes for which the trust has been created may be reasonably thought to promote the social interest of the community. This is the case even if a majority of people believe that the specific purpose is unwise or not well suited to its social objective. Restatement (Third) sets forth the standard to be applied by the courts in such cases to be "not to attempt to decide which of conflicting views of the social or community interest is more beneficial or appropriate but to decide whether the trust purpose or the view to be promoted is sufficiently useful or reasonable to be of such benefit or interest to the community, including through a marketplace of ideas, as to justify the perpetual existence and other privileges of a charitable trust."[25] It notes that

18. Id., §28 cmt. h.
19. Restatement (Second) of Trusts, §370 cmt. e.
20. Restatement (Third) of Trusts, §28 cmt. l.
21. Restatement (Second) of Trusts, §374 cmt. g.
22. Restatement (Third) of Trusts, §28 cmt. l.
23. Restatement (Second) of Trusts, §370 cmt. i.
24. Restatement (Third) of Trusts, §28 cmt. h.
25. Restatement (Third) of Trusts, §28 cmt. a(2).

the difference between an irrational purpose and a valid one may be difficult to draw and that the line "may be drawn differently at different times and in different places."[26]

There is another category of purposes that may violate a standard of public policy that is not proscribed by a criminal statute but may nonetheless be outside the concept of valid charitable purposes. This category generated the greatest interest and the largest number of cases in the latter half of the twentieth century. The cases invariably involved trusts for valid charitable purposes such as education or relief of poverty that, however, restricted the class of beneficiaries on the basis of national origin, race, religion, gender, sexual preference, age, group, political affiliation, or other characteristics or background. The standards that the courts have applied to determine validity are whether the carrying out of the purposes involves state action or, where state action is not present, whether the trust involves invidious discrimination, for in both cases if the answer is yes, the trust will fail.[27]

The question of state action arises by virtue of the application to charitable trusts of the provisions of the Fourteenth Amendment of the United States Constitution prohibiting the state from discriminating on the basis of race or religion. Discrimination on the basis of race was the basis for challenges in two cases decided by the Supreme Court in 1957 and 1966. In the first case, the Court held that the Fourteenth Amendment prohibited the city of Philadelphia from acting as trustee of a trust created by Stephen Girard to establish and operate a school for poor white male orphans.[28] The Pennsylvania court, acknowledging that state action was involved, had removed the city officials and appointed individual trustees to carry out the trust. This action was upheld by the Supreme Court of Pennsylvania, and the United States Supreme Court refused to hear further appeal.[29]

The second case involved a devise in a will executed in 1911 to the mayor and council of Macon, Georgia, of a tract of land to be used as a park "for white people only," the trust to be under the control of a board of managers consisting of seven white persons.[30] The restriction was enforced until the 1960s when the city opened the park to all persons on the grounds that it was a public facility. In response, members of the board of managers brought suit requesting the court to remove the city as trustee and transfer title to the park to a court-appointed board of trustees that would carry out the original

26. Id.

27. See generally Restatement (Third) of Trusts, §28 cmt. f.

28. Pennsylvania v. Board of Directors of City Trusts, 353 U.S. 230 (1957).

29. In re Girard College Trusteeship, 138 A.2d 844 (Pa. 1958), cert. denied and appeal dismissed, 357 U.S. 570 (1958).

30. Evans v. Newton, 382 U.S. 296 (1966).

terms of the devise. The testator's heirs entered the suit claiming that the property should revert to them. The lower court accepted the city's resignation and appointed three individual trustees to operate the park under the terms of the gift, a decision that was affirmed by the Supreme Court of Georgia. On appeal, the United States Supreme Court reversed the lower courts, holding that the actions of the city in operating the park as an integral part of its activities could not be refuted by merely appointing new trustees.[31] The aftermath of this decision was a holding by the Georgia trial court that in view of the fact that the intended trust could not be enforced, the trust failed and the property therefore reverted to the testator's heirs, rejecting motions from the state attorney general and local citizens to apply the cy pres doctrine by striking out the racial restrictions. This decision was affirmed by the Georgia Supreme Court,[32] a decision that was in turn affirmed by the United States Supreme Court in *Evans v. Abney*.[33]

The *Evans* case had an unforeseen, but important, repercussion as regards the Girard Trust; the Federal Circuit Court for the Third Circuit in a suit brought after the *Evans* decision held that in light of the fairly comparable facts and trusteeship histories of the school and of the park, the latter decision governed the issue and required, cy pres, that the school admit applicants without regard to race.[34] The result in the *Evans* case reflected a rigid attitude toward application of the cy pres doctrine, discussed below. The outcome in the *Girard* case demonstrated that remedial action was available to remove restrictions that violate public policy even if state action was initially involved.[35]

The issue of what constitutes state action continued to be litigated with challenges to the affirmative action policies in admissions to educational institutions upheld in a number of cases decided between 1994 and 2002 by the federal district and appellate courts.[36] Appeals from two of these, in both of

31. Id.
32. Evans v. Abney, 165 S.E.2d 160 (Ga. 1968).
33. 396 U.S. 435 (1969).
34. Pennsylvania v. Brown, 392 F.2d 120 (3d Cir. 1968), cert. denied, 391 U.S. 921 (1968).
35. Restatement (Third) of Trusts, §28, Reporter's Notes, cmt. f; see also David Luria, "Prying Loose the Dead Hand of the Past: How Courts Apply Cy Pres to Race, Gender, and Religiously Restricted Trusts," 21 *University of San Francisco Law Review* 41 (1986).
36. Podberesky v. Kirwan, 38 F.3d 147 (4th Cir. 1994); Hopwood v. Texas, 78 F.3d 932 (5th Cir. 1996); Texas v. Lesage, 528 U.S. 18 (1999); Smith v. University of Washington Law School, 233 F.3d 1188 (9th Cir. 2000); Wooden v. Board of Regents of the University System of Georgia, 247 F.3d 1262 (11th Cir. 2001); Johnson v. Board of Regents of the University of Georgia, 263 F.3d 1234 (11th Cir. 2001); Gratz v. Bollinger, 135 F. Supp. 2d 790 (E.D. Mich. 2001), cert. granted, 123 S. Ct. 617 (December 2, 2002); Grutter v. Bollinger, 288 F.3d 732 (6th Cir. 2002), cert. granted, 123 S. Ct. 617 (December 2, 2002).

which the admissions policies of the University of Michigan were challenged, were decided by the Supreme Court in June 2003. One involved the admissions policy of the law school, in which race was considered to be one of a number of factors in a "highly individualized, holistic review of each applicant's file." In a five-to-four decision, the Court upheld the constitutionality of the policy, thereby effectively ruling that there was a compelling state interest in maintaining racial diversity in education.[37] The second case addressed the admissions policy of the undergraduate school, which used a point system based in part on race that had the effect of admitting nearly all qualified minority applicants while rejecting many qualified white students. The Court held that this policy did not meet the constitutional requirement adopted in the first case, namely, that there be individualized consideration of each candidate rather than a mechanical rule.[38]

Restatement (Third) noted that "there has been little suggestion so far of the possibility that 'state action' is inherently present in charitable trusts because of their dependence on enforcement by a state official and the array of special privileges bestowed by state and federal law."[39] In cases in which no state action has been involved, restrictions designed to favor minorities have been upheld as remedial measures designed to expand opportunities for disadvantaged classes. A majority of these cases have involved admission to educational institutions and financial aid, although some have dealt with facilities for the elderly and the poor. Thus the law of trusts does not prohibit use of a criterion such as gender, religion, or national origin "when it is a reasonable element of a settlor's charitable purpose and charitable motivation."[40]

Unlike racial and in some instances gender limitations, religious restrictions have generally been upheld. Thus in a 1977 case the Connecticut court lifted racial and gender restrictions on beneficiaries of a scholarship fund while maintaining a religious limitation.[41] Similarly, a South Carolina court in 1986 removed a racial restriction while retaining a religious one.[42]

Challenges to discrimination have also been brought as claims of violations of the freedom of association. One of the most important involved a charity. *Boy Scouts of America v. Dale,* decided in June 2000, challenged the organization's policy forbidding membership to homosexuals.[43] The New Jersey courts had held that this policy violated the state's public accommoda-

---

37. Grutter v. Bollinger, 123 S. Ct. 2325 (2003).

38. Gratz v. Bollinger, 123 S. Ct. 2411 (2003).

39. Restatement (Third) of Trusts, §28, Reporter's Notes, cmt. f.

40. Id., §28 cmt. f; see also Einat Philip, "Diversity in the Halls of Academia: Bye-Bye *Bakke?*" 31 *Journal of Law and Education* 149 (2002).

41. Lockwood v. Killian, 375 A.2d 998 (Conn. 1977).

42. Grant Home v. Medlock, 349 S.E.2d 655 (S.C. App. 1986).

43. 530 U.S. 640 (2000).

tions law. On appeal, the Supreme Court, in a five-to-four decision, ruled that New Jersey's interpretation of its public accommodation law violated the plaintiff's First Amendment right of expressive association. In short, it ruled that the Boy Scouts was an expressive association and that its board was entitled to define the membership as it saw fit.

Motives of Donors

The motive of the donor of a charitable trust is not usually a factor that the courts will consider in determining the validity of a charitable purpose. The effect of the gift is the controlling feature, not what the donor intended it to accomplish.[44] A request that a marker be placed on a building indicating the name of the donor, a stipulation that a foundation's title always have the donor's name in it,[45] or any other direction concerning administration that is aimed at keeping the name of the settlor for posterity does not affect the gift's validity.[46]

Gifts for Charitable and Noncharitable Purposes

Ordinarily a gift to charity never fails for uncertainty. If the gift is "for charity," whether in trust or not, the court will direct a scheme for the disposition of the property. If the gift is "to such charitable purposes as X shall select," and X fails to select, the court will either appoint a new trustee to make the selection or approve a scheme for the administration of the trust.[47]

The courts have not been as consistent in their treatment of cases where the gift has involved a choice between charitable and noncharitable objects. The situation in these cases is complicated by the fact that certain purposes, if not declared charitable, are not proper subjects for private trusts, in most instances because they do not meet the requirement that there be a beneficiary capable of enforcing every private trust. Particularly in England but to some extent in the United States, the courts historically have refused to uphold trusts where a donor coupled a valid charitable purpose with other purposes that, in the opinion of the court, were wider and less definite than "charitable" purposes. The most common cases have involved the presence of the word "charitable" with commonly accepted synonyms such as "benevolent," "public," "deserving," "philanthropic," and "patriotic." The courts have held in these cases that, in law, the words are not synonymous and, although

44. Restatement (Third) of Trusts, §28 cmt. a.
45. Taylor v. Columbian University, 226 U.S. 126 (1912).
46. Massachusetts Institute of Technology v. Attorney General, 126 N.E. 521 (Mass. 1920).
47. Scott and Fratcher, *Law of Trusts*, §§396–397.4; Kirwin v. Attorney General, 175 N.E. 164 (Mass. 1931).

the purpose is broad enough to include "charity," it does not limit the gift to charitable purposes in the legal sense.

In the United States some cases followed the strict English rule,[48] but in the majority of cases the courts have held that dispositions of this type were for charitable purposes, thereby upholding the trusts.[49] Restatement (Third) notes that charitable trusts are favored in matters of interpretation so that a trust for "charitable and benevolent purposes" or even a trust for "charitable or benevolent purposes" would likely be interpreted as intended to include only charitable purposes.[50] The wisdom of this liberal attitude is self-evident. It has been given further support in this country by the large number of statutes relating to charitable dispositions that use the word "benevolent," and by court interpretations holding that the two words "charitable" and "benevolent" are synonymous.[51]

Where a gift is for specific named purposes, some of which are charitable and others of which are clearly not, if the noncharitable purposes are also recognized in law and the trust does not involve a violation of the Rule Against Perpetuities, the trust will not ordinarily fail; if necessary, the court will order a division of the gift. If, however, the noncharitable purposes are not recognized in law as the proper subject of a private trust, or if the trust would violate the Rule Against Perpetuities, the courts have divided as to the proper disposition of the property. In some cases an apportionment has been made among the charitable and noncharitable purposes; those that were valid were upheld, and the rest were declared to revert to the testator's heirs. In other cases the court directed that all of the property be applied to charitable purposes with the exception of a maximum amount that could conceivably be required for the invalid purpose, ruling that the trust failed as to that amount. In some cases the entire disposition has been upheld as charitable, while in others the entire gift has failed. The deciding factor in each of these situations has usually been the nature of the disposition and the willingness of the court to apply liberal rules of construction.[52]

Charitable Purposes for Nonprofit Corporations

Sources for the definition of legal purposes for charitable corporations are initially to be found in the statutes authorizing creation of the corporations.

48. In re Hayward's Estate, 178 P.2d 547 (Ariz. 1947) (trust for the benefit of any purposes deemed by trustees beneficial to town failed).
49. See Scott and Fratcher, *Law of Trusts*, §398.1, for citations.
50. Restatement (Third) of Trusts, §28 cmt. a.
51. Id., §28, Reporter's Notes, cmt. a.
52. See generally Scott and Fratcher, *Law of Trusts*, §398.2.

Many of the early general incorporation statutes for nonprofit organizations contained lists of those purposes for which a corporation could be formed. The Illinois General Not For Profit Corporation Act of 1986, for example, provides that not-for-profit corporations may be organized for any one or more of "the following or similar purposes," and then lists thirty-two of them, with the final two referring to sections 501(c) and (d) and section 170(c) of the federal Internal Revenue Code.[53] Similarly, the Massachusetts statute permits incorporation for any one or more of thirteen purposes.[54] New York classifies nonprofit corporations by type, with Type B applicable to organizations with "nonbusiness" purposes that track section 501(c)(3) of the Internal Revenue Code.[55]

In contrast to the statutes described above, the Revised Model Nonprofit Corporation Act (RMNCA) states that "[e]very corporation incorporated under this Act has the purpose of engaging in any lawful activity unless a more limited purpose is set forth in the articles of incorporation."[56] This act then subdivides corporations into three categories, religious, public benefit, and mutual benefit, categories that must be declared in the articles of organization.[57] The RMNCA does not contain a definition of purposes. Rather, the test for determining if a corporation is "charitable" in the legal sense of the word is made by the courts by reference to the law of charitable dispositions discussed above.[58]

Requirement of Indefinite Beneficiaries

The Restatement definition of a charitable trust does not include the word "beneficiary,"[59] and therein lies an important distinction between a charitable trust and a private trust. For a private trust to be valid, there must be a named or ascertainable beneficiary who is capable of providing continuing scrutiny of the activities of the trustee and who is able to call abuses to the attention of the court for correction. The beneficiaries of a charitable trust, on the other hand, are in the broadest sense the public at large. There are no individuals who have enforcement powers comparable to those held by beneficiaries of a private trust, or there is no valid charity.

53. 805 Ill. Comp. Stat. 105/103.05.

54. Mass. Gen. Laws ch. 180, §4; see also Fla. Stat. ch. 617.0301.

55. N.Y. Not-for-Profit Corp. Law §201.

56. Revised Model Nonprofit Corporation Act (RMNCA), §3.01(a) (1987).

57. RMNCA, §2.02(2).

58. "The test of a charitable gift or use and a charitable corporation are the same." Matter of Rockefeller's Estate, 165 N.Y.S. 154 (App. Div. 1917), aff'd, 119 N.E. 1074 (N.Y. 1918).

59. Restatement (Second) of Trusts, §348.

Even if individuals receive direct benefits from a charitable trust, such as scholarship grants, money, food, clothing, or any other direct assistance, they are considered the "conduits of the social benefits to the public and are not in reality the beneficiaries of the trust."[60] This does not mean that at certain times and in certain circumstances there cannot be individuals who would have a right similar to that of the beneficiaries of a private trust to sue for enforcement. For example, charitable trusts for the benefit of the minister of a particular church have been upheld on the ground that, although the direct beneficiary for a certain finite time is a specific ascertained individual, the underlying and main purpose of the trust is to promote religion, and the total number of beneficiaries over a long period of time is not ascertainable.[61]

This same reasoning has been applied to uphold trusts the income of which is to be used for a prize or an award,[62] research or scholarship grants to individuals meeting certain requirements,[63] prizes to winners of competitions, or awards to a specified number of individuals to be picked each year by the trustee.[64] In addition, a donor may direct that certain individuals shall be preferred as beneficiaries, so long as the primary purpose can be considered of public benefit. For example, a trust for the poor with instructions that it be applied first to the donor's poor relatives was upheld in *Bullard v. Chandler*,[65] but a trust solely for the descendants of a donor who may be in need is not usually considered a valid charitable gift.[66]

As with the determination of charitable purposes, judicial interpretation of the requirement of indefiniteness has varied considerably. Whereas the English courts tend to exclude trusts to aid special groups not open to the general public, the United States courts have usually considered these trusts to be valid. For example, an English trust for the benefit of workers in a factory employing 110,000 was held to be invalid as benefiting too narrow a class,[67] but trusts for even smaller groups of employees have been upheld in the United States.[68] The rulings of the Commissioner of Internal Revenue on trusts of

60. George G. Bogert and George T. Bogert, *The Law of Trusts and Trustees,* §362 (St. Paul: West Group, 3d ed., 1977).

61. Curtis v. First Church in Charlestown, 188 N.E. 631 (Mass. 1934); see also Scott and Fratcher, *Law of Trusts,* §375.1.

62. Powell's Estate, 71 Pa. D. & C. 51 (1950).

63. Hoyt v. Bliss, 105 A. 699 (Conn. 1919).

64. Sherman v. Shaw, 137 N.E. 374 (Mass. 1922).

65. 21 N.E. 951 (Mass. 1889).

66. Kent v. Dunham, 7 N.E. 730 (Mass. 1886); see also Scott and Fratcher, *Law of Trusts,* §375.3.

67. Oppenheim v. Tobacco Securities Trust Co., [1951] A.C. 297.

68. In re Fanelli's Estate, 140 N.Y.S.2d 334 (Surr. Ct. 1955); In re Scholler's Estate, 169 A.2d 554 (Pa. 1961).

this type are generally stricter than the court decisions on validity; but the denial of exemption has usually been based on the fact that there would be inurement to the donor, not that the class was too definite.[69]

Trusts established to provide relief to victims of disasters have caused problems under both state law and federal tax law. It has not been uncommon for business corporations to establish trusts to aid the families of persons who have died during the course of their employment. In most cases these will not qualify as charitable trusts. The legal difficulty lies in determining the dividing line between an identifiable class of beneficiaries and the indefinite class required under the law of charitable trusts, and often the determination will be made more on the basis of sentiment than of adherence to a strict legal definition.[70]

The terms of some charitable trusts require the trustees to manage the capital fund and pay over income to a charitable corporation or association for its general purposes or for a specific limited purpose. In these cases the beneficiary of the first trust is a definite, identifiable legal entity. However, the trust is valid as a charity since the ultimate benefit will be to the community at large.

The rules requiring dedication to public purposes applicable to charitable trusts are also applicable to charitable corporations and are construed without distinction as to the form of the charity. The trust law requirement that the beneficiaries must constitute an indefinite class does not arise at the time of creation as it does with a charitable trust, which can last in perpetuity only if the class of beneficiaries is sufficiently indefinite. In fact, organizations that will benefit only a limited class of members are usually organized under general nonprofit laws; examples include a mutual benefit association, a social club, or a trade association. The charitable nature of the corporation, and therefore the question of the nature of its beneficiaries, will be considered by tax officials and by the courts in actions to determine disposition of the assets on dissolution or merger. The question of whether the class of beneficiaries is sufficiently indefinite may also arise whenever there is a question of compliance with laws imposing a duty on charitable entities to file reports with the state, such as the Massachusetts law applicable to all "public charities" incorporated within the Commonwealth[71] or the provision of the California statute for the supervision of trustees for charitable purposes that defines a charitable corporation as "any nonprofit corporation organized under the laws of this State for charitable or eleemosynary purposes and any similar for-

69. See Chapter 5.

70. See Chapter 5 for tax treatment of organizations providing relief to victims of disasters, including the families of individuals killed on September 11, 2001.

71. Mass. Gen. Laws ch. 12, §8(f).

eign corporation doing business or holding property in this State for such purposes."[72]

Definitions in State Tax Laws

A parallel set of definitions of charitable purposes is to be found in the laws granting exemption to charities from inheritance, estate, income, and property taxes imposed by the various states. Decisions as to imposition of tax are made by the state courts by reference to the statute granting exemption. There is little uniformity in these taxation statutes.

Some state constitutions authorize exemption of charities from taxes of various kinds. In others, the exemption may be mandatory. If the constitution is silent, exemption will be determined by the legislature.[73] Exemption from taxes on real property is usually granted only to property actually occupied and in use for the charitable purpose of the organization, and exemption is rarely allowed for income-producing property even if the income is applied to the charitable purpose.[74] Often the exemption is not available to a foreign corporation without a showing that a substantial portion of its activities is carried on within the state. In some jurisdictions a further distinction is made between property owned by a charitable corporation, which is granted exemption, and property owned by a trust, which may not be.[75]

The wording used in the statutes to describe the "purposes" of institutions eligible for tax exemption also varies from state to state. Usually it takes the form of a statement like that of the New York statute, which exempts the property of corporations or associations organized for any of twenty-two different specific charitable purposes.[76] The Pennsylvania statute exempts institutions of purely public charity.[77]

It is, of course, possible to have a determination that property of a particular institution is not eligible for tax exemption, even though there may be a court determination, based on other issues, that the institution is a valid charity. A classic case of this nature involved the Boston Symphony Orchestra.

72. Cal. Gov. Code §12582.1.

73. Janne Gallagher, "The Legal Structure of Property-Tax Exemption," in *Property-Tax Exemption for Charities: Mapping the Battlefield,* 3, 4 (Evelyn Brody ed., Washington, D.C.: Urban Institute Press, 2002).

74. For a discussion of state property tax laws and the business activities of charities, see Andras Kosaras, Comment, "Federal and State Property Tax Exemption of Commercialized Nonprofits: Should Profit-Seeking Art Museums Be Tax Exempt?" 35 *New England Law Review* 115 (2001).

75. See, for example, Mass. Gen. Laws ch. 59, §5; N.Y. Real Prop. Tax Law §§402, 438.

76. N.Y. Real Prop. Tax Law §402.

77. Pa. Stat. Ann. tit. 72, §3244.

The Massachusetts court held that the orchestra was subject to a property tax on its hall, since it charged admission and permitted certain renewable season ticket privileges.[78] This decision was criticized by Scott on the grounds that the fact that admission is charged is not sufficient to deny status as charitable to an organization.[79] In 1961 the Massachusetts court determined that the orchestra was not subject to tort liability on the basis that it was a valid charitable organization.[80]

The state courts are more frequently liberal in cases involving the validity of a charity than in cases interpreting tax laws.[81] The provision in the Ohio property tax law grants exemption only if the property is used for the charitable purpose.[82] In *Wehrle Foundation v. Evatt*,[83] the Ohio court ruled that property used as offices by a foundation that was engaged solely in making grants to other charitable organizations was not property used for charitable purposes within the meaning of the statute.

Challenges to the exemption of health care organizations became a major issue in Utah and Pennsylvania in 1985. In the Utah case, although the statute provided that property used for a hospital would be deemed to be used for charitable purposes, the court ruled that the burden was on the charity to prove that it operated for charitable purposes.[84] As a result of the case, the state's hospitals and nursing homes collaborated with the state tax commission to develop standards for determining eligibility for tax exemption. They required provision of charity care, publicity of the availability of this care, and demonstration that the value of unreimbursed gifts to the community exceeds the value of the exemption. These standards were held constitutional by the Utah Supreme Court in 1994.[85]

In Pennsylvania, exemption is available under the constitution to "institutions of purely public charity."[86] At dispute was exemption from the sales tax of a jointly owned hospital support facility. In its decision the court framed a five-part test to determine whether an organization met the constitutionally required definition. The five requirements were that the organization advance a charitable purpose, donate or render gratuitously a substantial portion of its services, benefit a substantial and indefinite class of persons who

78. Boston Symphony Orchestra, Inc. v. Board of Assessors, 1 N.E.2d 6 (Mass. 1936).

79. Scott and Fratcher, *Law of Trusts,* §375.2 n.28.

80. Boxer v. Boston Symphony Orchestra, Inc., 174 N.E.2d 363 (Mass. 1961).

81. Rivers Oaks Garden Club v. City of Houston, 370 S.W.2d 851 (Tex. 1963); but see Samarkand of Santa Barbara v. County of Santa Barbara, 31 Cal. Rptr. 151 (Cal. Ct. App. 1963).

82. Ohio Rev. Code §5709.12.

83. 49 N.E.2d 52 (Ohio 1943).

84. Utah County v. Intermountain Health Care, 709 P.2d 265 (Utah 1985).

85. Howell v. County Board of Cache County, 881 P.2d 880 (Utah 1994).

86. Pa. Const. art. VIII, §2(a)(vi).

are legitimate subjects of charity, relieve the government of some of its burdens, and operate entirely free from private profit motive.[87] As reported by Gallagher, the lower court in a series of decisions denied exemption to virtually every charity that came before it, reading each of the requirements as narrowly as possible.[88] In 1994 the state supreme court reversed a lower court ruling denying exemption to a nursing home with a large population of Medicaid patients and formulated modifications to the five tests.[89] In a second decision rendered in 1997, the state supreme court affirmed a lower court decision granting property tax exemption to a small independent school, finding that an institution that is open to all benefits a charitable class.[90] Shortly before the decision was rendered, the legislature adopted a statute that was designed to broaden the five standards in the *Hospital Utilization Project* decision, thereby resolving the controversies in a manner favorable to the charities.[91]

The most noteworthy case involving exemption from real property taxes was *Camps Newfound/Owatonna, Inc. v. Town of Harrison*,[92] decided by the Supreme Court in 1997. At issue was the constitutionality of the Maine property tax, which provided beneficial tax treatment for organizations that served mostly state residents and penalized those that conducted principally interstate business. Most of the children who attended the camps in question were from out of state and, under the restrictive provisions of the statute, the camps were not eligible for exemption. The Court held that the statute violated the dormant provisions of the commerce clause and was accordingly unconstitutional. In 2002, relying on this decision, the supreme court of Minnesota found unconstitutional a provision of Minnesota law denying deductions for contributions to non-Minnesota charities for purposes of the state's alternative minimum tax.[93]

The matter of exemption from state inheritance, gift, and income taxes is also important to many charities, and there was wide variation in the statutory language among the states. At one time it was the general rule that deductions would be permitted only for transfers to institutions and corporations located in the state granting the deductions and that all exempt trusts must be limited to use within the state. Often these restrictions were not based on express statutory language, but were the result of court determina-

---

87. Hospital Utilization Project v. Commonwealth, 487 A.2d 1306 (Pa. 1985).
88. Gallagher, "The Legal Structure of Property-Tax Exemption," 13.
89. St. Margaret Seneca Place v. Board of Property Assessment Appeals and Review, 640 A.2d 380 (Pa. 1994).
90. City of Washington v. Board of Assessment Appeals, 704 A.2d 120 (Pa. 1997).
91. Institutions of Purely Public Charity Act, Pa. Stat. Ann. tit. 10, §371 et seq.
92. 520 U.S. 564 (1997).
93. Chapman v. Commissioner of Revenue, 651 N.W.2d 825 (Minn. 2002).

tions that exemption statutes should be strictly construed and that the state should not be presumed to authorize exemption for purposes having little or no relation to the welfare of its residents. Exemption was also granted for legacies to nonresident charities if there would be no tax under the laws of the state where the foreign charity was located or if that state granted reciprocity. The issues became essentially moot, however, during the latter half of the twentieth century as all but a handful of states repealed their individual tax provisions and imposed instead an estate tax equal in amount and determined in relationship to the state tax credit allowed under the Internal Revenue Code.[94]

The Trust Form for Charities

A private trust is a device for making dispositions of property whereby the legal title and the duties of management are given to a trustee who is charged with managing the property and applying it for the benefit of named beneficiaries. The right to enjoyment or the beneficial interest in the property belongs to the beneficiaries who can enforce their rights against the trustees and the donor through appropriate court action.[95]

A charitable trust is similar to a private trust in that a trustee holds and manages the property not for the benefit of specified individuals but for certain defined purposes that are considered to be of benefit to the public at large. The Restatement (Second) of Trusts defines a charitable trust as follows:

> [A] charitable trust is a fiduciary relationship with respect to property arising as a result of a manifestation of an intention to create it and subjecting the person by whom the property is held to equitable duties to deal with the property for a charitable purpose.[96]

This definition indicates the specific elements required by law for the creation of a charitable trust and the nature of the legal duties of the trustee that the law will enforce.

---

94. See *Inheritance Estate and Gift Tax Reporter, State* (CCH), vol. 5, at 70,111 to 70,633 (2002), for provisions in all states.

95. Trusts are peculiar to Anglo-American law; although there are analogous institutions in other legal systems, none is as flexible. Maitland has said: "If we were asked what is the greatest and most distinctive achievement performed by Englishmen in the field of jurisprudence I cannot think that we should have any better answer to give than this, namely, the development from century to century of the trust idea." Frederic W. Maitland, *Equity,* 23 (Cambridge: University Press, 2d ed., 1936).

96. Restatement (Second) of Trusts, §348.

Creation of Charitable Trusts

There are three requirements for creating a charitable trust: (1) property that is to become the subject matter of the trust; (2) evidence of an intention to create the trust; and (3) devotion to a purpose that the courts of the state where the trust is created will recognize as charitable.

The evidence required to establish an intent to create a charitable trust is usually a written declaration or deed, called the trust instrument or trust indenture. A written instrument may be required by law if the subject matter of the property is land and if the state where the land is situated has enacted a statute called the Statute of Frauds, which requires that a transfer of land is not valid unless it is in writing. Aside from this, there is no need for a written instrument, just as there is no need for consideration. An individual may create a charitable trust by declaring orally that he holds certain specific property as trustee for the benefit of some specific charitable purpose. This is rarely done, however, since the problem of proof is often difficult, particularly in connection with tax questions; and a donor will usually desire to specify provisions for administering the trust.

Inter vivos trusts created during the lifetime of a donor may be formed without recourse to any court or state authority. In some states a donor may have the instrument recorded in a local court, although this again is rarely done. Testamentary trusts in contrast are created by will, and come into existence only after the death of the donor. The document evidencing the creation of these trusts must conform to the requirements established for all testamentary dispositions in the state in which the will is executed. The trust will later be established under the supervision of the court of the state where the testator was domiciled at his death. This court will then oversee the disposition of the testator's entire estate and in many instances will retain power over the trust for its duration.

Restrictions on the Amount of Charitable Bequests

The common law placed no restrictions on the amount of property that a testator could dispose of by will for charitable purposes. In England and in some states, however, statutes were enacted that restricted the power to make charitable dispositions, whether they were to be in trust or not. The early statutes, particularly in England, were designed to prevent property from being kept out of commerce in perpetuity. The restrictions in the United States statutes were directed primarily toward preventing a testator from disinheriting his or her family by so-called deathbed provisions. This legislation is of two types. In some states a gift to charity in a will executed within a certain time before the testator's death is invalid.[97] The second type places a limit on the proportion of an estate that a testator can leave to charity if he is survived by certain near relatives.[98]

Duration and Restrictions on Remoteness of Vesting

A private trust is distinguishable from a charitable trust in terms of its duration. Private trusts have generally been subject to the so-called Rule Against Perpetuities. The classic statement of the Rule, given by Professor Gray, is that "No interest is good unless it must vest, if at all, not later than twenty-one years after some life in being at the creation of the interest."[99] The purpose behind the Rule was to prevent the withdrawal of property from commerce. The public interest in encouraging charitable dispositions led to their exclusion from the provisions of this rule in all states by either case law or statute.[100]

Starting in the 1990s, a number of states undertook to modify the Rule Against Perpetuities, first, by permitting trusts to continue for the greater of 100 years or the period of the Rule. Then, in 1997, South Dakota, Alaska, and Delaware enacted legislation abolishing the Rule.[101] Since then it has been abolished or modified to make it optional in another twelve states.[102]

The Rule Against Perpetuities is applicable to noncharitable dispositions where there is a contingent gift over to charity on the happening of some future event. If the gift to charity will not vest within the period of the Rule, it fails. It also fails if there is an attempt to create a charitable trust to last for a period longer than the Rule with a gift to individuals at the end of the period. A gift over from one charity to another, however, is valid regardless of the time at which a change of beneficiary may occur.

---

97. See Bogert and Bogert, *Law of Trusts and Trustees*, §326, and Scott and Fratcher, *Law of Trusts*, §362.4, for citations and further discussion.

98. In re Estate of Moore, 219 Cal. App. 2d 737 (1963).

99. John Chipman Gray, *The Rule Against Perpetuities*, §202 (Boston: Little, Brown, 4th ed., 1942).

100. "The cases so holding are so numerous that it is unnecessary to cite them; indeed, most charitable trusts are of indefinite duration." See Scott and Fratcher, *Law of Trusts*, §365 n.1, which also includes a partial list of citations; Restatement (Third) of Trusts, §28 cmt. d.

101. Joel C. Dobris, "The Death of the Rule Against Perpetuities, or the Rap Has No Friends—An Essay," 35 *Real Property, Probate and Trust Journal* 601 (2000).

102. As of June 2003, the Rule has been abolished in the following additional states: Arizona, Florida, Idaho, Illinois, Maine, Maryland, New Jersey, Ohio, Rhode Island, Virginia, Washington, and Wisconsin. See Note, "Dynasty Trusts and the Rule Against Perpetuities," 116 *Harvard Law Review* 2588 (2003); T. P. Gallanis, "The Future of Future Interests," 60 *Washington and Lee Law Review* 513 (2003).

In addition to restrictions on the duration of trusts that arise from the operation of the Rule Against Perpetuities, there are statutes in a number of states that prohibit the suspension of absolute ownership or limit the power of alienation to a certain period of time. The time given in these statutes is usually measured in the same terms as the Rule Against Perpetuities, but the statutes operate to prevent restrictions on the disposition of property by an owner; they do not act on the question of whether an interest will vest within the given period.

It is not, of course, essential to the validity of a charitable trust that it exist for an indefinite term. Some American foundations, such as the Rosenwald and the Alton Jones, were created with the express purpose of distributing all of their capital funds within a finite period. Some writers have advocated that there be a limit on the duration of charitable trusts on grounds of public policy.[103] The law, however, takes no position as to the desirability of existence in perpetuity as opposed to limitation on existence, and permits both without distinction.

Termination

It is the intent of the settlor that determines the duration of charitable trusts, and a court will not usually order termination where such action could be considered to be against the intent of the settlor. Thus, in cases where there has been a gift to trustees to hold property and pay the income to a charitable corporation, the courts have refused to turn over the trust to the corporation to manage.[104]

An interesting example of this rule involved a trust created in the will of Benjamin Franklin. Franklin directed that the fund was to accumulate for two one-hundred-year periods, during which time loans were to be made to young artificers on certain specified conditions, and after which time the principal and accrued income were to be paid to the Commonwealth of Massachusetts and the city of Boston. In the early twentieth century it became impossible to make loans under the terms of the will, and the funds were invested. In 1959 the state legislature and the city both agreed to turn their interest in the gift over to the Franklin Foundation, which had been created to manage the distribution under the trust after the first one hundred years. The Foundation then brought suit as the sole beneficiary to have the trust termi-

103. Arthur Hobhouse, *The Dead Hand* (London: Chatto and Windus, 1880); Courtney Stanhope Kenny, *Property Given for Charitable or Other Public Use* (London: Reeves and Turner, 1880); Julius Rosenwald, "Principles of Public Giving," *Atlantic Monthly,* vol. 143, at 599 (1929).

104. Winthrop v. Attorney General, 128 Mass. 258 (1880).

nated, but the court refused, holding that the testator's purpose was not merely to aid citizens but to accumulate funds for the commonwealth and the city for the one-hundred-year period.[105]

The rule as to termination is applied in cases of partial termination. However, if the reason for duration of the trust is no longer valid, the court may permit termination. This was exemplified in the case of *State Historical Society v. Foster*,[106] where a testator left property in trust to pay an annuity to his son and, if he should marry, to his wife, with a gift over to a charitable corporation on his death without issue. The son died without issue leaving a wife, and the court permitted the corporation to compel the trustees to convey the trust property to it subject to a duty to pay the annuity to the son's widow.[107]

In a case decided in Illinois in 2003, the court was called upon to interpret a provision in a charitable trust directing that it be terminated not later than fifty years after the date of its creation and that any then-remaining funds be distributed for the original broad charitable purposes of the trust. The trustees sought declaratory judgment that they were empowered to distribute the trust assets to a charitable foundation of which they were among the trustees. The attorney general challenged this action, claiming it violated the terms of the trust. The court upheld the proposed action of the trustees, finding that the terms of the trust did not preclude the proposed disposition, nor did the trustees have unclean hands by virtue of the fact that they would serve as trustees of the transferee charity.[108]

A charitable trust may be created with a provision that on the happening of a certain event the trust will terminate and the funds will revert to the donor or his heirs. Such a condition or limitation must be clearly stated; it will not be implied. There will be no reversion merely for breach of trust unless that condition is explicitly stated. Furthermore, such limitations are strictly construed by the courts and may even be disregarded if, under all the circumstances, it would be inequitable to abide by the condition.[109] The Rule Against Perpetuities is not applicable to gifts subject to conditions or limitations where the property is to revert to the donor or his heirs.[110]

---

105. Franklin Foundation v. Attorney General, 163 N.E.2d 662 (Mass. 1960). Following a suggestion made by the court in this case, the Foundation in 1962 successfully brought suit for application of the cy pres doctrine to the loan provision, so that loans could be made to needy medical students and others studying in technical or scientific schools.

106. 177 N.W. 16 (Wis. 1920).

107. See also Armstrong Estate, 29 Pa. D. & C.2d 220 (1963).

108. Brown v. Ryan, 788 N.E.2d 1183 (Ill. App. Ct. 2003).

109. Scott and Fratcher, *Law of Trusts*, §§401–401.4.

110. See the discussion of the cy pres doctrine in this chapter as it applies to terminations.

Accumulation of Income

Just as the Rule Against Perpetuities is an expression of public policy, so is the rule that income from property in trust may not be allowed to accumulate for a period longer than that of the Rule Against Perpetuities. This is the general rule in regard to private trusts in both England and a majority of the states. In regard to charitable trusts, however, English and American rules are somewhat different. In England directions to accumulate income of a charitable trust for a fixed period are invalid, no matter what the purpose, and the court may direct immediate application of income to the beneficiary.[111] In the United States, on the other hand, where the courts have been more disposed to upholding a donor's wishes, the rule has developed that provisions for accumulation of income will be upheld if they are not to continue for an unreasonably long time.[112] The fact that the period may be longer than the period of the Rule Against Perpetuities is not fatal. Thus in one case the federal Circuit Court of Appeals upheld the validity of a trust that was to accumulate income for five hundred years after which the principal and accumulated income were to be paid to the state of Pennsylvania for the purpose of concentrating the wealth of the world in a single governmental unit. The court stated that the provision for accumulation, while not invalidating the entire trust, was to be given effect only so far as public policy permitted.[113] In those states where statutes prohibit accumulation in private trusts for certain periods, exceptions are made for charitable dispositions.[114]

Administrative Duties of Trustees

The rules of law imposing specific duties on trustees are to be found in the statutes and case law in all of the states. They are important not only for determining the nature of a charitable trust; they contain the limits on the enforcement powers of the state against the trustees of charitable trusts. Some of them can be characterized as administrative in nature, while others are ba-

---

111. Wharton v. Masterman, [1895] A.C. 186. Today in England a provision for accumulation often will not cause an otherwise valid charitable trust to fail, but the court, on application by the Attorney General, may compel the trustees to make immediate application of the trust property in spite of a provision made by a donor postponing such application and providing for accumulation of the income in the meantime. Scott and Fratcher, *Law of Trusts*, §401.9.

112. Restatement (Second) of Trusts, §442.

113. Holdeen v. Ratterree, 292 F.2d 338 (2d Cir. 1961), rev'g 190 F. Supp. 752 (N.D.N.Y. 1960).

114. Pa. Stat. Ann. tit. 20, §6106; Note, "Accumulations in Charitable Trusts," 41 *Harvard Law Review* 514 (1927).

sic to the concept of trust and fiduciary relations. Those duties that are basic to the assurance of faithful performance by the trustees—loyalty and prudence—are discussed in Chapter 4.

The principal administrative duties of a trustee are the following.

DUTY WITH RESPECT TO DELEGATION. Under the common law, a trustee was under a personal duty to administer the trust.[115] Although he could delegate the performance of administrative tasks to others, could employ counsel, attorneys, accountants, or stockbrokers to assist him and entrust them with trust property, he was prohibited from delegating to others "the doing of acts which the trustee can reasonably be required personally to perform." Specifically prohibited was delegation of the power to select investments. This was the rule adopted in Restatement (Second) of Trusts, although it was severely criticized. As noted in the comments of the Commissioners on the provisions of the Uniform Prudent Investor Act, "The rule put a premium on the frequently arbitrary task of distinguishing discretionary functions that were thought to be nondelegable from supposedly ministerial functions that the trustee was allowed to delegate."[116]

The Uniform Trustees' Powers Act, adopted in 1964, effectively rejected the common law nondelegation rule by conferring in section 3(c)(24) the power to delegate trustees' administrative duties, to act without independent investigation upon agents' recommendations, and to permit agents to perform any act of administration, whether or not discretionary.[117] Section 4 of the act, however, prohibited a trustee from delegating the entire administration of the trust to a co-trustee or another.[118]

The Prudent Investor Rule adopted in 1990 as Restatement (Third) of Trusts included a section on delegation that provided that a trustee was under a duty to personally perform the responsibilities of trusteeship except as a prudent person might delegate those responsibilities to others.[119] This section was revised and renumbered as section 80 in Preliminary Draft No. 6 of the Restatement (Third) dated May 23, 2003.[120] In this draft the Prudent Investor Rule was incorporated as section 90 of what would become the expanded Restatement (Third).[121] The new section 80 recited the following rule as to delegation:

115. Restatement (Second) of Trusts, §171.
116. Uniform Prudent Investor Act, §3 cmt. (1994).
117. Uniform Trustees' Powers Act, §3(c)(24) (1964).
118. Id., §4.
119. Restatement (Third) of the Law of Trusts: Prudent Investor Rule, §227(c)(2) (1992).
120. Restatement (Third) of the Law of Trusts, §80 (Preliminary Draft No. 6, 2003).
121. Id., §90.

1. A trustee has a duty personally to perform the responsibilities of trusteeship except as a prudent person of comparable skill might delegate those responsibilities to others.

2. In deciding whether, to whom, and in what manner to delegate fiduciary authority in the administration of a trust, and thereafter in supervising or monitoring agents, the trustee is under a duty to the beneficiaries to exercise fiduciary discretion and to act as a prudent person with comparable skills would act in similar circumstances.[122]

Section 9 of the Uniform Prudent Investor Act (1994) codified the rule of Restatement (Third), thereby authorizing a trustee to delegate investment and management functions that a prudent trustee of comparable skills could properly delegate under the circumstances, subject, however, to the trustee's duty to exercise reasonable care, skill, and caution in selecting an agent, establishing the scope of the delegation, and reviewing periodically the agent's performance.[123] The Commissioners' comments on this new definition noted that it reflected an attempt to resolve the tension between the desire to provide flexibility to a trustee in administering his trust and protecting beneficiaries from the misuse of his position. The solution chosen by the drafters of the new rules was to rely on the trustee's duties of loyalty and prudence to prevent overbroad delegation. It gave as an example of improper delegation an investment management agreement containing an exculpation clause that left the trust without recourse against reckless mismanagement, an arrangement that would be inconsistent with the duty to exercise care and caution.[124] Section 807, Delegation by Trustee, of the Uniform Trust Code was derived from this section of the Uniform Prudent Investor Act.[125]

DUTY TO KEEP AND RENDER ACCOUNTS. Generally, trustees are under a duty to keep and render clear, complete, and accurate accounts and records with respect to the trust property and the administration of the trust,[126] and to provide accountings or reports to the beneficiary on request at reasonable intervals.[127] This includes records of all receipts and expenditures, gains and losses, and allocations of funds to principal or income.

If a reasonable request for information is refused, the court may order a trustee to account to his beneficiaries. In the case of charitable trusts, unless

122. Id., §80.

123. Uniform Prudent Investor Act, §9. See Chapter 4 for discussion of the duties of loyalty and prudence.

124. Uniform Prudent Investor Act, §9 cmt.

125. Uniform Trust Code, §807 cmt.

126. Restatement (Third) of Trusts, §83 (Preliminary Draft No. 6, 2003).

127. Id., §82.

another charity is the named beneficiary, an action for an accounting can be brought only by the attorney general or by the court on its own motion. The requisites for an action for an accounting were discussed in *State v. Taylor*,[128] a case involving a charitable trust created in 1939 to establish and endow a charitable institution. By the terms of the trust, the trustees were required to keep full and accurate accounts, to direct an audit of their accounts at the end of each fiscal year, and to publish a condensed statement of the condition and assets of the trust immediately thereafter in a local newspaper. In 1958 the attorney general of Washington wrote to the trustees requesting a complete history of the trust, including records of income and distributions, all property, and changes in administration; legal actions relating to the trust; and present status. He also requested notification of future changes in administration. The trustees refused to supply the requested information, and the attorney general brought an action for an accounting. The attorney general's bill contained no allegation that the trustees had failed to follow the requirements of the trust instrument regarding accounts. The court dismissed the action on the basis that the letter from the attorney general was not a reasonable and proper request, and was insufficient to constitute a proper demand for a full-scale accounting, which is the prerequisite for court action. The court, however, refused to accept the arguments of the trustees that a showing of mismanagement or breach of trust was also a prerequisite for court action.

This duty to account may extend to the trustee's personal affairs and actions if they have a bearing on the trust property. It also extends to the administration of a corporate business managed by the trustee. For example, a New York court held in 1961 that where a trustee owned 56% of the stock of two business corporations personally and held the balance as trustee of a charitable trust, he was required to account to the attorney general for the management of these business corporations. The court stated that the fiduciary duty extended not only to the trust estate but to the entire operations of the corporation.[129] This doctrine is of particular importance when a charity owns stock in a closely held corporation.

Complete relief from a duty to account may be included as a term of a trust. In some instances such a clause has been interpreted as indicating an intention by the donor to give the entire interest to the trustee and therefore to

---

128. 362 P.2d 247 (Wash. 1961).
129. Matter of Luce, 224 N.Y.S.2d 210 (1961), aff'd, 230 N.Y.S.2d 45 (App. Div. 1962). See also In re Hubbell's Will, 97 N.E.2d 888 (N.Y. 1951); Note, "The Trust Corporation: Dual Fiduciary Duties and the Conflict of Institutions," 109 *University of Pennsylvania Law Review* 713 (1961).

negate the creation of any trust. In other cases the courts have refused to recognize the provision and have required trustees to account.[130]

ADDITIONAL DUTIES. In addition to the administrative duties relating to delegation and accounting, there are other specific duties imposed on trustees on the basis that they arise from the trust relationship. Restatement (Second) of Trusts enumerated nine of these in separate sections: the duty to administer the trust; take and keep control of the property; preserve the trust property; enforce claims; defend actions; keep the trust property productive; keep the trust property separate; keep the trust property apart from the trustee's own property; and use care in selecting a bank as depository for trust funds and properly earmark bank deposits.[131]

Preliminary Draft No. 6 of 2003, in section 76, simplified the prior version by deleting the separate sections and reciting a single duty to administer the trust in accordance with its terms. Specifically, it provided: "The trustee is under a duty to the beneficiaries to administer the trust, diligently and in good faith, in accordance with the terms of the trust and applicable law."[132] This is described as an affirmative duty, which implies that an improper failure to act constitutes a breach of trust.[133] The duty to administer the trust thus encompasses the performance of the basic management functions that had been separately enumerated in Restatement (Second), although they are described in this revision in the comments.[134] The formulation conforms with the parallel provisions in section 801 of the Uniform Trust Code.[135]

An exception to the duty not to mingle funds (as well as to the duty not to delegate) was effected with the passage of statutes in almost all the states authorizing trustees to make investments in so-called common trust funds. These funds are exempt from federal income tax and, when administered by national banks, must conform to rules prescribed by the Federal Reserve Board of Governors covering their administration and the amounts that may be so invested. A Uniform Common Trust Fund Act was approved by the Commissioners on Uniform State Laws in 1952 and has been enacted in thirty-five states. These funds are an effective means for diversifying investments and securing diversification and simplifying the administration of smaller trusts.[136]

130. Scott and Fratcher, *Law of Trusts,* §172.

131. Restatement (Second) of Trusts, §§169, 175–180.

132. Restatement (Third) of Trusts, §76 (Preliminary Draft No. 6, 2003).

133. Id., §76 cmt. b.

134. Id., §76 cmts. b–g.

135. Uniform Trust Code, §801 (amended 2001).

136. Annotation, "Construction of the Uniform Common Trust Fund Act," 64 *American Law Reports 2d* 268 (1959).

In England, by the terms of the Charities Act of 1960, a new duty was imposed on all trustees of trusts for charitable purposes, namely, "where the case permits and requires the property or some part of it to be applied cy pres, to secure its effective use for charity by taking steps to enable it to be so applied."[137] There is no similar legislation in effect in any of the states, although the duties to administer a trust and the duty of loyalty could well give rise to such an obligation.

Of particular importance to trustees of charitable trusts is the question of whether they are under a positive duty to assure that they do not by their actions jeopardize the tax-exempt status of the trust. Some commentators believe this duty is implicit in the fiduciary concept, but it has not been the subject of either legislation or court decision. The Uniform Trustees' Powers Act, drafted and approved by the National Conference of Commissioners on Uniform State Laws in 1964 and now in force in eleven states, includes the following section:

> In the exercise of his powers including the powers granted by this Act, a trustee has a duty to act with due regard to his obligation as a fiduciary, including a duty not to exercise any power under this Act in such a way as to deprive the trust of an otherwise available tax exemption deduction or credit for tax purposes.[138]

As explained by the executive director of the Conference of Commissioners, the purpose of this provision was "to avoid the possibility that ordinary trusts might inadvertently run afoul of some provision of the revenue laws because of the existence of unusual administrative provisions."[139] Its ramifications for charitable trustees may be even more far-reaching.[140]

Administrative Powers of Trustees

The law of trusts does not merely impose negative restraints; it also grants powers to trustees to carry out their duties. A trustee may execute any powers specifically conferred on him by the terms of the trust so long as they are not contrary to law or public policy. Additional powers considered necessary and appropriate to the accomplishment of the trust purposes are conferred by law, although a settlor may forbid the exercise of powers that, without such

137. Stat. 8 & 9 Elizabeth 2, ch. 58, §13(5) (1960).

138. Uniform Trustees' Powers Act, §3(b).

139. Allison Dunham, "Uniform Laws on Estates," 103 *Trusts and Estates* 818 (1961).

140. The definition of trust in section 1 of the act states that the trust must be for the benefit of a named or otherwise described income or principal beneficiary or both, which would seem to preclude charitable trusts and corporations. Clarification of this would be desirable.

express provision, would normally be inferred from the nature of the trust.[141] In some instances, however, under the doctrine of deviation, the court may disregard these prohibitions if their exercise will impair accomplishment of the trust purpose.

The powers ordinarily conferred by law are closely related to the trustees' duties. For example, a trustee must make the trust property productive. Accordingly, he is granted a power to invest and reinvest. Similarly, he has the power to incur expenses, to lease and to sell property, to compromise, arbitrate, or settle claims, and to vote stock so long as it is not done against the interests of the beneficiary.[142]

The powers of trustees of charitable trusts may in some cases be more extensive than those of trustees of private trusts as a result of the indefinite duration of the charitable trust. This is particularly true of the power to make long-term leases. Where land is the subject of a charitable trust, the courts have granted power to sell, even where it was expressly forbidden by the terms of the trust. However, if no power to sell can be inferred expressly or by implication, a court order authorizing sale is required, and the attorney general is ordinarily a necessary party to the suit.[143]

In general, the powers to mortgage or to pledge securities are not as broad as the powers to sell or lease. It is improper for a trustee to mortgage or pledge property unless the authority can be clearly implied from the purposes of the trust or from specific provisions therein, such as those granting a trustee power to deal with the property in his own discretion.[144]

As in the case of sales, the court may disregard an express prohibition and permit the mortgaging of property if it is necessary to carry out the purpose of the trust. For example, the New York Estates, Powers and Trusts Law permits New York's Supreme Court to authorize the sale or mortgage of real estate held for charitable purposes when the property has or is likely to become unproductive, has depreciated or is likely to depreciate in value, when it is advisable to raise money to improve or erect buildings upon the property, or when it is expedient for any other reason.[145]

141. Restatement (Second) of Trusts, §380.

142. Id., §227; §§188–193; §§380(b)–(d), (f)–(g).

143. Congregational Church Union of Boston v. Attorney General, 194 N.E. 820 (Mass. 1935); Trustees of Sailors' Snug Harbor v. Carmody, 105 N.E. 543 (N.Y. 1914). If the trust instrument expressly provides for a reversion of the property to the donor or his heirs in case of sale, the court will not permit the sale in spite of a change of condition. Roberds v. Markham, 81 F. Supp. 38 (D.D.C. 1948). Conditions of this type are usually strictly construed, however.

144. Annotation, "Powers of Trustees of Charitable Trusts to Mortgage Trust Property," 127 *American Law Reports* 705 (1940).

145. N.Y. Est. Powers & Trusts Law §8-1.1; see also Scott and Fratcher, *Law of Trusts*, §§191, 191.2.

As trusts have come to be used for a growing variety of purposes, the powers of trustees have been expanded to make the trust device better suited to modern use. In some states this has been made possible with the enactment of statutes granting to trustees greater powers than those traditionally conferred by equity courts. They are generally applicable to trustees of charitable as well as private trusts.[146] Even where these statutes are in force, however, the trend is to write into trust instruments broad powers to deal with the trust property, as well as to limit to the extent possible the liability of the trustees.

Discretionary Powers of Trustees

Often a trust instrument confers broad discretionary powers on a trustee as to both the administration of the trust and the application of its funds, particularly in regard to the fulfillment of its charitable purposes. Courts do not interfere with exercises of discretion unless it can be clearly shown that the exercise was not within the bounds of reasonable judgment. The duty of the court is not to substitute its own judgment for that of the trustee but to consider whether he has acted in good faith, from proper motivation, and within the bounds of judgment that appear to the court to be reasonable:

> [I]n determining whether the trustee is acting within the bounds of a reasonable judgment the following circumstances may be relevant: (1) The extent of discretion intended to be conferred upon the trustee by the terms of the trust; (2) the existence or non-existence, the definiteness or indefiniteness of an external standard by which the reasonableness of the trustee's conduct can be judged; (3) the circumstances surrounding the exercise of the power; (4) the motives of the trustee in exercising or refraining from exercising the power; (5) the existence or non-existence of an interest in the trustee conflicting with that of the beneficiaries.[147]

The courts will not relinquish all powers to supervise a trustee no matter how broad a grant of freedom is incorporated in a trust instrument. For example, in the case of *Conway v. Emeny*, a testator who created a trust for the benefit of a museum gave to the trustees "absolute" discretion to determine a certain matter. The court stated, "It is apparent from the presence of the word 'absolute' that she intended to give them considerable discretion. The

---

146. William F. Fratcher, "Trustees' Powers Legislation," 37 *New York University Law Review* 627 (1962), contains a listing and discussion of many of these statutory provisions.

147. Scott and Fratcher, *Law of Trusts*, §187.

use of the qualifying adjective, however, did not give unlimited discretion and the grant of authority, broad as it was, did not necessarily remove the trustees from judicial supervision."[148]

In decisions rendered in 1964 and 1965,[149] the Massachusetts Supreme Judicial Court reiterated the position that the exercise of even the broadest of discretionary powers is still subject to supervision under principles of equity:

> [I]ndeed, even with respect to very broad discretionary powers "a court of equity may control a trustee in the exercise of a fiduciary discretion if its acts beyond the bounds of a reasonable judgment or unreasonably disregards usual fiduciary principles, or the purposes of the trust, or if it fails to observe standards of judgment apparent from the applicable instrument." Such fiduciary powers cannot be used arbitrarily, capriciously, or in bad faith, but must be "exercised after serious and responsible consideration, prudently, and in accordance with fiduciary standards."[150]

In the 1965 case the court expressed open disagreement with the decision of the United States Court of Appeals for the First Circuit in *State Street Bank and Trust Company v. United States*,[151] a case that was decided on the basis of Massachusetts law and held that powers given to trustees under the trust in question were so broad and all-inclusive as to nullify effective court supervision and to permit the trustees to shift the economic benefits of the trust.

Exercise of Powers by Majority of Trustees

There is a very important difference between the administration of charitable trusts and that of private trusts. In a private trust powers can be exercised only with the concurrence of all the trustees; in a charitable trust, the affirmation of a majority is sufficient unless there is a provision in the trust instrument requiring unanimity.[152] A trustee who refuses to join with the majority in an action that constitutes a breach of trust is not liable for the conse-

148. 96 A.2d 221 (Conn. 1953); see also In re James' Estate, 119 N.Y.S.2d 259 and 130 N.Y.S.2d 691 (App. Div. 1953), involving a charitable foundation.

149. Copp v. Worcester County National Bank, 199 N.E.2d 200 (Mass. 1964); Boston Safe Deposit and Trust Company v. Stone, 203 N.E.2d 547 (Mass. 1965).

150. Boston Safe Deposit and Trust Company v. Stone, 203 N.E.2d 547 (Mass. 1965).

151. 263 F.2d 635 (1st Cir. 1959).

152. Scott and Fratcher, *Law of Trusts*, §383; Restatement (Second) of Trusts, §383 (1965); City of Boston v. Doyle, 68 N.E. 851 (Mass. 1903); Morville v. Fowle, 10 N.E. 766 (Mass. 1887).

quences of the majority action, but he may have a duty to apply to the court to prevent the action.[153]

Compensation of Trustees

Trustees of all trusts are permitted reasonable compensation for services rendered in the course of their administration of the trust, as well as remuneration of expenses incurred. The amount of a trustee's fee is often stated in the trust instrument, and, in fact, the English rule is that the trustee is not entitled to compensation unless the instrument so provides. There is no such restriction in the United States, however, where the matter is controlled by statute in almost all jurisdictions. Most of these statutes merely provide that the court may direct compensation reasonable in amount, although some include a fixed schedule. In certain states the statute refers only to executors but has been held by the courts to govern trustees as well.[154]

In the case of charitable trusts, it is customary for corporate trustees to be compensated at a rate comparable to that paid to trustees of private trusts. Until the late 1990s individual trustees of charitable trusts rarely received compensation other than reimbursement for expenses incident to meetings or for travel. However, there was some evidence in 2003 that this had changed, at least in regard to foundations. A survey of 1998 information returns by 176 of the largest grant-making foundations, conducted by the Center for Public and Nonprofit Leadership at the Georgetown Public Policy Institute and published in September 2003, found that 64% of them compensated their trustees. A similar survey of 62 small foundations found that 79% of them paid fees to trustees. In both cases the amount of compensation varied widely.[155] There was no published information as to whether there had been a change in regard to fees being paid to directors and trustees of charities other than foundations.

Exculpatory Clauses

One of the most common provisions found in trust instruments today is the so-called exculpatory clause, designed to relieve a trustee from liability for

153. Sheets v. Security First Mortgage Co., 12 N.E.2d 324 (Ill. App. Ct. 1937); Heard v. March, 66 Mass. (12 Cush.) 580 (1853); Comstock v. Dewey, 83 N.E.2d 257 (Mass. 1949).

154. See Scott and Fratcher, *Law of Trusts*, §242, for a summary of the statutory provisions in the various states.

155. Christine Ahn, Pablo Eisenberg, and Channapha Khamvongsa, *Foundation Trustee Fees: Use and Abuses* (Center for Public and Nonprofit Leadership, Georgetown Public Policy Institute, September 2003).

certain breaches of trust. Provisions of this nature are strictly construed by the courts. In addition, no clause in a trust instrument is effective to relieve a trustee from liability for a breach of trust that is committed in bad faith, intentionally, with reckless indifference to the interests of the beneficiary, or for a breach of trust from which the trustee personally profits.[156] New York has gone further and by statute has declared that an attempted grant to an executor or trustee of a testamentary trust of exoneration of his fiduciary liability for failure to execute reasonable care, diligence, and prudence shall be deemed contrary to public policy and void.[157] This statute was applied in the case of *In re Schechter's Estate*,[158] where a clause in a trust for religious purposes stating that the trustee should be neither responsible for any loss or injury to the property nor accountable for its distribution was declared void as against public policy.[159] However, the presence of an exculpatory clause does relieve a trustee from the strict personal liability often associated with the office of trustee, and thereby affords protection similar to that given to directors of charitable corporations.[160]

Liability to Third Persons

It is not unusual to read that the chief disadvantage of forming a charitable organization as a trust is that the trustee is personally liable for all actions taken by him as trustee and legal actions may be brought against him personally. Until the 1960s the courts held that all obligations arising out of either contracts or torts made in the course of administration of a trust rested upon, and only upon, the trustee personally. If the trustee was not personally at fault, he was entitled to repayment, or indemnity, from the trust estate, but the legal action had to be brought against the trustee. Starting in the mid-1950s, this rule was relaxed, noticeably in court decisions and statutes alike, so that today it is possible under many circumstances for a plaintiff to bring an action in equity directly against the trust estate.[161] Section 7-306(a) of the Uniform Probate Code, in effect in sixteen jurisdictions, states the current rule:

> Unless otherwise provided in the contract, a trustee is not personally liable on contracts properly entered into in his fiduciary capacity in the

---

156. Restatement (Second) of Trusts, §222; Scott and Fratcher, *Law of Trusts*, §§222–222.3.

157. N.Y. Est. Powers & Trusts Law §11-1.7

158. 229 N.Y.S.2d 702 (Surr. Ct. 1962).

159. Scott and Fratcher, *Law of Trusts*, §222; Bogert and Bogert, *Law of Trusts and Trustees*, §542.

160. Trusteeship of Williams, 591 N.W.2d 743 (Minn. 1999); Petty v. Privette, 818 S.W.2d 743 (Tenn. 1989).

161. Restatement (Second) of Trusts, §262; Scott and Fratcher, *Law of Trusts*, §262.

course of administration of the trust estate unless he fails to reveal his representative capacity and identify the trust estate in the contract.[162]

A trustee may be relieved of his personal liability if there is a provision in the contract specifically stating this fact. Often such a provision is included in the trust instrument itself, but the courts require that the other party to the contract have notice of the provision.[163]

If a trustee commits a tort during the course of administration of the trust, the question of the trustee's liability will depend upon whether the trustee himself was personally at fault. Until the mid-twentieth century, in many states an injured party was unable to recover tort damages from the trust directly. The rationale was similar to that used to prohibit suits against government agencies, and it was based in part on the notion that trusts were quasi-public funds. By the end of the century, Massachusetts was the only state in which the rule was still in effect. In the states that do not grant immunity to charities, recovery is allowed out of the trust estate.[164]

Court Supervision of Trusts

In many states testamentary trustees are required to present accounts to the overseeing court at regular intervals for allowance. For example, in Ohio a fiduciary is required to file at least once in each two years an account that includes itemized statements of receipts, disbursements, distributions, assets, and investments.[165] In other states trustees may in their discretion present accounts for allowance, but they are not required to do so until they resign or are removed, or the trust is ready for termination. Only four states have no provision regarding accounts of trustees. The Uniform Trustees' Accounting Act, which has been enacted in Nevada,[166] requires testamentary and nontestamentary trustees to file detailed financial accounts annually with the probate court. These accounts must also include proof of no self-dealing; a statement of unpaid claims; and such other facts as the court may require. The act specifically states that it applies to charitable trusts.

The Corporate Form for Charities

The popularity of the corporate form for establishing charitable organizations can be attributed, in large part, to the pervasiveness of this legal form in

162. Uniform Probate Code, §7-306(a) (1969).
163. Scott and Fratcher, *Law of Trusts*, §262.2.
164. Id., §402.2
165. Ohio Rev. Code Ann. §2109.30.
166. Nev. Rev. Stat. §§165.010–165.250.

American business life and to the familiarity of the creators of charities with corporate operation. The corporation became popular in this country because it provided the means whereby large amounts of capital could be raised from investors whose ownership would be divorced from the responsibility of management and the liability for debt of the organization.

The most widely quoted definition of a corporation is that of Chief Justice Marshall in the case of *Trustees of Dartmouth College v. Woodward:*

> [A] corporation is an artificial being, invisible, intangible, and existing only in contemplation of law. Being the mere creature of law, it possesses only those properties which the charter of its creation confers upon it, either expressly or as incidental to its very existence. These are such as are supposed best calculated to effect the object for which it was created. Among the most important are immortality, and, if the expression may be allowed, individuality; properties by which a perpetual succession of many persons are considered as the same, and may act as a single individual. They enable a corporation to manage its own affairs, and to hold property without the perplexing intricacies, the hazardous and endless necessity, of perpetual conveyances for the purpose of transmitting it from hand to hand. It is chiefly for the purpose of clothing bodies of men, in succession, with these qualities and capacities, that corporations were invented, and are in use. By these means, a perpetual succession of individuals is capable of acting for the promotion of the particular object, like one immortal thing.[167]

This definition may be more appropriate for a charitable corporation than for its business counterpart, since the primary reason for the increase in the use of corporations for business purposes was the limited liability it offered to shareholders.

The two most important elements in this definition are that a corporation exists only by virtue of law and that it is treated in law as an entity capable of acting in many respects as a single individual. The right to existence as a corporation can be granted only by an act of the state. As was noted earlier, the original "franchises" granted by the King and later by Parliament to groups of men were accompanied by privileges, usually a monopoly to trade in certain areas or to operate a local "public work" such as a ferry, or in the case of charitable corporations, freedom from taxation. Implicit in the act of the sovereign was the assumption that some return would accrue to the public good from the grant of corporate existence. As the law of business corporations developed, the concept of the public good became less predominant, and with

167. 17 U.S. (4 Wheat.) 518, 636 (1819).

wider recognition of the advantages of corporate organization, the requirements for creation were gradually liberalized by the legislatures.

During the period when general incorporation statutes were enacted to liberalize the method of creating corporations, there was uniformity among the states in the provisions adopted for incorporation of business organizations, but not in the provisions for charitable and other nonprofit organizations. In some states a section of the general business corporation act was applicable to nonprofit corporations; in others, legislation regarding religious and educational corporations was separate from legislation for other types of nonprofit activities; and in still others, no mention of nonprofit organizations appeared in the statute books at all. The last case is still true in Delaware, the state that was the leader in the development of business corporation law but has no separate statute governing the creation and operation of nonprofit corporations.[168]

Development of a Model Nonprofit Corporation Act

General statutes governing the creation and operation of nonprofit corporations now exist in all but two states. Prior to the 1980s they varied greatly. However, in 1981 the American Bar Association formed a committee to spearhead a nationwide revision of the laws governing business corporations, which culminated in adoption of a Revised Model Business Corporation Act in 1984. This effort, in turn, spurred interest in the parallel provisions for nonprofit corporations.[169]

A Model Non-Profit Corporation Act had been promulgated in 1952 by the Committee on Corporate Laws and the Committee on Non-Profit Corporations of the American Bar Association. Minor revisions were made in 1957 and again in 1964. In 1987 a major revision was drafted by a subcommittee of the Committee on Nonprofit Corporations of the American Bar Association's Section on Business Law. The Revised Model Nonprofit Corporation Act (RMNCA) was based in large part on a revised version of the California nonprofit statute enacted in that state in 1985, although the ministerial provisions, particularly in connection with the power of the secretary of state, closely followed the Revised Model Business Corporation Act.[170]

The major changes in the RMNCA were the classification of nonprofit corporations into three categories—public benefit, mutual benefit, and religious corporations—and the codification of the enforcement powers of the attor-

168. See Appendix, Table 3.

169. Lizabeth Moody, "The Who, What and How of the RMNCA," 16 *Northern Kentucky Law Review* 251 (1989).

170. Id. at 306.

ney general. The drafters also adopted standards of conduct for directors that mirrored the provisions in the Revised Model Business Corporation Act, rejecting the standards of trust law that had theretofore been the law in a number of jurisdictions. However, directors of public benefit corporations, a category that was designed to encompass all charitable corporations other than religious ones, were to be held to a higher standard in regard to conflicts of interest than those applicable to business corporations.[171]

As of January 1, 2003, forty-eight states and the District of Columbia had enacted nonprofit corporation acts, with twenty-three of these being in the form of the Revised Model Act or a modified version of it, and seven others adopting the terms of the original Model Act.[172] Delaware and Kansas do not have a nonprofit corporation act. In these states charitable corporations are formed under the provisions of the business corporation act, but the articles of organization of a nonprofit organization must contain a recitation affirming that the corporation is not created for private profit and prohibiting the distribution of dividends to shareholders.

Creation of Charitable Corporations

Unlike a trust, a corporation cannot come into existence without authorization from the state. Its existence depends upon a specific grant of authority from the sovereign. The method for receiving that authorization is today in almost all jurisdictions a matter of complying with a statutory requirement that certain papers be placed on file with an appropriate state official, usually the secretary of state. In some states instruments must also be filed with an official in the county or district in which the office of the corporation is to be located. In many states the application requires only one incorporator and basic information such as the purposes, powers, and the names and addresses of the directors, and members, if there are any.[173]

Upon receipt of the application and a filing fee, if one is required, in all but two states a state official automatically issues a charter or certificate of incorporation to the incorporators or their representatives.[174] The corporation will then be in existence for all legal purposes. In several states the appropriate state official may be directed by statute to inquire as to whether the articles conform to law, and he may refuse to issue a certificate if they do not. This re-

171. See Chapter 4 for discussion of the duties of loyalty and prudence contained in the RMNCA.

172. See Appendix, Table 3.

173. See Appendix, Table 1, Column 5.

174. Utah and Wisconsin require filing with additional state agencies before the certificate can be issued.

view is ordinarily cursory, however, and although the secretary of state or commissioner of corporations retains some residual power, it cannot be considered in the nature of a true regulatory power.

In addition to Delaware and Kansas where there are no statutes specifically applicable to nonprofit corporations, it is possible for a nonprofit corporation to issue stock in Pennsylvania[175] and Michigan.[176] However, it is the accepted practice in these states, as it is in Delaware and Kansas, to affirm the nonprofit nature of the organization, a requirement that would be necessary in any event in order to obtain a determination of federal income tax exemption.

Power of the Legislature to Modify Corporate Charters

In some states incorporation can be effectuated by means of special acts of the legislature as well as under general corporation laws. Throughout most of the nineteenth century, this was the only method of incorporation, but with the enactment of general statutes prescribing administrative methods for incorporation, it fell into disuse and has actually been prohibited by the constitutions of many states. Where a state legislature retains the power to create corporations by special act, its authority is of course broad enough to enlarge the class of charitable purposes. Once a corporation is created by means of a special act, its existence, powers, capacities, and mode of exercising them will be dependent on the law creating the corporation, not on the general body of law relating to charitable corporations of the state unless the special act is silent as to the matter.[177]

The power of the legislature is not absolute, however. Once a charitable corporation is formed, no legislature may change its initial purpose or control the method of administration designated in its charter. The limits on legislative power stem from Article I, Section 10 of the United States Constitution, which prohibits a state from passing any law impairing the obligation of contract. The constitutional provision was first applied to corporations in the case of *Trustees of Dartmouth College v. Woodward*,[178] involving an attempt by the legislature of New Hampshire to alter the charter of a charitable corporation, Dartmouth College, which had been created by special act. The Supreme Court held that there was an implied contract on the part of the state with every benefactor who should give money to the corporation. An alteration of the charter without the consent of the trustees would be a violation of this contract and therefore an unconstitutional act.

175. Pa. Stat. Ann. tit. 15, §5306.
176. Mich. Comp. Laws §450.2303.
177. Penobscot Boom Corporation v. Lamson, 16 Me. 224 (1839).
178. 17 U.S. (4 Wheat.) 518 (1819).

Today the statutes providing administrative methods for incorporation include clauses that reserve a power to amend charters granted thereunder. While these have minimized the effect of the *Dartmouth College* case, they have been held to be applicable to changes in administration, but not to any "alteration that defeats or fundamentally changes the corporate purpose." Such a measure is unconstitutional, no matter what powers a legislature may attempt to reserve to itself at the time of creation.[179] However, if the governing body of the charitable corporation assents to an amendment, the constitutional bar is removed.[180]

In the absence of a specific legislative declaration, the method of creation and, therefore, the form of a charitable institution do not influence the courts in the determination of the validity of its purposes. Once the determination of validity has been made, the enforcement procedures, the application of the cy pres doctrine, and the eligibility for certain tax exemptions from both the state and federal governments are applicable to a corporation just as they are to a charitable trust.

Restrictions on Holdings of Charitable Corporations

The influence of the English mortmain laws limiting the amount of property charitable corporations could hold was seen in many of the earliest general incorporation acts, which restricted the power of corporations, whether or not charitable, to take real property by will unless specifically authorized to do so by their charter or by special act of the legislature.[181] No provisions of this nature remain in state laws today.

A second type of statutory restriction limited the amount of property a charitable corporation could own. The only state in which limitations of this nature exist is Rhode Island. Its statute provides that if property given to a charitable corporation exceeds the amount it is entitled to take, the corporation takes the property on a condition subsequent that it obtain within one year after the date of the gift authority from the legislature to take and hold the property.[182]

---

179. Board of Regents of the University of Maryland v. Trustees of the Endowment Fund of the University of Maryland, 112 A.2d 678, 684 (Md. 1955), cert. denied, 350 U.S. 836 (1955).

180. Matter of Mt. Sinai Hospital, 164 N.E. 871 (N.Y. 1928); see also Marion R. Fremont-Smith and Jill R. Horwitz, "The Power of the Legislature: Insurer Conversions and Charitable Funds," Seminar on State Authority over Charitable Assets (Milbank Memorial Fund, New York, November 2002).

181. N.D. Cent. Code §10-33-21; Okla. Stat. tit. 18, §588.

182. R.I. Gen. Laws §7-1-17; see also Scott and Fratcher, *Law of Trusts*, §362.4.

Duration

An essential feature of a corporation is that it may endure forever. This means that the Rule Against Perpetuities does not apply to gifts to charitable corporations, unless the gift is subject to a condition that could be exercised at a time that was later than that permitted under the Rule. In such a case, the legal outcome would not differ from that which would apply to a charitable trust.

If a settlor gives funds to trustees with a condition precedent that they form a charitable corporation at a specific time, or after the happening of a future event, such date or event must normally take place within the period of the Rule.[183] If the gift can be considered to be one to trustees for charitable purposes with a gift over to a charitable corporation to be formed at a later date, the courts do not apply the Rule, holding that the initial gift creates a valid charitable trust not subject to the Rule.[184]

Amendment, Merger, and Dissolution

There is an important distinction between the power of the state to amend the articles of organization of a charitable corporation, to permit it to merge, or to dissolve a charitable corporation, and the power of the directors or members to do so. As a general rule, once a charitable corporation has been created, changes that alter the contract of the corporation with the state, such as a change of purpose, of special administrative procedures, or of limitations mentioned in the charter, may not be altered by the legislature. There has been no consensus, however, as to whether the board or the members may change purposes or special administrative procedures or limitations as they affect or apply to the general assets of the corporation, as opposed to assets attributable to contributions given for the general purposes of the corporation or subject to restrictions (endowment funds). Some cases hold that all assets of a nonprofit charitable corporation, other than restricted gifts, may be freely changed under the general amending powers granted in the nonprofit acts. Others hold that this power extends only to funds earned in the course of carrying out the corporation's purposes, such as fees for services of a social service agency or school tuitions. This view was upheld in a 2003 case in North Dakota involving the disposition of the proceeds of sale of a hospital.[185] In contrast, in a case involving a proposed sale of a hospital in South

183. Note, "The Charitable Corporation," 64 *Harvard Law Review* 1168, 1170 (1951).
184. Brigham v. Peter Bent Brigham Hospital, 134 F. 513, 518 (1st Cir. 1904).
185. Banner Health System v. Stenehjem, 2003 WL 501821 (D.N.D. 2003).

Dakota owned by the same health care system, the court in that state held that all of the corporation's assets, regardless of their source, were subject to trust doctrine.[186] This is the English view. In the states in which the amending power is limited, it is the courts that have jurisdiction to determine the appropriate application of the cy pres doctrine to permit changes of purposes or to order administrative changes under the doctrine of deviation.

Amendments that do not alter the initial purposes of the corporation may be made by the corporation under a statutory power granted in all general incorporation statutes. The statutory requirements are precise; in most cases they follow the procedure for initial incorporation, but require in addition either a majority or two-thirds vote of the directors, or of the members if they have voting rights. The by-laws of some corporations may tighten the statutory requirements as to the required number of votes.

The Revised Model Nonprofit Corporation Act requires a two-thirds vote of all members having voting rights to amend the charter of a public benefit corporation; if there are no members, or no members with voting rights, a majority vote of the board of directors is sufficient to authorize an amendment.[187] In New York a majority vote of the members is required,[188] and in Texas and Illinois, a two-thirds vote of the members or, if there are none, a majority vote of the directors is necessary.[189]

The merger and consolidation of business corporations are common procedures that raise many problems concerning corporate holdings and acquisition of stock that do not ordinarily arise in the case of charitable corporations. For the latter, state statutes specify methods for either consolidation or merger that are similar to procedures for amendment. If the proposed application will affect property held under restrictions or will alter purposes, court application of the cy pres doctrine is necessary.[190] The Revised Model Nonprofit Corporation Act permits a public benefit or religious corporation to merge into any other corporation only if the surviving corporation is also a public benefit or religious corporation, unless a court has approved the merger in a proceeding in which the attorney general has been given notice, or unless prior to the merger, the assets of the corporation have been transferred to a public benefit or religious corporation.[191] The Massachusetts statute permits consolidation or merger only if the resulting or surviving

---

186. Banner Health System v. Long, 663 N.W.2d 242 (S.D. 2003).
187. RMNCA, §§10.20, 10.21.
188. N.Y. Not-for-Profit Corp. Law §802.
189. Tex. Rev. Civ. Stat. art. 1396-4.02; 805 Ill. Comp. Stat. 105/110.15.
190. Note, "The Charitable Corporation," 1179–1180.
191. RMNCA, §11.02.

corporation constitutes a public charity governed by the nonprofit corporation act.[192]

The foregoing discussion applies to amendments that do not change the charitable purposes of the corporation. The ability to make changes in purposes is limited, not by statute but by the terms of gifts to the corporation, whether received subject to restrictions that they be used only for specific purposes or from unrestricted donations made prior to the date of the amendment.[193]

Unlike a trust, a corporation may be dissolved by act of those who direct its affairs, although dissolution, like creation, involves authorization by the state. Usually a vote of the board of directors is sufficient, although in some cases approval of the members may also be required. Until the early 1970s, in the majority of states a cy pres application of funds on dissolution was required, but in most of them the administrative procedures were not designed to assure such a distribution. However, Treasury regulations require the inclusion of a provision assuring that on dissolution, the assets of the corporation will be distributed to other organizations exempt from tax by virtue of being described in section 501(c)(3).[194]

As with the statutory procedure for amendment or merger, a majority vote, or in some cases a two-thirds vote, of the directors or members approving a resolution to dissolve and a plan for distribution of assets are required. Six states have no further requirement.[195] The great majority of states require that the vote be filed together with a statement of debts and liability, and a plan for distribution of the corporation's assets, with the secretary of state or another state administrative official and in some cases a county clerk. In ten states the plan must be filed with a court official; only three of these require judicial approval, however. In New York and Massachusetts judicial approval must follow a hearing, notice of which must be given to the attorney general. In both of these states distribution of the assets of a charitable corporation must be made for other similar charitable purposes.[196] In Minnesota the authority to approve a petition for voluntary dissolution is placed in the county district courts, and the attorney general is specifically authorized to intervene in any proceeding if it is in the public interest to do so.[197] However, there is no statutory provision requiring notice to the attorney general of such a pro-

---

192. Mass. Gen. Laws ch. 180, §§10, 10A.
193. Attorney General v. Hahnemann Hospital, 494 N.E.2d 1011 (Mass. 1986).
194. Treas. Reg. §1.501(c)(3)-1(b)(4); see also Chapter 5.
195. See Appendix, Table 1, Columns 9 and 10.
196. N.Y. Not-for-Profit Corp. Law §1005; Mass. Gen. Laws ch. 180, §11A.
197. Minn. Stat. §317A.

ceeding, although the cy pres doctrine has been made applicable to charitable corporations.[198] Rhode Island and Pennsylvania have similar procedures.[199]

In Texas directors are made personally liable for a distribution of the assets of an insolvent corporation or for a distribution that would render the corporation insolvent. They are excused for liability only if they have used diligence, acted in good faith, or relied in good faith on financial statements of the corporation represented as correct by either the president, an officer in charge of the corporation's books or records, or a certified public accountant. The Texas statute also permits reliance on a written opinion from an attorney.[200]

Charitable corporations may also be dissolved involuntarily by action of the state in a proceeding, often entitled *quo warranto,* that may be brought by the attorney general or other state official. These proceedings usually require a showing of public injury or failure to comply with statutory requirements concerning the filing of reports.

Accumulation of Income

The validity of provisions for the accumulation of income of charitable corporations is decided on the same basis as for charitable trusts. In some states the statutes regulating accumulations are applicable to all charitable dispositions. Until 1963 Arizona had explicit provisions concerning charitable corporations under which accumulations of income for charitable purposes for twenty-one years were allowed.[201] Until 1961 New York placed a statutory limit on the amount that could be accumulated by charitable corporations, but the provision was repealed, and directions for accumulation are now valid subject to court supervision.[202]

Internal Organization

Since a corporation is, in one sense, an association of individuals, it follows that certain legal rights and duties arise from the relationship of these individuals to the corporate entity. Membership in a business corporation arises through the purchase of shares of stock issued by the corporation. Each share represents a part interest in the corporation's assets and entitles the stock-

---

198. See the discussion of cy pres in this chapter.
199. R.I. Gen. Laws §7-6-50; Pa. Stat. Ann. tit. 15, §5971.
200. Tex. Rev. Civ. Stat. art. 1396-2.26.
201. Ariz. Rev. Stat. §71-118, repealed by 1963 Ariz. Sess. Laws ch. 25.
202. N.Y. Est. Powers & Trusts Law §8-1.7.

holder to share in profits, participate in management, and receive a pro rata share of corporate assets on dissolution.

The governance of charitable corporations is initially determined by the incorporators, who specify in the articles of organization the basic framework under which the corporation will operate. Aside from determining the charitable purposes, the most important decision will be whether control of the corporation is to be in the board of directors or whether it will be divided between directors and members. The majority of charitable corporations are governed by a self-perpetuating board of directors, often called trustees. For the minority that do have members, in many instances the members and directors will be the same persons, and when they cease to hold one office, they also cease to hold the other.

In those instances in which a charity has both members and directors who are not the same persons, the position of member and the powers that attach to that office are analogous to the position and powers of stockholders, except that the members have no financial interest in the assets or income of the corporation. The articles and by-laws will specify the terms of office and qualifications, if any, for the members, and any powers they may retain other than those granted by law, namely, the power to elect directors and to approve amendments to the by-laws. Members do have a right to see books and records, a right that is usually conferred by statute. In a Florida case decided in 2002, this right was affirmed for members even after they had been removed and the corporation had changed its articles of organization to do away with the position of member.[203]

In the 1980s and 1990s, most of the large health care organizations and hospitals throughout the country underwent reorganizations in which certain components were established as separate corporations, each of them having a sole member "parent," which might be the original organization or a newly organized charitable corporation. This sole-member parent corporation, in addition to retaining the inherent powers of a member to elect directors and approve by-law changes, would have the power to ratify budgets, appoint or elect the officers, and approve changes in activities, dissolutions, or disposition of assets.[204]

The majority of nonprofit corporations that are not charities do have members. If created under a statute modeled on the Revised Model Nonprofit Corporation Act, they will be organized as mutual benefit, not public benefit

203. Raffinan v. Philippine Cultural Foundations, Inc., 821 So. 2d 1272 (Fla. Dist. Ct. App. 2002).

204. Dana Brakman Reiser, "Decision-Makers without Duties: Defining the Duties of Parent Corporations Acting as Sole Corporate Members in Nonprofit Health Care Systems," 53 *Rutgers Law Review* 979 (2001).

corporations, and their members in most instances will have a right to share in the assets of the corporation on termination. Membership in a private benefit corporation is more analogous to that of stockholders of a business corporation. The existence of members, whether there will be different classes of members, and if so their respective powers and duties are set forth in the articles of organization.

It was not uncommon at one time for corporations, charitable and otherwise, to issue transferable certificates of membership that could be bequeathed by will, although in most jurisdictions a transfer of this nature would have been specifically prohibited. In 1963 Illinois enacted legislation designed to prevent the sale of membership certificates.[205] The desirability of a statute specifically prohibiting this type of transaction came to light when a tax case was brought by the federal government against members of the corporation of a charitable hospital who had sold their certificates for $710,000, the buyers obtaining the sales price by mortgaging the hospital property.[206]

There are few statutory rules prescribing the identity of and the powers of directors. The provisions governing public benefit corporations in the California Nonprofit Corporation Act are an exception. They require that not more than 49% of the persons serving on the board of any corporation organized under this section may be "interested persons," a term defined as (1) one who is currently being compensated by the corporation for services rendered within the previous twelve months (including full- or part-time employees, independent contractors, or otherwise), other than reasonable compensation paid to a director as director, and (2) a family member of such director, defined as siblings, ancestors, descendants, or the spouse of a director or of any of the defined family members.[207]

In 2002 Maine adopted a requirement that no more than 49% of a public benefit corporation's board membership may constitute "financially interested" persons. A "financially interested" person is defined as (1) any individual receiving or entitled to receive compensation from personal services rendered within the previous twelve months to the corporation (including full- or part-time employees, independent contractors, or otherwise), other than reasonable compensation paid to a director as director; this also includes any individual entitled to receive net income from a business entity providing services for consideration to the corporation (excluding income received as a shareholder of a publicly traded corporation); or (2) a family member of any

---

205. 805 Ill. Comp. Stat. 105/107.03.

206. Grace Sharf's Estate v. Commissioner, 316 F.2d 625 (7th Cir. 1963), aff'g 38 T.C. 15 (1962).

207. Cal. Corp. Code §5227.

such individual, defined as a spouse, brother, sister, parent, or child of that individual.[208]

New Hampshire also limits the identity of directors, providing as follows:

> In the interest of encouraging diversity of discussion, connection with the public, and public confidence, the board of directors of a charitable nonprofit corporation shall have at least 5 voting members, who are not of the same immediate family or related by blood or marriage.[209]

However, the requirement may be waived with the approval of the attorney general.[210] Sections 7:19(II) and 292:6-a also provide that directors, officers, and trustees of charitable organizations shall serve on governing boards only for the charitable purposes of the organizations. "[I]f such directors, officers or trustees are serving for any other expressed or intended reasons, they shall not serve on the governing board of the organization."[211]

Legal review of matters relating to the internal affairs of a corporation is difficult to obtain. The courts will, of course, intervene when there is a violation of statutory requirements. If the dispute relates to the internal affairs of the corporation, such as the expulsion of a member or the denial of a member's right to vote or participate, the courts will not take jurisdiction until the internal method for settling disputes specified in the corporation's legal instrument is exhausted or unless it is shown that the corporation delayed or denied a hearing or right of appeal. If all other resources are exhausted, the courts, under principles of equity, will nullify fraud, mistake, accident, or other inequitable conduct.[212]

Administrative Duties of Directors

The duties of directors of charitable corporations are to be found in the corporate statutes and case law and are embodied in the Restatement (Second) of Trusts, and, as of the end of 2003, were being revised.[213] They can be divided into the same two categories as the parallel duties of trustees: the first group includes the duties of loyalty and care, substantive provisions designed to assure adherence by the officers and directors to the purposes of the orga-

208. Me. Rev. Stat. Ann. tit. 13-B, §713-A.
209. N.H. Rev. Stat. §292:6-a.
210. Id.
211. N.H. Rev. Stat. §7:19(II).
212. Ralph Boyer, *Non-Profit Corporation Statutes: A Critique and a Proposal* (Ann Arbor: University of Michigan Law School, 1957).
213. Restatement (Third) of Trusts (Preliminary Draft No. 6, 2003).

nization. They are discussed in Chapter 4. The administrative duties of directors of charitable corporations are discussed below.

DUTY WITH RESPECT TO DELEGATION. In the management of a business enterprise, delegation of many functions by the board of directors to the officers and employees is not only desirable but necessary. Under the rule developed fairly early in the history of corporations, directors are permitted to delegate most management duties provided they retain general supervision over the business. Directors may not, however, abdicate their duty to direct, and they may be chargeable with losses resulting from failure to participate.[214] They may not agree to place authority in one person or under one group of members, or agree that a director be only nominal. Every corporation has an inherent power to appoint an executive committee to act at times when the board is not in session even if the power is not specifically granted by statute.[215] Ordinarily the president of a corporation has authority to execute notes or ordinary commercial contracts for the corporation, but this rule has not been applied to nonprofit corporations, and in order to hold the corporation liable, it is necessary to have proof of the authorization by the directors.[216]

The application of these principles to the directors of a charitable corporation as members of its managing body was specifically made in the case of *Ray v. Homewood Hospital, Inc.,*[217] where the court stated that there could be no dummy or nominal board of directors and therefore no delegation of a director's final responsibility to administer the corporation. This principle was also well illustrated in a Massachusetts case in which directors of a charitable corporation set up a separate trust to which they turned over certain assets that had been donated for the general purposes of the corporation. The court declared such a delegation to be illegal on the grounds that the charter provided that the corporation should be the sole custodian and manager of its funds.[218]

In the operation of the usual charitable corporation the question of a power to delegate arises most frequently in connection with investing the organization's funds. Until the later part of the twentieth century, a trustee was prohibited from delegating this function unless expressly authorized to do so

214. Henry Winthrop Ballantine, *Ballantine on Corporations,* §46 (Chicago: Callaghan Press, rev. ed., 1946).

215. See, for example, N.Y. Not-for-Profit Corp. Law §702.

216. Ballantine, *Ballantine on Corporations,* §52; see also People's National Bank v. New England Home for Deaf Mutes, Aged, Blind & Infirm, 95 N.E. 77 (Mass. 1911).

217. 27 N.W.2d 409 (Minn. 1947).

218. Massachusetts Charitable Mechanic Association v. Beede, 70 N.E.2d 825 (Mass. 1947).

in the trust instrument, although he was allowed to seek the advice of investment counsel before making his choice. A charitable corporation, on the other hand, was generally permitted to assign the making of investments to a finance committee and in some jurisdictions to outside investment counsel. The Restatement (Second) of Trusts used the right to delegate the choice of investments as an example of the difference between the duties of a trustee of a charitable trust and those of the director of a corporation.[219]

One of the major recommendations contained in the 1969 report on *The Law and the Lore of Endowment Funds,* which led to adoption of the Uniform Management of Institutional Funds Act (UMIFA), was that the "corporate standard" regarding delegation of investment authority should apply in the management of endowment funds, including specifically the power to delegate investment decisions to an outside investment manager.[220] This recommendation was adopted and appears as section 5 of UMIFA. Five years later, a follow-up study noted a marked change in practice, particularly among universities and colleges, and urged widespread liberalization of the laws, particularly in those states that had not adopted UMIFA.[221] The difficulty posed by these developments, however, has been that the provisions of UMIFA are applicable only to "institutional funds," and not to the general funds of the corporation including those that are characterized as "funds functioning as endowment" or "quasi-restricted," signifying that they are being treated by the corporation as permanent funds although legally they are not so restricted. This led to the anomalous situation of having one organization subject to duties that differed based solely on whether the funds being managed did or did not meet the definition of institutional funds.

Since the rejection of the common law constraints on delegation embodied in the Uniform Trustees' Powers Act, the Uniform Prudent Investor Rule, and Restatement (Third) of Trusts Preliminary Draft No. 6, the duties with respect to delegation by trustees of charitable trusts are virtually identical to the laws applicable to charitable corporations in all but a few states. In all states, legislation permitting trusts to invest in common trust funds applies to charitable corporations.[222]

DUTY TO KEEP AND RENDER ACCOUNTS. The Model Non-Profit Corporation Act did not require directors to make annual reports, although

219. Restatement (Second) of Trusts, §379(D).

220. William L. Cary and Craig B. Bright, *The Law and the Lore of Endowment Funds,* 61 (New York: Ford Foundation Press, 1969) (a report to the Ford Foundation).

221. William L. Cary and Craig B. Bright, *The Developing Law of Endowment Funds,* 48–49 (New York: Ford Foundation, 1974) (a report to the Ford Foundation).

222. See Chapter 4 for a discussion of investment duties of directors.

it specified that the corporation must keep correct and complete books and records of accounts and minutes of all its proceedings, and required that all books and records be open to inspection by any member or his agent or attorney "for any proper purpose at any reasonable time."[223] The Revised Model Act retained this requirement but added a provision requiring the corporation to provide on demand from any member or director the latest financial statements, accompanied by a statement of either a public accountant or the president or chief financial officer affirming the reasonable belief that the records were prepared on generally accepted accounting principles and declaring the basis of any inconsistencies from accounts of prior years.[224] When a corporation holds certain funds as trustee, it may be under additional duties to account. A Pennsylvania statute provides that the directors of a charitable corporation shall keep accounts of all trust funds separate and apart from other funds of the corporation and shall, unless the terms of the trust provide otherwise, make an annual report to the members concerning these funds.[225]

Where gifts are given to a charitable corporation by will or otherwise to be used for the general charitable purposes of the corporation, or with restrictions that are within the power of the corporation to follow, the corporation does not usually need to qualify in court as a trustee or to give bond. This specific issue was raised in the case of *American Institute of Architects v. Attorney General*.[226] A Massachusetts resident had left the residue of her estate to the American Institute of Architects, a New York charitable corporation, upon trust to maintain scholarships for advanced study by deserving architects and students of architecture. The court held that the corporation did not hold the property subject to a technical trust and was therefore not subject to the laws of Massachusetts requiring appointment and qualification of a trustee by the Massachusetts Probate Court. There have been similar holdings in other jurisdictions,[227] although in a Pennsylvania case the Orphans' Court directed that funds for an endowment of an incorporated school should be paid to the school as trustee so that the court might retain jurisdiction.[228]

Whether or not a charitable corporation is declared in a particular instance to be a technical trustee, it is nevertheless subject to the powers of an equity court, and on proper demand by the attorney general or a proper party, may

223. Model Non-Profit Corporation Act, §25 (rev. 1964).
224. RMNCA, §16.02.
225. Pa. Stat. Ann. tit. 15, §5548.
226. 127 N.E.2d 161 (Mass. 1955).
227. In re Estate of Bicknell, 160 N.E.2d 550 (Ohio Ct. App. 1958).
228. Wanamaker Trust, 7 Fiduciary Rptr. 486 (Pa. 1957).

be ordered to account in the same manner as a trustee.[229] There may also be a statutory source of court power to compel accounts.

ADDITIONAL DUTIES. There are other administrative duties of trustees that are applicable to directors, including the duties to administer the trust according to its terms, take and keep control of property, preserve the property, enforce claims, defend actions, and make the trust property productive. The need to keep property separate from that of the individual trustees is not applicable to directors, since assets of a charitable corporation are owned in the name of the corporation, and contracts made by the corporation are made in the name of the corporation, not in the name of the individual directors.

Administrative Powers of Directors

The concept of a corporation as a separate legal person entitles it to certain constitutional protections. It may not be deprived of liberty without due process of law nor denied the equal protection of the laws. The application of the constitutional prohibition against impairment of contract to corporate charities made by the Supreme Court in the *Dartmouth College* case has been discussed, but it should be noted that the Court reached its conclusion by treating the corporation as a person who was party to the contract.

Corporations possess under law all the powers of a natural person that are reasonably necessary for the accomplishment of their proper purposes, with the exception of those specifically forbidden by statute, the federal and state constitutions, or the terms of their charters. General corporation statutes in all states give certain powers to corporations. The courts also imply others that are regarded as incident to corporate existence. These latter are conferred by the mere creation of the corporation. Many of the state nonprofit corporation acts include these powers by reference to the business corporation act, specifically deleting those that would be inapplicable to a nonprofit corporation such as the power to issue stock.[230] Section 3.02 of the Revised Model Nonprofit Corporation Act provides that every corporation has perpetual duration and succession in its corporate name and "has the same powers as an individual to do all things necessary or convenient to carry out its affairs," but then specifies seventeen powers that are included "without limitation." Among them are the powers:

229. Healy v. Loomis Institute, 128 A. 774 (Conn. 1925); Brown v. Memorial National Home Foundation, 329 P.2d 118 (Cal. Ct. App. 1958), cert. denied, 358 U.S. 943 (1959).
230. See, for example, Mass. Gen. Laws ch. 180.

- to sue and be sued
- to have and use a corporate seal
- to make and amend by-laws
- to acquire and deal freely with all types of property or interests in property, including the powers to mortgage or pledge
- to make contracts, borrow and secure property, and make loans other than loans to any director or officer
- to act within or without the state
- to elect or appoint directors, officers, employees, and agents and fix their compensation
- to pay pensions
- to make charitable donations
- to establish conditions for admission of members, and impose dues or other fees on members
- to carry on a business.[231]

These powers are typical of those found in nonprofit corporation acts that are not otherwise adaptations of the Revised Model Act. One common divergence from the powers contained in the Revised Model Act, however, is that the power to indemnify directors is granted in a separate section,[232] while in many other states it is treated as an optional power that may be exercised only if it has been included in the corporation's articles or by-laws.[233]

Treasury regulations require that the articles of organization of a corporation seeking federal tax exemption contain no express powers that would allow the organization to engage to any substantial extent in activities that in themselves are not in furtherance of one or more exempt purposes. Furthermore, they warn that powers may not be granted that are inconsistent with the organization's exempt purposes.[234] These rulings serve as a useful warning to directors at the time of creation that their powers are limited to furtherance of the organization's charitable purpose. If a question of liability should arise for the doing of unauthorized acts, such a ruling may limit the possibility of using the defense of honest mistake.

Section 508 of the Internal Revenue Code contains another limitation on the powers of those organizations that are classified as private foundations.[235] This section, enacted in 1969, requires that the governing documents of a

---

231. RMNCA, §3.02. See Ballantine, *Ballantine on Corporations,* §§82–88, for typical powers of business corporations.

232. RMNCA, Subchapter E.

233. See, for example, Mass Gen. Laws. ch. 180, §6; N.Y. Not-for-Profit Corp. Law §722.

234. Treas. Reg. §1.501(c)(3)-1(b)(1)(i)(b).

235. I.R.C. §508(e)(1); Treas. Reg. §1.508-3(d). See also Chapter 5.

private foundation contain language specifically prohibiting it from entering into any of the transactions prohibited to such organizations. This requirement may be waived, however, if a state statute imposes these prohibitions on all foundations. Although shortly after passage of the Tax Reform Act of 1969, all of the states passed legislation containing the limitations, it is common practice to include them in the founding documents. The required language is also contained in section 1.50 of Subchapter E, Private Foundations, of the Revised Model Nonprofit Act. The purpose of the provision was to provide state attorneys general with sanctions that could be enforced in state courts as a complement to the federal sanction of loss of tax exemption.

Comparison of the specific powers of directors with those of trustees reveals that in the actual operation of a charity there is little difference. Thus the powers to invest and reinvest, incur expenses, lease and sell, compromise, arbitrate or settle claims, and vote stock would all be inferred from the nature of a charity's purposes. Generally the law restricts business corporations from binding the corporation by a contract as surety or guarantor and thereby lending its credit to a third party solely for his accommodation or benefit.[236] This limitation holds unless it can be shown that such act was for the benefit of the corporation or that it was specifically authorized by the terms of its charter. There is small likelihood that such an act would be held proper for a charity.

The powers of a charitable corporation to sell, lease, or mortgage realty were at one time limited by statute in some jurisdictions. Generally these restrictions required a two-thirds vote of the directors or members authorizing a mortgage or lease.[237] The New York Not-for-Profit Corporation Law requires a two-thirds vote of the directors for any purchase, sale, mortgage, or lease of real property.[238] In *Emmerglich v. Vogel*,[239] it was held that a cemetery corporation that constituted a charitable trust could not mortgage property except as security for the purchase price. Only rarely will there be a distinction in result in cases involving powers of this nature if they are based on corporate law rather than on trust principles.

Many of the state nonprofit acts impose a limit on the power of a nonprofit corporation to dispose of all or a substantial part of its assets. Generally, prior to such a transaction the corporation must give notice to the attorney general or another state officer, and there will be a waiting period after notice before the transaction can be consummated. Provisions of this nature represent a

---

236. Ballantine, *Ballantine on Corporations,* §87.

237. Ala. Code §10-3A-120 (two-thirds of members or majority of directors); Pa. Stat. Ann. tit. 15, §5546 (two-thirds of members).

238. N.Y. Not-for-Profit Corp. Law §509.

239. 24 A.2d 861 (N.J. Ch. 1942).

modification of the rules applicable to business corporations requiring notice to shareholders. During the 1990s when many health care organizations were selling their assets to for-profit entities, the notice requirement was instrumental in permitting the attorney general to be assured that a fair price was being paid for the assets.[240]

Discretionary Powers of Directors

The powers of an equity court to control the discretion of corporate fiduciaries are as extensive as they are in regard to trusts. In most states the directors of charitable corporations, just as trustees, may bring a petition for instructions to determine their duties or powers whenever they are in doubt as to a specific action.[241] Although a New York case has been cited as leaving this matter in doubt in that jurisdiction, the holding can be explained on the grounds that the request did not meet the requirements generally imposed by the courts before they will issue instructions; namely, there was no specific pending question before the court.[242]

As with trustees of a charitable trust, the board of directors of a charitable corporation ordinarily acts by majority vote, although the articles, the by-laws, or a statute may provide otherwise.[243]

Compensation of Directors

The questions that arise in regard to the compensation of directors of a charitable corporation are the same as those in regard to the compensation of trustees, although there may be no statutory provisions fixing any schedule of fees for the former. The custom is also the same. Generally, in the case of a charitable corporation that operates an institution, the trustees will serve without compensation while salaries will be paid to the executives who direct the day-to-day operations of the institution. There is ordinarily no ban against an executive's also serving as a trustee. The one caveat in all questions of compensation is that fees must be based on the reasonable worth of services and must not be a disguise for a distribution of profits.[244]

240. Marion R. Fremont-Smith, "The Role of Government Regulation in the Creation and Operation of Conversion Foundations," 23 *Exempt Organization Tax Review* 37 (1999).

241. Arkansas Baptists State Convention v. Board of Trustees, 189 S.W.2d 913 (Ark. 1945); Trustees of Princeton University v. Wilson, 78 A. 393, 395 (N.J. Ch. 1910).

242. Trustees of Sailors' Snug Harbor v. Carmody, 137 N.Y.S. 968 (Surr. Ct. 1912), rev'd on other grounds, 144 N.Y.S. 24 (App. Div. 1913), aff'd, 105 N.E. 543 (N.Y. 1914).

243. See N.Y. Not-for-Profit Corp. Law §708, regarding contracts with directors requiring two-thirds vote.

244. Bogert and Bogert, *Law of Trusts and Trustees,* §364. See Chapter 5 for a discussion of excess benefit limitations in I.R.C. §4958 (popularly known as "intermediate sanctions").

Ultra Vires Contracts

There is a doctrine unique to corporate law that holds that when a corporation performs an act or enters into an agreement that is outside the scope of its express or implied powers, the act, or agreement, is held to be ultra vires (that is, "beyond the powers granted") and may be challenged on that ground in certain cases. Formerly, when a corporation entered into an ultra vires contract, either party could avoid liability under the contract and refuse to carry it out. Today, however, most courts have restricted the use of this defense, and if the contract has already been carried out, neither party can object. If it has not been carried out in any way by either party, they are both prohibited from enforcing it or suing for damages. However, the courts do not agree as to the result if the contract has been performed by one party only. A majority of states hold that it should be rescinded and both parties put back in their original positions. In some states, however, the court will require that the contract be completed.[245]

Corporations Formed to Administer Charitable Trusts

In some instances charitable corporations are formed by trustees of a charitable trust after the trust has come into existence. Unless this is contrary to the express purposes of the settlor, trustees generally have the power to incorporate.[246] The provisions of the charter or articles of incorporation must conform to the provisions of the trust,[247] and the trustees will be governed by trust doctrine in their management of the property. In one case, the Massachusetts court refused to allow trustees to form a corporation where the charter provisions would result in the trustees' losing control of the trust.[248] The Franklin Foundation, Inc., formed by the trustees of the trust created under the will of Benjamin Franklin for the benefit of the city of Boston, has been the subject of several court proceedings, and in each case the Massachusetts Supreme Judicial Court disregarded the corporate entity on the grounds that "its purpose is to facilitate the administration and execution of the trust, not to relieve the individuals composing it from the obligations incident to their fiduciary obligation as managerial trustees."[249]

After property is conveyed by trustees of a charitable trust to a corporation formed to administer the trust, the trustees may be relieved of their duty to

245. Ballantine, *Ballantine on Corporations,* §92.

246. Nelson v. Cushing, 52 Mass. (2 Cush.) 519 (1848).

247. Appeal of Vaux, 109 Pa. 497 (1885); Curran Foundation Charter, 146 A. 908 (Pa. 1929).

248. Shattuck v. Wood Memorial Home, Inc., 66 N.E.2d 568 (Mass. 1946).

249. City of Boston v. Curley, 177 N.E. 557, 562 (Mass. 1931).

account to the courts as trustees, and appointments of successor trustees may be made according to the provisions of the charter, not under the court supervision normally applicable to trustees.[250] This is the case whenever the gift includes a direction to form a charitable corporation or specifically permits trustees to incorporate at a later date if they deem it desirable; it may also apply in the absence of such directions. In some jurisdictions there are separate statutory provisions for the incorporation of trustees of charitable trusts,[251] and in others the statutory powers of nonprofit corporations include the ability to receive funds to be held pursuant to a charitable trust created by will or instrument.[252]

Trust Rules Inapplicable to Corporations

The nature of a charitable corporation's interest in its assets has been the subject of conflicting decisions. Today directors of charitable corporations are generally considered to be quasi-trustees. They are endowed with most of the attributes of regular trustees but freed from almost all of the more stringent supervisory powers of probate courts, particularly in relation to the appointment of trustees and accounting procedures.

The distinction was brought out in the leading case of *Brigham v. Peter Bent Brigham Hospital,* where the residue of an estate was left to trustees who were directed to manage the estate and accumulate income for twenty-five years, at which time they were to form a corporation to maintain a hospital. The court, in holding that a valid trust was created, went on to state:

> [W]e should observe that the corporation contemplated by the will was not to hold in trust, in the technical sense of the word, the property which it might receive. It was to hold it for its own purposes in the usual way in which charitable institutions hold their assets. Such a holding is sometimes called a quasi-trust, and an institution like the one in question is subject to visitation by the state; but the holding does not constitute a true trust. On the transfer of the property devised by the fourteenth paragraph to a corporation as was anticipated, all technical trusts ceased.[253]

The basic problem raised by discussions of this nature is, of course, how far the application of trust rules should be foreclosed by the characterization of the interest of the corporation as absolute. As noted in one commentary,

250. Attorney General v. Olsen, 191 N.E.2d 132 (Mass. 1963).
251. See Mich. Comp. Laws §450.158.
252. See Mo. Rev. Stat. §352.030.
253. 134 F. 513, 517 (1st Cir. 1904).

[T]he difficulty seems ultimately one of semantics: is the danger that the use of the word "trust" would cause an application of all the rules normally associated therewith so great as to outweigh the economy of mental effort in using a term which is in general valid, though modification of certain of its consequences would be necessary?[254]

The courts have gone both ways in their rationalization, depending on the interests affected; this is evident in the cases dealing with the availability of assets to meet creditors' demands. For example, in a Nebraska case where general creditors were attempting to assert claims against the assets of a college, the court held that the endowment funds, although not technical trusts, were not accessible but that gifts without limitations were.[255]

In a case decided by the Delaware Supreme Court in 1963, this question arose in connection with the administration of a corporate foundation.[256] An action was brought by two members of the foundation against the foundation itself and two other members who were also officers and directors, charging that the action of the board of directors in agreeing to divide its assets and to donate 55% of them to a newly created foundation organized for similar purposes was improper, since it was taken without a vote of the members and was contrary to the general rule that a trustee cannot divest himself of trust funds. The action had been agreed upon by a majority of the foundation board as a method of settling a disagreement over the operation of the foundation, a disagreement that had persisted for seven years following the donor's death.

In this case the court noted that it was sometimes important to determine whether a gift to a charitable corporation was an absolute gift to be used by the corporation for one or more of its corporate purposes, or a gift of such a nature as to make the corporation a trustee of a charitable trust. If there were no trust and no restrictions as to the disposition of the funds, the corporation would be under a duty to use the property solely for its corporate purposes and not to commit an ultra vires act. The court found in this case that a charitable trust was not created so that corporate law applied.

It ruled that, in a loose sense, the assets of a charitable corporation are trust funds, but that the extent and measure of the trust is to be determined from the certificate and by-laws of the corporation.[257] The court found that the certificate of incorporation, as well as the by-laws, gave to the members only the right to expel present members and to elect new members. Furthermore,

254. Note, "The Charitable Corporation," 1173.
255. Hobbs v. Board of Education, 253 N.W. 627 (Neb. 1934).
256. Denckla v. Independence Foundation, 193 A.2d 538 (Del. Ch. 1963).
257. Del. Code Ann. tit. 8, §141(e).

it found that the action of the directors was within their power to make grants to other charities, as stated in the certificate, so that they possessed, as a matter of law, sufficient authority to make the grant in question. Finally, as to the size of the grant, the court again stated that this was a question of degree to be left to the judgment of the board under "familiar principles of corporate law" and that the amount in question did not represent an abuse of its judgment.

It will be seen in the ensuing discussion that the outcome in this case was in actuality not different from what it would have been under trust doctrine, if the trust instrument had contained authorization for grants similar to that found in the certificate of incorporation.

The Massachusetts court stated in a case dealing with property held by a nonprofit college:

> [T]he college is a charitable corporation and all of its property is held in trust in furtherance of the purposes for which it was organized . . . [W]hether the gifts were made for some specified purpose of the college or unconditionally for any general purpose of the college, the petitioner holds the property in trust to carry out the terms and conditions under which it was given and accepted. Where no conditions were imposed by the donor, then it holds and must apply the property in carrying out the charitable object for which it was incorporated.[258]

Restatement (Third) of Trusts deals with this problem as follows:

> An outright devise or donation to a nonproprietary hospital or university or other charitable institution, expressly or impliedly to be used for its general purposes, is charitable but does not create a trust as that term is used in this Restatement. A disposition to such an institution for a specific purpose, however, such as to support medical research, perhaps on a particular disease, or to establish a scholarship fund in a certain field of study, creates a charitable trust of which the institution is the trustee for purposes of the terminology and rules of this Restatement.[259]

Reporting Provisions

In twenty-five states the statutes relating to the creation of charitable corporations impose a duty on the corporation to report at certain intervals to a

258. Wellesley College v. Attorney General, 49 N.E.2d 220, 223 (Mass. 1943); see also Banner Health System v. Long, 663 N.W.2d 242 (S.D. 2003); In re Roxborough Memorial Hospital, No. 555, 17 Fiduciary Rptr. 2d 412 (Pa. C.P., Orphans' Ct. Div., September 30, 1997).
259. Restatement (Third) of Trusts, §28 cmt. a. See also Tauber v. Commonwealth, 499 S.E.2d 839 (Va. 1998); Blocker v. Texas, 718 S.W.2d 409 (Tex. 1986).

state official on the status of the corporation.[260] In fourteen states the report consists of information as to the location of the corporation and a list of its current officers or directors; in seven states it must contain financial information; and in four others, it consists of detailed financial reports submitted to the attorney general. Twenty-five states and the District of Columbia have no general reporting requirements for all charitable corporations. In thirty-nine states, however, detailed reporting of fund-raising solicitations is required.[261]

The Doctrines of Cy Pres and Deviation

Cy Pres

The doctrine of cy pres, originally formulated in the eleventh century, was the legal response to the problems inherent in permitting institutions to have perpetual existence. In its traditional iteration, it was applicable only after three conditions had been met: (1) there existed a valid charitable trust or corporation or a gift to be used for valid charitable purposes; (2) it was impossible or impractical to carry out the donor's original intention; (3) the donor had a general charitable intention, as well as the intention to benefit the particular charitable object he designated.[262] If these conditions were met, equity courts were empowered to modify the purposes to reflect current needs, choosing those as near as possible to the donor's original intent.

The doctrine is now generally accepted as part of the common or statutory law of all of the states except Alaska and North Dakota, although in Hawaii and Nevada it has been recognized only in dictum, while South Carolina uses the doctrine of "deviation" in its stead. The doctrine has a basis in statutory law in thirty of these states. The statutes in force in Maryland, Oklahoma, and Vermont follow the language of a Model Act Concerning the Administration of Charitable Trusts, Devises, and Bequests, which was recommended by the Commissioners on Uniform State Laws in 1944.[263] The Alabama statute follows the Model Act with some modification, and the statutes in Kansas and North Carolina have similar language.[264]

260. See Appendix, Table 1, Column 6.

261. See Appendix, Table 1, Column 15.

262. Edith L. Fisch, *The Cy Pres Doctrine in the United States*, 128–201 (New York: Matthew Bender, 1950); Restatement (Second) of Trusts, §399; Scott and Fratcher, *Law of Trusts*, §§399, 399.4.

263. Model acts adopted by the Commissioners on Uniform State Laws cover subject matter upon which the Commissioners do not believe uniformity among the states is necessary or desirable, but which would nonetheless promote uniformity if enacted.

264. See Appendix, Table 1, Column 11, and Table 2.

Section 67 of Restatement (Third) of Trusts stated a modern version of the doctrine:

> Unless the terms of the trust provide otherwise, where property is placed in trust to be applied to a designated charitable purpose and it is or becomes unlawful, impossible, or impracticable to carry out that purpose, or to the extent it is or becomes wasteful to apply all of the property to the designated purpose, the charitable trust will not fail but the court will direct application of the property or appropriate portion thereof to a charitable purpose that reasonably approximates the designated purpose.[265]

The Uniform Trust Code, adopted by the Commissioners in 2000, has the same formulation as Restatement (Third).[266] As of September 2003 the Uniform Trust Code had been adopted with this provision in four states, Arizona,[267] Nebraska,[268] New Mexico,[269] and Wyoming.[270] Delaware in 2002 also enacted a cy pres statute with language substantially similar to the UTC provision.[271]

To invoke the doctrine of cy pres, the trustees or the attorney general apply to the court for its permission or direction to modify the terms of the trust and to frame a scheme for the application of the property. The trustees or the attorney general often suggest a plan that the court may adopt. In complicated situations the court may appoint a master who will hear all interested parties and submit a proposal to the court. The attorney general is a necessary party to these proceedings. In states that follow the traditional version, notice to the heirs of the donor is required. Under the Massachusetts cy pres statute, the heirs or next of kin of the donor are not necessary parties to the suit; notice to them is not required unless the terms of the trust specify that the donor did not have a general intent or, if the Massachusetts statute pre-

---

265. Restatement (Third) of Trusts, §67. The comparable provision in Restatement (Second) of Trusts, §399, defines cy pres as follows: "If property is given in trust to be applied to a particular charitable purpose, and it is or becomes impossible or impracticable or illegal to carry out the particular purpose, and if the settlor manifested a more general intention to devote the property to charitable purposes, the trust will not fail but the court will direct the application of the property to some charitable purpose which falls within the general charitable intention of the settlor."

266. Uniform Trust Code, §413 (amended 2001).

267. S.B. 1351, 46th Leg., 1st Sess. (2003), to be codified at Ariz. Rev. Stat. §14-10413.

268. 2003 Neb. Laws, L.B. 130, §39, to be codified at Neb. Rev. Stat. §30-3839.

269. N.M. Stat. Ann. §46A-4-413.

270. Wyo. Stat. Ann. §4-10-414.

271. Del. Code Ann. tit. 12, §3541. Kansas has adopted the Uniform Trust Code without the cy pres provision. 2002 Kan. Sess. Laws ch. 133, §34, codified at Kan. Stat. Ann. §58a-413.

suming general charitable intent is held inapplicable, the court, upon a petition begun more than twenty years after the death of the donor, does not expressly find that the donor manifested a general intention.[272]

Illinois has gone further, permitting termination of trusts by the trustees with the consent of the attorney general, obviating recourse to the courts.[273] The Uniform Management of Institutional Funds Act, which applies to endowment funds held by charities, permits release of donor-created restrictions on use or investment policy with the assent of the donor, if living, otherwise by the court with the assent of the attorney general if the court finds that the restriction is "obsolete, inappropriate, or impracticable."[274]

The case of *Jackson v. Phillips*,[275] in which the court recited what is now considered the classic definition of valid charitable purposes, was brought by trustees seeking instructions as to the validity of a bequest in trust to create by various means "a public sentiment that will put an end to Negro slavery in this country." An additional sum was also left in trust to assist fugitive slaves. The testator died in 1861, and in 1865 the Thirteenth Amendment to the Constitution was adopted. The testator's heirs claimed that the trust failed, but the court held that the doctrine of cy pres was applicable: "Neither the immediate purpose of the testator—the moral education of the people; nor his ultimate object—to better the conditions of the African race in this country, has been fully accomplished by the abolition of slavery." The case was referred to a master, whose report was approved with minor changes by the Massachusetts Supreme Judicial Court. The trustees were directed to hold in trust the money left to create a public sentiment that would put an end to slavery and pay over in their discretion such sums, at such times as they thought fit, to the treasurer of the New England branch of the Freedmen's Bureau, to be expended to aid former slaves in the states in which slavery had been abolished by the Emancipation Proclamation or the Thirteenth Amendment. The money left to assist fugitive slaves was to be applied to the use of necessitous persons of African descent in the city of Boston and its vicinity, preference to be given to those who had escaped from slavery.

Criticism of the application of the cy pres doctrine in the United States during the latter half of the twentieth century centered on each of the three conditions listed above, and the Uniform Trust Code and Restatement (Third) reflected recognition of the need for change. Some critics believed that the requirement of a showing of general charitable intent should be

272. Mass. Gen. Laws ch. 214, §10B; ch. 12, §8K.
273. 760 Ill. Comp. Stat. 55/15.5; see also discussion below.
274. Uniform Management of Institutional Funds Act, §7 (1972).
275. 96 Mass. (14 Allen) 539, 556 (1867).

eliminated entirely.[276] They suggested that any gift for a charitable purpose should be, by implication, "for charity," and the only way to avoid this implication should be for a donor to affix a condition or limitation to the gift specifically calling for termination of the trust on failure to carry out the specific purpose.[277] In addition, they proposed that such a condition or limitation should be void unless limited to take effect within a fixed period of time, such as thirty or thirty-five years or within the time prescribed in the Rule Against Perpetuities.[278] However, the expansion or in some states the elimination of the Rule in the late 1990s made such a suggestion inappropriate.[279]

Posner in *Economic Analysis of Law* posited the argument for assuming general intent as follows: "since no one can foresee the future, a rational donor knows that his intentions might eventually be thwarted by unpredictable circumstances and may therefore be presumed to accept implicitly a rule permitting modification of the terms of the bequest in the event that an unforeseen change frustrates his original intention."[280]

There were a few cases in the latter half of the twentieth century in which the courts did broaden the application of the doctrine by assuming a general charitable intent from the existence of the gift in question, particularly if it was in the residue of a testator's estate. Thus the Massachusetts Supreme Judicial Court in a 1964 decision permitted the cy pres application of a gift of a testatrix's "homestead" and funds to establish a home for aged women in the town where she resided with a requirement that only women over sixty-five who did not smoke or drink be admitted. The bequest was not contained in the residuary clause. The court said:

> We accordingly attach no particular significance to the fact that the testatrix included a general residuary clause, naming as residuary legatees her closest relatives. The use of a residuary clause does not per se manifest a desire to benefit the residuary legatees if the trust cannot be executed in the precise manner described in the will. Per contra, the absence of a gift

276. Alex M. Johnson, Jr., "Limiting Dead Hand Control of Charitable Trusts: Expanding the Use of the Cy Pres Doctrine," 21 *Hawaii Law Review* 353 (1999); Rob Atkinson, "Unsettled Standing: Who (Else) Should Enforce the Duties of Charitable Fiduciaries?" 23 *Journal of Corporation Law* 655 (1998); Kenneth L. Karst, "The Efficiency of the Charitable Dollar: An Unfulfilled State Responsibility," 73 *Harvard Law Review* 433 (1960); Lewis M. Simes, *Public Policy and the Dead Hand*, 139 (Ann Arbor: University of Michigan Press, 1955).

277. Karst, "The Efficiency of the Charitable Dollar," 433; Simes, *Public Policy and the Dead Hand*, 139.

278. Simes, *Public Policy and the Dead Hand*, 139.

279. See discussion of the Rule Against Perpetuities in this chapter.

280. Richard A. Posner, *Economic Analysis of Law*, 520 (New York: Aspen Publishers, 6th ed., 2003).

over provision if the trust should fail does carry significance as indicating a general charitable intent.[281]

Moreover, the court did not consider either the request to restrict admissions or a further direction that the home be named for the testatrix to be evidence of lack of general intent.

An example of a gift that failed because the court refused to find a general charitable intent was a Connecticut case in which the court held that two charitable funds established in 1936 for the distribution of interest-free loans and food to needy Jews of Charrish, Poland, failed since the later extermination of the Jewish population in 1942 made it impossible to effectuate the trusts.[282]

The presumption of a general charitable intent was adopted in the Uniform Trust Code and the Restatement (Third) of Trusts.[283] They reflected changes in the law in several states. Thus, by June 2003, general charitable intent was presumed in cases in which a valid charitable trust or gift was created in Georgia,[284] Massachusetts,[285] and Virginia,[286] and in those states that had enacted the Uniform Trust Code.[287] The requirement was entirely eliminated in Delaware[288] and Pennsylvania.[289] In another fifteen states, the courts will infer a general charitable intent from evidence that the settlor left almost all of his estate to charity or similar evidence of intent in the document.[290] Furthermore, the absence of a gift over or a reversionary clause if a charitable gift failed was considered evidence of general charitable intent. For example, in a 2000 decision, the New York Surrogate Court found general charitable intent in a will in which the testators had left "all but an infinitesimal amount of their vast millions to numerous other charities."[291] The Uniform Trust Code contains a unique provision effectively prohibiting distributions on termination of a charitable trust to a noncharitable beneficiary unless there is a

---

281. Rogers v. Attorney General, 196 N.E.2d 855 (Mass. 1964).

282. Connecticut Bank & Trust Co. v. Coles, 192 A.2d 202 (Conn. 1963).

283. Uniform Trust Code, §413 cmt. (amended 2001); Restatement (Third) of Trusts, §67 cmt. b.

284. Trammell v. Elliott, 199 S.E.2d 194 (Ga. 1973).

285. Mass. Gen. Laws ch. 12, §8K (enacted in 1979).

286. United States, on behalf of the U.S. Coast Guard v. Cerio, 831 F. Supp. 530 (E.D. Va. 1993).

287. Arizona, S.B. 1351, 46th Leg., 1st Sess. (2003), to be codified at Ariz. Rev. Stat. §14-10413; Nebraska, 2003 Neb. Laws, L.B. 130, §39, to be codified at Neb. Rev. Stat. §30-3839; New Mexico, N.M. Stat. Ann. §46A-4-413; Wyoming, Wyo. Stat. Ann. §4-10-414.

288. Del. Code Ann. tit. 12, §3541.

289. Pa. Stat. Ann. tit. 20, §6110(A) (enacted 1947).

290. See Appendix, Table 2.

291. In re Estate of Othmer, 710 N.Y.S.2d 848 (Surr. Ct. 2000).

reversion to a living settlor or fewer than twenty-one years have elapsed since the creation of the trust.[292]

Major criticism has also been directed at the second requirement—that it must be impossible or impracticable to carry out the donor's purposes. Proponents of change have advocated that it should be sufficient to show that it is inexpedient or not in the public interest to carry out the stated purposes of the trust. This is the approach of the English law today.

In the United States, in forty-six states the standard for application of the doctrine remains that it has become impossible or impractical to carry out the original purposes, while ten of these have broadened the standard in various ways. In the four states that have adopted the cy pres provisions of the Uniform Trust Code[293] and in Delaware,[294] cy pres is available if a purpose becomes "unlawful, impracticable, impossible to achieve or wasteful."[295] The statute in New Hampshire also includes "prejudicial to the public interest to carry out."[296] In two states, Minnesota[297] and South Dakota,[298] the standards include "inexpedient."

The Illinois statute, enacted in 1997, permits application of the doctrine through termination of a trust and transfer of its assets if the trustees determine that the continued administration of the trust has become impractical because of changed circumstances that adversely affect the charitable purpose or purposes.[299] The term "changed circumstances" is defined as a condition in which the charitable purpose or purposes of the trust have in the judgment of the trustees become illegal, unnecessary, incapable of fulfillment, or inconsistent with the charitable needs of the community.[300] The Idaho statute uses the same phrase as the Illinois statute, but does not define "changed circumstances."[301]

The Illinois statute explicitly provides that the trustees need not obtain the approval of any court but must obtain the consent of the attorney general.[302]

---

292. Uniform Trust Code, §413(b) (amended 2001); see also Ronald Chester, "Cy Pres of Gift Over: The Search for Coherence in Judicial Reform of Failed Charitable Trusts," 23 *Suffolk University Law Review* 41 (1989).

293. Arizona, S.B. 1351, 46th Leg., 1st Sess. (2003), to be codified at Ariz. Rev. Stat. §14-10413; Nebraska, 2003 Neb. Laws, L.B. 130, §39, to be codified at Neb. Rev. Stat. §30-3839; New Mexico, N.M. Stat. Ann. §46A-4-413; Wyoming, Wyo. Stat. Ann. §4-10-414.

294. Del. Code Ann. tit. §12, §3541.

295. Uniform Trust Code, §413 (amended 2001).

296. N.H. Rev. Stat. Ann. §498:4-a.

297. Minn. Stat. §501B.31.

298. S.D. Codified Laws §55-9-4.

299. 760 Ill. Comp. Stat. 55/15.5.

300. Id., 55/15.5(b).

301. Idaho Code §68-1204.

302. 760 Ill. Comp. Stat. 55/15.5(a), (e).

It states, "The Attorney General shall consent to the termination of the trust and the transfer of the trust assets only after having determined that the termination and transfer are necessary or appropriate . . . because of changed circumstances, to fulfill the general intent of the donor of the trust as expressed in the governing instrument of the trust."[303] The Idaho statute also requires the consent of the attorney general.[304] The South Dakota statute requires the consent of the trustees and the donor if living and mentally competent.[305]

Another aspect of the question of impracticability is the problem raised by funds too small to be operated efficiently. Fourteen states, including those that have adopted the Uniform Trust Code, have recognized this problem and, by statute, have adopted expedited procedures to reform small charitable trusts.[306] Section 414 of the Uniform Trust Code provides that a trustee may modify or terminate a trust with assets less than $50,000 "if the trustee concludes that the value of the trust property is insufficient to justify the cost of administration."[307] However, notice must first be given to the attorney general and to any charitable organization expressly designated to receive distributions under the terms of the trust.[308] The court also is permitted to modify or terminate a trust "if it determines that the value of the trust property is insufficient to justify the cost of administration."[309]

In contrast, the Connecticut statute permits termination of charitable trusts with assets less than $150,000 when continuation would be uneconomic,[310] while the Illinois statute permits modification if continued administration of a charitable trust has become impractical because of its small size, which is defined as expenses exceeding 25% of trust income.[311] The New York statute applies to any charitable trust with a market value of $100,000 or less, if it has become "economically impracticable or is not in the best interests of the beneficiaries."[312] The Pennsylvania statute has two applicable provisions. One applies to charitable trusts with assets not exceeding $10,000, which may be terminated by the trustees with the consent of the attorney general and the beneficiaries.[313] The other provision allows for judicial termination where the administrative expense or other burdens are unreasonably out of

303. Id., 55/15.5(a).
304. Idaho Code §68-1204.
305. S.D. Codified Laws §55-9-4.
306. See Appendix, Table 2.
307. Uniform Trust Code, §414(a) (amended 2001).
308. Id., §§110(b)–(c).
309. Id., §414(b).
310. Conn. Gen. Stat. §45a-520.
311. 760 Ill. Comp. Stat. 55/15.5.
312. N.Y. Est. Powers & Trusts Law §8-1.1(c)(2)(i).
313. Pa. Stat. Ann. tit. 20, §6110(B).

proportion to the charitable benefits.[314] In Wisconsin the doctrine is applicable in any case in which the trust property is valued at less than $50,000.[315]

Under the terms of a New Hampshire statute, a judge of probate is authorized to appoint a public trustee to administer small charitable trusts assigned to him by the court upon a finding that the difficulties or expense involved in each trust would tend to defeat its purpose.[316] Consent of the trustee of the original trust is required.[317] The public trustee is authorized to establish common trust funds in which he may combine the trusts under his care, if the instruments contained no explicit prohibition. This legislation is similar to provisions in the English law. The enactment during the 1950s and 1960s of statutes in nearly every state permitting investment by trustees through common trust funds made it possible for trustees of private trusts voluntarily to combine funds for investment.[318] In the majority of states, however, compulsory poolings depend on court interpretation of its cy pres doctrine or its willingness to expand the doctrine of deviation.

The third requirement of the cy pres doctrine is that the property be applied to purposes as near as possible to those of the initial gift. Again, this requirement has been severely criticized, with advocates for change recommending that the standard be broadened to permit an application that observes the spirit of the donor's intention rather than narrow adherence to the original purposes of the gift. In some instances a scheme can be framed that permits application of funds given to a specific institution to be used for other purposes of the original donee. This was the result in an Ohio case in 1955 where permission was granted to use the income from three trusts established for the purchase of art objects for the Cleveland Museum of Art to help build an addition to the building.[319] Similarly, in a New Jersey case decided in 1949, funds left by a testator to be used to publish his scientific works, which turned out to have no scientific value whatever, were given by the court to Princeton University to hold and apply the income to support research in the philosophy department.[320]

The question of the degree to which the original intent of a donor must be respected in a cy pres application received a great deal of attention during the 1990s when a large number of charitable hospitals were sold to for-profit or-

314. Id., §6110(C).
315. Wis. Stat. §701.10(2)(c).
316. N.H. Rev. Stat. §564:2-a to §564:2-c.
317. Id., §564:2-a.
318. Uniform Common Trust Fund Act (amended 1952).
319. Cleveland Museum of Art v. O'Neill, 129 N.E.2d 669 (Ohio C.P. 1955).
320. Wilbur v. Owens, 65 A.2d 843 (N.J. 1949), aff'g Wilbur v. Asbury Park National Bank & Trust Co., 59 A.2d 570 (N.J. Ch. 1948).

ganizations and the courts were called upon to direct application of the proceeds of sale under the cy pres doctrine, in almost all instances in the form of a grant-making foundation. In California the attorney general took the position that the purpose of the surviving foundation be limited to support of hospitals.[321] In contrast, in Louisiana the proceeds of sale of the Tulane University Hospital were initially added to the endowment of the university to be used to support new programs at the medical school, while a Florida court permitted the proceeds of sale of its hospital by the city of Jacksonville to be used to build a new high school and for other capital improvements.[322] Even more remote from an organization's original purposes was the disposition of the sale of the assets of Trigon (Blue Cross Blue Shield of Virginia), in which the Virginia legislature passed a bill requiring the de-mutualization proceeds to be paid to the state treasury rather than to a new charity.[323] As a result, $175 million from the conversion was transferred to the Virginia treasury with the approval of the state attorney general.[324] The New York legislature enacted legislation in 2002 that would have had the effect of distributing almost $2 billion of the proceeds from conversion of Empire Blue Cross Blue Shield to the state.[325] At the close of 2003, the validity of this action was before the state courts.[326]

The comment to section 67 of Restatement (Third) of Trusts emphasizes that the substitute or supplementary purpose "need not be the *nearest possible* but one reasonably similar or close to the settlor's designated purpose, or 'falling within the general charitable purpose' of the settlor."[327] This is in accordance with the views of most commentators and reflects the modern English attitude.

Related to the issue of failed purposes is the question of the treatment of

---

321. Robert Kuttner, "Columbia/HCA and the Resurgence of the For-Profit Hospital Business (part 2)", 335 *New England Journal of Medicine* 446, 447–448 (August 8, 1996); see also Jill R. Horwitz, "Why We Need the Independent Sector: The Behavior, Law, and Ethics of Not-for-Profit Hospitals," 50 *UCLA Law Review* 1345 (2003).

322. General Accounting Office, *Not-for-Profit Hospitals: Conversion Issues Prompt Increased State Oversight* (GAO/HEHS-98-24), 21 (December 1997).

323. Va. Code Ann. §38.2-1005.1B.3, .4.

324. Prehearing Brief of the Division of Consumer Counsel Office of the Attorney General, Application of Blue Cross and Blue Shield of Virginia for Conversion from a Mutual Insurance Company to a Stock Corporation (August 30, 1996) (No. INS950103).

325. Health Care Workforce Recruitment and Retention Act, S.6084/A.9610, 2002 N.Y. Laws ch. 1.

326. Consumers Union of U.S., Inc. v. State, No. 118699/02 (N.Y. Sup. Ct. February 28, 2003); see also Consumers Union, Press Release, "Consumers Union Files Amended Complaint Challenging Constitutionality of Empire Blue Cross Deal" (March 31, 2003).

327. Restatement (Third) of Trusts, §67 cmt. d.

surplus funds. The case of *In re Estate of Buck,* which was heard in the California Superior Court for Marin County in 1986, presented the issue at its extreme.[328] It involved a gift that at the date of the donor's death was estimated to have a value between $7 to $10 million but due to outside and unforeseen circumstances had increased shortly after her death to $340 million. The original purpose of the gift was to benefit the needy in Marin County, an affluent suburb of San Francisco, and for the use of other charitable, religious, or educational purposes in that county. The donee trustee, the San Francisco Community Foundation, had petitioned the court to apply the cy pres doctrine to permit it to make grants within a wider geographic area. The case generated widespread interest in the San Francisco community and was ultimately settled by agreement of the attorney general, the County of Marin, and the Marin Council of Agencies, under which the Foundation resigned, new trustees were appointed, and it was agreed that the geographic limitation would remain with, however, a certain proportion of the income to be set aside for major projects of national and international importance administered from Marin County as determined by the court.[329] As noted by Simon, the court, while rejecting the Foundation's cy pres petition, ended by applying its own notion of cy pres.[330]

By far the most important issue relating to the application of the cy pres doctrine at the end of the twentieth century was in regard to trusts with discriminatory provisions. The clash was between donor intent and public policy—specifically prohibitions against discrimination, with the cases providing no clear precedent.[331] The disposition of cases challenging "affirmative action" policies and of the question of whether state action is involved in the administration of a charitable trust or corporation by reason of its exemption from federal income tax will signal the future direction of the law.

Deviation

As a complement to the doctrine of cy pres, equity courts have power to permit deviations from the terms of a trust if compliance appears to be impossible or illegal or if, owing to circumstances not known to the settlor and

---

328. In re Estate of Buck, No. 23259 (Cal. Super. Ct. 1986), reprinted in 21 *University of San Francisco Law Review* 691 (1987).

329. John G. Simon, "American Philanthropy and the Buck Trust," 21 *University of San Francisco Law Review* 641 (1987); see also Frederick D. Schrag, Comment, "Cy Pres Inexpediency and the Buck Trust," 20 *University of San Francisco Law Review* 577 (1986).

330. Simon, "American Philanthropy and the Buck Trust," 660–661.

331. Restatement (Third) of Trusts, §67, Reporter's Notes, cmt. c; David Luria, "Prying Loose the Dead Hand of the Past: How Courts Apply Cy Pres to Race, Gender, and Religiously Restricted Trusts," 21 *University of San Francisco Law Review* 41 (1986). See the discussion of charitable purposes in this chapter.

not anticipated by him, compliance will defeat or substantially impair the accomplishment of the purposes of the trust.[332] The most common types of deviations permitted have related to sales of real estate that were part of the original trust property and to removal of restrictions on investments, although the doctrine has also been used by courts to remove racial and gender restrictions.[333]

This power of the courts to permit deviations should not be confused with the cy pres power. The latter is applicable when the purposes are no longer capable of being accomplished. The power to permit deviations does not usually extend to the purposes of the trust, but is confined to matters relating solely to administration. In South Carolina, however, in which the doctrine of cy pres was not accepted, the courts have applied deviation to permit changes in purposes, discussing general charitable intent, impossibility or impracticability, and the similarity of the remedy to the original purposes of the gift.[334]

A Pennsylvania case that was characterized as a cy pres decision, although it more properly should have been adjudicated under the doctrine of deviation, involved a trust created in 1909 by Milton and Catherine Hershey. The purpose of the trust was to apply the income to support the Hershey Industrial School for the residence and accommodation of poor white male orphans. The trust terms were modified over the years to remove the racial and gender restrictions and enlarge the educational mission, and in 1963 to take $50 million from accumulated income to establish and support a medical school operated by Pennsylvania State University in Hershey, Pennsylvania. In 1999 when the accumulated income was close to $600 million, the Pennsylvania Orphans' Court denied a cy pres petition filed by the trustees asking permission to spend $25 million of accumulated and current income annually for the support of a child development institute.[335] The attorney general had originally assented to the petition, but later took the position that there had been no failure of the trust. The court found that the proposed plan was contrary to the dominant intent of the founders to care for as many children at the school as the income would permit. This conclusion was reached despite the fact that the school was spending $93,000 each year for the full support and free tuition of each of its 1,200 students and yet had more than $850 million of accumulated income on hand.[336] The decision is contrary to the

332. Restatement (Third) of Trusts, §66.

333. See Scott and Fratcher, *Law of Trusts*, §§167, 381, for collection of cases.

334. South Carolina National Bank v. Bonds, 195 S.E.2d 835 (S.C. 1973).

335. Milton Hershey School, No. 712, Year of 1963, slip op. (Pa. C.P., Orphans' Ct. Div., December 7, 1999) (Warren G. Morgan, J.).

336. Steven Pearlstein, "A Bitter Feud Erupts over Hershey Plant; Plan to Sell Candy Empire Divides a Company Town," *Washington Post*, September 2, 2002, at A1.

trend of contemporary cy pres and deviation decisions, and has been criticized as well in regard to the exercise of its power by the court in cases of this nature.[337]

Application to Charitable Corporations

Both Restatement (Second) and (Third) of Trusts make it clear that the cy pres doctrine is applicable to all funds devoted to charitable purposes, and therefore applies to gifts to and property held by charitable corporations.[338] This means that a gift to a corporation to be used for a limited purpose, as opposed to its general purposes, that cannot be carried out can be transferred to another institution that is able to meet the restrictions.[339] However, in many states the question is undecided. In the following eleven states, the cy pres doctrine has been applied to the general assets of a charitable corporation: Arkansas, California, Connecticut, Illinois, Maryland, Massachusetts, Minnesota, Missouri, New York, Pennsylvania, and Texas.[340]

It has been stated that at early common law, upon the dissolution of a corporation, its realty reverted to the grantor, and its personalty reverted to the Crown. The American cases rejected this view in relation to business corporations,[341] but a few followed it in regard to nonprofit corporations.[342] The question became the subject of a "scholarly controversy" when John Chipman Gray stated that the so-called common law doctrine rested on a dictum in a fifteenth-century case, was contrary to English law, and was "probably among those decantata which when carefully examined will be found not only 'obsolete and odious' but in fact to have never been law at all."[343] The issue was addressed in a 1911 South Carolina case, *McAlhany v. Murray*,[344] in which the court ruled that upon dissolution of a corporation

---

337. Evelyn Brody, "Whose Public? Parochialism and Paternalism in State Charity Law Enforcement" (on file with author); see also Ilana H. Eisenstein, Comment, "Keeping Charity in Charitable Trust Law: The Barnes Foundation and the Case for Consideration of Public Interest in Administration of Charitable Trusts," 151 *University of Pennsylvania Law Review* 1747 (2003).

338. Restatement (Second) of Trusts, §348 cmt. f; Restatement (Third) of Trusts, §67 cmt. e.

339. Restatement (Third) of Trusts, §67 cmt. e.

340. See Appendix, Table 2.

341. Note, "The Charitable Corporation," 35 *Harvard Law Review* 85 (1921). Ballantine points out that whether there is any real authority for this doctrine of reversion in the case of business corporations is very doubtful, but he notes that it has been applied in some American cases dealing with nonstock corporations. Ballantine, *Ballantine on Corporations*, §314.

342. Mott v. Danville Seminary, 21 N.E. 927 (Ill. 1889).

343. Gray, *Rule Against Perpetuities*, §51.

344. 71 S.E. 1025 (S.C. 1911).

formed to promote temperance that had certain characteristics of a fraternal-benevolent society, the assets were to be distributed to the members, rather than revert to the donors. This case was cited as representing a return to what was characterized as the "modern" view that rejected the rights of a donor, but only to the extent that it favored donors over members.

Most recent cases have tended to follow an early Pennsylvania decision that held that property of a charitable corporation is to be distributed on dissolution to another charitable corporation for similar purposes.[345] In *In re Los Angeles County Pioneer Society*,[346] the court said specifically that transfer of the assets of a charitable corporation to another similar organization was not a confiscation of members' property in contravention of the Fourteenth Amendment of the United States Constitution, since the members at no time had a right to receive the property. The court also rejected, in that case, the right of grantors or their heirs to receive the property.[347]

In twenty-three states the subject is now covered by specific legislation requiring distribution cy pres;[348] most of these statutes do not require a showing of general charitable intention, although they permit recognition of a right of reversion if it is expressly stated.[349] Scott suggested limiting any right of reversion to the duration of the period of the Rule Against Perpetuities,[350] a provision that would obviate the technical difficulties that arise when dissolution occurs many years after the death of the original donor.[351] The issue is in a certain sense moot in light of the requirement for exemption from tax under the Internal Revenue Code that there be a provision requiring that on dissolution or termination, a charity must distribute its assets to another organization then exempt under section 501(c)(3) of the Code.

The original iteration of the Uniform Management of Institutional Funds Acts contained provisions relaxing the rules under which restrictions on charitable gifts could be released, permitting release of a restriction with the consent of the donor.[352] A revision of the act adopted provisionally in August 2003 reflected the trend toward liberalizing the cy pres and deviation doctrines just described. Specifically, a new paragraph (b) was added to section 9

345. In re Centennial and Memorial Association, 83 A. 683 (Pa. 1912).

346. 257 P.2d 1 (Cal. 1953).

347. See also Kansas East Conference of the United Methodist Church, Inc. v. Bethany Medical Center, Inc., 969 P.2d 859 (Kan. 1998).

348. See Appendix, Table 1, Column 11.

349. McDonough County Orphanage v. Burnhart, 125 N.E.2d 625 (Ill. 1955).

350. Scott and Fratcher, *Law of Trusts*, §399.3 n.19.

351. Cases that have upheld a reversionary right include Industrial National Bank v. Drysdale, 114 A.2d 191 (R.I. 1955), aff'd, 125 A.2d 87 (R.I. 1956); Townsend v. Charles Schalkenbach Home for Boys, Inc., 205 P.2d 345 (Wash. 1949).

352. Uniform Management of Institutional Funds Act, §7 (1972).

under which a charity could release or modify the terms of a restricted fund (defined in the act as an "institutional fund") on its own if the value of the fund was small and the charity concluded that the restriction was unlawful, impracticable, impossible to achieve, or wasteful and if future use of the property would reasonably approximate the purposes of the original gift. The maximum size of a fund to which the provision would apply was left to the discretion of the legislatures in each state, with $50,000 as the suggested amount.[353] The standard for application of the release or modification was the same as that found in the Uniform Trust Code.

Community foundations are a subset of publicly supported charities that receive contributions from and conduct programs for the benefit of a defined community. One of the advantages that a community trust offers to its donors is assurance that their gifts will meet future needs of the community. This is accomplished through a "variance power" under which the foundation trustees retain a power to change the purpose of restricted gifts if circumstances change, based on a standard that was originally intended to be less restrictive than the traditional cy pres standard. The parameters of the variance power were the subject of litigation in New York in 2000, with the court affirming its power of review while finding that the suit was barred by the statute of limitations.[354]

353. Uniform Management of Institutional Funds Act, §9(b) (Draft, August 2003).

354. Community Service Society v. New York Community Trust, 713 N.Y.S.2d 712 (N.Y. App. Div. 2000); see also Mark Sidel, "Law, Philanthropy and Social Class: Variance Power and the Battle for American Giving," 36 U.C. Davis Law Review 1145 (2003).

4

Fiduciary Duties:
State Law Standards

The subject of this chapter is the laws that have been enacted to assure that those persons who have legal responsibility for the administration of charitable corporations and trusts will act to further those purposes and neither seek private benefit at the expense of the charity nor be reckless in its administration. The nature of the office of a charity trustee or director is described in law as a "fiduciary relationship." It refers to situations in which individuals have an affirmative duty to act for the benefit of other individuals as to matters within the scope of the relationship between the parties.[1] The duty of a fiduciary is, in essence, a duty of loyalty, and has as its corollary a rule that the fiduciary may not profit at the expense of the other party. It also requires that the fiduciary live up to certain standards in administering the property entrusted to him, a parallel duty known as the duty of prudence.

Dealings between partners, attorneys and clients, agents and principals, and corporation directors and stockholders are all examples of fiduciary relations, although the relationship is found in a peculiarly intense degree in a trust. The popular nonlegal meaning of the word "trust" is, in fact, almost synonymous with the concept of fiduciary relations. Even though the vast majority of charities are organized as corporations, the source of the duties of corporate directors is to be found in the law of trusts. Accordingly, the duties of trustees are set forth briefly to provide an understanding of the evolution of the duties of their corporate counterparts as well as a summary of the rules applicable to those charities that are operated as trusts.

Fiduciary Duties of Trustees: Prudence and Loyalty

The characterization of a trustee as a fiduciary is crucial to an understanding of his duties, and underlies the extent, as well as the limit, of all of his

---

1. Restatement (Third) of the Law of Trusts, §170 cmt. b (1996); Austin W. Scott, "The Fiduciary Principle," 37 *California Law Review* 539 (1949).

powers. The act of creating a trust imposes certain duties on the trustee. These duties have two sources: the terms of the trust instrument or indenture (conferred by the donor) and a set of well-established rules of law that apply to all trustees.

The settlor of a charitable trust may eliminate or limit the application of certain of these rules of law. The courts, however, interpret such provisions strictly and do not infer them from unclear language. Furthermore, a donor may not impose duties on a trustee that will be impossible to accomplish or will require him to perform acts that are illegal or inconsistent with public policy. The trust instrument cannot relieve a trustee from responsibility for performing any of these acts, and the trustee commits a breach of trust if he complies with the instrument. For example, a provision in a trust instrument relieving a trustee from all duty to account to the courts has been declared inconsistent with public policy, and in some states it may be illegal.[2]

Modern trust documents invariably include both relief from the strict trustee duties of care and loyalty as well as provisions for exculpation in the event of their breach. Accordingly, it is rare that the strict liability embodied in the law of trusts described herein is enforced by a court. The importance of these strict standards lies in the approach the law has taken to assure appropriate behavior for fiduciaries.

Duty of Prudence

The modern formulation of the duty of prudence was set forth in section 77 of the Preliminary Draft No. 6 of Restatement (Third) of Trusts as follows: "The trustee is under a duty to the beneficiaries to administer the trust as a prudent person would, in light of the purposes, terms, and other circumstances of the trust; prudence requires the exercise of reasonable care and skill and of a degree of caution suitable to the particular trust's objectives, circumstances, and overall plan of administration."[3]

In the two earlier versions of the Restatement, the duty was phrased in terms of a requirement to use the reasonable care and skill of a man of ordinary prudence in dealing with his own property. The newer version first appeared as section 227 of the Prudent Investor Rule of the Restatement (Third) of Trusts, approved in 1990;[4] it was renumbered as section 90 in the

2. Austin W. Scott and William F. Fratcher, *The Law of Trusts,* §172 (Boston: Little, Brown, 4th ed., 1987); George G. Bogert and George T. Bogert, *The Law of Trusts and Trustees,* §973 (St. Paul: West Group, 3d ed., 1977); Restatement (Second) of the Law of Trusts, §§165, 166 (1959); Restatement (Third) of Trusts, §187.

3. Restatement (Third) of the Law of Trusts, §77(1) (Preliminary Draft No. 6, 2003).

4. Restatement (Third) of Trusts: Prudent Investor Rule, §227 (published 1992).

2003 draft.[5] It appears as section 2 of the Uniform Prudent Investor Act[6] and section 804 of the Uniform Trust Code.[7]

The duty of prudence was first applied to charitable and private trusts alike in the 1830 case of *Harvard College v. Amory,* where it was stated that a trustee must "observe how men of prudence, discretion and intelligence manage their own affairs, not in regard to speculation, but in regard to the permanent disposition of their funds, considering the probable income as well as the probable safety of the capital to be invested."[8]

The duty of prudence requires a trustee to exercise at a minimum the skill of an ordinary prudent person. However, if a trustee has greater skill than others, he is under a duty to use such skill. Some cases hold corporate trustees such as banks to a higher degree of performance based on their particular qualifications and on the fact that they hold themselves out to the public as possessing extraordinary skill and receive compensation for such skill.[9]

A donor may in the trust instrument relax or modify the requirement of care and skill ordinarily required of a trustee. Such a clause will relieve a trustee from a duty that would otherwise be imposed on him. It differs, therefore, from an exculpatory clause, which relieves a trustee from liability if he does commit a breach of trust.

Investment of Trust Funds: The Modern Prudent Investor Rule

In the majority of the states, the standard as to investments of trust funds has traditionally been governed by statutes, and the majority of these laws recited this standard in terms of the prudent man rule.[10] However, prior to 1950, it was not uncommon in a number of states for trustees to be required to invest only in those securities enumerated in a statute called the "legal list,"[11] although in some states the statute combined a legal list with a standard of prudence. Confining investments to those on a legal list will not, necessarily, protect a trustee from liability for failure to meet one or more of the underlying duties of loyalty and impartiality or of care, skill, and caution, as well as the duty to diversify.[12] These statutes regulating the investment of trust funds

5. Restatement (Third) of Trusts, §90 (Preliminary Draft No. 6, 2003).

6. Uniform Prudent Investor Act, §2 (1994).

7. Uniform Trust Code, §804.

8. 26 Mass. (9 Pick.) 446, 461 (1830).

9. Restatement (Third) of Trusts, §77(2) (Preliminary Draft No. 6, 2003). Scott and Fratcher, *Law of Trusts,* §174.1, contains a discussion of the standards commonly imposed on professional trustees. See also Bogert and Bogert, *Law of Trusts and Trustees,* §541.

10. See, for example, Cal. Civ. Code §2261.

11. See, for example, Iowa Code §682.23.

12. Restatement (Third) of Trusts: Prudent Investor Rule, §228(a).

varied in their application. Some extended to all fiduciaries, others to banks and trust companies. Some permitted a settlor to enlarge or restrict investment provisions, his statements being controlling.

In their practical application to specific situations, statutory requirements as to investments gave fairly broad leeway to the trustees to use their discretion in regard to individual purchases as well as the nature of the investments. However, as these statutes were interpreted by the courts,

> much of the apparent and initially intended generality and adaptability of the prudent man rule was lost . . . Decisions dealing with essentially factual issues were accompanied by generalizations understandably intended to offer guidance to other courts and trustees in like situations. These cases were subsequently treated as precedents establishing general rules governing trust investments. Specific case results and flexible principles often thereby became crystallized into specific sub rules prescribing the types and characteristics of permissible investments for trustees.[13]

Standards for Investments

Recognition by scholars and practitioners alike of this narrowing of the rules and increasing conflicts between the law and contemporary asset management practices led the American Law Institute to undertake a major revision of the prudent man rule. The culmination was the adoption by the Institute in 1990 of the Prudent Investor Rule, which now comprises "Topic 5. Investment of Trust Funds" of the Restatement (Third) of Trusts. As stated in the Introduction, "The objectives of the 'prudent investor rule' of this Restatement Third range from that of liberating expert trustees to pursue challenging, rewarding, non-traditional strategies when appropriate to the particular trust, to that of providing other trustees with reasonably clear guidance to safe harbors that are practical, adaptable, readily identifiable, and expectedly rewarding."[14]

The reporter of the revisions indicated that the new formulation was limited to principles supported by general consensus among various theories that would be adaptable to the differences among various trusts, trustees, and their needs and objectives.[15] Reinforcement of this precept was found in a revision of section 389, "Investments of Charitable Trusts," which stated, "In making decisions and taking actions with respect to the investment of trust

13. Id., §227 cmt. k.
14. Id. at Introductory Note.
15. Id.

funds, the trustee of a charitable trust is under a duty similar to that of the trustee of a private trust."[16]

The Introduction also contained a summary of principles of prudence designed to instruct trustees and courts that:

1. sound diversification is ordinarily required of trustees;
2. market risk is unavoidable in investing, requiring trustees to make a deliberate assessment and judgment about a suitable level of risk and reward to be considered in light of the particular circumstances of the trust and the trustees. Most important, "investments and courses of action are properly judged not in isolation but on the basis of the roles they are to play in specific trust portfolios and strategies";[17]
3. trustees have a duty to avoid fees and other costs that are not justified by the needs and realistic objectives of the trust's investment program;
4. the fiduciary duty of impartiality requires a balancing of the elements of return between production of current income and protection of purchasing power from the effects of inflation;
5. delegation of investment powers may be required in order to carry out the duty of investing prudently.[18]

As noted earlier, the Prudent Investor Rule of the Restatement (Third) appears in a revised section 227.[19] A new section 228 restates the principle contained in the prior version of section 227 that this duty is subject to a trustee's duty to comply with applicable statutes and the terms of the trust.[20]

Following adoption of the Restatement (Third), the National Conference of Commissioners on Uniform State Laws adopted a Uniform Prudent Investor Act that was based on the revised Restatement. It stated as its general principle that "[i]nvestment and management decisions respecting individual assets must be evaluated not in isolation, but in the context of the trust portfolio as a whole and as a part of an overall investment strategy having risk and return objectives reasonably suited to the trust."[21] It then set forth eight circumstances that to the extent relevant to the trust and its beneficiaries were to be considered by a trustee in investing and managing assets, among them the possible effect of inflation or deflation, the tax consequences of decisions or strategies, the role of each investment within the overall portfolio, the ex-

---

16. Restatement (Second) of Trusts, §389 (revised).
17. Restatement (Third) of Trusts: Prudent Investor Rule, Introductory Note.
18. Id.
19. Id., §227.
20. Id., §228.
21. Uniform Prudent Investor Act, §2(b).

pected total return from income and appreciation, and an asset's special relationship or value to the purposes of the trust.[22]

The act also enumerated certain phrases that, if included in a trust instrument, were to be construed as authorizing any investment or strategy permitted under the act, unless otherwise limited or modified in the instrument. The phrases considered sufficient to make the act applicable included: "investments permissible by law for investment of trust funds," "legal investments," "authorized investments," "using the judgment and care under the circumstances then prevailing that persons of prudence, discretion and intelligence exercise in the management of their own affairs, not in regard to speculation but in regard to the permanent disposition of their funds, considering the probable income as well as the probable safety of their capital," "prudent man rule," "prudent trustee rule," "prudent person rule," and "prudent investor rule."[23]

As of January 2003 the Uniform Prudent Investor Act had been adopted in thirty-five jurisdictions. Two states, Alabama and Kentucky, still limited investments to those on a legal list; New Hampshire, Ohio, and Wisconsin had comparable restrictions for certain portions of a trust estate, and North Dakota had a legal list for individual trustees and a proportionate limitation for corporate trustees.[24]

The trust requirement of diversification was the subject of a Pennsylvania case that received wide attention in 2002. It involved investment decisions by the trustees of a trust created in 1909 by Milton and Catherine Hershey, the income of which was to be applied to support the Hershey Industrial School for the residence and accommodation of poor white male orphans. In 1999 the attorney general's office had written to the trustees questioning whether their holding of stock in the Hershey Food Company might be in violation of their duty to diversify investments. In July 2001, the value of the trust assets was $2.6 billion, of which 52% was the Hershey stock. This holding represented 32% of the total stock of the company and 77% of the voting shares. One year later, in the summer of 2002, the Hershey Trust announced its intention to sell the company shares, a proposal that was opposed by the school's alumni association, residents of the town of Hershey, employees of the company, and the attorney general of Pennsylvania.[25]

The attorney general immediately brought suit to halt the sale, claiming that it was his duty to protect the public against any social and economic dis-

22. Id., §8(c).
23. Id., §10.
24. Bogert and Bogert, *Law of Trusts and Trustees,* §§613, 670; Scott and Fratcher, *Law of Trusts,* §227.13.
25. See also the discussion of the Hershey Trust in Chapter 6.

advantages that might be occasioned by the activities and functioning of public charities. A preliminary injunction was issued and upheld on an appeal brought by the Trust.[26]

During the hearing on the preliminary injunction the attorney general acknowledged that existing trust law required fiduciaries to make decisions that are in the best interests of the charity and announced that he was seeking legislation to require charitable fiduciaries to consider the impact of their investment decisions on the community. The Hershey trustees subsequently abandoned their plans to sell the shares and agreed to seek court approval, with notice to the attorney general, if sale of the company was considered in the future.[27] The bill submitted by the attorney general was adopted by the legislature and signed on November 6, 2002. It modified the provisions of the Pennsylvania Prudent Investor Rule, section 7203 of title 20 of the Pennsylvania Consolidated Statutes, by adding the following to the requirement that a trustee consider an asset's special relationship or special value to the purposes of the trust or of its beneficiaries:

> including, in the case of a charitable trust, the special relationship of the asset and its economic impact as a principal business enterprise on the community in which the beneficiary of the trust is located and the special value of the integration of the beneficiary's activities with the community where that asset is located.[28]

Although the provision will be of limited general application, it represents an unusual degree of interference with trustee discretion, not to say a perversion of the intent of many donors.

Provisions in trust instruments may either limit or enlarge trustees' investment powers. Thus, if the trust instrument contains a clause that a trustee may invest "in his discretion" or as he "deems advisable," the effect of this clause will depend in part on the tradition of the state. As provided in Restatement (Third) of Trusts, if the investment rule is narrow, these words ordinarily mean that the prudent man rule will then become applicable. If the prudent man rule is in force, however, the phrase may not enlarge the trustee's powers.[29] The trust instrument, however, may go further and specifically permit "speculative" investments or investments not ordinarily con-

26. In re Milton Hershey School Trust, 807 A.2d 324 (Pa. Commw. Ct. 2002).

27. Evelyn Brody, "Whose Public? Parochialism and Paternalism in State Charity Law Enforcement" (on file with author).

28. H.B. 2060 (Pa. 2002), amending Pa. Stat. Ann. tit. 20, §7203(C)(6). See Chapter 6 relating to the provisions of the act requiring court approval, after notice to the attorney general, prior to sale of certain control stock.

29. Scott and Fratcher, *Law of Trusts,* §227.14; Appeal of Davis, 67 N.E. 604 (Mass. 1903).

sidered proper for a trustee. In such a case, the courts are likely to interpret the provision strictly, although according to Scott, there is no rule of public policy that prevents the settlor from permitting the trustee to make speculative investments. The one case generally cited in support of this proposition, however, dealt with a trust of which the settlor was also trustee and had reserved a right to direct investments; the court discussed this power in relation to the purposes of the trust, of which the ability to speculate was an integral part.[30]

Investment of Trust Funds: Diversification

One component of the Prudent Investor Rule is consideration of whether investments should be diversified so as to minimize risk. Until 1969 when the federal tax laws imposed limits on the stock holdings of private foundations, the question of diversification was an important one for these organizations, particularly if they were the donees of large holdings of stock of closely held corporations. Unfortunately, the cases did not make clear how far a trustee would be subject to liability for failure to diversify investments. The requirement of diversification has been specifically recognized by the courts in some jurisdictions,[31] and has been imposed by statute in others.[32] The Restatement (Third) of Trusts in section 229 explicitly requires consideration of diversification,[33] and it is embodied in the following provision in section 3 of the Uniform Prudent Investor Act: "A trustee shall diversify the investments of the trust unless the trustee reasonably determines that, because of special circumstances, the purposes of the trust are better served without diversifying."[34]

Where the rule of diversification exists, it has traditionally been applied less strictly to retention of investments received at the inception of the trust than to the making of investments. However, Restatement (Third), in new section 229, imposes a duty on a trustee within a reasonable time after the creation of the trust to review the contents of the trust estate and structure the portfolio in order to conform to the rules of prudence set forth in sections 227 and 228. If a trustee is specifically permitted by the terms of the trust to retain certain securities, the rule of diversification will not apply. There are statutes

---

30. In re Greenhouse's Estate, 12 A.2d 96 (Pa. 1940).

31. Appeal of Dickinson, 25 N.E. 99 (Mass. 1890); Pennsylvania Company for Insurance on Lives and Granting Annuities v. Gillmore, 59 A.2d 24 (N.J. Ch. 1948); Knox County v. Fourth & First National Bank, 182 S.W.2d 980 (Tenn. 1944).

32. Scott and Fratcher, *Law of Trusts*, §229.

33. Restatement (Third) of Trusts: Prudent Investor Rule, §229 cmt. g.

34. Uniform Prudent Investor Act, §3.

in some jurisdictions, however, that do permit retention of inception assets. In a state that restricts investments generally, Restatement (Third) provides that the trustee's authority and duties are those of section 227 of the Prudent Investor Rule, while in other states the rules of section 227 and 228 are not changed.[35] In addition, a provision in the terms of the trust authorizing a trustee to retain securities in which the donor invested or which the donor has contributed to the trust does not justify the trustee in retaining them if such retention later becomes imprudent.[36]

Duty of Loyalty

The duty of loyalty embodies the fiduciary relationship.[37] The classic description of its scope was expressed by Judge Cardozo:

> Many forms of conduct permissible in a workaday world for those acting at arm's length, are forbidden to those bound by fiduciary ties. A trustee is held to something stricter than the morals of the market place. Not honesty alone, but the punctilio of an honor the most sensitive, is then the standard of behavior. As to this there has developed a tradition that is unbending and inveterate. Uncompromising rigidity has been the attitude of courts of equity when petitioned to undermine the rule of undivided loyalty by the "disintegrating erosion" of particular exceptions. Only thus has the level of conduct for fiduciaries been kept at a level higher than that trodden by the crowd.[38]

In its operation, a trustee is prohibited from dealing with the trust property on his own behalf. He cannot buy or sell trust property or appropriate opportunities available to the trust to himself. His interest must always yield to that of the beneficiary.

A trustee will not be absolved on the basis that his action was inadvertent or that he acted in good faith or that he was ignorant of the scope of his duties. Under pure trust doctrine, it is immaterial whether the beneficiary is damaged. A trustee will be liable to the trust estate for any loss from any act of self-dealing. Any benefit or profit he obtains belongs to the trust estate, regardless of whether the transaction involved a loss. The rule also prohibits a

---

35. Restatement (Third) of Trusts: Prudent Investor Rule, §229 cmt. g; see also discussion of the Hershey Trust in this chapter.

36. Scott and Fratcher, *Law of Trusts,* §230.3.

37. Restatement (Third) of Trusts, §78(1) (Preliminary Draft No. 6, 2003), Restatement (Second) of Trusts, §170, and Scott and Fratcher, *Law of Trusts,* §§170–170.25, deal in great detail with the many aspects of this question.

38. Meinhard v. Salmon, 164 N.E. 545, 546 (N.Y. 1928).

trustee's spouse and his relatives from benefiting from his trust relationship, and it applies equally to trust companies or banks acting as trustees. The only conditions under which the trustee of a private trust may obtain relief from this strict rule, other than under a specific provision in the terms of the trust, are those in which the trustee deals directly with the beneficiary, or where he makes full disclosure to him, takes no advantage of his position, obtains his consent, and where the transaction is in all respects fair and reasonable. In the case of a trust for charitable purposes, there are no beneficiaries capable of giving this consent. As Karst notes:

> [I]t might be more accurate to say that when a trustee is guilty of self-dealing which has not been ratified by the beneficiary (and in the case of a charity, there is no one to ratify), he is an insurer for losses incurred by the trust, and he is accountable for any gains which he receives.[39]

Specific exceptions to the absolute prohibition against self-dealing are set forth in Preliminary Draft No. 6 of Restatement (Third) of Trusts. They include payment of reasonable compensation for services rendered as a trustee, special services that are necessary and appropriate to prudent administration such as those of an attorney or real estate agent, and loans of a trustee's personal funds for proper expenses of administration or to protect the trust estate.[40]

A number of state statutes expressly prohibit self-dealing by fiduciaries.[41] For example, the California Probate Code states, "A trustee has a duty not to use or deal with the trust property for his own profit, or for any other purpose unconnected with the trust, in any manner."[42] The Ohio statute provides that court approval of a transaction involving self-dealing is necessary even if the terms of the trust allow self-dealing.[43] Section 802 of the Uniform Trust Code, adopted in 2000, follows the general principles of Restatement (Second).[44]

As noted earlier in this chapter, by the terms of the trust, a donor may relieve a trustee from the stringent effects of this duty of loyalty, and may permit a trustee to deal with the property on his own account unless this is expressly prohibited by statute. However, no matter how broad the power to deal with himself or wide the relief from liabilities contained in a trust instrument, a donor may not relieve a trustee from responsibility for willful and deliberate violation of his fiduciary obligations, for gross negligence, for actions

---

39. Kenneth L. Karst, "The Efficiency of the Charitable Dollar: An Unfulfilled State Responsibility," 73 *Harvard Law Review* 443, 449 (1960).

40. Restatement (Third) of Trusts, §78 cmts. c(4)–(6) (Preliminary Draft No. 6, 2003).

41. See Scott and Fratcher, *Law of Trusts*, §170, for statutory references.

42. Cal. Prob. Code §16004(a).

43. Ohio Rev. Code Ann. §2109.44.

44. Uniform Trust Code, §802 cmt. (amended 2001).

taken in bad faith or dishonestly, or for acts from which he has profited personally. Considerations of public policy are given by the courts as the basis for this rule.[45]

Liability of Trustees for Breach of Trust

When a breach of trust is committed, the redress provided by law varies with the nature of the breach. In severe cases a court may remove a trustee in a proceeding brought by the attorney general, or by his co-trustees if there are any. In addition, if a trustee fails to discharge one or more of his duties, or otherwise falls below the standard of care required of him, the law seeks to place the beneficiary in the position that he would have occupied had there been no breach of trust. The liabilities imposed on the defaulting trustee are designed to attain this objective.[46] The trustee, therefore, is liable to account for the trust property and all of its proceeds. He is chargeable for any loss of the trust property arising from a breach of trust. A breach of trust may consist of a violation of any duty owing to the beneficiary: ordinarily, it involves an act in which the trustee is personally at fault, but it can also consist of a failure to exercise the care and skill of an ordinary man of prudence that results in loss, even though the trustee has done the best he can. In general, reliance on legal counsel is not sufficient to relieve a trustee from liability.[47]

If a trustee has doubt as to his powers or duties, the law allows him to obtain instructions from a court. In following the instructions, he will be protected from a later charge of breach of duty. A trustee may present to the court any question involving a proper construction of the trust instrument or a determination between conflicting claims. The primary limitation on the use of this procedure is that the problem must be practical, not theoretical, and in need of prompt decision. If the question relates to an exercise of discretion, the court will not usually give instructions.[48] In a petition for instructions by trustees of a charitable trust, the attorney general is a proper party to the proceeding, and in many states he is a necessary party.[49]

If there has been a breach of trust, the beneficiaries of a private trust have three possible alternative monetary remedies. They may charge the trustee

---

45. Browning v. Fidelity Trust Co., 250 F. 321 (3d Cir. 1918); Matter of Andrus, 281 N.Y.S. 831 (Surr. Ct. 1935).

46. Charles E. Rounds, Jr., *Loring, A Trustee's Handbook*, §7.2 (New York: Aspen Publishers, 2003).

47. See Scott and Fratcher, *Law of Trusts*, §201, and Restatement (Second) of Trusts, §201, for further discussion.

48. Scott and Fratcher, *Law of Trusts*, §394; Kirwin v. Attorney General, 175 N.E. 164 (Mass. 1931).

49. See Appendix, Table 1, Columns 1 and 2, and Chapter 6.

(1) with any loss that resulted from the breach, (2) with any profits made through the breach, or (3) with any profits that would have accrued if there had been no breach of trust. Interest is awarded as a form of income not received, not as a penalty. In the case of a trust for charitable purposes, the interest paid by a trustee will become part of the trust fund and be distributed in accordance with the purposes of the trust. In most cases a trustee will be liable for simple interest, although in some cases of deliberate fraud or a violation of express instructions, the court has required a payment of compound interest.[50]

The accountability of trustees is not confined to cases where there has been a breach of trust. The duty of loyalty requires that even when the trustee has committed no wrong through intention or negligence, and even if he is unaware of any moral fault, he is under an obligation to avoid possible conflicts of interest. Therefore, if he makes any personal profit through, or arising from, the administration of the trust, he is accountable to the trust for the amount he receives. For example, if a trustee receives a commission or bonus from a purchase or sale of trust property that is not itself improper, he must nevertheless pass the profit on to the trust. If he buys with his own funds an encumbrance on the trust property, he is accountable for any profits he makes thereby.[51]

The remedies for breach of trust in the case of a charitable trust are equitable. They may include, in addition to restitution and accounting, a decree of specific performance, injunction, the appointment of a receiver, or the removal of the trustee. A trustee may also be guilty of a criminal offence such as embezzlement or larceny. Failure to comply with certain statutes requiring registration or licensing of trustees who are soliciting funds from the public for charitable purposes is in some states a criminal act.[52]

The power to remove trustees is, in a sense, the most extreme remedy the court can impose. The question of removal is ordinarily a matter for the exercise of a court's sound discretion, and in deciding this type of case, the court will take into account all circumstances relating to the matter. The mere fact that a trustee has committed a breach of trust is not necessarily a ground for his removal. Serious breaches of trust will be remedied by removal, however, even if they were not committed dishonestly. Refusal or neglect to obey court orders has been held to be a ground for a removal action,[53] as have instances

---

50. Lewis Prichard Charity Fund v. Mankin Investment Co., 189 S.E. 96 (W. Va. 1936); see also Scott and Fratcher, *Law of Trusts*, §207.1, for a list of cases.

51. Restatement (Second) of Trusts, §203; Russell Niles, "Trustee Accountability in the Absence of Breach of Trust," 60 *Columbia Law Review* 141 (1960).

52. See, for example, Mass. Gen. Laws ch. 68, §17; N.J. Rev. Stat. Ann. §2A:111-30.

53. Attorney General v. Garrison, 101 Mass. 223 (1869); Restatement (Second) of Trusts, §107. See Scott and Fratcher, *Law of Trusts*, §§107, 387, for a collection of cases.

of willful breach of trust, unfitness, long continued absence, or excessive use of the trustee's powers. The matter of removal is dealt with by legislation in many jurisdictions,[54] but in most cases these statutes merely set forth the powers of the court in general terms. This subject is discussed in Chapter 6 relating to enforcement procedures available to the attorney general as representative of the beneficiaries of charitable trusts.

Exculpatory Clauses

One of the most common provisions found in trust instruments today is an exculpatory clause, a provision designed to relieve a trustee from liability for certain breaches of trust. Provisions of this nature are strictly construed by the courts. In addition, no clause in a trust instrument is effective to relieve a trustee from liability for a breach of trust that is committed in bad faith, intentionally, with reckless indifference to the interests of the beneficiary, or for a breach of trust from which the trustee personally profits.[55] New York has gone further than the ordinary standard and by statute has declared that an attempted grant to an executor or trustee of a testamentary trust of exoneration of his fiduciary liability for failure to execute reasonable care, diligence, and prudence shall be deemed contrary to public policy and void.[56] This statute was applied in the case of *In re Schechter's Estate*,[57] where a clause in a trust for religious purposes stating that the trustee should be neither responsible for any loss or injury to the property nor accountable for its distribution was declared void as against public policy.[58] However, the presence of an exculpatory clause does relieve a trustee from the strict personal liability often associated with the office of trustee, and under certain circumstances may make the position more like that of a corporate director.

Fiduciary Duties of Corporate Directors: Care

The fiduciary relationship arises in many different situations, and although it is considered to be most intense in the trust relationship, directors and officers of corporations are also fiduciaries. Their legal duties have been developed from the same principles as those applicable to trustees. In fact, in the earlier cases directors of all corporations were commonly said to owe a duty to the corporation as *cestui que trust* similar to that which a trustee owes to

54. See Scott and Fratcher, *Law of Trusts,* §§107, 387, for citations.
55. Restatement (Second) of Trusts, §222; Scott and Fratcher, *Law of Trusts,* §§222–222.3.
56. N.Y. Est. Powers & Trusts Law §11-2.3.
57. 229 N.Y.S.2d 702 (Surr. Ct. 1962).
58. Scott and Fratcher, *Law of Trusts,* §222; Bogert and Bogert, *Law of Trusts and Trustees,* §542.

his beneficiary.[59] Because business reality required that in some instances a director be allowed greater freedom than a trustee to deal with the corporation, particularly in making loans to assist the corporation, the rules were gradually relaxed.

In defining the duties of corporate directors, the courts have sought to formulate rules that would ensure the preservation and proper use of others' funds while at the same time recognizing that directors' actions are monitored by stockholders with whom they share a profit motive. It has been argued that directors of charitable entities, being public-spirited citizens serving without compensation, should be held to standards of care that are less strict than those applied to the ordinary corporate director.[60] This attitude was evident in one or two court decisions,[61] but in the majority of cases the courts have imposed a high degree of care and a strict rule of loyalty, based on their belief that this was necessary in order to assure the preservation of funds held for the benefit of the general public rather than individuals.

The question of whether a trust or corporate statute was applicable was unanswered until the latter half of the twentieth century and, although in some jurisdictions the matter remains undecided, the majority of states have opted to apply the more lenient standards applicable to business corporations to their charitable counterparts.[62] However, as Goldschmid has aptly pointed out, the distinct obligation of nonprofit directors and officers with respect to the corporation's mission creates a more difficult and complex decision-making process for them than for their for-profit peers. "For-profit directors and officers are principally concerned about long-term profit maximization, while nonprofit directors and officers, while keeping economic matters in mind, are principally concerned about the effective performance of the nonprofit's mission."[63] In the ensuing discussion of current law, this is a distinction that appears to have been ignored by the courts in adjudicating cases involving breaches of the duty of care as well as of the duty of loyalty, which is discussed in a later section.

---

59. Burden v. Burden, 54 N.E. 17 (N.Y. 1899); A. A. Berle, "Corporate Powers as Powers in Trust," 44 *Harvard Law Review* 1049 (1931); Lawrence E. Mitchell, "Fairness and Trust in Corporate Law," 43 *Duke Law Journal* 425 (1993).

60. Frederic J. Taylor, "A New Chapter in the New York Law of Charitable Corporations," 25 *Cornell Law Quarterly* 382, 398 (1940); Note, "The Modern Philanthropic Foundation: A Critique and a Proposal," 59 *Yale Law Journal* 447, 483 (1950).

61. Murdoch v. Elliot, 58 A. 718 (Conn. 1904); George Pepperdine Foundation v. Pepperdine, 271 P.2d 600 (Cal. Ct. App. 1954).

62. Bogert and Bogert, *Law of Trusts and Trustees*, §395.

63. Harvey J. Goldschmid, "The Fiduciary Duties of Nonprofit Directors and Officers: Paradoxes, Problems, and Proposed Reforms," 23 *Journal of Corporation Law* 631, 639 (1998).

Duty of Care

The standard of care applied to directors of corporations has been described as that degree of care and diligence that ordinary prudent men, prompted by self-interest, would exercise under similar circumstances.[64] There have been other expressions of this standard, but Ballantine explains that the difference is more of words than of actual substance.[65]

The duty of care and diligence is proportionate to the circumstances—in one court's formulation, "What would be slight neglect in the case of a quantity of iron might be gross neglect in the case of a jewel."[66] This rule has been made applicable to all directors, whether or not they receive compensation.

> [O]ne who voluntarily takes the position of director and invites confidence in that relation; undertakes . . . with those whom he represents or for whom he acts, that he possesses at least ordinary knowledge and skill, and that he will bring them to bear in the discharge of his duties . . . It matters not that the service is to be rendered gratuitously.[67]

Thus the standard to be applied by a court when asked to determine whether there has been a breach of the duty of care by a director is not essentially different from that used to determine a similar breach by a trustee. It is a standard that allows a great deal of leeway to the court, based as it is on the facts of the particular situation and the nature of the enterprise. In the cases dealing with commercial enterprises the courts have so applied the standard of care that mere "negligence," which would subject a trustee to liability, is not considered as serious a deficiency in a director.[68]

The standard is generally higher when applied to directors of banks or similar organizations where there is responsibility for the care of personal property of others. This has led some commentators to argue that where charitable funds are involved and the ultimate purposes of directors and trustees are the same, the standards of care should also be the same.[69] The Pennsylvania court discussed this question in *Groome's Estate*,[70] saying that a board of trustees has no attributes of shareholders of a business corpora-

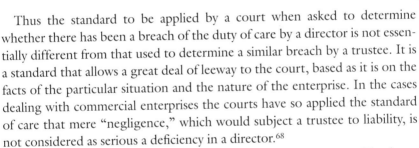

---

64. George D. Hornstein, *Corporation Law and Practice*, §445 (St. Paul: West, 1959).

65. Henry Winthrop Ballantine, *Ballantine on Corporations*, §63 (Chicago: Callaghan, 1946).

66. Hun v. Cary, 82 N.Y. 65, 71 (1880).

67. Id.; see also The Charitable Corporation v. Sutton, 26 Eng. Rep. 642 (1742).

68. Hornstein, *Corporation Law and Practice*, §445; Spiegel v. Beacon Participators, 8 N.E.2d 895 (Mass. 1937).

69. Note, "The Charitable Corporation," 64 *Harvard Law Review* 1168, 1174 (1951).

70. 11 A.2d 271 (Pa. 1940).

tion, but merely the position of trustees to whom the court would apply the standards governing trustees in determining the requirement of a duty of care.

Until the mid-1980s very few states had enacted statutes setting forth the duty of care applicable to directors of nonprofit corporations. According to one survey, as of 1987 only ten states had a statutorily defined standard of conduct.[71] Cases arising prior to the mid-1980s were decided under common law standards of care that were often uncertain or unsettled.[72] The major issue courts faced was whether to apply the standard of care applicable to trustees of charitable trusts or the standard applicable to directors of business corporations.[73] Implicit in this distinction was the question of whether directors of nonprofit corporations would be liable for ordinary negligence as trustees or only upon a showing of gross negligence that is required for directors of business corporations.[74] Much time was spent by courts and scholars debating which standard should be adopted.[75]

In 1974 the Federal District Court for the District of Columbia in the case of *Stern v. Lucy Webb Hayes National Training School for Deaconesses and Missionaries* came down strongly for adoption of the corporate standard to define the duty of care as well as the parallel duty of loyalty.[76] Commonly referred to as the "Sibley Hospital" case, the opinion constituted an unambiguous endorsement of a corporate standard of care. Soon afterward, New York and California adopted statutes containing narrowly defined standards of conduct for directors of nonprofit corporations, and in each case they codified the corporate standard.[77] The Revised Model Nonprofit Corporation Act (RMNCA), promulgated by the American Bar Association in 1987, also adopted the corporate standard.[78]

---

71. Thomas H. Boyd, Note, "A Call to Reform the Duties of Directors under State Not-for-Profit Corporation Statutes," 72 *Iowa Law Review* 725, 735 n.98 (1987).

72. Lizabeth Moody, "State Statutes Governing Directors of Charitable Corporations," 18 *University of San Francisco Law Review* 749, 753 (1984).

73. See, for example, Lynch v. John M. Redfield Foundation, 9 Cal. App. 3d 293, 298 (1970); Beard v. Achenbach Memorial Hospital, 170 F.2d 859, 862 (10th Cir. 1948).

74. Restatement (Second) of Trusts, §174; see also Bennet B. Harvey, Jr., "The Public-Spirited Defendant and Others: Liability of Directors and Officers of Not-for-Profit Corporations," 17 *John Marshall Law Review* 665, 679 (1984).

75. See, for example, Note, "The Fiduciary Duties of Loyalty and Care Associated with the Directors and Trustees of Charitable Organizations," 64 *Virginia Law Review* 449, 454 (1978); Harvey, "Public-Spirited Defendant," 675.

76. 381 F. Supp. 1003 (D.D.C. 1974).

77. Moody, "State Statutes," 762.

78. Revised Model Nonprofit Corporation Act (RMNCA), §8.30 (1987). In contrast, the Model Nonprofit Corporation Act, first promulgated in 1952, was silent on this issue.

The corporate standard of care as set forth in the RMNCA has three components, requiring a director to discharge his duties:

1. in good faith;
2. with the care that an ordinarily prudent person in a like position would exercise under similar circumstances; and
3. in a manner the director reasonably believes to be in the best interests of the corporation.[79]

There is some disagreement over whether the duty of care encompasses all three of these components. Some sources refer to the duties to act in good faith and in the best interests of the corporation as elements of the duty of loyalty. As a practical matter it would make little difference in the event of litigation as suits claiming breach of fiduciary duty invariably use both grounds.[80]

The official comment to section 8.30 of the RMNCA noted that the standard was designed to be broad and basic in order to preserve flexibility, leaving its exact meaning open to court decisions. Subsequent interpretations by courts and scholars have provided some amplification.[81]

The first component of the standard, "good faith," requires honesty of intention, openness, and fair dealing, thus embodying within it the duty of loyalty.[82] In evaluating whether a director acted in good faith, a court will look to the director's state of mind to see if it evidenced honesty and faithfulness to the director's duties and obligations, or whether, on the contrary, there was an intent to take advantage of the corporation.[83]

The "ordinarily prudent person" component mandates that directors of nonprofit corporations balance potential risks and rewards in exercising their decision-making responsibilities.[84] The director is not an insurer of results and is not liable for errors of judgment or mistakes so long as he acts with common sense and informed judgment.[85] Directors must spend enough time on the corporation's affairs to become reasonably acquainted with matters demanding their attention, and at a minimum must attend meetings and review and understand material submitted to the board. When a director has

79. RMNCA, §8.30(a); see also Principles of Corporate Governance, §4.01 (1992).

80. See, for example, RMNCA, §8.30 cmt. pt. 4.

81. RMNCA, §8.30 cmt. pt. 1.

82. Daniel L. Kurtz and Paula B. Green, "Liabilities and Duties of Nonprofit Directors and Officers," in *New York University Sixteenth Conference on Tax Planning for the Charitable Sector,* 11-9 (New York: Matthew Bender, 1988).

83. RMNCA, §8.30 cmt. pt. 5.

84. Id., pt. 2.

85. James J. Fishman, "Standards of Conduct for Directors of Nonprofit Corporations," 7 *Pace Law Review* 389, 399 (1987).

reason to believe a problem exists, the director must make reasonable inquiry into the surrounding facts and circumstances in order to resolve it.[86]

The concept of "like position" in the second component permits flexibility in the application of the standard of care by requiring a court to evaluate a director's conduct in light of the goals and resources of the particular organization that he serves rather than a hypothetical entity. Different goals and resources among nonprofit corporations will affect the calculation by which directors balance potential risks and rewards.[87] "Like position" also requires a court to be cognizant of the differences between nonprofit and for-profit entities in evaluating a director's conduct. For example, directors of nonprofit corporations generally attempt to promote the public good rather than to maximize the value of the corporation. The Massachusetts nonprofit corporation act attempts to address this issue by providing that a director must discharge his duties "with such care as an ordinarily prudent person in a like position with respect to a similar corporation organized under this chapter would use."[88]

The concept of "similar circumstances" in the second component enables a court to be mindful of the background, qualifications, and experience of an individual director and the role he plays in the corporation when measuring his conduct.[89] Although directors are not permitted to act as mere figureheads, a court may consider the reason for their election, such as fundraising skills or marketing experience, in determining whether they have satisfied their duty of care to the corporation.[90]

The concept of "similar circumstances" has been used by some courts to justify holding directors of nonprofit corporations who serve without compensation to a lower standard of care than directors who are compensated.[91] For example, in *George Pepperdine Foundation v. Pepperdine*,[92] the court ruled that holding volunteer directors liable for nonfeasance or neglect would constitute a "gross injustice." However, most courts have rejected this argument and have applied the same standards regardless of whether a director is paid.[93]

The final component of the corporate duty of care requires that a court determine whether the director, in fact, had a subjective belief that he was act-

---

86. RMNCA, §8.30 cmt. pt. 2.
87. Kurtz and Green, "Liabilities and Duties," 11-10.
88. Mass. Gen. Laws. ch. 180, §6C.
89. RMNCA, §8.30 cmt. pt. 2.
90. Id.
91. Kurtz and Green, "Liabilities and Duties," 11-10.
92. 271 P.2d 600, 604 (Cal. Ct. App. 1954).
93. See, for example, In re Neuschwander, 747 P.2d 104 (Kan. 1987); Lynch v. John M. Redfield Foundation, 9 Cal. App. 3d 293, 301 (Ct. App. 1970).

ing in the best interests of the corporation and whether that belief was objectively reasonable.[94]

The American Law Institute's Principles of Corporate Governance contains a description of the minimum duties of the board of directors of a publicly held business corporation. As set forth in section 3.02(a), the board of directors must:

1. Select, regularly evaluate, fix the compensation of, and, where appropriate, replace the principal senior executives;
2. Oversee the conduct of the corporation's business to evaluate whether the business is being properly managed;
3. Review and, where appropriate, approve the corporation's financial objectives and major corporate plans and actions;
4. Review and, where appropriate, approve major changes in, and determinations of other major questions of choice respecting, the appropriate auditing and accounting principles and practices to be used in the preparation of the corporation's financial statements;
5. Perform such other functions as are prescribed by law, or assigned to the board under a standard of the corporation.[95]

While section 3.02(a) was plainly drafted to apply to business corporations, the broad concepts apply equally well to the board of directors of a nonprofit corporation.

Reliance

In all jurisdictions in which the corporate standard of care for nonprofit corporations has been adopted, a director's right to rely on information, reports, and statements prepared by other directors, officers, employees of the corporation, or outside experts in discharging his duties is also recognized.[96] This right is set forth in the RMNCA, section 8.30, as follows:

(b) [I]n discharging his or her duties, a director is entitled to rely on information, opinions, reports, or statements, including financial statements and other financial data, if prepared or presented by:

1. one or more officers or employees of the corporation whom the director reasonably believes to be reliable and competent in the matters presented;
2. legal counsel, public accountants or other persons as to matters the

94. RMNCA, §8.30 cmt. pt. 6.
95. Principles of Corporate Governance, §3.02(a).
96. Id., §4.02 cmt. pt. A.

director reasonably believes are within the person's professional or expert competence;

3. a committee of the board of which the director is not a member, as to matters within its jurisdiction, if the director reasonably believes the committee merits confidence; or

4. in the case of religious corporations, religious authorities and ministers, priests, rabbis or other persons whose position or duties in the religious organization the director believes justify reliance and confidence and whom the director believes to be reliable and competent in the matters presented.

(c) A director is not acting in good faith if the director has knowledge concerning the matter in question that makes reliance otherwise permitted by subsection (b) unwarranted.[97]

Provisions authorizing such reliance, whether created by statute or common law, protect directors who properly rely on other persons and are subsequently sued for breach of the duty of care.[98] A director must "reasonably believe" that the party on whom he is relying for information is competent or merits confidence in order for the director to benefit from the safe harbor of the statute.[99] However, if the director is suspicious or has reason to be suspicious that the party on whom he is relying is not competent, he has a duty to make further inquiry.[100] In addition, if the director has actual knowledge concerning the matter in question that makes reliance unwarranted, the statute will not protect him.[101] Finally, if a director claims reliance on information provided to him by another person, he must in fact have relied on that information.[102]

One aspect of the duty of care that has important ramifications for charities is the manner in which inattention is treated. The Principles of Corporate Governance provides that the business judgment rule (described in a later section) affords protection only if there has been a conscious exercise of judgment. Its examples of situations in which the protection of the rule would not be available are directors who fail to oversee the conduct of the corporation's business by not considering the need for an effective audit process or who received but did not read financial information over a period of time and thus allowed the corporation to be looted. It then notes: "Of course, whether

97. RMNCA, §8.30(b), (c); see also Principles of Corporate Governance, §§4.02, 4.03.
98. Principles of Corporate Governance, §4.02 cmt. pt. C.
99. RMNCA §8.30(b); Principles of Corporate Governance, §§4.02, 4.03.
100. RMNCA, §8.30 cmt. pt. 7.
101. RMNCA, §8.30(c).
102. RMNCA, §8.30 cmt. pt. 7; Principles of Corporate Governance, 4.02 cmt. pt. C.

there has been a conscious decision or inexcusable inattentiveness may, at times, not be readily discernible."[103]

Review of Current Law

In 1987 a survey of state statutes revealed that only ten states had adopted a standard of conduct for nonprofit directors.[104] Since that time, state statutes governing a nonprofit director's duty of care have become the rule rather than the exception. As of January 1, 2003, thirty-seven states had adopted a duty of care provision in their nonprofit corporation acts.[105] Of the fourteen jurisdictions (thirteen states and the District of Columbia) without a duty of care provision in their nonprofit corporation act or without any nonprofit corporation act at all, an additional six states had adopted a duty of care provision in their business corporation acts.[106] In the absence of a provision in the nonprofit corporation statute the court will refer to the business corporation act for guidance.[107] Thus a total of forty-three states have codified the duty of care.

As to the substantive provisions, twenty-five of the forty-three states that have codified the duty of care have adopted the three components of the standard as set forth in RMNCA section 8.30(a), which requires a director to discharge his duties "in good faith; with the care that an ordinarily prudent person in a like position would exercise under similar circumstances; and in a manner the director reasonably believes to be in the best interests of the corporation." An identical standard is set forth in the Model Business Corporation Act, section 8.30(a), and Principles of Corporate Governance, section 4.01(a). The remaining states had adopted a standard of care with one or more material differences. Those states with statutes that differ from the RMNCA can be divided into three categories: (1) states that lack one or more of the three components of the duty of care standard; (2) states that have all three components, but one or more of the components differ materially; and (3) states that lack one or more of the three components, and one or more of the remaining components differ materially.

The "good faith" component of the standard of care as set forth in section 8.30(a) of the RMNCA appears in forty of the forty-three statutes while

---

103. Principles of Corporate Governance, §4.01(c).

104. Boyd, "Call to Reform," 735 n.98.

105. See Appendix, Table 3.

106. Delaware and Kansas are the only states that do not have a nonprofit corporation act.

107. Harvey, "Public-Spirited Defendant," 670; Moody, "State Statutes," 757; Goldschmid, "Fiduciary Duties," 641; see also Louisiana World Exposition v. Federal Ins. Co., 858 F.2d 233 (5th Cir. 1988).

three states do not explicitly require good faith; no state proposes an alternative formulation.

The "ordinarily prudent person" component of the standard of care set forth in section 8.30(a) of the RMNCA appears in thirty-eight of the forty-three statutes. Of these the majority recite the precise formulation of the RMNCA, while the remaining ones differ superficially but are substantively identical. This component of the standard of care is absent from the statutes in four states; only Texas has adopted an alternative standard requiring directors to discharge their duties "with ordinary care." The effect of this language is unclear.

The "best interests" component of the standard of care as set forth in section 8.30(a) of the RMNCA appears in just over half of the forty-three statutes and is absent from the statutes in four states. The remaining statutes differ in one or more ways. Some do not explicitly require a director to have an objectively reasonable belief that his actions are in the best interests of the corporation, with some adopting a more lenient standard that merely requires that the director have a subjective belief that his actions are in the best interests of the corporation or at most requires a showing that the director's belief is honest or in good faith. A few are silent on the issue of whether the director's belief will be evaluated by an objective or a subjective test, while some have adopted a different yet also lenient standard in that they do not impose an affirmative duty on directors to act in the best interests of the corporation. Other variations include a requirement that a director not act "in or not opposed to" the corporation's best interests or that he act "with a view to the interests of the corporation," a vague formulation that also appears to fall short of an affirmative duty to act in the best interests of the corporation.

All of the forty-three states that have adopted a duty of care standard have also adopted a provision recognizing a director's right to rely on information, reports, and statements prepared by other directors, officers, employees of the corporation, or outside experts. In contrast, Delaware, Kansas, and Missouri have codified a reliance provision but lack a statutory duty of care standard.[108]

Only a quarter of the states have adopted the standard for reliance set forth in sections 8.30(b) and (c) of the RMNCA. However, with the exception of clause (d) in the RMNCA, which permits reliance on religious authorities, the majority conform. Of the remaining statutes that do not conform, some differ only in that they do not mandate that the director's belief in the competence of his information source be objectively reasonable. Rather, they adopt a more lenient standard that requires that the director have a subjective

108. See Appendix, Table 3.

belief that his information source is competent or merits confidence. Six states have adopted reliance standards that differ more dramatically. For example, the Delaware business corporation statute provides that a director may rely

> in good faith upon the records of the corporation and upon such information, opinions, reports or statements presented to the corporation by any of the corporation's officers or employees, or committees of the board of directors, or by any other person as to matters the member reasonably believes are within such other person's professional or expert competence and who has been selected with reasonable care by or on behalf of the corporation.[109]

The Business Judgment Rule Limitation on Liability

The business judgment rule is a common law doctrine that has been described as a "judicial gloss" on the corporate duty of care that protects directors from hindsight reviews of their unsuccessful decisions.[110] If a director's decision qualifies as a "business judgment," a court applying the business judgment rule will not evaluate the director's decision under the corporate duty of care standard. Rather, the court will review the decision under a highly deferential standard that requires merely that the director had a rational belief that his decision was in the corporation's best interests. If a decision does not qualify as a business judgment, a court will evaluate the director's decision under the less deferential duty of care standard, which mandates a finding that the director had a reasonable belief that his decision was in the corporation's best interests. There is a sharp distinction between these two standards—rationality review and reasonableness review—and the former permits the director a significantly wider range of discretion.[111]

To qualify as a "business judgment," a director's decision must be made in good faith and without conflict of interest and on a reasonably informed basis.[112] In practice, this definition encompasses most of the decisions a director makes while performing his duties. The party challenging the director's decision sustains the burden of proving that the decision does not meet the criteria for protection under the business judgment rule. For example, the party

---

109. Del. Code Ann. tit. 8, §141(e).

110. Principles of Corporate Governance, §4.01 cmt. pt. D. In the nonprofit context, the business judgment rule is sometimes called the "best judgment rule." See, for example, Fishman, "Standards of Conduct," 400.

111. Principles of Corporate Governance, §4.01 cmt. pt. D.

112. Id., §4.01(c).

challenging the director's decision may show that a decision was not consciously made or that judgment was not, in fact, exercised. Alternatively, the party challenging the director's decision may prove that the director was not acting in good faith or with disinterest or was not reasonably informed. As a final resort, the party challenging the decision may attempt to demonstrate that the director did not actually believe, or did not rationally believe, that his decision was in the best interests of the corporation. As a practical matter, if a director's decision qualifies as a business judgment, it is virtually certain that he will not be found liable for breach of his duty of care to the corporation.[113]

In the nonprofit context, there is some debate whether courts should ever apply the business judgment rule. One commentator argues that application of the business judgment rule in the nonprofit context is overly permissive because the decisions of nonprofit directors are already free from scrutiny due to the absence of shareholders. More searching judicial review of directors' decisions reassures the public that charities are being properly managed and increases confidence in the nonprofit sector.[114] However, this appears to be the minority view, and most commentators argue that application of the business judgment rule to the decisions of nonprofit directors is justified. Thus the official comments to the RMNCA assert that the use of the rule "is consistent" with section 8.30.[115] These commentators point to the similarity of decisions made by nonprofit and for-profit directors and assert that applying the rule encourages nonprofit directors to engage in rational risk-taking and innovation; limits litigation and potential liability that would otherwise discourage people from serving as directors and are unfair to directors serving without compensation; and discourages inappropriate judicial interference in corporate governance.[116]

In practice, there are many examples of courts applying the business judgment rule to the decisions of nonprofit directors. For example, in the case of *John v. John,* decided in 1989, the court held that a director's actions are protected by the business judgment rule unless the plaintiff can show "gross misconduct" and thereby invoke the court's statutory power of removal.[117] In the earlier case of *Beard v. Achenbach Memorial Hospital,*[118] the court applied the business judgment rule to a board of directors' decision to pay bonuses to employees of a nonprofit hospital. Other courts have reached similar re-

113. Id., §4.01 cmt. pt. D.

114. Note, "The Modern Philanthropic Foundation," 464.

115. RMNCA, §8.30 cmt. pt. 3.

116. See, for example, Goldschmid, "Fiduciary Duties," 644–646; Kurtz and Green, "Liabilities and Duties," 11-11.

117. 450 N.W.2d 795, 801–802 (Wis. Ct. App. 1989).

118. 170 F.2d 859, 863 (10th Cir. 1948).

sults.[119] However, in other jurisdictions, including New York, the question whether the business judgment rule applies to the decisions of nonprofit directors is still unsettled.[120] The most recent case to affirm the applicability of the rule to nonprofit corporations was decided by the Minnesota Supreme Court in May 2003 in a case involving the decisions of a special litigation committee.[121]

The Duty of Care as Related to Investments

The Modern Prudent Investor Rule

The prudent man rule is applicable to the investment of funds by a charitable corporation unless there is a specific statute requiring a different standard.[122] In those states that do not follow the prudent man doctrine, but limit investments by trustees to a "legal list," the question of whether the statutory limitations on investments are applicable to charitable corporations is a matter of court interpretation. Scott states that if the statute is not considered applicable, the directors of a charitable corporation will be held to the prudent man rule.[123] For example, the Ohio court held that a cemetery corporation was not limited by the statute regulating investments by trustees but was bound to act with prudence.[124] An oft-cited case for this rule is *Graham Brothers v. Galloway Woman's College*,[125] where, due to the circumstances of the Depression, an investment that would otherwise have been improper was held not to be a violation of the prudent man rule.

The Restatement (Third) of Trusts, in comment b to section 389 on "Investments of Charitable Trusts," states:

> [I]n the absence of contrary statutory provision, or doctrine making general standards of corporation law applicable, funds held for investment by a charitable corporation for its general purposes are to be invested in accordance with the prudent investor rule of section 227. This

119. See, for example, Yarnall Warehouse & Transfer, Inc. v. Three Ivory Bros. Moving Co., 226 So. 2d 887, 890 (Fla. Dist. Ct. App. 1969); Beard v. Achenbach Memorial Hospital, 170 F.2d 859, 862 (10th Cir. 1948).

120. Scheuer Family Foundation v. 61 Associates, 582 N.Y.S.2d 662 (App. Div. 1992); see also ACTS for Children v. Galioto, 2002 WL 31525568 (Cal. Ct. App. 4th Dist. 2002); Summers v. Cherokee Children & Family Services, Inc., 2002 WL 31126636 (Tenn. Ct. App. 2002).

121. Janssen v. Best & Flanagan, 662 N.W.2d 876 (Minn. 2003).

122. Restatement (Second) of Trusts, §389 cmt. b.

123. Scott and Fratcher, *Law of Trusts*, §389.

124. Freeman v. Norwalk Cemetery Association, 100 N.E.2d 267 (Ohio Ct. App. 1950).

125. 81 S.W.2d 837 (Ark. 1935).

is so even in states in which the investment powers of trustees of charitable and private trusts are more restricted, by statute or otherwise, for the restrictions with respect to trustees are not applicable to charitable corporations.

Similarly, the reporter in comment b states that funds donated with a restriction as to the purposes for which they may be used, or that are to be held permanently and only the income to be expended, are not subject to statutory investment restrictions applicable to the investment of charitable or private trusts unless the terms of the transfer provide otherwise.[126]

The equity powers of the court are sufficient to permit a deviation from investment restrictions in a trust under which a charitable corporation was organized, or in the terms of a gift to a charitable corporation, when necessary owing to change of circumstances.[127] There are also some statutes specifically authorizing investment by charitable corporations in common trust funds or permitting collective investments.[128]

The questions of whether separate funds held by a charitable corporation may be mingled in the making of investments and whether the shares of the fund and its income may be allocated according to the various purposes for which they were donated have been a matter of particular interest to universities. The Restatement (Second) of Trusts took the position that such mingling was proper unless otherwise provided by the terms of a gift.[129] This position was reiterated in Restatement (Third), which provides that a charitable corporation may commingle separately contributed funds in making investments, allocating shares of the commingled fund and applying its income to the various purposes specified by the donors.[130]

The Uniform Management of Institutional Funds Act (UMIFA)

Many charitable corporations, particularly colleges and universities, museums, and hospitals, receive funds donated on condition that the principal be permanently invested and only the income may be expended by the corporation for its general purposes or for one or more of its specific purposes. The legal term used to describe such funds is "endowment," and they have been characterized as quasi-trust funds, carrying thereby the implication that a charitable corporation has duties with respect to them not applicable to

126. Restatement (Third) of Trusts, §389 cmt. b.
127. John A. Creighton Home for Girls' Trust v. Waltman, 299 N.W. 261 (Neb. 1941).
128. See, for example, Cal. Corp. Code §10250; Pa. Stat. Ann. tit. 15, §5548.
129. Restatement (Second) of Trusts, §389.
130. Restatement (Third) of Trusts, §389 cmt. b.

funds held for their general purposes without restriction as to the use of principal. During the late 1960s, the yield on common stocks dropped, and investors began to look primarily to appreciation in the value of capital rather than dividends for current funds. Concerned that this approach to investment and expenditure was not available to charitable corporations holding endowment funds, the Ford Foundation commissioned a study of corporate law principles relating to the use of capital appreciation. The result was a study entitled *The Law and the Lore of Endowment Funds*, which concluded that corporate law principles should be applied to the investment of endowment funds, thereby permitting expenditure of appreciation on assets.[131] It concluded with a recommendation that the states adopt legislation specifically permitting the use of realized and unrealized appreciation of endowment assets. This concept was embodied in the Uniform Management of Institutional Funds Act (UMIFA), adopted by the Commissioners on Uniform State Laws in 1972. It is now in effect in forty-eight states.[132]

UMIFA was made applicable to a newly defined category of charitable entity, denominated an "institution," which it defined as an incorporated or unincorporated organization designed and operated exclusively for educational, religious, charitable, or other eleemosynary purposes, or a governmental organization to the extent that it holds funds exclusively for any of these purposes.[133] It also defined an "institutional fund" as a fund held by an institution for its exclusive use, benefit, or purposes other than a trust for the benefit of an institution or a fund in which there is a noncharitable beneficiary.[134] UMIFA also identified an "endowment fund" as an institutional fund, or any part thereof, not wholly expendable by the institution on a current basis under the terms of the applicable gift instrument.[135]

A principal feature of UMIFA is a provision permitting the governing board of an institution to use for the purposes for which the fund was established that portion of the net appreciation, realized and unrealized, in the value of the assets over the historic dollar value of the fund as is prudent as determined by the governing board in accordance with a standard of conduct set forth in the act.[136] This standard is, in effect, a prudent business investor standard, calling for boards to "exercise ordinary business care and prudence

---

131. William L. Cary and Craig B. Bright, *The Law and the Lore of Endowment Funds* (New York: Ford Foundation, 1969) (report to the Ford Foundation); William L. Cary and Craig B. Bright, "The 'Income' from Endowment Funds," 69 *Columbia Law Review* 396 (1969).

132. See Appendix, Table 1, Column 17.

133. Uniform Management of Institutional Funds Act, §1(1) (1972).

134. Id., §1(2).

135. Id., §1(3).

136. Id., §2.

under the facts prevailing at the time of the action or decision."[137] In so doing they are directed to "consider long and short term needs of the institution in carrying out its . . . purposes, its present and anticipated financial requirements, expected total return on its investments, price level trends, and general economic conditions."[138]

In addition to reciting this standard of conduct, UMIFA authorizes the governing board to invest an institutional fund in any real or personal property deemed advisable whether or not it produces a current return, to retain contributed property so long as the governing board deems it advisable, and to co-mingle the fund in any pooled fund maintained by the institution or any other pooled investment vehicle.[139]

UMIFA preceded the Uniform Prudent Investor Act by more than twenty-one years, and because UMIFA's standards for investment differed from those applicable to an institution's other funds, it has been a source of confusion and uncertainty. This situation was further confounded for corporations categorized under the provisions of the Internal Revenue Code as private foundations, which under the terms of the Tax Reform Act of 1969 became subject to the provisions in section 4944 of the Code prohibiting the making of "jeopardy investments."

The provisions in UMIFA permitting use of unrealized appreciation were drafted at a time of dramatic growth in value of assets. They do not deal with the question of whether there is a duty to retain funds in the event that the value of the portfolio falls below its historic value. Implying such a duty would seem an inappropriate application of the statute. The Massachusetts version of UMIFA did modify the wording of the act by adding a provision authorizing fiduciaries to accumulate income in an amount that was reasonable if in the circumstances it appeared prudent to do so.[140]

In 2000 the Commissioners constituted a study committee to determine whether and to what extent changes should be made in UMIFA. The committee solicited views from the endowment world and the Joint Editorial Board for the Uniform Trust and Estate Acts, and made the following recommendations for amendments of UMIFA: conforming the investment provisions with those of the Uniform Prudent Investors Act; updating the cy pres regime to conform to the provisions in the Uniform Trust Act; resolving the tension between the provisions in UMIFA and the Uniform Trust Act relating to the power of a donor to enforce the terms of a gift; clarifying the definitions of "institution" and "institutional fund," which have caused dif-

---

137. Id., §6.
138. Id.
139. Id., §4.
140. Mass. Gen. Laws. ch. 180A, §4.

ficulties in the courts; and clarifying the definition of "appreciation" to remove a divergence between the term as used in the act and that of the accounting profession.[141] With the exception of a provision granting donor standing to enforce restrictions on institutional funds, these recommendations were accepted by the Commissioners at their August 2003 meeting; final approval would require an affirmative vote at the 2004 meeting.

Fiduciary Duties of Corporate Directors: Loyalty (Fair Dealing)

Duty of Loyalty (Fair Dealing)

Traditionally, directors of corporations were subject to a duty of loyalty analogous to that imposed on trustees. They "must subordinate their individual and private interests to their duty to the corporation whenever the two conflict."[142] In the earlier cases the trust prohibition against self-dealing was affirmatively applied to directors of business corporations simply on the ground that they were fiduciaries.[143] This remains the English rule.[144] In the United States, however, the absolute ban on dealings by a director of a business enterprise with his corporation has been relaxed, and the standard applied by the courts is described as a "fairness test," or to use the appellation adopted in the American Law Institute's Principles of Corporate Governance[145] and recent statutes, the "duty of fair dealing." It permits a director to deal with his corporation if a disinterested majority of the board approves the transaction and the contract itself is fair.[146] If the director participates in the vote, the transaction would be voidable by the corporation regardless of fairness, or at the least the burden will be on the directors to show the fairness of the transaction. If the vote was obtained through fraud or the transaction was unfair, the transaction is void.[147]

The most commonly cited early case applying the fairness test to a charitable corporation in the absence of a statute specifically reciting it was *Kenney Presbyterian Home v. State*.[148] In this case two members of the board of trust-

141. Uniform Management of Institutional Funds Act, §8 (Draft, August 2002); see also Memorandum from Susan Gary, Reporter to UMIFA Drafting Committee (October 20, 2002).

142. Winter v. Anderson, 275 N.Y.S. 373 (App. Div. 1934).

143. In re Taylor Orphan Asylum, 36 Wis. 534 (1875); State v. Ausmus, 35 S.W. 1021 (Tenn. Ct. Ch. App. 1895).

144. The Charitable Corporation v. Sutton, 26 Eng. Rep. 642 (1742).

145. Principles of Corporate Governance, §5.

146. Note, "The Fairness Test of Corporation Contracts with Interested Directors," 61 *Harvard Law Review* 335 (1948); Ballantine, *Ballantine on Corporations*, §67.

147. Ballantine, *Ballantine on Corporations*, §68.

148. 24 P.2d 403 (Wash. 1933).

ees of a charitable corporation formed to administer a trust dealt with the corporation, one by selling mortgages and the other by selling fire insurance to the corporation. The court found that the corporation was not subject to any additional expense because of the transactions, that the other directors had passed on the transactions, that there was no evidence of negligence or carelessness, and no loss. The directors were permitted to retain their commissions from both transactions. The court relied on the language of an earlier Washington case, which held that when a trustee performs services of a nature properly chargeable as current expenses, there is no reason not to pay.[149]

In the case of *Gilbert v. McLeod Infirmary*,[150] two members of a charitable corporation successfully brought suit against the corporation and the chairman of the board to have a conveyance of a part of the corporation's property to the chairman declared void. The court held that although there was no evidence of fraud or fraudulent intent, the conduct of the director was not up to the high standard required of the fiduciary relationship. It based its decision entirely on corporate law, although it cited the rule that a director stands in a fiduciary relationship to the corporation. The outcome in this case, therefore, although based on corporate law, would not have been different had trust standards been applied.

There were a few other cases decided in the 1950s and 1960s in which the court discussed the duties of directors solely in terms of trustee standards. Thus in *Eurich v. Korean Foundation*,[151] the Illinois Supreme Court ordered the dissolution of a charitable corporation in order to prevent "illegal and oppressive" acts by the president, who had attempted to handpick a board that would allow him to invest the corporate funds in his own property in violation of the duty of a trustee to refrain from self-dealings. In *Voelker v. St. Louis Mercantile Library Association*,[152] the Missouri court, dismissing a suit brought by members of a library who charged breach of trust, stated that the defendant was a public charitable corporation, which for the purposes of the suit would be considered subject to the principles applicable to a charitable trust.

Critics of these holdings argued that they created conditions detrimental to the efficient operations of nonprofit organizations and did not reflect the trends in the law relaxing standards of behavior for corporate directors. The 1974 "Sibley Hospital" case, noted above in regard to the duty of care, also involved charges that the directors had breached their duty of loyalty by

149. Id. at 418 (citing In re Cornett's Estate, 173 P. 44 (Wash. 1918)).
150. 64 S.E.2d 524 (S.C. 1951).
151. 176 N.E.2d 692 (Ill. App. Ct. 1961).
152. 359 S.W.2d 689 (Mo. 1962).

knowingly permitting the hospital to enter into frequent business transactions with corporations in which they had a financial interest, without disclosure to the board of those private interests.[153] In addition, certain directors had actively participated in and voted in favor of board and committee decisions to transact business with entities in which they had private interests, principally the banks and other institutions that handled the hospital's financial affairs. After reviewing both the trust and corporate standards for loyalty, the court adopted the corporate standard for the duty of loyalty.

Under the strict standards of fiduciary duty, directors are prohibited from engaging in transactions in which a conflict of interest could arise from their intimate knowledge of the corporation's affairs or from their position as director of the corporation. This ban has been likened to the rule that a trustee may not profit from any transaction arising from his relationship to the trust. The rule was applied by the Wisconsin court in a suit by a nonprofit corporation against a trustee who was charged with causing the corporation to engage in numerous buying and selling transactions through a corporation of which he was the president and majority stockholder. The court required the defendant to return to the corporation the sum he received personally as a commission on one particular transaction that plaintiff was able to prove. It refused, however, to charge defendant for any additional amounts merely because he was a majority stockholder and officer without proof of personal profit to him or loss to the corporation.[154]

Another specific form of self-dealing, the misappropriation of corporate opportunities, even when not the subject of specific statutory prohibitions, is considered by many courts to be a breach of the duty of loyalty. Thus, if a nonprofit director becomes aware of an opportunity that could be advantageous to the corporation he serves, the duty of loyalty requires that he disclose and offer the opportunity to the corporation before he takes it for himself. If the opportunity is rejected by the corporation after deliberation by the disinterested directors, only then may the director pursue it personally.[155]

Exactly which opportunities are subject to this common law rule is an unsettled question. In the for-profit context, some courts have applied the doctrine narrowly to opportunities in which the corporation has an already-existing interest or an expectancy growing out of an existing right.[156] Other courts have employed a broader "line of business" test, which states that a director must offer opportunities to the corporation that are sufficiently closely

153. 381 F. Supp. 1003 (D.D.C. 1974).

154. Old Settlers Club of Milwaukee County, Inc. v. Haun, 13 N.W.2d 913 (Wis. 1944).

155. Principles of Corporate Governance, §5.05.

156. See, for example, Lagarde v. Anniston Lime & Stone, Inc., 28 So. 199 (Ala. 1900).

related to its existing activities.[157] Finally, some courts have applied a fairness test that requires the court to evaluate the facts and circumstances surrounding the opportunity to determine whether it would be fair to require the director to make it available to the corporation.[158]

In the few cases arising in the nonprofit context, courts have applied various tests to determine whether the doctrine of corporate opportunity applies. For example, in *Valle v. North Jersey Automobile Club,* the court held that the doctrine applies to opportunities that a corporation is financially able to undertake, are in the corporation's line of business, and in which the corporation has an interest or reasonable expectancy.[159] And in *Mile-O-Mo Fishing Club v. Noble,* a director was held liable for purchasing certain real estate without ascertaining that the corporation he served had no desire or intent to acquire it.[160]

Statutory Formulations of the Duty of Fair Dealing

Until the mid-1980s very few states had codified procedures for validating conflict of interest transactions between interested directors and nonprofit corporations. According to one survey, as of 1986 only twelve states had statutes setting forth such procedures.[161] As of January 1, 2003, however, thirty-six states had adopted a duty of loyalty provision in their nonprofit corporation acts. Of the remaining fourteen states, as well as the District of Columbia, that had no statute governing the duty of loyalty in their nonprofit corporation act or that had no nonprofit corporation act, an additional twelve states had adopted a duty of loyalty provision in their business corporation acts.[162] These business corporation provisions are relevant as precedent in instances in which there is no statute applicable to nonprofit corporations.[163] Thus, as of January 2003, forty-eight states had codified the duty of loyalty in some form.[164] Four of these states follow the provisions in the Revised Model Nonprofit Corporation Act.[165]

157. See, for example, Guft v. Loft, Inc., 5 A.2d 503, 511 (Del. 1939).

158. Principles of Corporate Governance, §5.05.

159. 359 A.2d 504, 507 (N.J. Super. Ct. App. Div. 1976).

160. 210 N.E.2d 12 (Ill. App. Ct. 1965); see also Northeast Harbor Golf Club v. Harris, 661 A.2d 1146 (Me. 1995).

161. Fishman, "Standards of Conduct," 442 n.232.

162. See Appendix, Table 3.

163. See, for example, Oberly v. Kirby, 592 A.2d 445, 467 (Del. 1991) (applying Del. Code Ann. tit. 8, §144, to nonprofit corporation).

164. The District of Columbia, Massachusetts, and South Dakota are the only jurisdictions that have not codified the duty of loyalty.

165. RMNCA, §8.31. Montana, Nebraska, South Carolina, and Vermont have adopted this standard. See Appendix, Table 3.

Definitions of Conflicts of Interest

There are few statutes that use the terms "duty of loyalty" or "duty of fair dealing"; rather, the statutes refer to and limit dealings that involve a "conflict of interest." Thus the RMNCA provides in section 8.31(a), "A conflict of interest transaction is a transaction with the corporation in which a director of the corporation has a direct or indirect interest." Twenty-six states have similar definitions, while the statutes in Arizona, Connecticut, and Georgia apply to all transactions between a director and the nonprofit corporation or any subsidiary controlled by it.[166] The California Corporation Code applicable to public benefit corporations specifically excepts action fixing compensation of a director, as well as a transaction that is part of a public or charitable program of the corporation or a transaction of which the interested director or directors have no actual knowledge and that does not exceed the lesser of one percent of the gross receipts of the corporation for the preceding fiscal year or one hundred thousand dollars.[167]

Procedures for Validating Conflicts

The state statutes that govern the duty of loyalty set forth multiple procedures by which a conflict of interest transaction may be "validated." And, once validated, under the statutes in all forty-eight states that have codified the duty of loyalty and the RMNCA, the transaction is not voidable by the corporation. In addition, eighteen states and the RMNCA provide that upon validation the director may not be held liable to the corporation for damages resulting from the conflict of interest transaction.[168] In the thirty states that have not enacted such a provision, a director may be held liable to the corporation for damages even after validation.

A typical duty of loyalty provision contains at least three procedures for validating conflict of interest transactions between interested directors and the nonprofit corporations they serve. All of the state statutes prohibiting self-dealing and the RMNCA provide for validation by vote of the board of directors after disclosure of the interested director's conflict. Where validation by prior board approval is impossible, forty-five of the forty-eight states, as does the RMNCA, permit subsequent validation if the transaction was fair to the corporation as determined by a court.[169] In addition, the statutes in nine states and the comparable provision in the RMNCA provide for validation upon prior approval by the state attorney general or a court. Two states, Cali-

166. See Appendix, Table 3.
167. Cal. Corp. Code §5233.
168. RMNCA, §8.31.
169. Only Arkansas, California, and Kentucky lack such a procedure.

fornia and Nevada, provide for validation if the interested director was unaware of his conflict of interest when the transaction was approved, with California requiring that the amount of money involved in the transaction be de minimus. The third procedure for validating conflicts applies only to corporations that have members and permits approval by a vote of the disinterested members. In a majority of the states, the nonprofit corporation acts permit charities to be incorporated without members, which is the more common pattern of organization. This has meant that one method of validation is not available to the majority of charities.

Validation by Board Approval

VOTING AND QUORUM REQUIREMENTS. The specific requirements for validation by vote of the board of directors after disclosure vary from state to state. The statutes in thirty-five states and the RMNCA require that a transaction be approved by majority vote of the disinterested directors, with approximately half of these and the RMNCA providing that the majority of disinterested directors must constitute at least two votes.[170] Arizona has adopted the strict requirement that the majority of disinterested directors must constitute at least a majority of the entire board. In all but two of the thirty-five states and in the RMNCA quorum requirements are waived for the purpose of validation. In the remaining two states, Minnesota and North Dakota, a quorum is required for the vote of approval, and interested directors may not be counted towards it. The effect of this quorum requirement is to make it impossible to validate conflict of interest transactions by board approval where interested directors constitute more than a majority of the entire board. Half of the states require that a transaction be approved by "sufficient" vote of the board of directors, presumably as defined by the nonprofit corporation's by-laws. All of these states require a quorum to be present for the vote of approval, but interested directors may be counted towards it. Nearly all of them do not permit the votes of interested directors to count towards the actual vote while the remaining states permit the votes of interested directors to be counted.

REQUIREMENT OF FAIRNESS TO THE CORPORATION. Of the thirty-five states in which a conflict must be approved by a majority vote of the disinterested directors, five also mandate that the disinterested directors' approval must have been given in good faith.[171] Seven of them and the

170. RMNCA, §8.31.
171. Id.

RMNCA further require that the disinterested directors in good faith reasonably believed that the transaction was "fair," "not unfair," or "justified by the material facts."

Two of the states that require that a transaction be approved by "sufficient vote of the directors" and permit "interested directors to be part of the quorum" also require that the directors approve the transaction in good faith. One state also requires the board to ascertain that the corporation entered into the transaction for its own benefit and that the corporation could not have obtained a better deal elsewhere with reasonable effort. Two states, California and Alaska, have adopted a stricter rule, requiring that even after board approval the interested director must bear the burden of proving that the transaction was fair.

DISCLOSURE REQUIREMENTS.   There are two types of disclosure that a director will be required to make to avoid violation of his duty of loyalty—disclosure of facts regarding the director's interest in the transaction and disclosure of facts regarding the transaction itself.[172] Disclosure of facts regarding the director's interest would require, for example, that a director inform the board that he owns a 25% interest in real estate that the corporation is negotiating to purchase. All forty-eight states that provide for validation by vote of the board of directors require such disclosure. Disclosure of facts regarding the transaction itself would entail, for example, requiring that the director inform the board of rumors that the city may condemn the real estate to build a highway. This type of disclosure is required in thirty-eight states.

Disclosures of either type are typically limited to material facts. A fact is material if there is "a substantial likelihood that a reasonable person would consider it important under the circumstances in determining his course of action."[173]

RELIEF FROM LIABILITY.   As noted above, in thirty of the forty-eight states that have codified the duty of loyalty, it is provided by statute that a director may be held liable to the corporation for damages resulting from a conflict of interest transaction even though the transaction was properly disclosed, received board approval, and was believed by the noninterested directors to be fair if in fact it did not meet the standard of fairness. However, strict application of such a rule can be greatly relaxed by the courts through adoption of the business judgment rule under which, if a director exercised sound business judgment in entering into the transaction, he will not be held

---

172. Principles of Corporate Governance, §1.14; RMNCA, §8.31.
173. Principles of Corporate Governance, §1.14 cmt.; RMNCA, §8.31 cmt. pt. 4.

to have violated his duty of loyalty. Application of such a rule will almost invariably provide protection to an interested director, for it must be shown that the director did not rationally believe that the transaction was in the best interest of the corporation, a burden that is placed on the person challenging the transaction.[174]

Some courts impose a stricter requirement than the business judgment rule and, in the case of New York, the Appellate Division on one occasion rejected reliance on the business judgment rule, adopting instead a rule requiring close scrutiny of any self-dealing transaction. The court refused to rule, as requested by the plaintiffs, that the business judgment rule would never apply to a nonprofit corporation, leaving open the question as to whether it would be relied on if the disinterest of a majority of the directors was not in question.[175] Following the common law standards, these courts will require a director to sustain the burden of proving that the transaction in which he has an interest was inherently fair to the corporation.[176]

The Court of Appeals of Tennessee in a 2002 decision refused to apply the business judgment rule in a case in which the attorney general sought dissolution of two charitable corporations on the grounds that they had abandoned their charitable purposes and devoted themselves to private purposes.[177] The defendants had sought the protection of the business judgment rule, but the court ruled that, although it was generally applicable to nonprofit corporations, it was not a defense to dissolution for misapplication of corporate assets by operating for private gain, actions that it held to be violations of the duty of loyalty. The court stated, "While the business judgment rule reflects a judicial policy of declining to substitute a court's judgment for that of a corporation's directors when they have acted in good faith and in the exercise of honest judgment . . . that policy has no application to allegations that a public benefit corporation has abandoned any charitable purpose and has pursued private, rather than public, interests."[178]

A third group of courts have adopted a middle ground between the extremes of the business judgment and the inherent fairness rules. This intermediate standard was first explicated in *Oberly v. Kirby*,[179] where the Dela-

---

174. Deborah A. DeMott, "Self-Dealing Transactions in Nonprofit Corporations," 1993 *Brooklyn Law Review* 131, 134 (1993); Goldschmid, "Fiduciary Duties," 639; Kurtz and Green, "Liabilities and Duties," 11-9.

175. Scheuer Family Foundation v. 61 Associates, 582 N.Y.S.2d 662 (App. Div. 1992).

176. In effect, this is the rule adopted by Cal. Corp. Code §5233.

177. Summers v. Cherokee Children & Family Services, Inc., 2002 WL 31126636 (Tenn. Ct. App. 2002).

178. Id. at *32.

179. 592 A.2d 445, 469 (Del. 1991).

ware Supreme Court undertook to assess validated conflict of interest transactions under an intermediate standard of review—more searching than rationality review under the business judgment rule but less demanding than fairness review. The court also indicated that the party challenging the transaction would bear the burden of proof. The *Oberly* court's treatment of the effect of validation is similar to the recommendation of section 5.02 of the Principles of Corporate Governance. This section provides that the person challenging a validated conflict of interest transaction has the burden of proving that the terms of the transaction are "so clearly outside the range of reasonableness" that the disinterested directors who approved it could not reasonably have concluded that the transaction was fair to the corporation.[180]

Validation by Outside Authorities

There are some situations in which it will not be possible to validate an interested transaction because, for example, there are not enough disinterested directors to meet the voting requirements described above. In such cases a second procedure is available in forty-five of the forty-eight states and the RMNCA under which a court may validate the transaction if it finds that it is fair to the corporation.[181] The standard for determining fairness varies, however. In two-thirds of the statutes, the court must find that it was "fair"; in others the statute requires a finding that it was "fair and reasonable"; and one state requires the transaction to be "not unfair." The extent to which there are substantive differences among these standards is unclear. In two-thirds of the forty-five states, the time for determining the fairness of the transaction to the corporation is the time it was approved by the board of directors. In the remaining states, the statute is silent on the issue of when fairness should be evaluated.

The statutes in almost all of the forty-five states expressly require that the interested director bear the burden of proving fairness. In contrast, one state places the burden on the party challenging the transaction to prove by clear and convincing evidence that the transaction was unfair. In the majority of states in which there is no statutory provision, the courts have interpreted these statutes as placing the burden of proof on the interested director.

In determining the fairness of a conflict of interest transaction, a court must assess whether, under all the circumstances, the transaction carries "the earmarks of an arm's length bargain."[182] This analysis entails evaluating both

---

180. Principles of Corporate Governance, §5.02(a)(2)(B) cmt.
181. See Appendix, Table 3.
182. Pepper v. Litton, 308 U.S. 295, 306 (1939).

the procedural and substantive fairness of the transaction. This concept is sometimes referred to as "entire fairness," "inherent fairness," or "intrinsic fairness."[183]

PROCEDURAL FAIRNESS. Procedural fairness relates to the process by which a transaction was approved by the board. Procedural inquiries include:

> [W]hether corporate procedures for interested transactions have been established and whether they were followed in the particular transaction; whether the board environment was impartial and objective at the time the decision was made; whether the information relating to the transaction was fully disclosed by the interested director to the relevant decision-makers; and whether the interest of the director was disclosed to the relevant decision-makers.[184]

A director's failure to disclose a conflict of interest to the corporation is often sufficient grounds for a court to rule that a transaction was not procedurally fair. For example, in *Boston Children's Heart Foundation v. Nadal-Ginard*,[185] the defendant director failed to disclose to the corporation's board of directors material information relevant to the decision to set his compensation. As a result of this failure to disclose, the court held that the defendant director was liable to the corporation for the full amount of salary paid to him even though the salary was fair and reasonable. A similar result was reached in *Marist College v. Nicklin*,[186] where the court found a director liable for failing to disclose that his employer had a brokerage relationship with the investment advisor whom he recommended that the college employ.

Procedural fairness may also be achieved by having the board appoint an independent negotiator to represent the corporation in negotiating the transaction with the interested parties.[187] For example, in *Oberly* the court approved of the hiring of the nonprofit corporation's attorney to fill such a role. The independent negotiator must be instructed to seek out the best deal for the corporation, and the board of directors cannot impose preconceived notions of what the outcome of the negotiations should be. Absent special circumstances, seeking the best deal for the corporation should include the power to survey the market and consider transactions with other parties.[188]

---

183. Principles of Corporate Governance, §5.02(a)(2)(A) cmt.
184. Fishman, "Standards of Conduct," 424.
185. 73 F.3d 429 (1st Cir. 1996).
186. 1995 WL 241710 (Tex. App. 1995).
187. Principles of Corporate Governance, §5.02(a)(2)(A) cmt.
188. 592 A.2d at 455.

SUBSTANTIVE FAIRNESS. The requirement of substantive fairness pertains to the fairness of the consideration that the corporation receives in the transaction. The consideration must be at least that which an unrelated third party would have demanded in an arm's-length transaction.[189] While not required, in large or complex transactions a court will look favorably upon directors who seek a fairness opinion from a qualified outside appraiser such as an investment bank.[190] In addition to the fairness of the consideration, substantive fairness also requires the court to determine that the transaction was in the nonprofit corporation's best interests.[191] For example, a court may determine that real estate was purchased by a corporation from a director at a fair price, but that the purchase did not serve any corporate purpose.

Statutory Protection without Validation

Since the 1980s the standards under which directors may be held liable for breach of the duty of loyalty have been relaxed with the enactment of statutes explicitly limiting a director's liability even in situations in which the transaction was not validated. In addition, statutes authorizing indemnification and the purchase of directors and officers liability insurance have greatly increased the likelihood that nonprofit directors will not incur liability except in the most egregious circumstances. These statutes are described below.

Duty to "Mission" and the Cy Pres Doctrine

Kurtz has argued that there is a modern-day duty imposed on charitable fiduciaries in addition to those of loyalty and care.[192] He characterizes it as a duty of obedience, arguing that a trustee is under a duty to carry out the terms of the trust—and thus has a duty of obedience to the purpose specified by the donors. However, the duty of loyalty of the trustee of a private trust is to the beneficiaries, both those entitled to the current income as well as the remaindermen, and this translates into a duty of impartiality between them. With a charitable trust that is to last into perpetuity, the duty is to present and future beneficiaries. Implicit in this formulation is a duty to assure that the purposes of the trust can be and are being carried out effectively, so that if changed circumstances mean that the purposes are no longer capable of being fulfilled, or have become obsolete or impractical to carry out, the duty of

189. Principles of Corporate Governance, §5.02(a)(2)(A) cmt.
190. *Oberly,* 592 A.2d at 472.
191. Principles of Corporate Governance, §5.02(a)(2)(A) cmt.
192. Daniel L. Kurtz, *Board Liability: A Guide for Nonprofit Directors,* 84–85 (Mt. Kisco, N.Y.: Moyer Bell Ltd., 1989).

loyalty of the trustees to the ultimate beneficiaries encompasses a duty to seek deviation or cy pres application of the funds so that they may continue to be applied for public benefit. This duty is imposed on fiduciaries of charities in England.[193] To the extent the duty of obedience does not carry with it a duty to assure that the trust is meeting contemporaneous needs, it does not set forth an appropriate standard.

Prohibition against Loans to Directors

Loans to directors have been considered to be a particularly egregious instance of self-dealing, sufficiently so that such a transaction is regulated under a separate statute in thirty-seven states. Of these thirty-seven statutes, twenty-eight and the provisions of the RMNCA absolutely prohibit such loans.[194] In the remaining states loans by the corporation to its directors are permitted in a variety of circumstances. Among them are loans in the "usual course of the corporation's affairs"; ones that may be "reasonably expected to benefit the corporation"; and loans to finance a director's residence.

Statutory Relief from Liability

Codification of the Business Judgment Rule

In many states the business judgment rule has essentially been codified by adoption of statutes that provide that a director is not liable to the corporation for breach of his fiduciary duties unless his actions constitute bad faith, self-dealing, or gross negligence.[195] As of January 1, 2003, a total of thirty-one states had adopted statutes containing provisions of this nature, although sixteen of the statutes apply only if the director serves without compensation. One state limits application of the statute to directors who earn less than $5,000 per year for their services, and two states mandate that the nonprofit corporation carry general liability insurance.[196] The RMNCA does not contain a similar provision.

Although the specific requirements of these statutes vary considerably from state to state, a director's limited liability is generally subject to exceptions that fall under one of three broad categories—bad faith, gross negligence,

193. See Chapter 2.

194. RMNCA, §8.32.

195. Kurtz and Green, "Liabilities and Duties," 11-11. Such statutes are not to be confused with statutes that only protect directors from liability resulting from suits brought by third parties. See, for example, Cal. Corp. Code §5047.

196. See Appendix, Table 3.

and self-dealing.[197] These categories closely parallel the criteria for application of the business judgment rule. Of the states with statutes limiting a director's liability, nearly all have adopted an exception for actions that fall under the category of bad faith. This category includes stated exceptions for "willful and wanton misconduct"; "bad faith"; "knowing violation of the law"; "fraud"; "malice"; "intentional misconduct"; and other similar formulations.

Approximately one-half of these statutes do not offer protection in cases of "gross negligence" and "recklessness." A few except self-dealing, including "improper personal benefit" and "breach of the duty of loyalty." These statutes also contain a myriad of other acts that are not protected. Some statutes do not protect a director for conduct outside the scope of his duties; others exclude liability arising from the operation of a motor vehicle; other exclusions include criminal acts, unlawful distributions, and loans to directors.

Some states have gone even further in limiting a nonprofit director's liability. As of January 2003, nineteen states had adopted statutes that permit a director's liability for breach of the duty of care to be limited or entirely eliminated by a provision in the nonprofit corporation's articles of incorporation or by-laws.[198] None of these statutes extend protection to conduct that falls under the categories of bad faith or self-dealing. The category of bad faith includes "knowing violation of the law"; "bad faith"; "intentional misconduct"; and other similar formulations. The category of self-dealing includes "improper personal benefit"; "breach of the duty of loyalty"; "conflict of interest transactions"; and other similar formulations. However, only two states exempt from protection conduct that constitutes gross negligence. Thus, under the vast majority of these statutes, a director may be completely immunized from liability for actions that demonstrate "a manifestly smaller amount of watchfulness and circumspection than the circumstances require of a person of ordinary prudence."[199] An alternate provision in the RMNCA permits a corporation in its by-laws to eliminate or cap the personal liability of directors to the corporation and its members for breaches of the duty of loyalty or bad faith acts or omissions.[200]

Indemnification, Insurance, and Liability Shields

Thirty-one states have enacted statutes giving a nonprofit corporation the option of indemnifying a director who is sued by or on behalf of the corpora-

197. Some states' statutes contain multiple exceptions under one category.

198. See Appendix, Table 3. RMNCA §2.02(b)(5) is an alternative provision authorizing such limitations on liability.

199. *Black's Law Dictionary*, 1033 (6th ed. 1990).

200. RMNCA, §2.02(b)(5) (alternative provision).

tion for breach of his duty of care.[201] Twenty-two of the states plus the RMNCA limit indemnification to attorney's fees and court costs the director incurs in defending himself, although the California statute requires approval by the attorney general before indemnification for expenses incurred in settling a threatened or pending action. Nearly half of these states also allow the corporation to indemnify the director against amounts he pays to settle a suit. A few permit the corporation to indemnify the director against judgments and fines. All of the statutes and the RMNCA make indemnification against attorney's fees and court costs mandatory if the director successfully defends against the suit and is found not liable by a court.

Statutes authorizing optional indemnification are fairly uniform in the requirements they impose for eligibility. Almost all of them and the RMNCA prohibit indemnification without court approval if the director has been adjudged liable to the corporation for breach of his fiduciary duties, and all of them and the RMNCA permit indemnification only if the director acted in good faith. A little more than half of these and the RMNCA require a showing that the director reasonably believed that his actions were in the best interests of the corporation. The remaining states have an even more lenient requirement, namely, that the director reasonably believed his actions were "in or not opposed to" the corporation's best interests. One state permits indemnification only if the director acted with the care an ordinarily prudent person in a like position would exercise under similar circumstances.

The statutes in three states mandate indemnification, with two of these requiring that the indemnification extend to attorney's fees, court costs, amounts paid to settle a suit, judgments, and fines if the director acted in good faith, in a manner he reasonably believed to be in the best interests of the corporation, and did not receive an improper personal benefit. The remaining state provides that a nonprofit corporation must indemnify a director against attorney's fees, court costs, amounts paid to settle a suit, judgments, and fines unless his breach of the duty of care constituted willful misconduct or he received an improper personal benefit.

In states that do not expressly authorize indemnification by statute, directors may be entitled to indemnification under common law. However, in the majority of states the extent to which indemnification is permitted under common law is uncertain and depends on the "somewhat bizarre application of the principles of charitable trusts, agency, or contracts."[202] At least one court has held that there is no common law right to indemnification.[203]

---

201. See Appendix, Table 3.
202. RMNCA, §8.50 introductory cmt. pt. 1.
203. Texas Society v. Fort Bend Chapter, 590 S.W.2d 156 (Tex. Civ. App. 1979).

Directors who do not meet the statutory criteria of eligibility for indemnification for breach of their duty of care to the corporation or whose costs are not entirely covered under the applicable statute, may be entitled to coverage under the corporation's director and officer (D&O) insurance policy.[204] In many instances insurance coverage is more valuable to a director than indemnification since nonprofit corporations often lack sufficient funds to cover fully a director's expenses. Moreover, insurance coverage is guaranteed whereas indemnification may be unavailable when the corporation is dominated by a hostile board.[205] Even in cases where hostility is not a factor, the board may be reluctant to use charitable assets to satisfy judgments or to cover another director's attorney's fees.[206]

Thirty-three of the thirty-four states that permit or require indemnification have adopted statutes that authorize a nonprofit corporation to purchase insurance for claims asserted against a director.[207] Coverage depends on the terms of the privately negotiated insurance contract and is unrestricted by statute in all but one state. New York limits coverage to attorney's fees in cases where a director is adjudged liable to the corporation and found to have acted with deliberate dishonesty. However, in practice, New York's statutory limitation is superfluous since a typical D&O policy excludes dishonest acts from coverage in any event.[208] While statutory limits are virtually nonexistent, insurance coverage may also be limited by the common law doctrine that one may not contract to indemnify against one's own fraudulent or willful misconduct.[209]

In states that do not expressly authorize the corporation to purchase insurance by statute, the corporation may be authorized to do so under common law. However, in most states the extent to which common law permits the purchase of insurance is uncertain.[210]

Procedural Limits on Directors' Liability: Shifting the Burden of Proof

A small number of states limit a nonprofit director's liability for breach of the duty of care by placing procedural hurdles in the way of the party who brings

---

204. See generally Charles R. Tremper, *Reconsidering Legal Liability and Insurance for Nonprofit Organizations* (Lincoln, Nebr.: Law College Education Services, 1989).

205. Moody, "State Statutes," 775.

206. RMNCA, §8.50 introductory cmt. pt. 2.

207. Only North Dakota lacks such a provision. Wyoming also authorizes the purchase of insurance. Wyo. Stat. §17-19-857.

208. Moody, "State Statutes," 777.

209. Id. at 778.

210. RMNCA, §8.50 introductory cmt. pt. 1.

suit against the director. Most notably, four states have adopted a heightened evidentiary standard that requires the party bringing suit to prove a director's liability by "clear and convincing evidence" rather than by a "preponderance of the evidence" as is the norm in most civil suits. This standard of proof is typically reserved for cases involving serious matters such as libel, slander, and child custody proceedings.[211] Other states have made it more difficult to sue directors for breach of the duty of care by adopting a shorter statute of limitations period in which to file suit.[212]

State Prohibitions Based on Federal Tax Laws

In 2002 Maine adopted a far-reaching set of provisions revising the duty of care and conflict of interest provisions to follow the Revised Model Act, as well as regulating conversion transactions and enhancing the power of the attorney general to regulate breaches of duty.[213] A unique provision in the act was attributed to concerns of some of the legislative Judiciary Committee members that charitable organizations were paying excessive amounts as compensation and were investing charitable assets in for-profit subsidiaries and joint ventures.[214] Entitled "Misapplication of funds or assets of public benefit corporation," the new provision prohibits public benefit corporations (charities) from transferring or applying their assets, and their directors and officers from authorizing any such transfer if it meets any of the following four requirements: (1) the transfer constituted a conflict of interest transaction that was neither fair nor approved as required by statute under circumstances that include a showing of fairness; (2) the transfer misapplies the funds or assets in violation of statute, including the conversion statute; (3) the transfer is to a director or officer or another person in a position to exercise substantial influence over the affairs of the corporation and constitutes "private inurement or excess benefits that exceed the fair market value of the property or services" received in return; or (4) the transfer is to a "subsidiary or joint venture organized as a for-profit entity," unless the board of the charity determines in good faith under the facts and circumstances at the time of transfer or commitment to transfer that (a) the organization and operations of the for-profit entity will serve, further, or support a charitable purpose of the transferor; (b) the transfer is fair to the charity; (c) distribution of net income by the for-profit entity to its owners or investors will be proportion-

211. See Appendix, Table 3. See John J. Cound et al., *Civil Procedure: Cases and Materials,* 993 (St. Paul: West Group, 7th ed., 1997).

212. Michigan, South Carolina, and Tennessee.

213. 2001 Me. Laws ch. 550 (enacted March 25, 2002).

214. Donald E. Quigly, "The Rules for Managing Nonprofit Corporations Are Changing Fast," 17 *Maine Bar Journal* 156 (2002).

ate to their investment interests; and (d) the governing documents of the for-profit entity require that compensation transactions between it and its investors or directors and officers or other persons in a position to exercise substantial influence over the affairs of the entity do not provide excess benefits.[215]

These provisions were unique at the time of their enactment. By incorporating the prohibitions against private benefit in section 501(c) of the Internal Revenue Code and the limitations on excess benefit transactions in section 4958, they gave the state grounds for enforcing federal standards much as had been the case in connection with the adoption of restrictions on private foundations enacted in 1969. Furthermore, they addressed for the first time in state law the problems then being faced by the IRS in attempting to regulate joint ventures between charitable and for-profit investors. These provisions lay the groundwork for increased cooperation between the Service and state attorneys general, a development much desired by both government entities although much limited in application.[216]

In April 2003 a bill prepared by the New York attorney general was introduced in the legislature that took the approach of the Maine legislation, applying the conflict of interest provisions of section 4958 of the Internal Revenue Code to charitable corporations in the state. Specifically, a transaction between an interested director or officer and the corporation would be void or voidable by the corporation or the attorney general unless the parties established that the transaction was fair and reasonable to the corporation at the time it was entered into. The bill also contained provisions similar to those in the Internal Revenue Code under which the parties could take advantage of a presumption of reasonableness if certain procedures were followed, including a vote by disinterested directors based on information regarding comparable transactions. Unique was a provision empowering the attorney general to seek to recover from the interested director or officer or approving director restitution in amounts equivalent to the remedies that would be available to the Internal Revenue Service for violation of the provisions of section 4958. The power to seek restitution was stated to be applicable regardless of whether the charity was subject to section 4958 and whether the IRS pursued its remedies. Unlike the provisions in the Code, the bill would also apply to transactions between charities. A final provision would require thirty-day advance notice to the attorney general of any proposed payment of indemnification by a charity to an officer or director.[217]

---

215. Me. Rev. Stat. Ann. tit. 13-B, §§718, 721.
216. See Chapter 7.
217. S. 4836, 2003–2004 Reg. Sess. (N.Y. 2003).

Protection of Volunteer Directors from Tort Liability

Under common law and that of the majority of states, during the latter part of the nineteenth and the first half of the twentieth centuries, charitable trusts and corporations were immune from tort liability with the result that a person incurring injury due to the fault of the organization or one of its agents had no recourse against the charity's assets and would often look to the fiduciaries for redress. Reaction to the unfairness of the immunity doctrine led to its elimination during the 1940s and 1950s so that by 1985 almost every American jurisdiction had at least partially eliminated the protection afforded by the doctrine.[218] However, with an increase in the number of suits and the size of verdicts rendered against charities, judges and the legislatures in a number of states have revived the concept of immunity, granting either partial immunity or limited liability for organizations and attempting to shield individuals affiliated with them. The protection to officers and directors has been already noted. However, many of the statutes also protect volunteers, with separate statutes applying to specific groups of charities such as schools or colleges and other statutes applying to volunteers involved with sports programs or particular sporting events.[219]

The movement to legislate immunity for charity volunteers culminated in June 1997 with passage by Congress of a federal law preventing recovery of damages against a volunteer of a nonprofit organization for harm caused by his act or omission on behalf of the organization so long as the volunteer was acting within the scope of his responsibilities and the harm was not "caused by willful or criminal misconduct, gross negligence, reckless misconduct, or a conscious, flagrant indifference to the rights or safety of the individual harmed by the volunteer."[220] The act was a response to fears that frivolous lawsuits were keeping people from serving as volunteers for nonprofit organizations.[221] The act explicitly preempted state laws with contrary provisions. Individual states were given the option of making the limitation on liability applicable only if the nonprofit organization provided a financially secure source of recovery for individuals who suffer harm as a result of actions taken by a volunteer on behalf of the organization, such as an insurance policy or the sequestering of funds that would be available to meet claims.

218. Note, "Developments in the Law: Nonprofit Corporations," 105 *Harvard Law Review* 1578, 1680–1683 (1992).

219. Id. at 1695.

220. 42 U.S.C. §14503(a)(3), codified by Volunteer Protection Act of 1997, Pub. L. No. 105-199, §4, 111 Stat. 218, 219 (1997).

221. 104 Cong. Rec. H3118, 105th Cong. (May 21, 1997) (statement by Representative Inglis).

Dale criticized the provisions as encouraging irresponsibility on the part of nonprofit managers and deplored their long-term effects on the concept of fiduciary responsibility.[222]

Proposals for Reform

The power of the courts to enforce the duties of care and loyalty has been significantly undermined. This has come about with the passage of statutes limiting the grounds on which a director can be held to have breached his duties and permitting the corporation to indemnify a director found liable, absent a showing of bad faith, or to enter into a settlement even if there was bad faith. In addition, they permit a corporation to provide and pay for insurance protecting its fiduciaries from monetary loss. There are numerous critics of this trend, and their recommendations will be described in connection with each of the duties—care and loyalty.

Duty of Care

In regard to the duty of care, critics of the current trend toward relaxing the legal standards, like those who disapprove of the similar trend in regard to the duty of loyalty, express concern that it encourages recklessness in the handling of charitable funds. Fishman has proposed that the trustee standard be applied to decisions involving a corporation's charitable function or purposes, while the more lenient corporate standard be applied to less important ministerial and administrative decisions.[223] Similarly, Boyd would subject directors of public benefit corporations to the stricter trust standard while applying the corporate standard to directors of mutual benefit corporations.[224] As a third proposal, he suggested that the trust standard should govern "small" nonprofit organizations, leaving large ones subject to the corporate standard.[225]

Proponents of a more stringent standard of care also argue that nonprofit corporations, unlike their business counterparts, lack "watchdog" shareholders with an equity incentive to police the actions of board members, and point to the absence of an active plaintiff's bar that would profit by bringing

222. Harvey Dale, "Address before the Century Association on the Occasion of the Tenth Anniversary of Peter Swords as President of the Nonprofit Coordinating Committee" (New York, November 17, 1997) (transcript on file with author).

223. Fishman, "Standards of Conduct," 414.

224. Boyd, "Call to Reform," 744.

225. Id. at 745.

derivative suits on behalf of members in those states in which such suits are permissible.[226]

Brody has suggested codifying monetary limits on a director's liability. Maximum liability would be set at a level that would be low enough so that directors would continue to be willing to serve while making attorneys general and the courts more willing to find breaches, yet high enough to induce fiduciaries to take their tasks more seriously.[227]

Goldschmid, in contrast, refuted what he characterized as "the myth of 'quite low' standards," pointing out that during the 1980s and 1990s state courts had been applying duty of care standards in the for-profit sector in a demanding way, requiring directors to exercise a high degree of supervision and control over the policies and practices of the corporation. He concluded that it was not the "lowness" of care standards but rather the absence of enforcement that makes care standards "largely aspirational in the nonprofit context."[228]

Duty of Loyalty

DeMott formulated five normative alternatives for regulating self-dealing: (1) adopt an absolute prohibition on defined examples of self-dealing similar to those applicable under the Internal Revenue Code to private foundations, combined with financial penalties on the self-dealer, regardless of whether he realized a profit or caused a loss to the corporation; (2) make all transactions "tainted" by self-dealing voidable by the corporation regardless of whether there was benefit to the self-dealer or injury to the corporation; (3) adopt the business corporation standard making the transaction voidable unless its proponent establishes that it was intrinsically or entirely fair to the corporation; (4) provide that upon compliance with procedural safeguards, a self-dealing transaction would not be voidable, applying the business judgment rule to determine whether the approval of disinterested directors was sufficient; and (5) require administrative approval of defined instances of self-dealing, similar to SEC approval of investment companies.[229] She concluded that a fairness test, similar to that applicable to self-dealing controlling shareholders, would be the most effective deterrent in the context of nonprofit corporations, in light of the fact that it envisions judicial review of the merits of the transac-

226. Fishman, "Standards of Conduct," 408–409.

227. Evelyn Brody, "The Limits of Charity Fiduciary Law," 57 *Maryland Law Review* 1400, 1413 (1998).

228. Goldschmid, "Fiduciary Duties," 641.

229. Deborah A. DeMott, "Self-Dealing Transactions in Nonprofit Corporations," 1993 *Brooklyn Law Review* 131, 134 (1993).

tion and requires that the proponents affirmatively establish its fairness to the corporation at the time it entered into the transaction.[230]

Goldschmid favors adoption of either a fairness test or an intermediate test of judicial review based on section 5.02 of the Principles of Corporate Governance that would be more rigorous and intrusive than the "rationally believes" test of the business judgment rule.[231] He based this conclusion on a concern about "the tendency of nonprofit directors to defer to one another in an environment not characterized by skepticism and analytical rigor."[232] He noted that this was particularly the case given the absence of extensive disclosure requirements, enforcement machinery, and private litigation, and the fact that nonprofit institutions generally do not have voting rights, appraisal rights, and other protections found in the for-profit sector that would lessen the dangers, at least with respect to certain significant transactions.

> Reviewing courts should give enhanced scrutiny to allegations of conflict of interest or dominating influence in the nonprofit context. Business and familial relationships and "taints" to the process, for example, which might be considered of marginal concern in the for-profit context, should be resolved in favor of review under loyalty standards (not the business judgment rule) when nonprofit institutions are involved.[233]

In contrast, Hansmann in his 1981 study of nonprofit corporation law advocated an absolute prohibition on self-dealing,[234] although he subsequently revised this position, acknowledging its severity and instead proposing a more lenient standard.

Wolff, in a 1998 study,[235] recommended an approach similar to that in the California conflict of interest statute with its reliance on procedural safeguards, specifically that the corporation must conduct a reasonable investigation to determine that a transaction was the most advantageous arrangement that would have been attained at the time through reasonable efforts.[236] She

---

230. Id. at 143.

231. Goldschmid, "Fiduciary Duties," 639.

232. Id.

233. Id. at 651.

234. Henry B. Hansmann, "Reforming Nonprofit Corporation Law," 129 *University of Pennsylvania Law Review* 569–570 (1981); see also Henry Hansmann, "The Role of Nonprofit Enterprise," 89 *Yale Law Journal* 835 (1980); Ronald A. Brand, "Investment Duties of Trustees of Charitable Trusts and Directors of Nonprofit Corporations: Applying the Law to Investments That Acknowledge Social and Moral Concerns," 1986 *Arizona State Law Journal* 631, 658–659 (1986).

235. Beverly M. Wolff, "Conflict of Interest on Nonprofit Boards: The Law and Institutional Policy" (1998) (on file with author).

236. Cal. Corp. Code §5233.

urged amending nonprofit corporation laws to define conflicts more broadly to include, for example, conflicts with the interests of members of a director's household, situations in which a director may gain insider knowledge, and the competing interests of other nonprofits for which a director also acts as a fiduciary. Wolff's recommendations were to a certain extent enacted into law under the provisions of a statute adopted in Maine in 2002, which prohibited charities and their officers and directors from authorizing any distributions that would give rise to a violation of the prohibitions against private benefit and the excess benefit limitations in the Internal Revenue Code.[237] This approach has the advantage of coordinating state and federal standards, making compliance and regulation easier.

In summary, the majority of scholars who have analyzed modern formulations of the duty of loyalty as currently codified in the vast majority of states have decided that it is now too lenient. Their primary concern is the absence of judicial scrutiny of conflict of interest transactions that are validated by vote of disinterested directors and, if later challenged, will be weighed under the highly deferential rationality standard of the business judgment rule.

Proponents of the existing lenient standards argue that self-dealing by nonprofit directors is of more benefit to a charity than a prohibition on interested transactions. In many situations, self-dealing transactions are the only means by which a nonprofit corporation can gain access to goods and services that would otherwise be too expensive to afford. In particular, nonprofit corporations often have difficulty securing loans or credit from traditional lenders, and transactions with directors provide a crucial source of financing.[238] From an economic perspective, self-dealing is efficient. Transactions costs are low, and directors may be willing to give the best deal to the corporation because they have the most complete information about its financial situation.[239] Thus defenders of existing standards argue that increasing a director's risk of liability for self-dealing will result in fewer transactions that, on the whole, benefit nonprofit corporations.

Finally, the legal critics of the duty of loyalty, together with those who have analyzed the duty of care, conclude with a call for improved enforcement by the state attorneys general, often coupled with suggestions to expand the rules on standing to permit a larger group or class of individuals to bring enforcement suits, and a call for more detailed and widely disseminated disclo-

237. Me. Rev. Stat. Ann. tit. 5, §194-H.

238. Fishman, "Standards of Conduct," 424; Note, "The Fiduciary Duties of Loyalty and Care Associated with the Directors and Trustees of Charitable Organizations," 64 *Virginia Law Review* 449, 458 (1978); see also Harvey, "Public-Spirited Defendant," 683.

239. Fishman, "Standards of Conduct," 458; Note, "Developments," 1603.

sure of nonprofit financial dealings. These issues are discussed in succeeding chapters, as are the federal limits on self-dealing applicable to fiduciaries of tax-exempt charitable organizations that have had the effect of superseding state law in those states in which the federal prohibitions are more restrictive than the state standard.

5

The Internal Revenue Code

Charitable organizations have been afforded preferred status under the federal tax system since the first federal tax was enacted in 1909. That act contained exemption for "any corporation or association organized and operated exclusively for religious, charitable or educational purposes, no part of the net income of which inures to the benefit of any private stockholder or individual."[1] Similar phrasing has been in every federal income tax act adopted since that date, with corresponding provisions in the sections permitting deductions for income tax purposes for contributions to exempt organizations.[2]

Section 501(a) of the Internal Revenue Code confers exemption from income tax on a wide variety of organizations. The exemption for charities is set forth in section 501(c)(3), which describes:

> Corporations and any community chest, fund, or foundation, organized and operated exclusively for religious, charitable, scientific, testing for public safety, literary or educational purposes, or for the prevention of cruelty to children or animals, no part of the net earnings of which inures to the benefit of any private shareholder or individual, no substantial part of the activities of which is carrying on propaganda, or otherwise attempting, to influence legislation, and which does not participate in, or intervene in (including the publishing or distributing of statements), any political campaign on behalf of any candidate for public office.

There are twenty-three other types of organizations described in section 501(c) with a broad variety of purposes. All of them are exempt from income tax; however, only charities described in subsection (c)(3), certain cemetery companies, veterans organizations exempt under subsection (c)(19), and fra-

1. Corporation Tax Act of 1909, ch. 6, §38, 36 Stat. 11, 113 (1909).
2. See Chapter 2.

238

ternal organizations if the gifts are used for charitable purposes are eligible to receive contributions deductible for income tax purposes.[3]

Certain charitable organizations are granted exemption under other paragraphs of section 501; specifically, section 501(d) covers religious and apostolic associations, section (e) describes cooperative hospital service organizations, section (f) applies to cooperative service organizations of operating educational organizations, section (k) describes child-care organizations, and section (n) covers charitable risk pools of section 501(c)(3) charities. The remainder of section 501 contains provisions applicable to specific organizations.[4] For example, section (j) expands the definition of amateur athletic organizations that are described in section (c)(3), and section 501(k) similarly redefines eligible child-care organizations. Section (m), enacted in 1986, removed exemption from Blue Cross Blue Shield and other similar organizations providing commercial-type insurance.[5]

Social welfare organizations that are granted exemption under section 501(c)(4) may be considered charitable organizations under state law. Unlike section 501(c)(3) organizations, they are under no constraints in regard to lobbying activities, although the absolute prohibition against participation in elections also applies to them. Under section 504, adopted in 1976, an organization exempt under section 501(c)(3) that loses its tax exemption because of violations of the limits on lobbying under section 501(h) will not be eligible for exemption under section 501(c)(4) as a social welfare organization.[6]

Despite their eligibility for income tax exemption, the income from certain activities conducted by organizations described in section 501 may be taxed under other sections of the Code. For charities, section 511 imposes a tax on activities that are unrelated to the purpose for which they have received exemption;[7] similarly, political organizations,[8] social clubs,[9] and farmers cooperatives[10] are subject to income tax on their investment and certain other categories of their income.[11]

3. I.R.C. §170(c)(2), (3), (4), (5).

4. See James J. McGovern, "The Exemption Provisions of Subchapter F," 29 *Tax Lawyer* 523 (1976), for the history relating to the adoption and coverage of these provisions prior to 1976.

5. I.R.C. §501(m), codified by Tax Reform Act of 1986, Pub. L. No. 99-514, §1012(a), (b), 100 Stat. 2085, 2390–2394 (1986).

6. I.R.C. §504, codified by Tax Reform Act of 1976, Pub. L. No. 94-455, §1307(a)(2), 90 Stat. 1520, 1721–1722 (1976).

7. I.R.C. §511.

8. I.R.C. §527.

9. I.R.C. §501(c)(7).

10. I.R.C. §521.

11. I.R.C. §527(b); §1381; §512(a)(3)(A).

John Simon in his perceptive essay on "The Tax Treatment of Nonprofit Organizations: A Review of Federal and State Policies" characterizes four main functions served by the tax treatment of the nonprofit sector: support, equity, police or regulatory, and border patrol.[12] The border patrol function is part of the effort to keep nonprofit organizations from wandering into the territory of government and business. The government border is contained through the provisions in the federal tax code that limit the channels through which nonprofits can participate in public affairs activities—for private foundations an absolute limit, for public charities a more lenient one. The business border is maintained through limits on commercial activities of all charities and restrictions on ownership of business by private foundations.

The Code provisions circumscribing fiduciary behavior comprise Simon's regulatory function.[13] They appear (1) in the definition of charities in section 501(c)(3) that requires "exclusive" operation for exempt purposes, prohibits any degree of "inurement" to insiders, and limits conferring private benefit on any person, as well as in the regulations under that section establishing an "organizational" and an "operational" test for qualification for exemption; (2) in the prohibitions against self-dealing and the making of jeopardy investments and taxable expenditures applicable to a special category of charities defined as private foundations; and (3) in the excess benefit provisions of section 4958.

Those Code limitations that comprise the "border patrol function" of federal regulation include (1) the prohibition against political campaign activities, (2) limitations on lobbying, (3) the unrelated business income tax, and (4) certain constraints imposed through interpretation of the regulations, cases, and rulings on "commercial activities."[14] Although these provisions are not directly designed to limit fiduciary behavior as such, they affect fiduciary decisions as to how best to carry out an organization's exempt purposes. The scope and impact of these sections are discussed later in this chapter.

Basic to understanding the scope of the regulatory function is recognition that it does not treat the universe of charities uniformly. Nor is this universe divided, as under state law, according to the organizational nature of the entity—trust, corporation, or unincorporated organization. Rather the distinction was first made in the 1950s in regard to reporting requirements and then was formalized in the Tax Reform Act of 1969. It is based on the sources of support of the organization, with a group of organizations catego-

12. John G. Simon, "The Tax Treatment of Nonprofit Organizations: A Review of Federal and State Policies," in *The Nonprofit Sector: A Research Handbook*, 67, 68, 88–89 (Walter W. Powell ed., New Haven: Yale University Press, 1987).

13. Id.

14. Id.

rized as "private foundations" singled out for special and harsher treatment on the basis that they are free from the nonlegal constraints imposed on charities that must look to the general public for support.[15]

Additional and far-reaching restrictions on fiduciary behavior were enacted in 1996 as part of the Taxpayer Bill of Rights 2, with an effective date retroactive to September 14, 1995.[16] They apply to all organizations described in section 501(c)(3) that are not private foundations, thereby affecting approximately 93.5% of all organizations described in that section.[17] The taxes on excess benefit transactions in section 4958 also apply to section 501(c)(4) organizations. Referred to popularly as "intermediate sanctions," these rules represent an attempt to provide the Internal Revenue Service with a meaningful basis for enforcing a duty of loyalty similar in substance to that found under state law. The sanctions, which are in the form of excise taxes similar in application to those imposed on private foundations since 1969, apply to persons deemed to be in positions to exercise substantial influence over organizations described in section 501(c)(3) other than private foundations, and organizations described in section 501(c)(4), as well as on the fiduciaries of these organizations who knowingly approved a taxable transaction. Unlike the absolute prohibition on self-dealing applicable to private foundation fiduciaries, the penalties apply only to transactions in which excess benefits are received by insiders. They differ also in that the tax is on the excess benefits, not the entire transaction.

These rules comprise the federal tax counterpart of the state law duties of loyalty and care. They are by default the only restrictions on fiduciary behavior actively enforced. Equally important, they apply uniformly in all jurisdictions, thereby setting a nationwide minimum standard of behavior.

Permitted Purposes for Tax-Exempt Charities

Internal Revenue Service regulations, approved on June 22, 1959, define "charitable" as follows:

> The term "charitable" is used in section 501(c)(3) in its generally accepted legal sense and is, therefore, not to be construed as limited by the separate enumeration in section 501(c)(3) of other tax-exempt purposes

15. I.R.C. §§4940–4945, codified by Tax Reform Act of 1969, Pub. L. No. 91-172, §101, 83 Stat. 487, 499–515 (1969).

16. I.R.C. §4958, codified by Taxpayer Bill of Rights 2 Act, Pub. L. No. 104-168, §1311, 110 Stat. 1452, 1475–1479 (1996).

17. Murray S. Weitzman and Linda M. Lampkin, *The New Nonprofit Almanac and Desk Reference*, 125, Table 5.1 (New York: Jossey-Bass, 2002).

which may fall within the broad outlines of "charity" as developed by judicial decisions. Such term includes: relief of the poor and distressed or of the underprivileged; advancement of religion; advancement of education or science; erection or maintenance of public buildings, monuments or works; lessening of the burdens of government; and promotion of social welfare by organizations designed to accomplish any of the above purposes, or (i) to lessen neighborhood tensions; (ii) to eliminate prejudice and discrimination; (iii) to defend human and civil rights secured by law; or (iv) to combat community deterioration and juvenile delinquency.[18]

The influence of the Statute of Charitable Uses is evident in this enumeration, as is its similarity to state law definitions. Interpretations of the definitions in the Code are made by the federal courts, although they do not make them in a vacuum. Some cases even suggest that the federal decision was made on the basis of state law.[19] In the majority of these instances, the court referred to state law for an interpretation of the meaning assignable to particular words or terms in a charter or trust indenture of a particular charity.

Treasury regulation section 1.501(c)(3)-l(b)(5) states:

The law of the State in which an organization is created shall be controlling in construing the terms of its articles [that is, charter, trust instrument]. However, any organization which contends that such terms have under State law a different meaning from their generally accepted meaning must establish such special meaning by clear and convincing reference to relevant court decisions, opinions of the State attorney general, or other evidence of applicable State law.

The practice among the majority of the members of the bar who establish exempt organizations is to track the language in the Code and regulations, thereby avoiding controversy with revenue agents as to whether the organization will be eligible for exemption.

A basic issue that has permeated attempts to interpret the scope of the definition of charity has been whether exemption was available if the purpose of an organization entailed violation of principles of public policy. The issue came to the fore in the 1960s and 1970s in connection with the exemption of schools that discriminated on the basis of race, with the Service in 1967 adopting the position that exemption would not be granted to private

18. Treas. Reg. §1.501(c)(3)-l(d)(2) (T.D. 6391) (1959). Definitions of "educational" and "scientific" are contained in Treas. Reg. §1.501(c)(3)-l(d)(3), (5).

19. Gallagher v. Smith, 223 F.2d 218 (3d Cir. 1955); Schoellkopf v. United States, 124 F.2d 982 (2d Cir. 1942).

schools that so discriminated.[20] In 1983, in the case of *Bob Jones University v. United States*,[21] the Supreme Court affirmed this position, holding that exemption was available only to an organization meeting the common law standard of charity, a standard that required that its purpose not violate established public policy. The Court recognized that the determination of public policy could be difficult in some instances but that it was clearly within the power and the ability of the Internal Revenue Service to make determinations as to whether it was being violated in any specific instance. The Court further held that the constitutional guarantee of freedom of religion did not bar this holding, so its ruling applied to schools operated by religious organizations as well as to sectarian institutions.[22]

There are certain purposes that have always received close scrutiny by the Service. Among the more controversial has been the provision of health care. This was considered a charitable purpose under English common law, being mentioned in the Statute of Elizabeth.[23] Until the 1970s it was generally accepted that operation of a hospital came within the broad meaning of charitable as used in the regulations. Because, historically, the majority of hospitals primarily served the poor, there was no need to further define the scope of activities that would be required of a hospital in order for it to qualify for exemption.[24] Following the end of World War II, however, health care insurance payments and Medicare and Medicaid reimbursement became the primary sources of hospital support, and the Service was forced to reassess the standards under which a hospital would qualify for exemption, and to determine to what extent provision of services to the poor was a requisite to exemption.

The Service first addressed the issue directly in 1956 in a revenue ruling in which it held that to be charitable, a hospital "must be operated to the extent of its financial ability for those not able to pay for the services rendered and not exclusively for those who are able and expected to pay."[25] This came to be characterized as the "charity care standard"; it ignored the fact that provision of health care was one of the purposes considered charitable in the Statute of Elizabeth. In 1969 this earlier ruling was modified to provide that exemption

20. Rev. Rul. 67-325, 1967-2 C.B. 113.

21. 461 U.S. 574 (1983).

22. See Bruce R. Hopkins, *The Law of Tax-Exempt Organizations,* 98 n.86 (New York: John Wiley & Sons, 7th ed. 1998), for a list of articles discussing the case and its ramifications.

23. Stat. 43 Eliz. 1, ch. 4 (1601).

24. Jill Horwitz, "Corporate Form of Hospitals: Behavior and Obligations," 134–135 (2002) (Ph.D. dissertation, Harvard University) (on file with author); see also Charles E. Rosenberg, *The Care of Strangers: The Rise of America's Hospital System,* 244–248 (Baltimore: Johns Hopkins University Press, 1987).

25. Rev. Rul. 56-185, 1956-1 C.B. 202.

was available to a hospital that benefited the community if it served public rather than private interests and provided hospital care to all who could pay regardless of whether payment was made by the patient, his insurer, or the government.[26] Evidence that the hospital was providing community benefit could be established by a showing that it operated an emergency room open to all, that it had a disinterested board of trustees and an open staff, and that it provided programs designed to improve the health of the community.[27] In 1983 the requirements were further modified, with the Service ruling that a hospital located in an area with sufficient emergency room access did not need to operate one itself.[28] Almost ten years later, in 1992, the IRS issued guidelines reiterating as requirements for exemption the existence of a governing board comprised of civic leaders who were not primarily hospital administrators and doctors, an open staff, a full-time emergency room open to all in need, and nonemergency care for those who could afford it.[29] Although after that ruling a number of bills were introduced in Congress in the 1990s that would have mandated provision of charity care as a condition for exemption, none were enacted,[30] and the issue remained unresolved more than ten years later.[31]

The view that relief of the needy was a necessary component of the legal concept of charity also underlay a controversy that arose in late 2001 in connection with the disbursement of funds contributed to relieve the victims of the September 11 terrorist attacks. Not only were unprecedented amounts contributed to existing organizations, but hundreds of new organizations were formed throughout the country to assist in disaster relief, and the Service attempted to clarify the standards for exemption for new disaster relief organizations and for grant-making by existing organizations. In its first public announcement the Service implied that it was necessary to consider the needs of victims and their families in all instances.[32] This position was subse-

26. Rev. Rul. 69-545, 1969-2 C.B. 117.

27. Internal Revenue Manual (IRM) 7.25.3.11.1, available at *www.irs.gov/irm/index.html*; see also Rev. Rul. 83-157, 1983-2 C.B. 94.

28. Rev. Rul. 83-157, 1983-2 C.B. 94.

29. Audit Guidelines for Hospitals, Ann. 92-83, 1992-22 I.R.B. 59.

30. Charity Care and Hospital Tax-Exempt Status Reform Act of 1991, H.R. 790, 102d Cong., 1st Sess. (1991); H.R. 1374, 102d Cong., 1st Sess. (1991); see also Joint Committee on Taxation, *Proposals and Issues Relating to the Tax Exempt Status of Not-for-Profit Hospitals Including Descriptions of H.R. 1374 and H.R. 790* (JCX-10-91), 12–22 (July 9, 1991).

31. See, for example, IHC Health Plans, Inc. v. Commissioner, 325 F.3d 1188 (10th Cir. 2003).

32. Response by Charitable Organizations to the Recent Terrorist Attacks: Hearings before the Subcommittee on Oversight of the House Committee on Ways and Means, Serial 107-47, 107th Cong., 1st Sess. (2001) (statement of Steven T. Miller, Director, Exempt Organizations Division, Internal Revenue Service).

quently modified, to clarify that charities could provide financial assistance without regard to need if the purpose was to relieve distress and if the payments were made in "good faith using objective standards."[33] This standard was subsequently codified in the Victims of Terrorism Tax Relief Act, passed by Congress on December 20, 2001.[34] The act and the Service's rulings also addressed the circumstances under which private foundations could provide benefits to employees who were victims of the disaster, in this instance following the precedent found in rulings addressing the ability of company-sponsored foundations to provide benefits to employees and their families.[35]

Early in 2002, the Service issued a revised publication in which it attempted to clarify the general rules for charitable organizations providing disaster relief as modified by the 2001 Relief Act. It made clear that the prerequisites for distributions to victims of a disaster were that the victim was in financial need as a result of the disaster or was distressed and in need of crisis counseling, rescue services, or emergency aid.[36]

Other purposes that have been the subject of controversy include the provision of legal aid by public interest law firms,[37] the operation of day-care centers,[38] the activities of educational organizations that do not fit the definition of schools,[39] the conduct of scientific research,[40] publishing,[41] low-income housing and community economic development,[42] environmental preservation,[43] or promotion of the arts.[44]

Overall, the Service has been liberal in its interpretations of the definition of charity, expanding the category of public purposes to meet changing societal needs.

33. Notice 2001-78, 2001-50 I.R.B. 576.

34. Victims of Terrorism Tax Relief Act of 2001, Pub. L. No. 107-134, §104(a)(1), 115 Stat. 2427, 2431 (2002).

35. Rev. Proc. 76-47, 1976-2 C.B. 670; Rev. Rul. 81-172, 1981-2 C.B. 217; Rev. Rul. 86-90, 1986-2 C.B. 184; Rev. Rul. 2003-32, 2003-14 I.R.B. 689.

36. Internal Revenue Service, Publication 3833, *Disaster Relief—Providing Assistance through Charitable Organizations* (rev. ed. March 2002).

37. Rev. Rul. 75-74, 1975-1 C.B. 152.

38. I.R.C. §501(k), codified by Tax Reform Act of 1984, Pub. L. No. 98-369, §1032(a), 98 Stat. 494, 1033–1034 (1984).

39. Big Mama Rag, Inc. v. United States, 631 F.2d 1030 (D.C. Cir. 1980).

40. Rev. Rul. 65-60, 1965-1 C.B. 231; Treas. Reg. §1.501(c)(3)-1(d)(5)(iii)(c).

41. Rev. Rul. 67-4, 1967-1 C.B. 121.

42. Rev. Proc. 96-32, 1996-1 C.B. 717; Rev. Rul. 74-587, 1974-2 C.B. 162; Rev. Rul. 77-111, 1977-1 C.B. 144.

43. Rev. Rul. 76-204, 1976-1 C.B. 152.

44. Rev. Rul. 64-175, 1964-1 C.B. 185.

Basic Requirements for Exemption

The Organizational Test

The organizational test appears in the regulations as a restatement of the requirements of section 501(c)(3).[45] These regulations contain provisions that must be included in the governing documents of any organization that seeks exemption under section 501(c)(3).[46] They also identify provisions that, if included in these documents, will cause the organization to fail the test.[47] Although the regulations interpret the Code provision requiring that a charity be organized "exclusively" for exempt purposes to mean "substantially," they also provide that exemption will be denied if the organization's governing documents include a provision expressly permitting it "to engage in, or carry on, otherwise than as an insubstantial part of its operations, activities which in themselves are not in furtherance of one or more exempt purpose."[48] Thus exemption will be denied if the articles of organization empower the fiduciaries to engage in a manufacturing business or to operate as a social club.[49]

To meet the organizational test, the governing document must include a provision that, upon dissolution, the assets of the organization will be distributed to other organizations also exempt from income tax by virtue of being described in section 501(c)(3).[50] This test can be met if there is a similar requirement under state law that is enforced locally. In 1982 the Service issued a revenue ruling stating that nonprofit corporations organized in Arkansas, California, Louisiana, Massachusetts, Minnesota, Missouri, Ohio, and Oklahoma did not need a dissolution clause, while corporations organized in all other states and the District of Columbia would not meet the organizational test unless their articles of organization contained an express dissolution provision.[51] The ruling also listed certain states in which testamentary charitable trusts would meet the requirements, while expressly excluding inter vivos charitable trusts and unincorporated nonprofit associations. In practice, very few organizations rely on the state law exception, preferring the certainty afforded by having the restriction in their governing instruments.

In regard to fiduciary duties, the Service objects to inclusion of broad ex-

---

45. Treas. Reg. §1.501(c)(3)-1(b)(1)(iii).
46. Treas. Reg. §1.501(c)(3)-1(b)(1)(i)(a)-(b).
47. Treas. Reg. §1.501(c)(3)-1(b)(1)(iv), (b)(3).
48. Treas. Reg. §1.501(c)(3)-1(b)(1)(iii).
49. Id.
50. Treas. Reg. §1.501(c)(3)-1(b)(4).
51. Rev. Proc. 82-2, 1982-1 C.B. 367.

culpatory clauses on the grounds that they could excuse a trustee from any violations of the conditions for exemption. For example, a clause providing that the trustees should not be answerable for loss from investments made in good faith was acceptable, but if the following language would be added—"and for any cause whatsoever except his own willful misconduct"—exemption would be denied.[52]

The organizational test has had a dual effect. It has provided the basis for action by the Service to deny or revoke exemption; at the same time it has provided state enforcement officials grounds for action in state courts alleging breach of fiduciary duties due to the failure of trustees or directors to observe the requirements in the organization's governing documents.

The Operational Test

The operational test was adopted as part of the regulations under section 501(c)(3) in order to clarify that determinations of exemption would not be made solely on the basis of an organization's governing documents, but required a showing that the organization would meet the conditions for exemption in its ongoing activities.[53] One of the most important aspects of the test, as described in the regulations, was an acknowledgment that despite the fact that the Code requires that an organization be "operated exclusively" for exempt purposes, it will be considered to be so operated "if it engages primarily in activities which accomplish one or more of such exempt purposes specified in section 501(c)(3)."[54] The regulation further clarifies that the test will not be met if more than an insubstantial part of an organization's activities are not in furtherance of an exempt purpose, or if it violates the prohibition against private inurement.[55] Noteworthy is the fact that although the language of the Internal Revenue Code standard is "exclusively," the regulation in effect changed this to "primarily,"[56] a recognition on the part of the drafters that it would not be practicable to demand compliance with the stricter standard.

The question of whether pervasive commercial activities are compatible with exemption has been raised by the Service from time to time on the basis of what a few commentators characterized as a "commerciality doctrine" de-

52. Berrien C. Eaton, Jr. et al., "How to Draft the Charter or Indenture of a Charity so as to Qualify for Federal Tax Exemption," *Practical Lawyer*, October 1962, at 13, 15, and November 1962, at 87.
53. Treas. Reg. §1.501(c)(3)-1(c).
54. Treas. Reg. §1.501(c)(3)-1(c)(1).
55. Treas. Reg. §1.501(c)(3)-1(c)(1), (2).
56. Treas. Reg. §1.501(c)(3)-1(c)(1).

spite the fact that it is not articulated as such in the Code or regulations. Rather, it was extrapolated from cases upholding the Service's denial of exemption on the basis that the operation of the charity in question was more in the nature of a commercial business operating in competition with for-profit companies.[57] The case of *Better Business Bureau of Washington, D.C., Inc. v. United States*[58] was one of the earliest addressing this issue. More recently, the court upheld denial of exemption to an organization formed to provide consulting services to nonprofit organizations on the grounds that it operated in a manner identical to for-profit organizations and offered no services at a reduced rate or without charge.[59] In contrast, denial of exemption by the Service was overruled in the case of a charity that provided technical assistance to artisans in developing countries that would improve their ability to market their products and included the purchase, import, and sale of their handicrafts.[60] Similarly, the Court of Appeals overruled a Tax Court decision denying exemption to a religious publishing company that had greatly increased sales and revenue through the publication of the works of a popular author.[61] As of the end of 2002, the question of the extent of projected business activities that were permissible in order to meet the organizational test was unresolved.[62]

Prohibition against Private Inurement

The prohibition against private inurement was a part of that section of the first corporate excise tax that contained exemption for certain organizations with religious, charitable, or educational purposes.[63] The proscription against inurement applies to benefits that accrue only to persons who have an interest in the organization, such as directors, officers, or employees, and it comes into effect only when benefits conferred on the individual are not commensurate with the services he or she provides to the charity. Thus it is not an absolute ban on self-dealing; rather it is a standard based on reasonableness that can be substantiated by reference to the terms of an arm's-length transaction. Examples of inurement found in the cases include the following: payment of unreasonable compensation, whether in the form of excessive salary,[64] or a

57. Hopkins, *Law of Tax-Exempt Organizations*, 629–643.

58. 326 U.S. 279 (1945).

59. B.S.W. Group, Inc. v. Commissioner, 70 T.C. 352 (1978).

60. Aid to Artisans, Inc. v. Commissioner, 71 T.C. 202 (1978).

61. Presbyterian and Reformed Publishing Co. v. Commissioner, 743 F.2d 148 (3d Cir. 1984).

62. See this chapter for additional discussion of this issue.

63. Corporation Tax Act of 1909, ch. 6, §38, 36 Stat. 11, 113 (1909).

64. Incorporated Trustees of the Gospel Worker Society v. United States, 510 F. Supp. 374 (D.D.C. 1981), aff'd, 672 F.2d 894 (D.C. Cir. 1981), cert. denied, 456 U.S. 944 (1982).

salary based on a percent of "profits,"[65] or payment of personal expenses of an insider; payment of unreasonable rent;[66] loans to a donor or a corporation controlled by him with below-market interest or inadequate security;[67] payment of excessive prices for real or personal property;[68] and assumption by an organization of a private individual's indebtedness.[69]

Private inurement has also been found in one case in which the principal purpose of the organization was to promote its founder's ideas and writings for his own benefit,[70] and in another in which a charity was organized to provide personal assistance to performers who participated in a radio program directed by the founder of the charity.[71] A third example was the sale of an organization's assets to insiders at less than fair market value.[72] The Service found in this case that the sale constituted a breach of fiduciary duty under state law, and held that this was the basis for its finding of private inurement.[73]

Prohibited inurement arises only when benefits accrue to individuals who have a particular, close relationship to the organization. The term most commonly used to describe these persons is "insider," implying a relationship with the organization in which a private person has sufficient control or influence over the organization as to permit him to make use of the organization's income or assets for personal gain.[74] Insider status is not determined by reference to the amount of the benefit received. As Dale has pointed out, "If receipt of a sizeable benefit transforms the recipient into an 'insider,' the inurement prohibition would threaten to subsume the excess-private benefit rule. It is clear, however, that the two are distinct."[75]

65. Founding Church of Scientology v. United States, 412 F.2d 1197 (Ct. Cl. 1969), cert. denied, 397 U.S. 1009 (1970); Church of Scientology of California v. Commissioner, 823 F.2d 1310 (9th Cir. 1987), cert. denied, 486 U.S. 1015 (1988).

66. Texas Trade School v. Commissioner, 30 T.C. 642 (1958), aff'd per curiam, 272 F.2d 168 (5th Cir. 1959).

67. Lowry Hospital Association v. Commissioner, 66 T.C. 850 (1976).

68. Hancock Academy of Savannah, Inc. v. Commissioner, 69 T.C. 488 (1977).

69. Rev. Rul. 67-5, 1967-1 C.B. 123.

70. Rev. Rul. 55-231, 1955-1 C.B. 72.

71. Horace Heidt Foundation v. United States, 170 F. Supp. 634 (Ct. Cl. 1959). Cf. Bob and Dolores Hope Charitable Foundation v. Riddell, 61-1 U.S.T.C. ¶9437 (S.D. Cal. 1961).

72. Priv. Ltr. Rul. 82-34-084 (May 27, 1982); Priv. Ltr. Rul. 91-30-002 (undated).

73. State ex rel. Butterworth v. Anclote Manor Hospital, Inc., 566 So. 2d 296 (Fla. Dist. Ct. App. 1990); see also Est of Hawaii v. Commissioner, 71 T.C. 1067 (1979), aff'd, 647 F.2d 170 (9th Cir. 1981); Tech. Adv. Mem. 94-51-001 (December 23, 1994) (revoking exemption of LAC Facilities); LAC Facilities, Inc. v. United States, No. 94-604T (Fed. Cl. filed September 14, 1994).

74. Audit Guidelines for Hospitals, Ann. 92-83, §333.2(2), 1992-22 I.R.B. 59.

75. Harvey Dale, "Reflections on Inurement, Private Benefit, and Excess Benefit Transactions," n.75 (citing American Campaign Academy v. Commissioner, 92 T.C. 1053, 1068–1069 (1989)) (2001; on file with author).

Dale has called attention to the inherent ambiguities in the statutory language and concluded that the determination of the existence of inurement is inherently fact-specific. Despite the number of reported cases interpreting the proscription, he notes that there is little helpful guidance as to the application and meaning of the language: "It is often fairly easy to decide what is and what is not prohibited, even though it is quite daunting to try to describe the test."[76]

The sanction for violation of the private inurement prohibition is loss of exemption, a sanction that is applied no matter how small the amount involved. It is in large part because of the draconian nature of the sanction and the fact that it falls on the charity and not on those who have improperly received benefits at its expense that Congress was persuaded in 1996 to enact excess benefit limitations applicable to certain self-dealing transactions between public charities and their fiduciaries. The scope and effect of this legislation is discussed below.

Limitation on Private Benefit

The private benefit test was first formulated in the regulations under section 501(c)(3) that were promulgated in 1958 in T.D. 6301.[77] The pertinent section reads as follows:

> An organization is not organized or operated exclusively for one or more of the purposes specified in subdivision (i) unless it serves a public rather than a private interest. Thus, to meet the requirements of this subdivision, it is necessary for an organization to establish that it is not organized or operated for the benefit of private interests such as designated individuals, the creator or his family, shareholders of the organization, or persons controlled, directly or indirectly, by such private interests.[78]

Cases interpreting this regulation have treated it as a test separate from the private inurement proscription, and held that it will be violated only if the benefit conferred on a private individual is found to be more than incidental.[79] This is in direct contrast to the private inurement provision where loss of exemption follows the presence of any amount of prohibited benefit. A second distinction is that while inurement extends only to payments to "insiders," the proscription against private benefit applies to a benefit conferred

76. Id. at nn.67, 68.
77. 23 Fed. Reg. 5192 (T.D. 6301) (1958).
78. Treas. Reg. §1.501(c)(3)-1(d)(1)(ii).
79. *American Campaign Academy,* 92 T.C. 1053 (1989).

by the charity on any person. As stated in a general counsel memorandum issued in 1991, "the absence of inurement does not mean the absence of private benefit. Inurement, then, may be viewed as a subset of private benefit."[80]

Some of the cases interpreting the private benefit proscription have upheld denial of exemption on the basis that private entities unrelated to the charity will stand to benefit from its operations. Thus, in *American Campaign Academy v. Commissioner*,[81] the Tax Court upheld denial of exemption to a school that was organized by the Republican Party to train its candidates and campaign workers, noting that although the primary beneficiaries of the academy were its students (which included some candidates), the secondary beneficiary was the party's entities and all of its candidates, a private group earmarked and targeted by the organization. The court contrasted this relationship with the benefit conferred by organizations that provide training to individuals in a particular industry or profession, in that in the latter case, the benefits are broadly spread among a large class of individuals.

In contrast to the holding in *American Campaign Academy*, in 1980 the Tax Court upheld exemption for an organization that operated an art center in which it conducted classes, sponsored demonstrations, and operated a museum and two galleries in which it acted as a dealer in the sale of the works of local artists.[82] The Service had based its denial of exemption on the fact that the organization's activities were indistinguishable from those of a commercial, for-profit art gallery and provided more than incidental private benefit to designated individuals. However, the court found that the commercial activities of the center were incidental to its educational activities and that it was serving public, not private, purposes.

Until the end of the 1990s there had been a question as to whether a person receiving substantial benefits from a charity would by virtue of that fact become an insider and thereby bring the private inurement test, rather than the private benefit test, into play. In the case of *United Cancer Council, Inc. v. Commissioner*,[83] the court held that a fund-raising company that retained a large percent of the amounts raised did not by virtue of that fact become an insider, as the Tax Court had previously held. The question of the circum-

---

80. Gen. Couns. Mem. 39,862 (November 21, 1991) (citing *American Campaign Academy*, 92 T.C. at 1068–1069); see also *Founding Church of Scientology*, 412 F.2d 1197 (Ct. Cl. 1969); *Lowry Hospital Association*, 66 T.C. 850 (1976); People of God Community v. Commissioner, 75 T.C. 127 (1980).

81. 92 T.C. 1053 (1989).

82. Goldsboro Art League, Inc. v. Commissioner, 75 T.C. 337 (1980).

83. 165 F.3d 1173 (7th Cir. 1999), rev'g and remanding 109 T.C. 326 (1997). The case was remanded to the Tax Court for further consideration under the private benefit proscription. It was subsequently settled. Grant Williams, "IRS, Charity Settle Long-Standing Dispute," *Chronicle of Philanthropy*, May 4, 2000, at 39.

stances under which the private benefit provisions might conflict with excess benefit limitations is discussed below.

There are numerous cases and rulings dealing with allegations of private benefit. Among them are payments of unreasonable amounts, whether as compensation, rent, or loans with a low interest rate or interest-free to individuals who are not "insiders," as well as arrangements permitting individuals to retain interests in the organization's property. In a 1987 memorandum the Service described various compensation arrangements that did not constitute private benefit.[84] A number of recent cases have considered private benefit in connection with the operation of joint ventures between for-profit and nonprofit organizations in which private investors own equity interests in the venture and thereby stand to obtain financial benefit from its success. These are discussed below in the section on joint ventures.

It is to be noted that the private benefit proscription does not extend to acknowledgment of the gifts of donors. Thus charities are permitted to recognize contributors in ways that might confer nonmonetary benefits, such as naming a building, a university chair, or a restricted fund after the donor, without violating the private benefit proscription.[85]

Many of the rulings and cases alleging private benefit have also involved allegations of private inurement, and the court decisions often tend to use the language of the private benefit restrictions in cases involving insiders. With the passage of section 4958 prohibiting the provision of excess benefits to disqualified persons and the consequent diminution in the importance of the private inurement prohibitions as grounds for revocation of exemption, it is likely that the private benefit limitation may increase in importance as a regulatory tool for the Service.

Prohibition against Excess Benefit Transactions Applicable to Publicly Supported Charities

The most far-reaching change in the federal restrictions on fiduciary behavior of trustees and directors of tax-exempt charities occurred in 1996 with passage of section 4958 of the Internal Revenue Code.[86] The legislation provided for the imposition of excise taxes on certain persons who receive unearned benefits from public charities and on the fiduciaries who approved

---

84. Gen. Couns. Mem. 39,670 (October 14, 1987).

85. See discussion in this chapter on income tax treatment of sponsorship payments.

86. I.R.C. §4958, codified by Taxpayer Bill of Rights Act 2, Pub. L. No. 104-168, §1311, 110 Stat. 1452, 1475–1479 (1996); see also Steven T. Miller, "Easier Compliance Is Goal of New Intermediate Sanction Regulations," 2001 *Tax Notes Today* 14-148 (January 22, 2001) (written by Director, Exempt Organizations, Internal Revenue Service, Washington, D.C.).

the transaction knowing that it was prohibited. The legislation followed the format of the self-dealing provisions applicable to private foundations that were enacted in 1969, although with more lenient restrictions and sanctions.[87] It reflected an attempt to bring flexibility to the Internal Revenue Code, permitting correction of wrongdoing and avoiding the often inappropriate penalty of loss of tax exemption. Most important, the sanctions apply to those who benefit at the organization's expense, not to the organization itself.[88]

Excess benefit limitations are applicable in cases in which certain private individuals, described as "disqualified persons," receive "excess benefits" from "applicable organizations" in the course of dealing with them.[89] Each of these terms is defined below.

Disqualified Persons

Disqualified persons who may be subject to the sanctions are defined as those persons who at any time during the five-year period preceding the transaction in question were in a position to exercise "substantial influence" over the affairs of the exempt organization, certain of their family members, and corporations, trusts, and other entities over which they exercise more than 35% control.[90]

The regulations define disqualified persons to include voting members of an organization's board of directors or trustees or other governing body, its president, chief executive and chief operating officer, treasurer and chief financial officer, and persons with a material financial interest in certain health-care-provider-sponsored organizations in which an exempt hospital is a participant.[91] The regulations also include individuals with managerial control over a discrete segment of an organization, giving as an example a large university in which the dean of a school oversees faculty hiring for the department and exercises control over its budget, and concluding that he would be a disqualified person with respect to the university.[92]

The regulations specifically exclude from the definition of disqualified

87. I.R.C. §§4940–4945, codified by Tax Reform Act of 1969, Pub. L. No. 91-172, §101, 83 Stat. 487, 499–515 (1969).

88. Proposed regulations under section 4958 were issued by the Treasury Department on August 4, 1998 (63 Fed. Reg. 41,486); after periods for public comment and public hearings, temporary regulations were promulgated on January 1, 2001 (66 Fed. Reg. 2144); and final regulations became effective on January 23, 2002 (67 Fed. Reg. 3076).

89. I.R.C. §4958(a)(1).

90. I.R.C. §4958(f)(1)(A)-(C).

91. Treas. Reg. §53.4958-3(c).

92. Treas. Reg. §53.4958-3(g) (ex. 8).

persons other section 501(c)(3) organizations and employees who are not "highly compensated" and not substantial contributors to the organization, compensation being considered high if it exceeds $80,000, as adjusted for inflation.[93]

The regulations also list certain factors that will tend to indicate the ability to exercise substantial influence or its absence. Among those factors implying that a person should be included in the definition: the person was (1) a founder of the organization or a substantial contributor; (2) one whose compensation was based on revenues derived from activities of the organization that he controls; (3) the possessor of authority to control or determine a significant portion of the organization's capital expenditures, operating budget, or compensation for employees; or (4) one who has managerial authority or serves as a key advisor to a person with such authority, or owns a controlling interest in a corporation, partnership, or trust that is a disqualified person.[94]

In contrast, a person generally will not be considered to have substantial influence if he has taken a bona fide vow of poverty in connection with a religious organization; is an independent contractor such as an attorney, accountant, or investment advisor acting in that capacity; or receives preferential treatment also offered to other donors making similar contributions as part of a general solicitation campaign conducted by the organization.[95]

Family members of disqualified persons include the individual's spouse, ancestors, children, grandchildren, and great-grandchildren, the spouses of these descendants, his siblings and their spouses, corporations in which disqualified persons control 35% of the voting power, and partnerships, trusts, and estates in which disqualified persons own more than 35% of the beneficial interest. Voting rights held as a director or trustee are not considered in determining voting power.[96]

If an excess benefit transaction occurs, a separate, parallel set of excise taxes will be imposed on the organization's fiduciaries who have approved of the transaction knowing that it was prohibited, if their action was willful and not due to reasonable cause.[97] Organization managers include officers, directors, trustees, and other individuals who exercise similar powers regardless of their title.[98] The category does not include family members, controlled entities, or independent contractors. In addition, persons who serve as members of a committee that has power to approve a transaction for purposes of establishing a presumption that the organization did not confer an excess

---

93. Treas. Reg. §53.4958-3(d).
94. Treas. Reg. §53.4958-3(e)(2)(i)-(iv), (vi).
95. Treas. Reg. §53.4958-3(e)(3)(i)-(v).
96. Treas. Reg. §53.4958-3(b)(1), (2)(i)-(ii).
97. I.R.C. §4958(a)(2).
98. I.R.C. §4958(f)(2).

benefit are considered organization managers for the purposes of the statute.[99]

The final regulations also provided that organizations exempt from tax under section 501(c)(4) may under certain circumstances be considered disqualified persons with respect to all applicable organizations.[100] This extension of the coverage of the act was designed to prevent transactions in which a charitable organization described in section 501(c)(3) provided an excess benefit to a social welfare organization described in subsection (c)(4) in order to avoid limitations on the charity, such as limits on its lobbying activities.[101]

Excess Benefits

An excess benefit is the amount of an economic benefit provided directly or indirectly by an exempt organization to a disqualified person that exceeds the value of the property or services provided by the disqualified person to the organization in exchange for the benefit.[102] Fair market value, defined as the price at which property or rights would change hands between willing buyers and sellers, is the benchmark for determining whether payments have produced excess benefits.[103] The tax applies to sales, loans, or any other type of payment by an exempt organization to or for the benefit of a disqualified person, as well as to compensation and certain revenue-sharing arrangements.[104]

The regulations contain three specific exclusions from the definition of excess benefit: reimbursement for reasonable expenses of attending meetings; benefits provided to members of the public or volunteers in exchange for a membership fee not exceeding $75 per year; and economic benefits that the disqualified person receives by virtue of being a member of a charitable class that the organization benefits in the course of carrying out its charitable purposes.[105]

There are circumstances in which a benefit is paid to a disqualified person that would not constitute an excess benefit if the charity treated the payment as taxable compensation to the person receiving the benefit, but if not so treated would be in the nature of a gratuitous payment for which the payee provided no return benefit.[106] Under these circumstances payments will be considered compensation only if, at the time of payment, the organization

99. Treas. Reg. §53.4958-1(d)(2)(ii).
100. Treas. Reg. §53.4958-2(a)(4).
101. 67 Fed. Reg. 3076, 3078 (2002).
102. I.R.C. §4958(c)(1)(A).
103. Treas. Reg. §53.4958-4(b)(1)(i).
104. Treas. Reg. §53.4958-4(a).
105. Treas. Reg. §53.4958-4(a)(4)(i)-(iv).
106. Treas. Reg. §53.4958-4(b)(1)(ii).

can demonstrate by clear and convincing evidence that it intended to treat the benefit as compensation.[107] The regulations contain examples of acceptable ways of establishing such intent.[108]

If a charity purchases insurance that covers the liability of an officer, director, or employee who is a disqualified person for taxes imposed under section 4958, the cost of the insurance premiums will not be an excess benefit as long as it is treated as additional compensation to the disqualified person and his total compensation is reasonable.[109] In contrast, purchase of directors and officers liability insurance that would cover other potential liabilities would not come under the provisions of section 4958 and would not need to be included in compensation.

Prior to promulgation of the temporary regulations in 2001, it was uncertain whether a person would be considered disqualified in relation to the first contract he made with an exempt organization or whether that status would arise only after the contract was executed. The final regulations contained what was referred to as an "initial contract exception" under which a person will not be deemed "disqualified" while he is negotiating terms of employment, and benefits under that contract will not be subject to the excess benefit limitations.[110] However, the exception will not be available if the initial contract is materially modified or the person does not substantially perform his obligations under it.[111] Thus a person is free to negotiate the terms of an employment contract with an exempt organization without fear that he will subsequently be held to have incurred an excess benefit.

Payment of compensation is the most common transaction in which excess benefits can be conferred. Accordingly, the regulations contain detailed provisions regarding this aspect of section 4958. The general rule is that compensation will be considered reasonable if it is the same as would ordinarily be paid for comparable services by like enterprises, whether tax-exempt or taxable.[112] The original versions of the excess benefit limitations legislation prepared by the Treasury, as well as another version submitted by Independent Sector to the Ways and Means Committee, had provided that comparable data would be limited to compensation arrangements made within the tax-exempt sector,[113]

107. Treas. Reg. §53.4958-4(c)(1).

108. Treas. Reg. §53.4958-4(c)(3)(i)(A).

109. Treas. Reg. §53.4958-4(b)(1)(ii)(B)(2).

110. Treas. Reg. §53.4958-4(a)(3)(iii).

111. Treas. Reg. §53.4958-4(a)(3)(iv).

112. Treas. Reg. §53.4958-4(b)(1)(ii).

113. Tax Administration of Public Charities Exempt under Section 501(c)(3): Hearings before the Subcommittee on Oversight of the House Committee on Ways and Means, Serial 103-39, 103d Cong., 1st Sess. (1993); Serial 103-72, 103d Cong., 2d Sess. (1994); Subcommittee on Oversight, House Ways and Means Committee, *Report on Reforms to Improve the Tax Rules Governing Public Charities* (WMCP 103-26), 103d Cong., 2d Sess. (1994).

but the House Report stated explicitly that it was the broader universe of for-profit and nonprofit organizations that was to be considered,[114] thereby considerably weakening the impact of the act.

The concept of compensation is broad, including cash and noncash transfers, salaries, fees, bonuses and severance payments, deferred compensation, premiums for insurance coverage and reimbursements for liabilities, and other fringe benefits whether taxable or nontaxable, including medical, disability, and life insurance. It does not include, however, working-condition or de minimis fringe benefits such as parking, transit passes, occasional meals, or personal use of employer facilities. Included are payments from the exempt organization as well as economic benefits provided by other entities related to it.[115]

The timing of a determination that compensation is excessive is the date on which the contract is made unless it does not fix a specific amount of compensation, in which case the determination will be made in light of all the circumstances up to the date of payment. If a contract is subsequently modified, the determination will be made as of the date of modification.[116]

Revenue-Sharing Arrangements

Section 4958(c) identifies as an excess benefit transaction any transaction in which the amount of any economic benefit is determined in whole or in part by the revenues of one or more activities of the exempt organization providing the benefit where the transaction results in impermissible inurement under sections 501(c)(3) or (4), but only if regulations prescribed by the Treasury so provide.[117] The proposed regulations issued in August 1998 contained standards identifying when a revenue-sharing transaction constituted excess benefits.[118] In response to many conflicting comments on this formulation, in the temporary regulations issued in 2001 this section of the regulations was reserved, and the Treasury announced that until specific rules were issued dealing with revenue-sharing arrangements, all such transactions would be evaluated under the general rules governing excess benefit transactions.[119] In the final regulations this section remained "reserved";[120] it was accompanied by a comment to the effect that the Treasury and the IRS would continue to monitor revenue-sharing arrangements and would consider issu-

114. H.R. Rep. No. 104-506, 104th Cong., 2d Sess., at 56 n.5 (1996).
115. Treas. Reg. §53.4958-4(b)(1)(ii)(B)(1)-(2).
116. Treas. Reg. §53.4958-4(b)(2).
117. I.R.C. §4958(c).
118. 63 Fed. Reg. 41,486, 41,492, 41,503 (1998).
119. 66 Fed. Reg. 2144, 2152–2153 (2001).
120. Treas. Reg. §53.4958-5.

ing separate rules if they should later become appropriate.[121] The regulations and the Treasury explanation made clear that the general exempt standards of sections 501(c)(3) and (c)(4) would continue to apply so that inurement may exist although a disqualified person receives a reasonable amount from a revenue-sharing arrangement. The regulations state, "However, most situations that constitute inurement will also violate the general rules of regulation section 53.4958 (e.g., exceed reasonable compensation)."[122]

Rebuttable Presumption of Reasonableness

The House Committee Report accompanying passage of the Taxpayers Bill of Rights 2 suggested that the final regulations include a presumption of reasonableness that organizations could rely on in establishing that benefits paid to disqualified persons did not violate the provisions of section 4958.[123] The final regulations contain a procedure that, if followed, will establish a presumption in favor of the organization that the Service would have to overcome in establishing that a payment represented an excess benefit.[124] In order to avail itself of the presumption, an organization must follow certain prescribed steps when determining the amount of compensation of a disqualified person or conferring any monetary or other benefit on him. They are as follows: (1) The organization must obtain information on comparable transactions while determining the amount of consideration or compensation. If an organization's annual gross receipts are less than $1 million, it will be sufficient if it obtains information on the compensation paid by three other comparable organizations in the same or similar communities.[125] (2) Concurrently with approval of the transaction, the organization must document its terms, the date of approval, the individuals present at the meeting at which the vote was taken, and all circumstances surrounding the vote, including whether they disclosed any personal conflicts of interest, and the comparability date obtained. A record will be considered to have been approved concurrently if it is prepared prior to the next meeting of the board or committee after the approval and reviewed and approved by the board or committee within a reasonable time after it has been prepared.[126] (3) The transaction must be approved by the governing body, or a committee thereof, with the

---

121. 67 Fed. Reg. 3076, 3082 (2002).
122. Id.
123. H.R. Rep. No. 104-506, 104th Cong., 2d Sess., at 56 (1996).
124. Treas. Reg. §53.4958-6.
125. Treas. Reg. §53.4958-6(c)(2)(ii).
126. Treas. Reg. §53.4958-6(c)(3)(i)(A)-(D).

voting members consisting only of persons who do not have any interest in the transaction.[127]

If these conditions are met, the tax under section 4958 can be imposed only if the Service has assembled additional information to show that the compensation was not reasonable or the transfer was not at fair market value. Failure to follow the procedure will not have any adverse consequences for an organization, but it will have the burden of establishing the reasonableness of the transaction, whereas, if it establishes the presumption, the burden is on the Service.[128]

Excise Taxes on Disqualified Persons

Section 4958 provides for imposition of an initial excise tax on a disqualified person equal to 25% of the excess benefit that he received.[129] However, if the transaction was due to reasonable cause and not to willful neglect and it was corrected within the correction period, the Secretary of the Treasury is authorized to abate the initial tax and interest on it.[130] The correction period is defined as a period beginning on the date of the transaction and ending on the earlier of the date of mailing of a notice of deficiency or the date on which the first-tier tax is assessed.[131]

If an initial tax is imposed for an excess benefit transaction and it is not timely "corrected" or abated, a second-tier tax equal to 200% of the excess benefit will be imposed on the disqualified person.[132] Correction can be achieved by undoing the benefit to the extent possible and taking any other measures necessary to put the organization in a position that is no worse than that in which it would have been if no excess benefit had been paid. This can be achieved by returning the money with interest, by returning property if the benefit involved a transfer of property, or in the case of compensation, adjusting any ongoing compensation agreements to prevent them from resulting in additional excess benefits. If the organization to which a correcting payment is to be made is not in existence at the time for correction, the amount may be paid to a publicly supported charity that has been in existence for at least sixty months ending on the correction date.[133]

If correction is made within ninety days after the date of mailing by the

127. Treas. Reg. §53.4958-6(c)(3)(ii).
128. Treas. Reg. §53.4958-6(b).
129. I.R.C. §4958(a)(1).
130. I.R.C. §4962(a).
131. I.R.C. §4963(e).
132. I.R.C. §4958(b); Treas. Reg. §53.4958-7(a).
133. Treas. Reg. §53.4958-7(e).

Service of notice of deficiency with respect to the second-level tax, the tax will not be assessed; if assessed it will be abated and, if it has already been collected, it will be refunded.[134]

Excise Tax on Manager

The tax on organization managers is equal to 10% of the excess benefit. As noted, it may be avoided upon a showing that the manager did not know that the transaction provided an excess benefit and that his participation was not willful and was due to reasonable cause.[135] The tax on a manager is limited to $10,000, and there is joint and several liability in the case of several managers.[136] Managers may protect themselves from liability for the tax by demonstrating either that they did not approve of the transaction or that they relied on an opinion of counsel or of an accountant or appraiser that the transaction did not constitute an excess benefit.[137]

Applicable Organizations

Section 4958 as enacted was made applicable to organizations described in sections 501(c)(3) and (c)(4), but it was unclear prior to issuance of regulations whether this was meant to include a governmental entity that was exempt or was not subject to tax without regard to section 501(a), such as an organization described in section 115.[138] The final regulations provided that a governmental unit or an affiliate of a governmental unit will not be subject to section 4958 as an applicable exempt organization if it is exempt from, or not subject to, taxation without regard to section 501(a), or is not required to file an annual return pursuant to the authority of regulations under section 6033.[139]

Early Experience Applying Excess Benefit Limitations

In the first three years following passage of section 4958 excess benefit limitations, the IRS assessed more than $93 million on three for-profit companies and five individuals. All of these penalties arose in connection with the conversion of several related tax-exempt health care organizations to for-profit

134. Treas. Reg. §53.4958-1(c)(2)(iii); I.R.C. §§4961(a), 4962(a), 6212.
135. I.R.C. §4958(a)(2).
136. I.R.C. §4958(d)(1), (2).
137. Treas. Reg. §53.4958-1(d)(4)(iii).
138. 67 Fed. Reg. 3076, 3077 (2002).
139. Treas. Reg. §53.4958-2(a)(2)(ii); see also 67 Fed. Reg. 3076, 3077 (2002).

entities controlled by disqualified persons, the sole consideration being the for-profit organization's assumption of the exempt organizations' assets and liabilities. This "price" was based on a negative-valuation by a certified public accountant. The Service also revoked the exemption of the nonprofit organizations on the basis that the sales at less than fair market value resulted in private inurement. On May 22, 2002, the Tax Court upheld the imposition of excise taxes on the individual directors and the transferee for-profit home health care agencies, but refused to sustain the revocation of the transferor organization's tax exemption.[140]

The Service had also imposed intermediate sanctions on the trustees of a Hawaiian trust that operated the Kamehameha Schools (known as the Bishop Trust) in addition to revoking the trust's tax exemption retroactively to 1990. On December 1, 1999, the Hawaii Probate Court approved a settlement agreement between the IRS and temporary trustees appointed by the court to replace five trustees it had removed for breaches of trust. Under the terms of the settlement, tax exemption was preserved, but the question of intermediate sanctions was unresolved. In October 2000 the press reported that an insurance company for the trust would pay $25 million to settle the dispute between the attorney general and the former trustees, thereby ending this aspect of the dispute.[141] Then, in January 2001, as reported in the *Honolulu Star-Bulletin*, the former trustees

> each paid the Internal Revenue Service several thousand dollars to settle the federal agency's claims that the former board members received excessive compensation . . . The former trustees did not disclose the amount that they had paid, but sources familiar with the IRS investigation said that the agency had recently assessed each trustee with an excise tax of about $40,000.[142]

According to this report, the IRS had claimed that the former trustees should have been paid no more than $160,000 per year between 1990 and 1996, rather than the more than $1 million they had received annually.

In July 2002 the Service released a technical advice memorandum ruling that the founder, president, and executive director of an exempt organization

140. Caracci v. Commissioner, 118 T.C. 379 (2002).

141. Stephen G. Greene, "Insurer to Pay $25-Million to Settle Dispute in Hawaii," *Chronicle of Philanthropy*, October 5, 2000, at 42.

142. Rick Daysog, "Ex-Bishop Trustees Pay IRS in Settling Tax Claims," *Star-Bulletin*, January 4, 2001, at 1; see also Carolyn D. Wright, "IRS Assesses Intermediate Sanctions against Bishop Estate Incumbent Trustees," 31 *Exempt Organization Tax Review* 155 (2001); Evelyn Brody, "Troubling Lessons from the Bishop Estate Settlement for Administering the New Intermediate Sanctions Regime," 32 *Exempt Organization Tax Review* 431 (2001).

that was formed to receive deductible donations of used automobiles and distribute the proceeds from their sale to other exempt charities had entered into ten excess benefit transactions involving payment of excessive salary, repayment of undocumented loans, and a number of other instances of self-dealing, all of which subjected him to tax under section 4958 as a disqualified person as well as an organization manager.[143]

Section 4958 and Revocation of Exemption

The House Ways and Means Committee Report accompanying passage of the excess benefits provisions stated that the sanctions may be applied either "in lieu of (or in addition to) revocation of an organization's tax-exempt status."[144] In an accompanying footnote, however, the report stated that while, in general, intermediate sanctions were to be the sole sanction imposed in cases in which an excess benefit did not rise to the level where it calls into question the organization's tax-exempt status, "[i]n practice, revocation of tax-exempt status, with or without the imposition of excise taxes, would occur only when the organization no longer operates as a charitable organization."[145]

The preamble to the August 1998 proposed regulations listed four factors that the IRS would consider in determining whether to revoke an applicable tax-exempt organization's exempt status: (1) whether the organization had been involved in repeated excess benefit transactions; (2) the size and scope of the transaction; (3) whether the organization implemented safeguards to prevent future recurrences; and (4) whether it was in compliance with other applicable laws.[146] The preamble to the temporary regulations indicated that the Internal Revenue Service would publish additional guidance as it gained more experience in enforcing sections 4958, 501(c)(3), and (c)(4).[147]

In the preamble to the final regulations issued in January 2002, the IRS stated that it would continue to consider suggested additions and revisions to the list of factors and, until it published a revised or expanded list of factors, it would consider all relevant facts and circumstances in the administration of section 4958 cases.[148] These final regulations also provided that all substantive requirements for exemption would continue to apply so that, regardless of whether a particular transaction was subject to excise taxes under section

143. Tech. Adv. Mem. 2002-43-057 (July 2, 2002); see also Tech. Adv. Mem. 2002-44-028 (June 21, 2002).
144. H.R. Rep. No. 104-506, 104th Cong., 2d Sess., at 59 (1996).
145. Id. at 59 n.15.
146. 63 Fed. Reg. 41,486, 41,488–41,489 (1998).
147. 66 Fed. Reg. 2144, 2155 (2001).
148. 67 Fed. Reg. 3076, 3082 (2002).

4958, existing principles and rules may be implicated, such as the limitation on private benefit.[149] For example, if a transaction would not be subject to excess benefit limitations because the initial contract exception in section 53.4958-4(a)(3) applied, the transaction might, under certain circumstances, jeopardize the organization's exempt status under the private benefit proscription.

In the case of *Caracci v. Commissioner,*[150] described above, while upholding the IRS imposition of excise taxes on disqualified persons for violation of section 4958, the Tax Court overruled the decision of the Service revoking the exemptions of the organizations involved in the excess benefit transactions. The court noted that the question of revocation had been affected by the passage of section 4958, and relied on the legislative history indicating that after its passage, both revocation and the imposition of intermediate sanctions would be an unusual case. The court called particular attention to the fact that the transfer giving rise to the excess benefits was a single transaction for each of the exempt organizations and that, since the transfers, the organizations had not operated contrary to their tax-exempt purposes. Most important appeared to be the fact that maintenance of the tax exemptions would enable the petitioners to make permissible corrections by returning the assets of the transferee for-profit organizations to the tax-exempt entities, an alternative that would not be available if the transferors lost their tax exemptions. Accordingly, leaving the exemptions intact would be consistent with the legislative history and the provisions for abatement in sections 4961 through 4963. The Service filed an appeal from this aspect of the decision but seven months later the appeal was withdrawn.[151]

The addition of excess benefit limitations to the Code represented a major expansion of the power of the Service to regulate the behavior of charitable fiduciaries, remedying a long-recognized impediment to effective policing of the sector. Nonetheless, as finally enacted, the excess benefit provisions contained sufficient ambiguity and, more particularly, loopholes, to warrant concern as to their ultimate effectiveness in preventing breaches of the duty of loyalty. There are two major limitations: first, by setting the standard against which excessive compensation is to be measured to those in the for-profit sector, Congress effectively removed meaningful limits on the amount that can be paid to disqualified persons. Second, by permitting charities to purchase insurance to cover excise taxes on disqualified persons, Congress effectively assured that wrongdoers would not personally be liable for their payment. This was the outcome of the IRS settlement with the trustees of the Bishop

---

149. Treas. Reg. §53.4958-8.

150. Caracci v. Commissioner, 118 T.C. 379 (2002). See text accompanying note 140.

151. "Government Drops Appeal in EO Revocation Case," 2002 *Tax Notes Today* 237-6 (December 10, 2002).

Trust where, although the Service had initially sought to impose $65 million in taxes,[152] the trustees ultimately paid $40,000 each, with the insurance provider paying the balance.[153] These provisions should be amended to place the burden directly on the wrongdoers. In the meantime, the existence of the sanctions should serve to deter directors, trustees, and other disqualified persons from attempting to benefit unfairly from their dealings with the charity they serve, if only to avoid adverse publicity.[154]

Restrictions on Private Foundations

The Tax Reform Act of 1969 contained sweeping changes in the manner in which the Internal Revenue Code treated private foundations. For the first time, penalties were imposed on transactions involving these organizations and their managers and substantial contributors for certain activities determined by Congress to be incompatible with exempt status. These limitations appear in five sections of the Code described below. Section 4941, which replaced section 503, mandated a federal duty of loyalty; section 4942 replaced section 504, which had prohibited unreasonable accumulations of income. Sections 4943 superseded the limitations on investments in section 504 and, together with section 4944, in effect established a federal prudent investor rule for foundations. Finally, section 4945 contained limits on program activity and the process of grant-making, limits not theretofore a part of federal regulation.

Section 4940 added another unprecedented provision to the Code in the form of a 4% excise tax on the net investment income of all private foundations. The original bill had set the tax at 7½%, but this was reduced and characterized as an audit fee. As explained by the Joint Committee on Taxation, "The Congress has concluded that private foundations should share some of the burden of paying the cost of government, especially for more extensive and vigorous enforcement of the tax laws relating to exempt organizations."[155] However, the tax has never been earmarked for this purpose within the IRS budget.

---

152. Stephen G. Greene, "Bishop Estate to Pay IRS $9-Million but Retain Its Tax-Exempt Status," *Chronicle of Philanthropy*, January 13, 2000, at 50.

153. Daysog, "Ex-Bishop Trustees Pay IRS in Settling Tax Claims."

154. Evelyn Brody, "A Taxing Time for the Bishop Estate: What Is the IRS Role in Charity Governance?" 21 *University of Hawaii Law Review* 537 (1999); Evelyn Brody, "Troubling Lessons from the Bishop Estate Settlement for Administering the New Intermediate Sanctions Regime."

155. Joint Committee on Taxation, *General Explanation of the Tax Reform Act of 1969* (JCS-16-70), 29 (December 3, 1970).

The amount of the tax was reduced in 1978 to 2% after evidence that it was producing more than twice the revenue that was expended on regulation of exempt organizations.[156] In 1984 Congress further amended section 4940 to permit foundations to reduce the tax to 1% if they made additional distributions for charitable purposes.[157] Complaints that the two-tier tax provisions were poorly designed and overly complicated have led to proposals for change.[158] The most recent were proposals to reduce the tax to 1%, which were part of the CARE Act of 2003 and of a companion bill introduced in the House.[159] The Clinton administration in its 2001 budget proposal suggested replacing the two-level tax with a flat 1.25% tax, a proposal that was not adopted.[160]

With the exception of the taxes on investment income and on self-dealing, violation of these provisions results in imposition of excise tax on the foundation and on those foundation managers who approved the expenditure knowing that it was prohibited. In the case of self-dealing, the sanctions apply in a manner similar to the excess benefit limitations applicable to public charities, imposing excise taxes on the self-dealer and on the foundation managers. As is the case with excess benefit limitations, the prohibitions against self-dealing and jeopardy investments are the federal law counterparts of state law duties of loyalty and care, in both instances imposing uniform, nationwide standards of behavior on tax-exempt foundations.

Internal Revenue Code Definition of Private Foundations

The current Code definition of a "private foundation" was formulated in the Tax Reform Act of 1969 in section 509(a) and has remained unchanged since that time.[161] As noted, private foundations are defined in section 509(a)(1) by exclusion. Thus the term includes all organizations described in section 501(c)(3) other than

---

156. Revenue Act of 1978, Pub. L. No. 95-600, §520(a), 92 Stat. 2763, 2884 (1978).

157. Deficit Reduction Act of 1984, Pub. L. No. 98-369, §303(a), 98 Stat. 494, 781–782 (1984).

158. Reed Abelson, "Some Foundations Choose to Curb Donations and Pay More Taxes," *New York Times*, February 24, 2000, at C1.

159. S. 1924, 107th Cong., 2d Sess., §105 (2002); H.R. 7, 108th Cong., 1st Sess., §105 (2003).

160. Joint Committee on Taxation, *Description of Revenue Provisions Contained in the President's Fiscal Year 2002 Budget Proposal* (JSC-2-00), 231–235 (March 6, 2000).

161. I.R.C. §509, codified by Tax Reform Act of 1969, Pub. L. No. 91-172, §101, 83 Stat. 487, 496–498 (1969). See Chapter 2 for the development of the distinction under prior statutes.

1. churches and conventions and associations of churches;[162]
2. educational organizations with regular faculty, curriculum, and a regularly enrolled student body in attendance at the place where the educational activities are regularly carried on;[163]
3. organizations whose principal purpose or function is to provide medical or hospital care and medical education or research if a hospital, and endowment funds of state colleges or universities;[164]
4. governmental units;[165]
5. organizations that normally receive a substantial part of their support from governmental units or direct or indirect contributions from the general public, excluding, however, income received from activities that entail the carrying out of the organization's exempt purposes[166] (the regulations define "substantial" as meaning more than one-third of qualified support, while "qualified support" includes all contributions received from other publicly supported charities and the government, but no more than 2% of total support from any single individual contributor or private foundation; there is also a facts and circumstances test that can be met so long as at least 10% of support is from the general public);[167]
6. organizations that receive more than one-third of their total support from a combination of exempt function income and public support, and no more than one-third from investment income, but with a limit of 1% for exempt function income from any single entity or person;[168]
7. supporting organizations of other public charities, more specifically organizations that are organized and operated exclusively for the benefit of, to perform the functions of, or to carry out the purposes of one or more specified organizations that are not themselves private foundations, that are operated, supervised, or controlled by or in connection with one or more supported organizations, and that are not controlled by disqualified persons;[169]
8. organizations whose exclusive function is testing for public safety.[170]

There is also a separate category called a private operating foundation,[171] an entity that is eligible for the favorable contribution deductions available to

162. I.R.C. §509(a)(1); §170(b)(1)(A)(i).
163. I.R.C. §509(a)(1); §170(b)(1)(A)(ii).
164. I.R.C. §509(a)(1); §170(b)(1)(A)(iii).
165. I.R.C. §509(a)(1); §170(b)(1)(A)(v).
166. I.R.C. §509(a)(1); §170(b)(1)(A)(vi).
167. Treas. Reg. §1.170A-9(e)(2)-(3), (6)(i), (7).
168. I.R.C. §509(a)(2); Treas. Reg. §1.509(a)-3(a)(2)(ii), (3).
169. I.R.C. §509(a)(3).
170. I.R.C. §509(a)(4).
171. I.R.C. §4942(j)(3).

public charities while being subject to the Chapter 42 restrictions, although the payout requirement is less restrictive than that applicable to other private foundations.

Governing Instrument Requirements and Termination Rules

As an adjunct to the limitations on private foundations, the 1969 Tax Reform Act contained provisions designed to assure that foundations would be identified. This was accomplished by means of a presumption that all organizations in existence on the effective date of the act (October 9, 1969) that were then exempt under section 501(c)(3) other than churches and organizations with gross receipts that were normally less than $5,000 annually were private foundations unless they filed appropriate notice with the Service rebutting the presumption within fifteen months.[172] Those organized after that date were given fifteen months within which to file an application for exemption that includes the notice required under section 507.[173] However, an additional twelve months are available if an extension is requested.[174]

In an attempt to improve compliance with the new rules, private foundations were required as a condition of exemption to include in their governing instruments provisions mandating that they meet the payout rule of section 4942 and barring them from taking any action described in sections 4941 and 4943 through 4945.[175] Under regulations adopted in 1972, if a valid state law imposes these requirements on all private foundations, foundations within its jurisdiction will be considered to have met the Code requirement.[176] By 1975, forty-eight states and the District of Columbia had passed such legislation, and the Service acknowledged that foundations within their jurisdictions were deemed to have conformed with section 508(e).[177] This requirement has provided state regulatory officials with grounds for prosecuting failures to comply with federally imposed rules, an unprecedented example of coordination of the two regulatory schemes.[178]

Section 507 also embodies an attempt to integrate state and federal regulation. It imposes on any private foundation that terminates under certain circumstances a tax equal to the value of all tax benefits received by the foundation since its creation, whether income tax deductions or exemptions or relief

---

172. I.R.C. §508(a); Treas. Reg. §1.508-1(a)(1), (2).

173. Treas. Reg. §1.508-1(a)(2).

174. Rev. Proc. 92-85, §4.01, 1992-2 C.B. 490.

175. I.R.C. §508(e).

176. Treas. Reg. §1.508-3(d) (T.D. 7232) (1972).

177. Rev. Rul. 75-38, 1975-1 C.B. 161. Arizona and New Mexico are the only states without such legislation.

178. See Chapter 7.

from gift and estate taxes—in effect, a confiscatory tax.[179] Relief from the confiscatory termination tax can be obtained in one of two ways: either (1) the foundation distributes its assets to a public charity that has been in existence with that status for sixty consecutive months prior to the date of distribution;[180] or (2) following notice by the Service to an appropriate state officer, he notifies the Service within one year that corrective action has been taken under state law to ensure that the assets of the foundation have been preserved for charitable purposes under order of a state court, and the Service receives notice that this has been accomplished.[181]

The application of these provisions is ambiguous and has led to an inordinate number of requests for private letter rulings involving terminations and mergers of private foundations. In May 2002 the Service issued a revenue ruling designed to clarify the circumstances under which a private foundation may distribute all of its assets to one or more other private foundations and dissolve without incurring the termination tax under section 507(e). It provided that this would be the case so long as one of the transferee foundations agrees to continue monitoring all outstanding grants made by the transferor as if they had been made by the transferee.[182] The import of the ruling was that so long as the foundation did not provide the Service with formal notice that it was terminating or, if it had no assets on the day it provided notice, the tax would be zero. In January 2003 the Service issued a second revenue ruling dealing with termination of private foundations, this time attempting to clarify the provisions under which the termination tax under section 507 can be avoided by distribution of assets on dissolution or termination to a preexisting public charity.[183]

Disqualified Persons

For purposes of the private foundation excise taxes, disqualified persons include foundation managers; substantial contributors to the foundation; owners of more than 20% of the voting power of a corporation, the profit interest in a partnership, or the beneficial interest in a trust or unincorporated enterprise that was a substantial contributor to the foundation; specified family members of any of these individuals; and corporations and other business entities in which any disqualified persons have more than a 35% interest in voting power, profits, or beneficial interests.[184]

179. I.R.C. §507(a).
180. I.R.C. §507(g)(1).
181. I.R.C. §507(g)(2).
182. Rev. Rul. 2002-28, 2002-20 I.R.B. 941.
183. Rev. Rul. 2003-13, 2003-4 I.R.B. 1.
184. I.R.C. §4946(a); see also Treas. Reg. §53.4946-1(a).

There is one more category of disqualified persons that applies only for purposes of the prohibitions against self-dealing in section 4941—namely, government officials. This term is defined in section 4946(c) to include elected public officials in the United States Congress or executive branch, presidential appointees in the executive or judicial branch, certain higher compensated or ranking employees in any of the three branches, employees of the House or Senate earning at least $20,000 annually, and the personal or executive assistant or secretary to any of these.[185]

A substantial contributor is any person (which includes, in addition to an individual, a corporation, partnership, trust, or estate) who has contributed more than $5,000 to the foundation if the total of his contributions exceeded 2% of the total contributions received by the foundation from its date of creation to the end of the year in which the $5,000 limit was met.[186] Under the original legislation passed in 1969, a person who became a substantial contributor retained that status for life. In 1984 this provision was amended to permit termination of status as a substantial contributor if an individual and persons related to him have made no contributions to the foundation nor acted as a manager during a ten-year period, and the aggregate contributions made by him and his family members are determined by the Service to be insignificant.[187]

Family members include the spouse, ancestors, children, grandchildren, and great-grandchildren of the disqualified person, as well as the spouses of children, grandchildren, and great-grandchildren. The term "spouse" includes divorced spouses, whether or not they have remarried, and widows and widowers. Unlike the excess benefit limitations provisions, it does not include siblings and their spouses.[188]

Self-Dealing

The self-dealing rules are derived in large part from prior section 503 but contained different sanctions. Thus self-dealing transactions include the following transactions between a private foundation and a disqualified person: the sale or exchange or leasing of property, the lending of money or other extension of credit, the furnishing of goods, services, or facilities, the payment of compensation, and the transfer to or use by or for the benefit of a disqualified person of the income or assets of the foundation.[189]

185. I.R.C. §4946(c); Treas. Reg. §53.4946-1(g).
186. I.R.C. §507(d)(2).
187. I.R.C. §507(d)(2)(c), codified by Deficit Reduction Act of 1984, Pub. L. No. 98-369, §313(a), 98 Stat. 494, 786–787 (1984).
188. I.R.C. §4946(d); see also Treas. Reg. §53.4946-1(h).
189. I.R.C. §4941(d)(1).

There are a number of important exceptions to these rules: a disqualified person may lease property to a private foundation if the lease is without charge; similarly, a disqualified person may extend credit to a foundation if no interest or other charge is made and the proceeds are used exclusively for charitable purposes; and a disqualified person may furnish goods, services, or facilities to a foundation if there is no charge, and they are used exclusively for charitable purposes. Conversely, a private foundation may furnish goods, services, or facilities to a disqualified person if the furnishing is made on a basis no more favorable that that available to the general public. Although compensation to a disqualified person is enumerated as a self-dealing transaction, an exception is made for the performance of personal services to the foundation by a person other than a government official if the services are reasonable and necessary to carrying out the charitable purposes of the foundation and the amount is not excessive. Finally, the receipt by a disqualified person of an incidental or tenuous benefit from his use of a foundation's income or assets, such as naming a special fund or building after a donor, is not by itself considered self-dealing.[190]

The initial tax on a disqualified person for an act of self-dealing is 5% of the amount involved; for the manager who approved the transaction knowing it was an act of self-dealing, unless the action was not willful and due to reasonable cause, the tax is 2½% of the amount involved, with a cap of $10,000.[191] If correction is not timely made, there is an additional tax on the disqualified person equal to 200% of the amount involved, and 50% on a manager who refuses to agree to the correction, again with a cap of $10,000.[192]

The amount involved is the greater of the amount of money and the fair market value of any other property given or received, except in the case of rent where it is the difference between the amount paid and a fair market rental. It differs, therefore, from section 4958 under which the tax is applied only to the amount of the excess benefit, not the entire amount of the transaction that gave rise to the benefit. The initial tax is imposed for each year or part of a year between the initial act of self-dealing and either its correction or receipt from the Service of a notice of deficiency or imposition of the additional tax.[193]

Correction requires undoing the transaction to the extent possible and in all events assuring that the foundation is in no worse financial position than if the disqualified person had been dealing under the highest fiduciary stan-

190. I.R.C. §4941(d)(2).
191. I.R.C. §4941(a), (c)(2).
192. I.R.C. §4941(b).
193. I.R.C. §4941(e).

dards. Finally, a foundation manager may rely on advice of counsel, rendered in a reasoned, written, legal opinion, that the transaction did not constitute an act of self-dealing.[194]

If there have been willful, repeated violations of these rules and of any of the other private foundation limitations, section 507 provides that the tax-exempt status of the foundation may be involuntarily terminated and, should that occur, the foundation will be subjected to what is in effect a third level of excise taxes equal in amount to all tax benefits received by the foundation since its inception. This provision operates therefore as a confiscatory tax.[195] Unlike the other taxes on private foundation activities, there is no provision permitting abatement of the section 4941 first-level tax.[196]

There are distinctive differences between section 4958 and section 4941. Most basic is the fact that the prohibitions against private foundation self-dealing are absolute, while section 4958 applies only if a disqualified person receives an excess benefit. In line with this difference, as noted, the taxes under section 4958 are measured by the amount of the excess benefit while the section 4941 tax is imposed on the entire amount involved in the transaction. Furthermore, government officials are not subject to excess benefit limitations. Substantial contributors to private foundations include all persons coming within the limits, regardless of when the limits were met, as opposed to the excess benefit limitations provision under which substantial contributor status is determined for the five years immediately preceding the excess benefit transaction.

Critics of the self-dealing provisions point to the fact that the absolute prohibition has prevented foundations from participating in transactions involving disqualified persons that would be of obvious benefit to the foundation. A common example is a lease of property owned by a disqualified person to a foundation, which is prohibited even if the rent would be below market value. A Task Force established by the Exempt Organizations Committee of the Tax Section of the American Bar Association recommended in 2002 that the absolute prohibition be modified to permit transactions that can clearly be shown to benefit the private foundation and for which there is a readily ascertainable value. The Task Force also recommended adding an abatement procedure and modifying the penalty provisions so that they would apply, as do intermediate sanctions, to the amount of the excess benefit, not the entire amount involved. A final recommendation, reflecting wide-

---

194. I.R.C. §4941(e)(3); Treas. Reg. §53.4941(a)-1(b)(6).
195. I.R.C. §507(a)(2)(A).
196. I.R.C. §4962(a).

spread agreement, was repeal of the provisions applying this section to government officials.[197]

In an attempt to equate the penalties for self-dealing applicable to private foundations with those in section 4958 for publicly supported charities, a bill passed by the House of Representatives in September 2003 contained a provision that would have increased the initial excise tax on a self-dealer in section 4941 from 5% to 25%.[198] However, the private foundation tax would still be imposed on the entire amount involved, not the amount of the excess benefit, so that unless modified before final passage, the measure would not have the desired result.

Mandatory Distributions

Criticisms had been raised during congressional investigations of the 1950s and 1960s that many foundations were making no current distributions for charitable purposes.[199] In response to such criticism and in a trade-off for dropping a forty-year limit on the life of foundations, in the Senate version of what became the Tax Reform Act of 1969, Congress enacted section 4942, which requires minimum annual distributions by private foundations for their charitable purposes.[200] As originally enacted, section 4942 mandated annual distributions of amounts equal to the greater of the foundation's net income and a fixed percent of the fair market value of its assets held for investment. The initial payout rate was set at 6% of the value of the foundation's assets, but it was to be redetermined from time to time by the Treasury to reflect "a relationship to 6 percent which the Secretary or his delegate determines to be comparable to the relationship which the money rates and investment yields for the calendar year immediately preceding the beginning of the taxable year bear to the money rates and investment yields for the calendar year 1969."[201]

The payout rate remained at 6% for 1971; it was 5½% for 1972, and 5¼% for 1973; it rose to 6% for 1974 and 1975, and was set permanently at 5% for taxable years beginning after December 31, 1975.[202] In 1981, after a period

197. Exempt Organizations Committee, American Bar Association, "Report of Task Force on Revision and Simplification of Rules Applicable to Private Foundations," 36 *Exempt Organization Tax Review* 262, 267 (2002).

198. Charitable Giving Act of 2003, H.R. 7, §105(c), 108th Cong., 1st Sess. (2003).

199. See Chapter 2.

200. I.R.C. §4942, codified by Tax Reform Act of 1969, Pub. L. No. 91-172, §101(b), 83 Stat. 487, 502–507 (1969).

201. Tax Reform Act of 1969, Pub. L. No. 91-172, §101(b), 83 Stat. 487, 503 (1969).

202. Tax Reform Act of 1976, Pub. L. No. 94-455, §1303, 90 Stat. 1520, 1715 (1976); see also Treas. Reg. §53.4942(a)-2(c)(5).

of extremely high interest rates and relatively slow asset growth, section 4942 was amended by deleting the requirement to distribute an amount equal to a foundation's adjusted net income if it was higher than the minimum investment return and to require instead distribution of an amount equal to the foundation's minimum investment return, which was set permanently at 5% of the fair market value of investment assets.[203]

In determining minimum investment return, the regulations require that readily marketable securities must be valued monthly.[204] Blockage and similar facts may be considered in determining value, but blockage discounts may not exceed 10% of market value.[205] Assets that are not publicly traded may be valued less frequently than monthly, with the regulations sanctioning five-year intervals for appraisal of real property.[206]

Excluded from the computation of minimum investment return are assets held to carry out a foundation's exempt purposes[207] and program-related investments, a special category of assets that are exempt from the definition of jeopardy investments prohibited under section 4944.[208] Assets held for exempt purposes include real estate and tangible property used for an exempt activity such as a conference center, works of art made available to the general public, and real estate, or that portion of it, in which a foundation's exempt purposes are carried on.[209] The regulations also limit the amount of cash that can be excluded to 1½% of the fair market value of the investment assets, unless the foundation can demonstrate to the Service that a larger amount is necessary to have on hand to cover administrative expenses and other normal and current disbursements directly connected with the foundation's exempt activities.[210]

To meet the requirements of section 4942, a foundation must make qualifying distributions in the required amount by the end of the tax year following the year in which the required distributable amount was computed, in effect a two-year rule. If a foundation distributes an amount greater than its minimum distributable amount in one year, the amount of the excess may be applied to reduce the amount required to be distributed in the next five succeeding years.[211]

---

203. Economic Recovery Tax Act of 1981, Pub. L. No. 97-34, §823, 95 Stat. 172, 351–352 (1981).

204. I.R.C. §4942(e)(2)(A).

205. I.R.C. §4942(e)(2)(B).

206. Treas. Reg. §53.4942(a)-2(c)(4)(iv)(a), (b).

207. Treas. Reg. §53.4942(a)-2(c)(2)(v).

208. Treas. Reg. §53.4942(a)-2(c)(3)(ii)(d).

209. Treas. Reg. §53.4942(a)-2(c)(3)(ii).

210. Treas. Reg. §53.4942(a)-2(c)(3)(iv).

211. I.R.C. §4942(g)(2)(D).

Qualified distributions include amounts paid to organizations that are not themselves private foundations, other than private operating foundations, as well as reasonable and necessary administrative expenses incurred in connection with making the qualifying distributions.[212] Between January 1, 1985, and December 31, 1990, a limit was placed on the amount of administrative expenses that could be treated as "qualifying distributions" for purposes of determining compliance with section 4942. These distributions also include certain pass-through grants to private foundations.[213] The statute contained a sunset provision under which it would expire after December 31, 1990.[214] Because the formula was unnecessarily complicated and produced distortions for some foundations, it was accordingly allowed to expire on the sunset date.[215]

The initial tax on failure to make distributions is 15% of the required distributable amount that has not been distributed before the first day of the second or any succeeding taxable year. There is an additional tax equal to 100% of the amount remaining undistributed at the close of a correction period, which is measured from the first day of the taxable year in which the foundation failed to make the required distribution to the earlier of the date of the mailing of notice from the Service of imposition of the initial tax and one year from the date on which the initial tax was imposed.[216]

A foundation may request and receive advance permission from the Internal Revenue Service to "set aside" for future use certain amounts that will be excluded from its distributable amounts for a period not exceeding five years. To receive approval, it must demonstrate that the funds will be used for a project that can better be accomplished by accumulating the funds during that period or, if the foundation had made certain minimum distributions in prior years, it can demonstrate that the project will not be completed within the year in which the set-aside is made.[217] However, the number of ruling requests to approve set-asides has been sparse, and it is apparent that the vast majority of foundations have adjusted their giving patterns to comply with the payout requirements.

Section 4942 contains a less stringent payout requirement for a category of foundations that actively conduct programs that form the basis for their ex-

212. I.R.C. §4942(g)(1)(A).
213. I.R.C. §4942(g)(4).
214. I.R.C. §4942(g)(4)(F), codified by Deficit Reduction Act of 1984, Pub. L. No. 98-369, §304, 98 Stat. 494, 782–783 (1984).
215. See Chapter 2 for a description of legislative proposals introduced in 2003 to disallow all expenses in computing the minimum distributable amount.
216. I.R.C. §4942(a), (b).
217. I.R.C. §4942(g)(2)(B).

emption. Called "private operating foundations," they are defined as organizations that currently expend an amount equal to substantially all (for example, 85%) of their adjusted net income directly for active conduct of their exempt activities, as opposed to making grants to other organizations, and that also meet one of three tests relating to the nature of their assets or of their support.[218]

In addition to more lenient payout provisions, private operating foundations receive the more favorable income tax treatment afforded to gifts to publicly supported charities, notably the 50% limit on contributions of cash and ordinary income property, and the 30% limit on contributions of capital gains property, and donors are not required to reduce the value of their contributions to reflect unrealized capital gain.[219] In addition, grants from private foundations to operating foundations are treated as qualifying distributions for purposes of meeting the payout requirements under section 4942,[220] but they are subject to the expenditure responsibility limitations in section 4945.[221]

Finally, in 1984 Congress created a further subcategory of operating foundations, described as "exempt operating foundations,"[222] as a safe harbor for organizations that, having operated for a number of years as a public charity, have failed to meet the public support test, yet because of their history and the public nature of the services they provide, should not be automatically subject to the section 4940 excise tax[223] and the expenditure responsibility provisions of section 4945.[224] To qualify for this subcategory, a private operating foundation must have been publicly supported for at least ten years, and be governed by a board at least 75% of whose members are not disqualified persons and one that is representative of the general public, and that at no time within the year has had an officer who is disqualified.[225] There appear to be very few organizations to which this provision has been applied.

Under common law trust principles, a trustee is required to make trust property productive and, unless the terms of the trust provide otherwise, must distribute the income currently.[226] In 1969 when the payout rule was adopted, the terms of many charitable trusts prohibited distributions of prin-

218. I.R.C. §4942(j)(3).
219. I.R.C. §170(b)(1)(A)(vii).
220. I.R.C. §4942(g)(1)(A).
221. I.R.C. §4945(d)(4)(A).
222. I.R.C. 4940(d), codified by Deficit Reduction Act of 1984, Pub. L. No. 98-369, §302(a), 98 Stat. 494, 778–781 (1984).
223. I.R.C. §4940(d).
224. I.R.C. §4945(d)(4)(A).
225. I.R.C. §4940(d)(2).
226. Restatement (Second) of the Law of Trusts, §611.

cipal. The Tax Reform Act contained provisions that effectively required the trustees to seek court approval of amendments to the trust to permit compliance with section 4942.[227] Trusts created after the effective date do not qualify for exemption unless the trust documents mandate compliance with all of the private foundation restrictions so that state law is not a hindrance to compliance.[228] In fact, the concept of total return that underlies the Modern Prudent Investor Rule conforms to the approach of the payout provisions, while the Uniform Management of Institutional Funds Act permits distributions of unrealized appreciation.[229] However, the payout rule is inflexible, the rate itself is arbitrary, and the requirement imposes constraints on both investment policy and grant-making. It has been one of the more controversial of the private foundation restrictions, drawing criticism on the one hand from those who want to see more immediate benefits to society from assets that are tax-exempt, and on the other hand from those who would like the payout rate reduced so as to assure that future societal needs will be adequately met.[230]

Excess Business Holdings

Two provisions adopted in 1969 reflected congressional response to evidence that some foundation managers were investing foundation assets in enterprises in which their donors also had a personal interest and were operating them in a manner that provided more benefit to the donors than to the public. Section 4943 effectively prohibits a foundation from holding more than a de minimis interest in any donor-controlled business enterprise, while section 4944 restricts the nature of foundation investments.

Under section 4943, foundations, together with their disqualified persons, are prohibited from owning more than a 20% interest in any business enterprise. If effective control of the enterprise can be shown to be held by anyone other than the foundation and its disqualified persons, the limitation is increased from 20% to 35%.[231] There is also a safe harbor provision permitting ownership by a foundation, without regard to the holdings of others, of 2% of the voting stock and not more than 2% in value of all outstanding shares of a business enterprise.[232] In cases in which interests in a business enterprise

---

227. I.R.C. §508(e)(2), codified by Tax Reform Act of 1969, Pub. L. No. 91-172, §101(a), 83 Stat. 487, 499 (1969).

228. I.R.C. §508(e)(1).

229. See Chapter 4.

230. Donald W. Trotter et al., *Spending Policies and Investment Planning for Foundations: A Structure for Determining a Foundation's Asset Mix* (New York: Council on Foundations, 3d ed., 1999); Lester M. Salamon, *Foundation Investment and Payout Performance: An Update* (New York: Council on Foundations, 1991).

231. I.R.C. §4943(c)(2)(A)-(B).

232. I.R.C. §4943(c)(2)(C).

that will cause the foundation to exceed the limits are received by gift or bequest, the foundation has a five-year period from receipt to reduce its holdings to the minimum allowable limit. In addition, the Service may extend the five-year period for an additional five years if the foundation demonstrates that it has not been possible, despite its diligent efforts, to dispose of the interests during the initial five-year grace period.[233]

The act also contained detailed provisions governing the timing for disposition of business interests held on May 26, 1969, the effective date of the act.[234] Although these statutory provisions appear convoluted and difficult to comply with, there has been little controversy regarding their application.

The rules applicable to stock holdings also apply to interests in unincorporated businesses, while parallel rules apply to partnership interests and businesses that are conducted as sole proprietorships.[235] However, businesses that are considered "functionally related" to the foundation's exempt purposes, and those in which at least 95% of the gross income is derived from dividends, interest, rent, and other sources that are considered "passive," are excluded from the definition of business enterprise and thus not subject to the section 4943 limitations.[236]

The initial tax on an excess business holding is 5% of the value of the holding, with imposition of the tax made on the last day of a tax year but with the value of the holding determined as of the day during the year in which the value was the highest. An additional tax equal to 200% of the value of the excess holding will be imposed if it has not been disposed of during the correction period. There is no separate tax on foundation managers under this section.[237]

The excess business holdings provisions have been strongly criticized, notably by John Simon in congressional testimony during the hearings on private foundations conducted by the House Ways and Means Committee in 1973, and again in 1983, in which he expressed concern as to their adverse effect on the birth rate of foundations.[238] The members of the ABA 2002 Task Force were divided between some who saw no valid rationale for retaining the provisions, and the majority who believed there might be some

---

233. I.R.C. §4943(c)(6), (7).

234. I.R.C. §4943(c)(4).

235. I.R.C. §4943(c)(3)(B).

236. I.R.C. §4943(d)(3).

237. I.R.C. §4943(a), (b).

238. Private Foundations: Hearings before the Subcommittee on Oversight of the House Committee on Ways and Means, 93d Cong., 1st Sess., at 165–179 (1973); Tax Rules Governing Private Foundations, 1983: Hearings before the Subcommittee on Oversight of the House Committee on Ways and Means, Serial 98-32, 98th Cong., 1st Sess., pt. 2 (1984). See also John G. Simon, "The Regulation of American Foundations: Looking Backward at the Tax Reform Act of 1969," 6 *Voluntas* 243 (1995).

residual validity to the limits, but would like to see the 2% de minimis rule increased to at least 5%, and would change the definition of a business enterprise to permit investment in certain partnership and limited liability companies that serve as valid investment vehicles.[239]

Jeopardy Investments

Section 4944 imposes a tax on a private foundation that invests any amount in a manner that would jeopardize the carrying out of its exempt purposes. The regulations further define the prohibition by stipulating that the tax is to be imposed if the managers have failed to exercise ordinary business care and prudence under the facts and circumstances prevailing at the time the investment was made, and in providing for the long-term and short-term financial needs of the foundation in carrying out its charitable activities. Determinations are made on a case-by-case basis, looking, however, at the portfolio as a whole.[240] The regulations give as examples of speculative investments that are to receive close scrutiny: "trading in securities on margin, trading in commodity futures, investments in working interests in oil and gas wells, the purchase of 'puts,' 'calls,' and 'straddles,' the purchase of warrants, and selling short."[241] The regulations also provide that no state law could exempt or relieve any person from obligations under this section and vice versa.[242]

As noted in the description of the provisions of section 4942, exempt from the provisions of section 4944 are a category described as "program-related investments" (PRI), defined as investments, the primary purpose of which is to accomplish one or more of the exempt purposes of the organization and no significant purpose of which is the production of income or appreciation of property.[243] Examples of a PRI include investment in a business in a distressed area of an inner city, or a loan to an organization that will build and rent housing for the elderly. Classification as a PRI permits a foundation to disregard the gain from investments for purposes of determining the tax on net investment income under section 4940,[244] the foundation's minimum investment return under section 4942,[245] and excess business holdings under section 4943.[246]

---

239. Exempt Organizations Committee, "Report of Task Force," 268–269.
240. Treas. Reg. §53.4944-1(a)(2).
241. Id.; see also Staff of Treasury Department, *Report on Private Foundations*, 89th Cong., 1st Sess., at 53–54 (Committee on Finance, 1965).
242. Treas. Reg. §53.4944-1(a)(2).
243. I.R.C. §4944(c).
244. Treas. Reg. §53.4940-1(f)(1).
245. Treas. Reg. §53.4942(a)-2(c)(2), (3)(ii)(d).
246. Treas. Reg. §53.4943-10(b).

The regulations interpret the statutory language of section 4944 as requiring a foundation to apply a "but-for" test in regard to PRIs, thereby precluding investments that might have a reasonable possibility of success, regardless of their close connection to the carrying out of the organization's purposes.[247] The uncertainty regarding this standard has led many foundations to refrain from making PRIs, despite the fact that the investment would specifically be in furtherance of the organization's exempt purpose.

The excise taxes under section 4944 are imposed on the foundation itself, in an amount equal to 5% of the amount of the investment for each year or part thereof of the taxable period and, if there is no correction, there is an additional tax equal to 25% of the investment.[248] As with the other provisions in Chapter 42, the taxable period begins on the date on which the prohibited investment was made and ends on the earliest of the date of mailing of a notice of deficiency, the date on which the tax is assessed, or the date on which the amount is removed from jeopardy, which is the date of sale or other disposition of the improper investment and the reinvestment of the proceeds in assets that are not prohibited under the Code.[249]

There is also a tax on any manager who approved the investment knowing that it was a jeopardy investment, unless his participation was not willful and was due to reasonable cause. The tax is equal to 5% of the amount invested, with a limit for each jeopardy investment improperly approved of $5,000. If an initial tax is imposed and the manager refuses to agree to the correction, there is an additional tax equal to 5% of the investment with a limit of $10,000.[250] Managers are jointly and severally liable for the taxes, and the section 507 termination tax is applicable if there are repeated willful violations of the provisions.[251] As with the other provisions of Chapter 42, managers may rely on advice of counsel, in this instance both legal and investment counsel.[252]

Critics of this provision believe it is beyond the ability of the Service to administer, pointing to the paucity of rulings and cases involving violations. They also express concern that the current regulations are too far out of step with state law changes, particularly the standards of the Modern Prudent Investor Rule. Reflecting these views, the ABA 2002 Task Force recommended repeal of section 4944 or, as an alternative, eliminating reference to "close scrutiny" of any particular investment, as well as broadening the exception for program-related investments and clarifying that the presence of a seem-

247. Treas. Reg. §53.4944-3(a)(2)(i).
248. I.R.C. §4944(a)(1), (b)(1).
249. I.R.C. §4944(e).
250. I.R.C. §4944(a)(2), (b)(2), (d)(2).
251. I.R.C. §4944(d)(1).
252. Treas. Reg. §53.4944-1(b)(2)(v).

ingly high projected rate of return should not per se prevent an investment from qualifying as a PRI.[253]

Taxable Expenditures

Unlike the restrictions on foundations in sections 4941 through 4944 that define the duties of foundation managers in connection with their duties of loyalty and care, the restrictions under section 4945 relate to the manner in which they carry out the foundation's charitable purposes, restrictions that have no counterpart in state law. These limitations were not a part of the original recommendations made by the Treasury, nor did they surface in the reports of the Reece, Cox, and Patman Committees. Rather, as described in Chapter 2, they reflected adverse reactions of Congress to testimony presented during the hearings on the Tax Reform Act of 1969 to the effect that certain foundations were conducting activities considered inimical to their preferred status as charities eligible to receive tax-deductible contributions.

There are five categories of "taxable expenditures," the making of which will subject the foundation itself and its managers to excise taxes. They are as follows:

PROPAGANDA AND LOBBYING. Section 4945(d) prohibits foundations from expending any amount on grassroots lobbying or attempting to influence legislation through communication with any member or employee of a legislative body or any other government official or employee who may participate in the formulation of the legislation.[254] Legislation is confined to acts by a legislature—federal, state, or local—thereby exempting actions by executive, judicial, or administrative bodies as well as quasi-legislative entities whether elective or appointive.[255]

There are three important exceptions: lobbying communications do not include information containing nonpartisan analysis, study, or research, defined as communications to legislators and the public in which the foundation presents a "sufficiently full and fair exposition of the pertinent facts that enables the public to form an independent opinion."[256] Examinations and discussions of broad social, economic, and similar problems are likewise excluded from the definition of lobbying.[257] A second exception permits expenditure of amounts to provide technical assistance to a governmental body or

253. Exempt Organizations Committee, "Report of Task Force," 269–270.
254. I.R.C. §4945(d)(1).
255. Treas. Reg. §53.4945-2(a).
256. Treas. Reg. §53.4945-2(d)(1)(ii).
257. Treas. Reg. §53.4945-2(d)(4).

committee in response to a written request to the foundation from the governmental body.[258] The final exception is for expenditures made to influence proposed legislation that could affect the powers or duties of the foundation, its existence, its tax-exempt status, or the deductibility of contributions to it.[259] So long as a foundation's funds are not earmarked for prohibited activities, they will not put the foundation in jeopardy if the grantee uses them for expenditures that the foundation is prohibited from making.

INFLUENCING THE OUTCOME OF ELECTIONS.   The second category of taxable expenditures are those to influence the outcome of a specific public election or to carry on any voter registration drive.[260] The provision is redundant, in that it merely restates the basic requirements for exemption under section 501(c)(3). It was enacted to quiet congressional concerns raised after hearing testimony that foundation funds were being used to finance voter registration drives in certain sensitive areas and to publicize the views of certain political candidates.[261]

GRANTS TO INDIVIDUALS.   Section 4945(d)(3) does not prohibit grant-making activities, unlike the prohibitions against lobbying and political activities. Rather, a private foundation is precluded from making grants to individuals for travel, study, or similar purposes only if it has not obtained advance approval from the Service of a grant-making program that satisfies the Service that the grants (1) will constitute scholarships or fellowships that are not included in the gross income of the grantee by virtue of meeting the requirement under section 117(a) that the grant be used at an institution eligible for exemption and receipt of tax-deductible contributions and that the award procedure is objective and nondiscriminatory; (2) will constitute prizes or awards also eligible for exclusion from income of the recipient under section 74(b); or (3) are made to "achieve a specific objective, produce a report or other similar product or improve or enhance a capacity, skill or talent of the grantee."[262] The Senate Report explained that the provisions were designed to prevent foundations from using the grant-making process "to enable people to take vacations abroad, to have paid interludes between jobs, and to subsidize the preparation of materials furthering specific political views."[263]

---

258. Treas. Reg. §53.4945-2(d)(2).
259. Treas. Reg. §53.4945-2(d)(3).
260. I.R.C. §4945(d)(2).
261. S. Rep. No. 91-552, 91st Cong., 1st Sess., at 454 (1969).
262. I.R.C. §4945(d)(3), (g).
263. S. Rep. No. 91-552, 91st Cong., 1st Sess., at 69 (1969).

GRANTS TO OTHER FOUNDATIONS. As is the case with the restrictions on grants to individuals, there is no absolute prohibition in the section 4945 restriction on grants to organizations. In fact, all grants to public charities are exempt from the provisions of Chapter 42, unless earmarked for a noncharitable purpose.[264] Grants to other private foundations, however, are subject to excise tax unless the foundation exercises what is described as "expenditure responsibility" in connection with making the grant.[265] This entails investigating the reliability of the grantee prior to making the grant, requiring the grantee to agree to comply with the private foundation restrictions on expenditures and to use the grant only for the purposes for which it was made, and mandating that the recipient will provide reports on its progress in carrying out the terms of the grant. The grantor foundation must, in turn, report to the Service on the expenditures made by the grantee.[266]

In response to this limitation, a large number of foundations have adopted policies precluding the making of grants to any but publicly supported organizations, a practice that has persisted despite the fact that compliance is not as great a burden as was originally feared. One of the greatest difficulties has been with respect to grants to foreign charities that are required to establish that such charities meet the tests for an organization that is not a private foundation. Equally burdensome has been the requirement that the foundation must continue to exercise expenditure responsibility until the funds are fully expended, a rule that has been inconsistently applied in connection with grants for endowment or capital equipment.[267]

EXPENDITURES FOR NONCHARITABLE PURPOSES. The fifth category of expenditures characterized as "taxable" under section 4945 is in the nature of a "catchall," applicable to expenditures "for any purpose other than one specified in section 170(c)(2)(B)," that section of the Internal Revenue Code containing the definition of charitable purposes in connection with the income tax deduction for charitable contributions.[268] The regulations under section 4945 contain exceptions for reasonable administrative expenses, payment of taxes, or purchase of investments.[269] The prohibition applies to any grant to an organization that is not exempt under section 501(c)(3) unless the following conditions are met: (1) the making of the grant constitutes a direct charitable act or a program-related investment; (2) the grantor exer-

264. I.R.C. §4945(d)(4)(A).
265. I.R.C. §4945(d)(4)(B).
266. I.R.C. §4945(h).
267. Exempt Organizations Committee, "Report of Task Force," 270.
268. I.R.C. §4945(d)(5).
269. Treas. Reg. §53.4945-6(b).

cises expenditure responsibility in connection with the grant; and (3) the grantee agrees to continuously maintain the grant funds or other assets in a separate fund dedicated exclusively to exempt purposes.[270]

The penalties for violation of section 4945 may be imposed on the foundation as well as its managers. The initial tax on the organization is equal to 10% of the amount expended, while the second-tier tax is equal to 100% of the amount involved.[271] The first-level tax on a manager who knowingly approved the expenditure is equal to 2½% of the amount involved, with a $5,000 ceiling, and the second-tier tax is 50%, with a $10,000 ceiling.[272] Managers are not subject to tax if their participation was not willful and was due to reasonable cause.[273]

There are elements of section 4945 that reflect what can best be described as "overkill" that could be repealed without weakening the Service's ability to monitor foundation behavior. Modification of others would go far to lowering grant administrative costs and permitting foundations to be more effective. The ABA Task Force recommended adoption of a provision that would permit abatement of penalties upon a showing that an expenditure was made in good faith and in the belief that it was not a violation of the Code; reconcile the distinction between grants for travel, study, and so on, and other grants to individuals; eliminate the advance approval requirement for individuals; and repeal the expenditure responsibility requirement applicable to grants to other private foundations and in all events limit its duration. It also called for repeal of the restrictions in section 4945 on lobbying, noting their redundancy, and finally called for a provision permitting abatement of the tax for technical violations.[274]

Impact of Chapter 42 on Charitable Fiduciaries

Some insight into the effect of these provisions on the behavior of exempt organization fiduciaries can be garnered from the statistics on collection of the Chapter 42 taxes. The Internal Revenue Service chart of exempt organizations excise tax collections on page 284 shows the amount of excise taxes collected in the years between 1971 and 1997 under sections 4941 through 4945, as reported on Form 4720, the return that is required to be filed in all cases in which violation of the provisions of these sections is reported on the annual information return, Form 990PF, by a foundation. The amount of

270. Treas. Reg. §53.4945-6(c)(2).
271. I.R.C. §4945(a)(1), (b)(1).
272. I.R.C. §4945(a)(2), (b)(2), (c)(2).
273. I.R.C. §4945(a)(2).
274. Exempt Organizations Committee, "Report of Task Force," 270–271.

Exempt organizations excise tax collections (in thousands of dollars)

Fiscal year	IRC 4941	IRC 4942	IRC 4943	IRC 4944	IRC 4945
1971	8	*	27	*	1
1972	45	*	51	*	7
1973	78	94	13	16	1
1974	229	160	3	8	8
1975	324	360	6	*	1
1976	310	950	9	102	95
1977	212	809	3	*	103
1978	6,110[a]	1,265	*	2	79
1979	234	1,306	24	3	130
1980	239	976	67	2	117
1981	2,576[b]	1,158	44	4	150
1982	227	1,619	36	4	142
1983	438	1,041	61	8	119
1984	192	1,184	118	1	292
1985	N/A	N/A	N/A	N/A	N/A
1986	N/A	N/A	N/A	N/A	N/A
1987	N/A	N/A	N/A	N/A	N/A
1988	597	1,640	37	53	143
1989	1,574	718	11	8	251
1990	171	1,133	235	13	635
1991	695	4,797	26	4	81
1992	1,523	1,388	19	1	137
1993	441	906	14	*	86
1994	449	3,094	10	3	295
1995	293	633	1	2	113
1996	4,308	641	3	117	35
1997	286	1,912	51	*	42

Notes:
IRC 4941: Tax on Self-Dealing
IRC 4942: Tax on Undistributed Income
IRC 4943: Tax on Excess Business Holdings
IRC 4944: Tax on Investments That Jeopardize Charitable Purpose
IRC 4945: Tax on Taxable Expenditures
N/A: not available
* = less than $1,000
a. Includes tax payment in excess of $4.1 million in one case.
b. Includes tax payment in excess of $2 million in one case.

taxes levied for failure to comply with section 4943, excess business holdings, and section 4944, jeopardy investments, was minimal, as were the corresponding taxes imposed on foundation managers under these sections. This would seem to indicate that managers have learned the rules and that compliance has not been overly difficult. However, this does not appear to be the case with the tax on undistributed income, where the taxes far exceeded those collected under any other section. In contrast, the taxes collected for violation of taxable expenditures were relatively smaller.[275]

Reconciling Chapter 42 and the Excess Benefits Provisions

Aware of the fact that there was overlap between the private foundation and the excess benefit rules, in April 2002 the Service requested comments from the public as to whether the regulations under Chapter 42 dealing with the private foundation excise tax provisions should be revised to conform with the final regulations under section 4958.[276] Specifically singled out were the safe harbor rules for foundation managers who rely on advice of counsel that a particular transaction was not prohibited, which are more narrow in scope than those under section 4958.

Prohibition against Participation in Political Campaigns

The prohibition against participation in political campaigns is absolute. It was enacted in 1954, having been proposed by Senator Lyndon B. Johnson to curb the activities of a private foundation in Texas that he believed had provided financial support to his opponent in an election.[277] Although on its face it appears to be an absolute prohibition, and it is so viewed by the Service, the Commissioner of Internal Revenue, in a statement before Congress in 1987, acknowledged that there could be circumstances in which the activity was so trivial as to be without legal significance and, therefore, de minimus.[278]

In 2000 the United States Court of Appeals for the District of Columbia Circuit affirmed the revocation of the exemption of a church that had placed advertisements in two nationally distributed newspapers opposing a candidate four days prior to the presidential election and soliciting tax-deductible contributions. The court held that the revocation was not a violation of the church's free exercise of religion and did not constitute selective prosecution in violation of the equal protection clause.[279] The Circuit Court decision noted that the church could establish an affiliate exempt under section

275. IRS Statistics of Income, "Exempt Organizations Excise Tax Collections" (fiscal years 1971–1997) (original on file with author).

276. Ann. 2002-47, 2002-18 I.R.B. 1.

277. 100 Cong. Rec. 9604 (1954).

278. Lobbying and Political Activities of Tax-Exempt Organizations: Hearings before the Subcommittee on Oversight of the House Committee on Ways and Means, Serial 100-5, 100th Cong., 1st Sess., 96–97 (statement of Lawrence B. Gibbs); see also Joint Committee on Taxation, *Lobbying and Political Activities of Tax-Exempt Organizations* (JCS-5-87) (March 11, 1987).

279. Branch Ministries, Inc. v. Commissioner, 40 F. Supp. 2d 15 (D.D.C. 1999), aff'd, 211 F.3d 137 (D.C. Cir. 2000).

501(c)(4), which could in turn establish a separate segregated fund or political action committee to participate in campaigns without jeopardizing its own exempt status.

The limitation on political activity is applicable to the organization itself and not its officers, directors, and employees acting in their individual capacities, unless the organization has directly or indirectly authorized or ratified their activities.[280] For example, in 1986 the Service revoked the exemption of the Jimmy Swaggart Ministries attributing to the organization statements of its president, Jimmy Swaggart, that were made at an official meeting of the organization and in its newsletter endorsing Pat Robertson for president.[281]

In addition to the specific prohibition against campaign intervention, violation of which is grounds for revocation of exemption, section 4955, enacted in 1987, provides for imposition of excise taxes on organizations that make "political expenditures" and on their managers who approve the expenditures knowing they are political expenditures, unless the approval was not willful and was due to reasonable cause.[282] As with the private foundation taxes, an additional tax is imposed if there is no timely correction.[283]

Restrictions on Lobbying Activities

The limitation on lobbying that was enacted in 1934[284] has been attributed to congressional reaction to the activities of an organization known as the National Economy League.[285] McGovern observed that both the lobbying and the campaign prohibitions have had far greater impact than curbing of the specific abuses as intended by their sponsors.[286] It is to be noted that tax law differs most markedly from substantive property law in its denial of exemption to organizations whose purpose is to change existing laws. Thus the border patrol function of the federal government regulates an area for which there is no state parallel and no state precedents.

Constitutional challenges similar to those made to the political campaign prohibition have also been brought in regard to the limitations on lobby-

280. Gen. Couns. Mem. 33,912 (August 15, 1968).

281. The matter was subsequently settled and exemption reinstated, with the terms of the closing agreement requiring Mr. Swaggart to issue a public statement. "Public Statement: Jimmy Swaggart Ministries," 92 *Tax Notes Today* 31-31 (February 11, 1992).

282. I.R.C. §4955, codified by Omnibus Budget Reconciliation Act of 1987, Pub. L. No. 100-203, §10712(a), 101 Stat. 1330, 1330-465.

283. I.R.C. §4955(b).

284. Revenue Act of 1934, Pub. L. No. 73-216, §101(6), 48 Stat. 680, 700 (1934).

285. 78 Cong. Rec. 5861 (1934).

286. James J. McGovern et al., "The Final Lobbying Regulations: A Challenge for Both the IRS and Charities," 48 *Tax Notes* 1305 (1990).

ing.[287] The leading case is *Regan v. Taxation With Representation,* in which the Supreme Court found that the limitation on lobbying as applied to a charitable organization did not violate either the right of free speech nor the right to equal protection.[288] It held that both tax exemption and the ability of donors to make deductible contributions are in the nature of federal subsidies, and that Congress could choose to support one type of activity and not another without violating a constitutional right.[289]

In the earlier case of *United States v. Christian Echoes,* decided by the Court of Appeals for the Tenth Circuit in 1972,[290] the court upheld the revocation of exemption of a religious organization that published a periodical and other literature urging its readers to take action in regard to a number of legislative matters on the grounds that the limitations on lobbying did not violate the organization's rights under the First and Fifth Amendments. Fishman and Schwarz report that prior to the 1960s the lobbying limitations were only periodically enforced, but that during the early days of the Kennedy administration an "ideological organizations" project was instituted, of which this case was an outgrowth.[291]

In response to widely expressed concerns that the "substantiality test" was too vague, thereby discouraging charities from engaging in any but a minimal amount of lobbying, in 1976 Congress adopted section 501(h) under which charities may elect to be subject to a mathematical test to determine the amount they may expend for lobbying, rather than attempting to comply with the vague standard of the substantiality test.[292] Charities exercising the election are subject to a two-part test to determine whether they are in compliance with the lobbying limits, one applicable to total expenses[293] and a second equal to 25% of the first, for attempts to influence the general public in regard to legislation.[294] The limits are based on a sliding scale applied to the

287. Frances R. Hill and Douglas M. Mancino, *Taxation of Exempt Organizations,* ¶5.02 (New York: Warren, Gorham & Lamont, 2002).

288. 461 U.S. 540 (1983).

289. Hill and Mancino, *Taxation of Exempt Organizations,* ¶5.02 n.33; Kathleen M. Sullivan, "Unconstitutional Conditions," 102 *Harvard Law Review* 1415 (1989).

290. 470 F.2d 849 (10th Cir. 1972).

291. James J. Fishman and Stephen Schwarz, *Cases and Materials on Nonprofit Organizations,* 524 (New York: Foundation Press, 2d ed., 2000).

292. Tax Reform Act of 1976, Pub. L. No. 94-455, §1307(a), 90 Stat. 1520, 1720–1721 (1976). See Joint Committee on Taxation, *Description of Present-Law Rules Relating to Political and Other Activities of Organizations Described in Section 501(c)(3) and Proposals Regarding Churches* (JCX-39-02) (May 14, 2002), for a summary of the limits on lobbying under the substantiality test and section 501(h).

293. I.R.C. §4911(c)(2).

294. I.R.C. §4911(c)(4).

total amount of the organization's expenditures. Calculations are made on a four-year average; there is a cap of $1 million on total expenditures during any one calendar year.[295] An organization that exceeds these limits is subject to a 25% excise tax on the amount of excess expenditures,[296] and tax exemption will be lost if the organization expenditures averaged over a four-year period exceed 150% of either the total limit or the grassroots limit.[297]

The definition of lobbying under sections 501(h) and 4911 is to be found in the regulations under section 4911.[298] These regulations are also looked to by the Service when making determinations under the substantiality test of section 501(c)(3) and are similar to those under section 4945 applicable to private foundations. Direct lobbying is defined as an attempt to influence any legislation through a communication making reference to specific legislation and including a view on it to any member of a legislative body or other government official who may participate in the formulation of that legislation.[299] Grassroots lobbying is an attempt to influence legislation through communications that are aimed at influencing the general public or a segment of it. As with direct lobbying, it requires reference to specific legislation that has already been introduced and must reflect a view as to the legislation. It differs in that it includes a call to action by contacting a government official, provides information identifying legislators to contact and material to be used in making the contact, or identifies the positions of specific legislators in regard to the legislation.[300]

There is an important exception to the "call to action" definition: if within two weeks before a vote by a committee or the legislature on a "highly publicized piece of legislation," the charity communicates in the mass media a "point of view" on the general subject of the legislation and refers to the legislation or encourages the public to communicate with their legislators on the general subject of the legislation, the charity is presumed to have engaged in grassroots lobbying. The presumption may be rebutted if the organization can demonstrate that the communication is of a type that it regularly makes in the mass media without regard to the timing of the legislation.[301]

Not included within the definition of lobbying are five types of communications that together comprise major exceptions to the rules. They are (1) making available the results of nonpartisan analysis, study, or research, which

295. I.R.C. §4911(c)(2).
296. I.R.C. §4911(a)(1).
297. I.R.C. §501(h)(1).
298. Treas. Reg. §56.4911-0 to -10.
299. Treas. Reg. §56.4911-2(b)(1).
300. Treas. Reg. §56.4911-2(b)(2).
301. Treas. Reg. §56.4911-2(b)(5)(ii).

may include advocating a position on legislation so long as there is sufficient information presented to allow the recipients to form their own conclusions, and also permits wide distribution so long as the study is not targeted only to those interested in one side of the issue;[302] (2) discussion of broad social economic or similar problems so long as they do not relate to the merits of specific bills or directly encourage recipients to take action;[303] (3) provision of technical advice to a governmental body or committee in response to a written request;[304] (4) "self-defense" lobbying in connection with any action that might affect the charity's existence, its powers and duties, its tax-exempt status, or its eligibility to receive tax-deductible contributions;[305] and (5) communications with members so long as they are not directly encouraged to engage in direct or grassroots lobbying themselves, although they may be indirectly encouraged to do so by virtue of the inclusion of names and addresses of legislators.[306]

Far fewer organizations have made the election under section 501(h) than the sponsors of the legislation had anticipated. This may have been due in part to the complicated record-keeping needed to assure compliance, although some believe it is attributable to the fact that the large majority of organizations do not engage in lobbying to any extent. Unfortunately, there is no available information on the amount of excise taxes collected for violation of the lobbying limitations, making it difficult to assess the impact of the provisions.[307]

Unrelated Business Income Tax

In 1950, in response to charges that exempt charitable organizations were competing unfairly with private business, Congress enacted legislation applicable to organizations exempt under section 501 subjecting to income tax certain of their activities that were not "related" to the carrying out of the purposes that formed the basis for their exemption.[308] Although not directly regulating fiduciary behavior, these provisions are important in the decision-

302. Treas. Reg. §56.4911-2(c)(1).
303. Treas. Reg. §56.4911-2(c)(2).
304. Treas. Reg. §56.4911-2(c)(3).
305. Treas. Reg. §56.4911-2(c)(4).
306. Treas. Reg. §56.4911-5(f)(6).
307. Report on Strengthening Nonprofit Advocacy Project (May 2002) (joint project by OMB Watch, Tufts University, and Charity in the Public Interest).
308. I.R.C. §§511–513, codified by Revenue Act of 1950, Pub. L. No. 81-814, §301, 64 Stat. 906, 947-952 (1950).

making of exempt organization fiduciaries, influencing the activities that they authorize and the manner in which these activities will be pursued.

An activity is considered "unrelated" if it does not contribute importantly to the achievement of exempt purposes other than through the production of income, and it will be deemed substantially related only if there is a clear nexus between the business activity and the exempt purpose of the organization.[309] To be subject to tax, the activity in question must have the characteristics of a trade or business, and be "regularly carried on" rather than conducted on an intermittent basis.[310]

Excepted from the tax, although they might otherwise be considered "unrelated," are receipts from the following sources: (1) dividends, interest, payments with respect to securities, loans, annuities, royalties, income from notional principal contracts, and other income from ordinary and routine investments;[311] (2) rents;[312] (3) income from a trade or business in which substantially all of the work is performed by volunteers,[313] or is carried on primarily for the convenience of its members, students, patients, officers, or employees;[314] and (4) income from the sale of merchandise, substantially all of which has been received by the organization as gifts and contributions.[315]

The tax may be imposed on income from advertising, certain trade shows, distribution of low-cost articles, rental and exchange of member lists with for-profit entities, and income from property the acquisition of which was debt-financed.[316] It also extends to activities that, while they might otherwise be considered to be carrying out exempt purposes, are exploited in commercial endeavors beyond the scope necessary to carry out exempt functions.[317] The regulations give as an example of exploitation an organization that operated a public radio station that contributed importantly to the accomplishment of its exempt purposes but that also regularly sold advertising time and services to commercial advertisers. The example noted that the income from the commercial advertisers was income from an unrelated trade or business. This was in contrast to the operation by an exempt college of a campus newspaper operated by its students who solicited advertising, the distinction being

309. Treas. Reg. §1.513-1(a), (d)(1).
310. Treas. Reg. §1.513-1(a), (c)(1), (c)(2)(ii)-(iii).
311. I.R.C. §512(b)(1); Treas. Reg. §1.512(b)-1(a)(1).
312. I.R.C. §512(b)(3).
313. I.R.C. §512(a)(1).
314. I.R.C. §513(a)(2).
315. I.R.C. §513(a)(3).
316. I.R.C. §513(c), (d), (h), (i); I.R.C. §514.
317. Treas. Reg. §1.513-1(d)(4)(iv).

that the advertising business contributed to the students' education in connection with one aspect of the newspaper business.[318]

Section 512(b)(13) modifies the provisions of sections 512(b)(1)–(3) by denying the exemption for interest, dividends, rents, and royalties in cases when this income is received from a controlled organization.[319] Until the end of 1997, control was defined as an 80% interest. Amendments to the Code enacted in that year reduced the percentage to 50% for future years, and also extended the definition of control to include constructive ownership rules, thereby subjecting to tax income not only from a first-tier controlled subsidiary, but from a second-tier subsidiary controlled by the first-tier corporation.[320] These provisions substantially limited the ability of charities to avoid the unrelated business income tax (UBIT) by transferring unrelated business activities to controlled subsidiaries.

Under section 514, the breadth of the UBIT provisions extends to instances in which an exempt organization borrows funds to acquire income-producing property, with exceptions for property that is to be used in the performance of its exempt functions.[321] This section was enacted as part of the Tax Reform Act of 1969 in response to evidence presented to Congress that a number of individuals were trading on the exemption of charities they controlled by purchasing property on credit and leasing it back to the seller.[322]

Section 514 denies the exemption from unrelated business taxable income (UBTI) for passive income to income derived from debt-financed property. Thus an organization must include in its UBTI a percentage of income from property subject to indebtedness equal to the "average acquisition indebtedness" for the year in question over the average amount of its adjusted basis in the property during that year.[323] There are a number of important exceptions to the rule, specifically for property substantially all the use of which is substantially related to the organization's exempt purposes and property used in a trade or business the income from which is also exempt from UBIT.[324] This

318. Treas. Reg. §1.513-1(d)(4)(iv) (exs. 4, 5).

319. I.R.C. §512(b)(13).

320. Taxpayer Relief Act of 1997, Pub. L. No. 105-34, §1041(a), 111 Stat. 788, 938–939 (1997).

321. I.R.C. §514(b)(1), codified by Tax Reform Act of 1969, Pub. L. No. 91-172, §121, 83 Stat. 487, 543–548 (1969).

322. S. Rep. No. 91-552, 91st Cong., 1st Sess., at 62–63 (1969); H.R. Rep. No. 91-413, 91st Cong., 1st Sess., at 44–46 (1969); see also Suzanne Ross McDowell, "Taxing Leveraged Investments of Charitable Organizations: What Is the Rationale?" 39 *Case Western Reserve Law Review* 705, 712–714 (1988); Suzanne Ross McDowell, "Taxation of Unrelated Debt-Financed Income," 34 *Exempt Organization Tax Review* 197 (2001).

323. I.R.C. §514(a)(1).

324. I.R.C. §514(b)(1).

affects real estate holdings but also may extend to other special investments involving debt.

In 2000 the Court of Appeals for the Second Circuit ruled that income derived from securities purchased on margin was subject to UBIT, rejecting the charity's arguments that the activity was substantially related to its exempt function of providing financial support to another charity.[325]

The exemption from the definition of unrelated business taxable income for royalties has been a difficult one for the Service, resulting in a larger proportion of court decisions than has been the case with the other exemptions. Neither the Code itself nor the legislative history has provided guidance. The most contentious issues involved affinity credit card programs and rentals of mailing lists. The Service's position was that a payment is not a royalty if the subject of the payment is not "passive," and thus a royalty cannot include compensation for services rendered by the owner of the property.[326] After a series of defeats in the court,[327] the Service announced in December 1999 that it was suspending further litigation in cases involving credit cards and mailing lists with facts similar to those decided in favor of taxpayers, thereby resolving the issue in favor of the charities.[328]

Another area of contention involved advertising in magazines published by exempt organizations. The first major case, decided in 1986, dealt with the question of whether advertising in a periodical containing articles and editorials relating to the publisher's exempt purpose constituted unrelated business income, specifically whether receipts from sale of advertisements in a medical journal contributed importantly to the carrying out of the purposes of the American College of Physicians, the publisher of the journal. The Supreme Court, while finding that receipts from the sale of advertisements that contained information on medical subjects might be considered related if linked to editorial content, held that the receipts in question were subject to tax, rejecting the per se approach of the Service.[329]

An integral part of this approach is what is referred to as the "fragmentation rule," under which the components of a business activity will be treated individually, and determinations of relatedness made on the basis of individ-

325. Henry E. and Nancy Horton Bartels Trust for the Benefit of the University of New Haven v. United States, 209 F.3d 147 (2d Cir. 2000).

326. Sierra Club, Inc. v. Commissioner, 86 F.3d 1526 (9th Cir. 1996).

327. Id.; Mississippi State University Alumni, Inc. v. Commissioner, T.C. Memo 1997-397 (1997); Oregon State University Alumni Association v. Commissioner, 193 F.3d 1098 (1999); Common Cause v. Commissioner, 112 T.C. 332 (1999); Planned Parenthood Federation of America, Inc. v. Commissioner, 77 T.C. Memo 1999-206 (1999).

328. Memorandum from Director, Exempt Organizations Division, to Acting EO Area Managers (December 16, 1999).

329. United States v. American College of Physicians, 475 U.S. 834 (1986).

ual items rather than on the totality of the activity.[330] It has been applied by the Service in a number of instances in addition to advertising. It has had a major impact on the operation of retail stores, such as museum shops and college bookstores, which must determine and be prepared to demonstrate the connection of each item sold to the exempt purpose of the organization.[331]

Corporate sponsorships also proved particularly difficult for the Treasury and the Service. Proposed regulations were first issued in January 1993 on this activity.[332] Adverse reaction led to enactment in the Taxpayer Relief Act of 1997 of section 513(i), which provided that certain sponsorship payments would not be subject to UBIT.[333] New proposed regulations were then issued on March 1, 2000,[334] with final regulations promulgated on April 24, 2002, overall a period of almost ten years.[335] In these regulations a sponsorship payment will not be considered UBTI if there is no arrangement or expectation that the sponsor will receive any substantial return benefit in exchange for its payment.[336] "Substantial return benefit" is in turn defined as any benefit other than a use or acknowledgment of the payor's name or logo by the exempt organization in the course of its activities or one that will provide certain goods and services having an insubstantial value as determined under then existing IRS guidelines and defined minimum standards.[337] An important aspect of the regulations was a determination that use or acknowledgment of the name or logo of the payor's trade or business will not give rise to UBIT so long as the logos and slogans do not compare the payor's products or services with those of its competitors.[338] If a sponsorship agreement gives the payor an exclusive right to the sale, distribution, availability, or use of its products, services, or facilities, the portion of the payment attributable to the exclusive provider arrangement will not be considered a qualified sponsorship payment.[339]

Travel and tour activities also received the attention of the Service in the

330. Treas. Reg. §1.513-1(b).

331. Rev. Rul. 73-105, 1973-1 C.B. 264.

332. 58 Fed. Reg. 5687 (1993).

333. I.R.C. §513(i), codified by Taxpayer Relief Act of 1997, Pub. L. No. 105-34, §965, 111 Stat. 788, 893–894 (1997). See Fishman and Schwarz, *Cases and Materials on Nonprofit Organizations,* 795–797, for background to the legislation.

334. 65 Fed. Reg. 11,012 (2000).

335. 67 Fed. Reg. 20,433 (2002) (effective April 25, 2002, for payments solicited or received after December 31, 1997).

336. Treas. Reg. §1.513-4(c)(1), 67 Fed. Reg. 20,433 (2002).

337. Treas. Reg. §1.513-4(c)(2)(i), 67 Fed. Reg. 20,433 (2002).

338. Treas. Reg. §1.513-4(c)(2)(iv), 67 Fed. Reg. 20,433 (2002).

339. Treas. Reg. §1.513-4(c)(2)(vi), 67 Fed. Reg. 20,433 (2002).

late 1990s, with proposed regulations issued in 1998,[340] and final regulations promulgated effective as of February 7, 2000.[341] They provided examples of related tours, apply a fragmentation rule, and rely on facts and circumstances rather than enumerating specific factors to determine relatedness.[342]

In October 2000 the Service announced that it was seeking comments from the public on a range of questions relating to Internet activities conducted by exempt organizations, focusing particularly on the application of the unrelated business income rules to certain Internet activities and the relationship of these activities to the limitations on lobbying and political campaign activities. The announcement posed a wide range of questions and indicated that the Service hoped to develop new policies based on existing principles in a manner that would permit exempt organizations to take advantage of new technologies to their benefit.[343]

The extent of unrelated business activities conducted by charitable organizations is difficult to estimate. It appears to be relatively small, or at the least not very profitable. Total UBIT paid by all exempt organizations was $56 million in 1986, $132 million in 1992, $191.5 million in 1994, and $277.5 million in 1995, with less than one-fourth of this coming from charitable organizations. The average UBIT return filed by charities in 1995 was less than $400,000; after deductions were taken, only 3,187 charities paid any tax.[344]

Writing in 1999, Hines called for caution in relying on these figures, alleging that the combination of self-reporting and the improbability of audit may have led organizations to underreport business activities or make them appear less profitable than is the case.[345] The distortion is further increased with the increased use of taxable subsidiaries for the conduct of unrelated activities, in that the taxable income is isolated in those returns and they are not available to the public.

340. 63 Fed. Reg. 20,156 (1998).

341. 65 Fed. Reg. 5771 (2000).

342. Treas. Reg. §1.513-7; see also Sean Barnett et al., "UBIT: Current Developments," in *2002 IRS Continuing Professional Education Text*, 195, 195–196.

343. Ann. 2000-84, 2000-2 C.B. 285; see also Catherine E. Livingston, "Tax-Exempt Organizations and the Internet: Tax and Other Legal Issues," 31 *Exempt Organization Tax Review* 419 (2001).

344. Evelyn Brody and Joseph Cordes, "The Unrelated Business Income Tax: All Bark and No Bite?" in *Urban Institute-Hauser Center Emerging Issues in Philanthropy Brief* (April 1999); Margaret Riley, "Unrelated Business Income of Nonprofit Organizations, 1994," *IRS Statistics of Income Bulletin* (Spring 1998), 111–132; Cecilia Hilgert and Melissa Whitten, "Charities and Other Tax-Exempt Organizations, 1995," *IRS Statistics of Income Bulletin* (Winter 1998–1999), 105–125.

345. James R. Hines, Jr., "Non-Profit Business Activity and the Unrelated Business Income Tax," 13 *Tax Policy and the Economy* 57 (1999).

In 2000 Steuerle called attention to the fact that, despite a general belief in the business community that UBIT gives nonprofits an unfair advantage, there were flaws in this rationale. Noting that an income tax exemption is not an input subsidy in that it does not reduce the charity's cost of purchasing goods, a zero tax rate for charity is no more "unfair" to a 35%-taxed competitor than are the progressive income tax rates on individuals who conduct business activities in a sole proprietorship or through a form of organization in which income is passed through to the owners, such as a partnership.[346] Nor did he believe it likely that a nonprofit organization would underprice its for-profit competitor any more than it would accept a lower return on a passive investment.[347] Thus a more appropriate rationale for UBIT is that it provides a single level of tax that parallels the tax levied on corporate profits in taxable corporations the stock of which is owned by exempt organizations.

At a 1999 conference on the unrelated business income tax, the participants concluded that UBIT has in effect "become a voluntary tax and has served, at most, as an 'intermediate sanction' short of the loss of tax exemption for charities earning 'too much' commercial income."[348] The conferees also agreed that it was unlikely that Congress would repeal the tax or adopt major reforms. Nonetheless, certain improvements could be made. The most needed is adoption of workable guidelines governing allocation of income and costs between taxed and untaxed activities, an area in which the rules are unclear and practice varies greatly. Other suggestions were to increase the $1,000 standard deduction, modify the definition of excluded royalties, and clarify the determination of when a business is "regularly carried on," a determination that is of particular pertinence in connection with Web-based commerce.

Joint Ventures and Taxable Subsidiaries Conducting Exempt Activities

Simon, writing in 1984, made the following comments on commercial activity:

> The commercial activity issue has come increasingly to the fore in the 1980s as voluntary organizations of all kinds have scrambled to cope

346. Eugene Steuerle, "When Nonprofits Conduct Exempt Activities as Taxable Enterprises," in *Urban Institute-Hauser Center Emerging Issues in Philanthropy Brief* (November 2000).

347. Id.; see also Joseph J. Cordes and Burton A. Weisbrod, "Differential Taxation of Nonprofits and the Commercialization of Nonprofit Revenues," 17 *Journal of Policy Analysis and Management* 195 (1998).

348. Brody and Cordes, "The Unrelated Business Income Tax," in *Emerging Issues in Philanthropy Brief.*

with the combined impact of government reductions in the rate of social service and cultural spending, . . . government reductions in the rate of grant and contract support for the nonprofits themselves, and charitable giving levels that [had] not increased fast enough to make up the gap. The nonprofits' course, predictably enough, has been a rush toward earned income—increased reliance on fees for services, entry into new or expanded forms of commercial operations (whether or not related to the nonprofit's charter purposes), and acquisition of revenue-producing assets distinct from traditional passive investment holdings.[349]

At that time, interest was primarily directed toward creation of limited partnerships that a nonprofit formed and joined as a general partner, attracting for-profit investors into housing or theatrical ventures in which they could shelter personal taxable income with partnership write-offs.

The scope and size of commercial activities, particularly those involving joint ventures with for-profit investors, increased substantially in the next fifteen years. This was particularly the case with hospitals and other health care entities, although in the late 1990s a number of exempt organizations outside of the health care field established joint ventures to conduct exempt activities in controlled taxable corporations and partnerships.[350] In some instances, the impetus was to permit the payment of higher salaries within the taxable organization than would be considered appropriate for the parent charity. In others, it was to permit officers and directors to participate through stock ownership in the venture. In many, the sole motive was to attract private capital.

In the health care field the nature of the arrangements became increasingly complicated, with the creation of subsidiary organizations, some exempt and some not, designed to protect the parent charity. This trend culminated in what came to be termed "whole hospital joint ventures," arrangements under which the entire assets and operation of the hospital would be transferred to a commercial entity of which the hospital and private investors were joint owners and which would thereafter operate the hospital as a taxable enterprise. Although these arrangements have received much notoriety, it appears that so-called ancillary joint ventures, involving one or more of the many aspects of hospital operations, are more representative of the types of ventures being conducted in the health care, as well as the larger tax-exempt, field.

349. John G. Simon, "The Tax Treatment of Nonprofit Organizations: A Review of Federal and State Policies," in *The Nonprofit Sector: A Research Handbook,* 67, 91.

350. Michael I. Sanders, *Partnerships and Joint Ventures Involving Tax-Exempt Organizations,* 1 (New York: John Wiley & Sons, 2d ed., 2000).

One problem posed for the Internal Revenue Service by joint ventures has centered on interpretation of the "exclusiveness test" for exemption, with the Service first taking the position that if a charity controlled a business venture, whether through majority vote or stock holdings, it would not be operating exclusively for exempt purposes. It also held that if a venture operated in the form of a partnership in order to provide the greatest benefit to the for-profit investors, partnership law imposed a duty on the charity to act for the private partners that prevented the charity from complying with the private benefit test.

In the leading early case, *Plumstead Theatre Society, Inc. v. Commissioner,*[351] the Tax Court overruled the Service's revocation of exemption of a charity that, in order to raise funds to produce a play, formed a limited partnership of which it was the general partner and then sold limited partnership interests to individual investors. Of importance in the decision was the fact that the charity maintained control of the partnership, the activities of which were furthering the charity's exempt purposes. This case in effect provided a blueprint for charities wishing to enter a safe joint venture, with the requisites being retention of control of the commercial entity by the charity and assuring that the purposes of the subsidiary were in themselves charitable.

In 1998, responding to ever-increasing interest in the creation of joint ventures, uncertainties as to the extent that they would jeopardize exemption, and the difficulty the Service was having dealing particularly with whole hospital joint ventures, the Service issued a revenue ruling in which it attempted to clarify its position.[352] The revenue ruling described two arrangements that involved the transfer of the assets and operations of the hospital to a joint venture with for-profit organizations, one of which was characterized as "good," the other "bad." The distinguishing features were the degree of control exercised by the exempt organization over the subsidiary and whether the charity would be able to assure that the exempt mission of the subsidiary would not be subverted.

The Service's position on whole hospital joint ventures, as set forth in the revenue ruling, was upheld by the Appeals Court for the Ninth Circuit in 2001 in the case of *Redlands Surgical Services v. Commissioner,*[353] with the court finding that an arrangement in which a wholly owned subsidiary of the charity and a for-profit organization each held a 50% interest in a limited liability company (LLC) conferred impermissible private benefit on the for-profit members of the LLC, thereby rendering the charity's subsidiary ineli-

351. 74 T.C. 1324 (1980), aff'd, 675 F.2d 244 (9th Cir. 1982).
352. Rev. Rul. 98-15, 1998-1 C.B. 718.
353. 113 T.C. No. 3 (1999), aff'd per curiam, 242 F.3d 904 (9th Cir. 2001).

gible for exemption on the basis that it would not be operating exclusively for charitable purposes.

In June 2002 a federal district court reversed the Service's revocation of exemption of a charitable hospital that had entered into a limited partnership with a for-profit health care organization to which the charity contributed all of its hospital and medical assets.[354] The hospital and a subsidiary of the for-profit organization were the two general partners, with the for-profit serving as managing partner. Both parties also held limited partnership interests, with the hospital's combined interests comprising 45.9% of the total. Under the agreement each of the general partners appointed half of the members of the board of the hospital, but the chairman's position was to be filled by the charity and it also retained the power to unilaterally remove the chief executive officer. The charity also retained the power to dissolve the partnership if the hospital failed to operate in accordance with the community benefit standard set forth in Revenue Ruling 69-545 as a condition for exemption as a hospital.[355] The Service's position was that the partnership arrangement did not constitute a valid charity because St. David's was unable to cause the partnership to initiate activities that would further charitable purposes, it did not meet the community benefit standard, and there was no express duty on the manager to operate the facilities in conformance with the community benefit standard.

In granting summary judgment for the charity, the court ruled that maintaining and controlling a community board was not a prerequisite for exemption as a hospital, but that if it were, the partnership agreement gave the charity the requisite control. The court held further, relying on the *Redlands* case, that the charity's control was sufficient to assure that it would protect its exempt purpose, and the hospital would, therefore, be operated exclusively for charitable purposes.

In addition to the increase in joint venture arrangements between exempt and for-profit organizations, during the late 1990s a number of tax-exempt organizations began conducting certain related activities as for-profit taxable enterprises even though they would not be taxable conducted by the charity itself. The primary motive appeared to be the ability to attract outside capital, but in some instances the motive was likely the ability to provide higher salaries and other compensation incentives to certain executives or to reapportion control among private and nonprofit participants. Examples of the types of activities being conducted as taxable enterprises included long-distance learning programs, Internet enterprises, sales of reproductions and other art-

354. St. David's Health Care System, Inc. v. United States, 2002 WL 1335230 (W.D. Tex. 2002).

355. Rev. Rul. 69-545, 1969-2 C.B. 117.

related objects by museums, and participation in low-income housing.[356] Although relatively small in size and in the value of assets involved, these new ventures received attention from the press and the bar, which raised concern as to whether they would ultimately call into question the exemption of certain nonprofit organizations, not to say the entire sector.[357]

A further problem facing regulators arose in part by virtue of the fact that the Internal Revenue Code is unclear as to whether there is a limit to the amount of commercial activity, both related and unrelated, beyond which an organization will not be entitled to tax exemption. Although commentators and representatives from small businesses have continued to criticize the amount of commercial activity, implying that there is a level beyond which it is not appropriate for an exempt organization to expand, there is no firm basis in the law for such a position. Spitzer, for example, argued that the absence of a per se limit "is appropriate, in that intermediate sanctions, private inurement, private benefit and 'exclusively operated' limitations are sufficient enforcement tools for the IRS."[358] He suggested, however, the need for application of these tools in a more coherent manner by the IRS and the courts, measuring whether related commercial activities are proportionate with exempt activities, and whether unrelated activities are commensurate in scope with the resources of the organizations, the test found in a 1964 revenue ruling.[359] In addition to this clarification, the long-standing position of the Service that related activities are to be encouraged should be reaffirmed, and the parameters of permissible joint venture activity need to be defined. Then, an approach such as that suggested by Spitzer may be sufficient as a policing tool.

The Role of the Internal Revenue Code in Assuring Compliance with Fiduciary Duties

The role of the Internal Revenue Service as regulator of charitable activities nationwide was certainly not within the vision of the members of Congress

356. Eyal Press and Jennifer Washburn, "The Kept University," *Atlantic Monthly*, March 2000, at 39; Stephen Schwarz, "Federal Income Taxation of Investments by Nonprofit Organizations: Beyond a Primer," in *Conference: Taxing Charitable Investments*, 32–33 (New York University School of Law, National Center on Philanthropy and the Law, 2000).

357. Steuerle, "When Nonprofits Conduct Exempt Activities as Taxable Enterprises," in *Emerging Issues in Philanthropy Brief*.

358. A. L. Spitzer, "'Milking the Cash Cow'; Commercial Activities Undertaken by Nonprofit Organizations: Analysis and Recommendations," in *Conference: Defining Charity—A View from the 21st Century* (New York University School of Law, National Center on Philanthropy and the Law, 2002); see also John D. Colombo, "Regulating Commercial Activity by Exempt Charities: Resurrecting the Commensurate-in-Scope Doctrine," 39 *Exempt Organization Tax Review* 341 (2003).

359. Rev. Rul. 64-182, 1964-1 C.B. 186.

who voted to grant tax exemption to charitable organizations from the originally enacted income tax. In fact, it is only since 1969 that the Service became an effective regulator of fiduciary behavior, and not until the end of the twentieth century that this power was extended to the vast majority of charitable fiduciaries. For a regulatory scheme that was never intended to perform this role and one that has grown in large part without conscious planning, it has proved to be more effective than might have been anticipated. This is due, in large part, to the flexibility that has been built into the law, in its reliance on common law principles, and in the slow pace in which changes have been adopted. One can view the development of charity regulation as having had three phases: in the first, broad definitional parameters were established and self-policing was relied on to assure accountability; in the second, a border between exempt and nonexempt entities was drawn when Congress enacted the unrelated business income tax and lobbying limitations; in the third phase the regulatory function was expanded, first with the adoption in 1969 of limitations on private foundations and their managers, and then in 1996 with the enactment of excess benefit limitations on charitable fiduciaries and certain related parties who violated the fiduciary duties of loyalty and care by providing excess benefits to insiders.

The process has been slow, and not without upheavals. Noteworthy is the fact that expanded regulation has not restricted entry into the sector; in fact, based on preliminary statistics as to the growth in numbers and value of assets at the end of the twentieth century, the regulatory environment could well be characterized as unusually nurturing.

This is not to imply that no improvements are needed. The limitations of the excess benefit provisions have been described, as have suggested changes to the private foundation rules. Repeal of the limitations on lobbying would permit charities to contribute more meaningfully to society, but if that is unacceptable, at a minimum Congress should repeal the distinction between direct and grassroots lobbying. Finally, clarity is needed with regard to the treatment of joint ventures so that charities will understand and can operate within the parameters of legitimate activity.

6

Regulation of Charities in the States

The rationale used by the courts to confer validity on a trust for charitable purposes was that the beneficiary was the public at large. Practicality dictated, however, that an amorphous mass of individuals could not properly perform the functions of a beneficiary of a private trust motivated by natural self-interest. Well before passage of the Statute of Elizabeth, the courts answered the need for a substitute for a private beneficiary by considering that it was lodged in the king, as *parens patriae,* or father of his country. In the language of trusts, this power is described as the power of enforcement. It implies the duty to oversee the activities of the fiduciary who is charged with management of the trust funds, as well as the right to bring to the attention of the courts any abuses that may appear to need correction. Thus a duty to enforce implies a duty to supervise (or oversee) in its broader sense. It does not, however, include a right to regulate, or a right to direct either the day-to-day affairs of the charity or the action of the court. Both the enforcement power, exercised by the attorney general, and the regulatory power, exercised by the courts, extend to all assets dedicated to charitable purpose, regardless of the legal form—corporation, trust, or voluntary association—in which they are held. The nature of these roles is to be found in the basic framework of the Anglo-American legal system.

There are other state agencies that have power to regulate specific aspects of the operation of charities, such as a board of education in relation to schools, colleges, and universities, or a department of health in regard to hospitals and other health care facilities. However, with rare exceptions, the courts are the only agencies of government empowered to assure devotion of the managers of charities to their fiduciary duties. And, as will be seen, the power of the attorney general is in almost all respects an exclusive one, so that the effectiveness of state regulation of charities depends primarily on the manner in which the state attorneys general carry out their enforcement duties. The respective roles of the courts and the attorneys general are described in this chapter as are the rules of standing, which limit the other individuals who may sue to enforce breaches of duty by charitable fiduciaries, and the limited regulatory role of other state agencies.

The Courts

The broad range of equity powers held by the courts give to the judiciary an inherently predominant position in determining the affairs of charity. Judicial decisions have framed the categories of valid charitable purposes. They have defined the limits of trustees' powers and the extent of their duties. Even when these powers must be carried out within the framework of the most extensive legislatively enacted codes of law, the courts still have a wide area for interpretation. Through their power to settle accounts, they have drawn the lines governing proper investments. It is the courts that appoint new trustees and in some cases new directors, order corporate dissolution or force transfer of corporate property, determine the extent of trustees' discretionary powers, and direct the framing of schemes for cy pres dispositions.

Most of these matters are heard in the state probate courts or in trial courts having equity jurisdiction where the procedural rules governing appeal are such that the lower court judges' findings of fact are given great weight and are rarely reversed without a showing that they were plainly wrong. Therefore, it is primarily at the lower level of the court system that the affairs of charity are determined.

In many states testamentary trustees are required to present accounts to the overseeing court at regular intervals for allowance. For example, in Ohio a fiduciary is required to file at least once in each two years an account that includes itemized statements of receipts, disbursements, distributions, assets, and investments.[1] In other states trustees may in their discretion present accounts for allowance, but they are not required to do so until they resign or are removed, or the trust is ready for termination. Only four states have no provision regarding accounts of trustees. The Uniform Trustees' Accounting Act, which has been enacted in Nevada,[2] requires testamentary and nontestamentary trustees to file detailed financial accounts annually with the probate court. These accounts must also include proof of no self-dealing, a statement of unpaid claims, and such other facts as the court may require. The act specifically states that it applies to charitable trusts.

Broad as the powers of the courts are in theory, they are only rarely called into action in practice. The average charity comes into existence and functions without any contact with a court. Inter vivos trusts and charitable cor-

1. Ohio Rev. Code Ann. §2109.30.
2. Nev. Rev. Stat. §§165.010–165.250.

porations can be created without reference to judicial power in all jurisdictions.[3] Testamentary trusts come within the purview of the court at the time of creation, but unless the heirs dispute the validity of the disposition, the court merely acknowledges the filing of the instrument and the transfer of funds to the trustee at the close of the probate proceedings. Even in those jurisdictions where a duty is placed on trustees of testamentary trusts to file accounts periodically with the court, the court's contact with the trustees is rarely more than routine. There is no procedure for identifying trustees who are remiss in their duty to account. Furthermore, the matter of allowance of accounts by the courts is in itself almost automatic. The courts do not have their own auditors to review accounts,[4] and unless objection is made by an interested party, approval is granted without question.

The power of the probate courts to regulate the administration of charitable trusts was reaffirmed in a Massachusetts case decided in 1994 in which the court held that the statute conferring enforcement powers over charitable trusts on the attorney general did not deprive the probate courts of their powers. Accordingly the probate court was not bound by the terms of a settlement reached between the attorney general and the trustees of a charitable trust charged with breach of fiduciary duty, and could not only require the trustees to account for their administration but also nullify the terms of the settlement with the result that the surcharge on the trustees was greatly increased.[5]

The source of the courts' power over charitable corporations has been attributed to two factors: (1) the existence of a trust for indefinite beneficiaries implicit in every charitable gift; and (2) the power of visitation over all corporations arising from the power to create them, which resides with the state. The latter concept originated under the Roman law and was adopted by the English kings.[6] It has been supplemented by statutes enacted in every American jurisdiction, which grant to the court the power to dissolve a corporation on a showing of certain actions that were in excess of the corporation's powers or purposes or were injurious to the public welfare.[7] Today, therefore, the courts have a dual source of power over charitable corporations.

As noted above, the powers of any court to act are limited by the fact that

3. Judicial approval was required until 1970 in New York and 1972 in Pennsylvania (formerly found at N.Y. Membership Corporation Law, §10; Pa. Stat. Ann. tit. 15, §2851).

4. With the exception of Indiana, where an audit section in each court passes on accounts. Ind. Stat. §30-4-5-12.

5. Matter of Trust under Will of Fuller, 636 N.E.2d 1333 (Mass. 1994).

6. Roscoe Pound, "Visitorial Jurisdiction over Corporations in Equity," 49 *Harvard Law Review* 369 (1936).

7. Model Business Corporation Act, §14.30(2) (1995 revision).

they may adjudicate only disputes brought to their attention by opposing parties and they are confined to the issues raised by these parties. There are two exceptions to this rule. One, universally available to charitable fiduciaries, is the right to request a court for instructions as to the extent or interpretation of their duties.[8] A second, recognized in some jurisdictions in the United States, permits the court, under equity power, to act in certain circumstances on its own motion (or *sua sponte*). The power is invoked only rarely, however. The Supreme Judicial Court of Massachusetts explained the nature of its exercise in a case involving the power of the court to remove a fiduciary:

> Ordinarily courts properly remain inactive unless and until judicial action is required by some party in accordance with recognized practice. But courts have a wide inherent power to do justice and to adopt procedure to that end. Where a court has once taken jurisdiction and has become responsible to the public for the exercise of its judicial power so as to do justice, it is sometimes the right and even the duty of the court to act in some particular sua sponte.[9]

Aside from this extraordinary jurisdiction, however, the Anglo-American judicial system relies on an individual's self-interest to assure compliance with the law. The existence of ascertained individuals who will look after their own interests is a basic component of all fiduciary relationships. The laws are so framed that reliance is placed on the beneficiaries of a private trust or on the shareholders of a business corporation to call into action the enforcement machinery of the courts. The trust developed as a legal device only after the Chancery Courts recognized the rights of beneficiaries and agreed to enforce them. Today the existence of a beneficiary capable of looking after his own interests is, in fact, a prerequisite to the validity of a private trust. Similarly, we look to the powers of trust beneficiaries and corporate shareholders for analogies to the role of the attorney general in enforcing proper administration of charitable trusts.

There is one area unique to charity law in which the courts have almost unfettered power, namely in the application of the related doctrines of cy pres and deviation. As explained in Chapter 3, the cy pres doctrine is applicable in cases where the purposes of a charity become impossible or impractical to carry out, and deviation is applied when the methods specified for carrying out the purposes become impracticable. Upon a showing to that effect, and evidence that no right of reversion was retained by the donor, the court is empowered to permit a change of purpose or method to one near to that of

8. Matter of Jacobs, 487 N.Y.S.2d 992 (Surr. Ct. 1985); see also Austin W. Scott and William F. Fratcher, *The Law of Trusts*, §394 (Boston: Little, Brown, 4th ed., 1987).

9. Quincy Trust Co. v. Taylor, 57 N.E.2d 573 (Mass. 1944); see also Scott and Fratcher, *Law of Trusts*, §200.4.

the original gift. The ability to choose a substitute is essentially unfettered, and the decision of a lower court will not be overturned unless it can be demonstrated that the judge acted recklessly or irrationally.

This has meant that there is wide variation in result among the cy pres and deviation decisions, with those subject to criticism being the ones in which the courts have refused to find impracticability or framed too narrow a scheme. For example, in 1999 the Orphans' Court in Pennsylvania refused to grant a petition brought by the trustees of a trust established to operate a school for "the maintenance, support, and education of as many white, orphan boys as it could afford." The court had nullified the racial restriction in 1970, and the trustees were now requesting the court for an additional modification. The trust was originally funded with stock representing the controlling interest in the Hershey Company and, at the time of the petition, the corpus had grown to $5 billion, producing income far in excess of the amount needed to support the 1,050-student school it was operating. The trustees requested court approval of a plan to use a portion of the income to establish a research institute on teaching needy children. Protests were heard from alumni and local residents, as well as from a large number of educational organizations that requested the court to divert funds to them. The attorney general joined with those opposing the petition, and the court rejected it.[10]

Charities and their fiduciaries may in some instances violate criminal statutes, the most common being theft and embezzlement. In cases of this nature, the powers of the courts are derived from statutes that define the crime and prescribe penalties for those found guilty. The criminal laws generally apply to all individuals and corporations; they do not treat charitable organizations differently from any others, nor distinguish charitable fiduciaries from their counterparts who administer property for private purposes. The sole exception is the restrictions on solicitation of funds for charitable purposes, which in some states contain criminal sanctions for misleading the public applicable to charities and to others who hold themselves out as charities. The sanctions for violation of these rules include the imposition of fines and imprisonment. In their application the courts generally have less leeway in framing remedies than they do when exercising equity powers.

The Attorney General

The duty of the attorney general to "enforce the due application of funds given or appropriated to public charities . . . and prevent breaches in the administration thereof," to quote from a section of the Massachusetts General

---

10. Daniel Golden, "Bittersweet Legacy," *Wall Street Journal*, August 12, 1999, at A23. See also *www.mhsaa.org/Lib/*; Chapter 4.

Laws first enacted in 1847,[11] is stated in the legal texts as an absolute duty and is recognized in almost all of the states either by statute or judicial decision. In thirty-seven states it is recited by statute, although in Indiana the power is limited to petitioning for a trust accounting, while in Mississippi, Missouri, Nebraska, and Wyoming the power can be invoked only in connection with specific corporate transactions, while the statute in Florida grants power to bring actions to enforce "impropriety of nonprofit corporations." In the four states in which the power is limited to dealing with specific corporate transactions, the attorney general's power to enforce charitable trusts is recognized in the case law, as it is in Indiana and Florida in respect to trusts. Enforcement power is conferred under the case law in twelve additional states.[12]

Until 1999 New Mexico was the only state in which there was no clear-cut statement, either in judicial decisions or statutes, that the duty to enforce charitable funds rested on the attorney general or another public officer. In that year the New Mexico statute regulating solicitation of funds for charitable purposes was amended to state as its purpose "to authorize the attorney general to monitor, supervise and enforce the charitable purposes of charitable organizations."[13] Similarly, in Louisiana, although there is no authorization in the statutes or case law for the attorney general to assume this role, the statute dealing with notice in cy pres proceedings requires that notice be given to the attorney general.[14]

In January 2002 the Supreme Court of Virginia held that the common law enforcement powers of the attorney general of the Commonwealth did not extend to charitable corporations and, accordingly, he had no power to bring suit seeking removal of the directors and other equitable relief on the grounds of self-dealing, wasting foundation assets, and breach of fiduciary duties.[15] The decision was based upon interpretation of statutes granting the state corporation commission exclusive jurisdiction over nonstock corporations and authorizing the attorney general to exercise common law and statutory authority over certain nonprofit health care entities but not other nonprofit corporations. According to the dissent in the case, this latter statute was adopted in 1997 to regulate the conversion of health care corporations from nonprofit to for-profit status and was not intended to modify the powers of the attorney general. The decision, however, had the effect of limiting the powers of the attorney general to enforcement of charitable trusts, not charitable corporations.

11. Mass. Gen. Laws ch. 12, §8.
12. See Appendix, Table 1, Column 1.
13. N.M. Stat. Ann. §57-22-9.
14. La. Rev. Stat. Ann. §9-2332.
15. Virginia v. The JOCO Foundation, 558 S.E.2d 280 (Va. 2002).

In a swift response to the case, the legislature on April 8, 2002, amended the Code of Virginia by adding a clause to the effect that

> the assets of a charitable corporation incorporated in or doing any business in Virginia shall be deemed to be held in trust for the public for such purposes as are established by the donor's intent as expressed in governing documents or by other applicable law. The attorney general shall have the same authority to act on behalf of the public with respect to such assets as he has with respect to assets held by unincorporated charitable trusts and other charitable entities, including the authority to seek such judicial relief as may be necessary to protect the public interest in such assets.[16]

A second section of the act affirmed that the circuit courts were to have the same subject matter jurisdiction over charitable corporations as they have with respect to other charitable entities, "including the power to require accountings, appoint receivers, award damages and enter injunctive relief against such charitable corporations, their officers, directors, agents, employees and others as may be necessary to protect the public interest in such assets."[17]

Generally the attorney general's duty to enforce charities extends equally to corporations and trusts. The enforcement power in regard to corporate charities exists in addition to a statutory power (granted in all but nine states in which the power is granted to another state official) to bring an action to dissolve a corporation for certain violations. Usually the dissolution proceeding is called a "proceeding *quo warranto*" (by what warrant). Among the grounds usually considered sufficient to warrant involuntary dissolution are (1) abuse of corporate powers (misuser); (2) failure to exercise corporate powers for a fixed number of years (nonuser); (3) fraud practiced on the state in procuring the corporate franchise; (4) failure to file an annual report for a given period of years; and (5) failure for a specified period to appoint and maintain a registered agent or to notify a state officer after change of registered agent.[18] In 2002 the Tennessee attorney general brought a successful petition to dissolve two charitable organizations and distribute their assets to other charities upon a showing of self-dealing and diversion of assets by the directors and officers of the defendant charities.[19]

The power of the California attorney general over charitable corporations

16. Va. Code Ann. §2.2-507.1, added by 2002 Va. Acts ch. 792 (April 8, 2002).

17. Va. Code Ann. §17.1-513.01, added by 2002 Va. Acts ch. 792 (April 8, 2002).

18. See, for example, Revised Model Non-Profit Corporation Act (RMNCA), §§14.20, 14.30 (1987).

19. Summers v. Cherokee Children and Family Services, Inc., 2002 WL 31126636 (Tenn. Ct. App. 2002).

was limited in 1983 when the California legislature amended the nonprofit corporation law to transfer regulation of health care service plans to the corporations commissioner.[20] The stated purpose was to end unnecessary duplication of responsibility with respect to regulation of this category of charities. Several years after passage of the act the attorney general brought suit against a health care plan to enforce a settlement agreement entered into prior to passage of the legislation, and in a 1990 decision the court held that the act superseded any of his common law or statutory powers in regard to health care plans.[21] The Virginia and California situations are unique; other situations resolved since 1990 have affirmed the powers of the attorney general and continued to uphold the doctrine of exclusive standing described below.[22]

The extent of the power of an attorney general to affect disposition of charitable property in a state other than his own is undecided. The issue was before the courts of Kansas and Missouri in 2002 and 2003 in two cases involving the sale and conversion of Health Midwest, the largest health care system in the area, which owned and operated hospitals in both states. The sales price was $1.13 billion, of which $800 million was to be used to fund a new foundation to meet health care needs in the region, the trustees of which were to be the directors of Health Midwest. Health Midwest originally sought court approval of the sale in both states, but when the terms were opposed by the attorneys general, the charity challenged their power to intervene. Each state then sought court orders to dissolve the charity, remove the directors, and appoint a receiver, and it appeared that each was prepared to fight to retain jurisdiction over the disposition of the proceeds of the sale.[23]

The matter was settled in the spring of 2003 with an agreement to establish foundations in each state and to divide the proceeds of the sale between them, although the purposes of the Missouri foundation were stated to be directed toward health care needs in the greater Kansas City metropolitan area, thereby encompassing potential beneficiaries in both states. The Missouri attorney general retained unusually broad, continuing supervisory powers over the Missouri foundation, as well as the power to appoint one-third of the members of the initial board.[24] The agreement between the Kansas attorney

20. California Assembly Bill 795, 1983 Cal. Stat. ch. 1085, §§10–14, at 3879 (rewriting Cal. Corp. Code §10821).

21. Van de Kamp v. Gumbiner, 221 Cal. App. 3d 1260 (1990).

22. In re Estate of York, 951 S.W.2d 122 (Tex. 1997); State v. Holden, 953 S.W.2d 151 (Mo. 1997).

23. For court documents filed by parties, see *www.ksag.org/contents/litigation/main.htm* and *www.moago.org/health/index.html*.

24. Office of Missouri Attorney General, News Release, "Nixon Announces Agreement with Health Midwest to Establish $700 Million Foundation for Health Care Needs" (January 22, 2003); see also Memorandum of Understanding (January 22, 2003), available at *www.ago.state.mo.us/lawsuits2003/012203healthmidwest.pdf*.

general and Health Midwest followed the terms of the Missouri settlement, but the beneficiaries were confined to those in Kansas.[25]

The range of court actions that an attorney general may request a court to take to enforce fiduciary duties is as broad as the power of the courts to devise remedies for breach of fiduciary duties. He may request accountings, removal of trustees, dissolution of corporations, forced transfer of corporate property, or a combination of these. He may ask the court to force charitable fiduciaries to restore losses caused by breach of duty and to return profits made in the course of administering the trust. He may seek to enjoin trustees from further wrongdoing or from continuing certain specific actions. Furthermore, transactions involving a breach of the duty of loyalty may be voided at the option of the attorney general unless he decides that it is in the public interest to affirm them. The attorney general, as well as trustees, may bring actions requesting modification or deviation from the terms of a trust or cy pres application of funds.[26] In 2002 the Maine legislature amended its provisions governing conflict of interest transactions to specifically empower the attorney general to bring court action to void any transaction as to which he had reasonable grounds to believe that a charity had engaged in a conflict of interest transaction that was neither fair nor properly approved as required by the statute. Advance notice of the action was to be given to the charity unless it was "necessary to prevent immediate irreparable harm to the public."[27]

There are at least a few cases in almost every jurisdiction that have involved one or more of these actions. In many of the early ones, the action was frequently brought by the attorney general at the relation of private individuals, but the use of relators, although favored by some commentators as a means of expanding the rules on standing, is rare.[28] As noted above, charitable fiduciaries are not immune from prosecution for violation of criminal laws and, in most instances, the attorney general, together with state district attorneys, is empowered to bring suit charging violations of these acts.

There are limits to the power of the attorney general, some based on a reading of his statutory powers, and others on the fact that protection of charitable funds does not permit interference in the internal matters of a charity. As to statutory limits, the Supreme Court of Connecticut in 2002 held that the attorney general had no power to pursue claims against the president and treasurer of a charter school for self-dealing in regard to tuition

25. Office of Kansas Attorney General, Press Release, "Attorney General Kline Announces Settlement with Health Midwest" (March 13, 2003).

26. Marion R. Fremont-Smith, "Enforceability and Sanctions," in *Conference: Governance of Nonprofit Organizations—Standards and Enforcement* (New York University School of Law, National Center on Philanthropy and the Law, 1997).

27. Me. Rev. Stat. Ann. tit. 13-B, §718(8).

28. See discussion of standing in this chapter.

payments provided by the state.[29] Rather, his powers under Connecticut law were limited to protecting donated funds, while the power to bring suit in regard to state payments rested with the state's attorneys. In regard to internal affairs, the New York Court of Appeals in 1980 held that the attorney general lacked standing to sue a business corporation and its director for breach of fiduciary duty by failing to declare dividends on shares that one of the defendant directors had given to a number of charitable organizations. The attorney general brought this action on behalf of several of the donee charities, claiming that he was acting on behalf of their ultimate beneficiaries. The court acknowledged the power of the attorney general to enforce a disposition or require its application for a charitable purpose. However, here he was attempting to enforce obligations purportedly owing to the charitable organizations. The court found nothing in the law that would "authorize a large scale intrusion into the everyday affairs of charitable corporations."[30]

Similarly, the California court limited the power of the attorney general in *City of Palm Springs v. Living Desert Reserve*,[31] a case that involved the right of a city to condemn a reversionary interest in real property it had accepted on the express condition that it be used in perpetuity as a desert wildlife preserve. The court held that the transfer did not create a charitable trust and, accordingly, the attorney general was not a necessary party to the action.

The Minnesota attorney general in 2001 was successful in an attempt to control the appointment of board members of a charity that he alleged had been mismanaged, while a similar attempt in 2003 had a mixed outcome. In the first case, under threat of suit the charity agreed to a settlement under which it would spin off certain operations to a subsidiary, the board of which was to be composed of eight "special administrators" appointed by the attorney general with approval of the court. When, two years later, the charity requested that the court terminate the settlement, the court refused, holding that the agreement could be terminated only with the assent of both the charity and the attorney general.[32] In the second case, the attorney general attempted to appoint two members of the board of a health maintenance organization, HealthPartners, one of whom he designated as chairman of the board despite the fact that the governing documents required that directors be plan members. The charity challenged the attorney general's proposal, and, in June 2003, the district court held that the chairman proposed by the

29. Blumenthal v. Barnes, 804 A.2d 152 (Conn. 2002).
30. Lefkowitz v. Lebensfeld, 415 N.E.2d 919, 922 (N.Y. 1980).
31. 82 Cal. Rptr. 859 (Cal. App. 4th Dist. 1999).
32. Glenn Howatt, "Medica Is Still Subject to Hatch," *Star Tribune*, August 16, 2003, at 1A.

attorney general should be appointed a special administrator, who would act as an advisor, and not a board member, for one year.[33]

Commenting on these actions, taken together with the actions of the attorneys general in Pennsylvania in connection with the Hershey Trust, described in Chapter 4, as well as in Massachusetts in regard to the sale of the Boston Red Sox, and in Illinois in regard to the Terra Foundation, both of which are described below, Strom observed that these attorneys general "are becoming headhunters as well, shaking up scandal-tainted charities with new board members and administrators they pick themselves—often friends, colleagues and even political contributors and allies."[34] Similarly, Brody noted that the proliferation of anecdotes in the area of charity enforcement indicated what she termed the outer limits of troubling state action. She concluded that if the proper bounds of legitimate enforcement did not become clearer, the role of charities in society could suffer. Of particular concern was the fact that charities confronted with attorney general inquiry will often agree to settlements rather than face loss of donations, contracts, and patronage, as well as staff and volunteers. She feared that if charities too quickly acceded to state demands over matters of discretionary governance, the sector would see a degradation in charities' willingness to take risks and in volunteer board members' willingness to serve.[35]

Statutes Enhancing Attorney General's Enforcement Powers

Prior to the end of World War II, little attention was paid in the legal literature to the enforcement powers of the attorney general, and cases brought against charitable trustees were rare. Interest in enforcement was spurred by an increase in the number of charities established after the war. In 1947 the Council of State Governments conducted a survey of all attorneys general as to their powers, duties, and operations in regard to "charitable trusts." Replies from thirty-three states were supplemented in a second survey conducted in 1952 of eighteen states. Until 1950 only New Hampshire had enacted legislation supplementing the common law enforcement duties of the attorney general with powers designed to provide information to his office as to the activities of the charitable organizations subject to his jurisdiction and

33. Patrick Reilly, "Health Plan Scrutiny; Ruling May Restrict Oversight by Attorneys General," *Modern Healthcare*, June 23, 2003, at 44.

34. Stephanie Strom, "Strong-Arm Shaking of Charities Raises Ethics Qualms," *New York Times*, May 11, 2003, at §1, pg. 22.

35. Evelyn Brody, "Whose Public?—Parochialism and Paternalism in State Charity Law Enforcement" (on file with author).

expanding his investigative powers.[36] Four other states reported some activity, but it was apparent that there was little or no involvement or interest in the activities of charities.

The New Hampshire Charitable Trustees Act had been adopted in 1943.[37] No similar legislation was enacted until 1950 when the Rhode Island legislature passed a bill similar to that in effect in New Hampshire.[38] These states were followed by South Carolina[39] and Ohio[40] in 1953 and Massachusetts in 1954.[41] During this same period the National Association of Attorneys General and the National Conference of Commissioners on Uniform State Laws collaborated in drafting a Uniform Act for Supervision of Trustees for Charitable Purposes.[42] It was adopted by the Commissioners and approved by the House of Delegates of the American Bar Association in 1954.[43]

California was the first state to adopt the Uniform Act, enacting it in 1955 for a two-year trial period, which was extended to 1959 and thereafter made permanent.[44] In 1959 Iowa adopted an act modeled on the Rhode Island legislation, but it was repealed in 1965.[45] The Uniform Act was adopted in Michigan[46] and Illinois in 1961,[47] and in Oregon in 1963,[48] bringing to ten as of that year the number of states with registration and reporting statutes. New York adopted a statute similar to the Massachusetts statute in 1967,[49] and Washington took similar action in that same year.[50] Although certain provisions of that act relating to investigative powers remain in effect, the responsibility for maintaining a registry of trustees was transferred in 1993 from the office of the attorney general to the secretary of state who was also

36. Eleanor K. Taylor, *Public Accountability of Foundations and Charitable Trusts,* 143 (New York: Russell Sage Foundation, 1953).

37. N.H. Rev. Stat. Ann. §7:19, codified by 1943 N.H. Laws ch. 181.

38. R.I. Gen. Laws §18-9-8, codified by 1950 R.I. Pub. Laws ch. 2617.

39. 1953 S.C. Acts 274.

40. Ohio Rev. Code Ann. §109.24, codified by 1953 Ohio Laws.

41. Mass. Gen. Laws ch. 12, §8C, codified by 1954 Mass. Acts ch. 529.

42. National Association of Attorneys General, *Conference Proceedings,* 91 (1946); id. at 184 (1951); id. at 155 (1952). See also Comment, "Supervision of Charitable Trusts," 21 *University of Chicago Law Review* 118 (1953).

43. Uniform Supervision of Trustees for Charitable Purposes Act (1954).

44. Cal. Gov't Code §12580 et seq., enacted by 1955 Cal. Stat. ch. 1820, extended by 1957 Cal. Stat. ch. 2024, codified by 1959 Cal. Stat. ch. 1258. See also Lisa M. Bell and Robert B. Bell, "Supervision of Charitable Trusts in California," 32 *Hastings Law Journal* 433 (1980).

45. 1965 Iowa Acts (61 G.A.) ch. 432, §69.

46. Mich. Comp. Laws §14.251, codified by 1961 Mich. Pub. Acts 101.

47. 1961 Ill. Laws 297.

48. 1963 Or. Laws ch. 583.

49. N.Y. Est. Powers & Trusts Law §8-1.4.

50. Wash. Rev. Code §11.110, codified by 1967 Wash. Laws ch. 53.

responsible for the regulation of solicitations.[51] In 1997 the provisions relating to the register of trustees were repealed.[52] There was no legislative activity in any state between 1969 and 1989 when Minnesota adopted a "Supervision of Charitable Trusts and Trustees Act," which, although making no reference to the Uniform Act, contained similar provisions.[53]

A major drawback to the implementation of several of these statutes, as well as to the Uniform Act, was their failure to specifically include charitable corporations in the definition of the charitable organizations to which the act applied. The New Hampshire and Rhode Island statutes defined "charitable trusts" narrowly. In contrast, the Massachusetts act applied to all "public charities within the Commonwealth" as well as to foreign charitable corporations engaged in charitable work or raising funds in the Commonwealth.[54]

Section 1 of the Uniform Act was made applicable to "all trustees holding property for charitable purposes over which [the State or] the Attorney General has enforcement or supervisory powers."[55] "Trustee" was defined as

(a) any individual, group of individuals, corporation, or other legal entity holding property in trust pursuant to a charitable trust, (b) any corporation which has accepted property to be used for a particular charitable corporate purpose as distinguished from the general purposes of the corporation, and (c) a corporation formed for the administration of a charitable trust, pursuant to the directions of the settlor or at the instance of the trustee.[56]

The drafters of the California version of the Uniform Act recognized the ambiguity in subparagraph (b) and changed the wording so that the act was made applicable to "all charitable corporations and trustees holding property for charitable purposes."[57] An added section defined charitable corporations as "any nonprofit corporation organized under the laws of this State for charitable or eleemosynary purposes and any similar foreign corporation doing business or holding property in this State for such purposes." The Oregon act adopted similar language.

The attorney general of Illinois attempted to resolve the definitional problem in his state's version of the Uniform Act by means of regulations promul-

51. 1993 Wash. Laws ch. 471 (amending Wash. Rev. Code §19.090, §11.110).
52. 1997 Wash. Laws ch. 124 (effective July 27, 1997, repealing Wash. Rev. Code §11.110.050, §11.110.073, §11.110.080).
53. Minn. Stat. §§501B.33–.45, codified by 1989 Minn. Laws ch. 340, art. 1, §25.
54. Mass. Gen. Laws ch. 12, §8.
55. Uniform Supervision of Trustees for Charitable Purposes Act, §1.
56. Id., §2.
57. 1959 Cal. Stat. ch. 1258.

gated in 1962 explicitly including in the coverage of the act any corporation, business or charitable, that has accepted property for charitable purposes unless it came within one of the exceptions in the act.[58] After the legitimacy of the regulation was successfully challenged in a lower court by a disaffected charitable corporation, the attorney general sponsored a bill to clarify the coverage of the act. This bill was passed in 1963, rendering the appeal of the court decision moot.[59] The Illinois act now applies to any legal entity "holding property for or solicited for any charitable purpose."[60] The New York and Michigan acts define trustees to include any individual, group of individuals, corporation, or other legal entity holding and administering property for charitable purposes. In contrast, the statutes in South Carolina and Rhode Island are applicable only to charitable trusts, and no attempt has been made to expand their coverage to charitable corporations, thereby severely limiting their effectiveness. The similar provisions in the New Hampshire act were expanded in 1997 so that registration and reporting are now required from all charities other than religious organizations and, in the case of reports, certain smaller charities.[61]

In addition to the sections setting forth the coverage of the Uniform Act, section 3 lists the categories of charities excluded from the act. They include governmental entities, officers of religious organizations holding property for religious purposes, and charitable corporations organized and operated primarily for educational, religious, or hospital purposes. Bogert attributes the exclusion of religious entities to the desire to avoid any question regarding the constitutionality of the legislation.[62] The result of this provision was to limit severely the applicability of the act in that the vast majority of charitable organizations were those covered in the third category.

The Minnesota act adopted the Restatement (Second) of Trusts definition of a charitable trust, stating, however, that "trustee" means "a person or group of persons either in an individual or a joint capacity, or a director, officer, or other agent of an association, foundation, trustee corporation, corporation, or other legal entity who is vested with the control or responsibility of administering property held for a charitable purpose."[63]

---

58. William G. Clark, "The New Charitable Trust Act," 50 *Illinois Bar Journal* 753 (1962).
59. 1963 Ill. Laws at 1462.
60. 760 Ill. Comp. Stat. 55/3.
61. N.H. Rev. Stat. Ann. §7:28(I), (II).
62. George G. Bogert and George T. Bogert, *The Law of Trusts and Trustees,* §411 n.40 (St. Paul: West Group, 3d ed., 1977).
63. Minn. Stat. §501B.35(4).

Registration and Reporting Requirements

One of the major substantive provisions in the Uniform Act and those similar to it is a requirement that charities subject to the act register with the attorney general upon creation, or within a short time after the effective date of the act, and thereafter file periodic financial reports with the office of the attorney general, thereby creating a registry of reports that are available to the public. The attorney general is authorized to determine the contents of the periodic financial reports and to issue rules and regulations relating to the filing requirements.

In addition to the organizations excluded from coverage under the general provisions of the Uniform Act, certain charities are exempted from the filing requirements, most commonly religious organizations and governmental entities. For example, in Massachusetts the general provisions apply to every public charity organized in the state or under the laws of any other state, with the exclusion of the American National Red Cross and eleven named veterans organizations.[64] However, registration and filing of annual financial reports are not required for "any property held for a religious purpose by a public charity, incorporated or unincorporated."[65] The language of the New Hampshire act is now similar to that of Massachusetts.[66]

The New York Supervision of Trustees for Charitable Purposes Act excludes eleven categories of organizations from the registration and reporting requirements: governmental entities; trustees required to report to the United States Congress or the state legislature; religious organizations; educational institutions; hospitals; fraternal and veterans organizations, student alumni associations, and historical societies chartered by the New York state Board of Regents; certain trusts with foreign corporate trustees; trusts with contingent or deferred charitable interests; supporting organizations of any organization exempt under the statute; cemetery corporations; and certain parent-teacher associations.[67]

The California act is similar to New York, excluding any religious organizations, as well as cemetery corporations, educational institutions, and hospitals, while adding health care service plans.[68]

Ohio requires registration and reporting from all charitable trusts with fully vested interests unless exempted by regulations issued by the attorney

64. Mass. Gen. Laws ch. 12, §8E.
65. Id., §8F.
66. N.H. Rev. Stat. Ann. §7:19(I), §7:28(I), (II).
67. N.Y. Est. Powers & Trusts Law §8-1.4.
68. Cal. Gov't Code §12583.

general. The reporting provisions, however, are not applicable to religious organizations, educational institutions with faculty and curriculum and a regularly organized body of pupils, or if an organization's gross receipts are less than $5,000 and gross assets less than $15,000.[69] Illinois has similar exclusions but the limit for small organizations applies to those with less than $15,000 in revenue or $15,000 in assets in any year.[70]

The Minnesota act excludes organizations with gross assets of less than $25,000, religious organizations and organizations that are exempt from federal income tax by virtue of their being considered supporting organizations described in section 509(a)(3) of the Internal Revenue Code maintained by a religious organization, and any organization that registers and files with the attorney general under the provisions of the Minnesota Charitable Solicitations Act. This act, in turn, exempts religious organizations, certain educational organizations, organizations that limit solicitations to members or solicit for a single person, and private foundations that did not solicit contributions from more than 100 persons during an accounting year.

When the first registration and reporting statutes were enacted, the scope of the financial reports was narrow and only rudimentary information was required. With the expansion of information required to meet federal reporting requirements, however, state offices realized the desirability of coordinating their reporting forms with federal Form 990, the federal information return required to be filed annually by all organizations exempt from federal income tax except religious organizations and charities with gross receipts of less than $25,000.[71]

Under the terms of the Tax Reform Act of 1969, all private foundations were required to file a separate information return, Form 990PF, with the Internal Revenue Service and also with the attorney general in the state in which they were located. In the states that do not require financial reports from charities, these returns are accepted but rarely filed so that they are not readily available for inspections. The states that maintain their own registries of charities have found it expedient to adopt the federal forms to meet their filing requirements, particularly those received from private foundations. However, in almost every state, additional information suitable for state enforcement purposes will be required.[72]

Unlike other states, Massachusetts requires audited financial statements for charities, other than trusts filing reports with the probate court, whenever their gross revenues exceed $250,000. Charities with gross revenues of more

69. Ohio Rev. Code Ann. §109.23.
70. 760 Ill. Comp. Stat. 55/4–6.
71. See Chapter 7.
72. See Chapter 5.

than $100,000 but not more than $250,000 may, in lieu of audit, submit a financial statement accompanied by a CPA's or public accountant's review report. Proponents of a requirement of this nature argue that it establishes a self-policing mechanism, thereby relieving the burdens of underfunded state agencies. Others argue that the requirement is extremely costly and inappropriately diverts funds away from programs, particularly for smaller charities.

There are thirty-nine states in which solicitation of funds for charitable purposes is regulated, with registration and financial reporting required of soliciting organizations as well as professional fund-raisers and solicitors. In some states the reports are filed with the secretary of state or another state agency.[73] These statutes are described in more detail below.

In thirty-nine states, including those that require filing with the attorney general, nonprofit corporations must file governing instruments on creation with the secretary of state. In five others, they must register with a corporation commission, while in several others they must register with a probate judge, the commissioner of commerce and economic development, the mayor, or the departments of finance and taxation. In California, Mississippi, Minnesota, and Oregon the attorney general must be notified upon the filing of an application for tax exemption.

In all but six states charitable corporations must periodically file a certificate of continuing existence. In some of these states, failure to file after a certain number of years will result in automatic dissolution, although it is possible for the corporate charter to be reinstated, usually upon filing the missing reports and paying delinquent filing fees.

Power to Conduct Investigations

Section 8 of the Uniform Supervision of Trustees for Charitable Purposes Act authorizes the attorney general to investigate transactions and relationships of organizations subject to the act to determine whether property held for charitable purposes is being properly administered.[74] Similar provisions appear in the acts in other states with registration and reporting provisions. The power to investigate includes the power to examine persons under oath and to require attendance at hearings and production of papers. The attorney general is also granted the power to issue rules and regulations to supplement his powers under the act. Although infrequently used, the power to conduct

73. Many of the statutes regulating solicitation of funds for charitable purposes do require submission of audited financial reports. See Appendix, Table 1, Column 15.
74. Uniform Supervision of Trustees for Charitable Purposes Act, §8.

formal investigations is considered a necessary adjunct to traditional enforcement powers.

A provision unique to California reflects the legislature's attempt to relieve the state of the costs entailed in carrying out the provisions of the act. It provides that in any case that is decided in favor of the state, the court is required to order the person having responsibility or duty to comply with the provisions of the judgment on behalf of any charity to pay the reasonable expense necessarily incurred by the state in the investigation and prosecution of the action.[75]

Required Notice to Attorney General of Judicial Proceedings

One of the provisions generally considered to be a prerequisite to effective enforcement of charities is a requirement that the attorney general be provided with notice of legal proceedings involving charitable interests. Thirty-seven states have enacted provisions of this nature. In the majority of these states, notice is required for cy pres proceedings and petitions for termination or dissolution. California, Massachusetts, New York, Rhode Island, and Texas require notice of virtually every suit involving the disposition or administration of funds held for charitable purposes, including proceedings for probate of wills, compromise of will contests, and administration and termination of estates. In Georgia, Mississippi, Missouri, Montana, Nebraska, Oregon, Tennessee, Vermont, and Wyoming, notice is required in the case of derivative suits but not otherwise.[76]

In fifteen states charitable corporations that intend to dissolve voluntarily must give advance notice to the attorney general and, in the case of New York and Massachusetts, they must also give notice to and obtain approval from the state supreme court. In California, notice is required for probate of wills with charitable interests, recording inter vivos transfers of property for charitable purposes, and by virtue of being a necessary party to termination or modification proceedings for charitable trusts and public benefit corporations.[77]

In Wyoming, notice must be given by the charity to the secretary of state who is, in turn, required to notify the attorney general.[78] In all other states, notice of dissolution is filed with the secretary of state or any other state official with whom instruments are filed upon creation. Thus in the vast majority of states there is no monitoring of dissolutions—and thus no oversight by a state official interested in preserving the assets of the terminating charity.

75. Cal. Gov't Code §12597.
76. See Appendix, Table 1, Column 2.
77. Cal. Prob. Code §17203.
78. Wyo. Stat. §17-19-630.

The only nationwide safeguard against diversion of charitable funds to private individuals during the course of a dissolution has come about by virtue of a federal regulation imposing as a condition for obtaining tax exemption that the governing instrument or state law require that, on dissolution, the assets be distributed to other organizations also exempt from federal income tax.[79] This requirement appears in the statutes in all but four states.

In regard to mergers, charities are explicitly prohibited from merging with for-profit organizations in twenty-eight states. In twelve others, court approval is required before such a merger can be consummated, and in some instances notice to the attorney general of the court proceeding is also required. In eight states there are no limits. One question that must be decided when corporations with legal situs in different states merge is the situs of the surviving corporation. In some states the merger provisions require that the surviving corporation remain under the jurisdiction of the state in which the charity was originally organized. If the statutes of two states contain this requirement, merger is effectively prohibited. In other states, the surviving corporation need not remain in the originating state so long as it constitutes a charity in the foreign jurisdiction.

In sixteen states notice must be given to a state official if a charitable corporation intends to dispose of substantially all of its assets, in all but one to the attorney general, and in Wyoming to the secretary of state who is in turn required to notify the attorney general. New York requires notice to the attorney general and court approval. Arizona requires public notice and a hearing if the purchaser is not tax-exempt or the use will be unrelated to the charitable purposes of the corporation.

Power of the Attorney General over Conversions

The statutes requiring advance notice to the attorney general of sale or other disposition of a substantial part of a charity's assets were an important enforcement tool for state officials during the mid-1990s when there was a dramatic increase in the number of charitable hospitals and health care plans that were selling their assets to for-profit corporations, or converting from nonprofit to profit status in transactions in which in a number of instances the assets of the charities ended up in private hands.[80] It was estimated that while there had been between twelve and eighteen hospital conversions in each of the years from 1990 through 1994, the number increased to forty-four in

79. Treas. Reg. §1.501(c)(3)-1(b)(4).

80. Harvey J. Goldschmid, "The Fiduciary Duties of Nonprofit Directors and Officers: Paradoxes, Problems, and Proposed Reforms," in *Conference: Governance of Nonprofit Organizations—Standards and Enforcement* (New York University School of Law, National Center on Philanthropy and the Law, 1997).

1995.[81] In 1997 there were fifty conversions; in 1998 the number dropped to twenty-nine, and in 1999 it dropped to nineteen. During the same period, the number of "reverse conversions," sales by for-profit chains to nonprofit hospitals increased markedly, with twenty-five occurring in 1998 and thirty in 1999.[82] There were further reductions between 2000 and 2002.[83] These figures apply only to hospitals and health care conglomerates. There have been similar developments in regard to conversion of Blue Cross Blue Shield plans and scattered examples of conversions of other types of charities, such as schools. In regard to Blue Cross Blue Shield plans, there were fourteen conversions during the period 1995–2002.[84]

In Massachusetts and New York, the office of the attorney general used the notice requirements applicable to disposition of assets, together with restrictions on merger, to regulate conversions. However, the magnitude of the dollars involved and the rate of increase in the number of transactions, combined in some states with uncertainty as to the extent of the state's enforcement power, led a number of attorneys general individually and working through the National Association of Attorneys General, to look for a legislative solution. The result was that between 1996 and 2000 twenty-five states enacted thirty statutes regulating conversions, several of them with provisions identical to those in a Model Act for Nonprofit Healthcare Conversion Transactions that was approved by the National Association of Attorneys General in 1998. The regulatory schemes and the identity of the regulators varied greatly from state to state, but in every instance they demonstrated a willingness to extend state regulation to transactions that had not previously been subject to government scrutiny.

The common element in these statutes was a requirement of advance review of a proposed conversion in which one or more state officials determined whether fair market value would be received by the nonprofit and were able to assure that there would be no element of private inurement. Eight of the states granted exclusive regulatory authority to the attorney general. In eleven others, the attorney general shared regulatory authority with the commissioner of corporations, the secretary of state, the insurance commissioner, or the state agency charged with overseeing public health care access. Although the decrease in the rate of conversions after 1997 was attri-

81. David Cutler and Jill Horwitz, "Converting Hospitals from Nonprofit to For-Profit Status: Why and What Effect?" in *The Changing Hospital Industry: Comparing Not-for-Profit and For-Profit Institutions,* 55–56 (David Cutler ed., Chicago: University of Chicago Press, 2000).

82. Deanna Bellandi, "Spinoffs, Big Deals Dominate in '99," *Modern Healthcare,* January 10, 2000, at 36.

83. Irving Levin Associates, Inc., *The Health Care Acquisition Report* (2002).

84. Information provided by Community Catalyst, Boston.

buted principally to economic factors, there is little doubt that increased state regulation was an important factor in many instances.[85]

In 2002 Maine enacted a conversion statute that gave power to the attorney general to approve of conversions where the value of the assets was between $50,000 and $500,000, but required court approval in a proceeding in which the attorney general was a necessary party if the value exceeded $500,000. For assets of less than $50,000, notice to the attorney general was sufficient. The statute defined conversions broadly and added cross-references to the provisions governing mergers, sale of substantial assets, and voluntary dissolutions as possibly being subject to the new provisions.[86]

The Role of the Attorney General in Interstate Disputes

Charities Operating in Several States

Changes in the nature of the delivery of health care during the 1990s led to numerous mergers of hospitals into large conglomerates that operated facilities in multiple states. Prior to this development, it was rare that attorneys general would be in conflict with each other in the exercise of their regulatory powers over charities. However, the likelihood for conflict was always present, and it surfaced in cases involving a health care system operating hospitals in Kansas and Missouri described above in this chapter as well as in three cases dealing with the disposition of the proceeds from the sale of health care facilities located in South Dakota, North Dakota, and New Mexico that were owned by an Arizona nonprofit corporation, Banner Health Systems. The attorneys general of the states in which the hospitals were located each took the position that the proceeds of the proposed sales were to be considered in part "community assets," in that they had been donated by individuals in the community in which the hospital was located or reflected the benefits of exemption from real property tax granted to a local hospital, which meant that the proceeds should be applied for the benefit of the community and not for that of the larger health care system itself.

Banner had itself instituted court actions in the appropriate federal districts seeking to enjoin the attorneys general from interfering with the sales and to

---

85. Marion R. Fremont-Smith, "The Role of Government Regulation in the Creation and Operation of Conversion Foundations," 23 *Exempt Organization Tax Review* 37 (1999); see also Marion R. Fremont-Smith and Jonathan A. Lever, "Analysis and Perspective: State Regulation of Health Care Conversions and Conversion Foundations," 9 *Health Law Reporter* (BNA) no. 19, at 714 (2000) (Idaho, Massachusetts, and New Jersey enacted statutes after publication).

86. 2001 Me. Laws ch. 550 (enacted March 25, 2002), codified at Me. Rev. Stat. Ann. tit. 5, §§194B–194K.

obtain declaratory judgment that the proceeds were not subject to charitable trust laws. In the South Dakota decision, the state supreme court, on certification from the United States District Court in the original suit, found that the assets were held subject to a constructive trust for the benefit of the community and could not be used for the general purposes of the parent corporation.[87] In contrast, in the case involving the sale of the hospital in North Dakota, the lower court held that there was no fiduciary or confidential relationship between Banner and the community, thereby undermining any trust claim.[88] The North Dakota attorney general announced his intent to appeal this decision, and as of October 1, 2003, the matter was pending.

In the third case, the attorney general of New Mexico and the corporation reached a settlement in May 2002 under which Banner agreed to commit $11.5 million from sale proceeds toward fulfilling its obligations in the state by distributing $4.5 million to health-related charities in the area of New Mexico served by the hospital that was being sold, the specific beneficiaries to be selected by the attorney general, applying $4.5 million to meet Banner's obligations in Los Alamos County, and providing $2.5 million for capital improvements at the Los Alamos Medical Center, as well as making a commitment to recruit physicians to the area.[89]

There is little that can be done to resolve disputes of this nature, dependent as they are on local law and the inclination of individual attorneys general. What is needed is greater uniformity among the states as to the principles governing the organization and operation of charities, and more particularly a refusal to grant governing boards unfettered freedom to change charitable purposes.

Charities Seeking to Move Out of the State of Origin

Another aspect of multistate conflicts relates to the question of whether the attorney general has a duty to insist that charitable assets administered within his jurisdiction be retained there, a position that Brody has characterized as "parochialism."[90] Two cases that were in negotiation in 2003 illustrate the problem. One involved a dispute among the directors of the Terra Museum of American Art in Chicago over the disposition of its art collection. The attorney general joined in a suit brought by members of the board against the widow of the founder and two other directors seeking to thwart their attempts to move the collection to Washington and close the museum. A settlement was reached in 2001 under which the entire board would be replaced

87. Banner Health System v. Long, 663 N.W.2d 242 (S.D. 2003).
88. Banner Health System v. Stenehjem, 2003 WL 501821 (D.N.D. 2003).
89. Julie Piotrowski, "Banner, N.M. Strike a Deal," *Modern Healthcare*, June 3, 2002, at 20.
90. Brody, "Whose Public?"

and the collection would remain in Chicago for at least fifty years. The defendants appealed the court decree approving the terms of the settlement. As of October 2003 that suit was still pending, despite the fact that in June 2003 the foundation had announced that the museum would close by the end of 2004 and that the major works from the collection would be placed on permanent loan at the Art Institute of Chicago.[91]

In the second case, the attorney general of Kansas took a position similar to that of his Illinois counterpart when he opposed a proposed transfer of certain assets and of the operations of the Menninger Clinic from Kansas to Houston, Texas, claiming jurisdiction on the basis that Menninger's assets were subject to a trust to be held, used, and applied for charitable purposes and to serve the population of patients for which it was originally established and operated.[92] A settlement was reached in May 2003 under which the clinic was allowed to transfer its operations to Texas while agreeing to distribute one-half of the proceeds of the sale of its Kansas real property to a new Kansas foundation and of certain other assets to charities in the state.[93]

Brody noted that the proper role of the attorney general is not defined. She considered most worrisome the lack of a state official charged with representing the beneficiaries of a national or international charity, observing that in terms of the national public interest, relocation could in many instances provide affirmative benefits.[94] These cases also underline the potential drawbacks to enforcement by state regulators who are publicly elected and thus in many instances will be inclined to adopt positions that will appeal to local communities, large or small, rather than appear to favor interests outside their jurisdiction. Such, of course, is the case in the forty-three states in which the attorney general is elected.[95]

Charities Operating Outside Their State of Origin

Conflict of laws doctrines apply when a charity organized in one state operates in another and the laws governing its creation in the state of origin differ from those in the state in which it conducts its operations. Under conflict of

91. Id.; Charles Storch and Jon Yates, "Terra Giving Up, Closing Doors in '04: Treasures to Go to Art Institute," *Chicago Tribune*, June 21, 2003, at C1.

92. Michael Hooper and Alicia Henrikson, "Stovall to Study Agreement," *Topeka-Capital-Journal*, December 6, 2002, at 11A.

93. Office of Kansas Attorney General, Press Release, "Attorney General Approves Menninger Settlement; Agreement Protects Interests of Kansas, Creates Mental Health Foundation" (May 14, 2003).

94. Brody, "Whose Public?" at 32.

95. In Alaska, Hawaii, New Hampshire, New Jersey, and Wyoming, the attorney general is appointed by the governor, and in Maine he is chosen by secret ballot of the legislature, and in Tennessee by the state supreme court. See *www.naag.org/naag/about_naag.php*.

laws doctrines applicable to trusts, the settlor may designate the state whose laws are to apply to the trust. Absent such a designation, the general rule is that the law of the trust's principal place of administration will govern administrative matters, and the law of the place having the most significant relation to the trust's creation will govern its dispositive provisions. Place of administration is determined by considering the domiciles of the trustees, the physical location of the assets, and the place where the business of the trust is carried out.[96] For business corporations, an "internal affairs doctrine" holds that the laws of the state of incorporation will apply to regulate the intracorporate matters of a foreign corporation (one authorized to act in a state other than that in which it was incorporated). However, the Restatement (Second) of Conflict of Laws does not apply to nonprofit corporations, and there is little case law on the matter.[97]

There is one California case in which an appeals court applied California law to a dispute over the power of a charitable corporation to remove a director.[98] The court noted that under California law, directors of charitable trusts are considered to be trustees in many respects, particularly in regard to their duties, and under trust law doctrine, the laws of California, the state of administration, would be applicable. The court also held that although under corporate law the laws of the state of origin would apply to internal affairs such as the election and removal of officers, for a charity organized by California residents, located in the state, and with all of its assets and most of its activities there, it should not escape the scrutiny of California law. Without additional precedents, the law remains uncertain.

This issue can be of great importance to an attorney general in a state in which the laws governing fiduciary duty are stricter than those in the state of origin of a foreign corporation operating within the attorney general's jurisdiction. It will also be acute if a conflict arises regarding the composition of the board of directors of a charity in a state such as California, Maine, or New Hampshire that requires a charity to have a certain number of independent directors.

Standing to Sue to Enforce Duties of Charitable Fiduciaries

The common law not only conferred supervisory powers and duties on the attorney general to enforce charitable funds, but it largely excluded other members of the general public from so doing. The reasons for this exclusion

96. Uniform Trust Code, §7 (amended 2001).

97. Restatement (Second) of Conflict of Laws, ch. 13 introductory note (1969).

98. American Center for Education, Inc. v. Cavnar, 80 Cal. App. 3d 476 (Cal. Ct. App. 1978).

were based not on a denial of the public's interest, but on the purely practical consideration that it would be impossible to manage charitable funds, or even to find individuals to take on the task, if the fiduciaries were to be constantly subject to harassing litigation. The rule developed that a person who was unable to show an interest other than as a member of the community would not be recognized by the courts as having capacity to maintain a suit for enforcement of a charity. His remedy was to bring the facts before the attorney general and attempt to persuade him that the suit should be filed. The attorney general had the power to designate such a person a "relator," and to authorize him to bring the suit. The attorney general could require the relator to pay the costs of litigation or require the individual's agreement to pay all costs as a condition for bringing suit.[99]

The attorney general in California codified the procedures for acquiring relator status by regulation.[100] A potential relator must apply for leave to sue to the attorney general, filing a verified complaint and a statement of facts justifying the suit. If the application is accepted, the relator must post a bond and agree to pay for any costs and expenses. The attorney general remains at all times in control of the action and can withdraw or discontinue the suit at any time, as well as take over its prosecution. As is the case with derivative suits, there are no reported cases in which suit was brought by a relator under this regulation. Fishman has suggested that this may be due to the requirement to pay attorney's fees.[101]

Exclusion of the General Public

Prior to the 1960s, the law was unclear as to whether a person with no standing to enforce a charitable trust himself could compel the attorney general to bring suit for enforcement.[102] The better view had been that individuals were precluded from bringing an action such as mandamus to compel an attorney general to institute enforcement proceedings or allow the use of his name by others,[103] nor could an action be brought to force him to reconsider a decision not to bring suit without a showing that his decision was capricious or

99. See James J. Fishman and Stephen Schwarz, *Nonprofit Organizations: Cases and Materials*, 258 (New York: Foundation Press, 2d ed., 2000), which lists cases in which relator status was granted to certain nonprofit, noncharitable organizations.

100. Cal. Admin. Code tit. 11, §§1–2.

101. James J. Fishman, "The Development of Nonprofit Corporation Law and an Agenda for Reform," 34 *Emory Law Journal* 617, 674 (1985).

102. John G. Lees, "Governmental Supervision of Charitable Trusts," in *Current Trends in State Legislation (1956–1957)*, 609, 621 (Ann Arbor: University of Michigan Law School Legislative Research Center, 1957).

103. Scott and Fratcher, *Law of Trusts*, §391.

not based on legitimate considerations of policy.[104] In dictum in the case of *Longcor v. City of Red Wing*,[105] decided by the Minnesota court in 1940, the court suggested that if the attorney general, after an adequate showing, had refused to act, an action might have been maintainable by a private person, but this would represent an exception to the general rule.

The possibility of bringing a writ of mandamus to compel an attorney general to reconsider a decision not to bring suit against a charity was first decided in the 1955 case of *Ames v. Attorney General*.[106] The plaintiffs, a group of alumni of Harvard College, had requested the Massachusetts attorney general to bring a suit, in which they would act as relators, against Harvard in its capacity as trustee of the Arnold Arboretum for breach of trust. The purpose of the suit was to prevent the university from removing from the Arboretum premises to the college a large botanical library and herbarium. The attorney general, after a hearing, decided that the proposed transfer was within the trustee's discretion, and refused to permit the plaintiffs to proceed in his name. The plaintiffs then brought suit against the attorney general to attempt to compel him to reconsider his decision on the basis of the law as they viewed it, but the court held that the attorney general's decision was not judicially reviewable and dismissed the case.

Karst pointed out that the plaintiffs made no attempt to force the attorney general to bring the suit, but merely requested that he reconsider his decision, thereby coming within the rule that permits mandamus actions to compel a "ministerial," as opposed to a "discretionary," act by a public officer. He inferred from the court's refusal to grant this relief that it would not compel the attorney general to commence a suit to enforce the charity.[107]

These same rules are applicable in the case of actions against charitable corporations. For example, in a 1964 case in New York, members of the public were precluded from maintaining an action to rescind the charter of a charitable corporation after the attorney general refused to bring or sanction such an action.[108]

A Wisconsin statute that was enacted in 1945 provided that an action to

104. Kenneth L. Karst, "The Efficiency of the Charitable Dollar: An Unfulfilled State Responsibility," 73 *Harvard Law Review* 433, 449 (1960).

105. 289 N.W. 570 (Minn. 1940).

106. 124 N.E.2d 511 (Mass. 1955).

107. Karst, "Charitable Dollar," 450. With a subsequent change in administration, a new attorney general permitted the plaintiffs, known unofficially as "The Friends of the Arnold Arboretum," to proceed as relators in his name. The court subsequently held for the defendant university. Attorney General v. President and Fellows of Harvard College, 213 N.E.2d 840 (Mass. 1966).

108. People v. American Society for Prevention of Cruelty to Animals, 247 N.Y.S.2d 487 (App. Div. 1964).

enforce a charitable trust could be brought in the name of the state by any ten or more interested parties on their own complaint if the attorney general refused to act; it defined "interested party" as a donor or a member or prospective member of the class for whose benefit the trust was established.[109] There were no reported cases of actions brought under the statute, and it was repealed in 1969.[110]

It is not unusual for an attorney general to have duties that conflict with his duty to protect charitable funds. It commonly occurs when a state revenue department challenges the deductibility under the state tax laws of a charitable gift, and the attorney general must choose whether to represent the state department of revenue or fulfill his role as protector of the public interest in the preservation of charitable funds. This was the situation in Virginia in 1996 when the legislature approved a bill requiring that upon the demutualization of health care insurance corporations, the proceeds be paid to the state treasury rather than be held for charitable purposes.[111] As a result, $175 million from the sale of Trigon (Blue Cross Blue Shield of Virginia) was transferred to the Virginia treasury with the approval of the state attorney general.[112]

In 2001 a situation similar to that in Virginia arose in New York when the legislature passed an act allowing the sale of Empire Blue Cross Blue Shield and directing that 5% of the proceeds be held as a charitable foundation and the remaining 95% be treated as a "public asset," to be used for state purposes, specifically for wage increases for health care workers.[113] The attorney general did not participate publicly in the deliberations leading to passage of the bill. After its passage, he declined requests from interested parties to challenge the legislation and opposed efforts of a group of subscribers and public benefit charities to have the matter determined by a court, siding with the Commissioner of Insurance in arguing that the plaintiffs lacked standing to bring the suit.[114]

One resolution to the dilemma posed when an attorney general is faced with a conflict as to his duties is for the state agency to be represented by its own staff attorneys or to retain outside counsel, freeing the attorney general

109. Wis. Stat. §231.34.

110. 1969 Wis. Laws ch. 283, §2.

111. Va. Code Ann. §38.2-1005.1B.3, .4.

112. Prehearing Brief of the Division of Consumer Counsel, Office of the Attorney General, Application of Blue Cross and Blue Shield of Virginia for Conversion from a Mutual Insurance Company to a Stock Corporation (August 30, 1996) (No. INS950103).

113. N.Y. Ins. Law §4301(j)(3), (4)(B), (5), §7317(k), codified by Health Care Workforce Recruitment and Retention Act, S.6084/A.9610, 2002 N.Y. Laws ch. 1.

114. Brief for Defendant at 17–21, Consumers Union of U.S., Inc. v. State, No. 118699/02 (N.Y. Sup. Ct., filed September 20, 2002).

to represent the charitable interests. The choice of which interest to represent is his and should not be dictated from outside. However, in any case in which he chooses to appear as an adversary to charitable interests, strict interpretation of the rule of exclusive standing will effectively assure that the public interest will be defeated. This was never the intent of the rule. Accordingly, this presents a clear case in which the standing rules need to be modified to permit a suit to be brought.

Standing to Sue Granted to Certain Interested Parties

Although members of the general public are not recognized by the courts as proper parties to bring suit against a charity for breach of duty nor can they force an attorney general to do so, the attorney general's power of enforcement is not exclusive. When a charitable trust is created for a group of beneficiaries who are ascertainable at a given particular time although they may not be ascertainable over a longer period, these individuals have been recognized by the courts as proper parties to bring enforcement actions. The general rule is that a person must be able to show that he is entitled to a benefit from the trust beyond the benefit to which members of the public in general are entitled.[115] Where a trust has been established for the needy of a particular town or parish, the courts have allowed suits to be brought by the town officials, church wardens, or even residents or church members acting on behalf of themselves and other potential beneficiaries. There are records of cases of this sort in the Calendars in Chancery that were brought prior to the enactment of the Statute of Charitable Uses in 1601, as well as more recent examples.[116]

Another group of cases in which certain groups of citizens have routinely been granted standing have involved suits against governmental entities, usually cities and towns, to enforce the terms of gifts of land for public parks.[117] The courts have been more willing to grant standing to abutters, and in some instances groups of citizens, to enforce the terms of gifts to establish and maintain public parks. The clearest case of a party having a special interest, of

115. Restatement (Second) of Trusts, §391 cmt. b.

116. See Scott and Fratcher, *Law of Trusts,* §391, for citations.

117. Mary Grace Blasko et al., "Standing to Sue in the Charitable Sector," in *Topics in Philanthropy,* vol. 4, at 27 (1993) (New York University School of Law, Program on Philanthropy and the Law), distinguished these cases from suits against charities "because they generally involve suits brought against a government or an entity closely related to a government, often acting as a trustee, rather than against a charity." Id. at n.369. However, charitable trust rules apply to any trust for charitable purposes regardless of whether the trustee is an individual or a governmental unit.

course, is a trust for the benefit of a charitable corporation. It is well settled that in such a situation the corporation can maintain a suit against the trustees for enforcement.

Suits have also been brought by a class who claim to be beneficiaries on the basis that they are patrons or employees of a charity and, in one case, by subscribers to a nonprofit health plan. Noteworthy are cases involving charities located in the District of Columbia. The first was *Stern v. Lucy Webb Hayes National Training School*,[118] decided by the District Court for the District of Columbia in 1974, a leading case on the extent of the duties of directors of a charitable corporation. This suit was brought as a class action under the Federal Rules of Civil Procedure by patients of the Sibley Hospital who were certified as a class without protest in a prior decision.[119] In the earlier decision, the court dismissed antitrust claims brought by the plaintiffs, but certified them as a class to bring suit for breach of the duties of care and loyalty while barring them from personal recovery of damages.

The decisions in the *Stern* cases featured importantly in a case dealing with the issue of standing decided by the Court of Appeals for the District of Columbia in 1982.[120] This suit was brought by subscribers to Blue Cross Blue Shield Health Plans against the Plans and three banks that served as their depositories. The Plans provided health benefits to all federal government employees who chose to subscribe under the terms of a contract with the federal government. The basis of the subscribers' claim was that their relationship to the insurers was in the nature of a trust in that the Plans were nonprofit corporations and as such owed fiduciary duties to the subscribers as beneficiaries of the corporate activity. The plaintiffs alleged that these duties had been breached by virtue of the fact that the Plans and their agents had maintained amounts in non-interest-bearing checking accounts that were too high. The lower court had dismissed the suit, finding that the contracts with the government did not create trusts but rather established third party beneficiary relationships in regard to the employees and, in view of the fact that the Plans owed no fiduciary duties to the plaintiff subscribers, they lacked standing to bring suit. At no point did the court refer to the Plans as charitable corporations or apply charity law principles.

In affirming this decision, the Court of Appeals first distinguished the case from a prior decision in which it upheld the power of the United States acting as *parens patriae* to bring suit against a charitable corporation, not to enforce a private right but a public one that arose by virtue of the nature of the cor-

118. 381 F. Supp. 1003 (D.D.C. 1974).
119. 367 F. Supp. 536 (D.D.C. 1973).
120. Christiansen v. National Savings and Trust Co., 683 F.2d 520 (D.C. Cir. 1982).

poration. The court then turned to the application of the decisions in the *Stern* cases, noting that in its memorandum opinion the lower court in the instant case gave considerable attention to their holdings. The appeals court stated:

> Judge Greene's memorandum opinion reflects the fact that he had considerable difficulty with his colleague's decision in the *Stern* case, both as to the question to whom the directors' duties were owed, and the related if not identical issue of who had standing to enforce them. He treats the *Stern* decision as constituting "novel precedent" and as representing the "outer limits of the imposition of liability on directors of non-profit corporations on trust theory grounds . . ."[121]

The appeals court then analyzed the first of the *Stern* cases in which the court held that the plaintiffs had no standing to bring suit alleging violation of the antitrust laws. It reflected: "But instead of dismissing the breach of trust counts also, the court allows them to stand but with all members of the class barred from personal recovery of damages."[122] The court noted that it was unclear from the record whether Judge Gesell had before him motions to dismiss any other than the antitrust counts, crediting Judge Greene's explanation in the present case to be "as plausible an explanation as we can devise; it was considered that someone ought to be able to enforce the trustee's duties in litigation, and if the patients could not, there was no one else . . . [F]or enforcing fiduciary duties, justice requires someone to have standing, and it was the patients or nobody."[123] The importance of the case lies in its critique of the *Stern* cases, particularly its observation that standing was granted in that instance primarily because if the plaintiffs could not challenge the directors' breaches of their duties, "no one else could."[124]

The third case from the District of Columbia was decided in 1990. There, the plaintiffs were residents of a home for elderly women who were granted standing to try to prevent its closing.[125]

Review of Recent Standing Cases

A review was conducted of cases involving standing decided between 1980 and 2001 to determine the factors that influenced the courts and whether there were any noticeable trends in the application of the rules. In twenty-

121. Id. at 527.
122. Id. at 528.
123. Id.
124. Id.
125. Hooker v. Edes Home, 579 A.2d 608 (D.C. 1990).

four cases decided between 1991 and 2001, the right to bring suit was granted to private individuals in six and denied in seventeen cases, while one was remanded to determine whether a public interest was involved. Among those in which standing was granted were the *Smithers* case in which the administrator of the estate of a donor sought to enforce the conditions of an inter vivos gift he had made,[126] a case involving park abutters,[127] two suits for enforcement of trust by named charitable beneficiaries,[128] the *Hill* case brought by the donor's grandson and former trustee,[129] and the *Washington Orphan Asylum* case, which involved an 1828 special act creating what were in effect two parallel boards of directors.[130] In the first two of these cases, the attorney general was a party to the litigation, in two he had declined to participate, and in two others he was not mentioned. In the *Hill* case the court held specifically that in the absence of a party who would protect the public interest, the petitioner had sufficient interest to give him standing.

Of the seventeen cases in which standing was denied, three involved suits by faculty and students,[131] four were brought by donors or their heirs,[132] four by park abutters,[133] two by citizens in the county in which a hospital was located,[134] one by members of a church,[135] one by the distribution committee of a foundation,[136] one by a former member and trustee of a church,[137] and one by a hospital seeking to enjoin the conversion of another hospital in regard to which it had not been the successful purchaser.[138] Three of the cases

126. Smithers v. St. Luke's-Roosevelt Hospital Center, 723 N.Y.S.2d 426 (Surr. Ct. 2001).

127. Grabowski v. City of Bristol, 1997 WL 375596 (Conn. Super.).

128. Parish of Jefferson v. Lafreniere Park Foundation, 716 So. 2d 472 (La. App. 5th 1998); In re Estes Estate, 523 N.W.2d 863 (Mich. Ct. App. 1994).

129. Matter of Hill, 509 N.W.2d 168 (Minn. Ct. App. 1993).

130. Board of Directors of Washington City Orphan Asylum v. Board of Trustees of Washington City Orphan Asylum, 798 A.2d 1068 (D.C. 2002).

131. Warren v. University System of Georgia, 544 S.E.2d 190 (Ga. Ct. App. 2001); In re The Barnes Foundation, 684 A.2d 123 (Pa. Super. Ct. 1996); Steeneck v. University of Bridgeport, 668 A.2d 688 (Conn. 1995).

132. In re Alaimo, 732 N.Y.S.2d 819 (App. Div. 2001); Russell v. Yale University, 737 A.2d 941 (Conn. App. Ct. 1999); Arman v. Bank of America, 74 Cal. App. 4th 697 (Ct. App. 1999); Carl J. Herzog Foundation v. University of Bridgeport, 699 A.2d 995 (Conn. 1997).

133. Homes v. Madison, 1998 WL 712343 (Conn. Super. Ct.); Three Bills, Inc. v. City of Parma, 676 N.E.2d 1273 (Ohio App. Ct. 1996); Hinton v. City of St. Joseph, 889 S.W.2d 854 (Mo. 1994); In re DeLong, 565 N.Y.S.2d 569 (App. Div. 1991).

134. Cook v. Lloyd Noland Foundation, Inc., 825 So. 2d 83 (Ala. 2001); Plant v. Upper Valley Medical Center, 1996 WL 185341 (Ohio Ct. App.).

135. Weaver v. Wood, 680 N.E.2d 918 (Mass. 1997).

136. In re McCune, 705 A.2d 861 (Pa. Super. Ct. 1997).

137. Brock v. Bennett, 443 S.E.2d 409 (S.C. App. Ct. 1994).

138. State ex. rel Adventist Health Care System/Sunbelt Health Care Corp. v. Nashville Memorial Hospital, Inc., 914 S.W.2d 903 (Tenn. Ct. App. 1995).

involved claims that the trustees had breached their duties of care or loyalty, while nine involved challenges to trustees' interpretation of the terms of a gift and one challenged the merger of a local hospital. The case remanded for further findings involved a suit by an environmental group claiming mismanagement of timber lands owned by an endowment trust.[139] The decisions denying standing did not appear, however, to rest on the nature of the claim but rather on the relationship of the claimant to the charity involved.

There were thirteen cases involving the issue of standing that were decided during the preceding years between 1980 and 1990. Standing was granted to individuals in six of these and denied in seven. The cases granting standing included the *Hooker* case described above in which the plaintiffs were residents of a nursing home,[140] a Hawaii case involving a city-owned park,[141] a suit by a charitable corporation established to benefit employees of any companies owned by the donor,[142] a suit by members of a YMCA seeking to prevent sale of real property,[143] one brought by trustees of a charitable trust seeking an accounting,[144] and one by a corporation alleging to be the beneficiary of another charity.[145] None of them involved allegations of breaches of the duties of loyalty or care, and the attorney general was not a participant in any of the suits. Of the cases in which standing was denied, one was brought by students,[146] two by members of a charitable corporation,[147] and one by taxpayers against museum trustees.[148] The remaining cases included the *Christiansen* case already described involving subscribers to the federal health insurance plans,[149] another by former employees of a hospital claiming that its successor owed them monetary damages as well as alleging that the successor was not carrying out the charitable purposes of the original institution,[150] and the last was a suit against a foundation by a disaffected grant-seeker.[151]

139. Selkirk-Priest Basin Association, Inc. v. State ex rel. Andrus, 899 P.2d 949 (Idaho 1995).
140. Hooker v. Edes, 579 A.2d 608 (D.C. 1990).
141. Kapiolani Park v. City and County of Honolulu, 751 P.2d 1022 (Haw. 1988).
142. Alco Gravure, Inc. v. The Knapp Foundation, 479 N.E.2d 752 (N.Y. 1985).
143. YMCA of the City of Washington v. Covington, 484 A.2d 589 (D.C. 1984).
144. Estate of Vanderbilt, 441 N.Y.S.2d 153 (Surr. Ct. 1981).
145. Valley Forge Historical Society v. Washington Memorial Chapel, 426 A.2d 1123 (Pa. 1981).
146. Associated Students of the University of Oregon v. Oregon Investment Co., 728 P.2d 30 (Or. Ct. App. 1986).
147. Nacol v. State, 795 S.W.2d 810 (Tex. 1990); Lopez v. Medford Community Center, 424 N.E.2d 229 (Mass. 1981).
148. Hardman v. Feinstein, 195 Cal. App. 3d 157 (Cal. Ct. App. 1987).
149. Christiansen v. National Savings and Trust Co., 683 F.2d 520 (D.C. Cir. 1982).
150. Stallworth v. Andalusia Hosp., Inc., 470 So. 2d 1158 (Ala. 1985).
151. Kemmerer v. John D. and Catherine T. MacArthur Foundation, 594 F. Supp. 121 (N.D. Ill. 1984).

The overriding factor in almost every one of the cases in which individuals were granted standing was the lack of effective enforcement by the attorney general or another government official. Decisions in the District of Columbia already described, notably the *Christiansen* case, as well as several in New Jersey where regulation of charities has also been minimal, are typical of these cases.

Another factor influencing the court to grant standing, present in the New Jersey cases and those in a few other jurisdictions, has been that the question before the court was an interpretation of the terms of a trust or a complaint for cy pres or deviation, cases that did not involve allegations that reflected negatively on the fiduciaries. In cases involving the application of the cy pres doctrine, it is not unusual for the courts to permit interested parties to intervene in the proceedings, particularly if there is a dispute as to the recipient of the property on a termination or dissolution.[152]

A third factor noted by the court in several of these cases has been the existence of an immediate threat of injury to the class of beneficiaries or of permanent loss of the charitable funds. Such a threat was present in the *Hooker* case in which the closing of the home was imminent.[153] It also was an important consideration in the New York case of *Alco Gravure, Inc.,* in which employees who were beneficiaries of a charitable corporation were granted standing to challenge the action of the trustees in dissolving the corporation and transferring its assets to another corporation.[154]

On the other hand, the courts have for the most part had no problem rejecting suits seeking monetary damages for personal claims that may include a claim that charitable funds are being diverted in order to bolster the suit. Examples include the *Kemmerer, Stallworth,* and *Nashville Memorial Hospital* cases cited above.

The problem faced by the courts in deciding the grounds on which to permit an interested party to bring suit to enforce a charity is, of course, the need to strike the difficult balance between the desire to assure that abuses will be corrected and the desire to permit fiduciaries to function without unwarranted abuse and harassment. Theoretically, the attorney general can serve the function assigned to him. In the great number of standing cases, it is only when he fails that the courts will feel compelled to broaden the class of parties who may take over his role.

There are instances in which the legislature has spoken so as to alter this balance, but they are rare. One example is a Massachusetts statute that per-

---

152. See, for example, Matter of Multiple Sclerosis Service Organization of New York, Inc., 496 N.E.2d 861 (N.Y. 1986).

153. Hooker v. Edes Home, 579 A.2d 608 (D.C. 1990).

154. Alco Gravure, Inc. v. The Knapp Foundation, 479 N.E.2d 752 (N.Y. 1985).

mits a suit by taxpayers to enforce gifts made for charitable purposes to any city, town, or other subdivision. The attorney general must, however, be notified of the action and given leave to intervene.[155] This is a specialized type of enactment, however. In the majority of states, if the attorney general does not act, there is no other potential beneficiary capable of doing so, and abuses will remain uncorrected if he is in default in carrying out his duty.

In the situations discussed thus far, the interest of the person seeking standing to enforce a charity has been that of a beneficiary or a fiduciary. There are other interests, however, that are sufficient to allow a court to confer standing to commence action. One of several trustees may bring a suit to enforce a charitable trust or compel the redress of a breach.[156] Similarly, a director may bring an action on behalf of a charitable corporation against a co-director.[157] There are cases in which a successor trustee has been permitted to bring suit upon learning of a predecessor's breach of duty.[158]

It would seem that an analogy from the trust cases could be made to the case of a successor director of a charitable corporation, but in 1954 the District Court of Appeals of California refused to allow a nonprofit corporation to sue its founder and former director, his wife, and five other former directors to recover over $3 million that it charged had been dissipated over an eleven-year period through speculation and mismanagement.[159] The decision was severely criticized by Karst,[160] and in 1964 the Supreme Court of California gave tacit recognition to this criticism by quoting extensively from him in a decision in which it upheld the rights of three trustees of a charitable corporation to bring suit against the twenty-three remaining trustees and the attorney general to enforce breach of duties.[161] The lower court had dismissed the suit on the basis of the holding in the *Pepperdine* case that the plaintiffs had no capacity to bring the action and that the complaint did not set forth a threatened breach of a charitable trust. The state supreme court specifically rejected the defendants' contention that the fact that the charity was a corporation required the application of a rule different from that which would apply to a charitable trust, and concluded that the *Pepperdine* case was disapproved "to the extent it is contrary to this opinion."[162]

As to the members of a charitable corporation, or shareholders if such are

---

155. Mass. Gen. Laws ch. 214, §3.
156. Eurich v. Korean Foundation, 176 N.E.2d 692 (Ill. App. Ct. 1961).
157. Gilbert v. McLeod Infirmary, 64 S.E.2d 524 (S.C. 1951).
158. Shattuck v. Wood Memorial Home, Inc., 66 N.E.2d 568 (Mass. 1946).
159. George Pepperdine Foundation v. Pepperdine, 271 P.2d 600 (Cal. 1954).
160. Karst, "Charitable Dollar," 444.
161. Holt v. College of Osteopathic Physicians and Surgeons, 394 P.2d 932 (Cal. 1964).
162. Id.

permitted by statute, there are cases in which suits by members against the corporation's directors have been permitted on the theory that the relationship gives rise to the same rights and liabilities as those arising from the relationship between directors and stockholders of a for-profit corporation.[163] However, in other cases the courts have refused to confer the right to sue, holding that the issues of proper management or breach of fiduciary duty involve not the members' private interest as members but matters in which only the public interest, as represented by the attorney general, is directly concerned.[164] This position was upheld in two Massachusetts cases decided in 1981 and 1997 respectively. In the first, the court made a distinction between the rights of members to question the actions of the directors in carrying out the organization's charitable purposes and their rights as members to vote at meetings of the corporation. The court held that members would have standing to protect rights personal to them that were conferred by the articles of organization or by-laws, but had no greater rights to call the board of directors to account than other members of the general public.[165] In the second case the court refused to grant standing to members of a church who claimed breaches of the duty of care.[166] The court noted that a distinction had to be made between members who have a right to participate in governance, and those for whom membership confers only a right to participate in the programs of the organization, such as the petitioners in this case or members of YMCAs who join to receive services and, in addition, the many organizations that confer the title of member on contributors.

Paralleling the business corporation statutes that grant shareholders the right to sue directors, the Revised Model Nonprofit Corporation Act permits derivative suits by members having 5% of the vote or fifty in number, whichever is less.[167] Section 5142 of the California Nonprofit Corporation Law grants standing to any member to bring actions to enjoin, correct, and obtain damages for or to otherwise remedy a breach of a charitable trust. Prerequisites to bringing suit are that the plaintiffs were members of the corporation at the time of the transaction being challenged; that they had attempted to secure from the board the action complained of or presented valid reasons for not so doing; and that the attorney general was notified of the action. The court may, on request from the defendants, order the plaintiffs to post a bond for no more than $50,000 to cover reasonable expenses, including attorneys'

---

163. Leeds v. Harrison, 72 A.2d 371 (N.J. Ch. 1950).

164. Dillaway v. Burton, 153 N.E. 13 (Mass. 1926); Voelker v. St. Louis Mercantile Library Association, 359 S.W.2d 689 (Mo. 1962).

165. Lopez v. Medford Community Center, 424 N.E.2d 229 (Mass. 1981).

166. Weaver v. Wood, 680 N.E.2d 918 (Mass. 1997).

167. RMNCA, §6.3; See Appendix, Table 1, Column 3.

fees of both parties.[168] New York permits a derivative action if brought by 5% or more of any class of members, but the statute does not contain any provisions relating to costs or bonding.[169] Similar provisions are to be found in the statutes in Georgia, Illinois, and Michigan.[170] There are no reported cases brought under these statutes.

Proposals for Reform of Standing Rules

Critics of the doctrine of exclusive standing argue the need for a relaxation of the doctrine, pointing to the fact that in those states in which the attorney general does not have an active enforcement program, there is no effective supervision of the administration of charities. Thus Hansmann would accord standing to all patrons of charities, by which he means donors and "beneficiaries," using that term to signify individuals who utilize the charity's services, such as hospital patients or university students.[171]

Blasko et al. proposed expanding the concept of special interest to include a larger class of individuals than present law would permit and establishing a Uniform Code defining the considerations that should be applied by the courts in deciding whether parties qualified for standing on the basis of their special interests. The Code would include those considerations the authors found to have been influential in cases in which the courts had granted standing on the basis of special interests, notably the existence of fraud or misconduct, and the fact that the attorney general was not available to bring suit.[172]

Goldschmid also argued for broadening the class of persons empowered to bring derivative suits to include donors, members, and beneficiaries, but he would require that any monetary recovery would be awarded to the charity except in unusual circumstances. He would limit court awards of legal costs and fees against plaintiffs and their attorneys only if the action was unreasonably brought or litigated. In addition, plaintiffs would be awarded fees only if they were successful and the result of the suit was to confer substantial benefit to the general public. Finally, he suggested that courts and state regulators should participate actively in reviewing the fairness of settlements and the appropriateness of any award of attorney's fees.[173]

168. Cal. Corp. Code §5710.

169. N.Y. Not-for-Profit Corp. Law §623(a).

170. Ga. Code Ann. §14-3-741; 805 Ill. Comp. Stat. 5/7.80; Mich. Comp. Laws §§450.2491–.2493.

171. Henry Hansmann, "Reforming Nonprofit Corporation Law," 129 *University of Pennsylvania Law Review* 497, 606 (1981).

172. Blasko, "Standing to Sue," 61–78.

173. Goldschmid, "Fiduciary Duties," 28.

Fishman advocated increasing the use of relators, suggesting the California approach as a model but with the establishment of a fund for the compensation of attorneys similar to those that have been established to provide counsel in criminal cases, but under the supervision of the attorney general. In addition, he suggested restructuring nonprofit boards by bifurcating them into two parts, with a board of director-managers responsible for day-to-day management and a supervisory board of advisors charged with oversight of the management board, owing primary fiduciary responsibility to the public, beneficiaries, and donors. Advisors would be subject to a lesser standard of conduct than directors. They would have the power to select and remove director-managers, set their salaries, bring suits on behalf of the charity, and report annually to funding sources and beneficiaries.[174]

Other suggestions for increasing standing include a proposal by Ben-Ner and Van Hoomissen to create a new class of "stakeholders," similar in some respects to legal "members" of a mutual benefit corporation, who would be empowered to elect directors, receive financial and programmatic information from the directors on an ongoing basis, and be empowered to bring suit to assure board compliance with the charity's mission.[175] Individuals would become stakeholders by virtue of their relationship to the charity as donors or as consumers of its services.

Another proposal, offered by Manne, would be the creation of for-profit corporations that would contract with charities to oversee their operations, with power to bring suit to correct breaches of duty, acting in a sense as "private attorneys general."[176]

Among those who favor retaining the common law doctrine of limited standing, Atkinson questioned whether the deficiencies in attorney general enforcement are as widespread and serious as have been charged. He believes that the doctrine shields charities from the dangers of overregulation and wasteful litigation and that in many instances the threat of enforcement is a sufficient deterrent to misbehavior.[177]

Brody likewise questioned the efficacy of broadening the rules of standing. She notes that information from dissatisfied insiders constitutes a major resource for state attorneys general and questions whether private parties

174. Fishman, "Development of Nonprofit Corporation Law," 672–684.

175. Avner Ben-Ner and Theresa Van Hoomissen, "The Governance of Nonprofit Organizations: Law and Public Policy," 4 *Nonprofit Management and Leadership* 393, 408–410 (1994).

176. Geoffrey A. Manne, "Agency Costs and the Oversight of Charitable Organizations," 1999 *Wisconsin Law Review* 227 (1999).

177. Rob Atkinson, "Unsettled Standing: Who (Else) Should Enforce the Duties of Charitable Fiduciaries?" 23 *Journal of Corporation Law* 655, 683 (1998).

would have a better chance of success than government officials. Further, she challenged the ability of private individuals to be effective prosecutors:

> The public appears uneducated about the fiscal needs of charities, as many people express surprise that nonprofit managers are paid at all and reveal ignorance of charities' productive demands . . . A public that does not understand constraints cannot perform effective oversight. A public whose oversight focuses on the wrong consideration induces charities to adopt inefficient and ineffective behaviors.[178]

The Power of Visitation: Reserved Rights of Donors and Heirs

Under certain circumstances donors or founders of charities may have enforcement powers similar to those accorded to the attorney general. Following the Roman law terminology, at one time a distinction was made between the *fundatio incipiens,* the granting of the charter by the state, and the *fundatio perficiens,* the donation of funds by individuals. The *fundators perficiens* were given the right to enforce the faithful execution of the charity. They were permitted not only to prescribe rules for the management and administration of the trust at the time of the donation, but to specify methods for the government and control of the trustees, for the inspection of their proceedings, and for the correction of abuses.[179] Similarly, where an individual founded and gave property to a charitable corporation, he was allowed to reserve or confer on others a power of visitation. As described in an early Massachusetts case,[180] this was a power and duty to hear and determine all differences of the corporation members among themselves and generally to superintend the internal government of the body, taking as a guide the rules laid down by the founder. So long as the visitor did not exceed his province, his decision was deemed final, but he would be subject to prosecution and removal in an action by the attorney general for acts that were in excess of his powers.

The visitorial power did not extend to heirs unless expressly reserved, and in most cases such reservations were narrowly construed, the attitude of the court being that the interests of heirs were usually inimical to that of the charity.[181]

178. Evelyn Brody, "Institutional Dissonance in the Nonprofit Sector," 41 *Villanova Law Review* 433, 502 (1996).

179. Carl F. G. Zollman, *American Law of Charities,* 418 (Milwaukee: Bruce Publishing, 1924).

180. Nelson v. Cushing, 56 Mass. (2 Cush.) 519, 530 (1848).

181. Scott and Fratcher, *Law of Trusts,* §391.

The Uniform Trust Code (UTC), promulgated in 2001, adopted a provision contrary to the general rule and that of Restatement (Second) of Trusts section 391. Section 405(c) of the UTC provides that "[t]he settlor of a charitable trust, among others, may maintain a proceeding to enforce the trust."[182] This provision may have signaled a loosening of the strict rules of donor standing. However, until adoption of section 405(c) of the UTC, the right of a donor or his heirs was rarely recognized.[183] In Maryland, the relatives of a testator or founder are given, by statute, the right to enforce gifts to educational or charitable corporations,[184] and in Wisconsin the donor of a trust is considered an "interested party" for the purposes of the statute, which permits ten interested parties to bring suit for enforcement when the attorney general refuses to act.[185]

As to recent cases, in 1993 the Minnesota Supreme Court granted standing to a grandson of the settlor of a charitable trust that had been incorporated to object to the granting of a petition by the trustees for approval of an amendment of the provisions in the articles of incorporation dealing with trustee succession. The decision rested in part on the fact that the attorney general had elected not to participate in the proceedings.[186] This case is in direct contrast to one decided in 1955 in which the Supreme Court of Iowa refused to grant standing to the widow and five children of a deceased donor to maintain an action against a college for transferring ownership of its property to another educational institution.[187]

Section 7 of the Uniform Management of Institutional Funds Act (UMIFA) permits the governing board of a charitable corporation, with the consent of the donor, to release, in whole or in part, a restriction imposed by the donor in the instrument of gift on the use or the investment of an endowment fund.[188] This provision was the basis of a suit brought in 1997 by a foundation against a university to which it had made grants totaling $250,000 to provide scholarships for medical-related education. Shortly after

---

182. Uniform Trust Code, §405(c) (amended 2001); see John H. Langbein, "The Uniform Trust Code: Codification of the Law of Trusts in the United States," 15 *Trust Law International* 66, 58 (No. 2, 2002); Ronald Chester, "Grantor Standing to Enforce Charitable Transfers under Section 405(C) of the Uniform Trust Code and Related Law: How Important Is It and How Extensive Should It Be?" 37 *Real Property, Probate and Trust Journal* 611 (2003).

183. Karst, "Charitable Dollar," 445.

184. Kerbow v. Frostburg State University Foundation, 40 F. Supp. 2d 724 (D. Md. 1999).

185. Wis. Stat. §701.10.

186. Matter of Hill, 509 N.W.2d 168 (Minn. Ct. App. 1993).

187. Amundson v. Kletzing-McLaughlin Memorial Foundation College, 73 N.W.2d 114 (Iowa 1955).

188. Uniform Management of Institutional Funds Act, §7 (1972); see also Chapter 4 and Appendix, Table 1, Column 17.

the grants were made, the university closed its nursing school and co-mingled the donated funds with its general funds. The court held that section 7 of the Connecticut UMIFA was not intended to alter the exclusive power of the attorney general to enforce restrictions on the use of charitable gifts and it did not confer additional enforcement powers on donors.[189]

Karst argued in 1960 for permitting a founder to sue, pointing out that he is the one person, other than the fiduciaries, who knows and cares the most about the charity's operations. He raises serious objection to the visitorial power, however, because of its tendency to undercut the responsibility of charitable fiduciaries.[190] Of course, if a founder has a property interest in the administration or operation of the charity, as for example when he has made a charitable gift on a condition that, if met, will result in a reversion of the property to his estate, then he or his heirs or personal representative can maintain a suit to recover the property. In such a case these individuals will be attempting to enforce rights adverse to the trust, not seeking to enforce it. The same rule applies where there is a contingent gift to another charitable institution.[191]

In a 1961 case that raised the question of the nature of an adverse interest, the Supreme Court of Oregon dismissed a complaint of mismanagement brought against trustees of a testamentary charitable trust by the employees and managers of a newspaper who were given by the terms of the trust a preference to purchase the stock of the paper held by the trustees in the event that it was to be sold. The court held that the plaintiffs' interest was not sufficient to maintain an enforcement action.[192]

The Uniform Management of Institutional Funds Act, in force as of 2003 in forty-seven states and the District of Columbia, permits a governing board with the written consent of the donor to release in whole or in part a restriction on the use or investment placed by the donor on an endowment gift. Suggested revisions to the act in 2002 by a drafting committee of the Commissioners on Uniform State Laws contained a provision similar to that in the Uniform Trust Code granting donors standing to enforce restrictions on institutional funds.[193] The drafting committee rejected this proposal, however, so it was not included in the draft approved at a first reading by the Commissioners in August 2003.[194]

189. Herzog Foundation v. University of Bridgeport, 699 A.2d 995 (Conn. 1997).

190. Karst, "Charitable Dollar," 446.

191. Trustees of Dartmouth College v. City of Quincy, 118 N.E.2d 89 (Mass. 1954).

192. Agan v. United States National Bank, 363 P.2d 765 (Or. 1961).

193. Uniform Management of Institutional Funds Act, §8 (Tentative Draft, November 2002).

194. Uniform Management of Institutional Funds Act (Draft, August 2003).

As noted in the preceding comments on standing, the right of a donor who is not a founder to bring enforcement action has been consistently denied by the courts.[195] Following the analogy to the rights of founders to sue for enforcement, Karst suggested consideration of legislation permitting substantial donors a similar right, but with several safeguards. He would include a requirement that the donor have contributed a certain dollar amount or a certain percentage of the charity's total contributions during a recent period. The donor-plaintiff would be required to post security for costs, including counsel fees, which would be paid to the fiduciaries if they prevailed in the suit. He would also be compelled to present the case to the attorney general, argue his view at a public hearing, and receive an adverse determination before proceeding on his own. Furthermore, Karst recognized that the plaintiff should be prevented from receiving any private gains for his action, such as a settlement for withdrawing the action, although he would favor the allowance of counsel fees to the plaintiff if successful.[196]

During the years 2002–2003 there appeared to be an increase in the number of instances in which donors brought suit to enforce the terms of restricted gifts. For example, in December 2002 the son of donors of a gift of $3 million in 1993 to the trustees of Boston University to expand its library threatened to bring suit to recover the assets on the grounds that the university had failed to fulfill the terms of the gift. The matter was settled when the university agreed to distribute an amount equal to the original gift to charities chosen by the donors' son.[197] In a similar case, legal representatives of a major donor to the Metropolitan Opera brought suit in July 2003 accusing the organization of failing to abide by the terms of her gifts,[198] while in a related case descendants of Avery Fisher threatened to sue the New York Philharmonic if it were to carry through with plans to rename the hall for a potential future donor if one came forward with a gift to renovate the building.[199] Also, during the summer of 2002 Princeton University was sued by relatives of a major donor requesting the court to order transfer of a $560 million endowment fund to another charity on the basis that the terms of the gift had not been observed.[200]

195. Zollman, *American Law of Charities,* 420.

196. Karst, "Charitable Dollar," 446.

197. Patrick Healy, "BU Agrees to Give $3M from Mugar to Charities," *Boston Globe,* December 18, 2002, at A1.

198. Robin Pogrebin, "Donor's Estate Sues Metropolitan Opera," *New York Times,* July 24, 2003, at B3.

199. Stephanie Strom, "Donors Add Watchdog Role to Relations with Charities," *New York Times,* March 29, 2003, at A8.

200. Stephen G. Greene, "Seeking Control in Court," *Chronicle of Philanthropy,* November 28, 2002, at 6.

All too often, particularly in the case of private foundations, the donor is one of a small number of fiduciaries; and in many cases the entire board of trustees, or at least the majority, will be members of one family. Furthermore, the danger of being found to have had a contributory role in the breach of duty, either through acquiescence or neglect, may well deter many co-fiduciaries. Conferring an enforcement right on a founder or substantial contributor, if accompanied by the safeguards suggested by Karst, would be of value in some instances. How widespread its use would be, however, is seriously open to question. It would perhaps have great merit in those instances in which an attorney general is completely inactive or unreceptive to the pursuit of his duties in regard to charities.

Parties to Suits Involving Charities

An important adjunct to the question of who may bring an enforcement action against a charity is the decision as to which parties must be joined when a suit involving a charity is before the court. If an enforcement action is brought by the attorney general, ordinarily it is brought against the trustees or corporate directors, or some of them. If the action is a petition for application of the cy pres doctrine, the heirs may also be required to be defendants, unless it is clear that they do not have a right to the property if the court refuses to apply the doctrine and declares that the trust fails. When an action is brought by the trustees or directors of a charity, the question of parties is more complicated. It is necessary to distinguish in this discussion between those who are considered "necessary" parties and those who may be deemed "proper" parties. A final court decree is binding only on those who have been joined in the action and have been afforded a chance to state their position. Once joined, they may not later question the decision by bringing another action on their own or by attempting to raise the same question in a suit on another, although related, matter. In other words, a question once decided by an appellate court, or by a lower court, and not taken by the parties to an appeal, is res judicata as regards those who were joined and as regards all matters shown to have been put in issue or to have been necessarily involved and actively tried and determined.[201]

Necessary Parties

The term "necessary party" refers to individuals who will be so closely affected by the outcome of litigation that it would be inconsistent with equity and good conscience to permit judicial action without their receiving notice

---

201. Restatement (Second) of the Law of Judgments, §84 (1980).

and being given the opportunity to participate. The term "indispensable parties" is also used to designate such persons.

In all states where the attorney general is recognized as having a duty to represent the public interest in the enforcement of funds devoted to charity, he is considered a necessary party to all actions brought to enforce the duties of charitable fiduciaries or to uphold the charitable intent. Tudor's classic treatise on charitable trusts states the rule as follows:

> The Attorney-General, as representing the Crown, is the protector of all the persons interested in the charity funds. He represents the beneficial interest; consequently, in all cases in which the beneficial interest requires to be before the court, the Attorney-General must be a party to the proceedings.[202]

This requirement that the attorney general be a "necessary" party to certain actions involving charitable interests may be imposed by statute,[203] by court rule,[204] or precedent.[205] The Massachusetts Supreme Judicial Court has from its earliest cases read the statute conveying enforcement duties on the attorney general[206] as meaning that he is a required party to a broad category of actions involving charitable interests.[207]

> No proceeding in regard to a public charity, no matter how general the assent of those beneficially interested, would bind him if not made a party; nor can any proceeding in regard to a public charity to which he has been made a party be invalidated by those beneficially interested, but having no peculiar and immediate interests distinct from those of the public.[208]

This requirement was, in effect, restated by the legislature in 1954 when a statute requiring compulsory reporting to the attorney general by all public charities was enacted. The legislation included a section that stated: "The attorney general shall be made a party to all judicial proceedings in which he may be interested in the performance of his duties under section

202. Owen Davies Tudor, *The Law of Charitable Trusts*, ch. 12, sec. II (London: Sweet and Maxwell, 5th ed. 1930).

203. See Appendix, Table 1, Column 2.

204. N.J. Superior Court Civil Practice Rule 4:28-4.

205. In re Pruner's Estate, 136 A.2d 107 (Pa. 1957); Trustees of New Castle Common v. Gordy, 91 A.2d 135 (Del. Ch. 1952); Slate ex rel. Emmert v. University Trust Co., 74 N.E.2d 833 (Ind. Ct. App. 1947), rev'd on other grounds, 86 N.E.2d 450 (Ind. 1949); Thurlow v. Berry, 25 So. 2d 726 (Ala. 1946); Dickey v. Voelker, 11 S.W.2d 278 (Mo. 1928).

206. Mass. Gen. Laws ch. 12, §8.

207. President and Fellows of Harvard College v. Society for Promoting Theological Education, 69 Mass. (3 Gray) 280 (1855).

208. Burbank v. Burbank, 25 N.E. 427 (Mass. 1890).

eight."[209] Similar provisions in the statutes expanding the attorney general's supervisory powers have been enacted in California, Iowa, Michigan, New Hampshire, Ohio, Oregon, Rhode Island, and Texas.[210]

There is no uniformity, however, either in these statutes or in the court decisions regarding the type of proceeding in which the attorney general will be declared indispensable. In Massachusetts the courts have interpreted the statutory provision very broadly, and the attorney general must be given notice of the probate of every will that includes a charitable gift, so that he participates at all stages of the proceedings for probate of wills and accounts of executors, as well as actions involving trusts.[211]

In New York statutory interpretation requires the attorney general's participation in suits involving petitions for instructions, construction of wills, approvals of compromises, settlement of accounts, and cy pres applications. The attorney general's participation is also specifically required by the statutes providing for court approval of the sale or mortgage of real property by charitable corporations, as well as for their creation and dissolution. The Surrogate's Courts of New York, however, have ruled that the attorney general is not a necessary party to a proceeding where there is a specifically named charitable beneficiary, such as a corporate institution. In an extension of that holding, in 1980 the New York Court of Appeals held that the attorney general had no standing as representative of the ultimate beneficiaries of charitable organizations to which a gift of corporate stock had been made to bring a suit against the corporation that issued the stock to compel it to declare and pay dividends and pay fair market value for shares being redeemed. The court stated that to allow such an action was tantamount to permitting the attorney general to stand in the shoes of a charity and enforce obligations it was under a duty to pursue.[212]

An unsuccessful attempt was made in New York in 1962 to obtain legislation to amend the Civil Practice Act and the Surrogate's Courts Act to include wording similar to that in the Tilden Act that the attorney general "represents the sole inherent and statutory power of the ultimate beneficiaries of a charitable trust," thereby ensuring that he would be considered a necessary party to all proceedings in which a charitable beneficial interest was involved. Despite the failure to pass these amendments, the attorney general's office is a party to numerous cases each year.[213]

In California, where the statutory requirement for participation by the

209. Mass. Gen. Laws ch. 12, §8G.
210. See Appendix, Table 1, Column 1.
211. Budin v. Levy, 180 N.E.2d 74 (Mass. 1962).
212. Lefkowitz v. Lebensfeld, 415 N.E.2d 919 (N.Y. 1980).
213. Marion R. Fremont-Smith, *Foundations and Government: State and Federal Law and Supervision*, 211 (New York: Russell Sage Foundation, 1965).

attorney general is broad, the courts have nevertheless held that he is a necessary party to probate of a will only when the gift creates a trust and the trustee is not a California resident or corporation, or is not named in the trust. This is also the position taken by the courts in Nebraska[214] and Kansas.[215]

The Illinois court in an early case stated that the attorney general was an indispensable party when the trustees were charged with a wrong, but that in other situations, if the gift were to named trustees, the attorney general was not a necessary party.[216] In New Hampshire, where the attorney general's powers over the administration of charitable trusts are exceptionally broad, the court nevertheless held in a 1947 case that he was not a necessary party to a case involving compromise of a will:

> Whether the Attorney General should be notified concerning such claims involves questions of policy and procedure on which the Legislature has remained silent. If notice to the Attorney General and his approval are necessary, it will require legislative authority therefore. We know of no decision which requires the Attorney General's approval of all Probate proceedings or the actions of executors in administering the estate before the charitable trust is in existence.[217]

Legislation was enacted in 1959, however, under which the attorney general was made a necessary party to any agreement between an executor, creditors, legatees, or heirs at law whenever such agreement may directly or indirectly affect a charitable interest.[218]

The Pennsylvania court has taken an opposite view from that of New Hampshire, stating in several cases that the attorney general must receive notice of all matters involving charities.[219] Following these decisions, each of the local orphans' courts promulgated rules, in cooperation with the attorney general's office, to facilitate administration of the requirement. The office receives from 50 to 100 notices each month and participates in all cases where the charitable interest is not represented by a named charitable beneficiary such as a corporation.[220]

214. Rohlff v. German Old People's Home, 10 N.W.2d 686 (Neb. 1943), criticized by Scott and Fratcher, *Law of Trusts*, §391.

215. Trautman v. De Boissiere Odd Fellows' Orphans' Home and Industrial School Association, 71 P. 286 (Kan. 1903).

216. Newberry v. Blatchford, 106 Ill. 584 (1882).

217. Burtman v. Butman, 54 A.2d 367 (N.H. 1947).

218. N.H. Rev. Stat. Ann. §556:27.

219. In re Pruner's Estate, 136 A.2d 107 (Pa. 1957); Garrison's Estate, 137 A.2d 321 (Pa. 1958).

220. Telephone interview with Larry Barth, Philadelphia Bureau Chief, Commonwealth of Pennsylvania Bureau of Charitable Trusts and Organizations (February 12, 2002).

In a Texas decision in 1941 the court held that the attorney general was not a necessary party to a suit to construe a will bequeathing property to a public charity where the bequest was to named trustees for the benefit of an unincorporated charitable foundation, although it added that he was a necessary party to proceedings affecting validity, administration, and enforcement when the public interest was involved.[221] Legislation modifying this rule was enacted in 1959, however. The attorney general was made a necessary party to suits for termination, cy pres application, and construction, or to will contests involving "charitable trusts," which for the purpose of the act are defined as "all gifts and trusts for charitable purposes."[222] A judgment rendered without service of process on the attorney general in any suit referred to in this article is void and unenforceable, and settlements or compromises of suits are binding only if the attorney general is a party and joins in the agreement. It is interesting to note that section 6 of the statute states:

> It is the purpose of this Article to resolve and clarify what is thought by some to be uncertainties existing at common law with respect to the subject matter hereof. Nothing contained herein, however, shall ever be construed, deemed or held to be in limitation of the common law powers and duties of the Attorney General.[223]

Until 1978 the Ohio Charitable Trusts Act contained a provision similar in its wording to the Texas statute,[224] but two lower court decisions, decided in 1956 and 1961 respectively, limited its application to situations where charitable trusts had already been created, holding that the attorney general was not a necessary party either to a will contest[225] or to an action to construe a will containing provisions for the creation of a charitable trust.[226] In a third case, decided by the court of appeals of a different county, the court reached the opposite conclusion in an action to construe a will.[227] In 1978 the statute defining the trust proceedings to which the attorney general was a necessary party was amended to include proceedings, the object of which was to "determine the validity of a will having provisions for a charitable trust."[228] However, a 1979 case held that this provision did not make the attorney general a

221. Miller v. Davis, 150 S.W.2d 973 (Tex. 1941).
222. Tex. Rev. Civ. Stat. Ann. §4412(a), now Tex. Prop. Code. Ann. §123.001.
223. Id.
224. Ohio Rev. Code Ann. §109.26.
225. Spang v. Cleveland Trust Co., 134 N.E.2d 586 (Ohio C.P. 1956).
226. Baily v. McElroy, 186 N.E.2d 213 (Ohio Prob. Ct. 1961).
227. Blair v. Bouton, 15 Ohio Op. 2d 474 (1956).
228. Ohio Rev. Code Ann. §109.25(D).

necessary party in a case in which the will in question contained an unconditional bequest to a trustee of a charitable trust on the grounds that a will with such a provision did not create a charitable trust.[229]

When an action is brought by trustees of a private trust seeking settlement or allowance of their accounts, the ordinary procedure is for the court to require written notice to named and ascertainable beneficiaries; publication in a newspaper if there are unknown beneficiaries; and appointment by the court of a guardian ad litem, who is a neutral third party, to represent the rights of unborn or unascertainable beneficiaries. If no objection is made, the accounts are then allowed without a hearing. Where a charitable interest is involved, unless the beneficiary is a named charitable corporation, it is difficult to assure proper review, unless the courts or state statutes include this type of proceeding in the category of actions for which written notice to the attorney general is required. Otherwise, the adversary procedure is insufficient to protect the charitable interest.

The jurisdictions that require such written notice to the attorney general are in the minority, however; and in some, notice will be required as regards trusts where the charitable interest is vested, but not where it is contingent or is a remainder interest following the termination of one or several life estates. The need for review in these situations, however, is no less acute. Several states do have statutes specifically requiring that a copy of all accounts be mailed to the attorney general. Indiana,[230] Wisconsin,[231] and Nevada,[232] for example, are states in which this rule is followed. Vermont requires trustees of charitable trusts to file accounts annually in the district court for the district in which the trustee resides, and failure to comply is deemed a breach of trust. The requirement is generally ignored, and neither the attorney general nor the courts make any effort to enforce it.[233]

In Virginia, the court having jurisdiction over probate of wills appoints a commissioner of accounts who has general supervision of all fiduciaries, including trustees. It is the commissioner's duty to make all ex parte settlements of accounts, review fiduciaries' bonds, receive inventories, and report to the court on account of the transactions of all such fiduciaries.[234] Trustees of charitable trusts are required to settle accounts with him annually.[235] This would seem to be an adequate substitute for the attorney general, in theory,

229. O'Neal v. Buckley, 425 N.E.2d 924 (Ohio Ct. App. 1979).
230. Ind. Stat. §30-4-5-12.
231. Wis. Stat. §701.16(4).
232. Nev. Rev. Stat. §165.230.
233. Vt. Stat. Ann. tit. 14, §2501.
234. Va. Code Ann. §26-8.
235. Va. Code Ann. §55-29.

and it is at least preferable to the situation in other states where no provision whatsoever is made for representation of charitable interests.

Proper Parties

The determination of whether the attorney general is a proper as distinguished from a necessary party to a proceeding involving a charity is even more difficult. By definition, a "proper" party is one with no interest in the controversy between the immediate litigants, but with an interest in the subject matter that may be affected during the course of the suit. A proper party may be joined by the plaintiff in any action. When charitable fiduciaries bring suit, a failure to join the attorney general may result in a failure to resolve all the issues in the case, but will not prevent the attorney general from raising them in a subsequent action.

Occasionally, an attorney general has requested permission of the court to intervene in a case involving a charity to which he was not made a party. In certain categories of cases the courts have denied this right. But there is no clear-cut rule on which decisions have been based. If a suit is brought by trustees or directors seeking to enforce a contract or to obtain damages for a tort, or if a suit of a similar nature is brought against them, the attorney general is neither a necessary nor a proper party.[236]

Usually actions to enforce corporation membership rights fall into the same category, but, again, the rule is not absolute. For example, in the case of *Leeds v. Harrison*[237] a group of members and nonmembers of a Young Men's Christian Association brought suit against the corporation, charging that one of the requirements for membership was inconsistent with the corporate charitable purposes. The court required that the attorney general be joined in the action to represent the indefinite beneficiaries of the corporation.

The outcome of cases of this nature will often depend on the general attitude of the court toward the role of the attorney general. A Kentucky case denied the right of the attorney general to intervene in a suit involving the compromise of a will;[238] yet the Massachusetts court in a case with similar facts declared that he was not only a proper but a necessary party and refused to render judgment until he was joined.[239] In a federal case decided on the basis of New York law, the court permitted a motion by the attorney general to join in an action by the settlor of an inter vivos trust to require the trustees

236. Scott and Fratcher, *Law of Trusts,* §391.
237. Leeds v. Harrison, 7 N.J. Super. 558 (1950).
238. Commonwealth v. Gardner, 327 S.W.2d 947 (Ky. 1959).
239. Budin v. Levy, 180 N.E.2d 74 (Mass. 1962); see also In re Roberts' Estate, 373 P.2d 165 (Kan. 1962).

to account and pay over to him the corpus and income.[240] However, in an Ohio case decided in 2002, the court held that in a suit brought by a hospital and a medical practice affiliated with the hospital, the attorney general was not a necessary party and the trial court's judgment was not rendered void due to his absence as a party.[241]

Statutes of Limitations and Laches as Bars to Actions

In the case of private trusts, an action for breach of trust may be barred if the beneficiaries have consented to the breach, acquiesced in it, or failed to bring suit against the trustees for so long a time and under such circumstances that it would be inequitable to hold the trustees liable.[242] This last circumstance is described in law as "laches." It is a principle of equity and subject to the flexibility of many equitable doctrines. The primary limitation on its use is that it will be applied only if the beneficiary knew or reasonably should have known of his cause of action. In the case of charitable trusts, the doctrine of laches is not usually applicable to actions against a trustee to recover misappropriated funds. As the Massachusetts Supreme Judicial Court has said:

> Generally it is true that no length of time of diversion from the plain provisions of a charitable foundation will prevent its restoration to its true purpose.[243]

Similar holdings are to be found in decisions of the courts of Texas,[244] the District of Columbia,[245] and California.[246]

A further restriction on the time in which suits may be brought is to be found in the statutes of limitations of all states and the federal government. Although the first statutes of limitations enacted in the United States applied only to actions at law and not to proceedings in equity, the removal of the distinction between equity and law in many states, and the wording of the particular statute of limitations in still others, has led to the extension of the provisions of these statutes to both types of actions in all but a few jurisdictions.[247] When a statute of limitations applies to cases involving breach of

240. Grace v. Carroll, 219 F. Supp. 270 (S.D.N.Y. 1963).

241. University Hospitals of Cleveland, Inc. v. Lynch, 772 N.E.2d 105 (Ohio 2002).

242. Restatement (Second) of Trusts, §§216, 218, 219.

243. Trustees of Andover Seminary v. Visitors, 148 N.E. 900 (Mass. 1925).

244. The William Buchanan Foundation v. Shepperd, 283 S.W.2d 325 (Tex. Civ. App. 1955), rev'd by agreement of parties, 289 S.W.2d 553 (Tex. 1956).

245. Mt. Vernon Mortgage Corp. v. United States, 236 F.2d 724 (D.C. Cir. 1956).

246. Brown v. Memorial National Home Foundation, 329 P.2d 118 (Cal. Ct. App. 1958).

247. Note, "Developments in the Law of Statutes of Limitations," 63 *Harvard Law Review* 1177 (1950).

fiduciary duty, an exception is made to its unequivocal operation, and the period of the statute starts to run only after a defendant knew or reasonably should have known of the facts that constituted a breach of duty. A similar exception is made in cases of fraud. Both exceptions have obvious roots in the doctrine of laches.

The applicability of statutes of limitations to actions involving charitable trusts has not been clearly decided in many jurisdictions. Scott states that neither laches nor the statute of limitations is an absolute bar to actions brought to recover charitable funds that have been misapplied.[248] This was the holding of the federal court for the District of Columbia in the case of *Mt. Vernon Mortgage Corporation v. United States,*[249] and it has also been stated by the Massachusetts court.[250] Bogert explains that the exception arose because of "the indefinite nature of those persons who are to be benefited by a charity, and the probability that breaches of trust may easily be unnoticed by the Attorney General or any interested party, unless there is a record of all existing charities and periodic accountings are strictly enforced."[251]

This quotation has led to some speculation as to whether the filing of financial reports with the attorney general in compliance with the provisions of a supervisory statute is sufficient to start the running of a statute of limitations with respect to those matters included in the report, or whether the filing of reports would even constitute sufficient notice to the attorney general to warrant a finding of laches if he delayed bringing suit for an unreasonably long period of time. Fear of such an effect, combined with apprehension that an attorney general's staff may not be adequate to review reports properly, has been given by some state officials as the reason for opposing registration and reporting statutes. On the other hand, it is the rare breach of fiduciary duty that will clearly appear on the face of a report filed with the state.

In England all trustees, including trustees of charitable trusts, are entitled to plead the statute of limitations as a defense to suits brought after six years have elapsed since the action in question, but the statute is specifically inapplicable to claims of fraudulent breach of trust and to actions to recover trust property the trustee has received and converted to his own use. However, if the misapplication of charitable funds was due to honest mistake only, the trustees will not be compelled to refund payments made wrongfully before action was brought or before they received notice that their conduct was open to question.[252]

248. Scott and Fratcher, *Law of Trusts,* §392.

249. Mt. Vernon Mortgage Corp. v. United States, 236 F.2d 724 (D.C. Cir. 1956).

250. Trustees of Andover Seminary v. Visitors, 148 N.E. 900 (Mass. 1925).

251. Bogert and Bogert, *Law of Trusts and Trustees,* §399.

252. George W. Keeton, *Modern Law of Charities,* 208 (London: Sir Isaac Pitman and Sons, 1962).

The scarcity of cases dealing with the application of statutes of limitations has caused uncertainty in many states. In California in 1985 the Uniform Supervision of Trustees for Charitable Purposes Act was amended to limit to ten years after the cause of action accrues the time in which the attorney general can bring suit to enforce a charitable trust, impress property with a trust for charitable purposes, or recover property of a charity.[253] Uncertainty as to whether an action will be barred by the statute impedes enforcement efforts and gives fiduciaries no assurance of their rights. Legislation to settle this question may be desirable in certain states.

Effective State Enforcement Programs

The Uniform Supervision of Trustees for Charitable Purposes Act and acts with similar provisions provide for the establishment of a regulatory bureau in the office of the attorney general with which certain charities are required to register and file financial reports. The bureaus that administer these programs are headed by an assistant attorney general and may be staffed with lawyers, paralegals, auditors, and in some instances investigators. A registry of charities is maintained in each of these offices at which members of the public may review financial reports filed by charities subject to reporting requirements.

The work of these offices falls into a number of categories: maintenance of the registry; review of financial reports; investigation and prosecution of breaches of trust; participation in court proceedings in which the attorney general is a named party, such as cy pres and dissolution proceedings; regulation of solicitation, including oversight of solicitors and education; and efforts to protect the sector and improve performance of fiduciaries.

Examples of efforts to improve practices in the sector can be found in publications issued by the office of the attorney general in a large number of states, most often available on the Internet. They include summaries of the duties of fiduciaries and instructions for complying with registration and reporting requirements. An example of the positive role an attorney general may play in support of the sector involved a situation in which the Financial Accounting Standards No. 117 appeared to be in conflict with state law as set forth in the Uniform Management of Institutional Funds Act.[254] This act permits charities to expend a portion of the appreciation on their endowment funds, thereby modifying traditional trust law, which limited expenditure from endowment funds to ordinary income. Under the Generally Accepted

---

253. Cal. Gov't Code §12596.

254. Financial Accounting Standards Board, Statement of Financial Accounting Standards No. 117, "Financial Statements of Not-for-Profit Organizations," ¶22.

Accounting Provisions, however, the accounting profession interpreted this provision to mean that all appreciation on endowment funds was available for current use and, accordingly, available to creditors.

In response to requests from the charitable sector for clarification of this interpretation, the attorneys general in Massachusetts in 1995[255] and New York in 2002[256] issued position papers affirming that under the state statute, the only amounts available for expenditure, and thereby available to creditors, were amounts that the governing board had explicitly appropriated for specific current use and that, until such a determination was made, appreciation on endowment funds was not available to creditors. The Massachusetts position paper also held that sums appropriated but unexpended at the end of a year would no longer be available for expenditure, so that a board could not build up a reserve from appreciated assets for future use. Finally, it provided that appropriation could not be accomplished retroactively.

Based on descriptions of the operations of these offices published in 1965, 1977, and 1994, the nature of their activities has not changed markedly.[257] All of them operate with severely limited budgets, which has meant a shortage of legal and accounting support. Given these drawbacks, they have nonetheless had some success, particularly in preserving assets on dissolutions and conversions, encouraging termination or merger of small charities, and improving governance.

California

California enacted the Uniform Supervision of Trustees for Charitable Trusts Act in 1955.[258] All charities other than schools, hospitals, and churches register with the registry of charitable trusts. Annual financial reports are required of all registered charities unless their income or assets during the year do not exceed $25,000. Solicitations by charities are regulated at the county and city

255. "Attorney General's Position on FASB Statement of Financial Accounting Standards No. 117, ¶22 and Related G.L.c. 180A Issues," Office of the Attorney General, Massachusetts (June 7, 1995).

256. "New York State Attorney General Eliot Spitzer Advises Not-for-Profit Corporations on the Appropriation of Endowment Fund Appreciation," Office of Attorney General (rev. October 2002), available at *www.oag.state.ny.us/charities/endowment.pdf*.

257. Fremont-Smith, *Foundations and Government*, 198–200, 233–260; Office of the Ohio Attorney General, "The Status of State Regulation of Charitable Trusts, Foundations, and Solicitations," in Commission on Private Philanthropy and Public Needs, *Research Papers*, vol. 5, pt. 1, at 2705 (Department of Treasury, 1977); Harriet Bograd, *The Role of State Attorneys General in Relation to Troubled Nonprofits* (August 1994), available at *www.charitychannel.com/forums/cyb-acc/resources/agrept.html*.

258. Cal. Gov't Code §12580 et seq.

level, although professional fund-raising organizations are required to register, post bond, and file financial reports with the attorney general.

As of the end of 2002 there were 85,000 charities listed in the registry. Their total assets exceeded $202 billion, and they had revenues of $71.6 billion. There were 1,525 charities with assets over $10 million, 7,120 with assets over $1 million, and 13,041 reporting assets exceeding $250,000. The annual filing requirement is met with submission of the federal information return and a one-page state form. In 1999 the attorney general established a website containing copies of the most recently filed federal Forms 990, 990EZ, or 990PF in a searchable mode, the first state to provide easily accessible information to the general public.[259] In 2001 the office estimated recoveries of $50 million in charitable restitution and fraud cases, $2.7 billion in probate cases, and $34 million in recoveries and enhancement to sales prices in hospital conversion cases.

As of January 2003, the staff in the office of the attorney general included ten attorneys and ten auditors. Four attorneys, four auditors, and one administrative assistant were located in Sacramento; there were two attorneys, one paralegal, and one auditor in San Francisco, and four attorneys and four auditors in Los Angeles. In 1965 the total staff numbered four; in 1974 there were eight attorneys, ten accountants, and two registrars; in 1996 the number of attorneys had increased to eleven. These numbers do not include administrative staff at the registry, which is maintained in Sacramento.

New York

New York requires charities to register upon creation and file annual financial reports with the Charities Bureau in the office of the attorney general. Exempt from these requirements are religious organizations, educational institutions incorporated under the New York Education Law or by special act, hospitals, certain voluntary organizations, alumni associations, and historical societies, as well as organizations whose gross receipts and assets are less than $25,000. The term "charity" includes both trusts and nonprofit corporations with charitable purposes. Estates with charitable interests are also required to register. Until 1996 charities that solicited funds from the general public and fund-raising professionals were required to register and report to a separate bureau in Albany, a burden on the organizations as well as the regulators. Since that date, all registration and reporting have been centralized in New York City. Reporting charities are divided into three categories, each of which files separate forms: charities filing under the general reporting provisions;

259. *justice.hdcdojnet.state.ca.us/charitysr/default.asp.*

soliciting charities exempt from general filing; and charities that are subject to dual requirements. According to the New York State Department of Law Annual Report for 2000, 38,000 charities were registered with the Bureau; at the end of 2002 the number was estimated to be close to 40,000. Federal information Forms 990, 990PF, and 990EZ are required together with a state return, and a schedule of assets if securities are held at any time during the reporting period. These forms are available for public inspection.[260]

The Charities Bureau is located in New York City, and there is a branch in Albany staffed by one attorney. Although the numbers vary from time to time, the Bureau has been staffed since the late 1990s with eighteen attorneys and six accountants. This compares with ten staff members in 1974 and thirteen in 1996. The office of the attorney general maintains a website that contains copies of the required report forms as well as summaries of the applicable laws, guides for practitioners and fiduciaries, and a summary of recent developments in Charities Law Enforcement. The Bureau has also prepared for public distribution information on procedures for dissolution, guidelines for board members, and summaries of provisions affecting specific activities such as the conduct of raffles.[261]

Annual reports issued by the office of the attorney general contain descriptions of the activities of the Charities Bureau, including summaries of the major matters in which the Bureau was involved during the reporting year. The reports often include information about cases that were settled and were unlikely to have been reported elsewhere, although in some instances the attorney general will make public terms of a settlement, for example, a settlement with two directors of the Peter J. Schweitzer Foundation under which they paid $170,000 in restitution.[262]

With its limited staff, the Bureau has been forced to target certain specific areas for inquiry and investigation, relying on public education to reach the larger universe of charities. Among the issues receiving attention in 2001 and 2002 were reports of unusual or inappropriate expenditures, instances of private foundation self-dealing, failures to diversify investments, and payment of large salaries. Charities earmarked for inquiry were sent letters requesting additional information, and efforts were made to settle disputes without resort to litigation.

In June 2003 Attorney General Eliot Spitzer announced that a random check by four auditors from his Charities Division of the financial records filed with the state by some 46,000 nonprofit groups had turned up dozens

260. Department of Law, New York State, *Annual Report* (2000).

261. *www.oag.state.ny.us/charities/charities.html.*

262. Id.; see also William Josephson, "Recent Developments in Charities Law Enforcement," *New York Law Journal* (February 20, 2001).

of cases that raised questions for the regulators and that investigations of more than thirty of them were underway. Examples of the findings included instances of excessive compensation, mismanagement of investments, violation of conflict of interest limitations, and loans to insiders. The announcement was accompanied by proposals to reform both federal and state laws regulating charities, aimed primarily at fund-raising practices.[263] As noted in Chapter 2, during this same period the attorney general had drafted a bill, introduced in the New York state senate, that would have tightened the state rules relating to conflicts of interest and increased his enforcement powers in the event of breach.

The office of the attorney general played an important and unusual role in connection with the response of charities to the terrorist attacks on September 11, 2001. On September 26, the attorney general undertook to coordinate financial relief efforts. He proposed a limited-access database of victims designed to address fairness and avoid duplication, overlapping, and fraud during the relief effort. IBM had volunteered the equipment and services necessary to establish the database, and two other companies, McKinsey & Company and Accenture, volunteered their assistance. The regulators recognized that the government was legally prohibited from providing information from its records for such an effort, and had anticipated that the companies whose employees were among the victims and the major charities would provide the information for the database. However, the American Red Cross, which was reported to have the largest list of victims and had received the largest amount of contributions, refused to cooperate on the grounds that it would violate its clients' privacy and might deter victims from asking for assistance. During the ensuing month the president of the Red Cross resigned, and after other changes in its governance, the board adopted a new policy toward privacy. The Red Cross then entered into an agreement with the attorney general under which it would participate in establishing the database on the condition that the process would not be regulated by the public sector. On December 14, 2001, a group of nonprofit organizations formed a coalition, the 9/11 United Service Group, to coordinate the relief efforts. Although it took a number of months before it was operational, it ultimately was able to serve the role envisioned for it.[264]

The initial reaction to the attorney general's proposal to assist in the coor-

263. Grant Williams, "Making Philanthropy Accountable: New York's Top Regulator Pushes for Far-Reaching Changes," *Chronicle of Philanthropy*, June 26, 2003, at 23; Frank Brieaddy, "Small Private Charities Targeted: Attorney General Says Some Foundations Need Better Administration," *Syracuse Post-Standard*, July 28, 2003, at A1.

264. Victoria B. Bjorklund, "Reflections on September 11 Legal Developments," in *September 11: Perspectives from the Field of Philanthropy* (New York: Foundation Center, 2002), 11–47.

dination effort demonstrated widespread misunderstanding of his duties and power in connection with charitable activity. The final resolution of the dispute went far toward dispelling suspicion of the office and demonstrated the unique advantage of cooperation between government and the charitable sector.

Ohio

The Charity Law Section of the Ohio attorney general's office maintained a registry of approximately 18,000 active charitable organizations as of December 2002. Prior to 1995 there were 10,780 registered charities, and an annual average of 1,000 were added in the ensuing years. Exempt from the registration and filing requirements are religious organizations, schools, and organizations with gross receipts of less than $5,000 or assets of less than $15,000.

The duties of the staff include representing the attorney general in all civil litigation and administrative proceedings arising under the state laws regulating charitable organizations, including solicitations. The Section is also charged with supervising licensure requirements for charitable bingo games, a responsibility that accounted for a large proportion of staff time. However, in January 2003 legislation was enacted under which the attorney general was authorized to delegate to any other state agency the administration of the licensing requirements, which had been expanded under the terms of the act, a change that would greatly ease the burden on the division.[265]

The Section is staffed with six attorneys, five accountants, seven investigators, eight members of an account clerk unit, and five support staff. They are active in all aspects of the Section's activities. This has included publication of guides for board members and directories of charitable foundations in Ohio.

Hospital conversions became a major focus of the work of the Charity Section in the 1990s. As of 1997 the office had reviewed the sale of nine nonprofit hospitals and two HMO conversions and claimed to have protected over $600 million for charitable health care. In one instance a proposed sale of a community hospital was rescinded after concerns were raised by the attorney general of a conflict of interest on the part of a board member who subsequently resigned. The Section was instrumental in passage of conversion legislation in 1997.[266] Noteworthy has been the position taken by the attorney general that proceeds of sale in conversion transactions are to be

---

265. 2001 Ohio H.B. 512 (enacted January 2, 2003).
266. Ohio Rev. Code Ann. §109.35.

applied to further a broad spectrum of charitable health care purposes, including preventive health care for the indigent and other community health programs. This contrasts with the position taken in other states such as California that proceeds from conversions of hospitals must be used to support the provision of hospital care rather than broader purposes.

Massachusetts

The Massachusetts Division of Public Charities in the office of the attorney general was established in 1954. Massachusetts has the widest coverage of any state reporting program; all charities other than those with religious purposes are required to register and file annual financial reports with the Division. In addition, charities that solicit funds from the general public must file a separate registration statement and supplementary information relating to their fund-raising activities. Federal information forms are accepted. However, charities with gross support and revenue in excess of $100,000 and not more than $250,000 are also required to file financial statements accompanied by a report from a licensed CPA or public accountant. If gross support and revenue total more than $250,000, audited financial statements are required together with an independent auditor's report. Exempt from these requirements are private foundations, trusts filing probate accounts, and trusts audited by certain state and federal agencies. Filing fees range from $35 for charities with gross support and revenue under $100,001 to $250 if gross support and revenue exceed $500,000.[267] At the close of 2002, the director of the Division of Public Charities estimated that there were approximately 40,000 charities listed in the Division's files, but only 22,000 were active. The annual reports are open to the public during business hours at the Division's offices in Boston where copying facilities are available.

Massachusetts differs from the other states with mandatory annual reporting by requiring more specific information to supplement the federal information returns. This includes summaries of contributions, gross support and revenue, program services and grants, fund-raising expenses, management and general expenses, payments to affiliates, and year-end net assets or fund balances. Also required are the names and amount of compensation paid and the nature of services rendered by each of the organization's five highest paid consultants providing professional services, including attorneys, architects, accountants, management companies, investment advisors, and fund-raising solicitors and counsel. Similar information is required as to the compensation provided to the chief executive and four other current or former directors,

267. Mass. Gen. Laws ch. 12, §§8E, 8F.

officers, or employees who received the highest total compensation; information relating to payments or other transfer to related parties not included with the information relating to compensation; detailed information as to transactions with related parties and related organizations; whether any restrictions were removed during the year from donor-restricted funds; and whether any such funds have been loaned to unrestricted funds. A separate schedule is also required containing financial information, including compensation paid, by related organizations and other transfer of value not reported elsewhere such as in-kind gifts and waivers of interests. Related parties are defined as officers, directors, trustees, employees with management responsibilities, and their families, and any entity, whether nonprofit or for-profit, directly or indirectly owned or controlled by any of them. Ownership is defined as more than 35% of voting membership rights or voting stock, and an entity is considered "controlled" if the related individuals comprise over 35% of the fiduciaries of the entity.[268]

At the end of 2003 the Division was staffed with fifteen people, of whom five were attorneys, one of whom worked part-time, and two were paralegals. This was two fewer attorneys than reported in 1996, and the reduction was attributable to statewide budget cuts. The comparable numbers were two attorneys in 1965, four in 1974, and seven in 1996.

The Division of Public Charities pioneered in public outreach, establishing a committee in 1964 to advise as to the content of the original reporting forms, and then to assist in efforts to assure public understanding of the reporting requirement, the duties of directors and trustees, and the importance of consolidating small charities and seeking cy pres and deviation where appropriate.

The Division played an important role in the 1990s in two cases that received wide national press coverage. The first of these related to an investment made in 1985 by the trustees of Boston University in a privately held biotechnology company, Seragen, founded by scientists on the university faculty. In 1989 the *Boston Globe* reported that the university had invested approximately one-third of its general funds available for investment in the company and that it had written off $16.4 million of the investment.[269] Allegations were also made that the president of the university had purchased stock in a company spun off from the original biotech firm.[270] In April 1992 the press reported that the university was complying with a request from the

268. Massachusetts Office of Attorney General, Division of Public Charities, Form PC.

269. Peter G. Gosselin, "BU Writes Off $16M of Seragen Stake," *Boston Globe*, December 29, 1989.

270. Brian C. Mooney, "Silber Flip-Flops on Stock Ownership," *Boston Globe*, November 1, 1990.

attorney general's office to reduce its investment in Seragen by taking the company public.[271] At that time the *Globe* reported that the university owned 8.8 million shares of the 12 million shares outstanding, and that the value of the 8.8 million shares was $85 million.[272] Nearly one year later, the attorney general announced that he was instituting legal proceedings to force the university to make changes in its governance.[273] This was followed in December 1993 by an announcement of a settlement of the legal dispute under which the university agreed to a number of basic changes in its governance and in the manner in which compensation decisions were made.[274] Four years later the university's $85 million investment in Seragen was reported to be worth $3.5 million.[275] No action was taken against individual members of the board or the officers.

In 2002 the Massachusetts Division of Public Charities was again involved in a dispute that received national press coverage. The controversy arose when the attorney general objected to the terms of a sale of the controlling interests in the Boston Red Sox baseball team. The owner of these interests had left them at her death to a testamentary trust under the terms of which the trustees were to sell them and distribute the proceeds to a charitable foundation that the owner had created during her life. The trustees had adopted a bidding process that was widely publicized. After they announced the identity of the buyer, the attorney general objected on the grounds that the selected bid was not the highest, and he threatened to seek an injunction to block the sale. Because of the timing, near the start of a season, this would have been very detrimental to both the sellers and the purchasers. Ultimately, the designated buyers agreed to pay an additional $30 million, which would go directly to the foundation and not to the minority owners of the team. The foundation trustees also agreed to increase their number from four to nine members, with the new members broadly representing the general public.[276]

271. Joan Vennochi, "The Private Sector," *Boston Globe*, April 3, 1992.

272. Ronald Rosenberg, "Silber Invests $1M of Own Funds in Seragen Inc.," *Boston Globe*, May 22, 1992.

273. Stephen Kurkjian and John H. Kennedy, "AG Pushes BU Reform, Rebuts Silber on Funds, $386,700 in Proceeds Cited," *Boston Globe*, March 16, 1993.

274. Alice Dembner, "BU Trustees Agree to Increase Control," *Boston Globe*, December 15, 1993.

275. Ronald Rosenberg, "Despite Losses, BU and Seragen Plow On," *Boston Globe*, December 21, 1997, at G1.

276. "AG Reilly Announces Agreement to Bring $30 Million More to Charities from Sale of Red Sox," Office of Attorney General, News Release (January 16, 2002), available at *www.ago.state.ma.us/press_rel/bosoxdeal.asp;* Beth Healy, "Foundation Faces Greater Oversight," *Boston Globe*, January 18, 2002, at C1.

The greatest concern of the Division in 2002 was the marked increase in the number of charities seeking permission to establish subsidiaries, both tax-exempt and for-profit, to which they would transfer some of their functions and which, in the case of taxable entities, would have private investors. Although health care organizations had for a number of years been participating in joint ventures of all sorts, charities with other purposes were seeking approval of entering into joint ventures. The Division's concerns related to the relationship of the parent and the subsidiary, with compensation being paid to the same individuals from the parent and one or more subsidiaries. The detailed information about related parties and total payments to them required in the annual financial reports was designed to provide sufficient information to determine whether corrective action was needed.

Other Jurisdictions

The Illinois Division of Charitable Trusts reported in 1998 that the number of charitable fraud cases it had prosecuted had increased by 64% over the prior decade, from 81 in 1988 to 133 in 1997.[277] A great number of them involved thefts of funds from community groups, a situation that was attributed to lack of experience on the part of the founders and board members and a failure to monitor the financial accounts properly. The Illinois office of the attorney general maintains a registry of approximately 20,000 charities and investigates an average of 500 allegations of fraud annually.

There is no law requiring charities to register and file financial reports in Texas, so that the office of the attorney general relies on information provided voluntarily by charities and the watchdog organizations that monitor solicitations. A bill to require registration and reporting was prepared and supported by his office in 1993 but, according to the attorney general, was opposed by certain religious organizations and did not pass. In testimony before the Ways and Means Committee's Subcommittee on Oversight in 1993, the attorney general identified what his office considered abusive practices by charities.[278] Included were instances of self-dealing, waste of charitable assets, failure of hospitals to provide charity care, hiding behind "church" status to claim no responsibility for public accountability or compliance with regulatory requirements applicable to other charities, and deceptive fund-raising

277. Darlene Gavron Stevens, "Club Treasuries Ripe for Raiding, Say Authorities; Fleecing of Non-Profit Groups Linked to Lax Financial Controls," *Chicago Tribune*, November 29, 1998, at C1.

278. Tax Administration of Public Charities Exempt under Section 501(c)(3): Hearings before the Subcommittee on Oversight of the House Committee on Ways and Means, Serial 103-39, 103d Cong., 1st Sess. (1993) (statement of Dan Morales).

practices. The attorney general's Charitable Trusts Section within the Consumer Protection Division was staffed with three lawyers, one investigator, and one accountant charged with regulating approximately 22,000 public charities.

There are thirty-nine states that have laws requiring registration and reporting from charities that solicit funds from the general public, but do not impose similar requirements on other charities.[279] They include Connecticut, Maryland, Minnesota, New Mexico, and Pennsylvania. In these states in particular, there has inevitably been increased regulation of nonsoliciting charities than in those with no reporting statutes and, consequently, no staff or budget to attend to charitable matters. In contrast, Arizona affords an example of a state in which charity regulation is virtually nonexistent. In an article in the *Chronicle of Philanthropy* on May 16, 2002, the chief counsel of the Consumer Protection and Advocacy Section in the Arizona attorney general's office was quoted as saying, "We don't regulate charities in Arizona . . . I'm not aware of any state law or regulation covering corporate governance of nonprofits."[280]

The Legislature

The determination of broad community policy through the enactment of laws and through the creation of the specific executive, administrative, and judicial machinery to administer them is the function of the legislative branches in the United States and England. In this sense, the legislature may be considered to have a more fundamental power to alter the course of charitable dispositions.

Legislative power is limited, however, by the federal and state constitutions, although it is generally broad enough to supersede, alter, revise, or reject judge-made law. The legislature can establish the arbitrary dividing lines so essential to a system of laws. An example is the enactment of a law that specifies the range of permissible trustees' fees; another is a law that lists specific categories of investments proper for a trustee. Furthermore, only the legislature can work out broad and sweeping solutions to problems covering an entire class of related situations and at the same time create new methods for administration of these solutions.[281]

In a majority of the states the laws of trusts are drawn from the com-

279. See Appendix, Table 1, Column 15.

280. Harvey Lipman, "A Risky Mix for Charity," *Chronicle of Philanthropy,* May 16, 2002, at 29.

281. J. Willard Hurst, *The Growth of American Law: The Law Makers* (Boston: Little, Brown, 1950).

mon law and are to be found in decisions of the state supreme court. In a few states, notably California, Georgia, Louisiana, Montana, North Dakota, Oklahoma, South Dakota, and Texas, the legislatures have attempted to reduce this common law of trusts to statutory form and to publish it as a code. In all of these states, however, with the exception of Louisiana, the common law is still drawn upon to interpret the code as well as to supplement it wherever it is silent.

The state legislatures also frame the tax laws conferring exemption for charitable funds under certain circumstances that they have defined. They prescribe procedures for creation and dissolution of corporations. In some jurisdictions they are specifically granted power to investigate the affairs of charitable corporations.[282] In all states the power of the legislatures to conduct investigations for the purpose of gaining information in regard to the need for legislation extends over the entire range of charitable activities.

The chief restrictions on the legislative power to enact provisions replacing common law rules are the prohibitions in the United States Constitution against impairment of contracts and deprivation of property without due process.[283] These restrictions usually apply to attempts to terminate trusts or corporations, or to modify charitable purposes. The enumeration of fiduciary duties and powers, however, does not usually involve these constitutional restrictions, and the legislature may freely regulate such provisions as the duty to account, the amount of trustees' compensation, the regulation of trust investments, and the determination of allocations between principal and income. One particular aspect of these constitutional restrictions raised by the enactment of statutes affecting charitable dispositions is their retroactive effect. There is no constitutional restriction against a statute having a retroactive effect so long as it does not thereby impair a contract already made or violate the due process clause. A statute that has a prospective effect only does not run afoul of this proscription. Therefore if the wording of the statute is unclear as to its intended effect, the question of legislative intent often arises. The result of a court determination that the statute has a retroactive effect may be that the statute will be unconstitutional in its entirety.

The power of the legislature to establish procedures for enforcement is as extensive as that to determine substantive law. Although in some states the creation of state courts is circumscribed by the state constitution, the legislatures in all states have the power to allocate jurisdiction, designate venue, fix the number and length of terms of court, create, modify, and abolish remedies, and regulate court procedure. It is within the power of the legislature,

---

282. Minn. Stat. §300.63; S.D. Code §11.0106.
283. Trustees of Dartmouth College v. Woodward, 17 U.S. (4 Wheat.) 518 (1819).

therefore, to decide which courts have jurisdiction over charitable funds and the extent of this jurisdiction.

The legislature may also determine how broad the authorization of the attorney general will be to enforce the administration of charitable funds; or it can remove this duty from him altogether and place it in a different state official, create an entirely separate agency to regulate charitable funds, or adopt any combination of these arrangements. It is only when the state constitution and the legislature have remained silent concerning the duties of the attorney general and the standing of other parties that the courts are able to adopt or reject the common law rules concerning enforcement of the rights of charitable beneficiaries.

The drawbacks to reliance on the courts to change existing law have been described. The legislature, too, is limited in its freedom to make major changes and innovations in ways that go beyond the constitutional restrictions and may often be decisive when it comes to enacting specific proposals. The limitations stem from the very nature of the legislative process. Since the major focus of legislators is on the operation and financing of government and on keeping in touch with their constituents, persuasive and articulate pressure is needed to induce them to take any action on matters affecting private transactions and relationships. The existence of organized and vociferous opposition to new measures often results in no action. Based on the experience of the states in which the Uniform Supervision of Trustees for Charitable Purposes Act was adopted, passage was secured only after the attorney general exerted strong support. Once such legislation is enacted, if the attorney general initiates changes, they will be adopted if he has a strong voice in the legislature, but not otherwise.

The political climate and the political problems peculiar to each state will, of course, influence the attitude of the legislature toward regulation of charitable funds. There is, however, sufficient evidence to conclude that general lack of interest can be overcome only by forceful presentation from several sources. In Ohio the attorney general, the banking interests, and the judiciary combined to support enactment of reporting provisions;[284] and in Illinois the Trust Committee of the Chicago Bar Association assisted the attorney general in a successful attempt to amend the Illinois Uniform Act for Supervision of Trustees for Charitable Purposes in 1963.

Although it is more common for legislatures to resist expansion of state regulatory powers, the opposite occurred in the late 1990s and by early 2001 when legislatures in twenty-five states passed legislation regulating the con-

---

284. Ralph Klapp and Neva Wertz, "Supervision of Charitable Trusts in Ohio," 18 *Ohio State Law Journal* 181 (1957).

version of hospitals and health care organizations from nonprofit to for-profit status in transactions in which the proceeds from sale were not preserved for charitable purposes and the managers of the health care systems profited personally from the conversion.[285]

In sum, unless these political realities are taken into account in assessing new solutions to the problem of regulating charitable activities that require legislative action, the proposals may be meaningless.

Supervision by Other State Agencies

Secretaries of State and Corporation Commissions

In addition to the office of the attorney general, several other executive agencies of state government are empowered to supervise at least some aspects of the administration of charities. Administrative control over many charities was at one time exercised in the first instance through the state agencies that grant corporate charters and oversee corporate activities. The primary purpose of present-day corporation chartering laws is not regulatory, although they were originally conceived of as providing that function. These laws are more in the nature of enabling acts, and they were designed to afford an easy means for the state to confer authority on businessmen to organize and operate their businesses, large and small, with the advantage of the corporate mechanism. Gradually the concept of general chartering provisions was extended to include not-for-profit organizations. All of the statutes were drawn with a view toward facilitating the act of obtaining a corporate charter.

The mandatory reporting provisions contained in the corporation statutes of almost all states represent a second source of supervisory power over charitable corporations.[286] In all but a few states, however, corporations are required to report no more than a list of current officers and their addresses. Even in states where greater information is required, no separation of charitable from other not-for-profit corporations is made, and little if any evaluation of either the contents of the reports or their veracity is undertaken. The fact that failure to file may result in involuntary dissolution has actually created situations where dissolution of charitable corporations by the state has been done without any guarantee of cy pres distribution of funds, or even any investigation of the disposition of funds before the corporation became inactive.

Although in most states it is the attorney general who, on recommenda-

285. Fremont-Smith and Lever, "Analysis and Perspective: State Regulation of Health Care Conversions," at 718–719 (Idaho, Massachusetts, and New Jersey enacted statutes after publication).

286. See Appendix, Table 1, Column 6.

tion by other state officials, brings actions for dissolution of inactive corporations, he rarely has information as to whether a particular corporation was created for charitable purposes, and ironically it may be he who requests court action to dissolve a corporation without cy pres proceedings. Provisions for dissolution represent the area wherein the state regulatory powers are completely inadequate to achieve a suitable aim. The states lack adequate administrative arrangements and even the machinery for the cooperation between state agencies that would be necessary to assure proper disposition of funds on termination.

The states also lack adequate administrative machinery for enforcing provisions that impose restrictions on the fiduciary duties of corporate directors such as those forbidding loans to corporate officers and directors or a distribution of dividends to members or directors. In several states the secretary of state is given specific authority to propound interrogatories to any corporation formed under the provisions of the nonprofit corporation act, so long as they are reasonable and proper, to enable him to ascertain whether the corporation has complied with all provisions of the act.[287] These statutes usually provide that answers to interrogatories shall be confidential and that the secretary of state shall certify to the attorney general any answers that disclose violations of law. In other jurisdictions this power to examine the affairs of corporations is given to the attorney general, the legislature, the governor, or a combination of these.[288] They are rarely called into action, however.

A number of the statutes enacted in the late 1990s to regulate conversion of hospitals and other types of health care systems conferred regulatory power on state corporation commissioners. For example, in California, although regulation of hospitals was assigned to the attorney general,[289] the corporation counsel was given exclusive power to regulate the conversion of HMOs and Blue Cross Blue Shield organizations.[290]

Departments of Education, Health, and Similar Agencies

In some jurisdictions state regulatory boards, such as boards of education, health, social services, or insurance, have power to enforce standards of performance sufficiently broad to be coterminous with the power of the attorney

287. 85 Ill. Rev. Stat. 105/101.40; N.C. Gen. Stat. §55A-1-31; N.D. Cent. Code §10-33-141; see also RMNCA, §87.

288. Wis. Stat. §182.220 (the governor may request the attorney general to investigate and present findings to legislature); Minn. Stat. §300.63 (similar to Wisconsin but legislature may also conduct examination); Nev. Rev. Stat. §82.536 (attorney general); S.C. Code Ann. §33-31-171 (attorney general).

289. Cal. Corp. Code §§5914–5919.

290. Cal. Health & Safety Code §§1399.70–.76.

general to enforce fiduciary standards of trustees and directors. The Board of Regents in New York is one of the most powerful, having jurisdiction to "remove any trustee of a corporation created by them for misconduct, incapacity, neglect of duty, or where it appears to the satisfaction of the regents that the corporation has failed or refuses to carry into effect its educational purposes."[291] This power was invoked in 1996, in a suit filed with the Regents by faculty, students, and alumni of Adelphi University alleging that the president and members of the board of trustees of the university had breached their duties of care and loyalty. The university, its president, and members of its board challenged the power of individuals to petition the Regents and also the power of the Regents to delegate their investigative powers to private individuals.[292] The court dismissed this challenge, and at the conclusion of the Regents' hearings the president and all but one of the nineteen trustees were removed.[293] Subsequent litigation brought by the attorney general resulted in a settlement in which the university received a total of $3.4 million, $1.4 million of which came from the trustees.[294]

In the statutes enacted in the 1990s to regulate conversions, state commissioners of public health and of insurance were assigned regulatory power in six instances, while in twelve others, power was assigned to the attorney general acting with another state agency.[295]

The difficulties in multistate enforcement were illustrated in a controversy that arose in 2003 involving CareFirst, a Maryland nonprofit health insurance company that was the sole member of Blue Cross Blue Shield plans in Maryland, Delaware, and the District of Columbia. The corporation had sought approval of a conversion from the Maryland Insurance Commission. However, the Commission denied the application, finding that the board had breached its fiduciary duties under the statute and Maryland common law by failing to obtain fair value, not exercising due diligence, and not addressing conflicts of interest.[296] The Maryland General Assembly affirmed the Commission's position when in April it unanimously passed a bill requiring

291. N.Y. Educ. Law §226(4).

292. Adelphi University v. Board of Regents of the State of New York, 647 N.Y.S.2d 678 (Sup. Ct. 1996).

293. The Committee to Save Adelphi v. Diamandopolous, Board of Regents of the State of New York, 652 N.Y.S.2d 837 (App. Div. 1997); see also N.Y. Not-for-Profit Corp. Law §715.

294. Samuel Maull, "Adelphi and Vacco Announce Financial Settlement with Former Trustees," *Associated Press,* November 18, 1998.

295. Fremont-Smith, "Conversion Foundations," 47–51.

296. Order In Re the Consolidated Application for the Conversion of CareFirst, Inc. and CareFirst of Maryland, Inc. to For-Profit Status and the Acquisition of CareFirst, Inc. by Well-Point Health Networks, Inc., MIA No. 2003-02-032 (March 5, 2003), available at *www.mdinsurance.state.md.us/documents/MIA-2003-02-032CareFirstconversion.pdf.*

CareFirst to remain nonprofit for five years, and providing a schedule for removal of the twelve Maryland members of the twenty-one-person board, and their replacement by a nominating committee appointed by the governor, the speaker of the House, the president of the Senate, and one other.[297] National Blue Cross Blue Shield then terminated CareFirst's right to use its trademark, and CareFirst in turn sued the state challenging the constitutionality of the statute. A settlement was subsequently reached and approved by the federal district court that modified somewhat the nominating process.[298]

However, this did not settle the matter. The Delaware insurance commissioner scheduled a fall hearing to determine whether the Delaware plan should be required to sever ties with CareFirst on the grounds that the Maryland legislation and settlement require the corporation to favor Maryland subscribers over others. The insurance commissioner in the District of Columbia similarly contested the power of the Maryland legislature, particularly its power to prevent a sale should the District or Delaware order or approve one or should one prove necessary.[299] In this instance, unlike the situations involving Banner and the attorneys general in the Dakotas and New Mexico, the federal district court retains jurisdiction over all of the CareFirst entities.

Supervision of Bank and Trust Companies

Charitable trusts that are managed by bank and trust companies acting either as fiduciaries or as custodians of trust funds are subject to a degree of supervision under statutes in all states, as well as under federal laws, that require an annual audit of all accounts. In some states the banking laws include special sections relating to trust funds. For example, Indiana specifically makes it a routine duty of the state superintendent of banks to check all trusts, trust funds, and trust and estate accounts held in possession and control of banks.[300] Provisions in Ohio relate specifically to trust funds that have been held by a bank in its fiduciary capacity and not invested,[301] and the Mississippi statute requires separation of assets and the maintenance of separate books and records of all assets held in a fiduciary capacity.[302]

---

297. S.B. 772/H.B. 1179, 2003 Reg. Sess. (Md. 2003).

298. Dan Thanh Dang, "CareFirst Settlement Accepted by Judge; Parties Endorse Proposal for Reforms That Preserves Affiliation with Blue Cross," *Baltimore Sun,* June 7, 2003, at 1A.

299. Bill Brubaker, "CareFirst Oversight Questioned: District Wary of Maryland Control over Nonprofit Health Insurer," *Washington Post,* July 7, 2003, at B1.

300. Ind. Stat. §5-1025.

301. Ohio Rev. Code Ann. §1111:13.

302. Miss. Code Ann. §81-5-33.

Departments of Tax and Revenue

State tax authorities have a less pervasive influence on charitable activities than do their federal counterparts. This is due in part to the nature of state tax exemption statutes in which exemption is granted at creation based primarily on the purposes of the organization, with little or no attention paid to the manner in which it is subsequently operated. In comparison to federal code requirements, it is the organizational test that controls while the operational test is ignored.

Cooperation between state tax departments and other branches of state government is rare. An appeal from an adverse ruling by state tax authorities is, of course, heard by the courts. In almost all jurisdictions the attorney general's office serves as legal counsel for all actions involving the state, so that it is conceivable that an attorney general's duty to represent the state's interest in taxation will conflict with his duties to enforce charitable funds. Procedural conflicts are in some instances solved by having the state agency involved appoint its own attorney, or use one of its own legal officers to represent it in such a situation, leaving the attorney general free to represent the charitable interest. More often, however, the charitable gift in such cases is to a named charitable corporation capable of representing its own interests, so that there is not as great a need for the attorney general to intervene to protect the charitable interest.[303]

Exemption for charitable organizations from state corporate income and franchise taxes is granted in all states. Most of them have adopted the same qualifications for exemption as those in the Internal Revenue Code. Some, such as California, although using federal criteria, require charities to file and obtain a separate state determination of exemption.[304] In Delaware, exemption from federal tax carries with it exemption from the state tax, and no separate application for determination is required.[305]

Arizona is the only state that requires the filing of tax returns from exempt organizations. Its statute covers all charitable organizations except religious and educational corporations, charitable organizations supported by funds from the government or general public, and organizations whose gross income does not exceed $25,000. An organization may comply with the statute by filing a copy of its federal information return.[306] There is, however, no

---

303. See, for example, James E. Carroll v. Commissioner of Corporations and Taxation, 179 N.E.2d 260 (Mass. 1961).

304. Cal. Rev. & Tax. Code §23701.

305. Del. Code Ann. tit. 20, §1-314(b)(6).

306. Ariz. Rev. Stat. Ann. §43-1242.

apparent cooperation between the tax department and the office of the attorney general.

Cooperation between the offices of the attorney general and state tax officials is implicit in a section of the Uniform Act for Supervision of Trustees for Charitable Purposes as enacted in California, Michigan, and Oregon. It requires all agencies of the state receiving applications for tax exemption of any charitable trust subject to the act to file annually with the attorney general a list of all applications received in that year.[307] Furthermore, in California and Oregon, failure to file annual reports with the attorney general in compliance with the Supervision of Trustees for Charitable Purposes Act is made a mandatory ground for removal of tax exemption for the year or years in which the charity is in default.[308] It is obvious that statutory provisions requiring this type of cooperation increase the efficiency and effectiveness of state regulation by the attorney general.

In states that rely on a sales tax for the major part of their revenue, charitable organizations generally are exempted from payment of the tax for purchase of goods used in carrying out their charitable purposes. In the majority of states, exemption from sales tax as with exemption from other state taxes will be granted upon a showing that the organization is exempt from federal income tax by virtue of being described in section 501(c)(3) of the Internal Revenue Code. There is no evidence that it is difficult to obtain these exemptions.

Exemption from state and local real property taxes undoubtedly has the most important impact on the vast majority of charities, far more than exemption from state corporate income taxes. Exemption from local real property tax is granted under the constitutions in thirty-eight states and left as a matter for the discretion of the legislature in the rest.[309] Recent controversies generated by attempts in a number of states to interpret narrowly the group of charities eligible for exemption by adopting an exceedingly narrow definition of "charity" are described in Chapter 2. They are illustrative of the power of state tax authorities. This power also extends theoretically to enforcing fiduciary duties as they are implicit in the definition of charities eligible for tax exemption. The failure of tax officials to police this aspect of charitable activity is attributable more to budget constraints than to any other

307. Cal. Gov't Code §12594; Mich. Comp. Laws §14.254; Or. Rev. Stat. §128.730.

308. Cal. Rev. & Tax. Code §23703; Or. Rev. Stat. §128.740.

309. Janne Gallagher, "Recent Challenges to Property-Tax Exemption," in *Property Tax Exemption for Charities: Mapping the Battlefield* (Evelyn Brody ed., Washington, D.C.: Urban Institute Press, 2002); see also Evelyn Brody, "Of Sovereignty and Subsidy: Conceptualizing the Charity Tax Exemption," 23 *Journal of Corporation Law* 585 (1998).

factor. Yet it remains an important residuary source of control should a tax official decide to exercise it at any future time.

Regulation of Charitable Fund-Raising

Traditionally, regulation of solicitations made by charitable organizations was conducted by cities and towns. A growing awareness of the need for broader regulation of this type of activity at the state level was evident after the Second World War. By the mid-1960s, twenty-six states had adopted regulatory legislation. In seventeen of them, annual or special financial reports were required from soliciting organizations, and separate reports were called for from paid solicitors or promoters. Twenty-one states required either a license or registration before solicitation could be undertaken. It was also common for cities and towns to require door-to-door solicitors to register and obtain permits before conducting any solicitations. Some of the state statutes and ordinances contained limits on the amount that could be spent for fund-raising expenses or required that a certain amount be spent on the soliciting organization's charitable purposes.[310]

State attempts to limit the amount charities could spend on fund-raising were the subject of four cases decided by the United States Supreme Court between 1980 and 2003. The first case, decided in 1980, was *Schaumburg v. Citizens for a Better Environment*,[311] in which the Court held that an ordinance prohibiting door-to-door solicitation by any organization that did not spend at least 75% of the amounts it collected for "charitable purposes" was unconstitutional on the basis that it violated the First Amendment guarantee of free speech. This case was followed in 1984 by *Secretary of State of Maryland v. Munson*,[312] in which the state statute limited the amount that a charity could expend on fund-raising to 25% of the funds raised but permitted the secretary of state to waive the limitation if the charity could prove that it would effectively prevent it from raising contributions. Again, the Court found that the statute infringed free speech guarantees and that the waiver provision did not cure the defect.

In the third case, *Riley v. National Federation of the Blind of North Carolina, Inc.*,[313] the Court struck down several provisions of the North Carolina solicitation statute regulating professional fund-raisers. The statute

310. Ellen Harris et al., "Fundraising into the 1990s: State Regulation of Charitable Solicitation after *Riley*," in *Topics in Philanthropy*, vol. 1, at 20–22 (1998) (New York University School of Law, Program on Philanthropy and the Law).

311. 444 U.S. 620 (1980).

312. 467 U.S. 947 (1984).

313. 487 U.S. 781 (1988).

(1) contained a presumption that a fund-raiser whose fee exceeded 35% of gross funds raised was unreasonably enriched, and he would accordingly be required to return the excess to the charity; (2) required professional solicitors to disclose at the point of solicitation the professional's recent history as to the percentage of funds he raised that was actually turned over to charitable clients; and (3) required professional solicitors to obtain a license before soliciting, and contained no provision for expeditious administrative or judicial review if an application for a license was denied. The Court found each of these requirements constituted violations of the First Amendment: the first because it was not sufficiently narrowly tailored to the state's interest in preventing fraud; the second because it infringed on free speech rights; and the third because of the failure to provide remedies in the event of delay and abuse of discretion.

The fourth case, *Madigan v. Telemarketing Associates, Inc.*, which was decided on May 5, 2003,[314] was an appeal by the attorney general of Illinois from a decision of the state supreme court upholding the dismissal of a suit he had brought on the basis that no cause of action had been stated.[315] The grounds of the suit were that the defendants, professional, for-profit fund-raising corporations, in making telephone solicitations on behalf of a charity, represented that the funds would further its charitable purposes but, because the fees charged by the defendants were "excessive in amount and an unreasonable use and waste of charitable assets," and because the defendants did not advise donors that only 15% of the funds raised would go to the charity, the solicitations were "knowingly deceptive and materially false." The complaint was later amended to allege that the solicitations violated the terms of the Illinois statute governing solicitation of charitable funds, which required that professional fund-raisers identify fully and accurately the purpose for which funds are solicited. It was alleged that by failing to reveal to donors the percentage of the contribution that would actually go to the charity, the solicitors had obtained money under false pretenses, thereby also violating the Illinois Consumer Fraud and Deceptive Business Practices Act.

The defendants argued in their motion to dismiss that the solicitations were protected speech and that, pursuant to the *Riley* case, a claim of fraud could not be maintained where the basis for the complaint was the percentage of proceeds going to the fund-raisers and the failure to volunteer this information. The Illinois Supreme Court had found the attorney general's

---

314. Illinois ex rel. Madigan v. Telemarketing Associates, Inc., 123 S. Ct. 1829 (2003).

315. People ex rel. Ryan v. Telemarketing Associates, Inc., 763 N.E.2d 289 (Ill. 2001), cert. granted, 123 S. Ct. 512 (2002).

complaint to be "at its core, a constitutionally impermissible percentage-based limitation on the fund-raisers' ability to engage in a protected activity."[316] It held that the complaint incorrectly presumed a nexus between high solicitation costs and fraud, despite the fact that the fund-raisers also produced materials designed to increase community awareness of the charity.

The United States Supreme Court in a unanimous decision reversed the Illinois Supreme Court, holding that the First Amendment does not shield fraud and that the attorney general's claim for relief presented sufficient evidence of possible deception on the part of the defendants to survive a motion to dismiss. The Court noted that there were critical differences between fraud actions trained on representations made in individual cases and statutes that categorically ban solicitations when fund-raising costs run high. Based on the decisions in *Schaumburg, Munson,* and *Riley,* the latter type of restrictions are protected by the First Amendment, but it does not shield fraud actions based on intentional deceptions. The Court stated:

> High fundraising costs, without more, do not establish fraud. And mere failure to volunteer the fundraiser's fee when contacting a potential donee, without more, is insufficient to state a claim for fraud. But these limitations do not disarm States from assuring that their residents are positioned to make informed choices about their charitable giving. Consistent with our precedent and the First Amendment, States may maintain fraud actions when fundraisers make false or misleading representations designed to deceive donors about how their donations will be used.[317]

Although the first three Supreme Court decisions limited a state's ability to regulate charitable solicitations, regulation of fund-raising activities by non-profits and for-profit corporations has remained a major focus of state activity, and the *Madigan* decision renewed interest in pursuing cases involving fraud.[318] The interest in policing fraudulent solicitations reflected in part a more general interest in consumer protection, which is a major activity in the offices of the attorney general throughout the country.

As of 2003, thirty-nine states were actively regulating charitable solicitations. The duty to administer these programs was assigned to various state officials. In sixteen states, reports on solicitation activities are filed with the attorney general; in fifteen they are filed with the secretary of state, although the enforcement power is placed with the attorney general; and in eight oth-

---

316. Id., 763 N.E.2d at 363.

317. *Madigan,* 123 S. Ct. at 1842.

318. Williams, "Making Philanthropy Accountable," 23; Brieaddy, "Small Private Charities Targeted," A1.

ers it is the consumer protection agency that carries out the statutory duties, although in five of these, the attorney general retained his common law enforcement powers.[319]

A Model Act regulating solicitation of funds for charitable purposes was adopted in 1986 by the National Association of Attorneys General that contains the pattern of enforcement found in almost all of the state statutes.[320] Charities intending to solicit funds in the state are required to register and file financial reports either at the conclusion of a campaign or annually. Twenty-two states require audited reports from organizations receiving more than a fixed amount of revenue during the reporting period that ranges between $100,000 and $250,000. In some states there is a minimum threshold under which charities are exempt from reporting. Professional solicitors and fund-raising counsel are also required to register and report and, in some instances, file bonds. More recently, the scope of the statutes has been extended to cover commercial co-venturers, defined as persons who for profit conduct fund-raising activities or provide goods or services advertised in conjunction with the name of a charity or of a charitable purpose.[321]

As noted, enforcement power is given either to the attorney general or to another state officer, most often the secretary of state, and in some instances it may be given to both. In New Mexico, the solicitation statute applies to all charitable organizations other than religious organizations regardless of whether they conduct public solicitation, and the only exemptions from the registration and reporting requirements are educational organizations and certain solicitations for individuals or groups that suffered from medical or other catastrophes.[322] The *Continuing Professional Education Text* issued by the Internal Revenue Service for fiscal year 2001 contained an article on state charitable solicitation provisions written by Karl E. Emerson, director of the Bureau of Charitable Organizations of the Pennsylvania Department of State. It contains a detailed description of the provisions in Pennsylvania law and the manner in which they are administered, providing insight into the extent of activities and the problems faced by regulators.[323]

The multiplicity and diversity of filing requirements and the existence of greatly differing exemptions place a heavy burden on charities that solicit in more than a few states. In response to the problem of multiple filings, the National Association of Attorneys General (NAAG) and the National Associ-

---

319. See Appendix, Table 1, Column 16.

320. Model Solicitations Act (1986).

321. See, for example, Mass. Gen. Laws ch. 68, §18.

322. N.M. Stat. §57-22-4.

323. Karl E. Emerson, "State Charitable Solicitation Statutes," 155–167, in *2001 IRS Continuing Professional Education Text.*

ation of State Charity Officials (NASCO) cooperated with representatives of several national organizations representing charities that conduct solicitations to create a Unified Registration Statement (URS) as part of a Standardized Reporting Project, the purpose of which is to simplify and economize compliance under the states' solicitation laws.[324] As of January 2003, thirty-six states had agreed to use the URS, although four of them also required supplemental information. In addition, twelve states were participating in the project to encourage electronic filing that was being coordinated by the National Center for Charitable Statistics and NAAG/NASCO.

The solicitation statutes all exempt religious organizations from their scope, and the majority of them also relieve educational organizations and hospitals from their provisions. Exemptions in some states are also granted to museums, membership organizations soliciting only among their members, veterans organizations, volunteer fire or rescue groups, and parent-teacher organizations. California also exempts corporate trustees subject to the jurisdiction of other state agencies.[325] In contrast, Massachusetts exempts only religious organizations.[326]

One issue that remained unresolved after the *Riley* decision was whether the state could require any form of point-of-solicitation disclosure. Maryland, New York, and Pennsylvania are among the states that attempted to avoid the constitutional uncertainty by requiring that all solicitation materials contain a statement to the effect that financial information about the charity was available on request either from the charity or from the state regulatory agency, with the address where the information could be obtained.[327] These requirements are often difficult to comply with.

The most recent development at the state level in connection with solicitation is the use of the Internet for fund-raising. The National Association of Attorneys General and the National Association of State Charity Officials in 2000 circulated for public comment a document referred to as "The Charleston Principles," which is a codification of the circumstances under which Internet fund-raising activities would be considered sufficient in scope to require the charity conducting them to come within the ambit of a state solicitation statute.[328]

---

324. The Multi-State Filer Project, *The Uniform Registration Statement,* available at *www.nonprofits.org/library/gov/urs/.*

325. Cal. Gov't Code §12583.

326. Mass. Gen. Laws Ann. ch. 68, §20.

327. N.Y. Exec. Law §174(b); Pa. Stat. Ann. tit. 10, §162.13; Md. Bus. Reg. §6-101.

328. Charleston Principles, available at *www.nasconet.org/stories/storyReader$10.*

Proposals for Independent Boards for Charity Supervision

Karst, in an article written in 1960, proposed the creation of independent state boards of charity to bear primary responsibility for supervising charitable activities and administering the various state controls over their operation. His enumeration of the duties of such a board provided a useful catalog of the possibilities for effective state action. The proposed board would:

(1) replace the attorney general in his supervisory capacity, by (a) maintaining a registry of all charities operating in the state, (b) collecting and evaluating periodic reports to be required of all charities required to register, perhaps with some exemptions, (c) investigating possible breaches of fiduciary duty, and (d) calling abuses of fiduciary responsibility requiring remedial action directly to the attention of the proper court; (2) advise and consult with charity managers in (a) planning for future programs of operation and selection of projects, and (b) organizing the management and investment of funds; (3) take responsibility for effectuating new schemes for the operation of obsolete charities and the consolidation of charities of uneconomical size; (4) administer a statewide system of control over the solicitation of funds, which would either coordinate or supersede municipal control; (5) cooperate with tax officials, both state and federal, by reporting to them abuses which appear to call for withdrawal of tax exemption.[329]

In the years since this suggestion was made, there has been no overt public interest in establishing separate regulatory agencies in the states. In fact, since 1960, the date of the Karst proposal, only three states adopted legislation enhancing state enforcement powers, while two statutes passed in the 1960s that increased state enforcement programs were repealed and other programs were vastly curtailed. As of 2003, interest shifted to the federal government, with the Internal Revenue Service extending its enforcement role and with scholarly attention turning to consideration of establishing a centralized federal charity agency. The lack of interest in increasing state oversight of fiduciary duties is in contrast to the growth of state programs regulating solicitations of charitable funds. Even so, and despite efforts by the states and sector representatives to coordinate state regulatory programs, which has resulted in widespread acceptance of the Unified Registration Statement, the difficulty of policing Internet solicitation by the states has led to reconsideration of federal regulation.

329. Karst, "Charitable Dollar," 449.

The most far-reaching proposal for federal regulation of solicitation came as a suggestion from the New York attorney general to the House Ways and Means Committee in spring 2003. He proposed legislation that would amend the Code to deny a deduction for any part of a charitable contribution that represented payment to a professional fund-raiser, and would require charities to disclose to potential contributors the percentage of their contribution that would be denied deduction because of such payments.[330] This measure would impose restrictions through the tax laws that were prohibited under the *Riley* case and its predecessors, thus raising the validity of the doctrine of constitutional conditions, an issue that was unresolved as of that date.[331]

330. Williams, "Making Philanthropy Accountable," 23; Brieaddy, "Small Private Charities Targeted," A1.

331. See generally *Conference: Emanations from Rust: The Impact on the Nonprofit Sector of the Doctrine of Unconstitutional Conditions* (New York University School of Law, National Center on Philanthropy and the Law, 1992); see also Kathleen M. Sullivan, "Unconstitutional Conditions," 102 *Harvard Law Review* 1415 (1989).

7

The Role of the Federal Government in the Regulation of Charities

Charities are the creatures of the states, and the laws governing their establishment, their right to continuous existence, their freedom to operate, any limitations on the nature of their holdings, and the conditions for their dissolution have been and continue to be determined at the state level. However, since the 1950s the regulatory power of the federal government has been expanded so that it is effectively the primary source of regulation, extending to matters that had previously been the exclusive province of the states and, in many instances, preempting state regulation by conditioning tax exemption upon compliance with federal standards of behavior.

The substantive provisions of the federal tax law have been described in Chapter 5. This chapter contains a description of the methods by which these substantive laws are enforced. The federal role has three major aspects. In the first instance, the Congress determines the nature and scope of regulation. It has a dual role, conducting investigations to obtain information on which to determine whether changes are advisable, and enacting substantive provisions designed to effectuate these changes. Second, the Treasury Department prepares legislative proposals and congressional actions through the promulgation of regulations. The Internal Revenue Service, which is a branch of the Treasury, has direct responsibility for administering these laws and regulations. Third, the federal courts interpret the laws and regulations and determine their constitutionality. The judiciary thus holds the ultimate power, although the issues that are decided by the courts are a small segment of the universe of government regulation.

The Congress

The nature and scope of federal regulation of charities is determined in the first instance by the Congress and reflects its concern as to the importance of policing the charitable sector as compared with other segments of society. The fact that the federal role has evolved within the tax policing system is a matter of historical accident rather than a conscious assignment of responsibility to the tax authorities. Policing of charities (and other tax-exempt entities) could have been—and still could be—assigned to the Justice Department, thereby following the state pattern of regulation, or to another cabinet department; it could have been made the responsibility of a separate, independent agency such as the Securities and Exchange Commission or the Federal Trade Commission.[1] It is interesting to speculate whether, with a change of that nature, the role of the IRS would be entirely subsumed or whether, because of the underlying federal concern for the integrity of the tax system, the regulatory function would be bifurcated, as it is in Britain.

The history of federal regulation described in Chapter 2 illustrates a lack of deliberation in the development of the Service as regulator, with this role evolving over half a century from 1950 to 2000 in parallel with the growth of the sector and its consequent potential impact on the larger economy. Although the sector has grown, congressional attention to the operations of charities has not increased proportionately. This is due in part to a diminution of congressional power as exercised through its investigatory activities and in part to a transformation of the tax-writing process that has curtailed the power of the House Ways and Means and Senate Finance Committees, along with that of the Treasury.[2]

One aspect of the change in the tax-writing process that has affected the pace of enactment, as well as the substance of tax law changes, was the adoption in 1974 of a comprehensive budget process under which aggregate spending and revenue targets were established annually, budget committees were created to assist Congress to manage budget limits, and a process called budget reconciliation evolved to assure that spending limits were observed.[3] The result has been that, more often than not, efforts to increase regulation of tax-exempt organizations have been thwarted because they will not provide the additional revenue to cover the cost of enhanced regulatory programs. This change also provides an interesting contrast to the contentious history surrounding the enactment in 1969 of the private foundations excise tax provisions, as well as demonstrating the shift that has taken place within Congress.

The most recent change in the Code affecting charities, the passage in

1. David Ginsburg et al., "Federal Oversight of Private Philanthropy," in Department of Treasury, Commission on Private Philanthropy and Public Needs, *Research Papers*, vol. 5, pt. 1, at 2575 (1977).

2. Elizabeth Garrett, "The Congressional Budget Process: Strengthening the Party-in-Government," 100 *Columbia Law Review* 702 (2000).

3. Congressional Budget and Impoundment Control Act of 1974, Pub. L. No. 93-344, 88 Stat. 297 (1974).

1996 of intermediate sanctions for engaging in excess benefit transactions, provides an excellent example of the process by which tax legislation that is not contentious is formulated, refined, and enacted, with the Service, the Treasury, the Ways and Means and Finance Committees, and ultimately both houses of Congress agreeing on the need for legislation, the scope it would encompass, and the specific provisions that would be enacted. This legislation offers, therefore, a useful case study of the process involved in enacting new regulatory legislation and its subsequent implementation through regulations and rulings.

In 1989 an Internal Revenue Service Penalty Task Force issued a report recommending amendment of the Code to provide sanctions for violation of the conditions for tax exemption similar to those applicable to private foundations that would ensure correction without the need to revoke exemption.[4] The Commissioner included this recommendation as a formal request to Congress in testimony presented to the Oversight Subcommittee of the House Ways and Means Committee on June 15, 1993.[5] Prior to this request, several proposals to impose intermediate sanctions on health care organizations for self-dealing[6] or failure to provide emergency care[7] were included in bills introduced by several congressmen in 1991, although they received little attention at the time.

The first response to the Commissioner's testimony from the nonprofit community came from Independent Sector, whose board of directors approved a draft of legislation containing intermediate sanctions in October 1993.[8] Then on November 22, 1993, a Ways and Means Committee member, Congressman Fortney "Pete" Stark, offered a revision of a bill he had introduced in 1991 that would impose excise taxes in instances of private inurement and self-dealing.[9] Treasury officials weighed in the following March with testimony before the Oversight Subcommittee calling for limitations in the form of excise taxes on transactions involving excess benefits provided by organizations exempt under sections 501(c)(3) and (4) to insid-

4. Executive Task Force, Commissioner's Penalty Study, Internal Revenue Service, *Report on Civil Tax Penalties*, ch. 9, sec. III (1989).

5. Tax Administration of Public Charities Exempt under Section 501(c)(3): Hearings before the Subcommittee on Oversight of the House Committee on Ways and Means, Serial 103-39, 103d Cong., 1st Sess. (1993).

6. H.R. 4042, 102d Cong., 1st Sess. (1991).

7. Charity Care and Hospital Tax-Exempt Status Reform Act of 1991, H.R. 790, 102d Cong., 1st Sess. (1991); H.R. 1374, 102d Cong., 1st Sess. (1991).

8. Independent Sector, "Independent Sector Position on Possible Legislation Related to Performance and Accountability of Public Charities," 9 *Exempt Organization Tax Review* 151 (1994).

9. H.R. 3697, 103d Cong., 1st Sess. (1993).

ers.[10] This proposal was endorsed by the Oversight Subcommittee in a report issued in May 1994 in which it summarized testimony received at its 1993 and 1994 hearings on public charities.[11] One month later, the Senate Finance Committee released a summary of the version of health care reform upon which it had reached tentative agreement. This contained a provision applying intermediate sanctions to health care providers for breach of fiduciary duty as well as failure to provide community benefits.[12] No action was taken, however, until 1996 when the Treasury version of intermediate sanctions with some revisions was passed as part of the Taxpayer Bill of Rights 2.[13] Of note is the estimate of projected revenue that would result from its passage, specifically, $4 million in 1996, 1997, and 1998, $5 million in 1999, 2000, and 2001, and $6 million in 2002, a total of $33 million.[14]

The Ways and Means Committee and the Finance Committee have permanent staff who prepare reports to accompany all revenue bills. These comprise the official explanation of the provisions in the bills and the reasons for their inclusion. The House Report on intermediate sanctions provides an example of documentation relied on by the Treasury, the Service, and the courts not only to interpret the legislative language but to flesh out certain provisions. As an example, the House Report on the intermediate sanctions provisions contained a directive to the Treasury to develop regulations providing for a presumption of reasonableness in regard to compensation of disqualified persons, thereby establishing an agenda for the Treasury and the IRS.[15] In addition to the staffs for the full committees, various subcommittees are established from time to time to address specific issues. The Patman Committee is one example, as are the House Subcommittee on Oversight under Chairman Pickle, which was active in 1993,[16] and most recently the Senate Oversight Subcommittee led by minority member Senator Charles Grassley, who during a period of twelve months requested the General Accounting Office to conduct two major studies on different aspects relating to

10. Improved Compliance by Tax-Exempt Organizations: Hearings before the Subcommittee on Oversight of the House Committee on Ways and Means, Serial 103-72, 103d Cong., 2d Sess. (1994) (statement of Leslie B. Samuels, Assistant Secretary, Department of Treasury).

11. Subcommittee on Oversight, House Committee on Ways and Means, *Report on Reforms to Improve the Tax Rules Governing Public Charities*, WMCP 103-26 (1994).

12. Health Care Reform, Chairman's Mark (June 9, 1994) (Senate Finance Committee Print); see also Health Security Act, H.R. 3600, 103d Cong., 1st Sess. (1994); Health Security Act, S. 2351, 103d Cong., 2d Sess. (1994).

13. Taxpayer Bill of Rights 2, Pub. L. No. §1311, 110 Stat. 1452, 1475–1479 (1996).

14. H.R. Rep. No. 104-506, 104th Cong., 2d Sess., at 64 (1996).

15. Id. at 57.

16. See Chapter 2.

the accountability of charities and the role of the Internal Revenue Service in regulating their activities.[17]

The Joint Committee on Taxation serves as a permanent resource for the House Ways and Means Committee and the Senate Finance Committee, advising on technical matters, preparing estimates of the revenue effect of proposed legislation, preparing background information for use by the committees and subcommittees during hearings, and providing summaries of tax legislation that thereafter are incorporated in the tax history of the legislation.[18] As an example, the Joint Committee prepared a report issued in May 2002 describing the rules limiting political and lobbying activities, together with summaries of two pending bills that would have exempted churches from the prohibition against intervention in political campaigns, bills that were to be discussed at a hearing of the Ways and Means Oversight Committee.[19]

In 2000 the Joint Committee issued a major study of confidentiality and disclosure provisions in the Internal Revenue Code, a study mandated by the Internal Revenue Service Restructuring and Reform Act of 1998. Volume II of this report contained a 208-page study of disclosure provisions applicable to tax-exempt organizations together with extensive recommendations for expanding the availability of information relating to Service determinations affecting charities.[20] During the course of preparation of draft legislation, the staff of the Joint Committee works closely with the staff of the House and Senate Legislative Counsels to assure that the wording of proposed legislation accurately reflects congressional policy decisions.

General Accounting Office

The General Accounting Office (GAO) serves as the investigative arm of Congress charged with improving the performance and accountability of the federal government. Its stated mission is to examine the use of public funds,

---

17. General Accounting Office, *Tax-Exempt Organizations: Improvements Possible in Public, IRS, and State Oversight of Charities* (GAO-02-526) (April 2002); General Accounting Office, *September 11: More Effective Collaboration Could Enhance Charitable Organizations' Contributions in Disasters* (GAO-03-259) (December 2002).

18. Revenue Act of 1926, Pub. L. No. 69-20, §1203, 44 Stat. 9, 127–128 (1926).

19. Joint Committee on Taxation, *Description of Present-Law Rules Relating to Political and Other Activities of Organizations Described in Section 501(c)(3) and Proposals Regarding Churches* (JCX-39-02) (May 14, 2002).

20. Joint Committee on Taxation, *Study of Present-Law Taxpayer Confidentiality and Disclosure Provisions as Required by Section 3802 of the Internal Revenue Service Restructuring and Reform Act of 1998*, vol. 2 of *Study of Disclosure Provisions Relating to Tax-Exempt Organizations* (JCS-1-00) (January 28, 2000).

evaluate federal programs and policies, and provide analyses, recommendations, and other assistance to Congress.[21] The GAO accepts assignments from chairmen of subcommittees of the tax-writing committees. From its inception it has responded to requests for information about nonprofits on numerous occasions. Its 1987 study of the unrelated business activities of exempt organizations, prepared at the request of the Joint Committee on Taxation, was influential at the time,[22] as was a report issued in April 2002, requested by the ranking minority member of the Senate Finance Committee, that reviewed IRS and state oversight of charities and contained suggestions for improvement.[23]

The Treasury

The Treasury Department has dual roles in the regulation of charities. It is responsible for formulating and drafting proposals that reflect the administration's positions on tax and fiscal policy, and it directs the operations of the Internal Revenue Service, participating in all of its major policy decisions and actions, approving regulations, published rulings, and IRS forms, and assisting and cooperating on legal and legislative matters that affect the Revenue Service. These functions are carried out through the Office of the Assistant Secretary (Tax Policy).[24] This office, in turn, supervises the operations of the Office of the Tax Legislative Counsel, which provides legal and policy analysis and assistance on matters of domestic taxation, including formulating the administration's tax initiatives, commenting on tax proposals formulated by other executive departments, preparing testimony on domestic tax issues for presentation before congressional tax-writing committees, working with congressional staff in drafting language and legislative history, and assisting in the development of regulations, published rulings, and other administrative assistance.[25] Personnel in this office work closely with their counterparts in the IRS as regulations and rulings are developed.

It is during the budget process that the administrative decisions relating to specific legislative proposals are developed. Thus Code amendments relating to exempt organizations will only be developed within Treasury if they have been approved as part of the administration's annual budget. Outside events may, of course, require modification of the budget, but that would occur

21. Budget and Accounting Act of 1921, Pub. L. No. 67-13, §312, 42 Stat. 20, 25–26 (1921).

22. General Accounting Office, *Tax Policy: Competition between Taxable Business and Tax-Exempt Organizations* (GAO/GGD-87-40BR) (February 1987).

23. General Accounting Office, *Improvements in Public, IRS, and State Oversight of Charities.*

24. Treasury Directive 27-10 (October 15, 1990).

25. Id.

only in rare circumstances. This means that the public will know well in advance Treasury policy affecting the regulation and administration of charities.

Treasury review of regulations involves assuring that they are substantively correct, but the staff also looks to assure clarity and consistent style. Its review of published rulings is designed to ensure that they are substantively correct and are consistent with all relevant tax policy considerations. As noted in its official description, several hundred rulings are published each year. However, a substantial number of others referred initially to the Office of Tax Policy are not published after being questioned by Tax Legislative Counsel. It has been the custom to have one member of the staff of Tax Legislative Counsel responsible for exempt organization matters.[26]

Under the provisions of the 1998 restructuring of the Internal Revenue Service, its Chief Counsel reports exclusively to the General Counsel of the Treasury with respect to legal advice or interpretation of the tax law relating solely to tax policy, such as proposed legislation and international tax treaties.[27] However, he has dual reporting responsibilities, to the Commissioner of the Internal Revenue Service and the General Counsel of the Treasury, with respect to legal advice or interpretation of the tax law not relating solely to tax policy and tax litigation.[28] As explained in the House Conference Report accompanying the restructuring act, this would include drafting regulations, revenue rulings and revenue procedures, technical advice and other similar memoranda, private letter rulings, and other published guidance.[29] Personnel in the office of the IRS Chief Counsel report to him and not to other persons either at the IRS or at the Treasury.[30]

Promulgation of Regulations

There are four sources of law that determine the scope of a taxpayer's federal tax liability on any given matter—statutes, court decisions, regulations, and administrative rulings. Regulations are promulgated by the Treasury Department as Treasury Decisions, although they are originally prepared by the Service in cooperation with Treasury personnel. Tax regulations are specifically authorized by law and have the force and effect of law in the dealings of all taxpayers with the Treasury Department and the Service.[31]

Proposals for new Treasury regulations are first published in the Federal

---

26. Id.

27. I.R.C. §7803(b)(3)(B), codified by Internal Revenue Service Restructuring and Reform Act of 1998, Pub. L. No. 105-206, §1102(a), 112 Stat. 685, 698 (1998).

28. I.R.C. §7803(b).

29. H.R. Conf. Rep. No. 105-599, 105th Cong., 2d Sess., at 209 (1998).

30. I.R.C. §7803(b)(4).

31. I.R.C. §7805(a).

Register. A period of at least thirty days follows, during which interested parties may submit views, data, and arguments concerning the proposals. Final promulgation may occur immediately following the expiration of this thirty-day period, although in some cases the proposed regulations will be revised or republished. In the case of new laws or major revisions of existing provisions, it has become common practice for the Treasury Department to hold public hearings on the proposed regulations, affording interested members of the public the chance to present their views, and in some instances it has issued revised proposed regulations that have been submitted for further public comment. In addition, when the effective date of a tax act is close to or, as sometimes happens, has preceded passage of the legislation, the Treasury will issue temporary regulations containing immediate guidance on which taxpayers can rely pending issuance of proposed and final regulations. In many instances, particularly in the case of regulations that have been controversial, the Treasury may include preambles to proposed and, often, to final regulations, which adds useful elaboration of the evolution of the drafts and the Treasury response to public comments.

The importance of Treasury regulations cannot be overemphasized. They may be challenged by a taxpayer in a proceeding brought before the Tax Court or the Court of Claims to contest a deficiency, or in a suit for a refund in the federal district courts. Although they are not controlling on the courts, they may not be overruled unless the court finds that they are arbitrary or capricious, or contrary to the intent of Congress. Otherwise regulations have the same authority as law, binding on taxpayers and the Internal Revenue Service alike. Instructions on tax returns have the weight of regulations.

The authority of the Treasury Department to issue regulations is, in effect, a quasi-legislative power. It is a necessary adjunct to the taxing process and, when properly utilized, should keep litigation to a minimum. Following the intent of Congress is not always easy, however, and this has been particularly true of the regulations relating to the business activities of exempt organizations. Under the "organizational test,"[32] no more than an "insubstantial" amount of unrelated business activity may be permitted in the organization's charter or it will not qualify for exemption. However, the regulation defining the "operational test"[33] embodies both a primary activity test and an insubstantial activity test, whereas section 1.501(c)(3)-1(e) retains the primary purpose test, permitting substantial business operations in furtherance of exempt purposes if the primary purpose is not the carrying on of an unrelated trade or business.[34] This internal inconsistency in the regulations has created

---

32. Treas. Reg. §1.501(c)(3)-1(b)(iii).
33. Treas. Reg. §1.501(c)(3)-1(c).
34. Treas. Reg. §1.501(c)(3)-1(e).

problems for both the Service and tax-exempt organizations; yet without further congressional definition of the extent to which business activities should be permitted before exempt status may be denied, it is likely that the regulations will remain inconsistent.

Treasury Oversight of Published Rulings

The Treasury must approve the subject matter of rulings that will have precedential status before being developed by the Service. Each year representatives from the Service and the Office of Tax Policy develop a Priority Guidance Plan, also referred to as the Business Plan, which contains a list of those ruling areas that will receive priority for the forthcoming fiscal year. The plan for fiscal year 2002–2003 under the heading "Exempt Organizations" listed seven items that were to receive priority guidance. Five of these were holdovers from earlier Business Plans, including one on private foundation terminations, while two were new—guidance on joint ventures between exempt organizations and for-profit companies, and on the application of existing unrelated business income tax rules to Internet activities.[35] The plan for fiscal year 2003–2004 contained no major changes affecting organizations exempt under section 501(c)(3).[36]

The actual drafting of proposed revenue rulings and revenue procedures is undertaken within the Service, although there is close cooperation between Tax Legislative Counsel in the Treasury and Service personnel. No rulings may be issued, however, without specific approval by the Secretary of the Treasury.[37]

Treasury Inspector General for Tax Administration

Prior to the restructuring of the IRS in 1998 the Treasury Office of Inspector General was charged with conducting, supervising, and coordinating internal audits and investigations relating to all programs of the Treasury, including the Internal Revenue Service.[38] However, the actual internal investigations and internal audits of the Service were the responsibility of the Office of the Chief Inspector of the Service.[39] Under the restructuring the Office of the Chief Inspector was eliminated, and all of its powers and responsibilities were transferred to a newly established Treasury Inspector General for Tax Admin-

35. Notice 2002-22, 2002-14 I.R.B. 731.
36. Notice 2003-26, 2003-18 I.R.B. 885.
37. T.D.O. No. 111-2, 1981-1 C.B. 698.
38. Inspector General Act Amendments of 1988, Pub. L. No. 100-504, §102(f), 102 Stat. 2515, 2518–2520 (1988).
39. H.R. Conf. Rep. No. 105-599, 105th Cong., 2d Sess., at 218, 220 (1998).

istration, which operates in addition to and independent from the Treasury Inspector General.[40] The purpose was to provide the Service with greater insulation from political pressures and to do away with a situation in which the lines of authority between the Treasury and the Service were blurred.[41]

Treasury Department Antiterrorist Activities

After the terrorist attacks on September 11, 2001, the government seized the assets of a number of charitable organizations because of their financial ties to terrorist groups.[42] Court actions seeking release of the funds have not been successful, but there has been no public information indicating that there is to be a change in the tax-exempt status of the organizations.

In November 2002 the Treasury Department released an "Official Announcement" entitled "Treasury Guidelines to Prevent Diversion of Funds to Terrorists." The announcement contained what was described as a "voluntary set of best practices guidelines for U.S.-based charities to follow to reduce the likelihood that charitable funds will be diverted to finance terrorist activities."[43] In a separate press release, the Treasury Department reported that it had developed the guidelines at the request of Muslim groups concerned about future government action and faced with declining contributions.[44] Their formulation also included consultation with a number of exempt organizations that serve as watchdogs for charities that solicit contributions from the general public.

The content of the guidelines is described in Chapter 2. It was unclear from the announcement and the press release whether the Internal Revenue Service had participated in the preparation of the guidelines. Commentators thought it unlikely, in view of the fact that the text contained no cross-references to the Code and was recommending adoption as "voluntary" of certain provisions that are required of exempt charities. To that extent, the guidelines were seriously misleading, and further clarification would be needed.[45]

40. 5 U.S.C. §§2, 8D, 9, codified by Internal Revenue Service Restructuring and Reform Act of 1998, Pub. L. No. 105-206, §1103, 112 Stat. 685, 705–708 (1998).

41. H.R. Conf. Rep. No. 105-599, 105th Cong., 2d Sess., at 217–225 (1998).

42. Hanna Rosin, "U.S. Raids Offices of 2 Muslim Charities; Groups Accused of Funding Terror," *Washington Post*, December 16, 2001, at A28.

43. "U.S. Department of the Treasury Anti-Terrorist Financing Guidelines: Voluntary Best Practices for U.S.-Based Charities" (November 7, 2002).

44. Alan Cooperman, "In U.S., Muslims Alter Their Giving; Those Observing Islamic Tenet Want to Aid Poor but Fear Prosecution," *Washington Post*, December 7, 2002, at A1.

45. "Guidelines for Charities on Terrorist Funding May Be Costly, Impractical, Say EO Reps," 2002 *Tax Notes Today* 224-5 (November 20, 2002).

The Internal Revenue Service

Until the 1970s the Internal Revenue Service regulated tax-exempt charitable organizations as part of its regulation of all taxable entities. The Service itself was organized along functional lines with initial responsibility for determinations and audits located in district offices under a district director who reported to a regional commissioner. Agents who were specialized in exempt organization matters handled determinations and audits, but with performance measured in terms of revenue raised, many agents were reluctant to accept assignment in this area. Technical advice was provided within the Office of the Assistant Commissioner (Technical) at national headquarters where there were few, if any, exempt organization specialists.

In the course of drafting the Tax Reform Act of 1969, certain members of Congress recognized the large administrative task of dividing section 501(c)(3) organizations into private foundations and public charities and the added burden occasioned by the need to administer the new, complicated provisions applicable to private foundations. One response to the need for greater oversight was adoption of section 4940, imposing a 4% annual excise tax (later reduced to 2%) on the net investment income of all private foundations, in order that they would "share some of the burden of paying the cost of government, especially for more extensive and vigorous enforcement of the tax laws related to exempt organizations."[46] In operation, the tax produced substantial revenues, but none were allocated directly to staffing personnel dealing with exempt organizations.[47]

The Employee Retirement Income Security Act of 1974 (ERISA) included a major restructuring of the Internal Revenue Service designed to improve regulation of employee benefit plans and exempt organizations.[48] Oversight of these two areas of tax regulation was assigned to a separate office under an Assistant Commissioner for Employee Plans and Exempt Organizations (EP/EO). However, according to James McGovern, former Assistant Commissioner and Associate Chief Counsel for tax-exempt organizations, there were serious shortcomings with the organizational structure. He assigned the problem to the fact that, although the assistant commissioner had programmatic and budgetary authority over the EP/EO regulatory program, he had no authority to oversee personnel located outside of the Washington office who were responsible for delivering the program:

46. Joint Committee on Taxation, *General Explanation of Tax Reform Act of 1969* (JCS-16-70), 29 (December 3, 1970).

47. H.R. Conf. Rep. No. 105-599, 105th Cong., 2d Sess., at 210 (1998).

48. Employee Retirement Income Security Act of 1974, Pub. L. No. 93-406, §1051, 88 Stat. 829, 951–952 (1974).

For example, . . . EP/EO revenue agents who examined exempt entities reported to an EP/EO branch chief, who reported to an EP/EO division chief, who reported to a district director, who reported to a regional commissioner. Under this structure, the assistant commissioner (EP/EO) had no line authority over the revenue agents or their superiors who were responsible for delivering the EP/EO regulatory program. Similarly, the assistant commissioner had no authority over the service center directors or their employees who delivered the EP/EO program by processing EP/EO returns.[49]

Despite these shortcomings, the office of the assistant commissioner was credited with establishing education, outreach, and innovative voluntary compliance programs of great import.[50]

Beginning in 1997, a major effort was undertaken to restructure the tax administrative system with a stated aim of making the Service more responsive to the needs of the taxpayers. A preliminary step had been taken in 1995 with the establishment of a National Commission on Restructuring the Internal Revenue Service that was to last for one year.[51] The committee conducted twelve public hearings and over 500 private consultations. Its report, published in June 1997, called for structural changes in the IRS and increased congressional and executive branch oversight of its operations.[52] Bills containing provisions to carry out the recommendations were submitted to the House and Senate, and the House passed its version in November 1997.[53] Before the Senate completed work on the bill, the Finance Committee held a series of public hearings on the IRS in which serious allegations were made of abuse of taxpayers by IRS personnel. As summarized in a Congressional Research Service Report to Congress, dated March 22, 2001, on the Status of Restructuring and Reform at the opening of the 107th Congress, the hearings "effectively altered the tenor of the legislation, adding to measures to protect taxpayers."[54]

49. James J. McGovern, "The Tax Exempt and Government Entities Division—The Pathfinder," 27 *Exempt Organization Tax Review* 239, 243 (2000).

50. James J. McGovern and Phil Brand, "EP/EO—One of the Most Innovative and Efficient Functions within the IRS," 76 *Tax Notes* 1099 (August 25, 1997).

51. H.R. 2020, §637, Pub. L. No. 104-52, 104th Cong., 1st Sess. (1995).

52. National Commission on Restructuring the Internal Revenue Service, *A Vision for a New IRS* (June 25, 1997).

53. Internal Revenue Service Restructuring and Reform Act of 1997, H.R. 2676, 105th Cong., 1st Sess. (1997).

54. Congressional Research Service, *IRS: Status of Restructuring and Reform at the Opening of the 107th Congress* (March 22, 2001).

Regulation of Exempt Organizations in the Restructured IRS

The amended and expanded bill restructuring the IRS was enacted in July 1998.[55] It modified the IRS three-tiered geographical structure, which had divided the country into thirty-three districts, four regions, and ten service centers, each dealing with every taxpayer within the geographic division, regardless of the size or the complexity of the problem, and with all of these under the authority of the national office.[56] Instead, four operating divisions were established, each designed to meet all of the needs of a particular group of taxpayers: individual taxpayers; small businesses; large corporations; and tax-exempt entities. The Tax Exempt and Government Entities Operating Division (TE/GE) was placed in charge of an assistant commissioner, who was given direct authority over all personnel assigned to that division. TE/GE was divided into four segments: employee plans, exempt organizations, government entities, and customer account services.[57]

Another integral component of the restructuring was a shift from addressing taxpayer problems after returns are filed to addressing them early in the process. To accomplish this, interaction with taxpayers was divided into three parts: (1) prefiling: customer education and assistance, which includes forms, publications, a website, education programs, telephone assistance, published guidance, private letter rulings, and determination letters; (2) filing: customer account services, including processing returns, crediting payments, advising taxpayers of errors, answering inquiries about accounts, making corrections, abating penalties, and paying refunds; and (3) postfiling: compliance, which includes auditing returns, dealing with collections, handling appeals, litigation disputes, and detecting and investigating fraud.[58]

Also established within the exempt organization section were three subunits responsible for customer education and outreach, rulings and agreements, and examinations.[59] Prefiling strategy was assigned to Customer Education and Outreach, which would in effect be continuing many of the outreach efforts that had been adopted by EP/EO prior to the reorganization.[60] Its major task was to address the notable lack of published guidance that had been a matter of serious concern to the tax-exempt bar as well as

55. Internal Revenue Service Restructuring and Reform Act of 1998, Pub. L. No. 105-206, 112 Stat. 685 (1998).

56. Id., §1001, 112 Stat. at 689.

57. See generally Internal Revenue Service, *IRS Organization Blueprint* (2000); Charles O. Rossotti, *Modernizing America's Tax Agency*, IRS Publication 3349 (1999).

58. Rossotti, *Modernizing America's Tax Agency*, 15.

59. Internal Revenue Service, *IRS Organization Blueprint*, 5–14.

60. Id.

Service personnel for a number of years.[61] It reflected, in fact, a perennial problem for exempt organization enforcement, namely that precedence has historically been given and will continue to be given to regulation of taxable entities.[62]

The Rulings and Agreements subgroup would in turn have two components: issuance of determination letters, which were to be centrally processed in Cincinnati, and private letter rulings and technical advice memoranda, which would continue to be processed in Washington, D.C.[63] Strategies adopted prior to the restructuring that were designed to foster voluntary compliance were to be continued and enhanced. The major difficulty anticipated was the lack of technical personnel to staff adequately the national office. In large part this was due to the fact that EP/EO was created in 1974 as a separate IRS function and thus was the only technical function subjected to IRS downsizing.[64] There were no meaningful hiring initiatives in the Rulings and Agreements area during the 1990s, resulting in a significant attrition of experienced professionals, a situation that was exacerbated by virtue of the fact that EP/EO attorneys were not part of the Office of Chief Counsel and thereby not compensated on an equal basis with their counterparts within the Chief Counsel's office.[65]

The examination function is considered the heart of the postfiling strategy, with the majority of personnel in offices throughout the country assigned to this task. Under the reorganization this work was assigned to six geographic areas, which replaced four key district offices, each one under the direction of a separate director solely responsible for EO matters. An Exempt Organizations Examination Headquarters was also established in Dallas to maintain national uniformity and keep the examination selection process outside of Washington.[66] Lack of adequate staff was also a problem for the examination function. In a report issued in September 1997, the Joint Committee on Taxation observed that although the number of pension plans and exempt organizations more than doubled since the EP/EO division was created in 1974, and responsibility for regulation of tax-exempt bonds was added to its jurisdiction, its staffing remained essentially

61. Id.; see also Committee on Exempt Organizations, American Bar Association, "Comments on Compliance with the Tax Laws by Public Charities ('White Paper')," 10 *Exempt Organization Tax Review* 29 (1994).

62. McGovern, "The Tax Exempt and Government Entities Division—A Pathfinder," 244–246; Brian J. Menkes, "A Conversation with Evelyn Petschek," 25 *Exempt Organization Tax Review* 215 (1999).

63. Internal Revenue Service, *IRS Organization Blueprint*, 5–22.

64. McGovern, "The Tax Exempt and Government Entities Division—A Pathfinder," 246.

65. Id.

66. Internal Revenue Service, *IRS Organization Blueprint*, 5–27.

EP/EO staffing and budget authority

Fiscal year	Funded positions	President's budget authority ($ millions)
1975	2,075	N/A
1976	2,175	N/A
1977	2,202	N/A
1978	2,292	62.2
1979	1,945	64.1
1980	1,870	66.9
1981	1,738	68.9
1982	1,640	55.0
1983	1,770	80.8
1984	1,906	90.4
1985	1,902	94.3
1986	2,099	99.0
1987	2,311	104.9
1988	2,562	120.9
1989	2,573	125.8
1990	2,423	132.8
1991	2,336	132.3
1992	2,461	140.9
1993	2,331	143.1
1994	2,305	129.8
1995	2,304	132.5
1996	2,197	128.8
1997	2,112	132.5
1998	1,980	132.8
1999	1,989	138.1

Source: Internal Revenue Service.

unchanged.[67] Similar observations were made in March 2000 in another report from the Joint Committee,[68] and again in April 2002 in a report issued by the GAO.[69] The accompanying chart summarizes staffing and budget authority for fiscal years 1975 through 1999 contained in the Joint Committee's March 2000 report.

67. Joint Committee on Taxation, *Description and Analysis of Proposals Relating to the Recommendations of the National Commission on Restructuring the Internal Revenue Service on Executive Branch Governance and Congressional Oversight* (JCX-44-97), 60–62 (September 16, 1997).

68. Joint Committee on Taxation, *Report of Investigation of Allegations Relating to Internal Revenue Service Handling of Tax-Exempt Organization Matters* (JCS-3-00), 120–121 (March 2000).

69. General Accounting Office, *Improvements in Public, IRS, and State Oversight of Charities*, 23.

The restructuring included two other major components. First, all customer account services were to be centralized in the newly established TE/GE headquarters, thereby focusing functions related to filing in Ogden, Utah.[70] Previously, returns were filed at various service centers across the country where information returns such as Form 990 were considered low-priority work.[71] Second, a new position, the Operating Division Counsel, was established within the Office of Chief Counsel to provide legal advice to TE/GE from attorneys with expertise in exempt organization law.[72] McGovern characterized this as a "very significant change," aimed at ensuring a closer working relationship between legal counsel and the regulators, one that would encourage accountability.[73]

The revised structure for TE/GE was carried out in December 1999, the first of the new divisions to be established, and the former assistant commissioner of EP/EO was named as its head.[74] Prior to the restructuring, the Service had adopted a plan to centralize the determination function in a newly established office in Cincinnati. Shortage of personnel and funds delayed implementation, and the problem remained unresolved after the change. In response, personnel were shifted from the audit division to determinations, and the determinations function was again decentralized among agents across the country. The result was that personnel without experience in exempt organization matters were assigned to handle Form 1023 submissions, which resulted in bottlenecks in processing and inconsistencies in outcome. One reason for the continuing difficulty was that the grade structure for IRS personnel remained unchanged. This meant that there was lower promotion potential for personnel in determinations than for those in audit, making recruitment difficult, and there was no change in the amount of resources available to the Service to recruit additional personnel.

In an attempt to rectify the situation, the Service reassigned determination work, which had been conducted by personnel assigned and reporting to the Director of Examinations, to dedicated determination groups reporting to Rulings and Agreements. This initiative was given first priority in the fiscal year 2002 and 2003 lists of initiatives for the Office of the Director, Exempt Organizations, in the EO Implementing Guidelines for those years. Another initiative in the plans for both years was the redesign of the determination letter system to improve handling of determination

70. Internal Revenue Service, *IRS Organization Blueprint*, 5–15.

71. McGovern, "The Tax Exempt and Government Entities Division—A Pathfinder," 249–250.

72. Internal Revenue Service, *IRS Organization Blueprint* (1999, Phase IIA), 87–95.

73. McGovern, "The Tax Exempt and Government Entities Division—A Pathfinder," 250.

74. IRS News Release, IR-99-101 (December 12, 1999).

matters.[75] The Implementing Guidelines provide a blueprint for Service activities each year, and as such are important for the public as well as the Service. All of these developments are illustrative of the difficulties inevitably encountered in effecting major changes within a large bureaucracy, particularly for a branch with specialized functions and goals that do not fit easily within the framework of the larger entity.

Role of IRS Counsel

The Chief Counsel is the chief law officer of the IRS, appointed by the President with the advice and consent of the Senate.[76] His duties and powers are prescribed by the Secretary of the Treasury and include acting as legal advisor to the Commissioner, furnishing legal opinions for the preparation and review of rulings and technical advice memoranda, participating in the preparation of proposed legislation, treaties, regulations, and executive orders relating to laws that affect the Service, representing the Commissioner in cases before the Tax Court, determining which civil actions should be litigated, and preparing recommendations for the Department of Justice, which will do the actual prosecution.[77]

As noted, the 1998 reorganization called for establishment of a new position within the Office of Chief Counsel in Washington, the Operating Division Counsel, who would provide legal advice and representation to TE/GE. The person holding this position reports to the Chief Counsel, but is "co-located" within and operates in partnership with the TE/GE division and participates in its planning and management. The Office of the Operating Chief Counsel is assigned twenty-five trial attorneys who are located in four cities, as well as specialists in Washington. This arrangement brought legal counsel into closer relationship with the regulatory staff than previously, a change that it was thought would bring accountability to the relationship.[78]

Two years after establishment of the TE/GE division, the director of the EO division, Steven T. Miller, listed as the challenges facing the organization the need to reorganize the determination process again and to develop an e-filing program for Form 990. The handling of determinations was hampered by a disparity between workload and budget allocations. Exemption applica-

---

75. Exempt Organizations Division, Internal Revenue Service, *Exempt Organizations (EO) Implementing Guidelines (FY 2002)*, 14 (October 2001); Exempt Organizations Division, Internal Revenue Service, *Exempt Organizations (EO) Implementing Guidelines (FY 2003)*, 26–32 (September 2002).

76. I.R.C. §7803(b)(1).

77. I.R.C. §7803(b)(2).

78. Internal Revenue Service, *IRS Organization Blueprint* (1999 Phase IIA), 87–95.

tions rose from 52,000 in 1990 to 86,000 in 2001, while the plan to centralize operations in Cincinnati had not been fully carried out due to serious
understaffing. The shift of personnel from examinations to determinations
"gave rise to a perception that the Service is not out there looking, which impedes voluntary compliance," according to Miller.[79]

Commissioner's Advisory Committee on Tax-Exempt and Government Entities

In July 1999, as an important component of the restructuring, the Service
announced that it was creating a Tax-Exempt Advisory Committee to provide an organized public forum for the IRS and representatives of the customer groups that fall within the jurisdiction of the TE/GE division, namely
employee plans, tax-exempt organizations, tax-exempt bonds, and state, local, and tribal governments. There were to be eighteen members who would
be appointed by the Secretary of the Treasury to serve two-year terms, and
the Service requested nominations from the public. Under the Federal Advisory Committee Act, the Advisory Committee is required to hold public
meetings when it presents its advice to the IRS, and the date of its meetings
must be announced in the Federal Register at least fifteen days prior to the
meeting.[80]

The members of the Committee were announced in May 2001. The six
members of its subunit on exempt organizations included the chairman of
the Exempt Organization Committee of the Tax Section of the American Bar
Association, the director of the Pennsylvania Bureau of Charitable Organizations, and representatives of Independent Sector, the U.S. Catholic Conference, the Academic Health Center at the University of Michigan, and the
Heritage Foundation.[81] In May 2003 new members were appointed to fill va-
cancies due to rotation. Among them were two from exempt organizations,
one from a trade association and the other from a large foundation.[82]

The Committee held an orientation meeting in June 2001,[83] and in August the Service announced that it was renewing the Committee's charter
and changing its name to the Advisory Committee on Tax-Exempt and Government Entities to more accurately reflect its membership and purpose.[84]

---

79. Carolyn Wright LaFon and Christine J. Harris, "EO Division Faces Challenges Two Years
into Reorganization," 35 *Exempt Organization Tax Review* 16 (2002).

80. 64 Fed. Reg. 39,558 (1999).

81. IRS News Release, IR-2001-50 (May 8, 2001).

82. IRS News Release, IR-2003-62 (May 7, 2003).

83. IRS News Release, IR-2001-63 (July 16, 2001).

84. 66 Fed. Reg. 52,655 (2001).

The first public meeting of the Advisory Committee was held in June 2002, at which five project teams presented recommendations to the division commissioner and the senior leadership of the division. The projects relating to tax-exempt organizations covered the life cycle of a public charity, TE/GE external communication and outreach, and voluntary correction programs.[85] A second meeting was held on May 21, 2003, at which recommendations were made for improving the determinations process and for regulating abusive tax shelters involving tax-exempt organizations.[86]

Components of IRS Regulation

Revenue Rulings and Revenue Procedures

These are guidelines issued by the Internal Revenue Service to interpret the Code and the regulations, with revenue rulings dealing with points of law and revenue procedures providing rules of procedure for dealing with the Service.[87] They have the force of law, thereby binding the Service, but are subject to court review, which may find them overly broad or in rare cases unconstitutional. Revenue procedures issued annually at the start of the year set forth administrative rules governing issuance of determination letters and rules and information letters, as well as the procedural rules to be followed in order to obtain technical advice.[88] A persistent criticism of the Service since the 1990s has been the paucity of published rulings, a failing that Service personnel acknowledged, attributing it to lack of trained staff, which in turn was attributed to lack of funds and the hiring freeze that existed in the 1990s.[89] It was not uncommon for issues needing guidance to appear on the Priority Guidance Plan as rollovers for a number of years. Following the restructuring of the Service, a concerted effort was made to speed up the process, and, in fact, during 2002 the number of published rulings increased substantially, although five items remained as carryovers from prior years.[90]

---

85. *Report of the Advisory Committee on Tax Exempt and Government Entities (ACT)* (June 21, 2002).

86. *Report of the Advisory Committee on Tax Exempt and Government Entities (ACT)* (May 21, 2003).

87. 26 C.F.R. §601.201.

88. Rev. Proc. 2003-8, 2003-1 I.R.B. 236.

89. Committee on Exempt Organizations, American Bar Association, "Comments on Compliance with the Tax Laws by Public Charities ('White Paper')," 10 *Exempt Organization Tax Review* 29 (1994).

90. Department of Treasury and Internal Revenue Service, *2002–2003 Priority Guidance Plan* (July 10, 2002).

Information Releases and Notices

The IRS may also from time to time issue notices and announcements that also have the force of law. These are published permanently in the Cumulative Bulletin. Releases of this type will include requests for comments on proposed revisions to the Code or regulations, and contents of information returns or changes in policy, such as a decision made in 1999 to discontinue attempts to litigate the application of the unrelated business income tax to income from affinity credit cards and mailing lists.[91] The minutes of the June 21, 2002 meeting of the Advisory Committee on Tax-Exempt and Government Entities listed in an inventory of materials published by the EO division seven existing publications, five in process, and three in the planning stage.[92] The most recent was Publication 1828, Tax Guide for Churches and Religious Organizations, which became widely available the following August.[93]

Also available to the public are the Internal Revenue Manual and annual Continuing Professional Education texts prepared for IRS personnel, but used widely by practitioners. The IRS has also held regional conferences to educate exempt organizations and professionals on the intricacies of the tax practice in this specialized area. In the mid-1970s this was a major focus of the EO branch, one which subsequently lapsed primarily because of budget constraints, but was revived after the restructuring under a newly created Office of the Director, EO Customer Education and Outreach, which was charged with developing nationwide programs to promote voluntary compliance.[94] During fiscal year 2002, it planned to conduct one-day conferences for small and mid-sized organizations, plus a jointly held conference with charity officials in conjunction with the National Association of Attorneys General and the National Association of State Charity Officials, as well as "Issue Conferences" that would focus on technical issues relating to health care organizations and colleges and universities.[95]

Private Letter Rulings, General Counsel Memoranda, and Technical Advice Memoranda

Certain determinations issued by the Service are considered "private" in the sense that they are not precedential and they may not be cited as legal

91. 26 C.F.R. §601.201.

92. Mary Beth Braitman et al., "TE/GE Education and Outreach," in *Report of the Advisory Committee on Tax Exempt and Government Entities (ACT)*, Table V (June 21, 2002).

93. Internal Revenue Service, Publication 1828.

94. Exempt Organizations Division, Internal Revenue Service, *Exempt Organizations (EO) Implementing Guidelines (FY 2003)*, 19 (September 2002).

95. Id. at 19–24.

authority.[96] Prior to passage of the Freedom of Information Act in 1966, they were literally private, available only to the organization or individual to which they applied and to Service and Treasury personnel.[97] Their availability has been of far-reaching importance in changing the methods by which the Service handles all matters. Private letter rulings are issued in response to written questions submitted to the IRS by organizations and individuals seeking guidance on the tax effect of contemplated transactions.[98] In some instances, such as the provisions in section 4945(g) restricting private foundation grants to individuals, whereby grants can be made only after advance approval of a grant program by the Service, that approval will be issued in the form of a private letter ruling. Technical advice memoranda, in contrast, are rulings provided by the national office to a district office on questions as to which the district personnel seek guidance. General counsel memoranda are provided by the Office of Chief Counsel of the Service to personnel in the national office seeking legal guidance in preparing responses to requests for private letter rulings or technical advice. They relate in almost all instances to new issues as to which there is no precedential guidance. They are reviewed closely by practitioners seeking insight as to the Service's approach to controversial matters.

Limits on Disclosure of IRS Actions

Disclosure of IRS actions is governed under Code sections 6103, 6104, and 6110, and the Freedom of Information Act. The general rule is found in section 6103, which provides that tax returns and return information generally are not subject to public disclosure, and the word "return" is interpreted broadly in the Code to include

> any tax or information return, declaration of estimated tax, or claim for refund required by, or provided or permitted under, the provisions of this title which is filed by the Secretary by, on behalf of, or with respect to any person, and any amendment or supplement thereto, including supporting schedules, attachments, or lists which are supplemental to, or part of, the return so filed.[99]

Section 6104 contains an exception to section 6103 for returns from exempt organizations.[100] It was enacted in recognition that privacy accorded to individuals and corporations was not appropriate for these entities. Accordingly,

96. Treas. Reg. §301.6110-2(a).
97. 5 U.S.C. §552, codified by Act of July 4, 1966, Pub. L. No. 89-487, 80 Stat. 250 (1966).
98. Rev. Proc. 2003-8, 2003-1 I.R.B. 236, contains the schedule of fees for ruling requests.
99. I.R.C. §6103(b)(1).
100. I.R.C. §6104(d).

exemption to the confidentiality rule is allowed for approved applications for tax-exempt status, certain related documents, and annual information returns in unredacted form.[101] In addition, under section 6110, written determinations and related background files are open to public inspection in redacted form.[102] However, this section does not apply to matters covered by section 6104.[103]

The Freedom of Information Act, which applies to all government agencies, gives any person a right of access to federal agency records that are not protected from disclosure by one of nine exemptions or one of three special law enforcement record exclusions.[104] The question of whether section 6103 is one of the nine exemptions has been the subject of much litigation, and there are no clear-cut rules as to when it applies. Thus an IRS decision as to whether an organization was a private foundation was not subject to disclosure.[105]

Members of the general public can upon written request inspect an organization's Form 990 and related documents at the national office or in the district director's office.[106] The Secretary of the Treasury can deny public access to particular documents if disclosure would harm the organization or the national defense.[107] Organizations, however, can appeal an adverse determination of availability.[108] These rules apply to any papers submitted in support of Form 1023 by the organization, but not to papers submitted by other individuals.[109] Under section 6110, the text of any written determination and background file documents are also open to public inspections.[110] There has been controversy over whether "written determination" applies to rulings, determination letters, and settlement agreements (termed "closing agreement") under IRS procedure. As noted in a Joint Committee report, "In fiscal year 1999, the IRS finalized 78 closing agreements with section 501(c) organizations; in fiscal year 1998, the IRS finalized 72 closing agreements with section 501(c) organizations; and in fiscal year 1997, the IRS finalized 65 closing agreements with section 501(c) organizations."[111]

101. I.R.C. §§6104(a), 6104(d).
102. I.R.C. §6110(a)–(c).
103. I.R.C. §6110(l).
104. 5 U.S.C. §552.
105. Breuhaus v. IRS, 609 F.2d 80 (2d Cir. 1979); Belisle v. Commissioner, 462 F. Supp. 460 (W.D. Okla. 1978).
106. Treas. Reg. §301.6104(a)-6(b)(1).
107. I.R.C. §6104(a)(1)(D); Treas. Reg. §301.6104(a)-5.
108. Id.
109. Leherfeld v. Commissioner, 132 F.3d 1463 (D.C. Cir. 1998).
110. I.R.C. §6110(a).
111. Joint Committee on Taxation, *Study of Disclosure Provisions Relating to Tax-Exempt Organizations* (JCS-1-00), 38 n.97 (January 28, 2000).

As noted, the IRS interprets these provisions as excluding from disclosure any ruling denying exemption or revoking or modifying a prior exemption determination as well as technical advice relating to such actions, any letter rulings or documents relating to private foundation status, and any other ruling that, although relating to tax-exempt status, does not relate to an application for tax exemption.[112] In August 2002 the United States District Court for the District of Columbia upheld the Service's position, holding that the Freedom of Information Act did not extend to letter rulings denying or revoking exemption on the basis that they were not written determinations governed by section 6110, but rather constituted return information protected under section 6103.[113] The staff of the Joint Committee on Taxation in its 2002 report on disclosure had recommended that any action on an application for exemption should be disclosed.[114]

Another group of IRS actions that are not within the sweep of the Freedom of Information Act provisions includes closing agreements. These are documents memorializing the settlement of disputes between the Service and organizations and individuals that the parties have agreed to terminate without resort to the courts, or to further litigation in the case of disputes that have reached a lower court.[115] Three such matters involving questions of widespread import were settled in the late 1990s. The first related to the Church of Scientology. The second involved the United Cancer Council, and the third dealt with the revocation of tax exemption of the Bishop Estate. The texts of the closing agreements with the Church of Scientology and the trustees of the Bishop Estate were obtained by and reported in the press,[116] while the attorney for the United Cancer Council made public the terms of that settlement.[117] In contrast, in litigation involving a hospital, one of the conditions imposed by the IRS was that the terms of the settlement be made public.[118] In 1999 a tax-exempt organization sought unsuccessfully to force

112. Treas. Reg. §301.6104(a)-1(i).

113. Tax Analysts v. IRS, 2002 WL 1969317 (D.D.C. 2002).

114. Joint Committee on Taxation, *Disclosure Provisions Relating to Tax-Exempt Organizations*, 86–87.

115. 26 C.F.R. §601.202; see also *1993 IRS Continuing Professional Education Text*, 263–293.

116. "Scientologists and IRS Settled for $12.5 Million," *Wall Street Journal*, December 30, 1997, at A12; "Closing Agreement between IRS and Church of Scientology," 97 *Tax Notes Today* 251-24 (December 31, 1997); "Bishop Estate Settles Revocation Issues through Closing Agreement," 1999 *Tax Notes Today* 235-20 (December 8, 1999).

117. "United Cancer Council Closing Agreement Released," 2000 *Tax Notes Today* 75-12 (April 18, 2000).

118. "Hermann Hospital Closing Agreement Released," 94 *Tax Notes Today* 203-59 (October 17, 1994).

the IRS to release the texts of these agreements.[119] The Joint Committee on Taxation in its January 2000 report on disclosure had recommended that all closing agreements with exempt organizations be made available to the public without redaction, a recommendation that was not universally approved by the bar and was opposed by the Service.[120]

Department of Justice and the Solicitor General

Litigation on tax matters is bifurcated under the federal system. The Tax Division in the Department of Justice handles all civil litigation arising under the revenue laws other than those that are filed in the Tax Court. Thus attorneys from the Justice Department represent the IRS in suits for refunds in the federal district courts and the Court of Federal Claims, as well as in criminal tax prosecutions and all civil and criminal appeals, even if they were initiated in the Tax Court, as is the case in civil suits.

The civil trial work is performed by the Civil Trial Section in six regional trial sections as well as by the Court of Federal Claims Section.[121] An Appellate Section has the responsibility for making recommendations as to whether Tax Court and district court cases should be appealed, for handling cases in the Circuit Courts of Appeals, and for preparing recommendations for the Solicitor General as to whether an appeal should be taken to the Supreme Court.[122]

The Solicitor General has final say on all appeals to the circuits as well as to the Supreme Court. Litigation before the United States Supreme Court is supervised and conducted by the Office of the Solicitor General, which determines the cases in which review will be sought and the positions the government will take before the Court.[123]

In September 2002 the Fraud Section of the Criminal Division of the Department of Justice took an unusual step, issuing a special report on possible fraud schemes being conducted by organizations soliciting donations for victims of terrorist attacks. The announcement called attention to the fact that it was a federal crime to falsely solicit as a charity or to engage in mail fraud, wire fraud, or credit card fraud, and requested the public to report possible

---

119. Tax Analysts v. IRS, 53 F. Supp. 2d 449 (D.D.C. 1999).

120. Joint Committee on Taxation, *Disclosure Provisions Relating to Tax-Exempt Organizations*, 84–86.

121. Internal Revenue Manual (IRM) 35.16.2, available at *www.irs.gov/irm/index.html;* see also 28 U.S.C. §§516–519.

122. IRM 35.16.2.7.

123. IRM 35.16.2.3.

fraudulent schemes to the Federal Trade Commission. It concluded with a list of appropriate donee organizations.[124]

The Tax Division of the Department of Justice is also charged with assisting in the formulation of legislative and administrative policy in matters that may be the subject of litigation.[125]

The Courts

Private organizations and individuals have a right to appeal to the courts from decisions of the Internal Revenue Service in several ways, any of which may be determined by a number of factors, including the desirability of a jury trial, assessment of the familiarity of the court with the issues involved, and often whether it is feasible to pay the tax before suit or wait for the court's decision. There are two paths available to charities, one that is afforded to all taxpayers, the second unique to tax-exempt organizations.

Judicial Remedies Available Universally

Taxpayers and all tax-exempt organizations have two methods for seeking recourse in the courts once they have exhausted their administrative remedies within the Service. One requires paying any tax that has been assessed, filing a claim for a refund, and, if it is denied, filing suit for a refund in a district court or the Court of Federal Claims.[126] The second entails filing suit in the Tax Court.[127] Under the first alternative, the suit requesting a refund may be subject to the same administrative procedure that follows an unfavorable audit decision, namely, opportunity for an informal conference, receipt of a thirty-day letter, filing of a formal protest, an appellate division conference if desired, and issuance of the statutory notice of claim disallowance (a second, ninety-day, letter). However, if the Service takes no action for six months following receipt of a refund claim, a court petition may be filed without waiting for the ninety-day letter. The appeal may be to either a federal district court or the Court of Federal Claims. If it is to the district court, there is a right to a jury trial. Cases brought before the district court or the Court of Federal Claims are tried by the attorneys in the Tax Division of the Department of Justice.

The second method of appeal, which requires no advance payment of tax,

124. *www.usdoj.gov/criminal/fraud/.*
125. U.S. Department of Justice, *United States Attorneys' Manual,* Title 6.
126. I.R.C. §7422; 28 U.S.C. §§1346(a)(1), 1491.
127. I.R.C. §6213.

is to initiate suit in the Tax Court, an independent administrative board that functions as a court in all respects.[128] Suits in the Tax Court are handled by the legal staff of the Internal Revenue Service.[129] Cases must be filed in the Tax Court within ninety days of receipt of notice of deficiency, unless the organization has not already gone to appeals or received technical advice, in which case it can request transfer to appeals for settlement consideration.[130]

Declaratory Judgment Procedure on Denial or Loss of Exemption

Prior to 1976 an organization that was denied a determination of exempt status or was threatened with revocation of exemption had no effective method of appealing the Service's decision. The only available remedies entailed assessment of a tax deficiency or disallowance of a contribution deduction. Charities were forced to find some way to incur tax liability, whether income or, before 1983, FICA or FUTA tax, and even when this was possible, it entailed a delay of several years. Alternatively, donors whose deductions for contributions to the organization were denied could sue for refund or challenge the Service action in the Tax Court, but again this was a lengthy, expensive procedure and required a cooperative donor. It was also possible for the organization to operate as if it were tax-exempt for a year, hope to attract an audit by the Service, and, upon assessment of tax, file in the Tax Court or claim a refund in the Federal Court of Claims, neither of which afforded an expeditious remedy.

In two important cases decided in 1974 the Supreme Court, while holding that declaratory judgment suits were precluded under existing law, suggested that the situation should be remedied by statute.[131] In response to these decisions, and bolstered by the lobbying effort of a number of exempt organizations, Congress enacted section 7428 of the Code as part of the Tax Reform Act of 1976.[132] It authorized the Tax Court, the United States District Court for the District of Columbia, and the United States Court of Federal Claims to render declaratory judgments on determinations relating to the status of charities under section 501(c)(3), issues relating to charitable contribution

---

128. I.R.C. §7441.

129. I.R.C. §7452.

130. I.R.C. §6213(a).

131. Bob Jones University v. Simon, 416 U.S. 725 (1974); Alexander v. "Americans United," Inc., 416 U.S. 752 (1974).

132. I.R.C. §7428, codified by Tax Reform Act of 1976, Pub. L. No. 94-455, §1306(a), 90 Stat. 1520, 1717–1720 (1976).

deductions, and qualification as private foundations, private operating foundations, or public charities.[133]

Under the provisions of section 7428, recourse to the courts is available only after the organization has pursued all administrative remedies available to it within the IRS, or has appealed a proposed adverse ruling in cases involving exemption applications in which the national office had original jurisdiction.[134] Thus organizations are required to demonstrate that they have filed a substantially completed Form 1023, submitted all additional information requested by the Service in a timely fashion, and pursued appeal within the Service.[135] However, the statute imposes a time limit on the Service of 270 days within which it must issue a notice of final determination. If the IRS has not done so and if the organization has taken all reasonable steps to obtain the ruling or determination, it may then initiate a suit for declaratory judgment.[136]

The Tax Court has adopted procedural rules applicable to declaratory judgment suits under which, except in rare circumstances, it will rely solely on the administrative record and not accept additional evidence in a trial de novo.[137] The other courts with jurisdiction over declaratory judgment cases have adopted these rules on a case-by-case basis. The effect of these procedural rules is to make the administrative record that is compiled during the IRS appeals process all-important, a matter that is within the power of the charity to control.

A key aspect of the declaratory judgment procedure for new organizations is a provision under which, if the issue being litigated is revocation of an existing exemption determination, contributions to the organization not exceeding $1,000 made while the matter is being litigated will continue to be deductible until a final court decision is rendered, even if the decision is adverse to the organization.[138]

Appellate Courts

Decisions of the district courts may be appealed to the United States Circuit Court of Appeals for the circuit in which the district court is located.[139] Ap-

---

133. I.R.C. §7428(a).
134. I.R.C. §7428(b)(2).
135. Rev. Proc. 90-27, §12, 1990-1 C.B. 514; 26 C.F.R. §601.201(n)(7).
136. I.R.C. §7428(b)(2).
137. Rules of Practice and Procedure, U.S. Tax Court, Title XXI, Rule 217(a).
138. I.R.C. §7428(c)(2).
139. 28 U.S.C. §1291.

peals from the Tax Court are made to the circuit in which the organization's principal place of business is located.[140] Decisions of the Court of Federal Claims may be appealed only to the United States Court of Appeals for the Federal Circuit.[141]

If the Commissioner loses a case in the Tax Court and decides not to appeal, he may announce whether he will "acquiesce" in the decision. A decision to acquiesce means that the Service has accepted the legal interpretation made by the court as the correct one to be followed in future cases.[142] This may require amendment of the regulations, and notification of acquiescence often signals such a change. A notification of nonacquiescence, on the other hand, indicates that the Service does not concur in the court's interpretation and that future cases on the same issue may be brought to determine if the Tax Court will change its mind, or that an appeal may be later taken from a similar decision to the circuit court.[143]

The Commissioner is not bound to acquiesce in a single decision of the circuit court. If decisions in two circuits are conflicting, the Commissioner can appeal to the Supreme Court, which is likely to decide the issue. The grounds on which a Court of Appeals may overrule the Tax Court or a district court are that there was no opportunity for a fair hearing, insufficient evidence was presented to support the lower court's finding, or the lower court erred in its interpretation of the statute or the Constitution.

In 1999, following defeat in seven out of eight court cases dealing with the issue of whether the income from rental of mailing lists and affinity credit card arrangements is subject to the tax on unrelated business income, the Service announced in a memorandum to exempt organization area managers that they should not litigate similar cases and should resolve outstanding ones in a manner consistent with the existing court decisions. The memorandum described language in one of the cases indicating an alternative argument that was not made by the Service in the litigated cases, thus suggesting that this issue remained under consideration.[144] This situation is one in which an acquiescence might have been expected or could still be made.

Final appeal to the Supreme Court is not a matter of right, but is subject to its decision to grant certiorari to hear a particular case.[145] Generally, certiorari will be granted only in cases raising issues on which there is a conflict of statu-

---

140. I.R.C. §7482(b)(1).
141. 28 U.S.C. §1295(a)(3).
142. IRM 35.12.1.1.
143. Id.
144. Memorandum from Director, Exempt Organizations Division, to Acting EO Area Managers (December 16, 1999).
145. I.R.C. §7482(a); see also 28 U.S.C. §1254.

tory interpretation among the circuits, a substantial constitutional issue, or a question deemed to be of great public interest. The cases of *Bob Jones University v. United States*[146] and *Regan v. Taxation With Representation of Washington*,[147] both decided in 1983, are the most far-reaching decisions affecting charities decided by the Court in the latter part of the twentieth century.

Tax Regulation in Operation

Determinations of Exemption (Form 1023)

A new charitable organization seeking a determination that it is exempt from income tax by virtue of being described in section 501(c)(3) of the Code and eligible to receive contributions that are deductible for income, estate, and gift tax purposes must file Form 1023 with the Service. If filed within twenty-seven months from the date the organization was created, tax exemption will be retroactive to that date. If filed after that period, it will be effective on the date the determination is issued.[148] Form 1024 is used for organizations seeking exemption under section 501(c)(4).

Among the materials a charity must submit are certified copies of founding documents, statements describing the purposes and the manner in which the organization will carry out those purposes, the names of directors, officers, and trustees, and their projected compensation, if any, the relationship of the organization to any predecessor organizations and to other existing organizations, and actual financial data for years of operation or estimates for at least two future years—all designed to determine whether it will meet the operational test. If the organization is asserting that it is not a private foundation or will be a private operating foundation, it is also required to demonstrate that it will meet the tests for the appropriate categories, including financial data to support its status as a publicly supported organization.[149] Finally, there are nine schedules supporting compliance, with separate requirements for churches, schools, colleges, and universities, hospitals and medical research organizations, supporting organizations, private operating foundations, homes for the aged or disabled, child-care organizations, organizations providing scholarships, and successors to for-profit organizations.[150] In the fall of 2002, the Service released a draft revision of Form 1023 and requested

146. 461 U.S. 574 (1983).

147. 461 U.S. 540 (1983).

148. Treas. Reg. §1.508-1(a)(2)(i).

149. 26 C.F.R. §601.201(n); see also Internal Revenue Service, Publication 557, *Tax-Exempt Status for Your Organization*.

150. Form 1023, Schedules A through I.

public comments on it.[151] The changes were designed to make it more understandable and more easily adaptable for electronic filing.

As noted, until the early 1990s, applications for exemption were processed in the districts, unless they appeared to present novel or difficult issues, in which case they were sent to the national office for processing.[152] As of October 1997 all Forms 1023 (and Form 1024 for organizations seeking exemption under other sections of section 501(c)) are sent to Covington, Kentucky, or handled in the neighboring IRS office in Cincinnati.[153] Unless they require national office consideration, they are processed where received or forwarded to other regional offices.

It is not unusual for the examining agent assigned to process an application for exemption to contact the organization if he has additional questions, either by phone or mail. The Service has developed a number of form letters that are sent to elicit additional information, particularly in instances in which special requirements are imposed on the organization, such as those applicable to scholarship funds or schools.[154]

The GAO Report on Oversight of Charities, issued in April 2002, contained a detailed description of the procedures involved in handling exemption applications. It noted that the Service notifies organizations that the determinations process may take up to 120 days, but that the average time to approve an application was then 91 days. An expedited procedure has been available since 1994 for situations in which time is of the essence, such as disaster relief and emergency hardship programs. In those instances the revenue agent assigned to the case has the discretion to grant the request. The report stated that from September 11, 2001, to March 20, 2002, the IRS approved 262 applications for disaster relief organizations under the expedited processing, with an average time of seven days for processing.[155]

In addition to determining eligibility for tax exemption, Form 1023 also requires information sufficient to establish whether an organization is a private foundation as defined in section 509(a). Detailed information is required to establish qualification, and for organizations claiming public charity status on the basis of support from the general public, estimates of the extent of public support must be provided.[156] For these organizations, the determination is provisional, conditioned on their qualifying during an advance rul-

151. Ann. 2002-92, 2002-41 I.R.B. 709; Ann. 2002-103, 2002-45 I.R.B. 836.

152. 26 C.F.R. §601.201(n)(1)(i).

153. Ann. 97-89, 1997-36 I.R.B. 10.

154. IRM 7.4.

155. General Accounting Office, *Improvements in Public, IRS, and State Oversight of Charities,* 55–61.

156. I.R.C. §509(a)(1)-(2); §170(b)(1)(a)(vi).

ing period that will terminate five years after the date of organization. At that time they will receive from the service Form 8734, in which they must establish compliance with the applicable support tests. In August 2003 the Treasury Inspector General for Tax Administration issued a report evaluating the advance ruling follow-up process used to determine whether an organization had met the support tests to qualify as a public charity under section 509. Noting that it was inefficient, required information that duplicated data on Form 990, and that the IRS computer system did not always contain accurate information on the status of organizations that were reclassified during the process, the Inspector General recommended changes that it was claimed would reduce the number of personnel and make compliance easier.[157]

The advance ruling procedure has also caused administrative difficulties, a large number due to the fact that small organizations do not file the annual Form 990 or 990EZ, the information form, and it is not clear from the record whether they have not received the form, are no longer in existence, or have merely failed to respond. The situation is part of a larger problem that the Service has experienced in attempting to keep track of organizations that have filed Form 1023 but do not need to file annual returns because they do not meet the $25,000 gross receipts filing threshold. In 2002 Service representatives announced that they were looking at the problem and questioned particularly whether with electronic filing there was a need for an advance ruling period altogether, particularly in light of the fact that the support schedules are part of Schedule A of Form 990, which is filed annually.[158]

A special determination procedure permits the issuance of a group ruling to a central organization that acts as parent to a group of subsidiary organizations that are under its general supervision or control. The organizations that are part of the network must be exempt under the same paragraph of section 501(c)(3), although not necessarily the same one as that of the parent; they cannot be private foundations or foreign organizations; and they must have the same accounting period as the parent. Organizations participating in a group ruling must have an organizing document, although not necessarily articles of organization as a corporation, setting forth their affiliation with the parent, and must have agreed in writing to be included in the application for the group exemption. These subordinate organizations may, but are not required to, file separate information returns, so long as all information as to

157. Treasury Inspector General for Tax Administration, Department of Treasury, *The Tax Exempt and Government Entities Division Could Improve the Efficiency of Its Advance Ruling Follow-Up Process*, No. 2003-10-141 (August 2003).

158. "Roundtable Discussion with Tom Miller, Marc Owens, and Celia Roady," 7 *EO Tax Journal* 11, 17 (February 2002).

their finances and activities is reported to the Service as part of the parent's information return.[159]

Concern was expressed in 2002 with the possibility that some organizations were abusing the group ruling process by requesting its application to entities such as controlled hospital systems and limited liability companies with exempt and nonexempt members. The matter was placed on the "two-year" list of the IRS/Treasury Priority Guidance Plan for fiscal year 2002, a recognition of the Service's concern.[160]

A user fee must accompany Form 1023. Under the fee schedule in effect in 2002, the amount was $465 for organizations with gross receipts of more than $10,000, and $150 if the annual receipts were less. The fee for other ruling requests by exempt organizations in 2002 was $1,775, unless the organization's gross receipts were less than $150,000, in which event the fee was $500.[161]

Although there is no published precedent, the Service has taken the position than once an organization has received a determination of exemption, it cannot be relinquished voluntarily.[162] The legal basis for this conclusion is not explicit in the Code, the regulations, or the rulings, but as of the end of 2002 it had not been challenged.[163] Hill and Mancino compare the Service's position to that of the state attorneys general who impose a charitable trust on the assets of an organization formed for charitable purposes.[164] However, it is the law of trusts that protects in perpetuity property donated for charitable purposes, in contrast to the federal tax laws that afford no such protection and under which exemption can be revoked.

Given the unprecedented number of exemption applications filed in 2001 and 2002 and the paucity of trained personnel to process them, some commentators have suggested modifying the exemption process to permit attorneys or accountants to certify on Form 1023 that the organization is entitled to exemption. The suggestion did not receive widespread support in large part because the percentage of organizations represented by counsel who would be qualified to make the representation was relatively small and undoubtedly also due to the reluctance of professionals to take on the potential liability entailed in making such a representation.

159. Rev. Proc. 80-27, 1980-1 C.B. 677.

160. "Roundtable Discussion with Tom Miller, Marc Owens, and Celia Roady," 14; Department of Treasury and Internal Revenue Service, *2002–2003 Priority Guidance Plan* (July 10, 2002).

161. Rev. Proc. 2003-8, 2003-1 I.R.B. 236.

162. Priv. Ltr. Rul. 91-41-050 (July 16, 1991).

163. Gen. Couns. Mem. 37,165 (June 14, 1997); Priv. Ltr. Rul. 94-14-002 (June 29, 1993).

164. Frances R. Hill and Douglas M. Mancino, *Taxation of Exempt Organizations*, ¶32.02(1)(e) (New York: Warren, Gorham & Lamont, 2002).

Information and Tax Returns

Annual reporting by exempt organizations was instituted in 1942,[165] but it was not until 1950 that an information return, Form 990-A, a four-page precursor of the present-day Forms 990 and 990PF, was published by the Treasury and the forms were made available to the public as required by the Revenue Act of 1950.[166]

Form 990 is still in use, required to be filed by public charities exempt under section 501(c)(3) as well as almost all other organizations exempt from tax under section 501(a).[167] A supplement to Form 990, Schedule A, must accompany the form to report the compensation of the charity's five highest employees, the five highest-paid professional service providers, self-dealing transactions, grant programs, antidiscrimination rules, information regarding transactions with related organizations, and compliance with the requirements of section 501(h). Form 990 for the year 2002 contained a new Schedule B on which charities were required to report names, addresses, amounts, and other information regarding large donations received during the reporting period. The purpose was to permit the Service to separate more easily this information from the otherwise public information in Form 990 as it is required to do under Code section 6104(b) before making it public.

A public charity with gross receipts in a particular year that are less than $100,000 and total assets that are less than $250,000 at the end of the reporting year may file Form 990EZ, a two-page form, although if applicable, it may also be required to file Schedule A. Private foundations file Form 990PF.[168] Moreover, Form 4720 is required to be filed by private foundations that may be subject to Chapter 42 excise taxes, as well as by public charities incurring tax liability under section 4911 for excess lobbying expenditures and for reporting and payment of the section 4958 tax on excess benefit transactions by a disqualified person or organization manager.[169]

The filing of Form 990, 990EZ, or 990PF is sufficient to start the statute of limitations running in the event the organization's exemption is revoked retroactively or it is subject to Chapter 42 excise taxes. A timely filing is also sufficient to start the statute running for purposes of the unrelated business income tax, so long as it contains information disclosing the poten-

165. T.D. 5125, 1942-1 C.B. 101; T.D. 5177, 1942-2 C.B. 123.

166. Revenue Act of 1950, Pub. L. No. 81-814, §341, 64 Stat. 906, 960 (1950); see also Chapter 2.

167. I.R.C. §6033(a); see also IRM 7.8.2, ch. 48.

168. Treas. Reg. §1.6033-2(a)(2)(i).

169. I.R.C. §6033(b)(11); Peter Swords, "The Importance of the Form 990," 33 *Tax Exempt Organization Tax Review* 33 (2001).

tial existence of unrelated business income and the disclosure was made in good faith.[170]

One of the requirements under the Restructuring Act of 1998 was that 80% of all returns be filed electronically by 2007.[171] A preliminary survey by the Service indicated that 80% of Forms 990 and 990EZ were being prepared using software, leading it to conclude that the ability to file electronically would reduce the filing burden as well as provide easier and faster access to information for users of the data. Accordingly, in March 2002 the Service announced that it was requesting comments from tax-exempt organizations, state regulators, research and oversight organizations, practitioners, software vendors, and others as to the burdens, if any, that electronic filing would impose, what factors would encourage or discourage its use, whether it should be designed so that it could be used to satisfy multiple filings such as state requirements, and what specific changes should be made to the current form to facilitate electronic filing. The Service also announced that a test of an electronic form was planned for October 2003 and that it expected that it would begin processing 2003 returns in 2004.[172]

Exempt from filing Form 990 and 990EZ are organizations other than private foundations with gross receipts that do not normally exceed $25,000 in each taxable year,[173] using a broad definition of receipts[174] and making the determinations on the basis of receipts for the year of the return and the two preceding years.[175] Also exempt are churches and certain religious and church-affiliated organizations, and religious and apostolic organizations described in section 501(d).[176] An organization that has not received a ruling or determination letter recognizing its exempt status, but that has filed Form 1023, may file Form 990 or 990PF while awaiting determination.[177] However, until Form 1023 is filed, the IRS will accept only a tax return.[178]

All returns are due on or before the fifteenth day of the fifth month following the close of the organization's annual accounting period,[179] and the Service will accept requests for extension upon filing of Form 2758. A change in

170. Rev. Rul. 69-247, 1969-1 C.B. 303.
171. Ann. 2002-27, 2002-11 I.R.B. 629.
172. Ann. 2002-27, 2002-11 I.R.B. 629.
173. I.R.C. §6033(a)(2)(A)(ii), as modified by Ann. 82-88, 1982-25 I.R.B. 23.
174. Treas. Reg. §1.6033-2(g)(4).
175. Treas. Reg. §1.6033-2(g)(3)(iii).
176. I.R.C. §6033(a)(2)(A)(i).
177. Treas. Reg. §1.6033-2(c).
178. IRS Information Release, INFO-2000-0260 (August 31, 2000); Rev. Proc. 2003-4, 2003-1 I.R.B. 123; Rev. Proc. 2003-5, 2003-1 I.R.B. 163.
179. I.R.C. §6072(e); see also Treas. Reg. §1.6033-2(e).

accounting period can be effected with a timely filing of Form 990 or 990PF or EZ.[180] These returns are filed with the Ogden, Utah, Service Center.[181]

Form 990 plays what has been described as a "pivotal role" in financial reporting for nonprofit organizations. Not only is it the primary source of information for the Internal Revenue Service, but it is used as the basic annual report for state charities offices and as the basic data source for research on the sector, and also serves as the primary source of information for potential donors particularly since the late 1990s when copies of Form 990 became available over the Internet through GuideStar and some state charities bureaus. With the advent of electronic filing, this availability will increase exponentially.

The importance of Form 990 makes its shortcomings acute. The largest problem is that it is not consonant with audited financial reports. It provides information not found in them and omits information they contain. It presents information on a cash basis, while audited financial reports present information on an accrual basis, requiring organizations in effect to maintain two separate sets of accounts or, at the least, to transpose one to the other annually. In an effort to relieve this burden, a Unified Financial Reporting System for Not-for-Profit Organizations was published in 2000, with the support of a large number of nonprofit organizations.[182] It contained a Uniform Chart of Accounts designed to permit organizations to record on an ongoing basis information necessary to complete both Form 990 and an audited financial account. What the guide could not accomplish was closer integration of the two basic reporting systems, a development that was necessary if meaningful public information was to be made generally available.

A recurring problem with existing financial reporting by charities surfaced in connection with the issuance in September 2002 of proposed revisions to Form 990 that would have required compliance with certain auditing standards promulgated by the American Institute of Certified Public Accountants.[183] Of particular concern was a rule described as SOP 98-2, which applies to organizations that circulate appeals for contributions containing educational materials. Ordinarily, the solicitation would be considered a "joint activity," and the organization would allocate its cost between exempt activities and fund-raising expenses. Under this rule, however, if an organization employs fund-raisers whose compensation is based on the amount of contributions raised, and if that compensation is more than 50% of the cost of

180. Rev. Proc. 85-58, 1985-2 C.B. 740.

181. Ann. 96-63, 1996-29 I.R.B. 18.

182. Russy D. Sumariwalla and Wilson C. Levis, *Unified Financial Reporting System for Not-for-Profit Organizations* (San Francisco: Jossey Bass, 2000).

183. Ann. 2002-87, 2002-39 I.R.B. 624.

the solicitation, the entire cost must be allocated to fund-raising, and none may be allocated to exempt activites.[184] Objections were raised that this rule results in presentation of incomplete or inaccurate information regarding exempt activities and expenses and that it is exceedingly costly.[185]

Until 2000 a private foundation was required to publish a notice in a newspaper of general circulation of the availability for public inspection of its Form 990PF, and to append a copy of the notice to that form.[186] This requirement was deleted effective March 13, 2000, as part of the 1998 Tax Extension Act, which included new disclosure provisions.[187] There are special rules for certain charitable trusts that are treated as private foundations as well as for split-interest trusts that are subject to certain Chapter 42 provisions.[188]

Form 990T is required of all charitable organizations that receive $1,000 or more of gross income from an unrelated taxable business.[189] It is due on the same date as Form 990 and Form 990PF,[190] and is filed at the Ogden Service Center.[191] Both the unrelated business income tax and the private foundation tax on investment income are required to be estimated and paid quarterly.[192]

Changes in operations or organization must be reported as part of Form 990 or 990PF, as must any liquidation, dissolution, termination, or substantial contraction.[193] Public charities with gross receipts that are normally not more than $5,000 and churches and other religious organizations are exempt from this rule.[194]

The penalties for failure to file or for filing an incomplete or incorrect return are as follows: $20 per day for each day the form has not been filed, or filed with inadequate information, with a $10,000 cap unless gross receipts exceed $1 million in a year, in which case the daily penalty is $100, with a

184. American Institute of Certified Public Accountants (AICPA), "Accounting for Costs of Activities of Not-for-Profit Organizations and State and Local Governmental Entities That Include Fund Raising," SOP 98-2 (1998).

185. "Attorneys Ask IRS Not to Require Form 990 Filers to Follow SOP 98–2," 2003 *Tax Notes Today* 20–38 (January 30, 2003).

186. Tax Reform Act of 1969, Pub. L. No. 91-172, §101(e)(3), 83 Stat. 487, 523–524 (1969).

187. Tax Relief Extension Act of 1998, Pub. L. No. 105-277, §1004, 112 Stat. 2681, 2681-888 to 2681-890 (1998).

188. Rev. Proc. 83-32, 1983-1 C.B. 723.

189. I.R.C. §6012(a)(2); Treas. Reg. §1.6012-2(e); Treas. Reg. §1.6012-3(a)(5); see also Treas. Reg. §1.6033-2(j).

190. I.R.C. §6072(e).

191. Ann. 96-63, 1996-29 I.R.B. 18.

192. IRM 7.8.2., ch. 48.11.

193. I.R.C. §6043(b); Treas. Reg. §1.6043-3.

194. I.R.C. §6043(b)(1); Treas. Reg. §1.6043-3(b).

maximum of $50,000.[195] The Service may abate the penalty if the organization can show reasonable cause for the failure.[196] There are also penalties in the same amount on those individuals responsible for the failure to file, if the failure was not due to reasonable cause and the return remains unfiled following demand by the Service.[197] Tax-exempt charities are also subject to the accuracy-related penalties for underpayments, fraud penalties, and criminal penalties that apply to all taxpayers.[198]

The 2002 GAO Report contained a description of the IRS procedures for examining Form 990 submissions.[199] As of April 2000, as part of the restructuring of the Service, examination activities were centralized in Dallas. The stated purpose for the change was to improve consistency, coordination, and use of resources.[200] Returns are chosen for review in two ways. One occurs after automated analysis of basic information keypunched into a master file and analyzed electronically as to whether the returns are "likely to have issues" that will lead to a change in tax computation or revocation of exempt status.[201] The second method for selecting returns for examination is based on referrals from "the general public, corporations, and private and public sector employees." These referrals are analyzed in the office by a group of returns classification specialists who determine whether the information establishes a basis for a reasonable belief of noncompliance. Certain referrals are given a second review by a three-person committee that has the power to determine whether or not the returns will be examined. This category includes churches or "media attention," referrals from members of Congress, the White House, and the IRS, or referrals otherwise considered "political or sensitive."[202]

In 2000 Congress's Joint Committee on Taxation investigated allegations of undue influence on the Service in handling exempt organization matters. In its report the Committee exonerated the Service, stating that it could find no credible evidence that organizations were unfairly targeted for examination, or that examinations were conducted based on the views espoused by the organizations or related individuals, nor that Clinton administration officials had intervened in the selection process.[203]

195. I.R.C. §6652(c)(1)(A).

196. I.R.C. §6652(c)(3); Treas. Reg. §301.6552-2(f).

197. I.R.C. §6652(c)(1)(B).

198. I.R.C. §§6662, 6663, 6664, 7201, 7203, 7206, and 7207; see also Michael I. Saltzman, *IRS Practice and Procedure*, ch. 7A (Boston: Warren, Gorham & Lamont, 2d ed., 1991).

199. General Accounting Office, *Improvements in Public, IRS, and State Oversight of Charities*, 62–68.

200. Id. at 62.

201. Id. at 62–63.

202. Id. at 63.

203. Joint Committee on Taxation, *Investigation of Allegations Relating to Internal Revenue Service Handling of Tax-Exempt Organization Matters*, 7; see also Chapter 2.

An important development affecting the regulation of exempt organizations that followed the restructuring of the IRS was the division of the exempt organization universe into market segments that would be treated separately in an attempt to profile areas of noncompliant behavior. In announcing this development, the Service requested comments on the categorizations and announced that it had developed check sheets for various segments designed to provide organizations with guidance as to compliance as well as to assist agents examining organizations within a specific category.[204] As of April 2002, thirty-five segments had been identified, of which twenty were charities.[205] For fiscal year 2003, the Service planned to concentrate on seven of these latter segments: colleges and universities, hospitals, fraternal organizations, section 509(a)(3) supporting organizations, arts and humanities organizations, private foundations, and elder housing. For each the examinations would focus on foundation status, filing requirements, the unrelated business income tax, and lobbying and political activities.[206]

A second development was the establishment of an Exempt Organization Compliance Council designed to serve as an advisory body to the director of the Exempt Organizations Division. It was comprised of a diverse group of the division's employees, including managers and agents from examinations, from EO Rulings and Agreements, and TE/GE Counsel. The purpose was to integrate, develop, and recommend compliance activities for the exempt organization examinations group, and to prioritize and recommend market segment studies and compliance-education projects.[207]

Critics of the regulatory role of the Service in regard to charities throughout the 1990s and the succeeding years uniformly pointed to the dearth of examinations that were being conducted. The GAO as part of its 2002 study of exempt organizations reported that a comparison of fiscal years 1996 through 2001 indicated that the number of annual returns increased 25% while the number examined dropped by 25%.[208] The change was attributed to the need for the IRS to adjust overall priorities toward revenue-generating activities, the drop in resources provided to the Service during this period, and the reassignment of revenue agents from audits to process the increased number of applications for exemption that occurred during the period under

204. Announcement reprinted at 36 *Exempt Organization Tax Review* 73 (2002).

205. LaFon and Harris, "EO Division Faces Challenges," 17.

206. Exempt Organizations Division, Internal Revenue Service, *Exempt Organizations (EO) Implementing Guidelines (FY 2003)*, 47–48 (September 2002).

207. "Edited Transcript of the August 3, 2001 ABA Tax Section Exempt Organizations Committee Meeting," 34 *Exempt Organization Tax Review* 35 (2001).

208. General Accounting Office, *Improvements in Public, IRS, and State Oversight of Charities*, 21.

review. The report noted that the market segment approach was expected to reverse the situation.[209]

The Service announced in June 2003 that it was establishing a new compliance unit, the EO Compliance Unit (EOCU), to be located in Ogden. Its purpose was to increase the presence of the Service in the exempt organization community through the use of what it termed "soft contacts." These were described as letters that do not require a response, in which the Service would "point organizations to areas where they may want to review their operations and their compliance with a certain provision." The unit would also be empowered to conduct limited-scope examinations.[210] This represented another effort to deal with a shortage of personnel but did raise questions as to whether the letters or the examinations constituted audits, procedures that carry with them certain procedural requirements.

Record Retention

Section 6001 imposes record-keeping requirements for all organizations exempt from tax under section 501(a), specifically, permanent books of account or records sufficient to establish the items reported and the information required to be disclosed in the annual information return.[211] These records are generally required to be maintained by taxable organizations for at least three years after the later of the due date of the tax or the date it was paid.[212]

Document Availability and Disclosure Requirements

Once an organization has received a favorable determination letter, Form 1023, the application for exemption, together with the supporting documents filed with it, and all information returns subsequently filed by the charity are required to be made available by the IRS for public inspection.[213] They are available at an IRS Service Center or at the national office upon written request.[214] If an organization can demonstrate to the IRS that public access to information contained in Form 1023 or submitted with it that relates to a trade secret, patent, or similar material would adversely affect the organiza-

209. Id. at 23.

210. "Top IRS Officials Provide EO Outlook, Update," *Exempt Organizations Reports*, No. 347, at 1 (June 13, 2003).

211. Treas. Reg. §1.6001-1(c).

212. Treas. Reg. §31.6001-1(e)(2).

213. I.R.C. §6104(d).

214. Treas. Reg. §301.6104(a)-6(a).

tion, the IRS may withhold that information.[215] The text of any technical advice memorandum issued in connection with the issuance of a favorable ruling to an organization is also available for public inspection, in this case at the IRS Freedom of Information Reading Room at the national office.[216] However, unfavorable rulings in regard to Form 1023, any rulings revoking or modifying an original determination letter, and any letter filed with or issued by the IRS dealing with status as a nonprivate foundation or private operating foundation are not available to the public.[217]

Exempt charities are also required to make certain information available to members of the general public.[218] There are three aspects to this general rule: (1) Form 1023 and information returns must be made available without charge at an organization's principal office and any regional or district office during regular business hours, the annual returns to be available for three years after the later of the date they were required to be filed or the date actually filed; (2) the organization must provide copies without charge other than a reasonable fee for reproduction and actual postage costs of the documents required to be disclosed and supporting materials described in element (1) to any person who so requests them.[219] However, a charity need not comply with requests for copies if (3) it has made its documents "widely available," defined in the regulations to include posting on the organization's website or forming part of a database of similar documents of other exempt organizations that are posted on the website of another entity.[220] The regulations contain specific rules relating to the response time for meeting requests for copies and the parameters of the widely available exception. Furthermore, there are special rules under which an organization that demonstrates that it is subject to a harassment campaign may be relieved from the requirement.[221]

It was in recognition of the ever-expanding use of the Internet for dissemination of Form 990 that Schedule B was added to the 2000 Form 990 for reporting information about donors and the nature of their contributions. The purpose of using the separate schedule was to permit it to be withheld from public disclosure and that was so stated on its face. However, after its publica-

---

215. I.R.C. §6104(a)(1)(D); Treas. Reg. §301.6104(a)-5.

216. Notice 92-28, 1992-25 I.R.B. 5.

217. Treas. Reg. §301.6104(a)-1(i).

218. Treas. Reg. §301.6104(d)-1.

219. Treas. Reg. §301.6104(d)-1(a). Temporary and proposed regulations issued on July 9, 2003, clarified that exempt organizations were authorized to charge the same fee charged under the Freedom of Information Act. However, charities would not be required to make the first 100 pages available without charge, as is the case with government agencies. 68 Fed. Reg. 40,768 (2003).

220. Treas. Reg. §301.6104(d)-2.

221. Treas. Reg. §301.6104(d)-3.

tion, the Service ruled internally that it could not be withheld from public inspection, although names and addresses could be redacted.[222] This provoked a strong protest from the bar but no change in the policy.[223]

Penalties for failure to comply with the disclosure requirements are imposed on persons who knowingly fail to file a return. These penalties are equal to $20 per day for each day the failure continues unless a person can show reasonable cause, with a maximum of $10,000 per return,[224] and an additional penalty of $5,000 on any person who willfully fails to comply with the requirements.[225]

Audit Process

The Internal Revenue Service conducts different types of exams of exempt organizations. The least intrusive and most informal is a correspondence examination, conducted by mail by an agent located in the district office.[226] Office examinations are conducted at the district office, to which representatives of the charity are asked to appear with documents and supporting information requested by the agent in advance.[227] A field examination is conducted at the offices of the charity and consists of an in-depth examination of the books and records of the charity, including all information used as a basis for preparing the return being examined.[228] The focus of the exam is on whether the organization meets the tests for exemption, has any liability for unrelated business income taxes (UBIT) or for section 4958 or Chapter 42 taxes on private foundations, whether it is in compliance with other filing requirements or specific rules such as those relating to disclosure, and whether its returns are complete.[229]

The Coordinated Examination Program for exempt organizations (CEP) is designed to more appropriately examine organizations that have more than $50 million of assets and gross receipts, a number of controlled or related entities, and that possess national stature.[230] These audits involve a number of team members, including an active team manager, computer audit specialists,

222. Carolyn Wright LaFon, "Form 990 Schedule B Is Publicly Available, Despite Statements to the Contrary," 2001 *Tax Notes Today* 219-3 (November 13, 2001).

223. "Colvin Letter to Miller on Form 990 Disclosure," 2002 *Tax Notes Today* 31-41 (February 14, 2002).

224. I.R.C. §6652(c)(1)(C), (d).

225. I.R.C. §6685.

226. IRM 4252(2).

227. I.R.C. §7605(a); Treas. Reg. §301.7605-1(d)(2)(i).

228. I.R.C. §7605(a); Treas. Reg. §301.7605-1(d)(3)(i).

229. See generally IRM 7.8.1.

230. IRM 7.6.2, ch. 4.

economists, appraisers, international revenue agents, attorneys, and income tax revenue agents, together with traditional exempt organization revenue agents.[231] They review the organization chosen for examination as well as all of its effectively controlled entities, extending possibly to affiliated but uncontrolled organizations.[232] The individual income tax returns filed by employees of the organization may also be examined.[233] Area counsel will be involved in the audit, and representatives from the national office and Chief Counsel serve as advisors to the field agents.[234]

There is a prescribed planning procedure for CEP examinations. The organization's prior returns and other information available to the Service, including press coverage, are reviewed by the case manager to determine the scope and depth of the examination. The organization's books and records are then reviewed for noncompliance and unusual items. The case manager then establishes procedures for listing areas to be examined, as well as proposed audit procedures and a time estimate for each area. An examination plan is then produced, with one part sent to the organization.[235] The next step is a preexamination conference with the charity's representatives, at which time the organization is informed of the penalty for substantial underpayment under section 6662 and the procedure for avoiding the penalty by supplying information at the outset of the audit.[236] The charity is next given a written examination plan that contains agreements and arrangements made during the conference, a description of the scope of the examination, where and when it will take place, and a list of the records the charity is expected to make available. During the course of the audit, the Service will also deliver numerous information document requests to the organization as well as proposed adjustments.[237]

In CEP audits examining agents are urged to seek technical advice during the course of their examinations as issues arise, rather than at the conclusion of the audit. In general, after an EO examination, if the appeals office determines that it is likely to seek technical advice, it may request a presubmission conference if all parties agree that it should be requested. There are two areas where requests for technical advice are mandatory: the first is requests for relief under section 7805(b) and the second is cases concerning qualification for exemption or private foundation status for which there is no published

---

231. Id., ch. 4.3.
232. Id.
233. Id., ch. 4.8.5.
234. Id., chs. 4.1, 4.5.
235. Id., chs. 4.7.5.1, 4.12.
236. Id., chs. 4.12, 4.13.
237. Id.

precedent or for which there is no reason to believe that nonuniformity exists.[238] During the course of a CEP audit, the Office of Chief Counsel may provide field service advice without the taxpayer's knowledge or participation, although these memoranda are required to subsequently be disclosed in redacted form. The charity being examined may also request technical advice at any time during a field or CEP audit. The request may involve legal, engineering, or valuation questions, and it may be procedural as well as technical.

If the technical advice is adverse to the taxpayer, the examining agent must raise the issue, but an appeals officer can settle it subsequently based on the hazards of litigation. If, however, the advice is favorable to the taxpayer, the area appeals office must resolve the case in a manner consistent with the advice, and it is to be applied retroactively.[239] At the start of each calendar year, the Service issues a revenue procedure setting forth in question-and-answer format the rules governing when and how technical advice is given in regard to exempt organization matters and the rights of a taxpayer when technical advice is to be requested.[240]

An IRS official reported in 2001 that during the fiscal years between 1991 and 2001, the IRS identified $428,861,317 in deficiencies in the 202 CEP cases it closed, with the average deficiency being $2,123,072. Common issues occurring in at least ten exams included (1) allocation of losses in UBIT returns, (2) the treatment of employment taxes and employee versus independent contractor issues in employment tax cases, and (3) entertainment expenses on Form 990T, exemption from tax on corporations and certain trusts, and backup withholding.[241] The inference to be drawn from this, which is confirmed in other reports on the CEP audits of hospitals and universities, is that the IRS uncovered very few instances of abuse sufficient to warrant revocation of exemption; rather, the problems were related to employment tax and allocations under UBIT.

During the period between 1980 and 2002, the Service conducted what it described as a Taxpayer Compliance Measurement Program for exempt organizations (TCMP), under which it conducted audits targeted at specific categories of organizations. The purpose of these audits was to promote voluntary compliance, and it was to be accomplished by analyzing examination data to evaluate Service performance in reaching that goal. The data were also used to improve the selection of returns to examine, and to evaluate allocation of resources, educational programs, and the effectiveness of reporting

238. Rev. Proc. 2003-5, §5.04, 2003-1 I.R.B. 163.

239. 26 C.F.R. 601.106.

240. Rev. Proc. 2003-5, 2003-1 I.R.B. 163.

241. "IRS Officials Discuss Developments in Exempt Bond Office," *Exempt Organization Reports, Tax Exempt Advisor*, November 9, 2001, at 2.

forms.[242] A successful TCMP for private foundations conducted in the 1980s concluded that they were engaged in a high level of compliance, and, as a result, the Service was able to reduce the number of private foundation audits and use its resources in other areas.[243] However, in 2001 the Service announced that it was discontinuing the program, having found it to be insufficiently flexible to meet the new goals of the restructuring act.[244]

The Service has for many years prepared specialized audit guidelines for certain categories of organizations. Originally designed to provide internal guidance to its agents, since the application of the Freedom of Information Act provisions they are also relied on by affected organizations, even though they do not have precedential effect. Of particular importance have been the guidelines for audit of hospitals and colleges and universities.[245]

As noted earlier, a settlement that resolves disputes in the course of or at the conclusion of an examination is called a closing agreement. It is a final agreement on specific issues of liability.[246] It provides certainty as to the conclusion of issues raised on exam and guidance for the future.[247] If there is no closing agreement and no resolution of the issues raised during audit, the charity is given a copy of the examining agent's report and, after consideration of proposed resolutions, can agree to a settlement based on uncertainty as to the facts or interpretation or application of the law. Both parties can estimate litigation hazards.[248] If there is still no resolution, the organization will receive the agent's report and a thirty-day letter that must be in hand before the organization can request administrative review. To obtain review, the charity must protest the proposed adjustment to the regional appeals office in writing. However, if the organization determines not to seek review, it may request the Service to issue a statutory notice of deficiency, giving the charity ninety days to file a Tax Court petition. If no petition is filed, this letter is considered a final assessment.[249]

Audits of churches are governed by a separate set of rules set forth in section 7611 that limit the ability of the Service to inquire into eligibility for exemption, application of the unrelated business income tax, and the question of whether the organization is conducting any other taxable activi-

242. IRM 4860, MT 4800-146 (March 9, 1992).

243. Hill and Mancino, *Taxation of Exempt Organizations,* ¶34.05.

244. "Edited Transcript of the January 18, 2002 ABA Tax Section Exempt Organizations Committee Meeting," 35 *Exempt Organization Tax Review* 327, 341 (2001).

245. Examination Guidelines for Hospitals, Ann. 92-83, 1992-22 I.R.B. 59; Final Examination Guidelines Regarding Colleges and Universities, Ann. 94-112, 1994-37 I.R.B. 36.

246. I.R.C. §7121(b).

247. *1993 IRS Continuing Professional Education Text,* 263–293.

248. IRS Fact Sheet, FS-97-09 (February 26, 1997).

249. IRM 8.16.1.

ties.[250] The effect of the rules is to greatly circumscribe the ability of the Service to commence any inquiry of a church's tax status or liabilities and the extent of its examination.[251]

In the Joint Committee's March 2000 report on its investigation of IRS audit procedures, the staff noted that while the restrictions on church audits provide important safeguards against the IRS engaging in unnecessary examinations of churches, the procedures also made it more difficult for the IRS to initiate an examination of a church even where there was clear evidence of impermissible activity, as well as hampering IRS efforts to educate churches with respect to actions there were not permissible. The staff concluded that it would be beneficial to change the procedures to permit the IRS to undertake educational and outreach activities with individual churches without the need to initiate a full church tax inquiry.[252]

Appeals Process

The procedure for appealing the outcome of an audit, whether revocation or modification of exempt status, is set forth in regulations section 601.106.[253] As noted above, it entails written protest of the audit report and a request for referral to the regional appeals office filed within thirty days after the date of the key district's notice. The written protest must include a statement of the facts, applicable law and arguments in support of the charity's position, as well as an indication of whether a conference is requested. In addition, since the restructuring, a taxpayer may request an early referral of one or more unresolved issues from the Examination or Collection Division to the Office of Appeals. However, this procedure is not available in connection with exemption or private foundation status issues, issues relating to church audits, and examinations involving certain foundation provisions.[254]

The protest letter will be reviewed by the personnel in the key district in which a conference, if requested, will be held. The appeals process is informal, and testimony under oath is not required. The regional appeals office may reconsider the determination but, if it does not, will then send the matter to the chief of the appropriate appeals office. That office will then notify the organization of its decision and issue an appropriate determination letter.

250. I.R.C. §7611; Treas. Reg. §301.7611-1.

251. Joint Committee on Taxation, *Investigation of Allegations Relating to Internal Revenue Service Handling of Tax-Exempt Organization Matters*, 18–19, 22.

252. Id. at 22.

253. 26 C.F.R. §601.106, as amplified by Rev. Proc. 90-27, §10, 1990-1 C.B. 514, and Rev. Proc. 2003-8, 2003-1 I.R.B. 236.

254. Rev. Proc. 99-28, 1999-2 C.B. 109.

If the proposed action by the appeals office is contrary to a prior technical advice or ruling by the national office, the proposed decision must be submitted through the Office of the Regional Director of Appeals to the Commissioner (TE/GE). If Appeals believes the conclusion of the national office is wrong, it must promptly request reconsideration: in all events, it is bound by the decision of the Commissioner. One exception to the procedure just described is that an organization may not appeal a determination by the district that was based on technical advice issued to the district by the national office.[255]

One part of the restructuring of the TE/GE division of the Service was the creation in 1999 of a position of senior technical advisor who would provide advice to the assistant commissioner of the division and its other executives as well as an independent review of cases involving difficult or complex issues to ensure fairness and technical correctness.[256] The role of the advisor received extensive public attention in the spring of 2003 when it was disclosed that the Service had restored the exemption of two organizations with close ties to former House Speaker Newt Gingrich. The exemptions had been revoked in 1996 and 2000 on the grounds that the organizations had improperly furthered the interests of the Republican Party. The House Committee on Standards of Official Conduct in 1996 had held hearings on the connection of the Speaker with the organizations and had concluded that he had improperly used one of the organizations to fund a project that benefited his political action committee. The Service denied that political influence had played any part in its decision to restore the exemptions, but refused to release any internal documents relating to its decision.[257]

Standing to Sue

The rights of third parties to sue to enforce the federal tax laws governing exempt organizations is as circumscribed as the rights of third parties to enforce the actions of charitable fiduciaries under state law. Over the years there have been a number of attempts by interested third parties to challenge Service actions in regard to tax-exempt organizations, but none have succeeded, primarily due to the case and controversy requirements of Article III of the Constitution. The basic requirements that must be met in order to obtain standing are that the plaintiff has suffered an injury in fact that is concrete and traceable to his conduct; that the injury is fairly traceable to the

255. IRM 8.16.1.

256. IRS News Release, IR-2001-34 (March 14, 2001).

257. Christine J. Harris, "Talk with IRS Reps Offers More Insight into Review of Gingrich Groups," 2003 *Tax Notes Today* 118-4 (June 19, 2003).

defendant's conduct; and that the injury was redressable by removal of the defendant's conduct.

In the leading case of *In re United States Catholic Conference,* decided in 1989 by the United States Court of Appeals for the Second Circuit, as to which the Supreme Court denied certiorari,[258] the court reviewed these requirements and found that they were not met as applied to a consortium of abortion rights groups, civil liberties organizations, clergy, and individual taxpayers who challenged the tax exemption of the Roman Catholic Church on the grounds that it was engaging in political activities related to abortion issues in violation of the requirements for exemption. The court suggested that the lack of a plaintiff to litigate an issue might suggest that the matter was more appropriately dealt with by Congress. Given the scope of interests represented by the plaintiffs in this action, the possibility of a third party prevailing in a suit challenging deduction became extremely remote.

The barriers to private suits against charities were confirmed in a decision of the United States District Court for the Eastern District of New York rendered in 1998 dismissing a lawsuit filed by a private individual against two tax-exempt foundations seeking to force them to make their tax returns available for inspection by the public as required under Code section 6104. The court looked to the wording of the statute and the legislative history and found that Congress did not intend to create a private cause of action, and noted that the structure of the tax code weighed against the plaintiff's position in that the information being sought was available directly from the Service and because enforcement of the penalties could only be authorized by the Treasury.[259]

Other Federal Agencies That Regulate Charities

There are a number of federal agencies other than the Internal Revenue Service that oversee, or are implicated in, certain activities of charitable organizations. The GAO 2002 Report on Oversight of Charities contained a review of the activities of five federal agencies and the extent to which the IRS coordinated its oversight of charities with them.[260] It reported that the Federal Bureau of Investigation, through its Economic Crimes Unit, attempts to reduce the amount of economic loss by national and international telemarketing fraud. This activity may involve charities, as would FBI investiga-

---

258. 885 F.2d 1020 (2d Cir. 1989), cert. denied sub nom. Abortion Rights Mobilization, Inc. v. United States Catholic Conference, 495 U.S. 918 (1990).

259. Schuloff v. Queens College Foundation, Inc., 994 F. Supp. 425 (E.D.N.Y. 1998).

260. General Accounting Office, *Improvements in Public, IRS, and State Oversight of Charities,* 69–71.

tions of allegations of fraud related to federal government procurement, contracts, and federally funded programs. After September 11, 2001, the FBI instituted investigations of select charities for fraudulent activities related to terrorism. It has no charity-specific investigation classification and no ongoing relationship with the IRS.[261]

The work of the Federal Emergency Management Agency (FEMA) involves contacts with charities in its programs to coordinate disaster relief work.[262] This is done through the National Voluntary Organizations Active in Disaster, an independent tax-exempt organization, as well as other charities such as United Way. Although FEMA does not work with the IRS to assess charities or to make referrals to it, the IRS has held training sessions for FEMA relating to accounting for disaster donations.[263]

A third federal agency, the Federal Trade Commission, enforces both antitrust and consumer protection laws, but its mission has not traditionally extended to charity fraud.[264] One of the recommendations to the Filer Commission in 1977 was to extend the power of the FTC to regulate charitable solicitations, and this possibility has been raised from time to time since then but without generating congressional interest.[265] However, the USA Patriot Act of 2001 contained in section 1011, Crimes Against Charitable Americans, provisions extending the agency's authority regarding telemarketing and consumer fraud abuse to require any person engaged in telemarketing for the solicitation of charitable contributions to disclose promptly and clearly the purpose of the call.[266]

Subsequently, the FTC by regulation affirmed that the act did not amend the jurisdictional limitations of the Commission to extend to charitable orga-

261. Id. at 69.

262. Reorganization Plan No. 3 of 1978, 43 Fed. Reg. 41,943 (1978); Executive Order 12127, 44 Fed. Reg. 19,367 (1979); Federal Emergency Management Agency, 44 Fed. Reg. 25,797 (1979).

263. General Accounting Office, *Improvements in Public, IRS, and State Oversight of Charities,* 69–70.

264. 15 U.S.C. §45; see also Charitable Contributions for September 11—Protecting against Fraud, Waste, and Abuse: Hearing before the Subcommittee on Oversight and Investigations of the House Committee on Energy and Commerce, Serial 107-67, 107th Cong., 1st Sess., at 90–95 (2001).

265. Adam Yarmolinsky and Marion R. Fremont-Smith, "Judicial Remedies and Related Topics," in Department of Treasury, Commission on Private Philanthropy and Public Needs, *Research Papers,* vol. 5, pt. 1, at 2697, 2703–2704 (1977).

266. Uniting and Strengthening America by Providing Appropriate Tools Required to Intercept and Obstruct Terrorism Act of 2001 (USA Patriot Act), Pub. L. No. 107-56, §1011, 115 Stat. 272, 397 (2001).

nizations; rather, FTC regulation was to extend only to for-profit organizations soliciting funds for charities.[267] The FTC also participates in an online watchdog site, Consumer Sentinel, the members of which are primarily law-enforcement agencies.[268] The site lists consumer complaints and investigations relating to fraud, and the FTC may act on those complaints. The GAO reported that the Commission acts on referrals from state attorneys general, but that, except for occasional work on criminal investigations, it does not coordinate its enforcement activities with the IRS.[269] In February 2003 the FTC and the Department of Justice began the first of five public hearings on the implications of competition law and policy for health care financing and delivery. Among the subjects to be considered were hospital mergers, the significance of nonprofit status, the boundaries of state action, and the implications of the Commission's consumer protection mandate.[270] The FTC has played a major role in monitoring the antitrust implications of health care mergers and joint ventures, and this appeared to be a continuation of that role.

The United States Postal Inspection Service is also responsible for combating fraud, in this case fraud involving the mails.[271] Accordingly it has regulatory powers over charitable solicitations conducted through the mails. It also participates in the Consumer Sentinel effort, but does not coordinate its investigations with the IRS unless the validity of tax exemption of an organization being investigated is raised or if the expertise of the IRS is needed.[272]

The fifth agency described in the GAO Report, the Office of Personnel Management, oversees the Combined Federal Campaign and thus selects charities to which federal employees may make their charitable contributions through a coordinated appeal.[273] As reported by the GAO, OPM neither audits charities directly nor looks to the IRS to assist in identifying fraudulent charities.[274]

---

267. 67 Fed. Reg. 4492 (January 20, 2002) (proposed regulations); 16 C.F.R. pt. 310 (2002) (final regulations); see also *www.ftc.gov/opa/2002/12/donotcall.htm*.

268. *www.consumer.gov/sentinel/*.

269. General Accounting Office, *Improvements in Public, IRS, and State Oversight of Charities*, 70.

270. 67 Fed. Reg. 68,672 (2002); see also *www.ftc.gov/ogc/healthcarehearings/index.htm*.

271. 18 U.S.C. §1341.

272. General Accounting Office, *Improvements in Public, IRS, and State Oversight of Charities*, 70.

273. 5 C.F.R. §950.101 et seq.

274. General Accounting Office, *Improvements in Public, IRS, and State Oversight of Charities*, 71.

Federal-State Cooperation

Section 6104(c), enacted in 1969,[275] was designed to enhance regulation of charities by permitting exchange of information between the IRS and state attorneys general and other officials charged with their regulation. Prior to its enactment, the IRS was limited to providing information only to state tax officials who, in turn, were not authorized to share that information with other state officials. The statute required the IRS to notify the appropriate state officials charged with overseeing section 501(c)(3) organizations of its determinations made with respect to the denial or revocation of tax exemption. However, Treasury regulations promulgated under the section interpreted "determination" to mean a final determination, and that a determination was not final until all administrative review with respect to the determination was completed.[276]

This interpretation has meant that state officials cannot be notified in the majority of matters until a number of years after the Service has begun action to correct abuse, during which time the charities' fiduciaries could have disposed of its assets, transferred out of the jurisdiction, or taken other measures that made it impossible for the state to conduct appropriate corrective action. Furthermore, the inability to share information has made it exceedingly difficult for state officials to act against a charity at the same time as the Service. This problem was dramatically exemplified during the IRS audit of the Bishop Estate. As described by Evelyn Brody:

> Appearing on a recent panel discussing the relationship between state charity regulators and the IRS, former Hawai'i attorney general Bronster eloquently described her frustration at not knowing whether she was duplicating the efforts of the IRS in her Bishop Estate investigation; her belief that the Incumbent Trustees were providing conflicting information to her office and to the IRS; and her desire to obtain documents being denied her by the Incumbent Trustees (who initially claimed confidentiality under the tax laws!).[277]

Finally, as pointed out in the Joint Committee on Taxation's 2000 study of disclosure provisions relating to tax-exempt organizations, the IRS is not permitted to provide any notice when an organization withdraws an application

---

275. I.R.C. §6104(c), codified by Tax Reform Act of 1969, Pub. L. No. 91-172, §101(e)(2), 83 Stat. 487, 548 (1969).

276. Treas. Reg. §301.6104(c)-1(c).

277. Evelyn Brody, "A Taxing Time for the Bishop Estate: What Is the I.R.S. Role in Charity Governance?" 21 *Hawaii Law Review* 537, 547 (1999).

for tax exemption prior to an IRS determination because such a withdrawal is not considered a final determination.[278]

Legislation to correct these shortcomings was recommended by the GAO in its April 2002 report on exempt organizations.[279] It received a qualified approval from the Treasury, which expressed concern about the confidentiality of taxpayer information, together with an offer to work with the Congress, the IRS, and state charity officials to develop similar legislation in the future. A provision implementing the GAO recommendation was included in the Charity Aid, Recovery, and Empowerment Act of 2002 and received support from the Treasury and state officials; it was included as well in the CARE Act of 2003, passed by the Senate in April 2003. It would permit disclosure to an appropriate state officer of notices of proposed refusal to recognize exempt status, proposed revocation of exemption, or deficiencies under section 507 and under Chapter 42 governing private foundations and the excess benefit limitations in section 4958. However, information could be provided only upon written request by an appropriate state officer and only for the purpose of and to the extent necessary in the administration of state laws regulating such organizations. Additionally, the Secretary of the Treasury would be authorized to make available returns and return information of a charity if it was determined that the inspection or disclosure "may facilitate the resolution of Federal or State issues relating to the tax-exempt status of such organization." Accordingly, the statute would, once again, have limited effect by requiring a request from the state, and limiting disclosure of information to a state that may have no prior knowledge of existing problems to issues "relating to the tax-exempt status of such organization" where the state interest is not tax exemption but rather preservation of charitable interest, correcting wrongdoing by charitable fiduciaries, or regulating solicitation of contributions.[280]

278. Joint Committee on Taxation, *Disclosure Provisions Relating to Tax-Exempt Organizations*, 103–104.

279. General Accounting Office, *Improvements in Public, IRS, and State Oversight of Charities*, 34.

280. CARE Act of 2002, H.R. 7, §205, 107th Cong., 2d Sess. (July 16, 2002); CARE Act of 2003, S. 476, §205, 108th Cong., 1st Sess. (2003). See S. Rep. No. 107-211, 107th Cong., 2d Sess., 37–40 (2002).

8

Improving the Law and Regulation of Charities

Despite the breadth of the legal constraints on charitable fiduciaries, the law gives them an extraordinary degree of freedom in which to carry out their organization's mission. So long as fiduciaries are faithful to the purposes of the organization, the law keeps its hands off. It does not tell them how to operate; it does not set priorities for expenditures; it does not mandate any one method for achieving purposes. Of course, the same constraints placed on all members of society apply to charity fiduciaries. They may not steal nor otherwise transgress the criminal laws. They may not adopt measures that are contrary to public policy, such as invidious discrimination on the basis of race or religion. Except with respect to the doctrines of cy pres and deviation, the duties imposed on charitable fiduciaries are negative in nature. They must not benefit personally at the expense of the charity. They must not be reckless in carrying out its purposes. These are minimal obligations, and the strength of the charitable sector is attributable in large part to the fact that the restrictions on behavior are sufficiently lenient to encourage a high degree of compliance.

Evaluation of the effectiveness of the laws governing charities requires consideration of the degree to which they impinge on their freedom to operate while at the same time assuring that they will be administered for the benefit of the general public. How difficult will it be to comply with a particular restriction? Will it stifle innovation? Will it encourage support from the public? The preceding chapters have described the laws governing charities and the means by which they are enforced. In this chapter these laws will be revisited in an attempt to evaluate their effectiveness as well as to suggest improvements.

Effect of a Dual Legal System

A distinguishing feature of charity regulation is that it is a dual system, with state and federal rules and enforcement programs that parallel each other to a large degree. Accordingly, we will consider each set of rules separately and then look to where they diverge, where they can be brought together for more effective regulation, and, finally, whether a single system would be preferable and, if so, where it might be lodged.

Charities are creatures of state laws, established and dissolved under the jurisdiction and thus the laws of a particular state. These laws contain definitions of the purposes for which a charity may be established, as well as set limits on the behavior of its fiduciaries. State courts possess a wide range of sanctions that they can use to correct wrongdoing and assure future compliance.

State laws are permissive regarding the creation of charities. It is possible for an individual to execute a declaration of trust that recites a charitable purpose, name himself or another as trustee, donate as little as ten dollars to it, and thereby constitute a valid charity. To create a charitable corporation one or more persons submit to a state official a form stating a name, charitable purposes, names of directors and officers, acknowledgment of agreed-upon by-laws, the date for an annual meeting, and a choice of a fiscal year together with a filing fee. In some states this can be accomplished over the Internet. Upon receipt, the state official will approve articles of organization, thereby establishing a charitable corporation.

However, creating a charity under state law is merely the start. The overriding consideration for the majority of organizations, particularly small- to medium-sized ones, is to assure that they will be exempt from federal tax and eligible to receive tax-deductible contributions. Furthermore, since the criterion for exemption from income and sales taxes in almost every state is federal exemption, compliance with the federal tax requirements has particular importance. Even though exemption from local property tax may not follow the federal exemption, it is the rare charity that operates by choice without federal exemption. A final consideration for larger charities is the ability to issue tax-exempt bonds, one that in many cases is more important than exemption.

Until the 1970s the state and federal regulatory regimes operated with divergent aims and divergent enforcement methods. The state courts held the panoply of sanctions, while the only sanction available to the IRS was revocation of exemption, for many charities a sanction without clout. This shortcoming in the federal system was recognized by the mid-1960s. It was remedied to a limited extent in 1969 with respect to private foundations, a group that then comprised 5% of the universe of charities. The Tax Reform Act of that year provided for sanctions for self-dealing imposed on transgressors and on foundation managers who approved the transactions knowing they were prohibited. Congress also amended the Code to permit the IRS to abate a confiscatory termination tax that became payable in cases of repeated or egregious violation of the new limitations if a state court acted to preserve the foundation's funds—a clear recognition that the equitable remedies available in the states were far superior to the sanction of revocation of exemption, which confiscated charitable assets while leaving the wrongdoers in charge with no federal limits on their future behavior.

Almost thirty years later, the value of intermediate sanctions as a regulatory tool for all charities was acknowledged when Congress, in the Taxpayers Bill of Rights 2, imposed self-dealing limitations on publicly supported charities and on social welfare organizations described in section 501(c)(4). The sanctions for violations of these new rules are similar to those applicable in the case of private foundation self-dealing, namely excise taxes on insiders who receive excess benefits from dealings with the charity and on those managers of the charity who knowingly and willfully approved the transaction. The excess benefit rules represent a major extension of federal regulation, not just because of the nature of the remedies, but because they established what is in effect a universal fiduciary duty of loyalty that parallels the duty under state law, thereby bringing the two systems closer. With their focus on punishing individuals, not the charity, these provisions changed the regulation of tax-exempt charities from one framed primarily in terms of protecting the integrity of the tax system to one that also seeks to preserve charitable funds.

The 1969 Act also contained a provision aimed at improving charity regulation by encouraging cooperation between the IRS and the states. The general prohibition against any disclosure by the IRS of taxpayer information was amended to permit IRS personnel to provide information about specific cases involving charities to state attorneys general as freely as they could to state revenue department officials. However, the amendment did not achieve the intended result; rather, it was interpreted in the regulations to permit exchange of information only after a federal matter had been closed, a limitation that rendered the provision virtually meaningless. By the time information could be provided to a state attorney general, the charitable assets would have long since been expended or diverted for private purposes. Legislation to remedy this limitation was proposed by the Joint Committee on Taxation in 2000 in a report evaluating disclosure provisions in the Code, and a measure to further amend section 6104 was part of a bill before the Congress in 2002 but it failed of passage. The same provision was included in the CARE Act of 2003 passed by the Senate in April 2003.[1]

State Laws Governing Charities and Their Fiduciaries

Enabling Statutes for Charitable Corporations

All but two states have enacted statutes governing the creation, operation, and dissolution of nonprofit corporations. These statutes encourage creation

---

1. See Chapter 7.

of new organizations, providing straightforward, fairly uncomplicated rules. Although at one time in some states the courts or a state administrative official had power to refuse to grant a corporate charter, for example because the purposes were not considered charitable, there is now no jurisdiction in which a charity must obtain what was in effect a license from the state before it can come into being.

The Revised Model Nonprofit Corporation Act, adopted in 1987 by the American Bar Association, in effect in twelve states and in a modified form in eleven others, contains easily understandable rules governing the operation of charitable corporations. The model act divides the universe of nonprofit organizations into three distinct categories—public benefit, mutual benefit, and religious corporations. Individuals are granted wide freedom to choose the form of governance for a charitable corporation, including the number of directors or trustees, their terms of office, the rules relating to the calling of meetings, quorums, voting requirements, removal of officers and directors, and the degree to which they may be indemnified.

As of the end of 2002 only three states, California, Maine, and New Hampshire, imposed limitations on the composition of the board. California and Maine provide that no more than 49% of the directors can be persons who are being compensated by the corporation or members of their families. The New Hampshire statute requires that there be at least five directors of every corporation who are not of the same immediate family or related by blood or marriage.[2] It is likely that other states will adopt provisions of this nature, mirroring requirements imposed on publicly traded companies contained in the Sarbanes-Oxley Act passed in 2002, which requires that the audit committees of public corporations be comprised solely of "independent" directors.[3] A rule of this nature may be appropriate for large charities that operate complex enterprises such as hospitals and universities. However, for the vast number of charities it would constitute an unnecessary burden.

The powers granted to officers and directors under nonprofit corporation enabling statutes are designed to encourage independence. They affirm the ability of directors to delegate their duties, to establish committees, and to rely on their reports. They permit, but do not require, that there be an executive committee. The same is true in regard to audit committees, and, in fact, following passage of the Sarbanes-Oxley Act, many charities voluntarily established them.

Among the few restrictions on the operation of public benefit corporations are those governing the disposition of charitable assets on termination or substantial contractions. In the case of dissolution, statutes in sixteen states

2. See Chapter 3.
3. Sarbanes-Oxley Act of 2002, Pub. L. No. 107-204, 116 Stat. 745 (2002).

require prior notice to the attorney general, and in three court approval is necessary. In thirty-six states notice must be given to the secretary of state or other state official with whom governing instruments are filed upon creation, but, unlike the attorney general, this state official has no regulatory powers to assure that the corporation has distributed its remaining funds to another charity, thus rendering the provision ineffective. Sixteen states also require that notice be given to the attorney general of a proposed sale of substantially all of the assets of a charitable corporation.[4]

The importance of statutory restrictions of this nature that are designed to protect charitable assets was belatedly recognized in the 1990s when a large number of hospitals converted to for-profit status, selling assets at prices below fair market value in some instances and in others allowing the proceeds to pass into private hands.[5] Statutes in three states prohibit conversions to for-profit status, while in ten others approval from the court or the attorney general is required. These provisions apply to all charitable corporations. In addition, there are now twenty-five states with legislation dealing specifically with conversions of health care organizations.

Duty of Care

The duty of care, which in effect protects fiduciaries from liability for ordinary negligence, is a rational standard to which charitable managers and directors should be held. Shortcomings associated with enforcement of the duty of care do not arise from its formulation. Rather, it is the application of the business judgment rule to measure liability for failure to comply with this standard that is inappropriate. The result has been to discourage enforcement in all but the most egregious circumstances. This rule was developed in the context of the business corporation where directors are policed by shareholders who want to encourage risk-taking for their pecuniary benefit. It does not have a place in the context of a charity subject to the nondistribution constraint and with a mission that is not confined to private financial benefit. Furthermore, the business judgment rule, as formulated in section 4.01 of the American Law Institute's Principles of Corporate Governance, protects a fiduciary only when there has been a conscious exercise of judgment and then only if the director or officer is informed with respect to the subject of the business judgment to the extent he reasonably believes to be appropriate under the circumstances. Inattentive or uninformed directors are subject to the reasonable care standards of section 4.01(a).

4. See Appendix, Table 1, Columns 9 and 12.
5. See below and Chapter 6.

The issue of how much attention should be demanded of directors is a particularly acute one for a large number of charities. It is not uncommon to elect individuals to serve as directors because of certain unique contributions they are able to make by virtue of their particular expertise, standing in the community, or as potential donors. In many instances it is understood that these individuals will not be expected to attend meetings or give the affairs of the charity the degree of attention expected of other board members.[6] Suggestions have been made to redefine the duties of directors to permit what might be considered a special class that would not be held to the standards required of others. A better solution would be to provide these individuals with an honorary title or, if the corporation has members, elect them to that position, rather than diluting the overall standards appropriate for directors.

The duty of care applies to the investment of charitable assets as well as to the administration of the organization. The standards for investing were modified in 1990 with the adoption by the American Law Institute of a Modern Prudent Investor Rule, embodied in Restatement (Third) of the Law of Trusts and the Uniform Prudent Investor Act.[7] This formulation brought modern investment theory and practice to trust law and by extension to the investment policies of charitable corporations. It freed directors to invest in a wide range of assets and to delegate their powers to professionals. This does not, however, mean that it absolved them from exercising judgment or from the requirement of attention, failures exemplified in the case of the Foundation for New Era Philanthropy where a large number of charitable organizations were drawn into a Ponzi-type scheme that resulted in serious losses to the charities and the criminal conviction of the Foundation's organizer.[8]

The duty to diversify investments is recited in section 227(b) of the Restatement formulation of the Prudent Investor Rule as follows: "In making and implementing investment decisions, the trustee has a duty to diversify the investments of the trust unless, under the circumstances, it is prudent not to do so." Unfortunately, the commentary does not provide adequate guidance to make this a meaningful standard. There were a sufficient number of instances in the 1990s and early 2000s in which charities experienced severe losses from the failure to diversify to warrant concluding that the rule should be modified or at the least further clarified. Examples that were widely publicized involved Emory University, which was reported in 2000 to be invested

6. Judith R. Saidel, "Expanding the Governance Construct: Functions and Contributions of Nonprofit Advisory Groups," 27 *Nonprofit and Voluntary Sector Quarterly* 421 (1998).

7. See Chapter 4.

8. Joseph Slobodzian, "Bennett Gets 12 Years for New Era Scam," *National Law Journal,* October 6, 1997, at A8.

disproportionately in Coca Cola stock;[9] Temple University, which in 2000 had more than 50% of its portfolio in bonds;[10] the Art Institute of Chicago, whose board approved an investment of almost $400 million of its $650 million endowment in hedge funds, with one particular investment of $23 million reported in June 2001 to have nearly vanished and another $20 million to be at risk;[11] and the Packard Foundation, whose holding of stock in Hewlett Packard Company fell from $13 billion in 1999 to $3.8 billion as of October 2002.[12]

The Uniform Management of Institutional Funds Act (UMIFA) was formulated in 1972, twenty years before the Restatement (Third) of Trusts. This act was also designed to free fiduciaries to follow modern investment principles, specifically the concept of total return. However, it applies only to endowment funds, with the anomalous result that a charity will be governed by two different rules depending on whether its funds were subject to restrictions as to expenditure of principal or not. With adoption of the Modern Prudent Investor Rule, it is not appropriate to retain UMIFA in its original form, at least in regard to its formulation of an investment standard. Furthermore, UMIFA does not address the question of whether and in what circumstances endowment funds may be pledged as security for loans. In a number of jurisdictions approval by the attorney general and, in some instances, by the court is required. This requirement should be universal, particularly if no change is made in the liability provisions applicable in the case of breach of the duty of care. Finally, the provisions in UMIFA defining the charities to which it is applicable are confusing and have created uncertainty on the part of the regulators and charities. Recognizing the need for change, the Commissioners in 2003 approved in a first reading amendments to UMIFA designed to clarify and broaden the definition of "institutions." They also adopted the provisions of the Uniform Prudent Investors Act, but did not address the question of whether a charity could pledge endowment assets. Final approval requires a second vote in 2004.

Although the Sarbanes-Oxley Act, noted earlier, was directed at reforming the manner in which large, publicly traded corporations would be governed, a number of charities announced that they were voluntarily adopting provi-

9. John Hechinger, "Emory U Gets a Lesson in Subtraction as Coke's Stock Fails to Make the Grade," *Wall Street Journal*, January 28, 2000, at C1.

10. Holly M. Sanders, "Temple University Shifts Investments to Stocks," *Bloomberg News*, September 29, 2000.

11. Thomas A. Corfman and Barbara Rose, "Art Institute Investment Strategy Raises Questions," *Chicago Tribune*, December 16, 2001, at C1.

12. Stephanie Strom, "Cultural Groups and Charities Are Feeling Each Bump on Wall Street," *New York Times*, October 11, 2002, at A27.

sions that mirrored the restrictions in the act. Regulators were also analyzing the Sarbanes-Oxley rules to determine how they might improve compliance with fiduciary duties of charities.[13] Early in 2003, the New York attorney general introduced a bill in the state senate that would impose the Sarbanes-Oxley requirements on nonprofit organizations in the state. The bill was subsequently revised to meet objections from the sector, but in September 2003 the attorney general announced that he believed further study was needed before he would seek enactment.[14]

The provision in the Sarbanes-Oxley Act prohibiting loans to directors and executives is similar to laws applicable to nonprofit corporations in a number of states, and should be more widely adopted. Other provisions might provide meaningful limitations for large charities, but would be ineffectual or inappropriate, as well as costly, for smaller ones. The greatest danger was that these provisions would be considered a panacea that, if extended to nonprofits, would serve to divert attention from the more basic changes that are needed to make the regulatory process meaningful.

Duty of Loyalty

With few exceptions, state standards of behavior for officers, directors, and trustees are well tailored to prevent them from realizing personal benefit at the expense of the charity and to deter reckless behavior. They have failed, however, to impose meaningful penalties for noncompliance, a failure that has seriously undermined enforcement efforts. The principal shortcomings include (1) permitting self-dealing transactions to be ratified after the fact without a showing of fairness, (2) applying the business judgment rule to excuse all but extreme gross negligence, and (3) condoning broad indemnification, backed by insurance paid for by the corporation even in some circumstances in which there was bad faith. The rationales for the adoption of each of these measures include the old concept that it is not appropriate to ask too much of volunteers, and a more contemporary fear that unless shielded from liability, people will not serve as directors or trustees. There is no evidence that this latter concern is in fact true, yet it has persisted as a rationale for providing charitable fiduciaries an almost free rein.[15]

13. See, for example, John L. Pulley, "Drexel U. Adopts Provisions of a Tough New Corporate Financial-Reporting Law, but Skeptics Warn Colleges against Moving Too Fast," *Chronicle of Higher Education,* June 13, 2003, at 27.

14. National Association of Attorneys General and National Association of State Charity Officials, 2003 Annual Charitable Trust and Solicitations Seminar (Brooklyn, September 15, 2003); see also Chapter 2.

15. See Chapter 4.

Suggestions for reforming the duty of loyalty have ranged from calls to further loosen the standards to recommendations to prohibit any sort of self-dealing. Among them, the most balanced and likely to gain acceptance is that put forth by Goldschmid, requiring that the transaction be fair to the corporation and that court review of transactions be governed "under loyalty standards" and not the business judgment rule.[16] In addition, states should repeal statutes that prevent directors from voiding an approved self-dealing transaction if they subsequently find that it was unfair to the corporation. This rule is counter to the excess benefit transactions limitations in section 4958 of the Internal Revenue Code, which was enacted in 1996, and offers no protection to a charity that has been misled by an insider.

Other components of the duty of loyalty, or fair dealing as it is termed under business law, needing clarification are the definitions of "conflicts of interest" and of "independent" parties. The descriptions of "conflicts of interest" in the statutes do not always specify whether the term applies only to financial conflicts or rather extends to situations that involve nonfinancial relationships. A common example is a director who serves on the boards of two charities that are looking for major gifts from a specific donor or are interested in purchasing a specific parcel of real estate. In most instances conflicts arising from service on the boards of competing charities can be taken care of without legal subvention. It is rare to find the same individual serving on the boards of two hospitals, two art museums, or two schools in the same community. Nonetheless, there are situations in which conflicts of this nature pose difficult problems for charities, and the difficulties should not be ignored. A possible approach would be to follow the example of many state governments and some private institutions by adopting a code of ethics or other nonbinding statement to cover appearances of conflicts and those without financial ramifications.[17] Such a code or policy would contain sanctions, but they would be applied by the organization and not the courts.

The definition of "independent directors" is similarly in need of clarification, particularly as to whether it includes donors or other persons dealing regularly with the charity such as consultants and professionals. If any of these categories are to be included, the parameters of the relationships will need definition. The analogous provisions in the self-dealing and excess benefit provisions in Chapter 42 of the Internal Revenue Code and the regulations may provide models.

16. Harvey J. Goldschmid, "The Fiduciary Duties of Nonprofit Directors and Officers: Paradoxes, Problems, and Proposed Reforms," 23 *Journal of Corporation Law* 631, 651 (1998).
17. See, for example, Mass. Gen. Laws. Ann. ch. 268A, §23.

Indemnification, D&O Insurance, and Liability Shields

The ability to indemnify directors has been considered necessary in order for charities to obtain the services of knowledgeable volunteers to serve as fiduciaries. In thirty-one states, corporations are permitted to pay attorneys' fees and costs of its officers and directors in suits charging them with breaches of the duty of care. In a few states indemnification is permitted against judgments and fines, while nearly half permit indemnification for amounts paid in settlement of suits. A concomitant to the power to indemnify is the power of the corporation to purchase insurance to cover judgments against directors and officers and to pay attorneys' fees incurred in defending them. Except in instances of bad faith, the coverage will typically leave the charity and its fiduciaries harmless and in cases involving bad faith will cover the costs of attorneys' fees and other expenses. It is also permissible to advance sums to meet expenses. Brody has noted that attorneys general appear to be keeping an eye on policy limits in negotiating settlements, citing the settlement with the trustees of the Bishop Estate for $25 million, which was the limit of the directors and officers liability policy, half of which went to the charity and the remainder to attorneys' fees.[18]

It is possible in some jurisdictions to include in the articles of organization of a business corporation, with approval of the shareholders, a provision placing a cap on a fiduciary's financial liability or waiving it entirely, particularly in connection with breaches of the duty of care. The Revised Model Nonprofit Corporation Act contains an optional provision permitting inclusion of such a liability shield in the articles of organization. In cases involving breaches of the duty of care only, Brody suggests that such an approach might be salutary by making the risk low enough to attract directors while high enough to induce fiduciaries to take their tasks more seriously.[19] On the other hand, it is difficult to justify protection to any degree for gross negligence, which is what these limitations are attempting to accomplish.

According to press reports, in the settlement of the suit between the New York attorney general and the trustees of Adelphi University who were removed from office by the New York Board of Regents, the attorney general prohibited use of the university's directors and officers liability policy to pay the $1.23 million in fines imposed on the trustees and the $400,000 of legal

18. Evelyn Brody, "The Legal Framework for Nonprofit Organizations," 19–20 (on file with author).

19. Id. at 21.

bills they incurred.[20] Obviously, a cap would be of no avail where this approach is permissible.

The California nonprofit corporation act places special limits on the power of indemnification in enforcement proceedings involving the attorney general. As is the case in other jurisdictions, indemnification is mandatory if the defendant prevails on the merits. It he does not, again following the general rule, the court may permit indemnification for expenses in an amount it determines. In the case of a settlement, indemnification is allowed to cover costs and the amount of a settlement only if the attorney general approves and if a court or a majority of disinterested directors or members determine that the person acted in good faith and in a manner he reasonably believed to be in the best interests of the corporation. A provision of this nature would permit relief in appropriate cases while not affording blanket coverage regardless of the extent of the breaches of duty involved.

Cy Pres; Deviation; Amendment Powers

The doctrine of cy pres, applicable with some variations in forty-nine states to charitable trusts and to charitable corporations, empowers a court to modify the original purposes of a charity if they become illegal, impossible, impracticable, or, in some jurisdictions, as well as in the Restatement (Third) of Trusts and the Uniform Trust Code, wasteful to fulfill.[21] Under common law the new purposes were to be "as close as possible" to the original ones, but that rule has been relaxed so that the standard, as recited in the Restatement (Third) of Trusts, calls for application to a purpose that "reasonably approximates the designated purpose." Furthermore, the Restatement explicitly provides that the doctrine is applicable in the case of gifts to charitable corporations that subsequently are dissolved. Traditional law has also required a showing that the settlor/donor had a general charitable intent, a requirement that still obtains in twenty-three states but has been abolished in the others.

A companion to the cy pres doctrine is the doctrine of deviation, applicable to private and charitable trusts alike. It permits a court to modify an administrative or distributive provision of a trust or permit the trustee to deviate from such a provision if because of circumstances not anticipated by the settlor the modification or deviation will further the purposes of the trust. Furthermore, it places the trustee under a duty to petition the court for devi-

---

20. David M. Halbfinger, "Lawsuits over Ouster of Adelphi Chief Are Settled," *New York Times,* November 18, 1998, at B1.

21. See Appendix, Table 2.

ation if he knows or should know of circumstances that justify such action. The two doctrines are often confused, with the court in South Carolina rejecting the doctrine of cy pres but applying deviation to modify purposes.[22]

Although the Restatement formulation of the doctrine of deviation incorporates a duty to seek its application, there is no corresponding duty recited in regard to the cy pres doctrine. However, it is implicit in the duty of loyalty, which as originally formulated in the case of private trusts is a duty to the beneficiaries, while for a charity it was transposed into a duty to carry out purposes for the benefit of an indefinite class of beneficiaries. Thus, in situations where it becomes impossible, impracticable, or wasteful to continue to fulfill the original purposes, the trustee cannot fulfill his duty to the public beneficiaries unless he seeks modification under the cy pres doctrine. Statutory clarification in the various states would be helpful. In England, by statute charity trustees are under an affirmative duty to seek cy pres application of their trust assets when it becomes appropriate.

Kurtz has articulated a duty of obedience to the original mission of a charity, which was cited in one decision of a court in New York in which the trustees filed a petition seeking approval of a sale of assets.[23] Interpretation of the traditional duty of loyalty to make explicit that it includes the duty to seek revision of purposes when they can no longer be carried out would assure that charitable funds will be used for purposes beneficial to the public on a contemporaneous basis. It is true that an attorney general can bring a cy pres petition on his own motion if the prerequisites for application of the doctrine are met, but it would be preferable for trustees to understand this as one of their duties rather than let it pass to the state by default.

There has been a question as to whether directors or members may amend the original purposes of a charitable corporation without court approval, thereby in effect avoiding the need to apply to a court for application of the doctrines of cy pres or deviation. The limitations on the power of amendment were set forth in a Massachusetts case in which a corporation created to operate a hospital attempted to amend its purposes to permit it to conduct any activity that promoted the health of the public. The court held that the fact that the provisions in the corporation statute made no reference to limitations on the power to amend, meant that the corporation could change its purposes; however, the directors would be violating their fiduciary duty were they to apply funds given subject to restrictions or unrestricted donations made prior to the amendment to a new purpose. In rejecting the hospital's

---

22. See Chapter 3.

23. Daniel L. Kurtz, *Board Liability: A Guide for Nonprofit Directors*, 84–85 (Mt. Kisco, N.Y.: Moyer Bell, 1989); Matter of Manhattan Eye, Ear and Throat Hospital, 715 N.Y.S.2d 575 (Sup. Ct. 1999).

argument that it had unfettered power to amend its purposes, the court stated, "As the Attorney General, colorfully, but no doubt correctly observes in his reply brief, 'those who give to a home for abandoned animals do not anticipate a future board amending the charity's purpose to become research vivisectionists.'"[24]

Conflicting decisions rendered in 2003 in two cases involving conversions of hospitals reflected a division of authority on this question. At issue were general assets of the corporations, not restricted funds. In one of them, the court took a narrow view of the corporation's powers, subjecting them to the requirements of the doctrines of cy pres and deviation, thereby preventing proposed sales of assets without court approval, while in another the court applied general corporate law principles under which the directors are virtually unrestricted in their ability to direct disposition of the general funds of the corporation, whether they are amending its charitable purposes or selling its assets and directing disposition of the proceeds.[25] In states that have enacted conversion statutes, the matter is further compounded because these statutes impose limits on the power of health care organizations to amend their purposes or change their operations, restrictions that do not necessarily apply to other charities.

This matter has never been at issue in England where trust doctrine is applied uniformly to charitable corporations and trusts alike, but the legal history in the United States is not as clear. In terms of effective and efficient regulation of the charitable sector, the English rule that the assets of charitable corporations are subject to the doctrines of cy pres and deviation, regardless of their source, and regardless of whether they were given subject to explicit restrictions, is clearly preferable. However, unlike the manner in which the law developed in England, the doctrines of cy pres and deviation should be applied liberally. Charitable assets merit protection, and mere form should not determine their disposition.

Rights and Duties of Members

The majority of mutual benefit corporations are constituted by members who have certain rights in connection with the governance of the corporation. There are also uncounted public benefit corporations with members. In some instances members are individuals whom the directors wish to acknowledge for their contributions or other manner of support, but who for any number

---

24. Attorney General v. Hahnemann Hospital, 494 N.E.2d 1011, 1021 n.18 (Mass. 1986).

25. Banner Health System v. Long, 663 N.W.2d 242 (S.D. 2003); Banner Health System v. Stenehjem, 2003 WL 501821 (D.N.D. 2003).

of reasons are not appropriate persons to serve as directors, among them being a desire to keep the board relatively small. In some instances members are chosen to represent various constituencies of the corporation. State statutes and the case law hold that members have a right to vote for directors, to compel accountings, and to approve amendments to the by-laws. In some states they are also given the power to approve amendments to the articles of organization and changes of purposes. There are a large number of cases dealing with the rights of members to sue the directors for breaches of their duties or to protect the corporation's assets. These are discussed below.

There are no precedents and little commentary about the duties of members. During the 1980s and 1990s the extent of these duties assumed importance in an unanticipated context. During this period many charitable organizations, particularly hospitals, were reorganizing their corporate structures to provide for a central parent corporation controlling a number of subsidiary organizations, some taxable and some exempt. In the for-profit context, control would be exercised by virtue of the parent's ownership of stock in the subsidiary corporation. Following the analogy made between members of a nonprofit corporation and stockholders of a business corporation, a nonprofit parent corporation would be named the sole member of each of the nonprofit subsidiaries, with the right to elect directors, approve certain measures relating to the management of the subsidiary, and amend its articles and by-laws. Once in operation, conflicts arose in some of these arrangements between the interests of the parent and those of the subsidiary, with no rules prescribing to whom the sole member's duty of loyalty ran. The same question arose in regard to the duty of the directors of a subsidiary who were elected by the sole-member parent organization: is their loyalty to the parent or to the corporation for which they serve as fiduciaries? As of 2003, the problem was unresolved and the conflicting interests involved made it difficult to craft a solution.[26]

Powers of Donors

Under common law, donors have only the rights they may reserve at the time of their gifts. If none are reserved, once the gift is complete they have no standing to sue the corporation or the directors to enforce the terms of the gift. As a practical matter, if a donor reserves a right of reverter, unless the possibility of reversion is so remote as to be negligible, the gift will not be

---

26. Dana Brakman Reiser, "Decision-Makers without Duties: Defining the Duties of Parent Corporations Acting as Sole Corporate Members in Nonprofit Health Care Systems," 53 *Rutgers Law Review* 979 (2001); see also Chapter 3.

considered complete for purposes of the tax laws, so that the donor will not be entitled to a deduction from income, estate, and gift taxes for the contribution. Donors wanting to be assured that the terms of their gifts will be observed, but unwilling to risk loss of tax benefits, may provide in the deed of gift for a transfer of the assets to another charity if the original donee fails to carry out the terms of the gift, thereby making the alternative beneficiary the enforcer of the conditions.

The original version of UMIFA permitted donors to release restrictions they had placed on institutional funds, but gave them no right to agree to modifications or standing to sue to enforce restrictions. In contrast, the Uniform Trust Code, adopted in 2000, grants donors the right to modify gift terms and standing to sue. Proposed amendments incorporating the Trust Code rules were rejected by the UMIFA drafting committee in 2003, and thus did not appear in the draft that was approved in a first reading by the Commissioners in August 2003.

Community foundations have long had "donor-advised funds," a term signifying funds as to which they will consider the recommendations of a donor or his designee as to the identity of grantees of distributions from that specific fund. Since 1992 a number of commercial investment companies have followed this model, establishing donor-advised funds for which they serve as trustee and which, because of their size and the large number of contributors, qualify as public charities. A survey published in May 2003 estimated that $3.5 billion was held by twelve commercial donor-advised funds, of which $2.4 billion was held by Fidelity Investments Charitable Gift Fund, the originator of the concept. Another forty-nine community foundations offering donor-advised funds held an estimated $4.9 billion.[27] The Fidelity Charitable Gift Fund in 2001 and 2002 received $1 billion, second only to the Salvation Army in the amount of private donations received by charities that year as compiled by the *Chronicle of Philanthropy*.[28] This was an unprecedented record of growth, which signified the popularity of this vehicle for funneling charitable contributions.

During the 1990s it also became popular for some foundations and individual donors to characterize their grant-making as "venture philanthropy," differentiating it from "old-fashioned philanthropy" by the degree of involvement of the grantors who claimed to be applying the approach of ven-

27. Marni D. Larose and Brad Wolverton, "Donor-Advised Funds Experience Drop in Contributions, Survey Finds," *Chronicle of Philanthropy*, May 15, 2003, at 7.

28. Elizabeth Greene et al., "The Tide Turns: Donations to Big Charities in Uncertain Economic Climate," *Chronicle of Philanthropy*, October 31, 2002, at 28; Nicole Lewis and Meg Sommerfeld, "Donations to Big Groups Rose 13% in 2000," *Chronicle of Philanthropy*, November 1, 2001, at 35.

ture capitalists. This approach entails a high degree of involvement in the decisions of the company in which the venture funds are invested, as well as receipt of detailed current financial information as the project goes forward; in some instances a seat on the board of the grantee is required.[29]

Taken together these trends reflect a new attitude toward charitable giving and the disbursement of charitable assets, which emphasizes the ongoing importance of donors in a manner contrary to common law. If this continues, the limits on donors' powers that have been a basic component of charity law are likely to change, a development not without irony in light of the objections to donor control of foundations voiced by the Treasury Department and the Congress in the 1960s.

State Regulation of Charities

Regulation by the Office of the Attorney General

The duty to regulate charities in the states is imposed on the attorney general, acting as representative of the indefinite beneficiaries of these institutions. However, there are only twelve states in which this power is exercised in a manner that impacts positively on the behavior of charitable fiduciaries. In 1991 Dale characterized state enforcement as follows: "In most states, the Charity Bureau of the Attorney General's office is inactive, ineffective, understaffed, overwhelmed, or some combination of these."[30] Over ten years later, this characterization holds, particularly in regard to breaches of the duties of care and loyalty and in efforts to assure dedication of funds to charitable purposes. It is to be noted that this characterization does not apply to the same degree to regulation of solicitations of funds for charitable purposes, a separate aspect of charitable activity regulated under separate laws now in force in thirty-nine of the fifty states and the District of Columbia and enforced by the attorney general or a state charity official, often as part of the duties of a bureau of consumer protection. This aspect of charitable regulation is far better staffed and managed in most states than the efforts to police fiduciary duties. Furthermore, regulation of solicitation is better publicized and better understood by the general public.

The discussion that follows does not apply to regulation of solicitation ex-

---

29. Christine Letts et al., *High Performance Nonprofit Organizations: Managing Upstream for Greater Impact* (New York: Wiley, 1999); William P. Ryan et al., "Problem Boards or Board Problem?" *The Nonprofit Quarterly*, 1 (Summer 2003).

30. Harvey P. Dale, "Diversity, Accountability, and Compliance in the Nonprofit Sector," Norman A. Sugarman Memorial Lecture, Mandel Center for Nonprofit Organizations, Case Western Reserve University, Cleveland, Ohio (March 20, 1991).

cept to the extent that there is overlap in the programs and the reporting requirements. Thus, for example, in Illinois, Massachusetts, Michigan, New York, and Ohio, the attorney general is responsible for both aspects of charity regulation and his efforts are coordinated in the same office. In contrast, in Connecticut, Maryland, and Pennsylvania, only certain charities that solicit funds from the general public need register and file annual financial reports with the office of the attorney general. In these states the attorney general has no record of the universe of charities in his jurisdiction and no information on the financial activities of any of them other than private foundations, which are required to file duplicates of their federal information returns with the state, and those soliciting charities that are required to register and report. In contrast, in California, registration and financial reporting are required of all charities, as well as of professional fund-raisers, while soliciting charities are regulated by the cities and towns. In South Carolina and Rhode Island the registration and reporting requirements apply only to charitable trusts, not corporations, while in Minnesota soliciting charities are subject to detailed reporting requirements and other charities are required to file copies of their federal tax return or, if none, an audited financial report.[31]

Indicative of the low level of state interest in regulation of fiduciary duties is the fact that in 1965 the three New England states with reporting statutes, together with California, Illinois, Michigan, Ohio, Oregon, and South Carolina, required registration and reporting from charities and still do. Iowa had a similar statutory requirement, but it was repealed. Minnesota and New York are the only states to have adopted reporting provisions since 1965, with the result that there is now one more state regulating fiduciary duties than was the case forty years ago. It is true that the great majority of charities in the country are organized and operating in one of these states so that the statutes affect more organizations than might otherwise appear. The problem, however, is that the disparity between states with active programs and those without fosters forum-shopping and creates inconsistencies that make regulation exceedingly difficult.

The statutes establishing these state regulatory programs are for the most part adequate for their purposes. There is a Uniform Supervision of Trustees for Charitable Purposes Act, adopted by the National Conference of Commissioners on Uniform State Laws in 1954. However, the definition of the charities covered by the act is seriously flawed. It required amendment in Illinois and Michigan to clarify that it applied to charitable corporations as well as charitable trusts, while the California version was changed before enact-

---

31. See Chapter 6 and Appendix, Table 1.

ment for that purpose. The Oregon act adopted the same language used in the California act.[32]

The rationale for these statutes is that it is impossible for an attorney general to regulate charities in his jurisdiction if he has no record of their identity nor information about their operations. In addition to the registration and reporting requirements, the statutes provide his office with broad powers to investigate allegations of misappropriation of charitable funds, subpoena witnesses, hold hearings, and issue regulations to assist in carrying out his duties. Complementary provisions in other state laws require that the attorney general receive notice of all legal proceedings involving the disposition of charitable funds, and in some instances he is considered a necessary party to those proceedings. The latter is the case with petitions for cy pres or deviation in all but a few states. Finally, statutes in a number of states require either notice to or approval by the attorney general of dissolutions, mergers, and substantial contractions of charitable corporations.

In short, these laws give broad power to the attorney general to regulate charities, yet the few active programs in existence operate with limited staff and inadequate financial resources. The lack of support may reflect the disinterest of a particular attorney general, but that has not been the usual case. Rather, the principal reason is that all of these programs are underfunded. For example, New York has 40,000 charities registered and reporting to the attorney general's Charity Bureau, which is staffed with eighteen attorneys. In California, the attorney general maintains three offices, staffed by ten attorneys. A separate Registry of Charities is maintained in Sacramento with which all annual reports are filed. As of February 2003, there were 85,000 charities registered and filing with the state. These are the best-staffed and most active of the offices in the larger states, and offices in Illinois, Massachusetts, Michigan, and Ohio operate in a similar manner. In contrast, one attorney is assigned on a part-time basis to handle trust matters in Rhode Island.

In addition to the eleven states just described, there are twenty-two others with statutes requiring registration and reporting by certain charities that conduct public solicitations for contributions. Some of these programs are conducted by the attorney general, others are under the jurisdiction of the secretary of state or another state official. In a number of these states, notably Pennsylvania, Connecticut, and New Mexico, the attorney general has instituted proceedings against individual charities on the basis of information obtained through the reports from soliciting organizations. The regulators in

32. See Chapter 6.

these states are knowledgeable as to the duties of charitable fiduciaries and willing in appropriate circumstances to bring actions to preserve charitable funds. However, it is far beyond the resources of any of these state officials to enforce breaches of fiduciary duty on a regular basis.

Suggestions have been made to fund state regulatory programs through filing fees, and a number of the states do require annual payments. However, as is the case with the federal excise tax on private foundations that was originally to be earmarked to provide funds for the IRS to audit exempt organizations, the Congress and state legislators routinely resist dedicating funds for specific purposes, preferring to retain control over their disposition as part of the general appropriations powers.

In assessing the effectiveness of the state programs, two disturbing trends have become apparent since the late 1990s. The first trend is increasing use by attorneys general of the threat of litigation to force charities to agree to settlements of disputes with conditions that are far more restrictive than the law requires or that would be imposed by a court. One widely publicized example was the terms of a settlement between the Massachusetts attorney general and the trustees of Boston University over a controversy relating initially to the investment of a large percent of the university's assets in a start-up venture. Under the terms of the settlement, the trustees agreed to reform the corporation's basic governing structure to mandate fixed terms for directors and trustees with limits on the number of consecutive terms they could serve, give alumni and faculty a voice in nominating and electing trustees, and require the board to adopt special procedures for approving the salary of the president. None of these limits are required of newly formed charities, nor is there precedent for the courts to impose them permanently.

This does not mean that settlements are per se undesirable. In many instances they assure reform while avoiding embarrassment to well-intentioned fiduciaries, and they save public and charitable funds. A major drawback to the use of settlements, however, is that their terms are rarely made public, so it is difficult to determine the extent to which they are correcting wrongdoing, as well as the degree to which the sanctions that are imposed go beyond those that might be ordered by a court.

The second trend is closely related to the first; namely, the politicization by the attorney general of his regulation of charities. An early example was the publicity generated regarding allegations of self-dealing by the president of Boston University at a time when he was running for governor of Massachusetts in 1990. More recently, the attorney general of Pennsylvania, while running for governor in the summer and fall of 2002, generated nationwide publicity when he successfully prevented the trustees of a school from selling their controlling interest worth $1.35 billion in the stock of the Hershey

Foods Corporation on the grounds that the trustees had a duty to the community in which the charity was located in addition to their duty to operate the school. As a result of the challenge the trustees abandoned the plan to sell the stock and then resigned to be replaced by a slate approved by the attorney general. Shortly thereafter the state legislature amended its prudent investor rule to require charitable fiduciaries in similar circumstances to consider the needs of the community in which they carry out their charitable purposes—a major departure from common law principles.[33]

A final area in which reforms are needed is one affecting both the states and the Internal Revenue Service, namely, the nature of the information that is required to be filed by the charities. Since the 1980s state attorneys general and state charity officials have cooperated with the IRS and each other in efforts to improve the content of the state and federal forms charities must file, and most states now accept the federal Form 990 with some supplemental information to meet state reporting requirements. In those states that regulate solicitation, thirty-three accept a uniform reporting form that uses Form 990 as its starting point. This has eased the burden on filers to a certain degree, although it has not obviated the need for charities that conduct interstate solicitations to file separate reports in as many as thirty-nine jurisdictions. The specific shortcomings related to the forms filed with the states, and more particularly the information required to be provided in them, are discussed below in connection with the federal information-reporting forms that are accepted by all of the states.

The nature of state charity oversight is regulatory, but it also has an ameliorative function. It is exemplified in the wording of the Massachusetts statute, which imposes a duty on the attorney general to "enforce the due application of funds given or appropriated to public charities . . . and to prevent breaches in the administration thereof."[34] In a few jurisdictions and during different periods, there have been attorneys general who viewed their role as that of an adversary and confined their activities to policing and prosecuting charities and their fiduciaries. However, in almost all of the states in which the attorney general is active in enforcement, he has viewed his role as that of supporter of the sector, placing upon him a duty to improve the administration of charities. When the first regulatory statutes were enacted between 1950 and 1970, efforts were made to identify charities and to educate fiduciaries as to their duties, including the duty to register and file financial reports. During this effort many small trusts were identified as having income that merely covered the fees and expenses of their fiduciaries. The states en-

33. See Chapter 4.
34. Mass. Gen. Laws ch. 12, §8.

couraged and in some instances initiated court actions to consolidate small trusts or apply them under the cy pres doctrine to other purposes.

A number of attorneys general have undertaken campaigns to educate trustees as to their duties and to improve reporting procedures. Attorneys general now regularly issue publications and newsletters, hold conferences for fiduciaries, and, with the advent of the Internet, post information about their activities and aids for compliance. The Massachusetts Division of Public Charities in 1962 established an advisory committee comprised of leaders in the charitable and financial communities, members of the bar and accounting professions, fund-raisers, and civic leaders who meet with the attorney general and his staff on a regular basis to discuss matters of concern and formulate measures to improve compliance. Succeeding attorneys general have continued this practice, and it has been replicated in a number of other states, most recently in Illinois. One of the most compelling examples of the benefits that can arise from cooperation between the attorney general and the charitable community is the group that was formed in the fall of 2001 in New York to assist in coordinating the disbursement of donated funds to victims of the September 11 disaster and their families.

Standing to Sue

Under the common law the attorney general is granted what amounts to virtually exclusive standing to sue to enforce charitable assets. Members of the general public, unless they can show a specific beneficial relationship to a charity, are not permitted to call charitable fiduciaries to account. The rationale is that if trustees and directors were open to suit by anyone, it would be impossible to find individuals to serve. Furthermore, members of the general public are not permitted to sue the attorney general to force him to take action. This has meant that in states in which the attorney general has no role in charity enforcement, in most instances there is no effective way to apply to the courts to correct abuses. Co-trustees and co-directors do have standing, as do members in a few states. The courts have also relaxed this rule of exclusive standing under some circumstances to permit donors or their heirs, hospital patients, park abutters, and alumni to bring suit, but the cases in which standing has been denied outnumber those in which it has been granted. In the majority of the cases allowing private parties to sue, a major factor in the court's decision has been the absence of any state official able or willing to act.[35]

The desirability of expanding standing has received much attention in the

35. See Chapter 6.

legal literature, with a number of suggestions to broaden the rules and a number of commentators concerned that to do so will encourage frivolous suits that will divert fiduciaries and deplete charitable funds in the defense of lawsuits. There can be no question that expanded standing will encourage disaffected persons, whether grantees, potential beneficiaries, or disgruntled members of the public, to use the courts to attempt to force trustees and directors to take desired courses of action. The best solution is to have an active and interested attorney general who will take action to correct abuses. There is also precedent for allowing him to let individuals bring suit in his name if he believes there is merit to the action but is disinclined to do so himself.

There is one situation in which relaxation of the rules of standing would be appropriate. That is in a situation in which the attorney general as part of his constitutional duties is called upon to represent a state agency that is party to a suit in which a charity is on the opposing side. In such a case the attorney general could agree to represent or defend the charitable interest and arrange for outside counsel to represent the state agency. If he chooses, however, to oppose the charitable interests, the doctrine of limited standing needs to be modified so that the charitable interests may be heard.

Other State Agencies Regulating Specific Charitable Activities

The office of the attorney general is not the only state office that regulates charitable activities and the actions of their fiduciaries, although its powers are broader than those of other state agencies. The secretary of state or corporation counsel in all jurisdictions issues articles of organization and monitors the existence of corporations through requirements to report active status annually. Boards of educations, or in New York the Regents, have broad supervisory powers over educational organizations. The extent of this power was demonstrated in the 1995 case of Adelphi University in which a class consisting of students, faculty, and staff brought suit against the trustees alleging violation of the duties of care and loyalty, the outcome of which was the imposition of fines and removal of all but one of the trustees.[36]

State tax departments have the power to grant exemption from state income and sales taxes, while taxation of real and personal property is governed at the local level. In almost every case, state exemption follows the federal determination. However, this is not necessarily the case in regard to property taxes, as the history of attempts to tax hospitals and other health care delivery

---

36. Jack Sirica, "Suit Filed against Adelphi President," *Newsday*, October 20, 1995, at A66; David M. Halbfinger, "Lawsuits over Ouster of Adelphi Chief Are Settled," *New York Times*, November 18, 1998, at B1.

systems in Pennsylvania and Utah, described in Chapter 3, substantiates. It is likely that local taxation will remain a major issue, not easily resolved other than through indirect pressure on institutions to make payments in lieu of taxes.

Regulatory powers are also exercised by state accrediting agencies, anti-trust divisions, bankruptcy courts, and consumer protection bureaus. None has power to effect change in the entire sector and should not be looked to for regulation of fiduciary behavior.

Federal Laws Governing Charities and Their Fiduciaries

Internal Revenue Code Provisions

Although state laws govern the creation and dissolution of charities and the duties and powers of their fiduciaries, in actuality it is the federal government and, specifically, the Internal Revenue Service that regulate this segment of the nonprofit sector today, as has been the case for the last half-century. The importance of the federal regulatory regime cannot be overemphasized. One has only to consider that in two-thirds of the states regulation of charities is minimal or nonexistent, and even in the eleven jurisdictions with active en-forcement programs, the federal rules set an important minimum standard for compliance.

Recommendations for Changes in the Code and Regulations

The provisions in the Internal Revenue Code that contain the requirements for exemption from income tax and eligibility for receipt of deductible con-tributions are described in Chapter 5, while the manner in which the Service regulates charities is summarized in Chapter 7. Many of the shortcomings in the regulatory scheme and recommendations for revision of the substantive provisions are described in those chapters. Like the state provisions, by and large the Internal Revenue Code limitations are adequate to protect charita-ble funds and, with some exceptions, do require high standards of fiduciary behavior. This was not the case until passage in 1996 of the excess benefit limitations. Prior to that, only private foundation managers and substan-tial contributors were prohibited from self-dealing, with penalties appropri-ately imposed on them and not the foundation itself. Private foundations, however, represented only 5% of the organizations exempt under section 501(c)(3). The fiduciaries of the remaining 95% of organizations described in section 501(c)(3) were subject to poorly articulated prohibitions against pri-vate inurement and private benefit, with the only sanction being revocation of exemption of the charity and no sanction on the individuals whose behavior led to the revocation. With the limits on the ability of the IRS to provide information to state attorneys general, there was no effective way in which one could assure that timely action would be brought against those individuals or that the assets of the charity would be protected.

The provisions in the Internal Revenue Code that limit the behavior of charitable fiduciaries are found in the first instance in the definition of organizations eligible for exemption from taxation and the regulations thereunder that prescribe that a charity must be organized and operated exclusively for exempt purposes in order to qualify. There is a prohibition in the Code itself against inurement of income to private individuals, and a similar prohibition against "private benefit" is found in the regulations.

The organizational test in a sense sets the ground rules for operation of a charity, requiring that governing instruments limit the manner in which fiduciaries may carry out the organization's purposes. The regulations do not permit broad exculpatory language and require inclusion of a provision assuring that upon dissolution, the organization's assets will pass to another exempt charity. They also identify provisions that, if included, will disqualify the organization from exemption. Thus they prohibit inclusion of a provision expressly permitting an organization to engage in activities that in themselves are not in furtherance of one or more exempt purposes unless the activity is an insubstantial part of its operations. The effect of this provision has been to alter the Code requirement that a charity be organized "exclusively" for exempt purposes, so as to read "substantially."

The operational test further expands on this distinction by providing that an organization will be considered to be operated exclusively for exempt purposes if it engages primarily in activities that accomplish exempt purposes and that the test will not be met if more than an insubstantial part of an organization's activities are not in furtherance of an exempt purpose or if it violates the prohibition against private inurement. The prohibition against private inurement applies to directors, officers, employees, and other "insiders," and to payments that are not commensurate with the services provided to the charity. There have been two difficulties in its application: uncertainty as to whom it applies and uncertainty as to the extent to which a benefit gives rise to the prohibition. The problem is compounded for the regulators because the existence of any amount of private inurement is grounds for revocation. This is in contrast to the limit on private benefit, which is violated only if the benefit is found to be more than insubstantial. The private benefit prohibition, however, applies to any person, not just insiders, so that the private inurement prohibition is in effect a subset of the private benefit rule.

Congress enacted the excess benefit provisions in recognition of the shortcomings inherent in relying on the provisions in the Internal Revenue Code defining exempt charities to police fiduciary behavior. With the passage of intermediate sanctions for violation of the excess benefit limitations, it was anticipated that the private inurement provisions would decrease in importance while the private benefit proscription, applying as it does to a greater universe than the excess benefit provisions, would assume more importance. This may not, however, be a satisfactory situation for the regulators in that the parameters of private benefit remain unclear and the ultimate sanction of revocation remains inappropriate.

In regard to the excess benefit prohibitions themselves, there are two major shortcomings that could not be resolved in the regulations. The first is that in determining whether the amount of compensation is excessive, the congressional history made it clear that the organization could rely on comparable data from the private sector and not just within the nonprofit universe. With the sharp rise in executive compensation that began in the late 1990s and, despite the subsequent economic downturn, did not abate proportionally, this provision effectively removed meaningful limits on the amount of compensation that most of the large charities may provide. There is already anecdotal evidence that the Code provisions have raised the level of payments. A balance needs to be found in which charities can compete with private employers, possibly by limiting comparables to the mean levels or, at the least, excluding the upper ranges of payments, which, evidence has shown, do not relate to performance as it is measured in the charitable sector.[37]

The second shortcoming relates to indemnification of disqualified persons, specifically managers. Payment of director and officer liability insurance premiums is not an excess benefit transaction nor is the application of insurance proceeds to pay excise taxes imposed for violations of the provisions so long as the payments are treated as compensation to the fiduciary. The distortion that results from permitting payments from insurance proceeds was exemplified in the settlement of the Bishop Estate dispute with the IRS under which the amount paid by each trustee was $40,000, while the reported total fines of $14 million came from the proceeds of insurance that had been owned by the estate.[38] Limitations in state law would be preferable, but it is unlikely that they would be universally adopted. Accordingly, it would be ap-

37. Peter Frumkin, "Are Nonprofit CEOs Overpaid?" *The Public Interest*, 83, 88 (Winter 2001); see also John Cassidy, "The Greed Cycle," *The New Yorker*, September 23, 2002, at 64; Patrick McGeehan, "Again, Money Follows the Pinstripes," *New York Times*, April 6, 2003, at §3, p. 1.

38. Rick Daysog, "Ex-Bishop Trustees Pay IRS in Settling Tax Claims," *Star-Bulletin*, January 4, 2001, at 1.

propriate to limit the use of insurance proceeds in cases where the person subject to tax has not prevailed in a court proceeding or the case has been settled but there was evidence of bad faith or harm to the corporation. The California statutory provisions applicable in enforcement proceedings involving the attorney general, described above, require approval of indemnification by the attorney general and a court or disinterested directors or members if they determine that there was good faith and a reasonable belief that the actions were in the best interests of the corporation. A similar standard in the Code would be an appropriate solution.

In addition to these modifications, guidelines are needed from the Service as to the application of section 4958 to revenue-sharing arrangements as well as the relationship between violation of the excess benefit provisions and revocation of exemption for violation of the private inurement or private benefit prohibitions. In the case of *Caracci v. Commissioner,* decided in 2002,[39] the Tax Court upheld the imposition of excise taxes on the disqualified persons but refused to approve revocation of exemption of the charities involved. The case signaled to the Service that the courts may well be reluctant to use revocation as a sanction, particularly if there is evidence that the situation has been corrected and is unlikely to recur. Such a result would be salutary.

In this case the court also invoked another provision in section 4958 that was precedent-setting and may signal a new appreciation of the value of preserving charitable assets. The defendants, family members and three S-corporations that had purchased the assets from the nonprofit corporations, were given the option of restoring the assets to the tax-exempt corporations within a ninety-day correction period, in which case the court indicated that it would consider abatement of the excise taxes. The IRS appealed the decision, but shortly thereafter the Justice Department filed a motion to withdraw the appeal. Some commentators raise serious objections to the abatement power, noting that if it is widely used, there is no effective sanction on the individuals who violated the Code provisions and, as with revocation, in many instances they will remain as managers of the charity. Thus, although the abatement provisions are a welcome addition to the Code to the extent they result in restitution and thereby preservation of charitable funds, this comes at the cost of having meaningful deterrents. The provisions in section 507 under which the private foundation termination tax can be abated if a state court has taken appropriate action, which could include removal of managers, would be preferable.

In 2002 the Service requested suggestions from the public for changes in

39. Caracci v. Commissioner, 118 T.C. 379 (2002).

the private foundation provisions in light of the parallel provisions applicable to publicly supported charities that provide excess benefits to insiders. Although it appeared unlikely that Congress would agree to any major changes to Chapter 42 that would allow private foundations to be treated on the same equal basis as publicly supported charities, it was possible that some minor revisions might be considered. Among many suggestions for amendment that have been offered, the definition of supporting organizations that are not private foundations is one of the most convoluted in the Code, and the regulations under that section seriously add to the complexity. In addition, there is no reason not to use the same definition of family members for both public charities and private foundations.

Instead of the current per se ban on self-dealing in the private foundation provisions, consideration should be given to applying the excise tax penalties for self-dealing to the amount of the excess benefit as is the case in section 4958. In regard to the minimum distribution rules in section 4942, prior to the economic downturn that started in 2000 a number of suggestions were made to increase the payout rate, either by increasing the percentage or by prohibiting administrative expenses from being treated as qualifying distributions for purposes of determining compliance with the rules.

The debate became heated in the spring of 2003 and split the charitable community between grantors and grantees. The controversy over an appropriate payout rate was not resolved and appeared unlikely that it would be, posing as it does the unanswerable questions as to whether one should save to meet future needs at the expense of current ones, and if so at what rate; how one measures the time value of money; and how the market will behave in the future. During the debate advocates of increasing the payout turned, as they had in the mid-1980s, away from these considerations and instead focused on and publicized examples of excessive compensation and benefits to board members, problems that would more properly be addressed by strengthening the provisions in sections 4941 and 4945 that limit self-dealing and define taxable expenditures.

Another recommendation for changing Chapter 42 has been to repeal the prohibition against making jeopardy investments under section 4944 on the basis that it does not lend itself to enforcement by the IRS and was a limitation best left to the states. In view of the fact that it might be enforced in no more than fourteen or fifteen states, it is unlikely that such an amendment would or should be adopted. There is pressing need, however, for the regulations to be amended to adopt the Modern Prudent Investor Rule as the standard for compliance. In addition, the taxable expenditure provisions should be relaxed to remove the distinction between grants and contracts, and to permit foundations to make grants to other foundations in the same manner as they make grants to publicly supported charities. Finally, the excise tax on foundation investment income should be repealed. It serves only to reduce the amount that is contributed to other charities or for direct public benefit. Alternatively, the tax should be earmarked, as was originally intended, to support IRS regulation of exempt organizations.

The most important revision that could be made to Chapter 42, however, relates not to the details of the prohibitions but to the sanctions applicable to violations of all but the prohibition against self-dealing. In each of these cases the punitive excise taxes are imposed on the foundation, thereby diminishing its grant-making ability. Repeal of these penalties is desirable, but it needs to be accompanied by adoption of more meaningful sanctions on foundation managers who have caused the foundation to enter into the prohibited transactions. The Code now does provide for imposition of taxes on managers who approve a transaction involving violation of the jeopardy investment and taxable expenditure provisions. However, these excise taxes apply only if the manager knew that the act involved was a violation of the Code prohibitions and his approval was willful and not due to reasonable cause, a heavy burden for the Service to prove. Far more meaningful would be sanctions applicable to managers who knew or should have known that they were approving prohibited transactions. Furthermore, there is no reason why similar sanctions should not apply in the case of failure to meet the payout provisions or the limit on business holdings, both of which are in the power of the managers. Finally, provisions permitting abatement of the excise taxes if restitution is made should be included in any revision, although it would be preferable to include measures similar to those in section 507 whereby it would be possible to effect removal of fiduciaries who have violated the Code provisions.

There are other Code provisions affecting charities that need amendment or repeal; although they are not directed at fiduciary behavior, they warrant mention. One of the most far-reaching would be to remove the limitations on lobbying so that charities may contribute more meaningfully to society. However, this is unlikely to be acceptable to the Congress, although, on the grounds of simplification, it appears to be willing to remove the distinction between direct and grassroots lobbying, a proposal to that effect having been passed by the House and the Senate in 2003.[40] The prohibition on participation in political campaigns is related to the lobbying limitations but seems to be considered quite differently. In 2002 a strong lobbying effort was made to permit churches to support candidates for public office. As the bill neared passage, a group of moderate church leaders joined to oppose it, expressing

40. Charitable Giving Act of 2003, H.R. 7, §206, 108th Cong., 1st Sess. (2003); CARE Act of 2003, S. 476, §303, 108th Cong., 1st Sess. (2003).

the belief that churches should remain separate from the political process. The bill containing the amendment was defeated in the House.[41]

Another measure requiring congressional action is the parameters of disaster relief that are considered charitable under the Code. The Victims of Terrorism Tax Relief Act of 2001 established a separate, distinct standard applicable only to the victims of the September 11, 2001 attacks and of anthrax. A distinction of this sort will inevitably be difficult to apply in the future, and the inconsistencies should be addressed before another acute situation arises.

Despite many calls for amendment of the unrelated business income tax provisions (UBIT), the overall scheme is effective. Two important improvements would be to clarify the scope of the exception for income from royalties and to establish uniform, meaningful rules governing the allocation of expenses between exempt activities and those subject to UBIT.[42]

Finally, there is a pressing need for clarification of the treatment of joint ventures between exempt and nonexempt entities. The problems in this area stemmed originally from a misunderstanding by the Service of partnership law, the duties of directors of business corporations, and the extent to which activities of a subsidiary corporation can be attributed to its parent.

Underlying the specific issues are unresolved questions as to the proper scope of "commercial activities" for an exempt charity. The arguments that are made against permitting charities to undertake unlimited "business activities" are based on fears of "unfair competition" and distraction of charitable fiduciaries from attending to exempt purposes. However, the unrelated business income tax provisions were designed to and can effectively deal with unfair competition, particularly if the modifications just described are effectuated, while an argument about distraction carries little weight. Based on existing precedents, there appears to be no per se limit to the amount of related or unrelated business activity that may be conducted by a charity, and that is appropriate. In the case of related activities, the Service's position is that once a business is determined to be related, the broader the market that is reached, the more the organization can fulfill its exempt function. In the case of an unrelated activity, it would be appropriate to apply the primary purpose test of the regulations together with a commensurate test based on the extent of the business activity vis-à-vis the related activities (and not the revenues generated). This will not answer the objections from the small business sector nor from commentators who believe that a distinction needs to be

41. Houses of Worship Political Speech Protection Act, H.R. 2357, 107th Cong., 1st Sess. (2001).

42. Henry Hansmann, "Unfair Competition and the Unrelated Business Income Tax," 75 *Virginia Law Review* 605 (1989).

made between the private and charitable sectors based on the manner in which they fulfill their purposes.

A different approach to the problem has been proposed by Hill to deal with what she terms a nondiversion constraint. This would take the form of a tax on "diversion transactions" within an organization, defined as expenditure of revenues on purposes other than those that form the basis for exemption.[43]

In his 2003 study of the commercialization of higher education, Bok recounted the increased attention to profit-making activities, notably in athletics, scientific research, and extension programs, from the view of a university leader concerned with the erosion of academic standards and institutional integrity, not from that of the tax administrator. There was some evidence that the enthusiasm for commercial venturing was abating with the change in the economy after 1999 and possibly reflecting recognition of the problems these ventures pose for the sector as well as for the organizations that comprise it.[44]

Financial Reporting

A major drawback to efforts to police charities that pervades both state and federal programs is the reliance of regulatory schemes on financial reporting from the sector. There is basic disagreement among the sector, the accounting profession, and the tax bar as to the way in which information should be reported; moreover, an unusually high percentage of the reports that are filed contain errors, while even more are incomplete. Despite public education efforts by the sector to improve the quality of reporting, particularly after 1990, there is little evidence of improvement. Furthermore, in two surveys of financial executives conducted by the Urban Institute in 2002, 72% of organizations reported using external professionals to prepare Form 990, virtually all of whom were certified public accountants; almost 70% of these worked for a local or regional accounting firm, which often had a nonprofit specialty practice.[45] Prior to this study, it had been assumed that the high incidence of error was attributable to the fact that most returns were prepared by the charities themselves. Based on the findings in the report, it appears that educational efforts need to be readdressed to the professional preparers.

43. Frances R. Hill, "Targeting Exemption for Charitable Efficiency: Designing a Nondiversion Constraint," 56 *Southern Methodist University Law Review* 675 (2003).

44. Derek Bok, *Universities in the Marketplace: The Commercialization of Higher Education* (Princeton: Princeton University Press, 2003).

45. Zina Poletz et al., *Charities Ready and Willing to E-file: Final Report* (Urban Institute, June 2002).

Financial reports that are prepared electronically are reported to be more accurate, and the software can be designed to assure that they are filled in completely. Accordingly, the Service's announcement in March 2002 that January 2004 had been set as the deadline for implementing universal electronic filing of Forms 990 and 990EZ was welcomed by the advocates of improved reporting. In preparation, under a program devised with the help of the National Center for Charitable Statistics and Guidestar, charities in Pennsylvania and Colorado were able to file their returns for the year ending 2001 electronically with both the state and the IRS, while ten other states are in the process of implementing electronic filing. Regulators anticipate that this will drastically reduce the number of incomplete forms as well as those containing inappropriate responses.

While electronic filing should improve error rates, it will not address the underlying flaws in the reporting systems. The lack of agreement as to the appropriate manner in which to report information stems from the application by the accounting profession of standards adopted for for-profit corporations to the nonprofit sector without recognition of the basic differences between them. Thus generally accepted accounting principles (GAAP) do not address many of the special situations applicable to charities, such as the appropriate manner in which to report restricted funds. Second, the information required on Form 990 is not consonant with that contained in audited financial reports. At the most basic level, Form 990 information is reported on a cash basis while audited financial reports provide information on the accrual basis; Form 990, in contrast to GAAP, does not require disclosure of problems identified in an audit, and information on officers and directors and their compensation is reported on Form 990 but not included in an audited financial statement.

In some states audited financial statements are required of all charities of a certain size or those that solicit funds from the general public. These reports must be filed together with a copy of Form 990 or other state reporting forms. In all of these states, the audited financial reports are made available to the public but they can be obtained only at the state charity offices. In contrast, the federal reports must be made available on request or through the Internet; they are also accessible to the public on the Internet through Guidestar and in a few states, including California and New Mexico, on the website of the state charity office.[46]

The requirement that certain charities provide audited financial statements has been considered a self-policing tool, and some state regulators believe it has enhanced performance. Others, however, are concerned about the bur-

46. See Chapter 6.

den the requirement places on smaller organizations that are in effect required to provide two sets of financials—one to meet audit requirements and one to meet state or federal provisions. That there is a need for uniformity is not disputed. Possible solutions are discussed below in connection with evaluation of the federal reporting requirements.

The Effect of Privatization on Nonprofits

A review by Fremont-Smith and Kosaras of wrongdoing among charitable fiduciaries as reported in the press between 1995 and 2002 identified a subgroup of charities formed to carry out, or receiving their sole support from, government-sponsored programs in a number of fields such as housing, mortgage assistance, and adult and children lunch programs.[47] The high incidence of criminal convictions of the managers of these programs, several of whom were repeat offenders, may be attributable to tighter monitoring of the programs, although it also suggests inadequate screening of the charities being funded. To the extent it is the latter, the problem warrants greater attention from the federal contracting agencies. It also needs to be addressed by the charitable sector itself, particularly in light of the increase in privatization that has marked the early 2000s and is expected to continue to expand.[48]

Federal Regulation of Charities: The Internal Revenue Service as Regulator

The members of Congress who voted to grant tax exemption to charitable organizations in the first income tax law certainly did not envision that the Internal Revenue Service would become the principal regulator of charitable activities nationwide. Federal regulation has, in fact, gone through four major phases. In the first, broad definitional parameters were established but self-policing was relied on for compliance. In the second, the enactment in 1950 of the unrelated business income tax reflected an attempt to define a border between exempt and nonexempt entities. In the third phase, the police function was enhanced with passage in 1969 of the private foundation limitations. Finally, in 1996 the police function was extended with adoption of intermediate sanctions for self-dealing transactions applicable to public

47. Marion R. Fremont-Smith and Andras Kosaras, "Wrongdoing by Officers and Directors of Charities: A Survey of Press Reports 1995–2002," 42 *Exempt Organization Tax Review* 25 (2003).

48. See generally Mark H. Moore, "Introduction to Symposium: Public Values in an Era of Privatization," 116 *Harvard Law Review* 1212 (2003); Martha Minow, "Public and Private Partnerships: Accounting for the New Religion," 116 *Harvard Law Review* 1229 (2003).

charities, provisions that are already changing the way in which charities make decisions on matters involving conflicts of interest.

Whether these limitations will ultimately improve fiduciary behavior will not be apparent for some time, but it would be surprising if this is not the case. The chances for improvement will be far greater if the Code is amended to permit the IRS to effectively cooperate with state officials in prosecuting cases involving breach of fiduciary duty. The abatement provisions in section 4958 can be meaningfully used if a state attorney general actively supervises the activities of an affected charity. State courts are in a position to complement federal action, whether through power to issue injunctions or remove fiduciaries or demand restitution. The ability to act in these matters may even be an impetus in some states to increase their regulatory programs, making regulation more effective at both the state and federal levels.

For a regulatory regime that was never intended to police fiduciary duty, and for one that has grown in large part without conscious planning, federal oversight through the Internal Revenue Service has proved far more effective than one might have anticipated. This is due to a number of factors: the requirements for organizing and operating a charity permit great flexibility as to the form of organization and the means of operating; federal law incorporates many of the common law principles found in state law, rather than establishing a separate set of standards; changes have been adopted at a slow pace with time for the sector to adjust to each change. The process has not been without upheavals. Notably, increased federal regulation has not restricted the growth of the sector; to the contrary, based on preliminary statistics as to the growth in numbers and value of assets at the end of the century, the regulatory environment could be best characterized as nurturing.

A major factor that has impeded the effectiveness of the IRS as regulator of fiduciary behavior is that it is a large, unwieldy bureaucracy, beset by inadequate funding, particularly since the early 1990s. Staffing for the exempt organizations branch was 2,075 in 1975. In 1997 this had grown by 25 employees to 2,100, a period during which the number of reporting tax-exempt organizations increased from 700,000 to 1.1 million. Unfortunately, when Congress passed the Internal Revenue Service Restructuring and Reform Act in 1998, it failed to increase the Service's appropriations commensurate with the growth in the sector, thereby impeding what would under the best of circumstances have been a difficult process. The exempt organizations branch has continued to deal with inadequate personnel and outmoded computer systems. Attempts to centralize the handling of exemption applications in one location, begun before the restructuring, had not been accomplished four years later. The result has been a dearth of guidance in the form of revenue rulings and procedures, failure to improve reporting forms, and a reduction in the number of audits to a level that has raised concern as to the integrity of the system. The lack of guidance provided by the Service since the early 1990s has been of particular concern. Of 433 exempt organization revenue rulings published between 1974 and 1997, 406 were published between 1974 and 1983, while 27 were published in the succeeding fourteen years.[49] Although efforts were made to increase the amount of guidance after the restructuring, there was no evidence that there would be rapid improvement.

Proposals to Change the Situs of Regulation

Given the shortcomings in both state and federal regulation, one is led to consider whether a different government agency would make regulation more effective. Although one might have considered delegating regulation to the states at some time during the 1950s, the growth of the nonprofit sector and its complexity since that time and the concomitant overriding federal interest in its operations, combined with the failure of the states to provide effective enforcement, have rendered this question moot. The question therefore is whether regulation of nonprofit organizations should be moved from the Internal Revenue Service to another existing agency or department or to a newly created agency or bureau. These possibilities received considerable attention from the Filer Commission in the early 1970s, and its final report, issued in 1975, contained a strong endorsement of the Internal Revenue Service as the appropriate body to regulate charities. The Commission did recommend certain changes in the Code to improve regulation, in particular adding a prohibition against self-dealing applicable to the trustees and directors of public charities. It also favored granting the federal courts equity powers to correct violations similar to those available in the state courts, including the power to remove trustees, appoint receivers, and enjoin certain actions. The Commission also called for legislation that would permit the Service to defer to state regulators in situations in which it was clear that the state courts would be able to correct violations and obtain restitution more effectively than the Service, provisions that to some degree are now in effect.[50]

The Filer Commission also recommended creation of an independent quasi-governmental agency, established by Congress but without governmental powers, that would support the sector by sponsoring research and serving as its voice before Congress and the administration, a proposal drawn from a re-

49. See Chapter 7.
50. See Chapter 1.

search paper prepared for the Commission by Yarmolinsky and Fremont Smith.[51] The charitable community was divided in its support of this recommendation but recognized the value of an advocate before Congress and the public. The outcome of the debate that ensued was the establishment in March 1980 of Independent Sector (IS), effected by the merger of two other organizations, the Coalition of National Voluntary Organizations and the National Council on Philanthropy. The mission of the new organization was that envisioned by the Filer Commission for a quasi-governmental agency, the difference being that IS was wholly voluntary. As of 2002, IS had approximately 700 members representing umbrella organizations for all aspects of the sector and a number of individual organizations. It has become the leading spokesman for the sector. Among the issues affecting regulation in which it has taken a major role are the enactment of section 501(h), which gives public charities a means for assuring compliance with the lobbying limitations, and the enactment of the excess benefit provisions in 1996.

The most often mentioned suggestion for improving regulation has been to move it from the Service to a new independent body similar to the Charity Commission in England or to a separate division within the Treasury Department, the Securities and Exchange Commission (SEC), or another federal agency. Alternatively, some commentators have suggested giving regulatory powers over organizations with specific purposes or conducting particular activities to another existing agency such as Health and Human Services for hospitals or the Department of Education for schools, colleges, and universities or to a new monitoring agency. Thus Keating and Frumkin called for establishment of an independent accounting board that would receive and review audited financial reports from charities,[52] while Goldschmid believed that SEC-type powers were required to control health care conversions and possibly other aspects of the operations of large health care organizations.[53]

51. Adam Yarmolinsky and Marion R. Fremont-Smith, "Preserving the Private Voluntary Sector: A Proposal for a Public Advisory Commission on Philanthropy," in Department of Treasury, Commission on Private Philanthropy and Public Needs, *Research Papers,* vol. 5, pt. 1, at 2857 (1977).

52. Elizabeth Keating and Peter Frumkin, "Reengineering Nonprofit Financial Accountability: Toward a More Reliable Foundation for Regulation," 63 *Public Administration Review* 1, 12–13 (2003); see also Regina E. Herzlinger and Denise Nitterhouse, *Financial Accounting and Managerial Control for Nonprofit Organizations* (Cincinnati: South-Western Publishing Co., 1994); National Health Council, *Standards of Accounting and Financial Reporting for Voluntary Health and Welfare Organizations* (1964).

53. Harvey J. Goldschmid, "The Fiduciary Duties of Nonprofit Directors and Officers: Paradoxes, Problems, and Proposed Reforms," 23 *Journal of Corporation Law* 631, 651 (1998).

Fleishman urged in 1999 that a change be made.[54] He preferred establishing an independent agency modeled on the SEC or the Federal Trade Commission (FTC), empowered with all aspects of the regulation of nonprofit organizations other than determinations of exemption, deductibility of contributions, and decisions relating to the tax on unrelated business income. As these were inextricably a part of the tax process and because it would not be good policy to lose the ninety years of IRS experience in the field, he recommended that they remain under the jurisdiction of the IRS but that a new U.S. Charities Regulatory Commission be established with the primary responsibility

> to keep tabs on the procedural—not substantive—functioning of not-for-profit organizations so as to assure the public that tax exemption is not used as a shield for fraudulent or illegal purposes. It would be empowered to investigate instances of alleged wrongdoing, it would have the power of subpoena, and it could institute civil or criminal proceedings as appropriate on its own motion. It would be charged with supervising interstate charitable solicitation, and creating the guidelines and disclosure requirements necessary to ensure that charitable solicitation is not used for fraudulent purposes. It would be responsible for monitoring the function of the NFP [not-for-profit] sector as a whole, gathering data and creating databases about the sector, commissioning studies on various aspects of the sector, reporting periodically to Congress on the operation of the sector, issuing regulations to guide the sector in conforming with applicable laws, and making recommendations for legislative changes that may be thought desirable.[55]

Under this proposal the IRS would have authority to certify tax exemption initially and be the primary recipient of financial reporting forms. Although he preferred that the separate agency be independent, Fleishman recognized that it would per force be small, and that it might thus be more effective if it were part of the SEC. His proposal entailed no change in state regulation, although it included a strong recommendation that any new agency be empowered to defer to the states if enforcement could best be provided at that level.

Fishman, in contrast, recommended expanding state regulation of charities through establishment of state, or in the case of the larger states such as New

---

54. Joel L. Fleishman, "Public Trust in Not-for-Profit Organizations and the Need for Regulatory Reform," in *Philanthropy and the Nonprofit Sector in a Changing America*, 172 (Charles T. Clotfelter and Thomas Ehrlich, eds., Bloomington: Indiana University Press, 1999).

55. Id. at 189.

York or California, regional Advisory Charity Commissions that would serve under the control and guidance of that state's attorney general. The commissions would be comprised of fifteen unpaid citizens, eight appointed by the governor and seven by the attorney general, with an assistant attorney general serving as administrator. Their principal role would be to filter citizen complaints, and to that end they would have powers to hold hearings, demand documents, and subpoena witnesses. They would be able to publicly exonerate a charity, agree to a settlement, or turn a matter over to the attorney general for prosecution.[56] Adoption of this proposal, however, would add to the lack of uniformity among the states. Furthermore, it is doubtful whether commissions could be established and operated at minimum cost as the author suggests. A more fundamental objection is that they would likely politicize the regulatory process more than it is under the present system in which the attorney general has exclusive regulatory power.

In regard to regulation of fund-raising activities, the Filer Commission had recommended establishment of a new federal agency within the Treasury Department to regulate interstate solicitation of charitable funds, as well as strengthen intrastate regulation of fund-raising. The Commission rejected giving additional power to the IRS in this area, or lodging it in an independent agency such as the SEC. Yarmolinsky and this author had recommended to the Filer Commission that the appropriate agency was the Federal Trade Commission, which was already empowered to deal with deceptive advertising.[57] A variant of this suggestion was revived in the late 1990s in regard to regulation of telemarketing. In October 2001, Congress enacted the USA Patriot Act, which contained provisions extending the jurisdiction of the FTC to telemarketing by for-profit entities that entailed fraudulent charitable solicitations. Final regulations, issued under the act in December 2002, contained an affirmation that the act did not amend the jurisdictional limitations of the Commission to extend to charitable organizations; rather, FTC regulation was to extend only to for-profit organizations soliciting funds for charities.[58]

For more than a century, charities in England have been regulated by an independent agency, the Charity Commission, which has broad regulatory as well as quasi-judicial powers over charitable fiduciaries. Its decisions are accepted by the Inland Revenue in regard to the eligibility of charities for

56. James J. Fishman, "Improving Charitable Accountability," 62 *Maryland Law Review* 218 (2003).

57. Adam Yarmolinsky and Marion R. Fremont-Smith, "Judicial Remedies and Related Topics," in Department of Treasury, Commission on Private Philanthropy and Public Needs, *Research Papers,* vol. 5, pt. 1, at 2697, 2703–2704 (1977).

58. 16 C.F.R. pt. 310 (2002).

tax benefits. Although a similar system might have great merit in the United States, it is naive to think that Congress would remove regulation of charities or other exempt entities from the Service. The integrity of the tax system rests in large part on assuring that it cannot be undermined through the use of exempt entities. In addition, as conceded by critics of the Service, tax exemption for charities is inextricably intertwined with administration of the tax on unrelated business income as well as with the deductibility of contributions for purposes of the income, estate, and gift taxes. Bifurcating regulation at the federal level would add a third regime of regulation that would add immeasurably to complexity and delay. Viewed from this perspective, the possibility of effecting major change is remote.

In making comparisons with the English system of charity regulation, one must also be aware that it is not administered by the Inland Revenue and that deductibility of contributions for English taxpayers is very limited in comparison with that allowed under United States law. As of the end of 2001, there were 188,000 charities registered with the Charity Commission, 27,000 of which were branches or subsidiaries of other registered organizations. Of these, 42,012 had an annual income of £1,000 or less while almost 60,000 had income between £1,001 and £10,000. In addition, universities, some schools, and churches, as well as very small charities are not required to register.[59] Thus the scale of the regulatory effort is far different from that of the Internal Revenue Service and is closer in some respects to that of California.

There are more positive reasons, however, for keeping regulation of charities in the Internal Revenue Service. A principal objection to the Service as regulator made prior to the early 1970s was that the personnel doing the regulating were trained to raise tax revenue, not oversee the activities of organizations that were not subject to tax. This changed when Congress established the Employee Plans/Exempt Organizations Division in the Employee Retirement Income Security Act of 1974. The new structure was created to assure adequate federal regulation of tax-exempt pension plans, and it was logical to group regulation of all exempt organizations together—which meant including charities and other nonprofit corporations. Under the 1999 restructuring the EP/EO division was retained as a separate administrative branch, to which was added responsibility for governmental entities, thereby leading to the creation of a new TE/GE (tax-exempt and government entities) branch under an assistant commissioner. This has ensured that personnel

59. Strategy Unit Report, Cabinet Office, *Private Action, Public Benefit: A Review of Charities and the Wider Not-for-Profit Sector*, 13–27 (September 2002), available at *www.strategyunit.gov.uk*.

have the understanding and experience to handle appropriately the special problems—and needs—of exempt organizations nationwide.

Finally, the record of the Service in resisting political pressures, despite challenges to the contrary, has been unusually unblemished. There can be no guarantee that a new agency, whether independent or part of another government branch, would be able to maintain the degree of independence exercised by the Service. It is an advantage that should not be lost. The Service's current efforts to improve the nature and extent of information provided to the public, to streamline administration, to provide more published guidance, and to cooperate more meaningfully with state regulators confirm the wisdom of retaining the present scheme of regulation.

The Role of the Charitable Sector

Discussion of regulation of any segment of society inevitably raises consideration of self-regulation as an alternative or, at the least, as a complement to government regulation. There are institutions within the charitable sector that do perform a regulatory function. Notable are the organizations that certify charities with common purposes such as educational institutions, hospitals and other health care facilities, specific professions, and fund-raising organizations. It is not surprising, however, that no single group has emerged with power to impose a self-regulating regime. Nor would it be advisable given the diversity of purposes of the components of the sector and the many methods employed to achieve them, unless the standards to be applied were so lenient as to be meaningless.

Nonetheless, voluntary organizations formed to improve the sector and its components can play an important role in educating the sector, as well as the general public, about its role and responsibilities, and in raising standards of practice.

Organizational Components of the Current Infrastructure

While the recommendation of the Filer Commission to establish a quasi-governmental agency to oversee and encourage the nonprofit sector met with general disapproval, it provided the impetus for creation of a new nongovernmental organization, the purpose of which was to fill the supporting role envisioned by the Commission. The new organization, Independent Sector, as described earlier, was established in 1980 through the merger of two existing nonprofits, the Coalition of National Voluntary Organizations and the National Council on Philanthropy.

Under the leadership of John Gardner as chairman and Brian O'Connell as president, Independent Sector set about to become the spokesman for the nonprofit sector, as well as its leader in improving practices and increasing giving and volunteering. Starting with 50 members, it had over 600 members five years later, and its funding was assured. At the end of 2002, the membership was 700, including almost all of the national organizations representing the various components of the sector. Independent Sector's lobbying efforts on behalf of nonprofits have been unusually successful. It has also submitted amicus briefs to the United States Supreme Court on issues affecting solicitation of funds for charitable purposes and conducted nationwide educational efforts to increase the amount of charitable giving. In 1991 the organization promulgated a code of ethics in a statement entitled "Obedience to the Unenforceable." It was republished in 2002 for wider dissemination, together with a compendium of Standards, Codes, and Principles and an exhaustive list of the wide variety of nonprofit and philanthropic organizations that had adopted these various standards.[60]

As a step toward improving self-regulation, Independent Sector adopted procedures in 1999 under which a member organization that was determined to have violated the principles set forth in its by-laws would be removed from membership. Little public information as to the success of efforts to implement the procedure has been available.

At the same time that Independent Sector was formed, the work of the Donee Group was taken on by the National Committee for Responsive Philanthropy under the leadership of Pablo Eisenberg, who had been the principal spokesman for the Donee Group. The Committee has continued the focus of the Donee Group as critic of foundations, corporate giving programs, and United Ways, with support from more than 200 members. In 2003 it took the lead in the effort to increase the foundation payout rate.

Other organizations at the national level addressing the entire nonprofit sector include Board Source, formerly the National Center for Nonprofit Boards, whose mission is to improve governance practices; the National Council of Nonprofit Organizations, which requires its members to meet standards of behavior and publishes a code of ethics; the National Center on Nonprofit Enterprise, formed in 2000 to improve management practices of nonprofits; and the Urban Institute Center on Nonprofits and Philanthropy and the Aspen Institute, both of which conduct and support important research on all aspects of the sector.

Organizations representing individual components of the sector on a na-

60. "Compendium of Standards, Codes, and Principles of Nonprofit and Philanthropic Organizations," available at *www.independentsector.org/issues/accountability/standards.html;* see also Evelyn Brody et al., "Selected Materials on Trustee Code of Ethics," in *Legal Problems of Museum Administration: ALI-ABA Course of Study Materials* (1998).

tional basis include the Council on Foundations, the Council for Advancement and Support of Education, the American Hospital Association, the National Health Council, the American Association of Museums, Catholic Charities, and Lutheran Services in America. Also operating at the national level are external review organizations, commonly referred to as charity watchdogs. These organizations monitor and disseminate information about charities that solicit from the general public. They include the BBBWise Giving Alliance, established in 2001 through the merger of the National Charities Information Bureau, which was founded in 1918, and the Philanthropic Advisory Service of the Council of Better Business Bureaus, established in the mid-1970s. The American Institute of Philanthropy, organized in 1992, and Charity Navigator, formed in 2001, analyze and disseminate information about soliciting charities taken from Internal Revenue Service Forms 990. This information became widely available after 1994 with the creation of GuideStar, a charitable organization that, in collaboration with the Urban Institute and the IRS, makes available on the Internet all filed Forms 990 with schedules.

There are also a number of regional, state, and local organizations formed to improve the performance of the sector, while the National Council of Nonprofit Associations is a state-by-state support network for nonprofit organizations that includes state and regional associations. It has a collective membership of more than 20,000 local associations of grantmakers and sets standards for membership. Power of Attorney was established in 1999 to assist in the creation of nonprofit organizations in other parts of the country to provide legal services and educational programs similar to those conducted by the Lawyers Alliance for New York.

Other national associations that require compliance with minimum standards are the Evangelical Council for Financial Accountability, with over 900 members; InterAction, a coalition of more than 150 United States-based international development, disaster relief, and refugee assistance agencies; the Association of Governing Boards of Colleges and Universities, founded in 1921, which is affiliated with 1,800 colleges and universities; and the Land Trust Alliance sponsored by 750 land trusts, which has set standards for more than 1,200 land trusts across the country. The Association of Fund Raising Professionals, formerly the National Society of Fund Raising Executives, is a professional association with more than 20,000 members in 154 chapters across the country that requires members to comply with its standards and certifies members of the profession.

A final aspect of self-regulation is improved reporting to the public. This includes improving the content of reports, both those required by government and those issued voluntarily, improving public understanding of that content, and expanding the availability of this information. In 1999 the IRS requirement that charities make their reporting forms available on request from the public was modified to permit compliance by making the return information available on the Internet. Although copies were available through GuideStar, this meant that more timely returns would be available. Paralleling these changes, the Urban Institute, together with Independent Sector, undertook a major public education effort to improve the quality of reporting on Form 990.

Organizations Monitoring and Studying Nonprofit Activity

The growth of the charitable infrastructure has been accompanied by growth in the number of organizations that monitor, promote, or study the sector. *Giving USA,* an annual report on philanthropy published by the American Association of Fund-Raising Counsel since 1955, listed in its 2003 report eighty sources of information on the nonprofit sector.[61] The first issue of *Chronicle of Philanthropy* appeared in 1988, and it has subsequently become the industry standard with approximately 45,000 subscribers. Its companion *Chronicle of Higher Education* serves the educational sector. *NonProfit Times* has 34,000 subscribers, while the smaller *Nonprofit Quarterly,* with 7,000 subscribers, is part of a broader educational program of Third Sector New England. The Council on Foundations and the National Committee for Responsive Philanthropy also publish journals, as does BoardSource. There are a number of Internet sites that provide information on the sector,[62] while, as noted, GuideStar makes available the information reports filed by nonprofit organizations with the Internal Revenue Service.

As of January 2003 there were seventy-two institutes and research centers devoted to the nonprofit sector, including thirty-eight members of the Nonprofit Academic Centers Council, among them the centers established at Yale, Johns Hopkins, Indiana, and Duke University, the Center on Philanthropy and Law at New York University, and the Hauser Center for Nonprofit Organizations at Harvard University. Independent research centers include the Aspen Institute, the Urban Institute, the Brookings Institution, and the Foundation Center, formerly the Foundation Library Center. Professional associations have also been established, including the Association for Research on Nonprofit Organizations and Voluntary Action (ARNOVA), which publishes the *Nonprofit and Voluntary Sector Quarterly,* and the Inter-

61. AAFRC Trust for Philanthropy, *Giving USA 2003,* 203–209.
62. For a list compiled by the *Chronicle of Philanthropy,* see *philanthropy.com/free/resources/social/.*

national Society for Third Sector Research, which publishes *VOLUNTAS, the International Journal of Voluntary and Nonprofit Organizations.*[63]

It was estimated that in September 2002 there were 240 colleges and universities offering courses in nonprofit management, with 66 offering noncredit courses, and 146 colleges and universities with at least one course within a graduate department. In addition, there were 700 unaffiliated management support organizations offering nondegree instruction and technical assistance.[64]

Measuring Performance

In the regulation of charities, the IRS and the states measure compliance by a set of standards that are framed in financial terms. Compliance with the duty of loyalty requires that one does not benefit financially at the expense of the charity. Compliance with the duty of care is similarly measured by the degree to which the funds of the charity are put at risk. Mention was made earlier of a new public interest in what is termed "venture philanthropy," a phrase that describes attempts to redefine the manner in which grantors interact with potential grantees, evaluating proposals as they would business investments, involving themselves with the day-to-day operations of the grantees, and subsequently evaluating their results as they would in the for-profit sector. It has become common to describe the process of making these final evaluations as "outcomes measurements"; many organizations are attempting to apply these measurements to determine the degree to which they are accomplishing their missions as well as the impact they are having on beneficiaries.

The trend toward conversion of hospitals and health care delivery organizations that peaked in the late 1990s was fueled in part by studies that compared nonprofit and for-profit hospitals and concluded either that there was no difference between them or that on the basis of financial data, for-profit corporations outperformed their nonprofit counterparts. These studies provided a rationale for denying tax exemption to nonprofit hospitals, sparking heated debate among legal and tax scholars. In a study published in August 2003, Horwitz compared nonprofit, for-profit, and government hospitals in terms of the services they provide to meet public needs. She concluded that corporate form accounts for differences in the provision of specific medical services sufficiently large to provide new justification for tax exemption for nonprofit hospitals. In addition to its importance in the debate over delivery

63. For a list compiled by Independent Sector, see *www.independentsector.org/pathfinder/resources/index.html.*

64. Roseanne M. Mirabella, "Nonprofit Management Education: Current Offerings in University Based Programs," available at *pirate.shu.edu/~mirabero/Kellogg.html.*

of health care, her study suggests an approach to measurement that could prove valuable when applied to other segments of the charitable sector.[65]

Some scholars and some of the organizations that evaluate charities for the benefit of potential contributors are calling for the addition of nonfinancial measurements to the information required by government. In other words, they want performance outcomes presented along with financial outcomes. At the extreme, some argue that charities should not be entitled to tax or other public benefits if they do not carry out their mission in accordance with standards that have to do with efficiency and impact. Adoption of a requirement of this nature would effect a major transformation of the sector and its relationship to government. In instances in which government itself is the grantor, this new requirement may be perfectly appropriate and can easily be accomplished under the terms of the grant or contract. In all other situations it would bring subjective analysis into the regulatory scheme, a development that would only stifle innovation and reduce charitable efforts to the safest, most pedestrian levels. Performance evaluation may be an appropriate function for self-regulation, particularly if the "science" of measuring outcomes is perfected. It is not a province for government except to the extent it entails evaluation of the effects of direct government support by the granting agencies.

The Future of the Law and Regulation of Charities

Suggestions for improving the laws and the regulation of charity are to be found throughout this study, and the majority are summarized in this chapter. In regard to the substantive laws prescribing fiduciary behavior, the most important change would be to remove the almost complete protection from liability given to fiduciaries in the latter part of the twentieth century. In regard to regulation, the greatest need is to provide regulatory agencies in the states and the IRS adequate funds to effectively carry out their enforcement duties. These two changes, moreover, are intertwined. Government will not step in to regulate if it does not have the tools to effect change. On the other hand, fiduciaries bent on reaping private benefit or careless in their management will not alter their behavior if they believe that government is not carrying out its regulatory function. Neither of these recommendations requires major changes in the behavior of the sector or in the role of government. They reflect, in fact, an affirmation of the rationale for the existing system, designed as it is to afford freedom to charitable fiduciaries to manage while

---

65. Jill R. Horwitz, "Why We Need the Independent Sector: The Behavior, Law, and Ethics of Not-for-Profit Hospitals," 50 *UCLA Law Review* 1345 (2003).

assuring the public that charitable funds will not be diverted for private gain or used recklessly. The nonprofit sector exists and thrives because the public believes in its integrity. Although other recommended changes will improve performance and provide a better regulatory environment, these two recommendations should be considered the minimum necessary to assure the public that the laws set high standards for fiduciary behavior and that regulators are enforcing those laws, thereby warranting its continued support.

Appendix

Index

Appendix

Table 1 State laws governing creation, administration, and dissolution of charities: Columns 1–8

State	1 Power of attorney general	2 Notice to atty. gen. required in suits involving charitable orgs.	3 Standing	4 Nonprofit corp. act distinguishes public benefit from other corps.	5 Filing governing instruments with state official on creation of charitable org.	6 Periodic corporate status reports to state official	7 Periodic reports to attorney general	8 State vested with power to dissolve nonprofit corporation
AL	To enforce a public charity is a common law duty. State ex rel. v. Bibb, 173 So. 74 (1937)	No	Members or directors may sue corp. on grounds of lack of capacity or power. §10-3A-21	No	Yes for nonprofit corps., w/prob. judge who must forward charter to sec. of state. §10-3A-62	No	No	Yes, cir. ct. in action by atty. gen. §10-3A-146; §10-3A-147
AK	To intervene in action on contract against trustee of charitable trust. §13.36.175	No	No statement in statute or case.	No	Yes for nonprofit corps., with comm'r of commerce and econ. dev. §10.20.156	Yes, to comm'r of commerce and econ. dev. §10.20.620	No	Yes, comm'r of commerce and econ. dev. §10.20.325
AZ	Collier v. Bd. of Nat'l Missions of the Presbyterian Church, 464 P.2d 1015 (1970) (failed to decide whether atty. gen. is proper party to enforce charitable trust but cited other cases holding that atty. gen. is proper party)	No	No statement in statute or case.	No	Yes for nonprofit corps., with corp. commission. §10-3201	Yes, to corp. commission. §10-11622	No	Yes, cir. ct. in action by atty. gen. §10-11430 Corp. commission. §10-11420

AR	To file suit for enforcement of public trust or charity. State v. Van Buren School Dist., 89 S.W.2d 605 (1936)	No	No statement in statute or case.	Yes	Yes for nonprofit corps., with sec. of state. §4-33-202	No	No	Yes, chancery ct. in action by atty. gen. §4-33-1430 Sec. of state. §4-33-1420
CA	To supervise charitable trusts. §12598 To investigate transactions and relationships of corps. and trustees. Gov't Code §12588	Yes, notice required to atty. gen. in prob. actions involving charitable interests. Prob. Code §17203	Corp. or member of corp., officer, or dir. may bring action to enjoin, correct, obtain damages, or remedy breach of charitable trust. Corp. Code §5142	Yes	Yes, charitable corps. and trustees of charitable trusts must file art. of inc. or trust instrument with atty. gen. Gov't Code §12585	Yes, statement of officers to sec. of state. Corp. Code §6210	Yes, for charitable corps., and trusts financial reports. Gov't Code §12586	Yes, super. ct. in action by atty. gen. for public benefit corps. Corp. Code §6511
CO	Statutory and common law powers regarding trusts for charitable, educational, religious, or benevolent purposes. §24-31-101(5)	No	A member or dir. may bring a proceeding against a nonprofit corp. or its officers or directors. §7-126-401	No	Yes for nonprofit corps., with sec. of state. §7-122-101	Yes, to sec. of state. §7-136-107	No	Yes, dist. ct. in proceeding by atty. gen. §§7-134-301-302 Sec. of state. §7-134-201
CT	To represent public interest in the protection of any gifts, legacies, or devises intended for public or charitable purposes. §3-125	Yes, for termination of charitable trust with assets under $150,000. §45a-520	Carl J. Herzog Foundation, Inc. v. University of Bridgeport, 699 A.2d 995 (1997)	N/A. State does not have separate nonprofit corp. statute, but has separate provision for nonstock corps.	Yes for nonprofit corps., with sec. of state. §33-1025	Yes, to sec. of state. §33-1243	No	Yes, super. ct. in action by atty. gen. in the nature of *quo warranto.* §33-1187

Table 1 Columns 1–8 (*continued*)

State	1 Power of attorney general	2 Notice to atty. gen. required in suits involving charitable orgs.	3 Standing	4 Nonprofit corp. act distinguishes public benefit from other corps.	5 Filing governing instruments with state official on creation of charitable org.	6 Periodic corporate status reports to state official	7 Periodic reports to attorney general	8 State vested with power to dissolve nonprofit corporation
DE	To see to the proper admin. of charitable corps. See Wier v. Howard Hughes Medical Inst., 407 A.2d 1051 (1979)	Yes, for cy pres proceeding or a proceeding to terminate a small trust. Tit. 12, §§3541-3542	Wier v. Howard Hughes Medical Inst., 407 A.2d 1051 (1979)	N/A	Yes for nonprofit corps., with div. of corps. Tit. 8, §101	Yes, annual report to sec. of state. Tit. 8, §502	No	Yes, chancery ct. in proceeding by atty. gen. Tit. 8, §284
DC	To bring action on behalf of unknown beneficiaries of charitable corp. U.S. v. Mount Vernon Mortgage Corp., 128 F. Supp. 629 (1954)	No	Hooker v. Edes Home, 579 A.2d 608 (1990); Stern v. Lucy Webb Hayes Training School, 367 F. Supp. 536 (1973) ("Sibley Hospital")	No	Yes for nonprofit corps., with mayor. §29-532	Yes, to mayor. §29-584	No	Yes, civil ct. §29-554
FL	To protect interest of public in insuring that charitable trusts are properly administered. Dicta in State of Delaware v. Belin, 453 So. 2d 1177 (1984)	No	State v. Anclote Manor Hosp., Inc., 566 So. 2d 296 (1990)	No	Yes for nonprofit corps., with dept. of state. §617.02011	Yes, to dept. of state. §617.1622	No	Yes, cir. ct. in proceeding by dept. of legal affairs. §617.1430 Dept. of state. §617.1420

GA	To represent interests of beneficiaries under charitable trusts and interests of state in all legal matters pertaining to administration and disposition of charitable trusts. §53-12-115	Yes, for cy pres by virtue of representing the interests of beneficiaries in all cases in which rights of beneficiaries under a charitable trust are involved. §53-12-115	Members and directors can bring derivative proceedings. §14-3-741	No, but distinction between charitable and nonprofit corp. relevant in voluntary dissolution, sale of assets, and merger provisions.	Yes for nonprofit corps., with sec. of state. §14-3-201	Yes, to sec. of state. §14-3-1622	No	Yes, superior ct. in action by atty. gen. §14-3-1430 Sec. of state. §14-3-1420
HI	To act as of *parens patriae* of charitable trusts. Kapiolani Park Preservation Society v. City and County of Honolulu, 751 P.2d 1022 (1988)	No	Kapiolani Park Preservation Society v. City and County of Honolulu, 751 P.2d 1022 (1988)	No	Yes for nonprofit corps., with dir. of dept. of commerce and consumer affairs. §414D-3	Yes, to dir. of dept. of commerce and consumer affairs. §414D-308	No	Yes, dir. of dept. of commerce and consumer affairs. §414D-248
ID	To supervise nonprofit corps., charitable societies, and persons holding property subject to any charitable trust. §67-1401	If estate involves or may involve a charitable trust, the ct. shall forward to atty. gen. a copy of decree of distribution. §15-3-1009	Dir. may bring derivative suit. §30-3-44	No	Yes for nonprofit corps., with sec. of state. §30-3-18	Yes, to sec. of state. §30-3-136	No	Sec. of state. §30-3-115A

Table 1 Columns 1–8 (*continued*)

State	1 Power of attorney general	2 Notice to atty. gen. required in suits involving charitable orgs.	3 Standing	4 Nonprofit corp. act distinguishes public benefit from other corps.	5 Filing governing instruments with state official on creation of charitable org.	6 Periodic corporate status reports to state official	7 Periodic reports to attorney general	8 State vested with power to dissolve nonprofit corporation
IL	To investigate transactions and relationships of trustees to determine whether the property held for charitable purposes is properly administered. Ch. 760, 55/9	For cy pres proceeding or proceeding to terminate small trust. Ch. 750, 55/15.5	Members can bring derivative suits. Ch. 805, 105/107.80	No	Yes, charitable orgs. and charitable trusts must register with atty. gen. Ch. 760, 55/5. Nonprofit corps. must register with sec. of state. Ch. 805, 105/102.10	Yes, to sec. of state. Ch. 805, 105/114.05	Trustees must file periodic annual written reports to atty. gen. Ch. 760, 55/7	Yes, cir. ct. in action by atty. gen. Ch. 805, 105/112.50 Sec. of state. Ch. 805, 105/112.35
IN	To petition for accounting of trust for a benevolent public purpose. §30-4-5-12 To maintain litigation involving public charitable trusts. Boice v. Mallers, 96 N.E.2d 342 (1950)	Yes. §30-4-6-6	No statement in statute or case.	Yes, but distinction between public benefit corps. and other nonprofit corps. is not relevant in voluntary dissolution or sale of asset provisions.	Yes, nonprofit corps., with sec. of state. §23-17-3-1	Yes for nonprofit corps., to sec. of state. §23-17-27-8	No, but if property or money is given for benevolent public purpose, trustee must file verified written statement annually w/ct. §§30-4-5-12, 13	Yes, cir. ct. in action by atty. gen. §23-17-24-1 Sec. of state. §23-17-23-1

IA	At any time when will creating charitable trust has been admitted to prob., atty. gen. may investigate to determine if estate or trust is administered in accordance with law. §633.303	No statement in statute or case.	No	Yes, for nonprofit corps., with sec. of state. §504A.30	Yes, to sec. of state. §504A.83	No	Yes, cir. ct. in action by atty. gen. §504A.53 Sec. of state. §504A.87
KS	To intervene to protect the estate if funds of public charity are in danger of being lost or poorly administered. In re Roberts, 373 P.2d 165 (1962), citing Troutman v. DeBoissiere, 66 Kan. 1 (1903)	No statement in statute or case.	N/A because no separate nonprofit corp. statute, but distinction between charitable corp. and nonstock corp. is relevant in merger provisions.	Yes for nonprofit corps., with sec. of state. §16-6001	Yes, to sec. of state. §17-7504	No	Yes, dist. ct. in action by atty. gen. quo warranto. §17-6812

Yes, for cy pres proceeding. §59-22a01

Table 1 Columns 1–8 (*continued*)

State	1 Power of attorney general	2 Notice to atty. gen. required in suits involving charitable orgs.	3 Standing	4 Nonprofit corp. act distinguishes public benefit from other corps.	5 Filing governing instruments with state official on creation of charitable org.	6 Periodic corporate status reports to state official	7 Periodic reports to attorney general	8 State vested with power to dissolve nonprofit corporation
KY	To supervise the administration of established charitable trusts, to prevent the mismanagement and waste of trust fund, to remedy malfeasance by trustees, and to see that purposes of trusts are fulfilled. Comm. ex rel. Ferguson v. Gardner, 327 S.W.2d 947 (1959)	No	No statement in statute or case.	No	Yes for nonprofit corps., with sec. of state. §273.243	Yes, to sec. of state. §273.3671	No	Cir. ct. in action by atty. gen. §273.320 Sec. of state. §273.318 Each year sec. of state may certify to atty. gen. names of all corps. that have given cause for dissolution. §273.323
LA	No statement in statute or case.	In cy pres petition if no heir in intestacy or special or universal legatee or donee is present or can be found. §9:2332	No statement in statute or case.	No, but distinction between public benefit and mutual benefit is relevant in merger and amendment provisions.	Yes for nonprofit corps., with sec. of state. §12:205	Yes, to sec. of state. §12:205.1	No	Ct. in action by atty. gen. §12:262.1 Sec. of state. §12:262.1

ME	To enforce the due application of funds given or appropriated to public charities and to prevent breaches of trust in the administration of public charities. Tit. 5, §194	No	No statement in statute or case.	Yes	Yes for nonprofit corps., with sec. of state. Tit. 13-B, §404	Yes, to sec. of state. Tit. 13-B, §1301	No	Yes, ct. of equity in action by atty. gen. Tit. 13-B, §1105
MD	To bring suit to enforce trusts for charitable purposes. Est. & Trusts §14-301	No	Person with interest in a charitable trust may bring action for enforcement. Est. & Trusts §14-301	N/A. State does not have nonprofit corp. statute, but business corp. act permits nonstock corp.	Yes for nonprofit corps., with dept. of taxation and assessment. Corps. & Ass'n §2-102	Yes, to dept. of taxation and assessment. Corps. & Ass'n §3-503	No	Dept. of assessment and taxation may annul the charters of corps. Corps. & Ass'n §3-503
MA	To enforce the due application of funds given or appropriated to public charities and to prevent breaches of trust in the admin. there. Ch. 12, §8	Atty. gen. shall be made party in all proceedings involving charitable trusts and charitable orgs. Ch. 12, §8G	Weaver v. Wood, 680 N.E.2d 918 (1997)	No, but distinction between public charities and nonprofit corps. is relevant in voluntary dissolution or merger.	Yes, public charities must file with atty. gen. (div. of public charities). Ch. 12, §8E Nonprofit corps. must also file with sec. of state. Ch. 180, §3	Yes, to sec. of state. Ch. 180, §26A	Trustees or governing board of every public charity must annually file a written report with atty. gen. Ch. 12, §8F	Yes, supreme judicial ct. in action by atty. gen. Ch. 180, §11B Sec. of state. Ch. 180, §26A

Table 1 Columns 1–8 (*continued*)

State	1 Power of attorney general	2 Notice to atty. gen. required in suits involving charitable orgs.	3 Standing	4 Nonprofit corp. act distinguishes public benefit from other corps.	5 Filing governing instruments with state official on creation of charitable org.	6 Periodic corporate status reports to state official	7 Periodic reports to attorney general	8 State vested with power to dissolve nonprofit corporation
MI	To control and represent the people of the state and the uncertain or indefinite beneficiaries in all charitable trusts and to enforce such trusts by proper proceedings in the courts. §14.254	Yes, atty. gen. is necessary party to proceedings to terminate a charitable trust or liquidate or distribute its assets, or modify or depart from the purposes of a charitable trust. §12.254	Members can bring derivative suits. §450.2491; In re Green Charitable Trust v. Jaffe, 431 N.W.2d 492 (1988)	No, but distinction between charitable corp. and nonprofit corp. is relevant in voluntary dissolution provisions.	Yes for nonprofit corps, with dir. of commerce. §14.255; §450.2201; §450.2131	Yes, to dir. of commerce. §450.2911	Yes. Trustees must submit periodic reports setting forth nature of assets held for charitable purposes and their admin. §14.256	Yes, cir. ct. in action by atty. gen. §450.2821 Dir. of commerce. §450.2831; §450.2922
MN	To conduct investigations for the administration of charitable trusts and trustees or for determining whether property held for charitable	Yes, atty. gen. must be notified of, and has the right to participate as a party in, all ct. proceedings. §501B.41	In re Hill, 509 N.W. 2d 168 (1993)	No, but distinction between charitable corp. and nonprofit corp. is relevant in voluntary dissolu-	Charitable trusts (including an org. with a charitable purpose that has gross assets of $25,000 or more at any	Yes, to sec. of state. §317A.823	A charitable trust (including an org. with a charitable purpose that has gross assets of $25,000) must annually file	Ct. in action by atty. gen. §317A.751 Sec. of state may administratively dissolve corp. but corp. continues for three years after

State								
	purposes is properly administered. §501B.40	tion, merger, and sale of assets.			time during the year) must register and file with atty. gen. articles of inc. or charitable trust instrument. §501B.37 Nonprofit corps. must also register w/ sec. of state. §317A.105		with atty. gen. a copy of its federal tax return; if it does not file a return it must file a balance sheet and a statement of income and expenses. §501B.38	dissolution for sole purpose of supervision, investigation, and other action by atty. gen. §317A.827
MS	To represent the public in proceedings involving charitable trusts. Mississippi Children's Home Society v. City of Jackson, 93 So. 2d 483 (1957)	Yes, in any proceeding that atty. gen. is authorized to bring under the nonprofit corp. act but that has been commenced by another person. §79-11-133	Members and directors can bring derivative suits. §79-11-193	No	Yes for nonprofit corps., with sec. of state. §79-111-139	Yes, to sec. of state. §79-11-391	No	Chancery ct. in action by atty. gen. §79-11-355 Sec. of state. §79-11-347
MO	To represent the public in matters pertaining to and connected with public charitable trusts. Murphey v. Dalton, 314 S.W.2d 726 (1958)	Yes, for proceeding brought in the right of a public benefit corp. or a mutual benefit corp. with assets held in charitable trust. §355.221	Proceeding may be brought in the right of a nonprofit corp. to procure a judgment in its favor by members or by any dir. §355.221	Yes	Yes for nonprofit corps., with sec. of state. §355.096	Yes, to sec. of state. §355.856	No	Cir. ct. in action by atty. gen. §355.726 Sec. of state. §355.706

Table 1 Columns 1–8 (*continued*)

State	1 Power of attorney general	2 Notice to atty. gen. required in suits involving charitable orgs.	3 Standing	4 Nonprofit corp. act distinguishes public benefit from other corps.	5 Filing governing instruments with state official on creation of charitable org.	6 Periodic corporate status reports to state official	7 Periodic reports to attorney general	8 State vested with power to dissolve nonprofit corporation
MT	To enforce charitable trusts. §72-35-315	Yes, for derivative proceedings involving a public benefit corp. or assets held in charitable trust by a mutual benefit corp. §35-2-1302	Atty. gen., a co-trustee, or person with a special interest can maintain a suit to enforce a charitable trust, but not persons with no special interest or the trustor or his heirs or personal rep. §72-33-503	Yes	Yes for nonprofit corps, with sec. of state. §35-2-212	Yes, to sec. of state. §35-2-904	No	District ct. in action by atty. gen. §35-2-728
NE	To bring action to enforce charitable trusts. In re Estate of Grblny, 147 Neb. 117 (1946)	Yes, for commencement of any proceeding that nonprofit corp. act authorizes atty. gen. to bring. §21-1918	By members or by any dir. in the right of a nonprofit corp. to procure judgment in its favor. §21-1949	Yes	Yes for nonprofit corps, with sec. of state. §21-1920	Yes, to sec. of state. §21-19,172	No	Dist. ct. in action by atty. gen. §21-19,141 Sec. of state. §21-19,137
NV	To ascertain on behalf of the state the condition of affairs of a corp. for pub-	Yes, in cause of action on a contract against a	Atty. gen. or person he appoints as relator may bring action to	No	Yes for nonprofit corps, with sec. of state. §82.081	Yes, to sec. of state. §82.193	No	Yes, dist. ct. in action by atty. gen. §82.486

	lic benefit or a corp. holding assets in charitable trust. §82.536	trustee of a charitable trust. §163.120	enjoin, correct, obtain damages for, or otherwise remedy breach of a charitable trust or departure from the purposes for which it was formed. §82.536		Yes, trustees receiving property for charitable purposes must file copy of trust instrument w/atty. gen. §7:28	Yes, to sec. of state. §292:25	Trustees must file annual periodic reports about trust assets and their administration w/atty. gen. §728	Sec. of state may revoke charter if corp. fails to renew. §292:25
NH	To exercise duties and powers in connection with supervision, administration, and enforcement of charitable trusts, charitable solicitations, and charitable sales promotions. §7:19	No charitable trust shall be terminated by decree of prob. ct. until atty. gen. has been given an opportunity to be heard. §7:29	No statement in statute or case.	No, but distinction between charitable and voluntary corp. is relevant in voluntary dissolution				
NJ	To enforce public charities is a common law duty. In re Grassman, 561 A.2d 1210 (1989)	Atty. gen. must be notified of the prob. of a will involving charitable purposes. §4:80-6	City of Patterson v. Patterson General Hosp., 235 A.2d 487 (1967).	No	Yes for nonprofit corps., with sec. of state who must forward copy to atty. gen. §15A:2-8b	Yes, to sec. of state. §15A:4-5	No	Super. ct. in action by atty. gen. §15A:12-11

Table 1 Columns 1–8 (*continued*)

State	1 Power of attorney general	2 Notice to atty. gen. required in suits involving charitable orgs.	3 Standing	4 Nonprofit corp. act distinguishes public benefit from other corps.	5 Filing governing instruments with state official on creation of charitable org.	6 Periodic corporate status reports to state official	7 Periodic reports to attorney general	8 State vested with power to dissolve nonprofit corporation
NM	Atty. gen. authorized to monitor, supervise, and enforce the charitable purposes of organizations. §57-22-9	No	No statement in statute or case.	No	Yes for nonprofit corps., to the corp. commission. §53-8-30	Yes, to corp. commission. §53-8-82	See col. 15	The dist. ct., but only on application by a member, dir., or creditor. §53-8-55
NY	To represent beneficiaries of charitable dispositions and to enforce their rights by proceedings in cts. Est. Powers & Trusts Law §8-1.1(f) To institute proceedings to secure compliance and to secure the proper administration of any charitable trust, corp., or other relationship to which charitable	Whenever any trustee of charitable trust files petition for instructions relating to the administration or use of trust property or income; or any accounting. Est. Powers & Trusts Law §8-1.4(e)	Members can bring derivative suits. Not-for-Profit Corp. §623; Alco Gravure Inc. v. Knapp Foundation, 479 N.E.2d 752 (1985)	Yes	Every trustee must file with atty. gen. copy of the instrument providing for his title, powers, or duties, unless already registered pursuant to statute regulating charitable solicitation. Est. Powers & Trusts Law §8-1.4 Not-for-profit corps. must also	No	Every trustee shall file periodic written reports about nature of assets held for charitable purposes and administration of such assets. Applies to trustees who are also required to file reports on charitable solicitation. Est. Powers & Trusts Law §8-1.4(f)	Atty. gen. may bring action. Not-for-Profit Corp. Law §112(2) Ct. in action by atty. gen. Not-for-Profit Corp. Law §1101

State								
	trust section applies. Est. Powers & Trusts Law §§8-1.4(m)							file cert. of inc. with sec. of state. Not-for-Profit Corp. Law §§402, 404
NC	To enforce any gift, transfer, grant, bequest, or devise for charitable uses or purposes. §36A-5	Atty. gen. must be given notice of any cy pres proceeding. §36A-53	A member or dir. has standing to bring a derivative action. §55A-7-40	No	Yes for nonprofit corps., with sec. of state. §55A-1-20	No	No	Yes, super. ct. in action by atty. gen. §§55-14-30
ND	Interested party to public or charitable trusts. §59-04-02 / Atty. gen. granted broad investigative powers. §10-33-123	By corp. or its members in a proceeding to remove a dir. §10-33-37	Nonprofit corp. and members have standing to bring action to remove a dir. §10-33-37	No	Yes for nonprofit corps., with sec. of state. §10-33-08	Yes, to sec. of state. §10-33-139	Charitable trust divesting itself of a banking institution shall file beforehand a commitment with atty. gen. §6-08.2-04	Yes, a ct. in action by atty. gen. §10-33-107 / Sec. of state. §10-33-13
OH	To institute and prosecute a proper action to enforce the performance of any charitable trust. §109.26	Atty. gen. is necessary party and shall be served with process in all judicial proceedings to terminate a charitable trust or distribute its assets or apply doctrine of cy pres. §109.25	Plant v. Upper Valley Medical Ctr. Inc., 1996 WL 185341	No, but distinction between charitable corps. and other nonprofits is relevant in merger provisions.	Every charitable trust established or active in the state shall register with atty. gen. §109.26 Nonprofit corps. must also register with sec. of state. §1702.04	Yes, statement of continued existence to sec. of state. §1702.59	Trustees of a charitable trust must register with atty. gen. and file annual reports or copies of annual federal tax returns. §109.31	Yes, by ct. in action quo warranto by atty. gen. or prosecuting atty. §1702.52

Table 1 Columns 1–8 (*continued*)

State	1 Power of attorney general	2 Notice to atty. gen. required in suits involving charitable orgs.	3 Standing	4 Nonprofit corp. act distinguishes public benefit from other corps.	5 Filing governing instruments with state official on creation of charitable org.	6 Periodic corporate status reports to state official	7 Periodic reports to attorney general	8 State vested with power to dissolve nonprofit corporation
OK	To enforce charitable trusts is a common-law duty and inferred from statute requiring notice to atty. gen. in action on a contract against a charitable trust. Sarkeys v. Independent School Dist. No. 40, Cleveland County, 592 P.2d 529 (1979)	In any action on a contract against a trustee of a charitable trust. Tit. 60, §175.18	Sarkeys v. Independent School Dist. No. 40, Cleveland County, 592 P.2d 529 (1979)	N/A. State does not have nonprofit corp. statute.	Yes for nonprofit corps, with sec. of state. Tit. 18, §1005	No	No	Yes, by dist. ct. in action by atty. gen. Tit. 18, §1104
OR	To investigate transactions and relationship of charitable corps. and trustees to ascertain whether the purposes of the corp. or trust are being carried out. §128.650	Yes, notice of the start of actions the nonprofit corp. act authorizes atty. gen. to bring but have been commenced by another person. §65.040	A member or dir. may bring a derivative suit in the right of a nonprofit corp. §65.174 A nonprofit corp.'s power to act may be challenged in a pro-	Yes	Every charitable corp. and trustee receiving property for charitable purposes must file with atty. gen. on receiving such property of art. of inc., trust	Yes, to sec. of state. §65.787	Every charitable corp. and charitable trustee shall file with atty. gen. periodic financial reports. §128.670	Cir. ct. in action by atty. gen. §65.661 Sec. of state. §65.647

		ceeding to enjoin the act by a member or dir. §65.084		agreement, or other instrument. §65.004			
PA	To intervene in any action involving charitable bequests and trusts. Tit. 71, §732-204	Notice of cy pres proceeding. Tit. 20, §6110	In re McCune, 705 A.2d 861 (1997)	No	Yes for nonprofit corps., with sec. of state. Tit. 15, §5308	Yes, to sec. of state. Tit. 15, §5110	No	Yes, by ct. in action by atty. gen. Tit. 15, §5502
RI	To supervise and enforce the due application of funds given or appropriated to charitable trusts and prevent breaches thereof. §18-9-1	Yes, for all judicial proceedings affecting a charitable trust. §18-9-5	No statement in statute or case.	No	Yes, charitable trusts register with atty. gen. §18-9-7. Nonprofit corps. must also file w/ sec. of state. §7-6-35	Yes, to sec. of state. §7-6-90	Yes, for charitable trusts. §18-9-13	Yes, sec. of state. §7-6-60
SC	To enforce the due application of funds given or appropriated to public charities and prevent breaches of trust in the administration thereof. §1-7-130	Notice of any proceeding that has been commenced by another person. §33-31-170	Derivative suits authorized but statute does not specify which parties may bring them. §33-31-630	Yes	Trustees file with atty. gen. within 60 days after creation of the trust. §62-7-501. Nonprofit corps. must file with sec. of state. §33-31-201	No	Trustees of charitable trusts shall submit annual report to atty. gen. §62-7-502	Ct. of common pleas in proceeding by atty. gen. §33-31-1430. Sec. of state. §33-31-1420

Table 1 Columns 1–8 (*continued*)

State	1 Power of attorney general	2 Notice to atty. gen. required in suits involving charitable orgs.	3 Standing	4 Nonprofit corp. act distinguishes public benefit from other corps.	5 Filing governing instruments with state official on creation of charitable org.	6 Periodic corporate status reports to state official	7 Periodic reports to attorney general	8 State vested with power to dissolve nonprofit corporation
SD	To represent beneficiaries of charitable trusts and to enforce such trusts by proper proceedings in the cts. §55-9-5	To atty. gen. in cause of action on a contract against a trustee of a charitable trust. §55-4-20	No statement in statute or case.	No	Yes for nonprofit corps., to sec. of state. §47-22-12	Yes, to sec. of state. §47-24-6	No	Cir. ct. in action by atty. gen. §47-26-16
TN	Ct. may require atty. gen. and reporter to be made party to represent beneficiaries, potential beneficiaries, and all citizens of the state. §35-13-110	Plaintiffs in a derivative action shall notify atty. gen. if it involves a public benefit corp. §48-56-401	Members or dirs. may bring derivative suits. §48-56-401	Yes	Yes for nonprofit corps., to sec. of state. §48-52-101	Yes, to sec. of state. §48-66-203	No	Ct. in action by atty. gen. §48-64-301 Sec. of state. §48-64-201
TX	To intervene in and to enter into a compromise, settlement agreement, contract, or judgment relating	Any party initiating a proceeding involving a charitable trust shall give notice of the	Gray v. Saint Matthews Cathedral Endowment Fund, Inc., 544 S.W.2d 488 (1976)	No	Yes for nonprofit corps., to sec. of state. Rev. Civ. Stat. art. 1396-3.03	Yes, if sec. of state requires them. Rev. Civ. Stat. art. 1396-9.01	No	Dist. ct. in action by atty. gen. Rev. Civ. Stat. art. 1396-7.01

to a proceeding involving a charitable trust. Prop. Code §123.002	proceeding to atty. gen. Prop. Code §123.003		No		No		Sec. of state. Rev. Civ. Stat. art. 1396-7.01
UT — To consent to a trustee's amending governing instrument and to petition court to relieve a trustee from restrictions on his powers. §§59-18-107, 108	Yes, for the release of a power to select charitable donees by a trustee. §59-18-109	No statement in statute or case.	No	Yes for nonprofit corps., to div. of corps. and commercial code. §16-6a-105	No	Yes, to div. of corps. §16-6a-107	Third dist. ct. in action by atty. gen. §16-6a-1414
VT — To take action to compel compliance with requirement that trustees holding property for charitable purposes annually file a financial report with prob. ct. Tit. 14, §§2501-2502	Complainants in a derivative action shall notify atty. gen. if court proceeding involves a public benefit corp. or charitable assets of a mutual benefit corp. Tit. 11B, §6.40.	Members and directors authorized to bring derivative suits. Tit. 11B, §6.40	Yes, but distinction between public benefit and other nonprofit corp. is not relevant in voluntary dissolution provisions.	Yes for nonprofit corps., with sec. of state. Tit. 11B, §2.01	No	Yes, to sec. of state. Tit. 11B, §16.22	Super. ct. in action by atty. gen. Tit. 11B, §14.30 Sec. of state, with notice to atty. gen. in case of a public benefit corp. Tit. 11B, §§14.20-.21
VA — To act on behalf of the public in matters involving charitable assets. Tauber v. Com., 499 S.E.2d 839 (1998)	Yes. §2.2-507.1	No statement in statute or case.	N/A. State does not have nonprofit corp. statute. Bus. corp. act permits nonstock corps.	Yes for nonprofit corps., with state corp. commission. §13.1-818	No	Yes, to state corp. commission. §13.1-936	State corp. commission. §13.1-915 Automatic termination for failure to file annual status report. §13.1-914

Table 1 Columns 1-8 (*continued*)

State	1 Power of attorney general	2 Notice to atty. gen. required in suits involving charitable orgs.	3 Standing	4 Nonprofit corp. act distinguishes public benefit from other corps.	5 Filing governing instruments with state official on creation of charitable org.	6 Periodic corporate status reports to state official	7 Periodic reports to attorney general	8 State vested with power to dissolve nonprofit corporation
WA	To investigate whether trust or other relationship is administered according to law and the terms of the trust, or compliance with the chapter pertaining to charitable trusts. §11.110.100	Yes for all proceedings involving or affecting a charitable trust or its administration in which, at common law, he is necessary or proper party as representative of the public beneficiaries. §11.110.120	No statement in statute or case.	Yes, but distinction between public benefit and nonprofit corp. is not relevant in sale of assets or merger provisions.	Yes for trustee with sec. of state. §11.110.051 Nonprofit corps. must register with sec. of state. §24.03.020	Every trustee required to file with sec. of state a copy of each publicly available tax return. §11.110.070	No	Super. ct. in action by atty. gen. §24.03.250 Sec. of state. §24.03.302
WV	To enforce charitable trusts. See dicta in Goetz v. Old Nat'l Bank of Martinsberg, 845 S.E.2d 759 (1954)	No	No statement in statute or case.	No	Yes for nonprofit corps., with sec. of state. §31E-1-120	Yes. §31D-1-101	No	Super. ct. in action by atty. gen. §31E-13-1330

WI	To enforce a charitable trust on atty. gen. information, or in atty. gen.'s discretion, on complaint by another person. §701.10(3)(a)(2)	Yes, in a proceeding affecting a charitable trust. §701.10(3)(a)(4)(b)	Members and directors may bring derivative proceedings. §181.0741	No	Yes for nonprofit corps., with dept. of financial institutions §181.0201	Yes, to dept. of financial institutions. §181.1622	A trustee of a testamentary charitable trust must file an annual account w/ the ct., a copy to atty. gen. §701.16(4)	Cir. ct. in action by atty. gen. §181.1430 Dept. of financial institutions. §181.1420
WY	Common law. Dicta in Town of Cody v. Buffalo Bill Memorial Ass'n, 196 P.2d 369 (1948)	Complainants in derivative action shall notify sec. of state if proceeding involves a public benefit corp. or assets held in charitable trust by a mutual benefit corp. Sec. of state shall then notify atty. gen. §17-19-630	Members and directors may bring derivative suits. §17-19-630	Yes	Yes for nonprofit corps., with sec. of state. §17-19-201	Yes, to sec. of state. §17-19-1630	No	Dist. ct. in proceeding by atty. gen. §17-19-1430 Sec. of state. §17-19-1420

Table 1 State laws governing creation, administration, and dissolution of charities: Columns 9–17

State	9 Notice to state official of voluntary dissolution	10 Assets must be distributed to other charitable corps. on dissolution	11 Cy pres	12 Notice to attorney general of sale of substantially all assets	13 Limits on mergers	14 Change from public benefit corp. to other corporate form limited	15 Solicitation statute requiring registration and/or annual filings	16 Situs of authority for enforcement of solicitation statute	17 Other statutes and notes
AL	Yes, to prob. judge. §10-3A-140	Yes. §10-3A-141	Yes. §35-4-251	No. §10-3A-120	Yes, nonprofit corps. may only merge with other nonprofit corps. §10-3A-100	N/A. §10-3A-80	Yes. §13A-9-70 to -76	Atty. gen.	UMIFA §§16-61A-1 to -8
AK	Yes, to comm'r of commerce and econ. dev. §§10.20.290, .315	Yes. §10.20.295	No statement in statute or case.	No. §10.20.280	Yes, nonprofit corps. may only merge with other nonprofit corps. §10.20.216	N/A. §10.20.171	Yes. §§45.68.010 to .900.	Atty. gen.	
AZ	Yes, to corp. comm., on filing art. of dissolution. §10-11401	Yes. §10-11405	Yes. §10-10413 (adopted Uniform Trust Code)	No. §10-11202	No. §10-11101	N/A. §§10-11001 to -11003	Yes. §§44-6551 to -6561.	Sec. of state; atty. gen.	UMIFA §§10-11801 to -11807

AR	Yes, to sec. of state, on filing art. of dissolution. §4-33-1401	Yes. §4-33-150	Yes. Lowery v. Jones, 611 S.W.2d 759 (1981) Applicable to corporations. Trevathan v. Ringgold-Noland Foundation, 410 S.W.2d 132 (1967)	No. §4-33-1202	Chancery ct. approval is required. §4-33-1102	No. §4-33-1001	Yes. §§4-28-401 to -410	Atty. gen.	UMIFA §§28-69-601 to -611
CA	Yes, public benefit corps. must file a cert. of election with atty. gen. upon electing to dissolve. Corp. Code §6611	Yes, all assets shall be distributed on dissolution according to articles or by-laws. Corp. Code §6716	Yes. In re Estate of Gatlin, 16 Cal. App. 3d 644 (1971) Applicable to corporations. Lynch v. Spilman, 431 P.2d 636 (1967)	Yes. Corp. Code §5913	Yes, atty. gen. consent required if public benefit corp. proposes to merge with an entity other than another public benefit corp. Corp. Code §6010	Yes, atty. gen. approval required if public benefit corp. proposes to amend its by-laws. Corp. Code §5813.5	Yes. Gov't Code §§12580-12599	Atty. gen.	UMIFA Prob. Code §§18500 to 18509 Alternate method of incorporation of religious orgs. Corp. Code §9130
CO	Yes, to sec. of state, on filing art. of dissolution. §§7-134-101 to -103	Yes. §7-134-105	Yes. In re Estate of Vallery, 883 P.2d 24 (1993)	No. §7-132-102	Yes, nonprofit corps. may only merge with other nonprofit corps. §7-131-101	N/A. §7-130-201	Yes. §§6-16-101 to -113	Sec. of state	UMIFA §§15-1-1101 to -1109

Table 1 Columns 9–17 (*continued*)

State	9 Notice to state official of voluntary dissolution	10 Assets must be distributed to other charitable corps. on dissolution	11 Cy pres	12 Notice to attorney general of sale of substantially all assets	13 Limits on mergers	14 Change from public benefit corp. to other corporate form limited	15 Solicitation statute requiring registration and/or annual filings	16 Situs of authority for enforcement of solicitation statute	17 Other statutes and notes
CT	Yes, with sec. of state, on filing cert. of dissolution. §§33-1170 to -1172 No notice required for religious corps. §33-264(e)	Yes. §33-1176	Yes. Smith Mem'l Home, Inc. v. Clarine Nardi Riddle, 1990 Conn. Super. LEXIS 1498 Applicable to corporations. MacCurdy-Salisbury Educational Fund v. Killian, 309 A.2d 11 (Super. Ct. 1973)	No. §33-1166	Yes, nonstock corps. may only merge with other nonstock corps. §33-1155	N/A. §§33-1140 to -1143	Yes. §§21a-190a to -190k	Dept. of consumer protection	UMIFA §§45a-526 to -534
DE	Yes, with sec. of state, on filing cert. of dissolution. Tit. 8, §§275-276	No. Tit. 8, §§275-285	Yes. Tit. 12, §3541	No. Tit. 8, §271	Yes. Tit. 8, §§255, 257	N/A	No	N/A	UMIFA Tit. 12, §§4701 to 4708 Alternate method of incorporation of religious orgs. Tit. 27, §101

DC	Yes. §§29-548 to -553	Yes. §29-549	Yes. Noel v. Olds, 138 F.2d 581 (1943)	No. §29-547	Yes, not-for-profit corps. may only merge with other not-for-profit corps. §29-540	N/A. §29-537	Yes. §§2-701 to -714	Mayor and council of district. §2-712	UMIFA §§44-1601 to -1609
FL	Yes, with dept. of state, on filing art. of dissolution. §617.403	Yes. §617.1406	Yes. In re Williams' Estate, 59 So. 2d 13 (1952)	No. §617.1202	Yes, not-for-profit corps. may only merge with other not-for-profit corps. §617.1101	N/A.	Yes. §§496.401 to .4255	Dept. of agriculture & consumer services. §496.420	UMIFA §240.127
GA	Yes, charitable corp. must notify atty. gen. §14-3-1403	Yes. §14-3-1403	Yes. §53-12-113	Yes. §14-3-1202	Yes. §14-3-1102	N/A. §14-3-1041(b)	Yes. §§43-17-1 to -23	Sec. of state	UMIFA §§44-15-1 to -9
HI	Yes, to dir. of dept. of commerce & consumer affairs. §414D-241	No	Yes. In re Estate of Chun Quan Yee Hop, 469 P.2d 183 (1970) (dictum)	No	No. §414D-201	N/A	No	Dept. of commerce & consumer affairs	UMIFA §§571D-1 to -11; Alternate method of incorporation of religious orgs. §§419-1 to -9

Table 1 Columns 9–17 (*continued*)

State	9 Notice to state official of voluntary dissolution	10 Assets must be distributed to other charitable corps. on dissolution	11 Cy pres	12 Notice to attorney general of sale of substantially all assets	13 Limits on mergers	14 Change from public benefit corp. to other corporate form limited	15 Solicitation statute requiring registration and/or annual filings	16 Situs of authority for enforcement of solicitation statute	17 Other statutes and notes
ID	Yes, to sec. of state, on filing art. of dissolution. §§30-3-110 to -112	Yes, if no provision in art. or by-laws, dissolving corp. may distribute its assets to 501(c)(3) entities or to its members. §30-3-113	Yes. §68-1204	No. §30-3-107	No. §30-3-100	N/A. §30-3-89	No	N/A	UMIFA §§33-5001 to -5008
IL	Yes, with sec. of state, on filing art. of dissolution. Ch. 805, 105/112.20	Yes. Ch. 805, 105/112.16	Yes. Ch. 760, 55/15.5 Applicable to corporations. Bertram v. Berger, 274 N.E.2d 667 (App. Ct. 1971); Riverton Area Fire Protection Dist. v. Riverton Volunteer Fire	No. Ch. 805, 105/111.60	Not-for-profit corps. may only merge with other not-for-profit corps. Ch. 805, 105/111.05	N/A. Ch. 805, 105/110.05	Yes. Ch. 225, 460/0.01 to /23	Atty. gen.	UMIFA Ch. 760, 50/1 to /10

				Dept., 566 N.E.2d 1015 (App. Ct. 1991)					
IN	Yes, with sec. of state, on filing art. of dissolution. §23-17-22-1	Yes, if corp. is public benefit or religious corp. and no provision in corp.'s art. of inc. or by-laws. §23-17-22-5	No. §30-4-3-27	Public benefit or religious corp. can merge without prior approval of the super. ct. only if it merges with another public benefit or religious corp. §23-17-19-2	No	No	N/A		UMIFA §§30-2-12-1 to -13
IA	Yes, with sec. of state, on filing art. of dissolution. §§504A.47 to .52	Yes. §504A.48	Yes. §633.5102	No. §504A.46	Nonprofit corps. may only merge with other non-profit corps. §504A.40	N/A. §504A.34	No	N/A	UMIFA §§540A.1 to .9
KS	Yes, on filing cert. of dissolution with sec. of state. §17-6805	Yes. §17-6805a	Yes. §59-22a01	No. §17-6801	A charitable nonstock corp. may not merge into a stock corp. §17-6707	N/A. §17-6602	Yes. §§17-1759 to -1775	Sec. of state; atty. gen., county or district atty.	UMIFA §§58-3601 to -3610
KY	Yes, on filing art. of dissolution with sec. of state. §§273.300 to .313	Yes. §273.303	Yes. Hampton v. O'Rear, 215 S.W.2d 539 (1948)	No. §273.297	Nonprofit corps. may only merge with other non-profit corps. §273.277	N/A	Yes. §§367.650 to .670	Atty. gen.	UMIFA §§273.510 to .590

Table 1 Columns 9–17 (*continued*)

State	9 Notice to state official of voluntary dissolution	10 Assets must be distributed to other charitable corps. on dissolution	11 Cy pres	12 Notice to attorney general of sale of substantially all assets	13 Limits on mergers	14 Change from public benefit corp. to other corporate form limited	15 Solicitation statute requiring registration and/or annual filings	16 Situs of authority for enforcement of solicitation statute	17 Other statutes and notes
LA	Yes, on filing cert. of dissolution with sec. of state. §12:250	Yes. §12:249	Yes. §9:2331	No. §12:247	Yes. §12:242	N/A. §12:237	No	N/A	UMIFA §§9:2337.1 to .8
ME	Yes, with sec. of state in advance of filing art. of dissolution. Tit. 13-B, §1101	Yes. Tit. 13-B, §1104	Yes. In re Estate of Thompson, 414 A.2d 881 (1980)	Yes. Tit. 13-B, §1001 Special limits on conversions. Tit. 13-B, §802(5)	Nonprofit corps. may only merge with other nonprofit corps. Tit. 13-B, §901	No	Yes. Tit. 9, §§5001–5016	Comm'r of business regulation; atty. gen.	UMIFA Tit. 13, §§4100–4110
MD	Yes, to dept. of assessment and taxation. Corps. & Ass'n §3-407	Yes. Corps. & Ass'n §5-209	Yes. Est. & Trusts §14-302; Corps. & Ass'n §5-209 Applicable to corps. Miller v. Mercantile-Safe Deposit & Trust Co., 168 A.2d 184 (1961)	No. Corps. & Ass'n §3-105	Nonstock corps. may only merge or consolidate with other nonstock corps. Corps. & Ass'n §5-207	N/A	Yes. Bus. Reg. §§6-101 to -701	Sec. of state; atty. gen.	UMIFA Est. & Trusts §§15-401 to -409

MA	Yes, to supreme judicial ct. setting forth grounds for application Ch. 180, §11A	Yes. Ch. 180, §11A	Yes. Ch. 214, §10B; Ch. 12, §8K Applicable to corps. Attorney General v. Hahnemann Hospital, 494 N.E.2d 1011 (1986)	Yes. Ch. 180, §8A	Yes, if one of the constituent nonprofit corps. to a merger or consolidation is a public charity, the surviving corp. must be a public charity. Ch. 180, §10	N/A	Yes. Ch. 68, §§18-35	Atty. gen. (div. of public charities)	UMIFA Ch. 180A, §§1-11
MI	Yes. §450.251	Yes. §450.2855	Yes. §14.254; In re Rood, 200 N.W.2d 728 (1972)	No. §450.2753	Nonprofit corps. may only merge with other nonprofits. §450.2701	N/A	Yes. §§400.271 to .293	Atty. gen.	UMIFA §§451.1201 to .1210
MN	Yes, to atty. gen. prior to filing art. of dissolution with sec. of state. §317A.811	Yes, assets held for charitable purpose subject to cy pres doctrine provisions dealing with charitable trusts (see Column 11). §317A.735	Yes. §501B.31 Applicable to corporations. Gethsemane Lutheran Church v. Zacho, 104 N.W.2d 645 (1960)	Yes. §317A.811	Charitable trusts and corps. exempt under 501(c)(3) must give notice to atty. gen. prior to merger. §317A.811	N/A	Yes. §§309.50 to .72	Atty. gen.	UMIFA §§309.62 to .71 Alternate method of incorporation of religious orgs. §315.21

Table 1 Columns 9–17 (*continued*)

State	9 Notice to state official of voluntary dissolution	10 Assets must be distributed to other charitable corps. on dissolution	11 Cy pres	12 Notice to attorney general of sale of substantially all assets	13 Limits on mergers	14 Change from public benefit corp. to other corporate form limited	15 Solicitation statute requiring registration and/or annual filings	16 Situs of authority for enforcement of solicitation statute	17 Other statutes and notes
MS	Yes, to sec. of state, on filing art. of dissolution. §§79-11-335 to -337	No. §79-11-341	Yes. Allgood v. Bradford, 473 So. 2d 402 (1985)	No. §79-11-331	None. §79-11-319	N/A.	Yes. §§79-11-501 to -529	Sec. of state; atty. gen., district attys., and county prosecuting attys. §79-11-519	UMIFA §§79-11-601 to -617. Alternate method of incorporation of religious orgs. §79-11-31
MO	Yes, to atty. gen. at or before filing art. of dissolution with sec. of state. §655.676	Yes, if public benefit corp. and no provision in governing instrument. §355.691	Yes. Comfort v. Higgins, 576 S.W.2d 331 (1979); St. Louis Mercantile Library Assoc., 359 S.W.2d 689 (1962)	Yes. §355.656	In a proceeding where atty. gen. is given notice, cir. ct. approval not required if pub. benefit corp. merges with another public benefit corp. §355.621	No	Yes. §§407.450 to .478	Atty. gen.	UMIFA §§402.010 to .060
MT	Yes, to atty. gen. at or before delivering art. of dissolution to	Yes. §35-2-725	Yes. §72-33-504	Yes. §35-2-617	In a proceeding where atty. gen. is given notice, dist. ct. approval not required if	No	No	N/A	UMIFA §§72-30-101 to -207

	sec. of state. §35-2-722				public benefit or religious corp. merges with another public benefit or religious corp. §35-2-609			N/A	
NE	Yes, to atty. gen. at or before delivering art. of dissolution to sec. of state. §21-19,131	Yes. §21-19,134	Yes. L.B. 130, Reg. Sess. (2003) (adopted Uniform Trust Code)	Yes. §21-19,126	In a proceeding where atty. gen. is given notice, dist. ct. approval not reqd. if pub. benefit or religious corp. merges with another pub. benefit or religious corp. §21-19,119	No	No	N/A	UMIFA §§58-601 to -609
NV	Yes, to sec. of state, on filing cert. of dissolution. §82.446	Yes. §82.461	Yes. Su See v. Peck, 160 P. 18 (1916) (dictum)	No. §82.436	No. §92A.160	N/A	No	N/A	UMIFA §§164.500 to .630
NH	Yes, to atty. gen., on application to the super. ct. or prob. ct. §292.9	No. §292.2	Yes. §547:3-d; §498:4-a	No	Voluntary corps. may only merge with other such corps. §292:7	N/A. §292:7	Yes. §7:24; §7:28; §7:28-b, -c, -d, and -f	Atty. gen.	UMIFA §§292-B:1 to B:9

Table 1 Columns 9–17 (*continued*)

State	9 Notice to state official of voluntary dissolution	10 Assets must be distributed to other charitable corps. on dissolution	11 Cy pres	12 Notice to attorney general of sale of substantially all assets	13 Limits on mergers	14 Change from public benefit corp. to other corporate form limited	15 Solicitation statute requiring registration and/or annual filings	16 Situs of authority for enforcement of solicitation statute	17 Other statutes and notes
NJ	Yes, on filing cert. of dissolution w/sec. of state who then forwards copy to atty. gen. §15A:12-7	Yes. §15A:12-8	Yes. Sharpless v. Medford Monthly Meeting of Religious Soc. of Friends, 548 A.2d 1157 (1988)	No. §15A:10-11	Nonprofit corps. may only merge with other nonprofit corps. §15A:10-1	N/A	Yes. §§45:17A-18 to -40	Atty. gen.	UMIFA §§15:18-15 to -24 Alternate method of incorporation of religious orgs. §16:1-1
NM	Yes, with corp. commission, on filing art. of dissolution. §53-8-52	Yes. §53-8-48	Yes. §46A-4-413 (adopted Uniform Trust Code)	No. §53-8-46	Nonprofit corps. may only merge with other nonprofit corps. §53-8-41	N/A	Yes. §§57-22-1 to -11	Atty. gen.	UMIFA §§46-9-1 to -12
NY	Yes, approval of supreme ct. and sec. of state required (with notice to atty. gen.) prior to dissolution. Not-for-Profit Corp. Law §1002	Yes. Not-for-Profit Corp. Law §1005	Yes. Est. Powers & Trusts Law §8-1.1(c) Applicable to corporations. Not-for-Profit Corp. Law §513(b), §522	Yes. Not-for-Profit Corp. Law §§510-511	Supreme ct. approval required after notice to atty. gen. Not-for-Profit Corp. Law §907	No	Yes. Exec. Law §§171-a to 177	Atty. gen.	UMIFA Not-for-Profit Corp. Law §§102, 512, 514, 522

NC	Yes. §55A-14-04	Yes. §55A-14-03	Yes. §36A-53	Yes. §55A-12-02	Approval of the super. ct. reqd. unless corp. merges w/another charitable corp. or religious corp. §55A-11-02	N/A	Yes. Ch. 131F	Sec. of state; atty. gen.	UMIFA §§36B-1 to -10
ND	Yes. §10-33-122	Yes. §10-33-95; §10-33-105	Undecided. Mercy Hosp. of Williston v. Stillwell, 358 N.W.2d 506 (1984)	Yes. §10-33-122	Nonprofit corps. may only merge with other nonprofit corps. §10-33-85	N/A. §10-33-14	Yes. §§50-22-01 to -05	Sec. of state; atty. gen. and state's atty.	UMIFA §§15-67-01 to -09
OH	Yes, on filing cert. of dissolution with sec. of state. §1702.47	Yes. §1702.49	Yes. §109.25	No. §1702.39	Charitable corps. may only merge with other charitable corps. §1702.41	N/A	Yes. §§1716.01 to .99	Atty. gen.	UMIFA §§1715.51 to .59
OK	Yes, on filing cert. of dissolution with sec. of state. Tit. 18, §1096	No. Tit. 18, §§1096–1099	Yes. Tit. 60, §602	No. Tit. 18, §1092	Charitable nonstock corps. may not merge into nonstock corps. Tit. 18, §1084	N/A	Yes. Tit. 18, §§552.1 to .18	Sec. of state; atty. gen. and district atty.	UMIFA Tit. 60, §§300.1 to .10
OR	Yes. §65.627	Yes, if no provision in by-laws, public benefit or religious corps. are limited to dist. to 501(c)(3)'s. §65.637	Yes. Good Samaritan Hosp. and Medical Center v. U.S. Nat'l. Bank, 425 P.2d 541 (1967).	Yes. §65.534	Public benefit or religious corp. can merge without consent of atty. gen. or prior approval of cir. ct. if it merges with another public benefit or religious corp. §65.484	Yes. §65.431	Yes. §§128.610 to .891	Atty. gen.	UMIFA §§128.310 to .355

Table 1 Columns 9–17 (*continued*)

State	9 Notice to state official of voluntary dissolution	10 Assets must be distributed to other charitable corps. on dissolution	11 Cy pres	12 Notice to attorney general of sale of substantially all assets	13 Limits on mergers	14 Change from public benefit corp. to other corporate form limited	15 Solicitation statute requiring registration and/or annual filings	16 Situs of authority for enforcement of solicitation statute	17 Other statutes and notes
PA	Yes, on filing art. of dissolution with sec. of state. Tit. 15, §5977	Yes. Tit. 15, §5547	Yes. Tit. 20, §6110(A) Applicable to corporations. Tit. 15, §5547	No. Tit. 15, §5930	Nonprofit corps. may only merge with other nonprofit corps. Tit. 15, §5921	N/A	Yes. Tit. 10, §§162.1 to .22	Sec. of state; atty. gen. and district attys.	
RI	Yes, on filing art. of dissolution with sec. of state. §7-6-55	Yes. §7-6-51	Yes. §18-4-1	No. §7-6-49	No. §7-6-43	N/A	Yes. §§5-53.1 to -18	Dept. of bus. regulation; atty. gen.	UMIFA §§18-12-1 to -9
SC	Yes, to atty. gen. at or before art. of dissolution delivered to sec. of state. §33-31-1406.	Yes, if corp. is a public benefit or religious corp. and no provision in governing instrument.	Doctrine consistently rejected by state courts. Collin McK. Grant Home v. Medlock, 349 S.E.2d 655 (App. Ct. 1986)	Yes. §33-31-1202	Yes. §33-31-1102	Yes. §33-31-1001	Yes. §§33-56-10 to -200	Sec. of state	UMIFA §§34-6-1- to -80

SD	Yes, on filing art. of dissolution with sec. of state. §47-26-10	Yes. §47-26-5	Yes. §55-9-4	No. §47-25-28	Nonprofit corps. may only merge with other nonprofit corps. §47-25-1	N/A	No. §37-3-1	N/A	N/A
TN	Yes, to atty. gen. at or before filing art. of dissolution with sec. of state. §48-64-103	Yes. §48-64-106	Yes. §35-13-106	Yes. §48-62-102	Public benefit corp. can merge w/o ct. approval if it merges with another public benefit corp. §48-61-102	No	Yes. §§48-101-501 to -521	Sec of state; atty. gen.	UMIFA §§35-10-101 to -109
TX	Yes, on filing art. of dissolution with sec. of state. Rev. Civ. Stat. art. 1396-6.06	Yes, unless provided otherwise in corp.'s art. of inc. Rev. Civ. Stat. art. 1396-6.02	Yes. In re Bishop College, 151 BR 394 (1993) Applicable to corporations. Blocker v. Texas, 718 S.W.2d 409 (App. Ct. 1986)	No. Rev. Civ. Stat. art. 1396-5.09	Nonprofit corps. may only merge with other nonprofit corps. Rev. Civ. Stat. art. 1396-5.01	N/A	Yes, for veterans orgs., public safety orgs., and telephone solicitations by charities relating to law enforcement. Rev. Civ. Stat. art. 9023e	Sec. of state; atty. gen.	UMIFA Prop. Code §§163.001 to .009
UT	Yes, on filing art. of dissolution with div. of corps. & commercial code. §16-6a-1403	Yes. §16-6a-1405	Yes. In re Gerber, 652 P.2d 937 (1982).	No. §16-6a-1201	Nonprofit corps. may only merge with other nonprofit corps. §16-6a-1101	No.	Yes. §§13-22-1 to -23	Div. of consumer protection of dept. of commerce	UMIFA §§13-29-1 to -8

Table 1 Columns 9–17 *(continued)*

State	9 Notice to state official of voluntary dissolution	10 Assets must be distributed to other charitable corps. on dissolution	11 Cy pres	12 Notice to attorney general of sale of substantially all assets	13 Limits on mergers	14 Change from public benefit corp. to other corporate form limited	15 Solicitation statute requiring registration and/or annual filings	16 Situs of authority for enforcement of solicitation statute	17 Other statutes and notes
VT	Yes, on filing art. of inc. with sec. of state. Tit. 11B, §14.01	Yes. Tit. 11B, §14.05	Yes. Tit. 14, §2328	Yes. Tit. 11B, §12.02	Yes. Tit. 11B, §11.02	No	No. Tit. 9, §2471	N/A	UMIFA Tit. 14, §§3401 to 3407
VA	Yes, on filing art. of dissolution with corp. commission. §13.1-904	Yes. §13.1-907	Yes. §55-31	No. §13.1-900	No. §13.1-898.1	N/A; conversion of nonstock corp. to stock corp. expressly permitted. §13.1-941	Yes. §§57-48 to -69	Comm'r of agriculture & consumer serv's.; atty. gen., atty. for Commonwealth, or atty. for any city, county, or town.	UMIFA §§55-268.1 to -.10
WA	Yes, to atty. gen. prior to filing art. of dissolution with sec. of state. §24.03.220	Yes. §24.03.225	Yes. Puget Sound Nat'l Bank of Tacoma v. Easterday, 350 P.2d 444 (1960)	Yes. §24.03.215	Nonprofit corps. may only merge with other nonprofit corps. §24.03.185	No	Yes. §§19.09.010 to .915	Sec. of state; atty. gen.	UMIFA §§24.44.010 to .900

WV	Yes, on filing art. of dissolution w/sec. of state. §31E-13-1303	Yes. §31E-13-1309	Yes. §35-2-2	No. §31E-12-1201	Nonprofit corps. may only merge with other nonprofit corps. §31E-11-1101	No	Yes. §§29-19-1 to -16	Sec. of state; atty. gen.	UMIFA §§44-6A-1 to -8
WI	Yes, on filing art. of dissolution with dept. of financial institutions. §181.1403	Yes. §181.1405	Yes. §701.10(2)(a)	No. §181.1202	N/A	N/A	Yes. §§440.41 to .48	Dept. of regulation and licensing; atty. gen.	UMIFA §112.10 Alternate method of incorp. of religious orgs. §187.01
WY	Yes, to sec. of state. §17-19-1403	Yes. §17-19-1406	Yes. §4-10-414 (adopted Uniform Trust Code)	Yes, via sec. of state. §17-19-1202	Public benefit or religious corp. can merge without dist. ct. approval if it merges with public benefit or religious corp. §17-19-1102	No	No	N/A	UMIFA §§17-7-201 to -205

Table 2 Cy pres doctrine applicable to outright transfers and trusts

State	Adopted by statute, case law, or dictum [49]	General intent			Standard		
		Required [23]	Presumed (P) or eliminated (E) [9]	Inferred [15]	Impossible or impractical [6]	Inexpedient, wasteful, other [10]	Expedited procedures for small trusts [14]
AL	X (S)(T)	X			X		
AK							
AZ	X (SU)		P		X	X	X
AR	X	X			X		
CA	X			X	X		
CO	X	X			X		
CT	X			X	X		X
DE	X (S)		E		X	X	
DC	X	X			X		
FL	X	X			X		
GA	X (S)		P		X		
HI	X (D)						
ID	X (S)[1]			X	X	X[2]	X
IL	X (S)[1]			X	X	X[3]	X
IN	X (S)(T)	X[4]			X		
IA	X (S)	X			X		
KS	X (S)			X	X		X
KY	X	X			X		
LA	X (S)			X	X		
ME	X (T)			X	X		
MD	X (S)	X			X		
MA	X (S)		P		X		
MI	X (T)			X	X		
MN	X (S)	X			X	X	
MS	X	X			X		
MO	X	X			X		
MT	X (S)(T)	X			X		
NE	X (SU)		P	X	X	X	X
NV	X (D)						
NH	X (S)(T)	X			X	X[5]	X
NJ	X			X	X		
NM	X (SU)		P		X	X	X
NY	X (S)			X[6]	X		X
NC	X (S)			X	X		
ND							
OH	X	X			X		
OK	X (S)	X			X		
OR	X (T)	X			X		
PA	X (S)		E		X		X
RI	X (S)			X	X		X
SC	X (DV)						
SD	X (S)(T)			X[7]	X	X	
TN	X (S)	X			X		
TX	X (S)	X			X		

Table 2 (*continued*)

State	Adopted by statute, case law, or dictum [49]	General intent			Standard		
		Required [23]	Presumed (P) or eliminated (E) [9]	Inferred [15]	Impossible or impractical [6]	Inexpedient, wasteful, other [10]	Expedited procedures for small trusts [14]
UT	X	X			X		
VT	X (S)			X	X		
VA	X (S)(T)		P		X		X
WA	X	X			X		
WV	X (S)	X			X		
WI	X (S)	X			X		X
WY	X (T) (SU)		P		X	X	X

Notes: In the following states the cy pres doctrine applies to the general assets of charitable corporations: AR, CA, CT, IL, MD, MA, MN, MO, NY ("quasi cy-pres"), PA, TX. Also, statutes in all states except DE, MS, and OK require distribution of assets upon dissolution to other charitable corps.

(S)—adopted by statute.   (SU)—Uniform Trust Code.   (T)—doctrine applicable to trusts only, not outright transfers.   (D)—approved in dictum.   (DV)—deviation used as substitute.

1. Trustee need not obtain the approval of any court but does need the consent of the attorney general.

2. "Impractical because of changed circumstances adversely impacting [trust] purposes."

3. "Inconsistent with charitable needs of community."

4. Living heir or named beneficiary may present evidence as to heir's or beneficiary's opinion of settlor's intent and heir's or beneficiary's wishes in regard to the property.

5. "Obsolete or ineffective or prejudicial to the public interest to carry out."

6. Donor consent required if living.

7. Donor consent required if living and mentally competent.

Table 3 Fiduciary duties under state laws

State	Nonprofit corporation act	Duty of loyalty (date adopted)	Loans	Duty of care (date adopted)	Reliance	Limited liability	Optional elimination of liability	Indemnification and insurance
AL	Tit. 10, Ch. 3A [MA]	§10-2B-8.60[b] et seq.	§10-3A-45	§10-2B-8.30[b]	§10-2B-8.30[b]	§10-11-3		§10-2B-8.51[b]
AK	Tit. 10, Ch. 20 [RMNCA]	§10.06.478[b]	§10.20.141	§10.06.450[b]	§10.06.450[b]		§10.20.151	
AZ	Tit. 10, Chs. 22 to 40	§10-3860 et seq. (1999)		§10-3830 (1999)	§10-3830		§10-3202	§10-3851 et seq.
AR	Tit. 4, Subt. 3, Ch. 33 [RMNCA]	§4-33-831 (1993)	§4-33-832	§4-33-830 (1993)	§4-33-830			§4-33-851 et seq.
CA	Corp. Code, Tit. 1, Div. 2 [RMNCA(mod)]	§5233 (1980)	§5236	§5231 (1980)	§5231			§5238
CO	Tit. 7, Art. 121 et seq. [RMNCA]	§7-128-501 (1998)	§7-128-501	§7-128-401 (1998)	§7-128-401	§13-21-116	§7-128-402	§7-129-102 et seq.
CT	Tit. 33, Ch. 602	§33-1127 et seq. (1997)	§33-1106	§33-1104 (1997)	§33-1104	§52-557m	§33-1026	§33-1117 et seq.
DE	None	Tit. 8, §144[b]			Tit. 8, §141[b]	Tit. 10, §8133	Tit. 8, §102[b]	
DC	Pt. 5, Tit. 29, Ch. 3 [MA]		§29-301.28			§29-301.113		
FL	Tit. 36, Ch. 617	§617.0832 (1990)	§617.0833	§617.0830 (1990)	§617.0830	§617.0834		§617.0831
GA	Tit. 14, Ch. 3 [RMNCA(mod)]	§14-3-860 et seq. (1991)		§14-3-830 (1991)	§14-3-830		§14-3-202	§14-3-851 et seq.
HI	Div. 2, Tit. 23, Ch. 414D [RMNCA(mod)]	§414D-150 (2002)	§414D-151	§414D-149 (2002)	§414D-149	§414D-32		§414D-160 et seq.
ID	Tit. 30, Ch. 3 [RMNCA(mod)]	§30-3-81 (1993)	§30-3-82	§30-3-80 (1993)	§30-3-80	§6-1605		§30-3-88

State	Statute							
IL	Ch. 805, Art. 105	§105/108.60 (1987)	§105/108.80			§105/108.70		§105/108.75
IN	Tit. 23, Art. 17 [RMNCA(mod)]	§23-17-13-2 (1991)	§23-17-13-3	§23-17-13-1 (1991)	§23-17-13-1	§34-30-4-1		§23-17-16-8 et seq.
IA	Tit. 12, Subt. 5, Ch. 504A	§490.831[b]	§504A.27	§490.830[b]	§490.830[b]	§504A.101		
KS	None	§17-6304[b]			§17-6301[b]	§60-3601	§17-6002[b]	
KY	Tit. 23, Ch. 273	§273.219 (1988)	§273.241	§273.215 (1988)	§273.215	§411.200	§273.248	
LA	Tit. 12, Ch. 2	§12:228 (1969)		§12:226 (1969)	§12:226	§9:2792.1		§12:227
ME	Tit. 13-B	Tit. 13-B, §718 (2002)	Tit. 13-B, §712	Tit. 13-B, §717 (2002)	Tit. 13-B, §717	Tit. 14, §158-A		Tit. 13-B, §714
MD	[RMNCA(mod)] Corp. Code Tit. 5, Subt. 2	§2-419[b]		§2-405.1[b]	§2-405.1[b]	§5-406	§2-405.2[b]	
MA	Pt. I, Tit. 22, Ch. 180			Ch. 180, §6C (1989)	Ch. 180, §6C		Ch. 180 §3	
MI	Ch. 450	§450.2545 et seq. (1983)	§450.2548	§450.2541 (1983)	§450.2541		§450.2209	§450.2561 et seq.
MN	Corp. Code, Ch. 317A [RMNCA(mod)]	§317A.255 (1989)	§317A.501	§317A.251 (1989)	§317A.251			§317A.521
MS	Tit. 79, Ch. 11 [RMNCA(mod)]	§79-11-269 (1988)		§79-11-267 (1988)	§79-11-267			§79-11-281
MO	Tit. 23, Ch. 355 [RMNCA]	§355.416 (1995)	§355.421	§355.426	§355.426			§355.476
MT	Tit. 35, Ch. 2 [RMNCA]	§35-2-418 (1991)	§35-2-435	§35-2-416 (1991)	§35-2-416	§27-1-732	§35-2-213	§35-2-447 et seq.
NE	Ch. 21, Art. 19 [RMNCA]	§21-1987 (1996)	§21-1988	§21-1986 (1996)	§21-1986			§21-1997 et seq.
NV	Tit. 7, Ch. 82	§82.226 (1991)		§82.221 (1991)	§82.221	§82.221		§82.541
NH	Tit. 27, Ch. 292	§293-A:8.31[b]		§293-A:8.30[b]	§293-A:8.30[b]			
NJ	Tit. 15A [MA]	§14A:6-8[b]	§15A:6-11	§15A:6-14 (1983)	§15A:6-14	§2A:53A-7.1	§15A:2-8	§15A:3-4

Table 3 *(continued)*

State	Nonprofit corporation act	Duty of loyalty (date adopted)	Loans	Duty of care (date adopted)	Reliance	Limited liability	Optional elimination of liability	Indemnification and insurance
NM	Ch. 53, Art. 8	§53-11-40.1[b]	§53-8-29	§53-8-25.1 (1987)	§53-8-25.1	§53-8-25.2		
NY	Ch. 35	Ch. 35, §715 (1969)	Ch. 35, §716	Ch. 35, §717 (1969)	Ch. 35, §717			Ch. 35, §§722, 726
NC	Ch. 55A [RMNCA(mod)]	§55A-8-31 (1986)	§55A-8-32	§55A-8-30 (1986)	§55A-8-30	§55A-8-60	§55A-2-02	§55A-8-51 et seq.
ND	Tit. 10, Ch. 33 [MA]	§10-33-46 (1997)	§10-33-82	§10-33-45 (1997)	§10-33-45	§10-33-47		§10-33-84
OH	Tit. 17, Ch. 1702	§1702.301 (1988)	§1702.55	§1702.30 (1988)	§1702.30	§1702.30		
OK	Tit. 18, Ch. 19	Tit. 18 §1030[b]				Tit.18, §867		
OR	Tit. 7, Ch. 65 [RMNCA]	§65.361 (1989)	§65.364	§65.357 (1989)	§65.357	§65.369	§65.047	§65.39 let seq.
PA	Tit. 15, Pt. 2, Subpt. C	Tit. 15, §1728[b]		Tit. 15, §5712 (1990)	Tit. 15, §5712		Tit. 15, §5713	Tit. 15, §5741 et seq.
RI	Tit. 7, Ch. 6	§7-6-26.1 (1989)	§7-6-32	§7-6-22 (1984)	§7-6-22	§7-6-9	§7-6-34	§7-6-6
SC	Tit. 33, Ch. 31 [RMNCA]	§33-31-831 (1994)	§33-31-832	§33-31-830 (1994)	§33-31-830	§33-31-834		§33-31-851 et seq.
SD	Tit. 47, Chs. 22 to 26					§47-23-29		
TN	Tit. 48 [RMNCA]	§48-58-302 (1987)	§48-58-303	§48-58-301 (1987)	§48-58-301	§48-58-601		§48-58-502 et seq.

TX	Civil Stat., Tit. 32, Ch. 9 [MA]	§1396-2.30 (1994)	§1396-2.25	§1396-2.28 (1994)	§1396-2.28	§1396-2.22	§1302-7.06	§1396-2.22A
UT	Tit. 16, Ch. 6a [RMNCA (mod)]	§16-61-825 (2001)	§16-6a-825	§16-6a-822 (2001)	§16-6a-822	§16-6a-822	§16-6a-823	§16-6a-901 et seq.
VT	Tit. 11-B [RMNCA]	Tit. 11-B, §8.31 (1997)	Tit. 11B, §8.32	Tit. 11-B, §8.30 (1997)	Tit. 11-B, §8.30			Tit. 11B, §8.51 et seq.
VA	Tit. 13.1, Ch. 10 [MA]	§13.1-871 (1950)		§13.1-870 (1985)	§13.1-870	§13.1-870.1		§13.1-876 et seq.
WA	Tit. 24, Ch. 24.03 [RMNCA]	§23B.08.700ᵇ et seq.	§24.03.140	§24.03.127 (1986)	§24.03.127		§24.03.025	§24.03.043
WV	Ch. 31E, Art. 1 [RMNCA (mod)]	§31E-8-860 (2002)		§31E-8-830 (2002)	§31E-8-830	§31E-8-831	§31E-2-202	§31E-8-850 et seq.
WI	Ch. 181 [MA]	§181.0831 (1999)	§181.0832	§181.0850	§181.0850	§181.0855		§181.0872 et seq.
WY	Tit. 17, Ch. 19 [RMNCA]	§17-19-831 (1992)	§17-19-832	§17-16-830ᵇ	§17-16-830ᵇ			

Notes: A superscript "b" indicates that a statute is from a state's business corporation act. Year of adoption is provided for nonprofit corporation acts only.

[MA]—Model Nonprofit Corporation Act (1952) adopted by state as promulgated or modified.
[RMNCA]—Revised Model Nonprofit Corporation Act (1987) adopted by state.
[RMNCA (mod)]—Revised Model Nonprofit Corporation Act (1987) adopted by state in modified form.

Index of Cases

519

General Index

46–47, 51, 52; state supervision of bank and trust companies, 367–368; termination of, 136–137, 179–180; Uniform Trust Code and, 177. *See also Appendix Table 3*

Charities. *See* Charitable corporations; Charitable trusts; Standing to sue

Charities Acts (England), 32, 33–34, 35, 41

Charities regulation, dual legal system of, 428–430

Charity: common law definition of, 101, 103; concept of, 3; cy pres doctrine and, 438–439; definition of under state law, 117, 119; evolution of, 3, 19–22; exemption from taxation, 19; general categories of, 3; legal definition of, 3–4; nomenclature of, 4; public benefit and, 4; public perceptions of, 2; and section 501(c)(3) of the IRC, 3, 4, 5, 238, 405; and section 501(c)(4) of the IRC, 239. *See also* Charitable corporations; Charitable purposes; Charitable trusts; *Appendix Table 1*

Charity Aid, Recovery, and Empowerment Act. *See* CARE Act

Charity care standard, for hospitals, 243. *See also* Hospitals

Charity Commission (England), 32–33, 34, 35, 38, 39, 41, 101

Charity Navigator, 468

Charity supervision by state agencies, 364–370; bank commissioners, 367–368; departments of education, health, and similar agencies, 365–367; departments of tax and revenue, 368–370; secretaries of state and corporation commissions, 364–365

Charter, corporate. *See* Incorporation

Chief Counsel, IRS, 393, 419. *See also* IRS

Chronicle of Higher Education, 469

Chronicle of Philanthropy, 469

Church: as early dispenser of charity, 51–52; the bishops and, 20–21, 22; dissolution of monasteries, 27; ecclesiastical courts, 22–23. *See also* Religious organizations

Church of Scientology, and IRS, 399

Çizakça, Murat, 22n

Clark, Elias, 117, 118n, 120

Clark, William G., 314n

Closing agreements with IRS, 398, 399–400, 420

Coalition of National Voluntary Organizations, 83, 462, 466

Colorado, regulation of fund-raising, 370–374, 444–445

Commercial activities, of charities, 247–248, 295–299; amount of, compatible with federal tax exemption, 107–108, 299; ancillary joint ventures, 297–298; commerciality doctrine, 247–248; competition with for-profit companies, 247–248; joint ventures with for-profit investors, 296–297, 298–299; subsidiary organizations, 296; whole hospital joint ventures, 296–298. *See also* Unrelated business income tax

Commissioner of IRS. *See* IRS

Commissioner's Advisory Committee on Tax-Exempt and Government Entities (2001), 394–395

Commissioner's Exempt Organization Advisory Group (1987), 106

Commissioners on Uniform State Laws, 173, 340

Commission on Foundations and Private Philanthropy (Peterson Commission), 80–81, 84

Commission on Private Philanthropy and Public Needs (Filer Commission), 81–84, 97, 352, 378, 424, 461–462, 466

Common law definition of charity, 101

Community chest or fund, described in IRC section 501(c)(3), 7, 58, 238

Community foundations or trusts, 186. *See also* Foundations; Public charity

Compensation: of directors, 168, 452; of trustees, 147

Confiscatory termination tax under IRC section 507, 429–430

Conflict of interest: clarification of definition needed, 436; definitions of, 219; disclosure requirements, 221; procedural fairness, 224; procedures for validating conflicts, 219–220; relief from liability for directors, 221–223; requirement of fairness to the corporation, 220–221; statutory protection without validation, 225; validation by board approval, 220; validation by outside authorities, 223–224. *See also* Duty of loyalty (fair dealing) of corporate directors; Duty of loyalty of trustees

Congress, U.S.: budgeting process and, 378–380; CARE Act (2002), 427, 430; CARE Act (2003), 265, 427, 430; church audits, 91–93; Crimes Against Charitable Americans Act (USA Patriot Act) section 1011, (2001), 424–425; enactment of first

Estates, Powers and Trusts Law, 144; exclusion of general public in actions against charitable corporations, 326; exemption from filing requirements, 315; indemnification, directors and officers insurance, 229, 437–438; judicial approval of corporate dissolutions, 157; limitations on power of attorney general, 310; notice to attorney general of disposition of assets, 319–320; parameters of variance power, 186; permission for derivative action, 336; proper parties to suits, 348–349; property tax exemption, 130; proposals to extend federal limits on business corporations to charities, 110; registration and reporting requirements for charities, 315; regulation of fiduciary duties by attorney general, 444; regulation of fund-raising, 370–374, 444–445; rejection of validity of charitable trusts, 46–47; response of charities to terrorist attacks (Sept. 2001), 355–356, 448; Tilden Act (1893), 46–47

New York University Center on Philanthropy and the Law, 469

Nongovernmental organizations (NGOs), 4

Nonprofit Academic Centers Council, 469

Nonprofit Almanac, 5

Nonprofit and Voluntary Sector Quarterly, 469

Nonprofit corporations: assets of, 155, 319–320; business judgment rule applied to directors, 210–211; charitable and noncharitable purposes for, 126–127; defining duties of directors, 200, 207–209; dissolution of, 184–186; limited partnerships and, 296; mutual benefit corporations, 127, 151; Principles of Corporate Governance and, 205–206; proposals to reform state laws governing, 431–432; public benefit corporations, 127, 151; religious corporations, 127, 151; restrictions on property holdings, 167–168; Revised Model Nonprofit Corporation Act (RMNCA), 127, 151, 156, 159–160, 165, 167, 205–206, 210, 431. *See also* Charitable corporations; Duty of care of corporate directors; Duty of loyalty (fair dealing) of corporate directors; *Appendix Tables 1 and 3*

Nonprofit sector, 1–2; arts and cultural organizations of, 11–12; assets of, 1, 319–320; challenges to specific components of, 9–13; contributions of, 1; convergence with taxable sector, 15–17; distinguishing feature of, 1–2; educational organizations of, 10; exemption from taxation, 4–7; foundations and other grantmakers of, 12–13; government regulation of, 2; government support of, 18; health care organizations of, 9–10; human and social service organization of, 10–11; number of organizations exempt from taxation, 7; policy issues of, 15–18; religious organizations of, 5, 9; resilience of, 16, 17–18; revenue growth of, 7, 300; tax treatment of, 58, 240; wrongdoing in, 13–15. *See also* Size and characteristics of nonprofit sector

NonProfit Times, 469

Non-section 501(c)(3) tax-exempt nonprofit organizations, 7, 58, 238

North Carolina: Model Act Concerning the Administration of Charitable Trusts, Devises, and Bequests, 173; regulation of fund-raising, 370–374, 444–445

North Dakota: assets of nonprofit charitable corporations subject to trust rules, 155; conflict between attorneys general and, 321, 322; regulation of fund-raising, 370–374, 444–445

Not-for-profit corporations. *See* Nonprofit corporations

Obedience to the Unenforceable, 467

O'Connell, Brian, 83, 466

Office of Employee Plans and Exempt Organizations (EP/EO), 97, 387–388, 389–391, 465

Office of Tax Legislative Counsel, 383

Office of the Operating Division Counsel in Office of Chief Counsel, IRS, 393

Ohio: attorney general as necessary party to suits, 346; Charitable Trusts Act, 346–347; Charity Law Section of, 356–357; denial of exemption from property tax to foundation, 131; effective enforcement program, 356–357; exemptions from filing requirements, 315–316; proper parties to suits, 349; registration and reporting by charities, 445; regulation of fiduciary duties by attorney general, 444; regulation of fund-raising, 370–374, 444–445; statutes supplementing common law enforcement duties of the attorney general, 312

Oklahoma: common law of trusts and, 362; regulation of fund-raising, 370–374, 444–445